A Macroeconomics
Reader

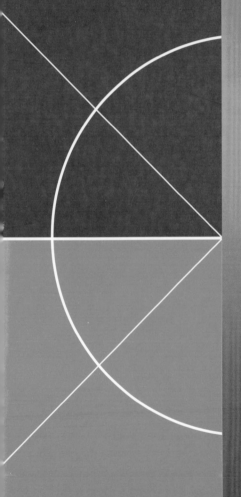

Contributors include:
Moses Abramovitz,
Robert Barro,
Alan Blinder,
Michael Carter,
Alan Coddington,
Steve Dowrick,
Milton Friedman,
Bill Gerrard,
Robert Gordon,
Bruce Greenwald,
David Laidler,
Robert Lucas,
Rodney Maddock,
Gregory Mankiw,
Thomas Mayer,
Franco Modigliani,
Don Patinkin,
Charles Plosser,
Edward Prescott,
Paul Romer,
Thomas Sargent,
Keith Shaw,
Robert Solow,
Lawrence Summers,
Joseph Stiglitz and
James Tobin.

Edited by **BRIAN SNOWDON & HOWARD R. VANE**

A Macroeconomics Reader

A Macroeconomics Reader brings together in a single volume a collection of key articles on developments and current debates in modern macroeconomics. The articles have been selected to provide the reader with an accessible and informative overview of a number of the most significant issues and controversies in macroeconomics.

Areas covered include:

Keynesian Economics and the Keynesian Revolution
The Monetarist Counter-Revolution
The Challenge of Rational Expectations and New Classical Macroeconomics
The Real Business Cycle Approach to Economic Fluctuations
New Keynesian Economics
The Renaissance of Economic Growth Analysis

Brian Snowdon is Principal Lecturer in Economics at the University of Northumbria. His previous books include *Markets, Intervention and Planning* (1987) and (with Howard Vane and P. Wynarczyk) *A Modern Guide to Macroeconomics* (1994).

Howard R. Vane is Reader in Economics at Liverpool John Moores University. His previous books (with J. Thompson) include *Current Controversies in Macroeconomics* (1992) and *An Introduction to Macroeconomic Policy* (1993).

A Macroeconomics Reader

Edited by

Brian Snowdon and
Howard R. Vane

London and New York

First published 1997
by Routledge
11 New Fetter Lane, London EC4P 4EE

Simultaneously published in the USA and Canada
by Routledge
29 West 35th Street, New York, NY 10001

Reprinted 1999

Routledge is an imprint of the Taylor & Francis Group

© 1997 BRIAN SNOWDON and HOWARD R. VANE

Typeset in Times by Pure Tech India Limited, Pondicherry
Printed and bound in Great Britain by TJ International Ltd, Padstow, Cornwall

British Library Cataloguing in Publication Data

A catalogue record for this book is available from the British
Library

Library of Congress Cataloging in Publication Data

A catalog record for this book has been requested

ISBN 0–415–15715–3 (hbk)
     0–415–15716–1 (pbk)

To Jean and Christine

Contents

Preface

Anyone who teaches 'intermediate undergraduate' macroeconomics can vouch that there now exist a large number of excellent textbooks they can choose from and direct their students to buy. This was certainly not the case when we were undergraduate and graduate students in the late 1960s and early 1970s. However, when it comes to recommending journal articles for students to read, two main problems arise. First, many important and/or seminal papers display a high degree of technical virtuosity and mathematical sophistication which most students find extremely demanding, to say the least. Second, students often experience difficulty in gaining access to popular articles which are inevitably in heavy demand.

The present volume seeks to alleviate these two problems. The main aim of the book is to bring together in a single volume a collection of insightful articles, for intermediate undergraduates, which shed light on the development of, and selected important controversies within, modern macroeconomics. As such the book will serve as a supplementary text to be read alongside a main macroeconomics textbook. The articles which make up this book of readings have been chosen to provide the reader with accessible and predominantly non-technical, reflective papers which critically assess and/or survey important areas/issues in the development of, and selected controversies within, modern macroeconomics. Choosing the final collection of twenty-six articles which make up this volume proved to be a more difficult task than we first anticipated (every economist would no doubt select their own favourite collection). One important criterion for selection has been the need to keep an ever watchful eye on production costs so that the book could be published at a price which is affordable to students. Our original proposal, which contained a collection of thirty-eight articles, would have been prohibitively expensive to produce, especially given the disproportionately high copyright permission fees levied by certain journals. The final selection of twenty-six articles chosen for this volume we believe are both thought provoking and insightful.

The book follows a structured direction, tracing the origins and development of modern macroeconomics in historical perspective around the main schools of macroeconomic thought through to the focus of much current debate and research, namely the issue of economic growth. In following this structured pattern we have consciously not included readings on such areas as, for example, consumption, investment, the demand for and supply of money, and open economy macroeconomics; topics which have previously occupied a significant proportion of macroeconomics readers. After an introductory chapter in which we present for the student reader a selective review of some of the most important developments in macroeconomics since the mid-1930s, the collection of articles is divided into six main parts covering

- Keynesian Economics and the Keynesian Revolution
- The Monetarist Counter-Revolution
- The Challenge of Rational Expectations and New Classical Macroeconomics
- The Real Business Cycle Approach to Economic Fluctuations
- New Keynesian Economics
- The Renaissance of Economic Growth Analysis

Each part starts with a brief introduction in which we place the articles included in an overall context. Our intention is not to comment in detail upon the central points raised in the articles concerned, merely to provide a frame of reference for the reader. In the introduction to each part we have included references which are particularly recommended for additional reading, together with some essay-style questions for review. Having completed such additional reading the reader will be in a much better position to make an informed answer to these and other questions in macroeconomics.

By bringing together in a single volume a collection of key supplementary readings we hope the book will attract a wide readership among intermediate undergraduates, as well as postgraduates and teachers, in the field of macroeconomics and the history of economic thought.

We wish to express our gratitude to all the authors, and journals, who have given their permission to reprint the collection of articles in this volume. Our final thanks to Katherine Eade, Kerry Douglas, Angie Dell and Sue Barlow for their patience, humour and co-operation in typing various parts of the final manuscript. Any remaining errors (few in number, it is hoped) are our responsibility.

Brian Snowdon
Howard R. Vane

1 The development of modern macroeconomics

A rough guide

Brian Snowdon and Howard R. Vane

Any economics student who graduated from university in the late 1960s and early 1970s, as we both did, would have found macroeconomics a much easier and far less controversial subject to study then than it is today. Since the breakdown of the Keynesian consensus in the early 1970s, macroeconomics has been in a 'state of disarray' (Brunner 1989) having witnessed the appearance of a number of conflicting and competing approaches. As a result modern macroeconomics is a rapidly changing diverse subject with a built-in tendency to generate deep divisions. These divisions have led to the formation of schools of thought consisting of economists who share a broad vision of how macroeconomic phenomena are generated. In order to better understand current controversies it is necessary, in our view, to know how macroeconomic thought has developed since Keynes's *General Theory* (1936) was published. In this opening chapter we briefly survey *some* of the important developments in the evolution of macroeconomics since the mid-1930s. Our purpose is not to critically assess in detail the central tenets underlying and policy implications of the main macroeconomic schools of thought, rather it is to provide a background discussion in order to help place the readings that follow in context (for a more detailed survey of competing schools of thought see Phelps 1990; Chrystal and Price 1994; Snowdon *et al.* 1994).

Although there are significant differences between the various schools of thought, the work of Keynes remains a central point of reference because, as Vercelli (1991) argues, all the schools define themselves in relation to the ideas originally put forward by Keynes in his *General Theory*, either as a development of some version of his thought or as a restoration of some version of pre-Keynesian classical thought. A unifying theme in the evolution of modern macroeconomics has been an 'ever-evolving classical Keynesian debate' (see Gerrard 1996). Although elsewhere (Snowdon *et al.*, 1994) we have identified seven schools of thought which have been influential in the development of macroeconomic analysis since the mid-1930s, each of these schools can be viewed as adhering to one of two basic positions in terms of broad vision. Gregory Mankiw (1989) – reprinted in Part IV – describes these two positions by distinguishing between the classical school and the Keynesian school with respect to their faith in the 'invisible hand'.

> The classical school emphasizes the optimization of private economic actors, the adjustment of relative prices to equate supply and demand, and the efficiency of unfettered markets. The Keynesian school believes that understanding economic fluctuations requires not just studying the intricacies of general equilibrium, but also appreciating the possibility of market failure on a grand scale.

Hence, although it is possible to distinguish between orthodox Keynesians, new Keynesians and post-Keynesians, all three groups are united in the belief that aggregate economic instability represents 'some sort of market failure on a grand scale' (Mankiw 1990). In contrast the majority of economists who have been prominent in the monetarist, new classical, real business cycle and Austrian schools have tended to place their faith in market forces as an equilibrating mechanism and question the capacity and desirability of government intervention as a means of achieving the major macroeconomic objectives. Following Gerrard (1996) the seven schools of thought identified above can also be differentiated and classified as orthodox, new or radical. The two 'orthodox' schools, 'IS-LM Keynesianism' and 'neoclassical monetarism', dominated macroeconomic *theory* in the period up to the mid-1970s. Since then three 'new' schools have been highly influential. The new classical, real business cycle and new Keynesian schools place emphasis on issues relating to aggregate supply in contrast to the orthodox schools which focused their research primarily on the factors determining aggregate demand and the consequences of demand-management policies. In particular the new schools share the view that macroeconomic models should be based on solid microeconomic foundations. The 'radical' post-Keynesian and Austrian schools are both critical of mainstream analysis whether it be orthodox or new. Since modern macroeconomics has been most influenced by the orthodox and new schools we will confine our discussion here to their contributions (see Davidson 1994 and Chick 1995 for a discussion of post-Keynesian macroeconomics; Garrison 1994 presents the case for the Austrian approach).

In the final section of this opening chapter we briefly review the renaissance of economic growth analysis which since the mid-1980s has moved into the centre stage of macroeconomic research after twenty years of relative neglect. The consequences of economic growth for economic welfare are so important that many prominent macroeconomists who previously concentrated their research efforts on the analysis of business cycles have now turned their attention to theoretical and empirical issues arising out of the burgeoning endogenous growth literature (see Barro and Sala-i-Martin 1995; Mankiw 1995).

KEYNESIAN ECONOMICS AND THE KEYNESIAN REVOLUTION

The birth of modern macroeconomics can be traced back to the 1930s, and in particular the publication of John Maynard Keynes's (1936) *General Theory of Employment, Interest and Money*. Prior to the 1930s the dominant view, in what we now call macroeconomics, was the classical approach that within capitalist market economies which are subject to periodic shocks the market mechanism would operate quickly and efficiently to restore full employment equilibrium. In such circumstances government intervention to stabilize the economy was believed to be neither necessary nor desirable. However, the experience of the 1920s and 1930s in Britain, and that of all major capitalist market economies during the 1930s, appeared to shatter the classical assumption that full employment was the normal state of affairs. In Britain the rate of unemployment never fell below 10 per cent between 1921 and 1938, and actually exceeded 20 per cent in 1931 and 1932. In the United States unemployment reached a peak of 25 per cent in 1933 and was still almost 10 per cent in 1941. Writing against this background Keynes (1936) put forward a new and revolutionary theory to explain, and provide a remedy for, the then-prevailing persistent and severe unemployment. In doing so Keynes was responding to what undoubtedly was the most significant macroeconomic event of the twentieth century; the Great Depression gave birth to modern macroeconomics.

The causes of the Great Depression are still the subject of considerable dispute and finding a plausible explanation for the global economic collapse during the early 1930s remains the 'Holy Grail' of macroeconomics (see C. D. Romer 1993; Bernanke 1995). In an extensive study of the US experience Gordon and Wilcox (1981) concluded that the cause of the Great Depression can be traced to a series of domestic spending shocks, both monetary and non-monetary. The initial decline in output during the 1929–31 period can be traced to a decline in consumption and residential investment expenditures. After September 1931 the recession was turned into the Great Depression by the perverse actions of the Federal Reserve in letting the money supply decline drastically (see Friedman and Schwartz 1963). Hence the Great Depression resulted from a shift of the aggregate demand curve to the left and the impact of the monetary contraction was transmitted worldwide via the operation of the gold standard (see Eichengreen 1992). The self-equilibrating tendencies of the market failed to come into play and as a result we have the best known example of massive monetary non-neutrality. In the face of enormous unemployment, nominal wages failed to adjust sufficiently to shift the aggregate supply curve so as to restore full employment (Bernanke and Carey 1996). The worldwide decline in aggregate demand as an explanation for the Great Depression has its origin in the work of Keynes, for it was his analysis in the *General Theory* which turned economists' attention away from the classical emphasis on supply-side factors. Although economists certainly examined (what we now call) macroeconomic issues prior to the publication of the *General Theory*, even Pigou argued that Keynes was the first economist to bring together real and monetary factors 'in a single formal scheme, through which their interplay could be coherently investigated' (quoted in Solow 1986). The dominance of Keynes in the field of macroeconomics prior to his death in 1946 is clearly illustrated by looking at data on citations for the period

Table 1.1 Most cited macroeconomists 1920–30

Rank	Name	Number of citations
1	Irving Fisher	30
2	W. C. Mitchell	24
3	A. C. Pigou	21
4	Alfred Marshall	15
5	W. S. Jevons	13
6	R. G. Hawtrey	11
	D. H. Robertson	11
8	H. L. Moore	10
	Carl Snyder	10
10	J. M. Keynes	9

Table 1.2 Most cited macroeconomists 1931–5

Rank	Name	Number of citations
1	J. M. Keynes	66
2	D. H. Robertson	44
3	F. von Hayek	33
4	R. G. Hawtrey	30
	I. Fisher	30
6	G. Cassel	22
7	A. C. Pigou	20
8	K. Wicksell	17
9	A. Hansen	14
10	A. Marshall	13

Table 1.3 Most cited macroeconomists 1936–9

Rank	Name	Number of citations
1	J. M. Keynes	125
2	D. H. Robertson	48
3	J. Hicks	33
4	A. C. Pigou	31
5	Roy Harrod	27
6	R. G. Hawtrey	25
7	F. von Hayek	24
	G. Haberler	24
9	Joan Robinson	20
10	J. M. Clark	18

Table 1.4 Most cited macroeconomists 1940–4

Rank	Name	Number of citations
1	J. M. Keynes	59
2	J. Hicks	30
3	G. Haberler	24
4	D. H. Robertson	22
5	R. G. Hawtrey	20
6	M. Kalecki	18
	J. Schumpeter	18
8	A. Hansen	17
	N. Kaldor	17
10	S. Kuznets	16
	A. Lerner	16

Source: Deutscher (1990)

1920–44 (see Tables 1.1–1.4). The outstanding feature of these tables is the extent to which Keynes had come to dominate macroeconomics by the mid-1930s.

In Solow's (1986) view, the *General Theory* 'has certainly been the most influential work of economics of the 20th century, and Keynes the most important economist'.

A central theme of Keynes's analysis is the contention that capitalist market economies are inherently unstable and are capable of coming to rest 'in a chronic condition of sub-normal activity for a considerable period without any marked tendency, either towards recovery or towards complete collapse' (Keynes 1936: 249). This instability was in Keynes's view predominantly the result of fluctuations in aggregate demand and the Great Depression resulted from a sharp fall in investment expenditure 'occasioned by a cyclical change in the marginal efficiency of capital'. The resulting unemployment was *involuntary* and reflected a state of deficient aggregate demand. Given the weak equilibrating powers of the market mechanism in these circumstances the implication of Keynes's analysis was that fiscal and monetary policy could correct the aggregate instability exhibited by market economies and help stabilize the economy at full employment. Once full employment is restored Keynes accepted that 'the classical theory comes into its own again' and Keynes was optimistic that limited government intervention could remedy the shortcomings of the invisible hand (see Keynes 1936: 379). Managed capitalism, with a commitment to full employment, was the kind of system Keynes had in mind when in the concluding section of his famous essay *The End of Laissez-Faire* (1924) he argued that:

> For my part I think that capitalism, wisely managed, can probably be made more efficient for attaining economic ends than any alternative yet in sight, but that in itself it is in many ways objectionable. Our problem is

to work out a social organisation which shall be as efficient as possible without offending our notions of a satisfactory way or life.

(reprinted in Keynes 1972: 294)

Keynes objected to mass unemployment which his analysis defined as largely *involuntary*. In such a situation the economy can be said to be operating in what Tobin (1992) refers to as 'the Keynesian regime'. Here aggregate economic activity is *demand constrained* and additional 'effective' demand creates its own supply since the economy has the necessary spare capacity during a recession. However, once full employment is restored, the economy operates in the *supply constrained* classical regime. Here supply creates its own demand. Whereas the classical model recognizes only the supply constrained regime, Keynes and Keynesians believe that the economy is capable, at different times, of being in either regime.

As early as the mid-1950s the consensus which was beginning to emerge in macroeconomics particularly in the USA was labelled the neoclassical synthesis by Samuelson:

In recent years 90 per cent of American economists have stopped being 'Keynesian economists' or 'anti-Keynesian economists'. Instead they have worked towards a *synthesis* of whatever is valuable in older economics and in modern theories of income determination. The result might be called *neoclassical* economics and is accepted in its broad outlines by all but about 5 per cent of extreme left-wing and right-wing writers.

(Samuelson 1955: 212, emphasis added)

The initial synthesis proceeded along two lines of inquiry. The first studied the long-run movement of output by identifying the determinants of the trend and ignoring fluctuations around the trend. Significant contributions were made during this period to the development of growth theory (see Hahn and Matthews 1964). The second line of inquiry concentrated on the analysis of short-run fluctuations around the trend. At the centre of this analysis lay the Hicks–Hansen IS-LM framework (Hicks 1937; Hansen 1953; Young 1987; Darity and Young 1995). During this period a great deal of macroeconomic research was devoted to refining the four basic building blocks of the IS-LM model, namely the consumption function, the investment function and the demand for, and supply of, money.

During the late 1950s and early 1960s a consensus emerged with respect to the 'Keynes v. Classics' debate in which it was generally accepted that at the theoretical level, once the Pigou or wealth effect of falling prices on consumption expenditure is taken into account, then unemployment equilibrium is possible in the Keynesian IS-LM model only where downward money wage rigidity prevents the classical automatic adjustment to full employment. Nevertheless at the practical policy level it was conceded that the process of adjustment via the Pigou effect might be so weak and slow that interventionist policies (notably expansionary fiscal policy) would be required in order to achieve the primary stated objective of full employment (see Snowdon *et al.* 1994: Chapter 3). With a relatively inelastic IS curve and a relatively elastic LM curve Keynesianism became synonymous with 'fiscalism' and policies to fine tune the macroeconomy.

The publication of the results of Bill Phillips's (1958) statistical investigation into the relationship between the level of unemployment and wage inflation, and Richard Lipsey's (1960) subsequent theoretical rationale for the curve, proved to be another important development during this period (see Santomero and Seater 1978; Wulwick 1987). The Phillips curve was quickly adopted by orthodox Keynesian economists for three main reasons. First, it provided an explanation of price determination, and inflation, which was missing in the then-prevailing macroeconomic model. Within the IS-LM model the price level is assumed to be fixed at less than full employment with the result that changes in aggregate demand affect only the level of output and employment. Up to full employment money wages are assumed to be fixed and unresponsive to changes in aggregate demand. The Phillips curve allowed the orthodox theory of output and employment determination to be linked to a theory of wage and price inflation (see Lipsey 1978). Second, the Phillips curve appeared to provide rare evidence of a stable relationship between unemployment and inflation that had existed for almost a century. Third, the curve provided an insight into the problem that policy-makers face of simultaneously achieving high levels of employment with price stability given the trade-off between wage inflation and unemployment. As such the Phillips curve was interpreted by many orthodox Keynesians as implying a stable long-run trade-off which offered the authorities a menu of possible inflation-unemployment combinations for policy choice (see for example Samuelson and Solow 1960). Up to at least the mid-to-late 1960s the prevailing Keynesian consensus in macroeconomics was one in which the IS-LM model was used to explain the determination of output and employment, while the Phillips curve enabled policy-makers to predict the rate of inflation which would result from different target levels of unemployment being attained by activist demand-management policies. This consensus position was first seriously challenged by Milton Friedman, who launched the monetarist attack against orthodox Keynesian analysis and policy-activism during the 1950s and 1960s.

THE MONETARIST COUNTER-REVOLUTION

Friedman's starting-point was one in which he sought to re-establish the quantity theory of money approach to macroeconomic analysis which had been usurped by the Keynesian revolution. In the mid-to-late 1940s and the 1950s the then-prevailing Keynesian orthodoxy emphasized real demand disturbances (notably fluctuations in investment and autonomous consumption) as the main cause of fluctuations in money or nominal income, predominantly in the form of changes in real income. In contrast, within the quantity theory approach, changes in the money stock are regarded as the predominant, though not the only, factor explaining changes in money income. Nevertheless Friedman (1956) initially presented his now famous restatement of the quantity theory of money as a theory of the demand for money rather than a theory of the general price level or money income. In his paper he asserted that the demand for money function was stable, an assertion which lies at the heart of the modern quantity theory approach to macroeconomic analysis. If the demand for money function is stable then velocity will also be stable, changing in a predictable manner if any of the limited number of variables in the demand for money function should change (see Laidler 1993). Over the period of the mid-to-late 1950s to the mid-1960s various empirical evidence was put forward in support of the belief that most of the observed instability in the economy could be attributed to factors which affected the supply of money independently of any change in the demand for money. In the latter case it was claimed that changes in the demand for money tend to take place gradually or result from events set in motion by prior changes in the supply of money.

The most persuasive evidence to support the belief that changes in the stock of money play a largely independent role in cyclical fluctuations was presented by Milton Friedman and Anna Schwartz (1963) in their influential study of the *Monetary History of the United States* (see Lucas 1994; Miron 1994). Friedman and Schwartz found that the only times when there was an *absolute* fall in the money stock corresponded with the six periods of major economic contraction over the period 1867–1960. Furthermore from studying the historical circumstances underlying the changes that occurred in the money stock during the six major recessions, they argued that the factors producing monetary contraction were mainly independent of contemporary or prior changes in money income and prices. In such circumstances Friedman and Schwartz interpreted monetary changes as the *cause*, rather than the consequence, of major recessions. For example, re-examining the monetary history of the period of the Great Depression, they argued that the depression became 'Great' only as a consequence of the failure of the Federal Reserve to prevent a dramatic decline in the money stock; between October 1929 and June 1933 the money stock fell by about a third. According to Friedman and his associates, the Great Depression demonstrated the potency, rather than the ineffectiveness, of monetary change and monetary policy (see Hammond 1996). However, because of the length and variability of the time lag involved between the implementation of monetary policy and its effects on money income (see Friedman 1958; 1961) it was suggested that discretionary monetary policy could turn out to be destabilizing. In consequence Friedman argued that the money supply should be allowed to grow at a fixed rate in line with the underlying growth of output to ensure long-term price stability.

The direction of the monetarist attack against the Keynesian demand-management policies and policy-activism changed at the end of the 1960s when Friedman (1968) augmented the basic Phillips curve with the expected rate of inflation as an additional variable determining the rate of change of money wages (Phelps 1967 provided a similar analysis from a non-monetarist perspective). While *A Monetary History* has undoubtedly been Friedman's most influential book in the macroeconomics sphere, his 1967 presidential address to the American Economic Association published as 'The Role of Monetary Policy' (1968) has certainly been his most influential article. In 1981 Robert Gordon described this paper as probably the most influential article written in macroeconomics in the previous twenty years. More recently James Tobin (1995), one of Friedman's most eloquent, effective and long-standing critics, has gone even further, describing the 1968 paper as 'very likely the most influential article *ever* published in an economics journal' (emphasis added). Friedman's utilization of Wicksell's concept of the 'natural rate' in the context of unemployment was in rhetorical terms a 'masterpiece of marketing' (see Dixon 1995) just as the application of the term 'rational' to the expectations hypothesis turned out to be in the rise of new classical economics during the 1970s. The impact of Professor Friedman's work forced Keynesians to restate and remake their case for policy-activism even before that case was further undermined by the penetrating theoretical critiques of Robert Lucas and other leading new classical economists. In line with orthodox neoclassical microeconomic analysis, Friedman suggested that the demand for and supply of labour should be specified in real not money terms. Friedman denied the existence of a permanent (long-run) trade-off between inflation and unemployment, and put forward the 'natural rate of unemployment' hypothesis. Five main implications for the role and conduct of stabilization policy derive from the view that the long-run Phillips curve is vertical at the natural rate of unemployment. First, the authorities can reduce unemployment below the natural rate only in the short run and then only because inflation is not fully anticipated. The assumption underlying orthodox monetarist analysis is that expected inflation adjusts to actual inflation only gradually in line with the so-called 'adaptive' expectations hypothesis. Second, any attempt to maintain unemployment permanently below the natural rate will result in accelerating inflation. Third, if governments wish to reduce the natural rate of unemployment in order to achieve higher output and employment levels they should pursue supply-management policies which are designed to improve the structure and functioning of the labour market and industry rather than demand-management policies. Fourth, the natural rate is compatible with any rate of inflation which in turn is determined by the rate of monetary expansion in line with the quantity theory tradition. Given the belief that inflation is essentially a monetary phenomenon (see Friedman 1970) propagated by excessive monetary growth monetarists argue that inflation can be reduced only by slowing down the rate of growth of the money supply. In monetarist analysis the output/employment cost of disinflation depends on three main factors namely: (1) whether the authorities follow a path of rapid or gradual monetary contraction (cold turkey v. gradualism); (2) the extent of institutional adaptations such as indexation (see Friedman 1974); and (3) the speed economic agents adjust their inflation expectations downwards which in large part depends on the credibility of any anti-inflation strategy. Finally, in a world of fixed exchange rates inflation is viewed as an international monetary phenomenon explained by an excess-demand expectations model. Monetarists attribute the acceleration of inflation that occurred in western economies in the late 1960s primarily to an increase in the rate of monetary expansion in the United States in order to finance increased spending on the Vietnam War (see for example Johnson 1972; Laidler 1976). In practice the US determined monetary conditions for the rest of the world, a situation which eventually proved unacceptable to other countries and helped lead to the breakdown of the Bretton Woods system in the early 1970s.

During the early 1970s the subject of the possible existence of a long-run vertical Phillips curve became a controversial issue in the Keynesian-monetarist debate and numerous empirical studies of the expectations – augmented Phillips curve were undertaken. However by the mid-to-late 1970s at least as far as the United States was concerned, the majority of mainstream Keynesians had come to accept that the Phillips curve was vertical in the long run (see Blinder 1988 – reprinted on pp. 109–34). While the controversy over the slope of the long-run Phillips curve was largely laid to rest, the associated controversy over the role for short-run interventionist stabilization policy continued unabated. Even if the long-run Phillips curve is vertical, Keynesian arguments justifying intervention to stabilize the economy in the short run can be made on the grounds of the length of time required for the economy to return to the natural rate of unemployment and the potential to identify and respond to economic disturbances.

The failure of inflation to slow down both in the US and UK economies in 1970–1, despite rising unemployment, and the subsequent simultaneous rise of unemployment and inflation during the 1970s destroyed the idea that there might be a *permanent* long-run trade-off between inflation and unemployment. These events also verified the predictions of Friedman's model and contradicted the then-prevailing Keynesian views. As a result of these developments there is little doubt that Milton Friedman became 'the most influential macroeconomist' from the late 1960s to the mid-1970s (see Snowdon and Vane 1997). With hindsight 1976, the year when he was awarded the Nobel Prize for Economics, probably marked the pinnacle of Friedman's influence in academia even if monetarism had yet to rise (and fall) in the policy-making arena following the initiation of the Volcker and Thatcher disinflations (see Friedman 1977; Blinder 1987).

Although within academia monetarism is no longer the influential force it was in the late 1960s and early 1970s, a large part of the reason for this apparent decline can be attributed to the fact that mainstream macroeconomics has absorbed the insights of monetarism with a small 'm'. The expectations-augmented Phillips curve is now a standard part of the Keynesian-monetarist synthesis, although modern hysteresis theories of unemployment challenge Friedman's natural rate hypothesis which denies the importance of aggregate demand factors in influencing the equilibrium rate of unemployment (see Cross 1995; 1996). Of enormous importance has been Friedman's numerous contributions which have succeeded in reminding economists that their knowledge of how the economy functions is limited. Friedman's view is that by claiming more than can be delivered economists have on too many occasions encouraged the general public 'to expect standards of performance that as economists we do not know how to achieve' (Friedman 1972). This was a lesson that monetarists themselves were to learn during the 'great velocity decline' during the 1979–82 period when the stable demand for money function began to suffer the same fate as had befallen the stable Phillips curve (see Laidler 1985; Modigliani 1988 – reprinted on pp. 247–61). As a result 'hard core' monetarism with a capital 'M' – devoted to Friedman's advocacy of a rigid monetary growth rate rule – has few remaining supporters. However, the majority of modern Keynesians recognizing the political, economic and informational constraints facing policy-makers also now accept that in practice the opportunity for frequently exploiting fiscal policy for stabilization purposes is extremely limited. In addition whatever controversies remain over aggregate fluctuations Friedman has undoubtedly won one important debate, that relating to the determinants of *sustained* inflation. A clear majority of economists and central banks emphasize the rate of growth of the money supply when it comes to explaining and combating inflation over the long run. This allows mainstream macroeconomists to attribute *temporary* bouts of inflation to non-monetary causes such as supply shocks.

During the 1970s theoretical developments in macroeconomics were dominated by the new classical school. The contributions of Lucas and his associates cast further doubt on the mature synthesis model even when modified to incorporate the expectations-augmented Phillips curve.

THE CHALLENGE OF RATIONAL EXPECTATIONS AND NEW CLASSICAL MACROECONOMICS

During the 1970s the new classical approach to macroeconomics replaced monetarism as the main rival to Keynesianism. Underlying the approach, which is often taken to be synonymous with the work most notably of Robert Lucas, Thomas Sargent, Robert Barro, Edward Prescott and Neil Wallace, is the joint acceptance of three main sub-hypotheses. First, the rational expectations hypothesis which is associated with the work of John Muth in the context of microeconomics. In his seminal article Muth (1961) suggested 'that expectations since they are informed predictions of future events are essentially the same as the predictions of the relevant economic theory'. In the Muthian version of the rational expectations hypothesis which has been incorporated into new classical models, economic agents' subjective expectations of economic variables will coincide with the true or objective mathematical conditional expectations of those variables, with the crucial implication that economic agents will not form expectations which are *systematically* wrong over time. Second, new classical models are Walrasian in that all observed outcomes are viewed as 'market-clearing' at each point of time, given the assumption that markets continuously clear all possible gains from trade have been exploited and utility has been maximized. Third, new classical models incorporate an aggregate supply hypothesis based on two orthodox microeconomic assumptions, namely that (1) rational decisions taken by workers and firms reflect optimizing behaviour on their part and (2) the supply of labour by workers, and output by firms, depends upon relative prices. The new classical approach to aggregate supply derives from the highly influential work of the 1995 Nobel Laureate Robert Lucas (1972, 1973). This work has given rise to the so-called Lucas 'surprise' supply function (in effect a restatement of the expectations-augmented version of the Phillips curve) where output deviates from its natural level only in response to errors in price (inflation) expectations (see Blanchard 1990).

By combining the Friedman-Phelps natural rate hypothesis with the assumption of continuous market clearing and the rational expectations hypothesis, Lucas was able to demonstrate rigorously how a short-run Phillips curve would result if inflation was unanticipated due to incomplete information. Since a short-run trade-off between a *real* variable (unemployment) and a *nominal* variable (inflation) breaks the classical dichotomy, the work of Lucas was crucial in that it demonstrated that the classical model is compatible with the Phillips curve phenomena providing the assumption of perfect information is abandoned. By invoking the Lucas aggregate supply hypothesis monetary shocks can have a *temporary* influence on real variables, that is unanticipated money is non-neutral. Within this framework Lucas (1975, 1977) was able to develop an *equilibrium* monetary explanation of the business cycle.

During the 1970s it would be no exaggeration to say that there was a 'rational expectations revolution' (Taylor 1989). The combination of the rational expectations, continuous market clearing and aggregate supply hypotheses within new classical models produces six highly controversial policy implications. The first of these, the policy ineffectiveness proposition, was initially presented in two influential papers by Thomas Sargent and Neil Wallace (1975, 1976). As 'forward-looking' rational economic agents will take into account any 'known' monetary rule in forming their expectations, new classical models predict that the authorities will be unable to influence output and employment even in the short run by pursuing a systematic monetary policy. Furthermore any attempt to affect output and employment by random or non-systematic monetary policy will, new classicists argue, only increase the variation of output and employment around their natural levels. Second, in contrast to both Keynesianism and monetarism the new classical approach implies that as long as announced monetary contraction is believed to be credible, rational economic agents will immediately revise downwards their inflation expectations enabling the authorities to engineer painless disinflation (see Blackburn and Christensen 1989). Only where policy announcements lack credibility will inflation expectations fail to fall sufficiently to prevent the economy from experiencing output/employment costs. Third, closely related to the importance of policy credibility is the problem of dynamic time-inconsistency first highlighted by Finn Kydland and Edward Prescott (1977) in support of monetary policy being conducted by rules rather than discretion. The problem can be illustrated as follows (see Fischer 1990). Suppose the authorities announce a policy of monetary contraction to reduce inflation. If the policy is believed and economic agents revise downwards their inflation expectations then authorities who are not bound by a fixed monetary growth rate rule will have an incentive to cheat or renege on their announced policy in order to reduce unemployment. In circumstances where the authorities have such discretionary powers, and have in consequence an incentive to cheat, the credibility of announced policies will be significantly weakened. Since the difficulty of gaining credibility derives from the authorities having discretionary powers with respect to monetary policy the problem could be overcome by transferring the responsibility of anti-inflation policy to an independent central bank. Fourth, associated with the work of Robert Barro (1974; 1989 – reprinted on pp. 314–33) is the highly controversial Ricardian debt equivalence theorem limiting the usefulness of tax changes as a stabilization instrument. According to this theorem a bond-financed tax cut will leave consumption unchanged as the private sector will fully anticipate the future tax liability required to meet interest-payments on, and repayment of, the debt. The fifth main policy implication of the new classical approach concerns what policies the authorities should pursue if they wish to increase output/reduce unemployment permanently. Given that changes in output and employment are held to reflect the equilibrium supply decisions of firms and workers, given their perceptions of relative prices, it follows from this view that the appropriate policy measures to increase output and reduce unemployment are those that increase the microeconomic incentives for firms and workers to supply more output and labour. The final implications of the new classical approach for the formulation of macroeconomic policy concerns what is known as the 'Lucas critique' of econometric policy evaluation after the title of Robert Lucas's (1976) seminal paper in which the proposition first appeared. Lucas concluded that macroeconometric models should not be used to predict the consequences of alternative policies since the parameters of such models may change as economic agents adjust their expectations and behaviour to the new policy environment.

Despite the enormous influence of these and other developments, by about 1980 the Barro-Lucas-Sargent-Wallace monetary surprise explanation of the business cycle had reached both a theoretical and empirical impasse. On the theoretical front the implausibility of the assumption relating to informational confusion was widely recognized (Tobin 1980). New classical theorists argue that *nominal* rigidities are implausible in a world of rational agents who will always exhaust the opportunities for mutually beneficial trade (see Barro 1979). With sticky prices ruled out on methodological grounds new classical models were left without an acceptable explanation of the business cycle involving money to output causality. On the empirical front while early work, in particular the seminal papers by Robert Barro (1977, 1978) seemed to support the policy ineffectiveness proposition, subsequent studies most notably by Frederic Mishkin (1982) and Robert Gordon (1982) found evidence that suggested that both unanticipated and anticipated monetary policy affects output and employment. The depth of the recessions in both the USA and UK in the 1980–2 period following the Reagan and Thatcher deflations provided further ammunition to the critics. In addition opponents of the new classical approach drew attention to aggregate price and money supply data which are readily available to economic agents at a relatively low cost and questioned how this could be reconciled with the magnitude and length of actual business cycles supposedly caused by incomplete information. These criticisms led a number of economists who were sympathetic to the new classical approach to develop a mark II version which, while maintaining the assumptions of rational expectations and continuous market clearing, has reverted to a full information assumption relating to monetary developments and views business cycles as being predominantly caused by persistent real (supply-side) shocks rather than monetary (demand-side shocks) to the economy. Leading exponents and/or contributors to the so-called real business cycle approach include John Long, Charles Plosser, Robert Barro, Robert King, Finn Kydland and Edward Prescott.

THE REAL BUSINESS CYCLE APPROACH TO ECONOMIC FLUCTUATIONS

During the 1970s, with the rebirth of interest in business cycle research, economists became more involved with research into the statistical properties of economic time series. One of the main problems in this work is to separate trend from cycle. The conventional approach has been to imagine that the economy evolves along a path reflecting an underlying trend rate of growth described by Solow's neoclassical growth model (Solow 1956). This approach assumes that the supply determined long-run trend component of GDP is smooth with short-run fluctuations about trend being primarily determined by demand shocks. This conventional wisdom was accepted by Keynesian, monetarist and new classical economists alike until the early 1980s. The demand-shock models of all three groups interpret output deviations from trend as *temporary*. Whereas Keynesians such as James Tobin (1987) feel that such deviations could be severe and prolonged and therefore justify the need for corrective action, monetarists, and especially new classical economists, reject the need for activist stabilization policy having greater faith in the equilibrating power of market forces. Nelson and Plosser's (1982) important paper challenged this conventional wisdom. The research of Nelson and Plosser into macroeconomic time series led them to conclude that

> macroeconomic models that focus on monetary disturbances as a source of purely transitory fluctuations may never be successful in explaining a large fraction of output variation and that stochastic variation due to real factors is an essential element of any model of macroeconomic fluctuations.

Nelson and Plosser reached this important conclusion because in their research into US data they were unable to reject the hypothesis that GDP follows a random walk. Nelson and Plosser argue that most of the changes in GDP that we observe are *permanent* in that there is no tendency for output to revert to its former trend following a shock.

These findings of Nelson and Plosser have radical implications for business cycle theory. If shocks to productivity growth due to technological change are frequent and random then the path of output following a random walk will exhibit features which resemble a business cycle. In this case however *the observed fluctuations in GDP are fluctuations in the natural (trend) rate of output not deviations of output from a smooth deterministic trend*. What looks like output fluctuating around a smooth trend is in fact fluctuations in the trend itself due to a series of permanent shocks with each permanent productivity shock determining a new growth path. Whereas following Solow's seminal work economists have traditionally separated the analysis of growth from the analysis of fluctuations, the work of Nelson and Plosser suggests that the economic forces determining the trend are not different from those causing fluctuations. *Since permanent changes in GDP cannot result from monetary shocks in a new classical world because of the neutrality proposition embedded in the natural rate hypothesis the main forces causing instability must be real shocks*. Nelson and Plosser interpret their findings as placing limits on the importance of monetary theories of the business cycle and that real disturbances are likely to be a much more important source of output fluctuations. If there are important interactions between the process of growth and business cycles then the conventional practice of separating growth theory from the analysis of fluctuations is illegitimate. By ending the distinction between trend and cycle, real business cycle theorists have begun to integrate the theory of growth and fluctuations (see Kydland and Prescott 1982). Hence the basic real business cycle model is a stochastic dynamic equilibrium growth model.

The starting-point of the real business cycle approach (see Plosser 1989 – reprinted on pp. 396–424; Stadler 1994) is the assumption that the economy is subjected to random supply-side shocks, most notably large random fluctuations in the rate of technological progress. These large and random shocks to the production function result in fluctuations in relative prices to which rational economic agents respond. According to this approach observed fluctuations in output and employment are equilibrium phenomena and are the outcome of rational economic agents responding optimally to unavoidable changes in the economic environment. For example the approach controversially assumes that fluctuations in employment reflect voluntary changes in the amount of labour people wish to supply. As fluctuations in output and employment are seen as Pareto efficient responses to shocks to the production function the approach implies that monetary policy is irrelevant in explaining such fluctuations (see Van Els 1995). However, the main policy implication of the approach is that because the existence of fluctuations in GNP do not imply the failure of markets to clear and are instead regarded as fluctuations in the natural (trend) rate of output, the government should not attempt to reduce these fluctuations through stabilization policy not only because such attempts are unlikely to achieve their desired objective, but also because reducing instability would reduce welfare (see Prescott 1986 – reprinted on pp. 366–88). While monetary policy has no real effects, the government could do a great deal of harm if its taxation and spending policies distorted output and employment from the optimal amounts chosen by firms and workers. Needless to say the approach is highly controversial and has been subjected to a number of criticisms (see Summers 1986 – reprinted on pp. 389–95; Mankiw 1989 – reprinted on pp. 425–36). One final feature of the approach worth noting is that concerning the development of the calibration method. Rather than attempting to provide models capable of conventional econometric testing, real business cycle theorists have instead developed the calibration method in which the simulated results of their specific models (when hit by random shocks) in terms of key macroeconomic variables are compared with the actual behaviour of the economy. Real business cycle theory therefore represents a specific approach to macroeconomic modelling (see Lucas 1980; Danthine and Donaldson 1993).

NEW KEYNESIAN ECONOMICS

The third approach which has dominated the more recent development of macroeconomics is new Keynesian economics. Since the mid-1980s the new Keynesian school has emerged as the main rival to the new classical approach. Leading exponents and/or contributors to the approach include Gregory Mankiw, Olivier Blanchard, George Akerlof, Janet Yellen, David

Romer, Joseph Stiglitz and Bruce Greenwald. While most new Keynesian analysis incorporates the rational expectations and natural rate hypotheses, it does *not* incorporate the new classical assumption of continuous market clearing. Indeed the central focus of one important strand of the burgeoning new Keynesian literature has been to explore a variety of reasons for wage and price stickiness that prevent market clearing. This has involved research into the causes of (1) nominal wage stickiness (e.g. via overlapping long-term wage contracts); (2) nominal price stickiness (e.g. arising from menu or adjustment costs faced by monopolistically competitive firms); (3) real rigidities in both the labour market (e.g. via efficiency wage, insider–outsider and implicit contract models) and product market (e.g. via customer markets); and (4) co-ordination failures (see for example Gordon 1990 – reprinted on pp. 478–551; Mankiw and Romer 1991; D. Romer 1993).

One problem with the new Keynesian developments is that there is no single new Keynesian model, rather the research programme has led to a multiplicity of explanations of wage and price rigidities, and their macroeconomic consequences. Although the numerous explanations to be found in the literature are not necessarily mutually exclusive and often complement each other, it is the case that different economists within the new Keynesian research programme emphasize various aspects and causes of market imperfections and their macroeconomic consequences (see Stiglitz 1992). Bearing this in mind we draw attention to three policy implications that derive from new Keynesian analysis. First, in new Keynesian models which emphasize wage and price stickiness money is no longer neutral and policy effectiveness is re-established. For example, Stanley Fischer (1977) and Edmund Phelps and John Taylor (1977) have shown that nominal demand disturbances are capable of producing real effects in models incorporating rational expectations providing the new classical assumption of continuous market clearing is abandoned. In such models systematic monetary policy can help stabilize the economy. Second, the gradual adjustment of prices and wages in new Keynesian models implies that any policy of monetary disinflation, even if credible and anticipated by rational economic agents, will lead to a substantial recession (sacrifice ratio) in terms of output and employment. Furthermore in some new Keynesian analysis the equilibrium rate of unemployment is affected by the path taken by the actual rate of unemployment so that the natural rate is affected by the aggregate demand (see Cross 1996). In circumstances where unemployment remains above the natural rate for a prolonged period the natural rate itself will tend to increase due to so-called hysteresis effects. Not only will those who are unemployed suffer a deterioration of their human capital (skills) exacerbating the problem of structural unemployment, but the number of long-term unemployed is also likely to increase. In the latter case it is claimed that such outsiders exert little influence on wages and are unable to price their way back into jobs, and as a result the natural rate of unemployment rises.

Such hysteresis effects provide new Keynesians with a strong case to boost aggregate demand during a protracted recession. While monetarism and new classical macroeconomics undermined the case for 'fine' tuning, new Keynesians have championed the case for 'rough' or 'course' tuning where policies are designed to offset or avoid the more serious macro-level problems. Lastly, contrary to the new classical approach, new Keynesian analysis has provided a rationale for the existence of *involuntary* unemployment as an equilibrium phenomenon. For example, in efficiency wage models (see Yellen 1984) firms are reluctant to cut wages even in the face of an excess supply of labour (persistent unemployment) since such a policy would be counter-productive as lower efficiency/productivity would result. In summary the bulk of new Keynesian research has sought to develop models with coherent microfoundations, in order to explain why prices and wages adjust only gradually, and in doing so have sought to re-establish a case for policy effectiveness and justify interventionist policies (both supply and demand – management policies) to stabilize the economy. However, it should be noted that a second strand of new Keynesian work demonstrates how money is not neutral even if prices and wages are perfectly flexible (see Greenwald and Stiglitz 1993 – reprinted on pp. 552–74). Greenwald and Stiglitz follow Keynes (1936) and argue that increasing price flexibility could well be destabilizing.

THE RENAISSANCE OF ECONOMIC GROWTH ANALYSIS

The causes of the enormous differences in living standards across time and space have long been of interest to economists. Since rising living standards depend in the long run on economic growth it is extremely important for economists to understand and quantify this process. The consequences of even small-differences in growth rates when compounded over time, are striking. The example provided by Barro and Sala-i-Martin (1995) clearly brings this point out. The 1.75 per cent growth rate of real per capita income in the USA between 1870 and 1990 enabled real GDP per head to rise from $2,244 to $18,258. If the growth rate had been 0.75 per cent over the same period, income per capita would have risen to $5,519. However, if the growth rate had been 2.75 per cent the real income per person in 1990 would have been an astonishing $60,841! While short-run fluctuations in output have important welfare consequences (in the opinion of the majority of mainstream economists) it is evident that 'the welfare implications of long-run growth swamp any possible effects of the short-run fluctuations that macroeconomics traditionally focuses on' (D. Romer 1996). As we have seen Keynesian, monetarist and new classical analysis was primarily concerned with trying to understand short-run instability of output, employment and the price level. Some prominent macroeconomists now seem to regard these previous efforts as perhaps misguided given that the economic instability since the second world war has been a relatively 'minor problem' (Lucas, 1987 p.30). Barro and Sala-i-Martin (1995) are more forceful and are worth quoting:

> if we can learn about government policy options that have even small effects on the long-term growth rate, then we can contribute much more to improvements in standards of living than has been provided by the entire history of macroeconomic analysis of countercyclical policy and fine-tuning. Economic growth . . . is the part of macroeconomics that really matters.

Given the importance of economic growth it is surprising that economists' interest in the theoretical and empirical issues relating to the causes and consequences of growth has itself been cyclical. Dynamic issues were of major concern to the classical economists who sought to understand the nature and causes of the 'Wealth of Nations'. But following the 'marginalist revolution' in the 1870s neoclassical economists turned the focus of their attention towards problems associated with static microeconomic issues relating to the efficient allocation of resources. With the onset of the Great Depression and the subsequent Keynesian revolution, economists quite understandably switched their interest towards the causes of short-run aggregate instability. However, some notable Keynesian economists (e.g. Hansen) feared that the Great Depression represented more than a severe example of a business cycle downswing. Rather it was feared that there may be a long-run tendency for capitalist economies to produce an actual rate of growth less than the underlying growth of productive potential. Hansen's stagnation thesis was an important contributing factor leading to a reawakening of interest in long-run issues in the post-war period (for a discussion of the stagnation thesis see Ackley 1966: Chapter 18).

Between 1956 and 1970 economists refined and developed the Solow-Swan neoclassical growth model (see Solow 1956; 1957; Swan 1956). But thereafter, until the mid-1980s macroeconomic research was predominantly concerned with business cycle issues in the wake of the 1973 oil shocks and theoretical developments which absorbed the rational expectations hypothesis into macroeconomic analysis. Following the contributions of Paul Romer (1986) and Robert Lucas (1988) the study of economic growth has once again become a vibrant research area. In 1996 the first issue of a new *Journal of Economic Growth* was launched and many well-known macroeconomics textbooks now have their discussion of economic growth at the beginning rather than at the end of the text (see Mankiw 1994; D. Romer 1996). Economic growth has returned as an active research area and is central to contemporary macroeconomics.

The essential starting-point to any discussion of economic growth is the Solow growth model which has as its centrepiece the standard neoclassical production function (see Solow 1994 – reprinted on pp. 649–59). This well-known framework illuminates how growth of the capital stock and labour force interact with technological progress to produce more output. Given a

Cobb-Douglas production function with diminishing returns to factors and constant returns to scale, economic growth is the result of changes in both the quality and quantity of factor inputs. Household savings are converted via investment into a higher capital stock which generates growth of output. However because of diminishing returns the marginal product of capital declines as the capital–labour ratio rises. The accumulation of reproducible inputs contributes less and less to growth and will approach zero unless population growth and technological change allow the quality and quantity of non-reproducible factors to rise. In Solow's model the long-run rate of growth is driven by the exogenous factors of labour force growth and technological progress and is independent of the rate of investment. A change in the savings rate can have only a temporary effect on growth although the savings rate does influence the *level* of output per head. The growth of long-run *income per head* depends on total factor productivity which is driven by *exogenous* improvements in technology. Hence long-run growth appears to be beyond the influence of government policy.

A striking implication of the Solow model is that if technical progress is regarded as a public good and freely available to all countries, rich and poor, there should be no cross-country divergence of growth rates of income per capita. Differences in the *level* of per capita income result from variations in the capital–labour ratio. Hence countries with low initial incomes per capita due to low capital–labour ratios have the potential for rapid growth which will allow them to *catch up* the high income countries. This *convergence hypothesis* is conditional on the underlying determinants of the steady state (see Abramovitz 1986 – reprinted on pp. 582–603; Baumol 1986). The empirical evidence on the extent of convergence suggests that this process has been present among some industrialized countries but apart from a limited number of 'star' performers (particularly in East Asia) the convergence between developed and developing countries has been limited or absent. As a result there is growing evidence of widening disparities of income across the world's economies (see Dowrick 1992 – reprinted on pp. 604–15).

Given the absence of convergence when a broad sample of countries are considered a number of theorists, notably P. Romer (1986) and Lucas (1988), have developed growth models where two essential assumptions of the Solow model are abandoned, namely that technological change is exogenous and that all countries have the same access to technological opportunities (see P. Romer 1994 – reprinted on pp. 628–48). These endogenous theories of growth have dominated the new literature since the mid-1980s (see Van de Klundert and Smulders 1992; Pack 1994). In some models of endogenous growth there are constant returns to broad capital accumulation and investment in physical and human capital can permanently raise the growth of output per head. Other models stress endogenous innovation and reject the idea of a universally available technology. In this case poor countries may fail to catch up the leading countries because of 'idea gaps' rather than 'object gaps' (see P. Romer 1993; Crafts 1996). Lucas (1993) has argued that 'the main engine of growth is the accumulation of human capital – of knowledge – and the main source of differences in living standards among nations is differences in human capital'. Endogenous growth theory also gives rise to important policy implications which imply that governments can influence the long-run growth rate (see Shaw 1992 – reprinted on pp. 616–27).

CONCLUSION

Since the mid-1930s there has been considerable progress in our understanding of macroeconomic phenomena. Following the monetarist contributions a consensus of economists now accept that sustained inflation is a monetary phenomenon. New classical theory has produced numerous insights with respect to the role and conduct of stabilization policy. Real business cycle theorists have caused everyone to rethink basic issues associated with economic fluctuations. The insights provided by new Keynesian economists have transformed the microfoundations of the supply side of models which stress the importance of aggregate demand disturbances in explaining aggregate instability. Finally economists are once more producing valuable research into the causes of economic growth. In the chapters which follow we hope the reader can capture some of the excitement which has been a constant feature of the controversies which have characterized macroeconomics since Keynes first stimulated its development.

REFERENCES

*Titles marked with an asterisk are particularly recommended for additional reading.
*Abramovitz, M. (1986) 'Catching Up, Forging Ahead, and Falling Behind', *Journal of Economic History* 46, June, pp. 385–406.
Ackley, G. (1966) *Macroeconomic Theory*, New York: Collier-Macmillan.
Barro, R. J. (1974) 'Are Government Bonds Net Wealth?', *Journal of Political Economy* 82, November/December, pp. 1095–117.
Barro, R. J. (1977) 'Unanticipated Money Growth and Unemployment in the United States', *American Economic Review* 67, March, pp. 101–15.
Barro, R. J. (1978) 'Unanticipated Money, Output, and the Price Level in the United States', *Journal of Political Economy* 86, August, pp. 549–80.
Barro, R. J. (1979) 'Second Thoughts on Keynesian Economics', *American Economic Review* 69, May, pp. 54–9.
*Barro, R. J. (1989) 'The Ricardian Approach to Budget Deficits', *Journal of Economic Perspectives* 3, Spring, pp. 37–54.
Barro, R. J. and X. Sala-i-Martin (1995) *Economic Growth*, New York: McGraw-Hill.
*Baumol, W. (1986) 'Productivity Growth, Convergence and Welfare', *American Economic Review* 76, December, pp. 1072–85.
Bernanke, B. S. (1995) 'The Macroeconomics of the Great Depression: A Comparative Approach', *Journal of Money, Credit and Banking* 27, pp. 1–28.

Bernanke, B. S. and K. Carey (1996) 'Nominal Wage Stickiness and Aggregate Supply in the Great Depression', *Quarterly Journal of Economics* 111, August, pp. 853–83.

*Blackburn, K. and M. Christensen (1989) 'Monetary Policy and Policy Credibility: Theories and Evidence', *Journal of Economic Literature* 27, March, pp. 1–45.

*Blanchard, O. J. (1990) 'Why Does Money Affect Output? A Survey', in B. M. Friedman and F. H. Hahn (eds) *Handbook of Monetary Economics*, Amsterdam: North Holland.

Blinder, A. S. (1987) *Hard Heads, Soft Hearts: Tough-Minded Economics for a Just Society*, New York: Addison-Wesley.

*Blinder, A. S. (1988) 'The Fall and Rise of Keynesian Economics', *Economic Record* December, pp. 278–94.

*Brunner, K. (1989) 'The Disarray in Macroeconomics', in F. Capie and G. Wood (eds) *Monetary Economics in the 1980s*, London: Macmillan.

Chick, V. (1995) 'Is There a Case for Post-Keynesian Economics?' *Scottish Journal of Political Economy* 42, February, pp. 20–36.

Chrystal, K. A. and S. Price (1994) *Controversies in Macroeconomics*, 3rd edn, New York: Harvester Wheatsheaf.

*Crafts, N. (1996) 'Post-Neoclassical Endogenous Growth Theory: What are its Policy Implications?', *Oxford Review of Economic Policy* 12, pp. 30–47.

Cross, R. (ed.) (1995) *The Natural Rate of Unemployment: Reflections on 25 Years of the Hypothesis*, Cambridge: Cambridge University Press.

Cross, R. (1996) 'The Natural Rate: An Attractor for Actual Unemployment or an Attractee?', *Scottish Journal of Political Economy* 43, August, pp. 349–64.

Danthine, J. P. and J. B. Donaldson (1993) 'Methodological and Empirical Issues in Real Business Cycle Theory', *European Economic Review* 37, January, pp. 1–35.

Darity, W. and W. Young (1995) 'IS-LM: An Inquest', *History of Political Economy* 27, Spring, pp. 1–41.

Davidson, P. (1994) *Post Keynesian Macroeconomic Theory: A Foundation for Successful Economic Policies for the Twenty-First Century*, Aldershot: Edward Elgar.

Deutscher, P. (1990) *R. G. Hawtrey and the Development of Macroeconomics*, London: Macmillan.

Dixon, H. (1995) 'Of Coconuts, Decomposition and a Jackass: The Genealogy of the Natural Rate', in R. Cross (ed.) *The Natural Rate of Unemployment: Reflections on 25 Years of the Hypothesis*, Cambridge: Cambridge University Press.

*Dowrick, S. (1992) 'Technological Catch Up and Diverging Incomes: Patterns of Economic Growth 1960–88', *Economic Journal* 102, May, pp. 600–10.

Eichengreen, B. (1992) *Golden Fetters: The Gold Standard and the Great Depression, 1919–1939*, New York: Oxford University Press.

Fischer, S. (1977) 'Long-Term Contracts, Rational Expectations and the Optimal Money Supply Rule', *Journal of Political Economy* 85, February, pp. 191–205.

Fischer, S. (1990) 'Rules Versus Discretion in Monetary Policy', in B. M. Friedman and F. H. Hahn (eds) *Handbook of Monetary Economics*, Amsterdam: North Holland.

Friedman, M. (1956) 'The Quantity Theory of Money: A Restatement', in M. Friedman (ed.) *Studies in the Quantity Theory of Money*, Chicago: University of Chicago Press.

Friedman, M. (1958) 'The Supply of Money and Changes in Prices and Output', in M. Friedman (1969) *The Optimum Quantity of Money and Other Essays*, Chicago: Aldine.

Friedman, M. (1961) 'The Lag in the Effect of Monetary Policy', in M. Friedman (1969) *The Optimum Quantity of Money and Other Essays*, Chicago: Aldine.

*Friedman, M. (1968) 'The Role of Monetary Policy', *American Economic Review* 58, March, pp. 1–17.

*Friedman, M. (1970) *The Counter-Revolution in Monetary Theory*, IEA Occasional Paper no. 33, London: Institute of Economic Affairs.

Friedman, M. (1972) 'Have Monetary Policies Failed?', *American Economic Review* 62, May, pp. 11–18.

Friedman, M. (1974) *Monetary Correction*, IEA Occasional Paper no. 41, London: Institute of Economic Affairs.

*Friedman, M. (1977) 'Nobel Lecture: Inflation and Unemployment', *Journal of Political Economy* 85, June, pp. 451–72.

Friedman, M. and A. J. Schwartz (1963) *A Monetary History of the United States, 1867–1960*, Princeton, NJ: Princeton University Press.

Garrison, R. (1994) 'Interview with Roger Garrison', in B. Snowdon, H. R. Vane and P. Wynarczyk, *A Modern Guide to Macroeconomics: An Introduction to Competing Schools of Thought*, Aldershot: Edward Elgar.

*Gerrard, B. (1996) 'Review Article: Competing Schools of Thought in Macroeconomics – An Ever-Emerging Consensus?', *Journal of Economic Studies* 23, pp. 53–69.

Gordon, R. J. (1981) 'Output Fluctuations and Gradual Price Adjustment', *Journal of Economic Literature* 19, June, pp. 493–530.

Gordon, R. J. (1982) 'Price Inertia and Policy Ineffectiveness in the United States, 1890–1980', *Journal of Political Economy* 90, December, pp. 1087–117.

*Gordon, R. J. (1990) 'What is New Keynesian Economics?', *Journal of Economic Literature* 28, September, pp. 1115–71.

*Gordon, R. J. (1993) *Macroeconomics*, 6th edn, New York: HarperCollins.

Gordon, R. J. and J. A. Wilcox (1981) 'Monetarist Interpretations of the Great Depression: An Evaluation and Critique', in K. Brunner (ed.) *The Great Depression Revisited*, London: Martinus Nijhoff.

*Greenwald, B. C. and J. E. Stiglitz (1993) 'New and Old Keynesians', *Journal of Economic Perspectives* 7, Winter, pp. 23–44.

Hahn, F. H. and R. C. O. Matthews (1964) 'The Theory of Economic Growth: A Survey', *Economic Journal* 74, December, pp. 779–902.

*Hammond, J. D. (1996) *Theory and Measurement: Causality Issues in Milton Friedman's Monetary Economics*, Cambridge: Cambridge University Press.

Hansen, A. H. (1953) *A Guide to Keynes*, New York: McGraw-Hill.

Hicks, J. R. (1937) 'Mr. Keynes and the "Classics": A Suggested Interpretation', *Econometrica* 5, April, pp. 147–59.

Johnson, H. G. (1972) 'Inflation: A Monetarist View', in H. G. Johnson (ed.) *Further Essays in Monetary Economics*, London: Macmillan.

Keynes, J. M. (1936) *The General Theory of Employment, Interest and Money*, London: Macmillan.

Keynes, J. M. (1972) *Essays in Persuasion*, vol. IX, London: Macmillan.

Kydland, F. E. and E. C. Prescott (1977) 'Rules Rather than Discretion: The Inconsistency of Optimal Plans', *Journal of Political Economy* 85, June, pp. 473–91.

Kydland, F. E. and E. C. Prescott (1982) 'Time to Build and Aggregate Fluctuations', *Econometrica* 50, November, pp. 1345–70.

*Laidler, D. E. W. (1976) 'Inflation in Britain: A Monetarist Perspective', *American Economic Review* 66, September, pp. 485–500.

Laidler, D. E. W. (1985) 'Monetary Policy in Britain: Successes and Shortcomings', *Oxford Review of Economic Policy* 1, pp. 35–43.

Laidler, D. E. W. (1993) *The Demand for Money: Theories, Evidence and Problems*, 4th edn, New York: HarperCollins.

Lipsey, R. G. (1960) 'The Relationship between Unemployment and the Rate of Change of Money Wage Rates in the UK 1862–1957: A Further Analysis', *Economica* 27, February, pp. 1–31.

*Lipsey, R. G. (1978) 'The Place of the Phillips Curve in Macroeconomic Models', in A. R. Bergstrom (ed.) *Stability and Inflation*, Chichester: John Wiley.

Lucas, R. E. Jr (1972) 'Expectations and the Neutrality of Money', *Journal of Economic Theory* 4, April, pp. 103–24.

Lucas, R. E. Jr (1973) 'Some International Evidence on Output-Inflation Tradeoffs', *American Economic Review* 63, June, pp. 326–34.

Lucas, R. E. Jr (1975) 'An Equilibrium Model of the Business Cycle', *Journal of Political Economy* 83, December, pp. 1113–44.

Lucas, R. E. Jr (1976) 'Econometric Policy Evaluation: A Critique', in K. Brunner and A. H. Meltzer (eds) *The Phillips Curve and Labor Markets*, Amsterdam: North Holland.

*Lucas, R. E. Jr (1977) 'Understanding Business Cycles', in K. Brunner and A. H. Meltzer (eds) *Stabilization of the Domestic and International Economy*, Amsterdam: North Holland.

*Lucas, R. E. Jr (1980) 'Methods and Problems in Business Cycle Theory', *Journal of Money, Credit and Banking* 12, November, pp. 696–715.

Lucas, R. E. Jr (1987) *Models of Business Cycles*, Oxford: Basil Blackwell.

Lucas, R. E. Jr (1988) 'On the Mechanics of Economic Development', *Journal of Monetary Economics* 22, July, pp. 3–42.

Lucas, R. E. Jr (1993) 'Making a Miracle', *Econometrica* 61, March, pp. 251–72.

Lucas, R. E. Jr (1994) 'Review of Milton Friedman and Anna J. Schwartz's A Monetary History of the United States, 1867–1960', *Journal of Monetary Economics* 34, pp. 5–16.

*Mankiw, N. G. (1989) 'Real Business Cycles: A New Keynesian Perspective', *Journal of Economic Perspectives* 3, Summer, pp. 79–90.

*Mankiw, N. G. (1990) 'A Quick Refresher Course in Macroeconomics', *Journal of Economic Literature* 28, December, pp. 1645–60.

*Mankiw, N. G. (1994) *Macroeconomics*, 2nd edn, New York: Worth.

*Mankiw, N. G. (1995) 'The Growth of Nations', *Brookings Papers on Economic Activity*, pp. 275–326.

Mankiw, N. G. and D. Romer (eds) (1991) *New Keynesian Economics*, Cambridge: MIT Press.

Miron, J. A. (1994) 'Empirical Methodology in Macroeconomics: Explaining the Success of Friedman and Schwartz's A Monetary History of the United States, 1867–1960', *Journal of Monetary Economics* 34, pp. 17–25.

Mishkin, F. S. (1982) 'Does Anticipated Monetary Policy Matter? An Econometric Investigation', *Journal of Political Economy* 90, February, pp. 22–51.

*Modigliani, F. (1988) 'The Monetarist Controversy Revisited', *Contemporary Policy Issues* 6, October, pp. 3–18.

Muth, J. F. (1961) 'Rational Expectations and the Theory of Price Movements', *Econometrica* 29, July, pp. 315–35.

Nelson, C. and C. I. Plosser (1982) 'Trends and Random Walks in Macroeconomic Time Series: Some Evidence and Implications', *Journal of Monetary Economics* 10, September, pp. 139–62.

*Pack, H. (1994) 'Endogenous Growth Theory: Intellectual Appeal and Empirical Shortcomings', *Journal of Economic Perspectives* 8, Winter, pp. 55–72.

Phelps, E. S. (1967) 'Phillips Curves, Expectations of Inflation and Optimal Unemployment over Time', *Economica* 34, August, pp. 254–81.

Phelps, E. S. (1990) *Seven Schools of Macroeconomic Thought*, Oxford: Oxford University Press.

Phelps, E. S. and J. B. Taylor (1977) 'Stabilizing Powers of Monetary Policy under Rational Expectations', *Journal of Political Economy* 85, February, pp. 163–90.

Phillips, A. W. (1958) 'The Relation between Unemployment and the Rate of Change of Money Wage Rates in the United Kingdom, 1861–1957', *Economica* 25, November, pp. 283–99.

*Plosser, C. I. (1989) 'Understanding Real Business Cycles', *Journal of Economic Perspectives* 3, Summer, pp. 51–77.

*Prescott, E. C. (1986) 'Theory Ahead of Business Cycle Measurement', *Federal Reserve Bank of Minneapolis Quarterly Review* Fall, pp. 9–22.

*Romer, C. D. (1993) 'The Nation in Depression', *Journal of Economic Perspectives* 7, Spring, pp. 19–39.

*Romer, D. (1993) 'The New Keynesian Synthesis', *Journal of Economic Perspectives* 7, Winter, pp. 5–22.

Romer, D. (1996) *Advanced Macroeconomics*, New York: McGraw-Hill.

Romer, P. M. (1986) 'Increasing Returns and Long-Run Growth', *Journal of Political Economy* 94, October, pp. 1002–37.

*Romer, P. M. (1993) 'Idea Gaps and Object Gaps in Economic Development', *Journal of Monetary Economics* 32, pp. 543–73.

*Romer, P. M. (1994) 'The Origins of Endogenous Growth', *Journal of Economic Perspectives* 8, Winter, pp. 3–22.

Samuelson, P. A. (1955) *Economics*, 3rd edn, New York: McGraw-Hill.

Samuelson, P. A. and R. M. Solow (1960) 'Analytical Aspects of Anti-Inflationary Policy', *American Economic Review* 50, May, pp. 177–94.

*Santomero, A. M. and J. J. Seater (1978) 'The Inflation–Unemployment Trade-Off: A Critique of the Literature', *Journal of Economic Literature* 16, June, pp. 499–544.

Sargent, T. J. and N. Wallace (1975) 'Rational Expectations, the Optimal Monetary Instrument and the Optimal Money Supply Rule', *Journal of Political Economy* 83, April, pp. 241–54.

Sargent, T. J. and N. Wallace (1976) 'Rational Expectations and the Theory of Economic Policy', *Journal of Monetary Economics* 2, April, pp. 169–83.

*Shaw, G. K. (1992) 'Policy Implications of Endogenous Growth Theory', *Economic Journal* 102, May, pp. 611–21.

*Snowdon, B. and H. R. Vane (1997) 'Modern Macroeconomics and its Evolution from a Monetarist Perspective: An Interview with Professor Milton Friedman', *Journal of Economic Studies* 24.

*Snowdon, B., H. R. Vane and P. Wynarczyk (1994) *A Modern Guide to Macroeconomics: An Introduction to Competing Schools of Thought*, Aldershot: Edward Elgar.

Solow, R. M. (1956) 'A Contribution to the Theory of Economic Growth', *Quarterly Journal of Economics* 70, February, pp. 65–94.

Solow, R. M. (1957) 'Technical Change and the Aggregate Production Function', *Review of Economics and Statistics* 39, August, pp. 312–20.

Solow, R. M. (1986) 'What is a Nice Girl Like You Doing in a Place Like This? Macroeconomics after Fifty Years', *Eastern Economic Journal* 12, July/September, pp. 191–8.

*Solow, R. M. (1994) 'Perspectives on Growth Theory', *Journal of Economic Perspectives* 8, Winter, pp. 45–54.

*Stadler, G. W. (1994) 'Real Business Cycles', *Journal of Economic Literature* 32, December, pp. 1750–83.

Stiglitz, J. E. (1992) 'Methodological Issues and the New Keynesian Economics', in A. Vercelli and N. Dimitri (eds) *Macroeconomics: A Survey of Research Strategies*, Oxford: Oxford University Press.

*Summers, L. H. (1986) 'Some Sceptical Observations on Real Business Cycle Theory', *Federal Reserve Bank of Minneapolis Quarterly Review* Fall, pp. 23–7.

Swan, T. W. (1956) 'Economic Growth and Capital Accumulation', *Economic Record* 32, November, pp. 334–61.

*Taylor, J. B. (1989) 'The Evolution of Ideas in Macroeconomics', *Economic Record* 65, June, pp. 185–9.

*Tobin, J. (1980) 'Are New Classical Models Plausible Enough to Guide Policy?', *Journal of Money, Credit and Banking* 12, November, pp. 788–99.

Tobin, J. (1987) *Policies For Prosperity: Essays in a Keynesian Mode*, Brighton: Wheatsheaf.

*Tobin, J. (1992) 'An Old Keynesian Counterattacks', *Eastern Economic Journal* 18, Fall, pp. 387–400.

Tobin, J. (1995) 'The Natural Rate as New Classical Economics', in R. Cross (ed.) *The Natural Rate of Unemployment: Reflections on 25 Years of the Hypothesis*, Cambridge: Cambridge University Press.

Van de Klundert, T. and S. Smulders (1992) 'Reconstructing Growth Theory: A Survey', *De Economist* 140, pp. 177–203.

Van Els, P. J. A. (1995) 'Real Business Cycle Models and Money: A Survey of Theories and Evidence', *Weltwirtshaftliches Archiv* 131, pp. 223–63.

Vercelli, A. (1991) *Methodological Foundations of Macroeconomics: Keynes and Lucas*, Cambridge: Cambridge University Press.

Wulwick, N. (1987) 'The Phillips Curve: Which? Whose? To Do What? How?', *Southern Economic Journal* 53, pp. 834–57.

Yellen, J. L. (1984) 'Efficiency Wage Models of Unemployment', *American Economic Review* 74, May, pp. 200–5.

Young, W. (1987) *Interpreting Keynes: The IS-LM Enigma*, Boulder, CO: Westview.

Part I

Keynesian economics and the Keynesian revolution

Introduction

Keynesian economics, in all its many forms, challenges the legacy of Adam Smith's basic theorem that competitive markets are capable of converting the self-interested behaviour of millions of individuals into a desirable macroeconomic outcome. To Keynes the 'invisible hand' mechanism is fundamentally flawed in that capitalist market systems seem incapable of generating the full utilization of societies scarce labour and capital resources except for limited periods of time. Given that the economic system is subject to periodic aggregate demand and supply shocks, a key question for macroeconomic theorists is: 'Will the economy, once displaced from its full employment equilibrium, return to that desirable state in a reasonable period of time via the normal functioning of the price mechanism operating without assistance from the "visible hand" of government intervention?' Keynesians of *all* persuasions share the view that some degree of selective government intervention, via fiscal and monetary policies, can improve upon the 'invisible hand' inspired non-interventionist stance of the classical economists and their modern day disciples (see Snowdon *et al.* 1994; Tobin 1996; Shaw 1997).

Although few, if any, economists have had an impact on the development of modern macroeconomics to compare with that of John Maynard Keynes, the essential message of his magnum opus, *The General Theory of Employment, Interest and Money* (1936), remains the subject of continuing controversy some sixty years following its publication. This is hardly surprising given the impact the *General Theory* has had in three important areas. First, the resultant theoretical revolution in the then newly created field of macroeconomics has inspired an ongoing theoretical debate concerning the equilibrating properties of the price mechanism. Second, in parallel to the theoretical revolution, it led to a policy revolution which represented a major shift in thinking which subsequently encountered political and intellectual resistance from those who remain wedded to the classical *laissez-faire* philosophy associated with the invisible hand doctrine (see Moggridge 1993; Skidelsky 1996). Third, as Colander and Landreth (1996) note, it led to a pedagogical (textbook) revolution which reflected the real need for economists to devise ways of distilling Keynes's ideas and presenting his theoretical innovations in a format which made them more accessible to a wider audience. In the latter case the rapid acceptance of Hicks's (1937) IS-LM model as the mainstream presentation of Keynes's ideas (e.g. Hansen 1953) and Samuelson's (1948) best-selling textbook were crucial in the 'Keynesianization' of academia. However, one unfortunate consequence of this pedagogical revolution was that it gave further impetus to the already growing separation of microeconomics from macroeconomics. Hence much of the modern debate between new Keynesians and new classical / real business cycle theorists has arisen from conflicting views about how to reconcile these two main branches of economics. The burgeoning literature on the microfoundations of macroeconomics since the early 1970s is testimony to the legacy of the Keynesian revolution (see Part V). The ongoing debate relating to the interpretation and relevance of Keynes's ideas remains an important source of controversy in macroeconomics and forms a major theme in the chapters which follow.

Alan Coddington's 1976 *Journal of Economic Literature* article, 'Keynesian Economics: The Search for First Principles' (reprinted on pp. 36–54) inquires into the various ways in which economic analysis has been used in an attempt to come to terms with Keynes's attack on classical economics and methods of analysis. Coddington identifies the classical method as 'reductionist' because the central idea is to analyse market phenomena on the basis of rational choices made by individual economic agents. Those Keynesians who see Keynes's work as a 'frontal assault' on the reductionist programme are classified as 'fundamentalists' by Coddington. Fundamentalist Keynesians place a great deal of emphasis on Keynes's 1937 *Quarterly Journal of Economics* article with its extensive discussion and focus on the influence of uncertainty, expectations and ignorance. Fundamentalist Keynesians regard Keynes as having liberated economic analysis from the strait-jacket of equilibrium theorizing. Coddington's second school of Keynesian thought is labelled 'hydraulic Keynesianism' and refers to the mainstream textbook Keynesianism associated with the neoclassical synthesis. The crucial feature of hydraulic (IS-LM) Keynesianism is the belief that stable relationships exist between variables at the aggregate level which provide governments with the potential leverage to influence real income and employment via fiscal and monetary policy. Coddington shows how this hydraulic approach to theorizing, by suppressing the role of price adjustment, is in conflict with reductionist market theory. Finally, Coddington discusses the contributions of Clower and Leijonhufvud, who argue that Keynesian economics is best understood within a disequilibrium trading framework. Their work is classified as 'reconstituted reductionism' and is important in that it challenges the neoclassical synthesis view which had downplayed Keynes's contribution as a pure economic theorist.

The second article reprinted in this part (pp. 55–94) is Don Patinkin's 1990 *Journal of Monetary Economics* article, 'On Different Interpretations of the General Theory'. Patinkin argues that it was not until the 1960s that major differences among the various interpretations of the *General Theory* began to appear. An important question is raised: Why are there so many 'vastly different' interpretations of the *General Theory*? Patinkin attributes this phenomenon to (1) the non-mathematical style of the *General Theory*; (2) its presentation of new and controversial ideas which contained 'some obscurities and even inconsistencies', (3) the failure of Keynes to pull together an explicit and complete model, this being left to numerous subsequent interpreters, and (4) the political implications and message of the *General Theory* which implied an extension of government intervention in the economy. Patinkin defends the IS-LM interpretation of Keynes which became the hallmark of mainstream Keynesianism in the 1950s and 1960s (see also Patinkin 1990; Darity and Young 1995). In doing so Patinkin provides a critique of the Post-Keynesian (fundamentalist) interpretation of the *General Theory* as well as the more recent reappraisal of Keynes by Allan Meltzer (1988). Patinkin rejects Meltzer's contention that Keynes favoured rules rather than discretion in the conduct of economic policy.

The chapters by Coddington and Patinkin show clearly that Keynes's *General Theory* has given rise to a number of different interpretations and generated a variety of research programmes. Bill Gerrard, in his article 'Keynes's General Theory: Interpreting the Interpretations' taken from the March 1991 issue of the *Economic Journal* (reprinted on pp. 95–108), puts forward the view that the reason why there is still so much controversy surrounding Keynes's *General Theory* is in part due to 'different presuppositions made about the nature of interpretation'. Gerrard argues that the study of hermeneutics (the study of interpretation) can help pierce the 'doctrinal fog' surrounding Keynesian economics. He presents two variants of the 'atomistic' approach to interpretation, namely the objectivist and relativist approaches. The former seeks to recover the author's original message which is hidden due to author- and reader-generated confusion, as well as disagreement over the stock of relevant textual evidence. The relativist approach treats interpretation as being determined by the worldview of the reader. Hence there is no single essential meaning. Gerrard argues that both varieties of the atomistic view of interpretation are flawed and suggests a second alternative, the 'organicist' approach. Of special interest, given our earlier discussion of the chapters by Coddington and Patinkin, is the proposition that *the existence of multiple interpretations is not a problem.* Multiple interpretation is taken as evidence of the high reference power and fertility of the text under examination. Indeed the main achievement of Keynes's *General Theory* 'was its ability to generate a diversity of research programmes'. Gerrard concludes that we should 'stop worrying about multiple interpretations of Keynes's *General Theory*' as it represents a strength rather than a weakness of his contribution.

During the 1970s Keynesian economics was generally regarded as exhibiting strong symptoms of crisis suggesting terminal decline. It was during this period that new classical economics (see Part III) began to provide penetrating critiques of both the theoretical and empirical foundations of Keynesian orthodoxy. In a highly entertaining and insightful article (reprinted on pp. 109–34) published in the December 1988 issue of the *Economic Record*, Alan Blinder surveys macroeconomic developments following the demise of the original stable Phillips curve analysis circa 1972. Blinder traces out the reasons for the declining influence of the Keynesian approach to macroeconomic analysis during the 1970s as well as the resurgence of Keynesian theorizing within academia during the 1980s (see also Blinder 1987). Blinder begins by discussing the essential characteristics which in his view identify what it means to be a Keynesian. Of particular importance is the emphasis placed on aggregate demand disturbances as a major source of aggregate fluctuations, the significance of wage and price stickiness, the need to reduce excessive levels of involuntary unemployment and the potential role for some degree of stabilization policy via 'coarse tuning'. Blinder goes on to argue that the fall of Keynesian economics had more to do with perceived theoretical shortcomings than empirical failure once the lessons of the expectations-augmented Phillips curve, and supply shocks of the 1970s, had been absorbed into mainstream macroeconomic analysis. In addition he identifies certain internal forces within academia which worked against the prevailing orthodoxy including the attraction that new classical economics generated for the new generation of technically sophisticated graduate students and faculty members seeking tenure (see Snowdon and Vane 1996). Finally, Blinder suggests that a fourth important factor contributing to the fall of Keynesianism was the resurgence of Conservative ideology in the United States and elsewhere. When it comes to explaining the resurgence of Keynesian economics in the 1980s Blinder draws attention to the growing body of empirical evidence mounted against the new classical model as well as theoretical deficiencies. At the same time new theoretical developments within the Keynesian paradigm have resulted in the re-emergence of Keynesian models with stronger microfoundations (see Part V). Important developments here include the use of imperfect competition as the basic microfoundation for Keynesian models, the use of efficiency wage theories to explain involuntary unemployment, the incorporation of costly price adjustment as an influence on optimal decision making and hysteresis models of unemployment which question Friedman's (1968) natural rate hypothesis (reprinted in Part II, pp. 164–79). As a result of these and other developments Blinder believes that once more Keynesian economics is on the 'ascendancy in academia'.

The final paper reprinted in this part (pp. 135–55) is by one of the world's foremost Keynesian economists, James Tobin. In an article entitled 'Price Flexibility and Output Stability: An Old Keynesian View', Tobin presents an articulate and spirited defence of what he considers to be the essence of Keynesianism. In proudly declaring himself to be an 'old Keynesian' Tobin is keen to distance himself from the new Keynesian views of economists such as Gregory Mankiw (see Part V and Tobin 1994). Tobin's article was originally published as part of a symposium on new Keynesian economics in the Winter issue of the *Journal of Economic Perspectives*, which also contains articles by D. Romer (1993), Greenwald and Stiglitz (1993 – reprinted on pp. 552–74) and King (1993). According to Tobin the central Keynesian proposition is not nominal price rigidity (as stressed by many new Keynesians) but the principle of 'effective' demand. Tobin argues that Keynesian economics in the spirit of Keynes's *General Theory* 'neither asserts nor requires nominal wage and/or price rigidity'. Tobin also differs from much new Keynesian analysis in stressing the importance of *real* shocks to aggregate demand rather than *nominal* disturbances. Given such disturbances Tobin shows how Keynes provided an explanation of aggregate fluctuations where greater wage and price flexibility would more than likely turn recession into depression due to the adverse expectational effects generated during a regime of deflation. Tobin dismisses the practical relevance of the Pigouvian real balance (or wealth) effect as an equilibrating mechanism relying as it does on a highly risky regime of deflation. Tobin concludes by restating the 'old' Keynesian policy position; 'that in the absence of activist "feedback" policies, monetary and fiscal, flexibility may well be destabilizing, both to prices and to real macro variables'.

REFERENCES

*Titles marked with an asterisk are particularly recommended for additional reading.

*Abel, A. B. and B. S. Bernanke (1995) *Macroeconomics*, 2nd edn, Chapter 12, New York: Addison Wesley.

*Backhouse, R. (1995) *Interpreting Macroeconomics: Explorations in the History of Economic Thought*, London: Routledge.

*Backhouse, R. (1997) 'The Rhetoric and Methodology of Modern Macroeconomics', in B. Snowdon and H. R. Vane (eds) *Reflections on the Development of Modern Macroeconomics*, Aldershot: Edward Elgar.

Barro, R. J. and V. Grilli (1994) *European Macroeconomics*, Chapter 21, London: Macmillan.

Blaug, M. (1990) *John Maynard Keynes: Life, Ideas, Legacy*, London: Institute of Economic Affairs.

*Blaug, M. (1994) 'Recent Biographies of Keynes', *Journal of Economic Literature* 32, September, pp. 1204–15.

*Bleaney, M. (1985) *The Rise and Fall of Keynesian Economics*, London: Macmillan.

Blinder, A. S. (1987) *Hard Heads Soft Hearts: Tough Minded Economics for a Just Society*, New York: Addison Wesley.

*Colander, D. C. and H. Landreth (eds) (1996) *The Coming of Keynesianism to America: Conversations with the Founders of Keynesian Economics*, Aldershot: Edward Elgar.

Darity, W. and W. Young (1995) 'IS-LM: An Inquest', *History of Political Economy* 27, Spring, pp. 1–41.

Davidson, P. (1994) *Post Keynesian Macroeconomic Theory: A Foundation for Successful Economic Policies for the Twenty-First Century*, Aldershot: Edward Elgar.

Fletcher, G. A. (1987) *The Keynesian Revolution and its Critics: Issues of Theory and Policy for the Monetary Production Economy*, London: Macmillan.

*Friedman, M. (1968) 'The Role of Monetary Policy', *American Economic Review* 58, March, pp. 1–17.

*Froyen, R. T. (1996) *Macroeconomics: Theories and Policies*, 5th edn, Chapters 6, 7 and 8, London: Prentice-Hall.

Gerrard, B. and J. Hillard (eds) (1992) *The Philosophy and Economics of J. M. Keynes*, Aldershot: Edward Elgar.

*Greenwald, B. C. and J. E. Stiglitz (1993) 'New and Old Keynesians', *Journal of Economic Perspectives* 7, Winter, pp. 23–44.

Hansen, A. H. (1953) *A Guide to Keynes*, New York: McGraw-Hill.

Hicks, J. R. (1937) 'Mr. Keynes and the "Classics": A Suggested Interpretation', *Econometrica* 5, April, pp. 147–59.

*Hillard, J. (ed.) (1988) *J. M. Keynes in Retrospect: The Legacy of the Keynesian Revolution*, Aldershot: Edward Elgar.

*Jansen, D. W., C. D. Delorme and R. B. Ekelund, Jr (1994) *Intermediate Macroeconomics*, Chapters 3, 4, 5 and 6, New York: West.

Keynes, J. M. (1936) *The General Theory of Employment, Interest and Money*, London: Macmillan.

Keynes, J. M. (1937) 'The General Theory of Employment', *Quarterly Journal of Economics* 51, February, pp. 209–23.

King, R. G. (1993) 'Will the New Keynesian Macroeconomics Resurrect the IS-LM Model?' *Journal of Economic Perspectives* 7, Winter, pp. 67–82.

*Mankiw, N. G. (1994) *Macroeconomics*, 2nd edn, Chapters 9, 10 and 11, New York: Worth.

Meltzer, A. H. (1988) *Keynes's Monetary Theory: A Different Interpretation*, Cambridge: Cambridge University Press.

*Moggridge, D. E. (1993) *Keynes*, 3rd edn, London: Macmillan.

Patinkin, D. (1990) 'In Defense of IS-LM', *Banca Nazionale Del Lavoro Quarterly Review* March, pp. 119–34.

Romer, D. (1993) 'The New Keynesian Synthesis', *Journal of Economic Perspectives* 7, Winter, pp. 5–22.

Samuelson, P. A. (1948) *Economics*, New York: McGraw-Hill.

*Shaw, G. K. (1988) *Keynesian Economics: The Permanent Revolution*, Aldershot: Edward Elgar.

*Shaw, G. K. (1997) 'How Relevant is Keynesian Economics Today?', in B. Snowdon and H. R. Vane (eds) *Reflections on the Development of Modern Macroeconomics*, Aldershot: Edward Elgar.

*Skidelsky, R. (1996) *Keynes*, Oxford: Oxford University Press.

Snowdon, B. and H. R. Vane (1996) 'The Development of Modern Macroeconomics: Reflections in the Light of Johnson's Analysis after Twenty-Five Years', *Journal of Macroeconomics* 18, Summer, pp. 381–401.

*Snowdon, B., H. R. Vane and P. Wynarczyk (1994) *A Modern Guide to Macroeconomics: An Introduction to Competing Schools of Thought*, Chapters 1, 2 and 3, Aldershot: Edward Elgar.

Tobin, J. (1994) 'Interview with James Tobin', in B. Snowdon, H. R. Vane and P. Wynarczyk, *A Modern Guide to Macroeconomics: An Introduction to Competing Schools of Thought*, Aldershot: Edward Elgar.

Tobin, J. (1996) *Full Employment and Growth: Further Keynesian Essays on Policy*, Aldershot: Edward Elgar.

QUESTIONS

1 Why are there so many different interpretations of Keynes's *General Theory*?

2 To what extent did Keynes make a distinct break from the classical economists and their methods of analysis?

3 'In the old Keynesian view there are two regimes: the Keynesian regime where demand creates its own supply and the classical regime where economic activity is supply constrained'. Explain and discuss.

4 Examine the importance of price flexibility in the Keynes v. Classics debate. Is price flexibility stabilizing?

5 What were the main reasons for the demise of Keynesianism during the 1970s? To what extent have Keynesian models been rehabilitated in recent years?

6 How relevant is Keynesian economics today?

7 'The era of discretionary demand management is over because the Keynesian view of governments as benign social welfare maximizers is discredited beyond repair'. Critically appraise this view.

8 How and why do the 'fundamentalist' and 'hydraulic' interpretations of Keynes differ?

9 To what extent did the neoclassical synthesis interpretation of Keynes introduce an artificial separation of microeconomics from macroeconomics?

10 'Creating visions is much more difficult than refining them'. What are the main features of Keynes's vision created in the *General Theory*?

2 Keynesian economics

The search for first principles

Alan Coddington
Journal of Economic Literature (1976) 14, December, pp. 1258–73

INTRODUCTION

In *The General Theory of Employment, Interest and Money* [13, 1936] and elsewhere, Keynes attacked a body of theory that he designated 'Classical'. In posing a threat to the 'Classical' system – or at least to a recognizable caricature of it – Keynes also called into question the method of analysis by which this system was constructed. The purpose of this article is to inquire into the various ways in which methods of economic analysis have come to terms with this threat, either by responding to it or by reinforcing it with further threats; it seeks to ask the question: 'What has to be changed or sacrificed in order to accommodate Keynesian ideas within standard methods of analysis?' Its theme will be the variety of ways in which this may be done: three broad types will be presented and the contrasts between them explored.

The first task accordingly is to characterize the method of analysis of that body of theory in opposition to which Keynes presented his own. Very broadly, this method consisted of analyzing markets on the basis of the choices made by individual traders. Thus, the resulting theory operates at two distinct levels – that of individual choice, and that of market phenomena – even though the connection between the two levels may be provided only by an analysis of the choices of a 'representative' trader. Moreover, in order to provide a basis for a manageable analysis of market phenomena, the analysis of individual choice has to be of a particularly stereotyped and artificial kind. This method of analysis, using market theory based on choice theory of a type that allows the two levels to be connected, I will refer to as 'reductionism', on the grounds that the central idea is the *reduction* of market phenomena to (stylized) individual choices.

Considerations of tractability impose restrictions on the kind of choice theory on which the market theory can be based: the theory cannot deal with choices in all the idiosyncratic detail in which actors conceive of them, nor in terms of the elusive and wayward manner in which actors make up their minds; stable objectives and well-defined constraints are needed to provide a firm enough foundation for market theory. And just as the choice theory has to be restricted in the interests of building up to market theory, so the market theory has to be restricted in the interests of working back to choice theory. Overwhelmingly, reductionist theorizing has confined its attention to situations of market equilibrium; for these situations a choice theory basis is relatively straightforward. There may be, in accordance with the standard schedules, a gap between market demand and market supply, but the choice theory from which each of these schedules is derived supposes that all choices are realizable; accordingly, the standard schedules can tell us nothing about what will happen when the traders attempt to do what, in the aggregate, is impossible; nor are the schedules likely to persist as the traders become aware of the difficulty of doing what they had regarded, in making their (intended) choices, as straightforward. Overwhelmingly, therefore, reductionist theory has been concerned with the connection between equilibrium states of market phenomena and the choice logic from which these states could be generated. It should be noted, however, that this concern with market equilibrium is not a defining characteristic of reductionism: it is rather a way in which reductionist theorizing has been rendered manageable.

FUNDAMENTALIST KEYNESIANISM

If Keynes's ideas are to be seen as a threat to the reductionist program, the question naturally arises of how serious a threat they are: of how fundamental the aspects are that are threatened. Those who have seen Keynes's work as a frontal assault on the whole reductionist program, I will refer to as 'fundamentalist Keynesians'. It is the purpose of this section to expound such an interpretation, to consider some of the difficulties in sustaining it, and briefly to discuss its significance for economic theorizing.

Like the interpretation of the work of any active mind, the interpretation of Keynes's writings requires the use of selection and emphasis: it requires a view as to what is central and what merely peripheral, what is essential and what merely incidental, in his writings; in this way apparent inconsistencies and obscurities may readily be resolved, at least to the satisfaction of those adhering to that interpretation. For fundamentalists, what is central and essential in Keynes's writing is to be found primarily in his article 'The General Theory of Employment' [14, 1937] in the *Quarterly Journal of Economics* of 1937, an article concisely restating the argument of the *General Theory* in response to various critics; in the *General Theory* itself, the essence is said to lie in Chapter 12, 'The State of Long-Term Expectations', and, to a lesser extent, in Chapter 17, 'The Essential Properties of Interest and Money'. The kind of considerations to be found in these places can be traced back at least to the work of ten years earlier in *The End of Laissez-Faire* [12, 1926] and, with hindsight, still further back.

An early statement of the fundamentalist position was provided by Hugh Townsend [28, 1937]. He argued that the kind of considerations raised by

Keynes in his theory of liquidity preference have quite devastating consequences for reductionist price theory if they are allowed to apply to all assets. Once all prices are seen as *money* prices, and all assets as bearing a liquidity premium, price theory becomes enmeshed in the same tangle of expectational and conventional elements that characterize Keynes's theory of the rate of interest. On this view, the hope of extracting 'real' (relative) prices from their monetary context looks bleak; although we should not, as Hicks [9, 1946: ch. 12] has pointed out, confuse Keynes's innovation in analytical procedure (in dealing with the rate of interest in association with money-holding decisions rather than with borrowing and lending) with his substantive contributions. Nevertheless, the threat to the reductionist program does, on this view, indeed appear to be a fundamental one.

Perhaps the most uncompromising, and certainly the most tirelessly eloquent, exponent of fundamentalist Keynesianism is G. L. S. Shackle [25, 1967; 26, 1972; 27, 1974]. His own work has centered on the irreducibly creative element in human choice: its basis in constructs of the choosing mind. His appreciation of Keynes's contributions to economic theory has, accordingly, centered around this same concern, and naturally he sees these matters of expectation, uncertainty, and ignorance – matters of the provision of knowledge-surrogates in the face of knowledge deficiency – as of the essence. A most succinct distillation of Shackle's reading of Keynes has been provided by B. J. Loasby [17, 1976].

One further line of thought must be mentioned in the present context: this is one that has attempted to use the fundamentalist aspect of Keynesianism as a way of clearing the ground to permit a return to a certain cluster of doctrines and concerns that are variously referred to as 'classical' (as distinct from 'neoclassical') or 'Neo-Ricardian'. The objective of this school, whose most distinguished practitioner is Joan Robinson, is to produce a hybrid of Keynesianism with those aspects of Ricardo's work that were appropriated by Marx: Ricardo minus Say's law and the quantity theory of money.

Keynes's *QJE* paper of 1937, to which fundamentalists attach such great importance, is, first and foremost, an attack on the kind of choice theory that is required for the reductionist program. As against the clearly specified and stable objectives and constraints required by reductionist theorizing, Keynes emphasizes that the basis of choice lies in vague, uncertain, and shifting expectations of future events and circumstances: expectations that have no firm foundation in circumstances, but that take their cues from the beliefs of others, and that will be sustained by hopes, undermined by fears and continually buffeted by 'the news'. He was drawing attention to both the importance and the elusiveness of the state of business confidence, and the way it unfolds. Keynes focused on the conventional element in valuation: the way in which valuations may persist to the extent that they are shared, but are thereby rendered sustainable in the face both of minor events and of changes in circumstances, but vulnerable to anything that threatens this conventional basis. In the course of a riot, for example, the moods and feelings of the rioters may be widely shared until, at a later stage when the riot has lost its force, the moods and feeling may generally and rapidly revert to normal. The coordination of such crowd behavior and its characteristic dynamics arise from the fact that the participants are taking their cues directly from one another. Reductionist choice theory as it has been developed does not shed any light on decisions involving such immediate and strong interdependence as this.

Once its choice-theoretic foundations are threatened, the whole reductionist program is called into question; for without them the market theory would have nothing on which to stand, nothing to which it could be reduced. The concept of market equilibrium is in this way left exposed to attack. For without a clearly-specified and stable basis in choice logic, the idea of market equilibrium is no longer connected to the realizability of individuals' intentions in the aggregate. This does not mean that market equilibrium cannot be rehabilitated; what it means is that the sustainability of equilibrium must depend on conditions that are confined to the level of the market. For the fundamentalist, however, Keynes's ideas require the rethinking and reconstruction of the whole body of reductionist theory: its choice-theoretic basis and the equilibrium theory of markets that rests on it.

The objections to equilibrium theorizing have been elaborated by fundamentalist Keynesians. Joan Robinson has shown that if the idea of equilibrium is pursued relentlessly, then as the concept becomes all-embracing it becomes paralyzed by its own logic: equilibrium becomes a state of affairs that is, strictly, unapproachable: unless it already exists, there is no way of attaining it [20, 1953]. Similarly, in the work of G. L. S. Shackle, the idea of general equilibrium is shown to require the *pre-reconciliation*, one with another, of all present and future choices of all economic actors [26, 1972]. On either ground it would follow that the standard use of the method of comparative statics (or, better, 'comparative equilibria') to analyze the effects of changes in circumstances, is strictly unwarranted and illegitimate.[1] Of course, this line of thought would have nihilistic consequences for the entire corpus of economic theory and in particular for its applicability; in this respect, the line of thought reaches a purist and impractical conclusion that is in marked contrast to Keynes's own highly eclectic approach to economic theory.

The concept of equilibrium is accordingly seen by fundamentalists not as a useful simplification for economic theorists, but as a distraction.[2] The essence of Keynes's thought is seen as the liberation from equilibrium theorizing, as an escape from the restrictions that it imposes on our thinking. This, however, is not so much a matter of what Keynes said, as of what we are led to if we follow his line of thought, taking the *QJE* article as the definitive guide to its direction.

Where we are led by a line of thought depends a great deal, of course, on where we are disposed to go. Fundamentalists have, correspondingly, contributed freely of their own preoccupations in arriving at interpretations of Keynes's thought. At their most uninhibited, fundamentalist Keynesians have presented Keynes's ideas as an escape from the essential 'timelessness' of the modes of thought he attacked. More concretely, they have presented his central message regarding employment as concerning the existence of a liquid asset in a world of uncertainty, thus providing a retreat from the holding of real assets and the associated commitment to (employment-generating) production of a particular output. This theme has been much elaborated by Shackle and is concisely expounded by Loasby; in Joan Robinson's work, however, we find its place taken by a preoccupation with the heterogeneity of capital goods: the fact that individual items of the capital stock that history bequeaths to us cannot be costlessly transformed into one another, but exist in particular forms, embodying particular techniques, reflecting the superseded expectations of the past. The problems raised by the existence of liquid assets and durable, functionally specific capital assets, are not, however, unrelated; the nature of capital goods means that holding them involves a kind of commitment, while the nature of liquidity allows an escape from that particular commitment.

Fundamentalist Keynesianism, in seeing Keynes's ideas as a wholesale onslaught on the reductionist program, does not see those ideas as providing a substitute for that program. Rather, it sees Keynes's own ideas as a *first step* in a thorough-going revision of economic theory. Accordingly, it sees what Keynes did *constructively* as merely a makeshift, an improvisation, a stop-gap. To take the constructive part of Keynes's work (in developing the consumption function, the marginal efficiency of capital schedule, etc.) as being the substance or result of 'the Keynesian Revolution' would therefore betoken a failure of nerve, a betrayal of fundamentalist principles.[3]

In order to sustain the fundamentalist interpretation, it is necessary to postulate that Keynes himself had occasional lapses. Thus, Joan Robinson [23, 1973: 3] writes:

> there were moments when we had some trouble in getting Maynard to see what the point of his revolution really was, but when he came to sum it up after the book was published he got it into focus.

Here she refers, of course, to the *QJE* article of 1937.

Again, she writes [21, 1964: 75]:

> The *General Theory* broke through the unnatural barrier and brought history and theory together again. But for theorists the descent into time has not been easy. After twenty years the awakened Princess is still dazed and groggy.
>   Keynes himself was not quite steady on his feet.

She then goes on to refer [21, 1964: 75] to Keynes's ('highly suspicious') remark about the timeless multiplier [13, 1936: 122].

A major embarrassment for fundamentalists is to be found in the final chapter of the *General Theory*. Here we find Keynes arguing as follows [13, 1936: 378–9]:

> if our central controls succeed in establishing an aggregate volume of output corresponding to full employment as nearly as is practicable, the classical theory comes into its own from this point onwards. If we suppose the volume of output to be given, *i.e.* to be determined by forces outside the classical scheme of thought, then there is no objection to be raised against the classical analysis of the manner in which private self-interest will determine what in particular is produced, in what proportions the factors of production will be combined to produce it, and how the value of the final product will be distributed between them.

This is abundantly clear, and in obvious conflict with the fundamentalist view of Keynes's thought being subversive of the whole classical ('reductionist') scheme. Accordingly, we find Joan Robinson writing [21, 1964: 92], in connection with this passage, of the 'fallacy' that Keynes fell into, and remarking sadly that, 'He was himself partly to blame for the perversion of his ideas' and 'Keynes himself began the reconstruction of the orthodox scheme that he had shattered' [22, 1971: ix].

A further embarrassment for fundamentalists is that Keynes indicated quite clearly that he found nothing to object to in Hicks's distillation [8, 1937] of the *General Theory* into the *IS-LM* framework, or what has come to be known as 'the income-expenditure model', quite devoid of any fundamentalist characteristics.[4] This again must be seen as some kind of momentary lapse on Keynes's part if the fundamentalist interpretation is to be sustained, at any rate if Keynes himself is to be allowed to be a fundamentalist Keynesian.

What, then, does fundamentalism add up to? It does not provide any sort of determinate theory or model of how the economy functions at the aggregate level; it does not enable one to make any definite predictions about the likely effects of alternative policies or circumstances. On the contrary, it is a viewing point from which such constructions would appear as rather desperate makeshifts of transient applicability. Fundamentalist Keynesianism is concerned with the texture rather than the direction, as it were, of the economic process.

To stress the basis of all economic activity in more or less uncertain expectations is precisely to emphasize the openness and incompleteness of economic theorizing and explanation. It does not itself provide any kind of fixed mechanism according to which the unfolding of events takes place; but it does show how one would set about constructing a narrative of events. It is a view about where the gaps are in the causal chains that can be identified in the economy: the points at which the economic process is susceptible to influence. We can accordingly begin to appreciate the deep ambivalence of this standpoint towards economic policy. On the one hand, it sees potentiality for enormous leverage, the whole economic process moving in response to changing states of mind and consciousness; on the other hand, the very precariousness of this vision leads very naturally to thoroughgoing scepticism about the predictability of the effects of deliberate attempts to apply leverage in pursuit of political objectives. The point of view in itself provides no guidance on whether the precariousness is so pervasive as to undermine the potential for political leverage. That is to say: the wayward and unruly character of individual choices – and in particular investment decisions – is seen as an impediment to economic functioning; but the question that must be faced from a policy point of view is whether it is a greater impediment to the self-regulation of the economy than it is to the workings of discretionary fiscal and monetary policy. This matter would involve not just the consideration of an impediment to economic functioning, but a comparison between its inhibiting effects on alternative modes of economic regulation. More broadly, the comparison also arises among the alternative effects of investment decisions taken within alternative institutional frameworks (various powers and responsibilities having been given to agencies of the State), whose regulative capacities then also become a part of the appropriate comparison.

In summary, we can say that fundamentalist Keynesians are united in seeing Keynesian ideas as posing a threat to the whole reductionist program; and that their primary concern has been to reinforce this threat with further threats. When it comes to providing an alternative to the reductionist program, however, matters are less unified. There is a marked contrast, for example, between the prospectus offered by Joan Robinson for the completion of the Keynesian revolution and the insight offered by Shackle into its integrity and essence. And when we move from the critical to the constructive aspects of fundamentalism, not only are matters less unified, they are also less definite. In Loasby's work, this indefiniteness is transformed into a methodological principle [17, 1976: 167]:

> If one can summarise in one sentence the theory of employment set forth by Keynes in his [*QJE*] article of 1937, it is this: unemployment in a market economy is the result of ignorance too great to be borne. The fully-specified macroeconomic models miss the point – which is precisely that no model of this situation can be fully specified.

HYDRAULIC KEYNESIANISM

During the 1940s and 1950s, there appeared a number of expositions of 'Keynesian economics', attempting to make the ideas accessible to students, and even to intelligent laymen. What these works had in common, quite apart from matters of substance, was an unmistakable enthusiasm for (what were taken to be) Keynes's ideas. This enthusiasm was at times unrestrained to the point of excitement; it was the authors of these works who spoke without reservation of a 'Keynesian Revolution', one of the books in fact having this title [15, Lawrence R. Klein, (1949) 1966]. It is some indication of the level of enthusiasm reached by these expositors and popularizers that one, Jan Pen, wrote a book setting out and discussing a particular specification of a static 'Keynesian' model of relationships between a small number of macroeconomic aggregates and gave it the title *Modern Economics* [19, 1965]. It is not my intention here, however, to attempt to chart the process of the diffusion and popularization of Keynes's ideas.[5]

The period of Keynesian enthusiasm was really the post-war period: the ideas went cantering briskly through the 1950s and early 1960s; faltered sometime in the mid-1960s and stumbled into the 1970s.[6] This, at any rate, is the picture as its emerges at the level of popular influence, at the level of widely and influentially held views on macroeconomic policy; at the level, that is, of Keynesianism as a doctrine about how a largely decentralized economy may be subject to broad (as opposed to detailed) central control or influence through the instrument of the budget. It is tempting to adopt the practice of referring to this doctrine as 'fiscalism' to show that it is a particular variant (and perhaps a corruption or vulgarization) of Keynes's ideas. At any rate, it is important to keep distinct the ups and downs of Keynesianism as a policy doctrine from those of Keynesianism as an academically respectable theory of the functioning of a capitalist economy at the aggregate level.[7] Indeed, the esteem in which the two aspects have been held has tended to move in opposite directions, the period when 'fiscalist' policy enthusiasm was at its height being a time at which the intellectual interest in the underlying theory had become moribund. Again, the demise of 'fiscalism' in the late 1960s and early 1970s was accompanied by a reawakening of interest in the underlying theoretical conceptions. (We shall have more to say about this revival in the next section.)

All this should not be allowed to give the impression, which would be quite mistaken, that the fiscal enthusiasm stemming from Keynes's ideas did not include, or could not provide, a theory in support of its policy doctrine. It could and it did. What, then, we are led to ask, is the theoretical basis for fiscalist enthusiasm? How is it to be characterized as one of the strands in the development of Keynesian thought? It is to these questions we now turn.

The theoretical content of the body of ideas that has been propagated through the educational system in the West since World War II as 'Keynesian Economics' (by, for example, Paul Samuelson's pedagogically authoritative textbook [24, 1973]) I shall proceed to refer to as 'hydraulic Keynesianism'. This designation reflects the view that the natural and obvious way to regard elementary textbook Keynesianism is as conceiving of the economy at the aggregate level in terms of disembodied and homogeneous flows. Of course, conceiving of the macro-economy in this way will be fruitful only to the extent that there exist stable relationships between these overall flows. And it is my contention that the central characteristic of 'hydraulic Keynesianism' is the belief that such stable relationships do exist at the aggregate level. It is this belief that gives some point to the hydraulic conception; without such a belief the conception would simply be a matter of national income accounting, not of economic theory.

It should be noted that the flows involved in this conception are flows of expenditure, income or output. That is to say, neither prices nor quantities per period make a separate appearance: they appear inextricably in the contribution each makes to the overall flows of spending and receipts. It should now be apparent why the belief in the existence of, and the attempt to establish, stable relationships between the overall flows is radically inconsistent with reductionism. For any reductionist program must give a crucial role in its theorizing to *prices as such* (not to the contribution they make to overall spending flows). The grounds for this view are that it is prices as such that provide the incentives that individuals face in making the choices on which the whole scheme is to rest. This does not mean that hydraulic Keynesianism can allow no part at all to be played by prices; when we come to think of such prices as embracing wage rates and interest rates, we can see that this cannot be so. Correspondingly, it does not mean that reductionism is incapable of allowing overall flows to play any part in its scheme. Since these are alternative programs for theorizing, rather than alternative theories, they revolve around matters of emphasis. They do not concern what can or cannot play a part in a theory, but what can or cannot play a *central* part.

In fact, contrary to the standpoint associated with reductionism, hydraulic Keynesianism is a scheme in which there is only one agency making deliberate acts of choice; that one agency is 'the government'. And it is the belief that there are indeed stable relations among the various overall flows in the economy that provides a basis for 'the government' to pursue its policy goals regarding the overall level of economic activity and hence, relatedly, of the level of employment. It is the stability of these aggregate relationships that provides 'the government' with the leverage it needs to influence those flows that are not under its *direct* control. By making deliberate choices for the flows it does control (via the budget), and bearing in mind the (allegedly) stable relationships between this and the other flows that are objects of concern for economic policy, 'the government' can, in principle, exercise an indirect control on the overall level (although not the composition) of the flows that are not the objects of anyone's deliberate choice. That is the story. On the face of it, it may appear a major triumph in the march of human reason: a dramatic and irreversible extension of the boundaries of political responsibility. Instead of unemployment and depression being seen and accepted passively, like the weather, they are to be seen as matters for human will and design, something that human agency, through the instrument of central government, could actually resist and remedy.[8] As an idea it looked both simple and good; accordingly, it was, at the end of the war, rapidly assimilated to both the policy statements and rhetoric of all major political parties.[9]

In summary, it can be seen that the hydraulic approach is in conflict with reductionist market theory. The hydraulic approach shows how things would work when market prices (and wages) will not, or will not quickly enough, or will not be allowed to, perform their allocative role; it analyzes a situation in which prices are failing, both as disseminators of information about relative scarcities and in the provision of incentives to act on the basis of that information.

If the central message of the *General Theory* is that overall employment is more a matter of the demand for output than of real wages, except when 'full employment' already obtains, then that message is certainly embodied in the hydraulic approach. As such, it is an audacious simplification, which is, on the face of it, in conflict with the corpus of reductionist theorizing. Furthermore, as a way of thinking about macroeconomic policy, it seems to work to some extent, sometimes. The intellectual problem that it raises, however, is that of its own *scope*. What we need to know are the circumstances in which, and the extent to which, the operation of an economy may be conceived of in hydraulic terms. There are various approaches to this question. A familiar one is provided by the *IS-LM* apparatus, within which it can be readily shown that the economy exhibits the characteristics of the hydraulic model to the extent that the interest elasticity of expenditure is low and of the demand for money is high; with a zero interest elasticity of expenditure and an indefinitely large interest elasticity of demand for money, the operation of the economy would be exactly in accordance with the hydraulic model: changes in expenditure flows would lead to changes in output flows without any repercussions on the rate of interest. In sum, it follows that the economy may exhibit the characteristics of the hydraulic model to the extent that the interest rate is impeded, for whatever reason, in its attempts to respond to changes in expenditure.

Since the *IS-LM* apparatus was put forward by Hicks, however, we have had something like 30 years' experience of demand management policies based on the assumption that the economy exhibits marked hydraulic characteristics in the short-run; and the question of why these policies have been less effective at some times than others naturally raises in a practical way the question of the scope of the hydraulic conception. It is therefore of considerable interest that Hicks, in a revision of Keynesian economics in the light of this experience, does not adopt his own *IS-LM* apparatus for the purpose [11, 1974: ch. 1]. Rather, he provides an alternative framework in which the possibility of an expansion in demand being translated into an expansion of output depends crucially on the structure of inventories at the outset of the process. In particular, it depends crucially on there being plentiful stocks of materials to sustain investment projects until decisions to increase the output of these materials are taken; or what amounts to the same thing, it depends on there being ample foreign exchange reserves representing command over foreign inventories of materials. Unless this condition is met, the attempted expansion can easily run up against bottlenecks and dissipate itself in the diversion of resources from other uses and, notoriously, in creating balance of payments problems. Of course, if the increase in investment expenditure *is* translated into a net increase in real investment, the multiplier process can set in, and adequate stocks of consumer goods will then be required to avoid bottlenecks at this stage and sustain the expansion.[10]

There are, of course, other approaches to the question of the scope of hydraulic theorizing. Indeed, the Monetarist arguments against Keynesian conclusions may be seen as one possible answer to this question: namely, that the scope of hydraulic theorizing is practically nonexistent. In these arguments the Keynesian conclusions are undermined by the reintroduction of a choice-theoretic basis of the standard reductionist type. As we shall see in the next section, the work of Clower and Leijonhufvud may also be seen as contributing to this question of scope, although this is not how either of them presented his work.

RECONSTITUTED REDUCTIONISM

During the 1960s there emerged a school of thought, associated primarily with the names of Robert W. Clower [2, 1969] and Axel Leijonhufvud [16, 1968], concerned with reappraising Keynes's contribution to economics. These writers presented their work as concerned with reestablishing and reasserting the discontinuity between Keynesian economics and its alternatives, a discontinuity that they saw as having been blurred and finally lost to view by the various activities of interpretation, condensation, and reconstruction that came in the wake of the *General Theory*. It is within this perspective accordingly that the contribution of Clower and Leijonhufvud to our understanding of Keynes has been discussed and appraised. My purpose here, however, will be to present the dispute between Clower and Leijonhufvud, on the one hand, and those whose views they were combating, on the other, as a family quarrel within the reductionist program. Most fundamentally, the family quarrel is about the expendability of the concept of equilibrium: the Clower-Leijonhufvud position being that the concept of equilibrium should be abandoned in the interests of a more thorough-going reduction of Keynesian ideas to choice logic. The thesis is that once equilibrium has been abandoned and one focuses on a process of trading at disequilibrium prices, then one has a framework that is entirely congenial to Keynesian ideas, unlike the framework of equilibrium theorizing which, on this view, leaves room for them in only the most attenuated and *ad hoc* form. The problem then becomes one of providing a more sophisticated specification of the constraints on individual choices, opening up the possibilities for theoretically novel and challenging forms of market interdependence arising from a schematization of the process of disequilibrium trading.

In order to lead up to my characterization of the work of Clower and Leijonhufvud, it is appropriate to begin by discussing each writer's own characterization of his work: how each of them conceived of the task he had set himself. I will argue that their own characterizations are in various respects unsatisfactory, and that my alternative is not therefore gratuitous. I shall not, however, attempt to substantiate the designation of the work of these writers as reductionist. I shall take it that once the idea of what is involved in the reductionist program is appreciated, it should be clear that this work falls within the program.

Let us take Clower first. Having advanced the 'dual decision hypothesis' as a basis for expecting consumer spending to depend on current income, Clower goes on to speak unguardedly of Keynes having had this theory of household behavior 'at the back of his mind when he wrote the *General Theory*' [2, 1969: 290]. Clower goes on immediately to admit that 'I can find no direct evidence in any of his writings to show that he ever thought explicitly in these terms.' After advancing what he takes to be 'indirect evidence' for this, he concludes that 'Keynes either had a dual-decision hypothesis at the back of his mind, or most of the *General Theory* is theoretical nonsense.' The picture here seems to be one of Keynes with a mind full of ideas, *some* of which he got onto the pages of the *General Theory*, the task being to work out what the remainder must have been. This is a problem of reading not so much between the lines as off the edge of the page. In his conclusion, however, Clower maintains, rather more soberly, that his purpose has been 'simply to clarify the *formal basis* of the Keynesian revolution and its relation to orthodox thought' (emphasis added) [2, 1969; 295]. This then leaves the task quite up in the air, for it is not explained to the reader how this relates to the previous concern with what Keynes had 'at the back of his mind'.

Turning to Leijonhufvud, we find that he is at some pains to try to make clear the task he has set himself. First, he makes it plain that the doctrine-historical question of 'what Keynes really said' is a strictly secondary matter for his purposes [16, 1968: 9]. 'The primary purpose,' he explains, 'remains ... to provide a fresh *perspective* from which the income-expenditure theory may be reconsidered' [16, 1968: 9–10]. (The 'income-expenditure theory' is Leijonhufvud's label for the 'conceptual framework which has crystallized out of the debate triggered by the *General Theory*' [16, 1968: 6].) This seems straightforward enough. The difficulty arises because what was presented was not just 'Leijonhufvud's fresh perspective', but rather the fresh perspective that Leijonhufvud claimed to have distilled from the *General Theory* itself. On the face of it, the task appears to be to get a perspective on the whole debate by going back to the origins of it. But the question arises of how the responsibility for this new perspective is to be apportioned between Keynes and Leijonhufvud. Keynes may well have provided the inspiration for the task, but if the product of the distillation is to be presented as a (purified) 'Economics of Keynes' to be contrasted with the (corrupted) 'Keynesian Economics', then we are back in the realms of mind-reading, especially as this 'Economics of Keynes' can be read into the *General Theory* only with what seems to me to be a great deal of ingenuity and determination. So although Leijonhufvud at first seems to be concerned with the rather modest task of finding *a* fresh perspective from which the development of Keynesian Economics can be surveyed or appraised, it turns out that he is in search of *the* one perspective from which the Keynesianness of these developments can be judged. What looks at first like a search for new angles turns out to be a search for authenticity.

But it is not just a matter of authenticity, for the fundamental presumption that underlies the work of Clower and Leijonhufvud is that Keynes said something important, not only for economic policy, but for economic theory. They are saying: 'Let us read the *General Theory* in a search for theoretical innovation.' In other words, far from being engaged in disinterested exegesis (as the concern for authenticity might suggest), they were concerned with reworking with a view to rejuvenating (by which standards they must be judged to have had some success).

How, then, is the task that Clower and Leijonhufvud set themselves to be expressed and understood? The view I want to advance is that they were setting themselves the task of constructing a framework that would provide room or scope for Keynesian ideas. This quite rightly takes it for granted that we already have a good rough idea what Keynesian ideas are: of what the *General Theory* was driving at. What was wanted was a theoretical niche in which what were taken to be Keynes's insights could take root and thrive. The motive for this search was evidently the recognition that the framework of general equilibrium theory that had been widely adopted for attempts at precise expression of Keynesian ideas leaves practically no room or scope for them: they may appear in only the most attenuated and *ad hoc* form.

On its own terms, then, the essence of the Clower-Leijonhufvud position is this: that in order to accommodate Keynesian ideas, we have to abandon equilibrium theorizing and address ourselves to an understanding of the process of disequilibrium trading. In my terms, however, it is not just equilibrium theorizing that has been shown to be uncongenial to Keynesian ideas, but rather equilibrium theorizing within the reductionist program. And one can see why this should be so without even taking any detailed view about the workings of the economy. For within reductionism everything boils down to acts of choice within a well-specified system of objectives, constraints and forms of interdependence; and in equilibrium theorizing we confine our attention to situations in which all the independently arrived at choices can be simultaneously realized. It then follows rather naturally, irrespective of any details of market forms or institutional arrangements, that such a system leaves no room for the 'unintended' and 'involuntary': for malfunctioning and disorder. It follows, however, from my characterization of such theorizing that there are two distinct possibilities for the accommodation of Keynesian ideas: (i) the abandonment of equilibrium and (ii) the abandonment of reductionism. Clower and Leijonhufvud consider only the former possibility. We can see, however, that the claim that equilibrium theorizing *must* be abandoned in order to accommodate Keynesian ideas postulates that theorizing *must* be carried out in accordance with the reductionist program; but this is something that Clower and Leijonhufvud simply take for granted.

The whole question of whether Keynesian ideas should be accommodated by abandoning equilibrium theorizing rather naturally raises the question of what use Keynes himself made of the concept of equilibrium.[11] It is certainly true that Keynes made use of the term 'equilibrium'. But before we conclude that if Keynes could express his ideas in these terms then they must be perfectly compatible with equilibrium theorizing, we must pause to consider the meaning of equilibrium and the uses to which an equilibrium concept might be put. We must bear in mind that it is entirely in keeping with Keynes's eclecticism that his use of the term equilibrium could have been a rather desperate improvisation at one stage in the 'long struggle of escape'.

An equilibrium is a configuration which, once attained, will be maintained provided the underlying circumstances (formally, the parameters and exogenous variables) remain unchanged. Accordingly, the interest and usefulness of an equilibrium construction, as an end in itself, depends on a question which is, in principle, an empirical one, namely: what is the range of variability of the underlying circumstances over the order of magnitude of the time involved in adjusting (near enough) to its equilibrium configuration?[12] That is to say, if the underlying circumstances are fairly stable relative to the speed of adjustment of the endogenous variables, the equilibrium configuration of the system becomes a matter of some interest in itself and may provide a reasonably useful substitute for becoming involved in the complexities of the adjustment process. It is something to know where we are heading, provided we have some grounds for believing that we will get most of the way there before we start heading somewhere else.

It is in the light of these considerations that we can say why Keynes's use of equilibrium constructions was a peculiar one: He was concerned with discussing, among other things, the instability of the underlying circumstances of his construction. That is, one of his focuses of interest was precisely the failure of his equilibrium construction to satisfy the conditions for the routine usefulness of an equilibrium construction. Therefore, in arriving at an appreciation of Keynes's method, it is not enough to ask the nature of his construction; we must enquire also into its mode of *animation*. When we have reason to expect relatively stable underlying circumstances, the construction may be animated according to the method of comparative statics. When the animation is endemic, when one is concerned, as it were, with the restlessness of the underlying circumstances, the use of the construction becomes less straightforward, and certainly less mechanical. Whether, in this case there is anything much left of the concept of equilibrium is a matter of no particular importance. What is important is to see that, just as one does not expect to quell a riot by taking a photograph of it, neither did Keynes's makeshift use of the equilibrium concept involve the expectation that he could freeze the economy in a particular state. Shackle has expressed this idea with characteristic elegance [25, 1967: 182]:

> At each curtain rise the *General Theory* shows us, not the dramatic moment of inevitable action, but a tableau of posed figures. It is only after the curtain has descended again that we hear the clatter of violent scene-shifting.

We have seen that Clower and Leijonhufvud's version of Keynesianism is a reconstituted reductionism: it addresses itself not to the state of equilibrium, but to the problem of attaining it.[13] It asks the question how a decentralized market economy might, with some degree of effectiveness, perform the task that the Walrasian auctioneer would perform smoothly. To ask this question, one needs a construction in which prices adjust less than instantaneously to economic circumstances, so that at any point in time the prices may be effectively providing incentives to act, but the information they reflect will not be appropriate for the equilibrium that is being approached.

Now it may well be that formulating this question raises some of the most profound questions in macro- and monetary economics; but we are still in need, for the practical deployment of Keynesian ideas, of a usable simplification such as the hydraulic approach provides. And the use of such a simplification will require an awareness of the circumstances under which it may be expected to work tolerably well: an awareness of its *scope*. This is where a reconstituted reductionism may play a part. For in order to examine the scope of a theory in which prices fail altogether to play their (ideal) allocative role, one needs a theory in which there is a *partial* failure in this respect. This latter theory could then be used to interpret the practical successes and failures of the hydraulic approach: as a way of trying to distinguish the circumstances conducive to its being an adequate simplification. Accordingly, we should see Leijonhufvud's book as not so much about the economics of Keynes as about the *scope* of the economics of Keynes. Clower and Leijonhufvud claim to have shown that Keynes was trying to adapt the reductionist method to the expression of his own ideas by refocusing it on situations of market disequilibrium. But in displaying the analytical unmanageability of such a program, they make it clear that, insofar as Keynes was able to come to any definite conclusions about economic functioning, he must have short-circuited such problems.

Within the hydraulic approach, employment problems are quite distinct from allocation problems; they arise at the aggregate level, and they are independent of relative prices and the composition of demand or output. The thrust of the reconstituted reductionist approach, however, is to present unemployment as a by-product or even a species of allocation problem. But if this formulation does not set any definite limits on the scope of the hydraulic simplification, all it can suggest is a general scepticism regarding the appropriateness of aggregate tools to deal with problems that are seen as involving the internal composition of those aggregates; this, however, adds nothing to what we already know, namely that the hydraulic approach *is* a simplification and abstracts from allocation problems. The question that still remains is essentially a question of *decomposability*. It is the question of the separability of employment problems from the allocation problems on which they are, in practice, superimposed. To what extent may we disregard the allocative structure of macroeconomic aggregates? Just how blunt an instrument is demand management? If the reconstituted reductionist approach could be made tractable without collapsing into the Monetarist simplification, it could be expected to shed some light on these matters (as indeed the Monetarist simplification itself has done).

CONCLUSION

In this paper we have considered three varieties of Keynesianism: the fundamentalist, the hydraulic, and the reconstituted reductionist approaches. Each one has been located in relation to the reductionist program: the fundamentalist approach by its rejection of the choice theory that is essential to and the (equilibrium) market theory that is typical of reductionist theorizing; the hydraulic approach by its short-circuiting of reductionist market theory and its eschewal of formal choice theory foundations; and the reconstituted reductionist approach by its attempt to make room for Keynesian ideas within the reductionist program by refocusing the market theory on disequilibrium states whilst retaining the standard choice-theoretic foundations.

It remains only to make some comments on the relationship of the approaches to one another; the thrust of these comments will be that the various approaches are, in their contribution to understanding, largely complementary.

The fundamentalist approach provides a very general critique of the methods of reductionism with regard to both its style of choice theory and the equilibrium theory of markets with which it is typically associated. As such it clears the ground for the introduction of Keynesian ideas; at the same time it forms a kind of backdrop against which hydraulic thinking can thrive, and, as it turns out, reductionism can reappear in a modified form. Hydraulic thinking can thrive because, in the absence of standard reductionist results, one needs some drastic simplification in order to say anything at all definite regarding forecasting or policy. (The alternative candidate is the drastic simplification provided by the quantity theory of money and its modern variants.) Reductionism can then reappear because, in making use of a drastic simplification, one is led to ask questions about its scope and limits; these questions will concern why the economy may not work in the way that standard reductionist theory indicates and are questions that could be formulated in a modified and expanded reductionist framework.

Thus, the fundamentalist approach clears the ground for Keynesian ideas, the hydraulic approach provides the dangerous simplification that makes them at all definite and manageable, and a loosened reductionism provides the reservations and qualifications that provide guidance on the scope of this simplification. The matter may be expressed cryptically in terms of Keynes's 'long struggle of escape'. We may say that what he escaped *from* was (unreconstituted) reductionism; what he escaped *to* was the hydraulic approach; and what he went through in the process of struggle has been preserved in the fundamentalist approach. For a generation brought up on Keynesian ideas, however, a sense of intellectual liberation is far more likely in the struggle of escape from hydraulic thinking into a reconstituted form of reductionism. In treading this particular path, Clower and Leijonhufvud were quite right to identify their work with that of Keynes; they differ from him only in their direction of travel.

ACKNOWLEDGEMENTS

I would like to acknowledge various forms of indebtedness in connection with this chapter: to, among others, Thanos Skouras, Alan Peacock, David Currie, and an anonymous referee of this journal for helpful comments on an earlier draft; to Michael Kennedy and Colette Bowe for indispensable guidance at various stages; and to the University of Manchester for the Hallsworth Fellowship in Political Economy, which made this work possible.

NOTES

1 This argument is elaborated in Coddington [3, 1975] and Loasby [17, 1976: ch. 3].
2 Thus: 'The argument stops when...the equilibrium lullaby hushes further inquiry' [Robinson, 21, 1964: 80]. But this soporific effect is never reconciled with the concurrently held view that 'The concept of equilibrium, of course, is an indispensable tool of analysis' [21, 1964: 78].
3 An immediate difficulty for fundamentalists is the fact that the *QJE* article of 1937, after having advanced the arguments already discussed, goes on to stress the importance of the consumption function, which is then deployed (anticipating terminology I will introduce at a later stage) in a thoroughly hydraulic fashion.
4 See Keynes's letter of 31 March 1937, to Hicks in Hicks [10, 1973: 9–10].
5 But see John Kenneth Galbraith's 'How Keynes came to America' for some interesting insights into the way Keynesian ideas made their entry into the US academic economics establishment [5, 1971].

6 For an attempt at intellectual stock-taking at that time, see my 'Rethinking Economic Policy' [4, 1974].

7 Reflecting on the fragmentation of Keynesian thought, Axel Leijonhufvud makes the following observation: 'For some time now, contentment with this state of the arts has rested on the motto "The Theoretically Trivial is the Practically Important and the Practically Important is the Theoretically Trivial." It is a disturbing formula which can hardly be a permanent basis for the further development of the field' [16, 1968].

8 This changed attitude did not come easily or quickly, and fundamental attitudes had been undergoing a process of erosion for some decades by the time Keynes came on the scene. For a painstaking documentation of this process in Britain, see José Harris [7, 1972].

9 The major bridge in Britain between Keynesian doctrines and political platforms was William Henry Beveridge [1, 1944]. The ideas were given official recognition in the White Paper *Employment Policy* [6, 1944].

10 This analysis can readily be transformed from a 'fixprice' basis to a 'flexprice' one; in which case the precondition for a successful expansion becomes that the prices of the various goods needed to sustain the expansion while changes in expenditure are being translated into changes in output are significantly below normal, so that as the expansion proceeds traders will release their stocks onto the market as prices rise. If this condition is not satisfied, the expansionary impetus will be *wholly* dissipated in price increases [11, Hicks, 1974: 23–30].

11 For a detailed exegesis of this point, see Don Patinkin [18, 1976: 113–19].

12 We are here avoiding the large question of whether the system may approach an equilibrium configuration without shifting the equilibrium that is being approached.

13 In order to do this, Clower and Leijonhufvud avoid Joan Robinson's ultra-strict logic of equilibrium according to which the equilibrium state is unapproachable and hence the problem of attaining it insoluble.

REFERENCES

1 Beveridge, William Henry [Sir], *Full Employment in a Free Society*, London: Allen and Unwin, 1944.

2 Clower, Robert W., 'The Keynesian Counter-Revolution: A Theoretical Appraisal', in *Monetary Theory*, edited by Robert W. Clower, Harmondsworth: Penguin, 1969.

3 Coddington, Alan, 'Creaking Semaphore and Beyond: A Consideration of Shackle's "Epistemics and Economics"', *British Journal for the Philosophy of Science* 1975, *26*(2), pp. 151–63.

4 —— 'Re-thinking Economic Policy', *Political Quarterly* Oct.–Dec. 1974, *45* (4), pp. 426–38.

5 Galbraith, John Kenneth, *A Contemporary Guide to Economics, Peace and Laughter*, Boston, MA: Houghton Mifflin; London: André Deutsch, 1971.

6 Great Britain Parliament, *Employment Policy*, Cmd 6527, London: HMSO, May 1944.

7 Harris, José, *Unemployment and Politics: A Study in English Social Policy, 1886–1914*, Oxford: Clarendon Press, 1972.

8 Hicks, John R., 'Mr. Keynes and the "Classics": A Suggested Interpretation', *Econometrica* April 1937, *5*, pp. 147–59.

9 —— *Value and Capital*, 2nd edn, Oxford: Clarendon Press, [1939] 1946.

10 —— 'Recollections and Documents', *Economica* Feb. 1973, *40*(1), pp. 2–11.

11 —— *The Crisis in Keynesian Economics*, New York: Basic Books, Oxford: Basil Blackwell, 1974.

12 Keynes, John Maynard, *The End of Laissez-faire*, London: Woulf, Hogarth Press, 1926.

13 —— *The General Theory of Employment, Interest and Money*, London: Macmillan, 1936.

14 —— 'The General Theory of Employment', *Quarterly Journal of Economics* Feb. 1937, *51*(2), pp. 209–23.

15 Klein, Lawrence R., *The Keynesian Revolution*, London: Macmillan, 1949; 2nd edn, 1966.

16 Leijonhufvud, Axel, *On Keynesian Economics and the Economics of Keynes*, New York: Oxford University Press, 1968.

17 Loasby, Brian J., *Choice, Complexity and Ignorance*, Cambridge: Cambridge University Press, 1976.

18 Patinkin, Don, 'Keynes' Monetary Thought: A Study of its Development', *History of Political Economy*, Spring 1976 *8*(1), pp. 1–150.

19 Pen, Jan, *Modern Economics*. Translated from the Dutch by Trevor S. Preston, Harmondsworth: Penguin, 1965.

20 Robinson, Joan, 'The Production Function and the Theory of Capital', *Review of Economic Studies* 1953–54, *21*(2), pp. 81–106.

21 —— *Economic Philosophy*, Chicago: Aldine, 1962; Harmondsworth: Penguin, 1964.

22 —— *Economic Heresies*, New York: Basic Books; London: Macmillan, 1971.

23 —— 'What has become of the Keynesian Revolution?', in *After Keynes*, edited by Joan Robinson, Oxford: Basil Blackwell, 1973.

24 Samuelson, Paul A., *Economics*, 9th edn of *Economics: An Introductory Analysis*, New York: McGraw-Hill, [1948] 1973.

25 Shackle, G. L. S., *The Years of High Theory*, Cambridge: Cambridge University Press, 1967.

26 —— *Epistemics and Economics*, Cambridge: Cambridge University Press, 1972.

27 —— *Keynesian Kaleidics*, Edinburgh: Edinburgh University Press, 1974.

28 Townshend, Hugh, 'Liquidity-Premium and the Theory of Value', *Economic Journal*, March 1937, *47*(1), pp. 157–69.

3 On different interpretations of the *General Theory*

Don Patinkin
Journal of Monetary Economics (1990) 26, October, pp. 205–43

During the first quarter-century after the publication of the *General Theory*, there were no significant differences among the various interpretations of this book. Such differences began to appear only in the 1960s. These interpretations are critically examined and an explanation given of their emergence.

I

To paraphrase Ecclesiastes, of making many interpretations of the *General Theory* there is no end, and that is what intrigues me. Why should there be different interpretations of this book? More to the point, what does it mean to provide a different interpretation of the *General Theory* thirty, forty, and even fifty years after it was published? What new information became available at those respective times to provide a basis for such new interpretations? And let me immediately say that one cannot answer that question by pointing to the hitherto unpublished or obscurely published materials in the Royal Economic Society's monumental thirty-volume edition of Keynes's *Collected Writings*. For the volumes of that edition which contain materials that relate to the *General Theory* (XIII, XIV, and XXIX) were not published until the 1970s, several years after different interpretations of the book had already been advanced. Furthermore, there is little reliance on these materials even in interpretations which appeared after the publication of these volumes. I might also add that the new classical macroeconomics has presented what it regards as fundamental criticisms of the *General Theory*, not different interpretations of it.

I am, of course, fully aware of the fact that much more than fifty years later we continue to get different interpretations of, for example, Smith, Ricardo, and especially Marx. But in these cases the difference in time is itself a partial explanation: for no matter how many and how detailed the studies we have of these writers and their respective periods, we still cannot have a feeling for the full social, political, and economic context in which they wrote. We still will not be aware of some of the events and / or discussions to which they alluded. We still will not fully know what mind-set on the part of their readers they took for granted and what details they accordingly did not bother specifying. And we also might be misled by words which today have a different meaning, a different connotation, from what they had at the time they were written.

The situation with respect to the *General Theory* is quite different. Here we know much more about the man and his times. Indeed, those of my generation and older may even have personal recollections of those times, those dark depression years during which the *General Theory* was written – even if (as in my case) they are recollections of adolescent days. And though there may be some exceptions (I shall return to this point later), there has been little if any change in the meaning of words since the time of the *General Theory*, and its historical allusions are ones that we are aware of and can (though sometimes only after close contextual study) identify.

So why are there such vastly different interpretations of the *General Theory*? Or to ask the question from another viewpoint: why are there not different interpretations of other classic works of the period? Why are there not different interpretations of John Hicks's *Value and Capital*, published three years after the *General Theory*,[1] or of Paul Samuelson's *Foundations of Economic Analysis*, published in 1947?

There are in part some obvious answers to this question, and I will ultimately come to them. At the moment, I would like to say that though the question of different interpretations of the *General Theory* has long intrigued me, it is with hesitancy that I undertake to discuss it – and this for two reasons. First, the question that I have raised is one in the field of literary criticism and hermeneutics, and hence a question which rapidly involves us in deep philosophical issues. And these are fields in which, to say the least, I have no expertise. Second, I do not undertake this discussion as a dispassionate observer, but as one who has over the past years himself presented an interpretation of the *General Theory*, and in this context even criticized other interpretations. So it is for you the reader to make whatever allowances you feel are called for by these facts.

I have, of course, tried to obtain a minimal outsider's understanding of the hermeneutical issues inherent in my inquiry. But as I have attempted to understand the successive waxing and waning of different theories of literary criticism and hermeneutics since World War II – of the New Criticism, of Reader-Response Criticism, of Deconstruction and so forth – I have again thought of Ecclesiastes and his conclusion that 'much study is a weariness of the flesh'. At the same time it has been most comforting for me to learn from my limited venture into this field that the half-life of a theory in literary criticism is even shorter than one in postwar macroeconomics, and that the debates between the protagonists of the various theories of interpretation are equally intense, protracted – and inconclusive.

There is one such debated issue which is of paramount importance for my purpose: namely, the question of the significance that we should attach to the intention of the author when we interpret a text. The views of the various schools of interpretation range here from the deconstructionists, who on philosophical grounds maintain that the meaning of a text is indeterminate and may always be construed by different readers in different ways – to which they add that the original intention of an author (even when he explicitly declares it) is again subject to different interpretations; to the approach of Stanley Fish (1980), who maintains that though in theory there are an unlimited number of possible interpretations of a text, in practice there are only a finite number of different 'interpretive communities', each with its own rules and conventions, and each accordingly with a 'legitimate' interpretation; to what I understand is today considered the conservative view of E. D. Hirsch (1967: ch. 5), who believes that though we cannot achieve absolute certainty, we can – by applying the inductive and probabilistic methods of all sciences – present a construal of the author's intention and explain why it is preferable to all others,[2] and who accordingly maintains (1976: 90–1) that *'unless there is a powerful overriding value in disregarding an author's intention (i.e., original meaning), we who interpret as a vocation should not disregard it.* . . . To treat an author's words merely as grist for one's own mill is ethically analogous to using another man merely for one's own purposes' (italics in original). As an example of such a 'powerful overriding value' Hirsch cites the possibility that 'one might fudge on original meaning for the sake of young, impressionable children' (ibid.: 90). I think that we here can safely ignore that danger.

I am obviously not qualified to express an opinion with respect to the validity of these and other theories of interpretation. I shall, however, take advantage of the degrees of freedom afforded by this lack of consensus among specialists in the field to choose among them and invoke the authority of Hirsch for the emphasis that I have always given in my interpretation of the *General Theory* on Keynes' intentions in writing it – its original meaning. I also invoke Hirsch's authority (1967: 209ff.; 1976: 124ff.) to justify my use of any evidence that throws light on these intentions: evidence not only from the text itself (*pace* the New Criticism, which contends that this should constitute the sole basis for interpretation), but also from the historical context in which the book was written, from the context of Keynes' other writings and activities, from the reactions of his contemporaries to the book, and so forth. I am also encouraged by the fact that this approach to the history of economic ideas accords with the one that Quentin Skinner (1969) has followed in his influential studies in the history of political ideas. I must admit that both Hirsch (1967: *passim*) and Skinner (1976: 68) emphasize that one cannot say that the original meaning of a text is the only possible reading. At the same time, I do think that this meaning can be used to justify the rejection of interpretations that differ greatly from it.

I would also like to say that whatever may be the proper hermeneutical principle to follow with respect to literary works, Hirsch's view is to my mind the correct one with respect to scientific writings – and for present purposes let me include economics as a science. As Robert Merton (1957) has emphasized, priorities play a major role in the reward system of science, so for this purpose alone the scientist writes with the intention of conveying to his profession a precise and definite message. And this is *a fortiori* so in the case of an economist whose message implicitly or explicitly includes the advocacy of certain policy measures. So in interpreting scientific writings, and especially writings in the social sciences, we should make use of all available evidence as to the author's intention.

II

Keynes' intention in writing the *General Theory* – its original meaning – is already indicated in its title, which lists 'Employment' as the first of the subjects to be dealt with. The *General Theory* (*GT*) is divided into six Books. In Book I – entitled 'Introduction' – Keynes presents 'a brief summary of the theory of employment to be worked out in the course of the following chapters' (*GT*: 27). This is his 'theory of effective demand', which in this introductory Book is presented under the explicit simplifying assumptions of a constant level of investment (which presupposes a constant rate of interest) and a constant money wage rate, an assumption with which Keynes tells us he will 'dispense later' (*GT*: 27–9). The central message of this theory and its analytical novelty (as I have shown on earlier occasions: Patinkin 1976: chs 8–9; 1982: ch. 1) is that changes in output themselves act as an equilibrating force to bring aggregate demand and supply – or, equivalently, planned investment and saving – into equality at a level that need not be one of full employment. In Keynes' words: 'The novelty in my treatment of saving and investment consists, not in my maintaining their necessary aggregate equality, but in the proposition that it is, not the rate of interest, but the level of incomes which (in conjunction with certain other factors) ensures this equality' (Keynes 1937a: 211; see also *GT*: 31, lines 16–23; 179: lines 2–6). And this was his explanation of the 'paradox of poverty in the midst of plenty' (*GT*: 30): his explanation of the seemingly endless depression in the Western world that was creating misery for millions of unemployed and even endangering the existence of its democratic institutions.

In this Book, Keynes also tells us that once his theory of effective demand is set out, 'we shall find that the theory of prices falls into its proper place as a matter which is subsidiary to our general theory' (*GT*: 31–2). I shall later indicate the specific sense in which it is subsidiary. Now, however, I would like to suggest that with this statement Keynes also intended to highlight the difference between the central message of the *General Theory* and that of his *Treatise on Money*, whose subject was indeed the price level as analyzed by what he termed 'The Fundamental Equations for the Value of Money' (so the title of Chapter 10 of that book).

After a 'digression' from the 'main theme' in Book II for the purpose of clarifying various concepts, Keynes devotes 'Book III: The Propensity to

Consume' and 'Book IV: The Inducement to Invest' to those two components of effective demand. In the latter Book, Keynes drops the assumption
of a constant level of investment and explains how this level is determined
by the marginal-efficiency-of-capital schedule in conjunction with the rate
of interest, which rate is in turn determined by the liquidity-preference
schedule in conjunction with the quantity of money.

Finally, in 'Book V: Money-Wages and Prices', Keynes drops (as he had
in Book I said he would) the assumption of a constant money wage and
devotes the first chapter of this Book (Chapter 19, entitled 'Changes in
Money-Wages') to an analysis of the effects of such changes – explaining at
the beginning of this chapter that 'it was not possible ... to discuss this
matter fully until our own theory had been developed' (*GT*: 257). And he
goes on in this chapter (which I have accordingly always regarded as the
apex of the *General Theory*) to tie together all the analytical elements of
the preceding chapters in order to argue that a decline in money wages in
the face of unemployment might create such perverse expectations and such
a wave of bankruptcies that the level of aggregate demand, hence effective
demand, and hence employment, would remain unchanged. From this
followed the main policy conclusion of the *General Theory*: namely, that
'there is, therefore, no ground for the belief that a flexible wage policy is
capable of maintaining a state of continuous full employment; – any more
than for the belief that an open-market monetary policy is capable,
unaided, of achieving this result. The economic system cannot be made
self-adjusting along these lines' (*GT*: 267). Consequently government must
take 'an ever greater responsibility for directly organising investment' (*GT*:
164; see also p. 378) in order to assure that total expenditures on investment
in the economy – augmented by the multiplier effect – will supplement
expenditures on consumption to the extent necessary to bring aggregate
demand to its full employment level.

Book V also contains 'Chapter 20: The Employment Function' and
'Chapter 21: The Theory of Prices', and I shall have something to say
about them later. I am also deferring until later some observations about
Book VI, entitled 'Short Notes Suggested by the General Theory', which is
the final one of the *General Theory*.

We can obtain a deeper understanding of Keynes' intentions in writing
the *General Theory* by reading it in the context of his earlier writings on the
problem of unemployment. Thus in his 1925 *Economic Consequences of Mr.
Churchill*, he attributed the increase in the level of unemployment that then
took place to England's return to the gold standard at prewar parity, thus
overvaluing the pound. The analysis of his 1930 *Treatise* was of a general
nature and attributed unemployment to entrepreneurial losses associated
with too high a real wage. In both cases Keynes contended that if only
nominal wages could be simultaneously and equiproportionately reduced,
the problem would be solved: in the *Economic Consequences of Mr. Churchill* this reduction was to be accompanied by one in domestic prices as well,

so that the real wage was to be reduced only in terms of international prices, thus offsetting the overvalued pound (Keynes, *Collected Writings*, hereafter *JMK* IX: 211, 228–9); in the *Treatise* it was to be a reduction of real wages in terms of domestic prices as well, thus eliminating business losses (*JMK*: 141, 151, 244–5, 265, 281). In both cases, however, the illocutionary force of Keynes' discussion was not to actually advocate a policy of dealing with unemployment by reducing nominal wages, but to highlight the fact that in practice the resistance of workers would make this impossible, so that the alternative policies that he was advocating were called for. (In the passages from the *Treatise* just cited, Keynes repeatedly expresses the view that only in a totalitarian state – 'in Bolshevist Russia or in Fascist Italy' (ibid.: 244) – could such a wage reduction be carried out.)

The unemployment of the 1930s, however, constituted (according to Thomas Kuhn 1970: chs 6–8) an 'anomaly' for Keynes' earlier analysis of the problem, and this for two reasons. First, unemployment had become a worldwide phenomenon, and so could not be explained in terms of the specific circumstances of Britain. Second, from 1929 to 1933 – that is, from the time of writing the *Treatise* to that of writing the *General Theory* – money wages had fallen in the United States by over a quarter, but to no avail insofar as unemployment was concerned. True, the price level had fallen even more, thus resulting in an increase in the real wage; but this too was part of the anomaly.

So in addition to the basic theoretical criticisms to which the *Treatise* was subjected (see Patinkin 1976: 54–8), this empirical experience necessitated two important revisions in Keynes' earlier views: it showed that in practice money wages could fall drastically (even if not simultaneously), but it also showed that this would not help to solve the problem of unemployment. It was to this experience that Keynes alluded when at the beginning of the *General Theory* he wrote that 'it is not very plausible to assert that unemployment in the United States in 1932 was due either to labour obstinately refusing to accept a reduction of money-wages or to its obstinately demanding a real wage beyond what the productivity of the economic machine was capable of furnishing' (ibid.: 9).

Keynes' new theory of effective demand, together with his acceptance of the 'first classical postulate' that 'the [real] wage is equal to the marginal product of labour' (*GT*: 5, italics deleted), provided the answer to both these anomalies. For if as a result of the adverse reactions described in Chapter 19, a reduction in money wages in the face of unemployment would actually be followed by a decrease in effective demand and hence in the level of output and corresponding input of labor, this would result in an increase in the marginal product of labor and hence in its real wage. And this is the meaning of Keynes' cryptic statement in 'Book I: Introduction' of the *General Theory* that 'there may exist no expedient by which labour as a whole can reduce its *real* wage to a given figure by making revised *money* bargains with the entrepreneurs' (*GT*: 13, italics in original). This was a specific instance of Keynes' general principle that 'the propensity to consume and the rate of new investment determine between them the volume of employment, and the volume of employment is uniquely related to a given level of real wages – not the other way round' (*GT*: 30).

III

I began this lecture by saying that I was intrigued by the existence today of widely different interpretations of the *General Theory*. In this connection there are two most significant facts: first, there were no such wide differences in the interpretations that were presented in the years immediately following its publication; and second, almost a quarter of a century was to elapse before such differences did appear.

The contemporary interpretations that I have in mind began with the 1935 'missionary' talk in which Robert Bryce (who had attended Keynes' lectures in the successive years 1932–4) brought the gospel according to Keynes to what he many years later described as 'the nearest concentration of heathen available from Cambridge' – namely, Hayek's seminar at the London School of Economics (Bryce 1977: 40, 129–45). It continued with Joan Robinson's 1937 book *Introduction to the Theory of Employment*; with the respective review articles that appeared in the years 1936 to 1938 by Champernowne (1936), Hansen (1936), Harrod (1937), Hicks (1936, 1937), Lange (1938), Lerner (1936), Meade (1937) and Reddaway (1936); and to the celebrated 1936 *Quarterly Journal of Economics* symposium with the participation of Leontief, Robertson, Taussig and Viner. This symposium concluded with a reply by Keynes (1937b) which has played a major role in other interpretations of the *General Theory* and which will be discussed in the next section.

In a letter that he wrote in August 1936 to Harrod commenting on a draft of the latter's review, Keynes identified the three major components of his book as being the theory of effective demand (with its 'psychological law' of a less-than-unity marginal propensity to consume), the marginal efficiency of capital, and the theory of liquidity preference (*JMK* XIV: 84–6). And almost a decade later, about a year before his death, Keynes (according to an entry from March 1945 in James Meade's diary) gave a 'lecture' to a government committee in which he once again designated these components as the main ones of the *General Theory*.[3] These are also the components – in varying ways and degrees of emphasis, and in some cases with explicit attention also being paid to Keynes' corollary discussions of the multiplier, of the inefficacy of a reduction in the money wage rate as a means of reducing unemployment, and of the determination of price given this rate – that we find in the foregoing contemporary interpretations.

What is even more important for my present purposes is what we do *not* find in them. Thus (with the exception of Robertson 1936: §I) we do not find discussions of the aggregate supply function: or of wage-induced cost inflation; or of the distribution of income; or of the 'animal spirits', the irrational aspects of economic behavior which influence economic decisions and thus allegedly make it impossible to speak – even in the short-run context which is the major concern of the *General Theory* – of a stable investment function and a corresponding equilibrium; or of the material contained in the chapter on social philosophy in Book VI. Nor do we find any discussions which interpret the *General Theory* as denying the possibility that proper government fiscal policy can assure full employment in a capitalist economy.

And what is equally significant is that though Keynes wrote letters to most of his reviewers, commenting on their respective interpretations, he generally approved of them, and in any event did not criticize them for omitting any of the foregoing points.[4] On the contrary, the only omission for which he criticized Harrod's review in the aforementioned August 1936 letter was precisely that it did not 'mention *effective demand* or, more precisely, the demand schedule for output as a whole, except in so far as it is implicit in the multiplier' (*JMK* XIV: 85, italics in original). And in essence this was also Keynes' major criticism of Lerner's review (which he otherwise termed 'splendid') in his letter to him two months before (*JMK* XXIX: 214–16).

Let me in particular emphasize that in his correspondence with Harrod, Reddaway, Meade, and Hicks on their respective review articles, Keynes did not express any objection to the fact that each in his own way had presented the analysis of the *General Theory* in terms of a general-equilibrium system of simultaneous equations. When in August 1935 Harrod had tried to convince Keynes that he should view his analysis in that way, Keynes vehemently rejected his suggestion (*JMK* XIII: 526–65, especially pp. 531–2, 545–6, 548, 553–4 and 557). But in the course of the year, Keynes had apparently come around to accepting it. Thus in his aforementioned 1936 letter to Harrod, Keynes wrote: 'I like your paper (may I keep the copy you have sent me?) more than I can say. I have found it instructive and illuminating, and I really have no criticisms. I think you have re-orientated the argument beautifully' (*JMK* XIV, p. 84). Similarly, in his March 1937 letter to Hicks on the latter's IS-LM interpretation, Keynes wrote that he 'found it very interesting and really have next to nothing to say by way of criticism'. And his main criticism was that Hicks' investment function depended only on current income, whereas Keynes felt that 'whilst it may be true that entrepreneurs are over-influenced by present income', nevertheless 'expected income for the period of investment is the relevant variable' (*JMK* XIV: 79–81). Again, he ended an August 1936 letter to Reddaway with 'I enjoyed your review of my book in the *Economic Record*, and thought it very well done' (*JMK* XIV: 70). And in a September 1936 postcard to Meade, Keynes wrote: 'Thanks for the copy of your paper. It's excellent. I have no criticisms to suggest' (cited by Young 1987: 34).

Furthermore, on at least one occasion, Keynes expressed his approval of a general-equilibrium interpretation of his book, not only in correspondence, but also in print. Specifically, in the course of an exchange with Robertson in the pages of the 1938 *Economic Journal*, Keynes described Lange's 1938 review article – which like those of Reddaway, Hicks and Harrod (as Lange himself pointed out in its opening footnote) presented such an interpretation – as one 'which follows very closely and accurately my line of thought' (*JMK* XIV: 232, n. 1).[5]

And now let me anticipate an issue that I will later discuss and emphasize that all of the above simultaneous-equation interpretations of the *General Theory* can essentially be regarded as variations of IS-LM: the distinctive feature of Hicks' version was that it also provided a diagrammatic presentation. Thus Keynes' approval of all these reviews also constituted his consistent approval of the IS-LM interpretation of the *General Theory*.[6]

The IS-LM interpretation was elaborated upon by Modigliani in his influential 1944 article; it appeared in Klein's classic 1947 work on *The Keynesian Revolution* (pp. 87–8); and it also played an important role in Hansen's *Guide to Keynes* (1953: 107, 143–8). And as we all know, the IS-LM interpretation became the standard representation of the Keynesian system in the macroeconomic textbooks that began to appear in the 1960s, and thereby became the hallmark of 'mainstream Keynesianism'.

I might also add that the interpretation presented in Chapters XIII: 4 and XIV: 1 and 3 of the 1956 and subsequent (1965 and 1989) editions of my *Money, Interest, and Prices* is essentially that of IS-LM – with the difference that I regarded its equilibrium position as being of a Marshallian short-run nature which, if disturbed by a decline in the money wage rate in the face of unemployment, might (in accordance with Keynes' argument in Chapter 19) bring the economy to a new short-run position of unemployment equilibrium, but would not restore full employment. In Keynes' words, in his chapter on 'The General Theory of Employment Re-stated',

> it is an outstanding characteristic of the economic system in which we live that, whilst it is subject to severe fluctuations in respect of output and employment, it is not violently unstable. Indeed it seems capable of remaining in a chronic condition of sub-normal activity for a considerable period without any marked tendency either towards recovery or towards complete collapse. Moreover, the evidence indicates that full, or even approximately full, employment is of rare and short-lived occurrence.
>
> (*GT*: 249–50)

This disequilibrium approach enabled me to dispense with the Hicks–Modigliani assumptions of a rigid money-wage rate (which, as emphasized in section II above, Keynes had dropped in Chapter 19 of the *General Theory*) and/or 'liquidity trap' [about which Keynes had said that 'whilst this limiting case might become practically important in future, I know of no example of it hitherto' (*GT*: 207)],[7] assumptions which are required if one interprets the *General Theory* as describing a position of long-run unemployment equilibrium, i.e. one which remains unchanged. Similarly, when in my *Keynes' Monetary Thought* I said that 'in most cases, I do not think that my views on these issues differ basically from the traditional ones' (Patinkin 1976: 10; see also p. 100), it was the IS-LM interpretation, with this difference, that I had in mind.

IV

When did significantly different interpretations of the *General Theory* begin to appear? There is no mention of them either in Schlesinger's (1956) survey article 'After Twenty Years: The General Theory' or in Harry Johnson's (1961) corresponding article on 'The General Theory after Twenty-Five Years'. And to the best of my knowledge, it is just about that time that such interpretations do begin to appear. I am referring in particular to Sidney Weintraub's (1961) *Classical Keynesianism, Monetary Theory, and the Price Level* and to George Shackle's survey article of the same year on 'Recent Theories Concerning the Nature and Role of Interest'. In the latter, Shackle (1961: 228) referred to Keynes' 1937 article in the aforementioned *Quarterly Journal of Economics* symposium and said that 'no reader of Keynes's article... will be in doubt that Keynes looking back saw as the main theme of his book the commanding importance of uncertainty and of the conventions by which the insoluble problems it poses, and the nonsense it makes of pure "rational calculation", can be shelved in order to make life possible at all'. And a few years later, in his book *Years of High Theory*, Shackle (1967) devoted a whole chapter to Chapter 12 of the *General Theory* (which bears the title 'The State of Long-Term Expectation') and to Keynes' 1937 article; subtitled his (Shackle's) chapter 'Keynes's Ultimate Meaning'; claimed that this theme is 'the message of the *General Theory*, and... the only part of it which Keynes troubled to reproduce' in his 1937 article (Shackle 1967: 130); and termed this article the 'third edition' of the *General Theory*, after having designated the *Treatise on Money* as the first one (Shackle 1967: 136; see also Shackle 1973). And in a still later article, Shackle (1982: 438) explicitly rejected Hicks' IS-LM interpretation on the grounds that 'the elemental core of Keynes' conception of economic society is uncertain expectation, and uncertain expectation is wholly incompatible and in conflict with the notion of equilibrium'.[8]

Weintraub's interpretation of the *General Theory* emphasized instead the analysis of the determination of the price level, particularly in the case of wage-induced cost inflation. He stated that he will 'make no effort to refer to Keynes even though I think the tenor and the text will sustain me' (1961: 3).[9] Weintraub also entered a plea for the abandonment of the IS-LM interpretation, as well as that of the 45°-cross diagram, on the alleged ground that these deal only with real quantities (ibid.: 5–10, 18–22). And he advocated instead the use of the aggregate demand and supply curves of Chapter 3 of the *General Theory*, which reflect changes in the price level by virtue of their being expressed in nominal money terms.

Let me begin with Shackle and say that there is no question that expectations and uncertainty play an essential role in the *General Theory*. But Shackle takes Keynes' discussion of uncertainty in the *Quarterly Journal* article somewhat out of the context in which it appears. Specifically, in the first part of this article, Keynes briefly discusses the criticisms of Leontief, Robertson, Taussig and Viner – and then states that Viner's is 'the most important of the four comments' (*JMK* XIV: 110). Now, Viner's major criticism was directed at Keynes' theory of liquidity preference. And this was the reason that Keynes went on to devote most of the second part of his reply to explicating the nature of the uncertainty that generates this preference. There is, however, little if anything in this exposition which differs from that of Chapter 12 of the *General Theory*. In particular, Keynes' well-known statement in the *Quarterly Journal* article that the uncertainty which characterizes so much of economic life is one for which 'there is no scientific basis on which to form any calculable probability whatever' (*JMK* XIV: 114) is equivalent to the at least equally well-known statement in Chapter 12 that 'our decisions to do something positive, the full consequences of which will be drawn out over many days to come, can only be taken as a result of animal spirits – of a spontaneous urge to action rather than inaction, and not as the outcome of a weighted average of quantitative benefits multiplied by quantitative probabilities' (*GT*: 161). Furthermore, contrary to Shackle's aforementioned statement in *Years of High Theory* (1967: 130), the discussion of uncertainty is not 'the only part' of the *General Theory* that Keynes reproduces in his 1937 article: for Keynes goes on in it to discuss both the theory of effective demand and the marginal efficiency of capital (*JMK* XIV: 119–23). In brief, Keynes' 1937 *Quarterly Journal* article emphasizes the same three basic components of the *General Theory* that he had emphasized in his 1936 letter to Harrod (see p. 61).[10]

I must also point out that Keynes concludes his discussion of 'animal spirits' in the *General Theory* with the statement that

> We should not conclude from this that everything depends on waves of irrational psychology. On the contrary, the state of long-term expectation is often steady, and, even when it is not, the other factors exert their compensating effects.
>
> (*GT*: 162)

Similarly, Keynes writes:

> There are not two separate factors affecting the rate of investment, namely, the schedule of the marginal efficiency of capital and the state of confidence. The state of confidence is relevant because it is one of the

major factors determining the former, which is the same thing as the investment demand-schedule.

(*GT*: 149)

Thus even after taking account of the major influence of 'the state of confidence' on expectations, Keynes still speaks of a determinate investment demand schedule in the short-run context which is the concern of the central message of the *General Theory*.[11] Needless to say, in a longer-run context Keynes emphasized that significant fluctuations 'in the market estimation of the marginal efficiency of different types of capital' would be 'likely' (*GT*: 164). Indeed, Keynes' explanation of the business cycle in Chapter 22 of the *General Theory* that he devoted to this subject was in terms of 'a cyclical change in the marginal efficiency of capital' (*GT*: 313).[12]

Let me finally note that the presentation of the nonprobabilistic nature of economic uncertainty can hardly be considered to be a contribution of the *General Theory*: it had been emphasized long before by Frank Knight (1921) in his classic *Risk, Uncertainty, and Profit*. Furthermore, as Samuelson (1946: 320) observed many years ago, the *General Theory* 'paves the way for a theory of expectations, but it hardly provides one' (see also Hart 1947).

I turn now to Sidney Weintraub's interpretation and first of all note that in contrast with his view that the aggregate supply curve is a basic component of the *General Theory*, this curve was not among the three such components of his book that Keynes set out in his August 1936 letter to Harrod, described in the preceding section. Similarly, as indicated in that section, this curve was not even referred to by any of the contemporary reviewers of the book, with the exception of Robertson; nor did Keynes complain about this in his correspondence with them. And to this I add that, as I have elsewhere shown (Patinkin 1982: 142–53), Keynes himself did not have a clear notion of the nature of this curve, and particularly about its mathematical properties (viz., its slope and convexity). Thus in Chapter 3 of the *General Theory* on 'The Principle of Effective Demand', the properties of this curve – in contrast with those of the aggregate demand curve – are not specified. Furthermore, in the only place in the book where they are specified (*GT*: 55, n. 2), Keynes does so incorrectly. And though Keynes devotes Chapter 20 to a discussion of what he calls the employment function, and which he defines as the 'inverse function' of the aggregate supply function (*GT*: 280), the various elasticity formulas which he presents do not explicitly describe the properties of the latter, beyond implying the obvious one that its slope is positive.

Insofar as Weintraub's emphasis on the price level is concerned, I have already noted Keynes' statement in Book I that 'the theory of prices falls into its proper place as a matter which is subsidiary to our general theory' (*GT*: 32). For if the level of employment and hence the marginal product of labor is determined by the level of effective demand, and if (as Keynes assumed) price is equal to marginal cost,[13] then for any given money-wage rate the level of effective demand also determines the price. In the words of Chapter 21 of the *General Theory* on 'The Theory of Prices': 'The general price-level (taking equipment and technique as given) depends partly on the wage-unit [i.e. on the money-wage rate] and partly on the volume of employment' (*GT*: 295). And I might also point out that, contrary to Weintraub's criticism, Hicks' IS-LM article deals not only with real quantities, but also with the respective price levels of consumption and investment goods as determined in this way (Hicks 1937: 103). Furthermore, the standard presentation of IS-LM includes a description of how changes in the price level cause shifts in the LM curve and hence affects the equilibrium position.

Note the parallel treatment in the *General Theory* of the determination of the real wage and the determination of the price level: in both cases this is achieved as a by-product of the theory that constitutes its central message – namely, the theory of effective demand that explains the level of output in the economy, hence its level of employment, and hence the marginal product of labor.

V

The quarter-century and more since the writings of Shackle and Weintraub in the early 1960s has seen the presentation of innumerable interpretations of the *General Theory*, far more than I could possibly discuss. My impression, however, is that most of them are variations on either the IS-LM interpretation of 'mainstream Keynesianism', or the interpretation of so-called 'Post-Keynesianism', to which I shall in a moment turn. I shall not, however, discuss such well-known works as those of Leijonhufvud (1968) and Chick (1983), for their avowed main purpose is to study the *General Theory* as the point of departure for their respective contributions to (in the words of the title of Chick's book) 'macroeconomics after Keynes'. Similarly, the subtitle of Leijonhufvud's book is 'A Study in Monetary Theory' (see also ibid., p. 9). Accordingly, I consider these works to be outside my terms of reference, strictly construed.[14]

Let me then briefly discuss Post-Keynesian economics. This is actually only in part concerned with the interpretation of the *General Theory*. In this context it is largely a combination of George Shackle's interpretation of the book in terms of the overriding impact of uncertainty on economic behavior, and Sidney Weintraub's interpretation in terms of the major importance in the book of the aggregate supply curve and of the analysis of the determination of the price level.[15] And I have nothing to add to my criticisms of these interpretations in the preceding section. In addition, Post-Keynesian economics – particularly as expounded by the so-called 'Modern Cambridge School' of Joan Robinson (in her postwar period), Piero Sraffa, and their followers – has a major concern with the development and elaboration of the theories of Marx, Kalecki, and Sraffa (see Harcourt 1987) and is in this respect also outside my terms of reference.[16] The same is true of the work of Nicholas Kaldor in taking the *General Theory* as his point of departure for developing theories of income distribution and growth, respectively – issues which were not among the concerns of the *General Theory* (see Patinkin 1976: 19–20; see also p. 80 of this chapter).

A Post-Keynesian *cum* Modern-Cambridge-School work that is however in large part devoted to an interpretation of the *General Theory* is Murray Milgate's 1982 book, *Capital and Employment: A Study of Keynes's Economics*. The Modern Cambridge School rejects both marginal analysis and the notion of capital as a factor of production, and then implicitly makes use of 'productivity ethics'[17] to deny the moral justification of profits in a capitalist economy. And a major purpose of Milgate's book is to attribute this rejection to the *General Theory* as well. Indeed, Milgate presents the transition from the *Treatise* to the *General Theory* as a transition from the marginal viewpoint to the nonmarginal one.

At first sight, this would seem to be 'mission impossible'. For whereas the theory of value *qua* marginal analysis – and even the term 'marginal' – is completely absent from the *Treatise* (see Patinkin 1976: 13, 47, 94), it is repeatedly and consistently applied in the *General Theory*: the marginal productivity of labor as determining its real wage, marginal cost as determining price, and the marginal efficiency of capital as determining investment decisions. And surely to speak of 'the marginal efficiency of capital' is to regard capital as a factor of production.

Milgate (1982: 166), however, explains that there is no reference to the theory of value in the *Treatise* because it is too 'obvious' to be mentioned. On the other hand, the notion of the marginal efficiency of capital – to which Keynes devotes a whole chapter in the *General Theory*, which he describes there as equivalent to Irving Fisher's (1930: 155, 159, 168) marginal rate of return over cost, and which in his aforementioned August 1936 letter to Roy Harrod (see p. 61 above) he listed as one of the three major analytical components of his book – that notion [tells us Milgate (1982: 91ff.)] is among the 'inconsistent' 'remnants of the orthodox position' that are to be found in the *General Theory*. Finally, Milgate interprets the *General Theory* as presenting a theory of long-run unemployment that necessarily exists in a capitalist economy, and (using a singular definition of the term) then interprets this view as constituting a rejection of 'orthodox marginalist theory' (1982: 96–7).[18]

In this connection I should also refer to Luigi Pasinetti – a leading member of the Modern Cambridge School – who contends that 'the marginal-efficiency-of-capital schedule, which might, at a first superficial look, appear as belonging to marginal economic analysis, when examined more deeply turns out to have a rather different origin' – namely, classical nonmarginal analysis (Pasinetti 1974: 43). Pasinetti also rejects Hicks' IS-LM general-equilibrium interpretation of the *General Theory* on the grounds that the correct interpretation of this book is in terms of a system of equations which is 'decomposed' into a causal chain by which the rate of interest is determined by the liquidity-preference equation alone (i.e. independently of the level of income), that the rate of interest so determined is then inserted into the savings = investment equation to determine the level of income, and that it was Hicks who has 'broken up Keynes' basic chain of arguments' by 'introducing income' into the liquidity-preference equation, thus yielding a system of equations which cannot be so 'decomposed' (Pasinetti 1974: 74). This contention stands in direct contradiction to the fact that the liquidity-preference function which Keynes presented and analyzed in Chapter 15 of the *General Theory* depends on both income and the rate of interest, and has the specific form $M = L_1(Y) + L_2(r)$ (see *GT*: 199).

The rejection of Hicks' IS-LM interpretation (though generally not on the grounds advanced by Pasinetti, but on those of Shackle – namely, on the grounds that it attributes to the *General Theory* the analysis of the determination of an equilibrium situation and of the equilibrium level of income in particular: see previous section) is another hallmark of Post-Keynesianism. Indeed, its rejection of this interpretation is so vehement as to bring it to follow Joan Robinson (1962a: 27–9; 1962b: 100–2; see also 1962c: 76; 1979: xi) in denouncing the kind of analysis which it represents as 'bastard Keynesianism'.[19] Some adherents of the Modern Cambridge School (see e.g. Harcourt 1980: 151) have even claimed that Keynes himself 'explicitly' rejected Hicks' interpretation in his 1937 letter to him. The discussion of this letter in section III above, as well as of Keynes' approval of what are essentially other 'IS-LM interpretations' of his book, shows how unfounded this claim is. And though that was probably not his intention in making it, Richard Kahn's (1984: 160) complaint that 'it is tragic that Keynes made no public protest when they [i.e. IS-LM interpretations of the *General Theory*] began to appear', is to my mind further evidence that Keynes basically accepted them.

Let me also note that the one diagram that we do find in the *General Theory* (p. 180) is logically equivalent to the IS curve. For though drawn with different axes, this diagram shows different combinations of the rate of interest and the level of income in which the commodity market is in equilibrium. Furthermore, Keynes goes on to say that this diagram alone cannot determine the equilibrium levels of these variables; 'if, however, we introduce the state of liquidity-preference and the quantity of money and these between them tell us that the rate of interest is r_2, then the whole position becomes determinate' (*GT*: 181). Here, then, is the spirit of IS-LM – the determination of the equilibrium level of income by the interaction between the markets for commodities and money – even if not its precise geometrical form.

In addition to making use of the aforementioned arguments of Shackle and Weintraub, Post-Keynesians have also attempted to support their rejection of IS-LM with the claim that Hicks himself has since then – to quote Joan Robinson (1978: xiv) – 'repented' (note the choice of language associated more with religious disputes than with scholarly disagreements: Hicks has not only been wrong, but like Jeroboam son of Nebat in the Book of Kings, he has sinned and made others to sin).[20] Robinson's claim was based on Hicks' statement in a 1976 article that the IS-LM diagram 'is now much less popular with me than I think it still is with many other people' (pp. 289–90). On this I have two observations: First, neither this article, nor Hicks' later article on 'IS-LM – An Explanation' (1981) – which Post-Keynesians also cite in this connection – say that IS-LM is not a proper interpretation of the *General Theory*: on the contrary, it seems to me that in both articles Hicks is actually very careful not to say this. Indeed, in the sentence immediately preceding the one from the 1976 article that Robinson quoted, Hicks referred to Keynes' March 1937 letter to him (see p. 62 above) and said: 'I think I am justified in concluding from that letter that Keynes did not wholly disapprove of what I had made of him'. Similarly, in his 1974 *Crisis in Keynesian Economics*, Hicks referred to his IS-LM interpretation and said:

> To many students I fear it *is* the Keynes theory. But it was never intended as more than a representation of what appeared to be a central part of the Keynes theory. As such I think it is still defensible.*
> *It would appear that Keynes himself accepted it as such. See his letter of March 1937 ... in *JMK* XIV, pp. 79–81.
>
> (Hicks 1974: 6, original italics and footnote)

(See also part 1 of Hicks' 1981 article, as well as Hicks 1973: 10.)

My second, and far more important point, however, is that whatever Hicks might have said or thought forty years after his 1937 article does not change the fact that at that time he presented IS-LM as an interpretation of the *General Theory*, and that Keynes accepted it as such. And let me immediately add that this last statement is not inconsistent with my emphasis on the importance of the author's intent in interpreting a text: for there is a fundamental difference between intent at the time of writing and 'retroactive intent' many years later.[21]

VI

In the opposite direction from Milgate's book on the political spectrum is that of the well-known conservative economist, Allan Meltzer, whose book is entitled *Keynes's Monetary Theory: A Different Interpretation* (1988). Almost one-third of the book is devoted to a chapter entitled 'The *General Theory*: A Different Perspective', which to a large extent repeats the contents of a 1981 article of his with an essentially identical title. In this chapter Meltzer contends that some of the major differences between his interpretation and others are that his does not depend on either money illusion in the labor market, or wage rigidity, or the 'liquidity trap', and that (on the other hand) it emphasizes the role of expectations. In a criticism of this article (Patinkin 1983), I showed (*inter alia*) that in point of fact Meltzer's interpretation does not differ in these respects from some earlier interpretations, and even from some macroeconomic textbooks – and I see no point in repeating that demonstration here. My present concern is instead with two of Meltzer's contentions that are indeed different from interpretations of Keynes hitherto. The first is his (Meltzer's) contention that a major objective of the *General Theory* was to stress the importance of 'a higher level of investment until the capital stock reached a social optimum' (1988: 300; see also pp. 7, 118, 185–6). The second is his attempt to create the impression that Keynes shared the conservative view in favor of rules in the present-day debate on 'rules *vs.* discretion', and that indeed this represents a consistent strand in Keynes' policy views from the 1920s on (Meltzer 1988: 8–9, 182–92, 200, 293–7).

Meltzer's first contention is based on Keynes' discussion in Chapter 24 of the *General Theory*, entitled 'Concluding Notes on the Social Philosophy towards which the General Theory Might Lead', in which Keynes says that if as a result of what he terms 'a somewhat comprehensive socialisation of investment' (*GT*: 378) a continuous state of full employment could be assured, then investment would proceed at such a rapid rate that the economy would achieve his 'aim of depriving capital of its scarcity-value within one or two generations' (*GT*: 377), with salutary consequences for the distribution of income.[22]

That here and in other writings Keynes considered it desirable to increase the stock of capital is a point of Meltzer's (1988: 186) that is well taken. But to contend that this was a major theme of the *General Theory* is to tear this book out of the historical context in which it was written, and to tear Chapter 24 out of its context in the book. For the *General Theory* was written at a time not only of idle men, but of idle factories; so it is surely far-fetched to think that a major concern of Keynes' at that time was to increase capital investment in order to further increase the stock of idle plant and equipment. Instead the crucial role of investment expenditures in the *General Theory* was to supplement consumption expenditures in order (with the help of the multiplier) to raise aggregate demand to its full employment level. In brief, the passage in Chapter 24 referred to in the preceding paragraph has to do, not with the major role of investment in the *General Theory*, but with its role (incidental to the central message of the book) in ultimately bringing about Keynes's version and vision of the classical stationary state.

Insofar as the context of Chapter 24 within the *General Theory* is concerned, let us remember that it appears in Book VI, the last one of the *General Theory*, and one that could have been omitted without affecting its central message. Of this there are several indications, of which the casual title of this Book – namely, 'Short Notes Suggested by the General Theory'

– is itself one. Further indications are provided by the nature of the three chapters which constitute this Book. Thus Keynes claims no novelty for the explanation of the cycle which he presents in Chapter 22, entitled 'Notes on the Trade Cycle' (*GT*: 314–15). Chapter 23 (entitled 'Notes on Mercantilism, the Usury Laws, Stamped Money and Theories of Under-Consumption') is, as its title indicates, a miscellanea. It is also significant that, in contrast with the careful procedure that he followed with other chapters of the *General Theory* (see *JMK* XIII and XXIX), Keynes apparently made little effort to subject the drafts and/or proofs of this chapter, as well as of Chapter 24, to the criticism of Kahn, Joan Robinson, Hawtrey, and Robertson. Indeed, it would seem that the proofs of these two chapters were sent only to Harrod, who sufficed with a brief comment on Chapter 23 (to which Keynes did not react), and none on Chapter 24 (see *JMK* XIII: 526, 542, 555; *JMK* XIV: 351).

In brief, Chapter 24 is part of a Book that is essentially an appendage to the *General Theory*, and one should not let the appendage to a text wag its body.

Let me turn now to Meltzer's contention that in his policy prescriptions throughout his career, Keynes was an advocate of rules as against discretion. Strictly speaking, that contention is outside my terms of reference: for as I have emphasized on earlier occasions (1976: 12–13, 135–6; 1982: 14, 212–13) – and as Meltzer (1988: 115) recognizes – the *General Theory* is (as indicated by its title) a book that is devoted almost entirely to theory. I wish nevertheless to deal with Meltzer's discussion of this point because it illustrates some additional pitfalls of interpretation.

To begin with, there is no evidence that Keynes ever gave specific thought to the issue of rules *vs.* discretion, and I share Quentin Skinner's (1969: 32–4) skepticism about attributing to earlier writers specific views about issues with which they were never concretely confronted. Furthermore, even if Keynes had thought of this issue, its meaning in his days was different from what it is today. Specifically, when in 1936 Henry Simons published his famous essay on 'Rules versus Authorities in Monetary Policy', the rule that he advocated as a contracyclical policy was that of stabilizing the price level by means of variations in the quantity of money – with no indication of how the extent of this variation should in each case be determined. Clearly, this policy would today be described not as one of rules, but of discretionary 'fine-tuning'.

Let me for the moment leave this fundamental point aside and consider the two pieces of evidence that Meltzer cites in support of his contention. The first is the fact that from his earliest writings on through Bretton Woods, Keynes advocated 'rules for international monetary arrangements' that called for 'fixed, but adjustable, exchange rates' (Meltzer 1988: 242–3; see also pp. 209–11)]. Without committing myself one way or the other on the validity of Meltzer's treatment of this subject – Moggridge's (1980: esp. 58–60) treatment of it provides somewhat different emphases – let me simply say that the policy issue of fixed *vs.* flexible exchange rates is one frequently considered to be in a category of its own, unrelated to the issue of rules *vs.* discretion. Suffice it to note the views of Milton Friedman (1953: 157ff.), who with equal forcefulness has advocated both a monetary rule and flexible exchange rates.

The second piece of evidence on which Meltzer attempts to base his contention that Keynes was an advocate of rules as against discretion consists of excerpts from Keynes' contributions to the wartime discussions that took place in the Treasury on the problem of maintaining full employment in the postwar period. In this connection, Meltzer (1988: 187) cites Keynes' statement in a 1943 letter to Meade (who played a major role in these discussions) that 'if the bulk of investment is under public or semi-public control and we go in for a stable long-term programme, serious fluctuations are enormously less likely to occur' (*JMK* XXVII: 326), and on the basis of this statement contends that 'Keynes's stabilization proposal did not depend on prompt changes in the amount of public works'. Similarly, at a later point in his book, Meltzer (1988: 294) refers to his discussion in Chapter 4 and writes: 'Keynes's postwar fiscal policy proposals... aim at stabilizing the rate of investment at a permanently higher level'.

Now, the passage in Keynes' letter to Meade which Meltzer cites is actually a loose quotation from a memorandum that Keynes had just written on 'The Long-Term Problem of Full Employment' and which he enclosed with his letter. In particular, this memorandum contains the following passage:

> If two-thirds of three-quarters of total investment is carried out or can be influenced by public or semi-public bodies, a long-term programme of a stable character should be capable of reducing the potential range of fluctuation [in the level of employment] to much narrower limits than formerly.
>
> (*JMK* XXVII: 322)

And what is significant about this passage for my present purpose is that it does not specify any rule for the government to use in determining its actual level of investment in the 'two-thirds to three-quarters [range] of total investment' or in the 'less than $7\frac{1}{2}$ per cent or more than 20 per cent [range] of the net national income' indicated in the passage in the memorandum which follows. In brief, what Keynes regards as 'stable' is not the level of 'public or semi-public' investment, but the need to carry it out. And in this he was reflecting the policy conclusion of the *General Theory* that 'a somewhat comprehensive socialisation of investment will prove the only means of securing an approximation to full employment' (*GT*: 378; see also p. 164).

That Keynes was not thinking in terms of a fixed rule that would determine the level of government investment is also clear from the fact that he goes on in the aforementioned memorandum to say that:

The main task should be to *prevent* large fluctuations by a stable long-term programme. If this is successful it should not be too difficult to offset small fluctuations by expediting or retarding some items in this long-term programme.

(*JMK* XXVII: 322, original italics)

Similarly, in a related 1943 memorandum, Keynes wrote:

if we can find ways of retarding or accelerating the long-term programme to offset unforeseen short-term fluctuations, all the better. No reason, surely, why the Treasury should not be fairly constructive and optimistic on this heading.

(*JMK* XXVII: 356; see also the similar statement on p. 323; see also the first paragraph of his letter to Meade reproduced on p. 319)

Thus, unlike many of today's advocates of, say, the constant-money-growth rule, Keynes' advocacy of a 'long-term programme of a stable character' did not exclude the desirability of also carrying out short-term discretionary policies when necessary.[23]

All this is brought out more clearly and systematically in the historic May 1944 White Paper on 'Employment Policy' which (I think it fair to say) largely reflected Keynes' view on how to carry out the full-employment policy that he advocated – or which (at the very least) advocated policies to which he had no basic objections. Indeed, not only did Keynes write the foregoing memoranda in the context of the Treasury discussions which culminated in this White Paper, but he even prepared notes for the Chancellor of the Exchequer to use in presenting it to the House of Commons (see *JMK* XXVII: 374–9). Now, Chapter V of the White Paper is entitled 'Methods for Maintaining Total Expenditure' at its full-employment level and *inter alia* outlines 'the measures by which the Government propose, *as part of their long-term policy*, to influence the volume of capital expenditure, private and public' (ibid., §57, italics added). The chapter then goes on to say that

for the purpose of maintaining general employment it is desirable that public investment should actually expand when private investment is declining and should contract in periods of boom.... The procedure which the Government have in mind is as follows. All local authorities will submit annually to the appropriate Department their programme of capital expenditure for the next five years.... These programmes will then be assembled by an appropriate co-ordinating body under Ministers and will be adjusted, upward or downward, in the light of the latest information on the prospective employment situation.... The machinery envisaged in this paragraph will enable the Government to set each year a target for the whole volume of public works in the succeeding year.

In order that public investment may be more quickly mobilized to redress the balance of private investment the Government also intend to seek means of reducing the time-lag which ordinarily intervenes between a decision to undertake public capital expenditure and the actual start of the work. Speed here is crucial, for if a decline in demand can be caught quickly enough and corrected, a comparatively modest amount of compensating expenditure will be sufficient to restore the balance.... The Government believe that in the past the power of public expenditure, skilfully applied, to check the onset of a depression has been underestimated.

(ibid. §§ 62–6)

And, significantly enough, this passage echoes one of the comments that Keynes made in February 1944 on what was essentially a draft of the White Paper.[24, 25]

I have quoted these passages *in extenso* in order to clarify the nature of Keynes' policy proposals, and in particular the meaning of the phrase 'long-term policy'. The picture that thus emerges from Keynes' wartime writings is quite at variance with Meltzer's contention (1988: 293) that they present Keynes as a 'proponent of discretionary action constrained by well-defined policy rules' – and my emphasis is of course on 'well-defined'. Thus, to say the least, Keynes' wartime memoranda and correspondence provide little if any support for Meltzer's repeated contention that they show that Keynes 'did not favor the discretionary policies to manage short-term changes in aggregate demand that are called Keynesian' (ibid.: 308; see also pp. 4–5, 122, 295) – whose nature Meltzer does not specify, but by which he presumably means policies of the kind advocated in the United States by (say) Robert Solow and James Tobin.

Meltzer (1988: 294) also tries to create the impression that Keynes was not in favor of 'deficit financing'. Here, however, Meltzer fails to take account of the fact that there is a fundamental difference between his usage of this term and Keynes'. For as part of his postwar proposals, Keynes recommended dividing the overall government budget into a current (or ordinary) budget (which ideally would be financed entirely by taxes) and a capital budget (within which framework the government would carry out its long-term program of investment, which would be financed primarily by borrowing). And he used the term 'deficit financing' only with respect to borrowing to finance a deficit in the ordinary budget.

This basic distinction is spelled out in the following passage from a 1945 memorandum in which Keynes advocated the establishment of a separate capital budget:

It is important to emphasise that it is no part of the purpose of the Exchequer or the Public Capital Budget to facilitate deficit financing, *as I understand this term*. On the contrary, the purpose is to present a sharp distinction between the policy of collecting in taxes less than the current non-capital expenditure of the state as a means of stimulating *consumption*, and the policy of the Treasury's influencing public capital expenditure as a means of stimulating *investment*.

(*JMK* XXVII: 406, first set of italics added)

Keynes then goes on in this memorandum (ibid.: 406–8) to list the various kinds of receipts on capital account to finance the capital expenditures, including, of course, loans from the public ('net receipts ... of public debt held by the private sector').[26]

And the distinctly different roles that Keynes assigned to these two budgets in his contracyclical policy is brought out most clearly in the following comment that he made in 1942 on proposed postwar budgetary policy: 'I should not aim at attempting to compensate cyclical fluctuations by means of the ordinary Budget. I should leave this duty to the capital budget' (*JMK* XXVII: 278; see also pp. 352–3). Thus it was only in his specific sense of the term that Keynes objected to 'deficit financing'. In, however, the sense in which it has been used in (say) the United States and the United Kingdom (where the budget is an overall one, which includes both current and capital expenditures), the contracyclical policy that Keynes advocated can only be described as one of deficit financing.

Let me now return to Meltzer's interpretation of Keynes' views on the issue of 'rules *vs.* discretion' and note that, over and above my foregoing criticisms, is the fundamental question that I raised above as to the meaningfulness of attributing to writers views about issues with which they were never concretely confronted. And in the case of Keynes, this question is particularly relevant. For Keynes was – and is – well known for the fact that he changed his policy recommendations in accordance with changing circumstances. Thus in 1929–30 he advocated public works, as against a lowering of the rate of interest, as the means of dealing with Britain's problem of unemployment; but after Britain abandoned the gold standard in 1931, he advocated doing so by lowering this rate (the 'cheap-money policy'); and when by 1933 this failed to produce the desired results, he returned to the advocacy of public works.[27]

Now, the postwar world which Keynes generally envisaged in the various wartime documents referred to above was one – in the words of the *General Theory* (p. 249) – 'capable of remaining in a chronic condition of sub-normal activity for a considerable period without any marked tendency either towards recovery or towards complete collapse'. So even if we accept the validity of Meltzer's interpretation of Keynes' views in these documents on the issue of 'rules *vs.* discretion' (and I have expressed serious doubts about that), there is little if any validity in his attempt to infer from it how Keynes would today regard this issue for the postwar world of vastly different circumstances that has actually emerged: a world which, far from remaining in *any* 'chronic condition', has experienced prolonged investment booms and unprecedented rapid growth in some periods, and unemployment and recessions in others; a world which in different periods has experienced different degrees of both demand-inflation and cost-inflation, accompanied sometimes by full employment and sometimes by different rates of unemployment; a world with an international monetary system which for the past two decades has been in a constant state of flux, and thus vastly different from the relatively stable system that Keynes envisaged at Bretton Woods.

Might I finally say that if one nevertheless insists upon making inferences from Keynes' writings about what his view would today be on the issue of 'rules *vs.* discretion' (and needless to say, I do not), then a more appropriate basis for such inferences is his 1930 *Treatise on Money*, which deals with a world that experiences significantly changing circumstances, a world subject to both booms and depressions, to both inflation and deflation. The contracyclical policy that Keynes advocated for this world was one that he termed 'The Management of Money' (title of Book VII of the *Treatise*) and described in the first chapter (31) of this Book as follows:

> Thus the art of the management of money consists partly in devising technical methods by which the central authority can be put in a position to exercise a sensitive control over the rate of investment, which will operate effectively and quickly, and partly in possessing enough knowledge and prognosticating power to enable the technical methods to be applied at the right time and in the right degree to produce the effects on prices and earnings which are desirable in the interests of whatever may be the prescribed ultimate objective of the monetary system which is being managed.
>
> (*Treatise* II: 189–90)

And the 'technical method' which Keynes went on to specify in Chapter 37 of the Book – after having taken due account of the fact that the monetary authorities could not produce effects 'instantaneously', and could not be 'expected always to foresee the operation of non-monetary factors in time to take measures in advance to counteract their influence on prices' – was to stabilize the price level by central-bank monetary policy in the form of variations of the short-term rate of interest, with the purpose of influencing the long-term rate and hence the level of investment (see ibid., especially pp. 304–5, 309–10, 315–16, 325–35): in brief, a policy that (like that of Henry Simons' described above) would today clearly be regarded as an example of discretionary 'fine-tuning'.[28]

VII

I conclude this chapter with an attempt to answer the question with which I began: why are there different interpretations of the *General Theory*? Why are there not different interpretations of *Value and Capital* and *Foundations of Economic Analysis*? All of these are canonical texts, and canonical texts attract different interpretations. A partial answer to this question is to be found in the fact that there is a fundamental difference between these texts. For without minimizing their basic contribution to our discipline, *Value and Capital* and *Foundations* were books that elaborated, rigorized and extended economic theory within the existing paradigm. Furthermore, they were books that presented their analysis in mathematical terms, thus leaving little if any ambiguity as to their intended meaning.

Not so the *General Theory*: here was a book which presented a new and at-the-time strange paradigm. It was a pioneering work that introduced new concepts (e.g. the very notion of an 'aggregate demand function') and new ways of thinking (see Patinkin 1976: 83, 98–9). And so it is not surprising that it left some obscurities and even inconsistencies, as well as some loose ends. Indeed, it never pulled together its various analytical components into an explicit and complete model: this task was left for its contemporary interpreters.

An equally if not more important difference is the fact that the works of Hicks and Samuelson had no political implications. This is not true from the Marxist viewpoint, which presumably regards them as rationalizing and hence justifying the functioning of a capitalist market economy. It is however true from the viewpoint of the Western democratic society to which these works were addressed: for neither of them expressed any specific view as to the extent and manner in which government should intervene in such an economy. In contrast, the *General Theory* had a clear political message: government intervention in the form of contracyclical public and semi-public investment was necessary to assure the existence of full employment in a capitalist economy; and only after full employment was thus assured could the market mechanism be relied upon to function without further intervention (*GT*: 378–9).

And these are the differentiae of the *General Theory* which have created fertile ground for different interpretations.

Now, with two of the contemporary interpreters of the *General Theory*, Joan Robinson at Cambridge and Roy Harrod at Oxford, Keynes had carried out intensive discussions of earlier drafts of the book (see *JMK* XIII and XXIX, *passim*). Three others (Bryce, Champernowne, Reddaway) had been students who had attended the lectures that Keynes had given in the process of writing it (see Rymes 1989: ix; *JMK* XIV: 59; Austin Robinson 1977: 33). Others (Hicks, Lerner, Meade) had in one way or another been aware of the work in progress.[29] And all of the contemporary interpreters were directly experiencing the seemingly endless years of the Great Depression which formed the background of the *General Theory*. So despite its ambiguities, there was little difference between them as to both its analytical and political message.

A quarter of a century later, however, and *a fortiori* half a century later, some of the interpreters and most of their readers were of a generation who knew not the Great Depression. Furthermore, the memories of those years had in general dimmed in a postwar world facing economic problems that were vastly different from the prewar one. And – no less important – Keynes was no longer around to defend himself against various would-be interpreters (as he had on at least one occasion, when in April 1938 he concluded a long correspondence with E. S. Shaw on a note that the latter had sent him on the 'finance motive', with the comment that 'there is a good deal in it which I cannot accept as anything like an accurate version of what I am driving at.... I am really driving at something extremely plain and simple which cannot possibly deserve all this exegesis' (*JMK* XXIX: 281–2). In these circumstances the obscurities and loose ends of the *General Theory* provided ample opportunities for different interpreters with different – and quite familiar – motivations: in particular, some interpreters wanted to invoke the authority of a canonical text in support of their prior theoretical views; and others wanted to invoke the authority of a canonical figure in support of their prior political views.[30]

Milgate, Shackle and Weintraub were clearly motivated by the first of these considerations. In section V above, I have said enough about Milgate's attempt to recreate Keynes in the image of the Modern Cambridge School. Insofar as Shackle is concerned, already in his 1938 book on *Expectations, Investment and Income* he had emphasized the importance of expectations and uncertainty in economic life; at the same time, while acknowledging his indebtedness to Chapter 12 of the *General Theory*, he did not claim that the 'animal spirits' of this chapter constituted the central message of that book. Quite the contrary: he went on to describe the analysis of the book in a way that is completely consistent with Hicks' IS-LM interpretation. In Shackle's words at that time:

> [Keynes'] *General Theory of Employment, Interest and Money* really deals with the formal interdependencies of economic variables at a moment of time. *Expectations*, the quantity of money, and the schedules of propensity to consume and of liquidity preference being all given, there is a certain level of the investment-flow, which, in view of the aggregate income corresponding to it, and the given quantity of money, will both evoke and be evoked by a certain rate of interest. In other words, from the knowledge specified we can determine values of certain main economic variables which are mutually consistent and can hold simultaneously.
>
> (Shackle 1938: 2, original italics)

Similarly, Shackle's 1949 book on *Expectation in Economics* (p. 60, footnote) contains only one passing reference to the *General Theory* and, what is even more significant, does not contain any reference to Keynes' 1937 *Quarterly Journal of Economics* article. To the best of my knowledge, it was only in a 1953 article on 'A Chart of Economic Theory' (pp. 217, 222–4) that we find the first indications of Shackle's interpretation of the *General Theory cum QJE* 1937 article that has been described in section IV above.

A similar story, albeit over a much shorter time span, and somewhat more complicated, holds for Sidney Weintraub and his wage-cost-markup theory of price. In order to present this story in its proper perspective, let me first note that there is little concern with the theory of price *per se* – and *a fortiori* little concern with this specific theory – in Weintraub's 1958 book on *An Approach to the Theory of Income Distribution*, whose main concern is precisely what its title says (but see p. 57, n. 16, and pp. 100–1). And though this book contains many references to the *General Theory*, I think it fair to say that Weintraub did not contend that the concern of his book was a major one of the *General Theory*. In any event, it is a fact that the latter contains no significant discussion of the distribution of income; and that, indeed, at the beginning of the *General Theory* (p. 4), Keynes distinguishes sharply between his concern with the level of total output and the 'Ricardian tradition ... [which] expressly repudiated any interest in the *amount* of the national dividend, as distinct from its distribution' (ibid., n. 1, original italics).

There is, however, one respect in which Weintraub's 1958 book foreshadows the interpretation of the *General Theory* that he was to present in his 1961 book on *Classical Keynesianism, Monetary Theory, and the Price Level*, for in Chapter 2 of the 1958 book, Weintraub develops the properties of what he denotes as aggregate demand and aggregate supply curves and states (ibid., p. 24) that 'in a way, then, this chapter constitutes a restatement of the main part of macroeconomic theory [and here a footnote provides references to various articles and notes on the aggregate supply curve]. Like all such analysis, its origin is to be found in Keynes's *General Theory*'.[31] On the other hand, and in sharp contrast with his 1961 book, Weintraub's 1958 book (ibid.: 153–6) presents Hicks' IS-LM analysis without in any way criticizing it.

We come now to Weintraub's 1959 book on the *General Theory of the Price Level, Output, Income Distribution, and Economic Growth*, whose central message is precisely his theory of price determination by wage-cost-markup. And in the Preface to the book, he describes this theory as 'a glimmer of an idea that had been stirring in [his] mind for some time ... a single idea ... able to unify important parts of the theory of the price level, output, income distribution and growth theory'. It is, however, most significant that Weintraub does not yet ascribe this theory to Keynes.

It is only in his article a year later on 'The Keynesian Theory of Inflation: The Two Faces of Janus?' (1960) that Weintraub (after referring to his 1959 book) does make such an ascription. And here he went on to describe the relation of his wage-cost-markup theory of price to Keynes' in the following words: 'I think I "know" what Keynes would have emphasized, but I refrain from any attempt at documentation, for it is equally possible for those who hold alternative views to find appropriate supporting passages in Keynes' *General Theory* or his later discussion in *How to Pay for the War* to sanction their doctrinal interpretation' (1960: 144). A year later this article was reprinted as Chapter 2 of his *Classical Keynesianism, Monetary Theory, and the Price Level* (1961), in which the foregoing quotation appears on p.

27. A similar ascription to Keynes – which has already been cited on p. 64 and in note 9 – also appears in Chapter 1 of the book (1961: 3). And in presenting his interpretation of the *General Theory* in both the article (1960: § § 1–2) and the book (1961: 5–10, 18–22, 35–8), Weintraub emphasizes the role of the aggregate supply curve in Keynes' analysis, and now firmly rejects both the 45°-cross diagram and the IS-LM one.

Needless to say, the distinction that I have made between theoretical and political motivations is not an absolute one. Thus Milgate's attempt to identify Keynes' theory with that of the 'Modern Cambridge School' is also an attempt to invoke Keynes' authority for the 'much more interventionist stance' of this School (Milgate 1982: preface). Similarly, Weintraub's 1961 interpretation of the *General Theory* as having a primary concern with wage-cost-push inflation was clearly related to his policy proposals – in opposition to those that he attributed to the 'Keynesians' – for dealing with the inflation of the 1950s (1961: 5–9).

Meltzer's book too reflects a combination of both motivations. Thus at many points in it (see e.g. Meltzer 9, 15, 177, 184, 207) he invokes Keynes' authority for his (Meltzer's) specific theoretical view of uncertainty as imposing on the economy an 'excess burden' that manifests itself in a lower rate of investment, and hence lower stock of capital, than would otherwise exist. But what stands out most in Meltzer's interpretation is his political motivation, and particularly his desire to claim the political mantle of Keynes for the conservative rules-as-against-discretion type of contracyclical policy that he advocates (see e.g. Meltzer 1983, 1987; Brunner and Meltzer 1983: esp. 97–100), and for the related conservative opposition to 'deficit financing'. And no less important is his desire to deny that mantle to the 'Keynesians': to drive a wedge between 'Keynes and the Keynesians' by denying that the latter are the legitimate heirs of the Master's views on the nature of the contracyclical policy that should be adopted.

Let me conclude this discussion of politically motivated interpretations by noting that the nature of such motivations is well illustrated by the following passage:

On questions of policy the differences can never be resolved. Even such an apparently simple problem as, for instance, the extension of public works as a remedy for unemployment, is found to give rise to violent conflicts of interest.... Revolutionaries who regard unemployment as only one of the evils of a system of private enterprise are not anxious for capitalist governments to learn the trick of reducing fluctuations in trade, and so deprive them of the most obvious, though not the most fundamental, of their objections to the system. The adherents of *laissez-faire*, on the other hand, fear that, if it once became clear to the public that state interference can reduce unemployment, the public might begin to think that state interference could do much else besides.

(Robinson 1937: 126–7)

This is a passage from the *Introduction to the Theory of Employment* by Joan Robinson – in her prewar period.

VIII

At the beginning of this chapter I expressed the view that though the original meaning which an author intended might not be the only legitimate one, at the same time this meaning can be used to justify the rejection of interpretations that differ greatly from it. And now I leave it for you the reader to decide which if any of the interpretations of the *General Theory* that I have discussed – including my own version of the IS-LM interpretation – should be rejected on those grounds.

ACKNOWLEDGEMENTS

This chapter originated in my Keynes Lecture delivered at the British Academy in November 1989. An augmented version of the lecture appears in the *Proceedings* of the Academy for 1989. The present chapter contains some minor changes and additions to that version, and is published here with the kind permission of the Academy.

Work on this lecture was begun while serving in September 1989 as the James S. McDonnell Scholar at the World Institute for Development Economics Research (WIDER) in Helsinki. During this visit I benefited greatly from discussions with my fellow McDonnell Scholars, Frank Hahn and Robert Solow. I am indebted to both the James S. McDonnell Foundation and WIDER for making possible this most fruitful visit.

Without in any way burdening them with responsibility for the end product, I wish to express my deepest appreciation to Menahem Brinker, Geoffrey Hartman and Ilana Pardes for guiding my reading in the field of hermeneutics, and for patiently discussing with me many of the problems that I there encountered. Again, without burdening them with any responsibility for the views expressed, I am also indebted to Brinker and Pardes, as well as to Chaim Barkai, Stanley Fischer, David Laidler, Donald Moggridge, Luigi Pasinetti, Robert Skidelsky, and Roy Weintraub, for valuable criticisms of earlier drafts of this chapter. Similarly valuable comments were received on the draft presented at the Department of Economics Seminar of the Hebrew University of Jerusalem. Finally, I wish to thank Vivian Nadir for her most pleasant and efficient technical assistance.

Reprinted articles are referred to by the date of original publication; for convenience, however, the page references to such articles are to the reprint. All references to the writings of Keynes are to the relevant volumes of the Royal Economic Society's edition of his *Collected Writings*. These volumes are, respectively, referred to as *JMK* XIII, *JMK* XXVII, and so forth. The

Treatise on Money is frequently referred to as the *Treatise*; and the *General Theory of Employment, Interest and Money* is referred to as the *General Theory* or *GT*.

This research was supported by the Basic Research Foundation administered by the Israel Academy of Sciences and Humanities, to which I express my thanks. I also wish to thank the Israel Academy itself for the pleasant and helpful atmosphere in which most of the work on this chapter was carried out.

NOTES

1 Note that the 1979 exchange between Coddington and Hicks deals – as indicated by the title of Coddington's article – with 'Hicks's Contribution to Keynesian Economics', and not with *Value and Capital* proper.

2 For an example of the use of probabilistic notions to draw a hypothetical regression line in order to determine what I have called the central message of a text, see Patinkin (1982, pp. 16–18).

3 The relevant passage in this entry reads: 'The meeting was devoted to a long academic lecture by Keynes on the whole of the *General Theory* – the equality between savings and investment; the inducement to invest; the propensity to consume; and liquidity preference' (Meade 1990: 48). See also Keynes' notes for this 'lecture' as reprinted in *JMK* XXVII: 388ff.

4 See the letters (written at various dates during the period 1935 to 1938) reproduced in *JMK* XIV to Joan Robinson (pp. 148–50), Harrod (pp. 84–6), Reddaway (p. 70) and Hicks (pp. 70–83); as well as the letters in *JMK* XXIX to Bryce (p. 150) and Lerner (p. 214–16). See also Hicks (1973).

Though in the correspondence with Robertson on his review Keynes did refer to the former's discussion of the aggregate supply curve (*JMK* XIV: 89), he did not do so in his published reply.

5 In this footnote, Keynes goes on to say: 'The analysis which I gave in my *General Theory of Employment* is the same as the 'general theory' explained by Dr. Lange on p. 18 of this article [corresponding to p. 176 of the reprint], except that my analysis is not based (as I think his is in that passage) on the assumption that the quantity of money is constant'.

6 Harrod, Hicks and Meade had all presented their reviews as papers at the September 1936 European meetings of the Econometric Society at Oxford: see the report by Phelps Brown (1937). For a fascinating behind-the-scenes account of these meetings, see Chapter 1 of Young (1987), who *inter alia* reproduces a letter from Hicks to Meade (ibid: 33 and 35) which shows that Hicks had read both Meade's and Harrod's papers before completing his own IS-LM paper, which is the one he presented at the meetings. Young (ibid.: 33 and 98 ff.), however, also emphasizes that Hicks never claimed originality for the IS-LM equations, but only for the diagram.

Having mentioned Young's book, I must add that at some points it reflects the 'Modern Cambridge School' *cum* Post-Keynesian interpretation of the *General Theory* which is criticized in sections V and VI of this chapter.

I might also note that in a March 1937 letter to Joan Robinson (reproduced in *JMK* XIV: 149), Keynes wrote that he did not 'feel any objection' to her publishing her *Introduction to the Theory of Employment* (1937), Chapter 2 of which presents an interpretation of the *General Theory* which is essentially a verbal rendition of the subsequent elementary-textbook 45°-cross diagrammatic explanation of the determination of the equilibrium level of income.

7 But see pp. 111–13 of my *Keynes' Monetary Thought* for a discussion of what may possibly be some ambivalence on this point in the *General Theory*.

8 It is this conclusion which led Coddington (1983: 93ff.) to designate the interpretation of Keynes by Shackle and those who have been influenced by him (see section V of this chapter) as 'fundamentalist Keynesianism', in the sense that it interprets the *General Theory* as being fundamentally opposed to traditional equilibrium theory. Coddington himself criticized this view (ibid.: 88, 97–100); see also note 10 below.

Coddington (1983: 102 ff., which reproduces the corresponding material of his 1976 article) contrasted this approach with that of 'hydraulic Keynesianism', which is essentially his term for mainstream Keynesianism as represented by (say) IS-LM. His explanation of his choice of this term is that it reflects the fact that this approach describes the macroeconomy 'in terms of disembodied and homogeneous flows' between which 'there exist stable relationships'. Readers of Coddington's posthumously published book have sometimes wondered whether his choice of this term was also influenced by the hydraulic mechanism that A.W. Phillips – with the assistance of W.T. Newlyn – constructed to illustrate the workings of what is essentially the IS-LM model of the *General Theory* (see Phillips 1950). In reply to a query of mine on this point, Mark Blaug has informed me that he once raised this question with Coddington and was told that 'the idea came from his memory of the Phillips machine, which he had never seen but which was legendary at L.S.E.' (cited from Blaug's letter with his kind permission). Susan Howson, however, has pointed out to me that Coddington might also have been influenced by Shackle's reference in his *Years of High Theory* (1967: 189) to the 'misleading' 'reduction of economics to hydraulics', and that Shackle himself, according to Arthur Brown (1988), was 'no doubt thinking of the Phillips–Newlyn model, which arrived in Leeds shortly before he did' (ibid.: 38). I am indebted to Howson for this additional information, as well as for referring me to Nicholas Barr's illuminating article on 'The Phillips Machine' (1988). Barr (ibid.: 330–4) reports that the machine fell into disuse in the late 1950s, but that a process of renovation was undertaken in 1987. Tony Atkinson has kindly informed me that the renovated machine was unveiled in 1989 and is on display once again at LSE (see postscript p. 94).

I might note that a hydraulic mechanism to illustrate the working of economic principles was first constructed by Irving Fisher in 1893 in connection with his 1892 doctoral dissertation on *Mathematical Investigations in the Theory of Value and Prices*. In Fisher's case, however, the principles illustrated were the utility-maximizing conditions of general-equilibrium analysis. Pictures of the 1893 mechanism, as well as a 'somewhat improved and simplified' one constructed in 1926, appear as frontispieces to the 1925 reprint of Fisher's dissertation. (The quotation is from Fisher's Preface to this reprint.)

9 In all fairness, I should add that this passage goes on to say:

> I am aware that other Keynesians can select other passages to corroborate their doctrinal position so that such controversies on 'what Keynes really meant', like those on 'what Marx – or Marshall – really meant', are likely to be peculiarly barren and futile. It is with Keynesianism then, not with Keynes, that I am concerned. For myself I acknowledge full indebtedness to his tremendous work, rather than to deny or camouflage it as is becoming fashionable. My ideas, like those of all modern Keynesians, emanate from it.

10 See also Coddington's (1983: 59–60) implicit criticism of Shackle's interpretation of Keynes' 1937 article.

11 For further evidence that in using the phrase 'animal spirits' Keynes did not intend to imply that 'the determination of investment is entirely arbitrary', see

Robin Matthews (1984: 209–12), who also cites supporting evidence from Joan Robinson. Matthews (ibid.) also reproduces the following interesting information on this phrase that he received from Donald Moggridge:

> The origins of 'animal spirits' seem to go a long way back in Keynes. The earliest reference comes in a set of lecture notes which are in the Marshall Library Collection, entitled 'Notes on Modern Philosophy I – Descartes, Leibnitz, McTaggart's Lectures, Ertemann's [*sic*] History – [includes Spinoza's Ethics]'. In the part concerning Descartes as regards life and biology the text runs: 'The body is moved by animal spirits – the fiery particles of the blood distilled by the heat of the heart. They move the body by penetrating and moving the nerves and muscles.... But does not this increase the amount of motion? No. for the animal spirits are always in motion – the will only directs them'.
>
> Keynes then adds a comment that reads 'unconscious mental action'.

In reply to a query from me, Moggridge has kindly supplemented this information with the following:

> The documents referred to are a set of handwritten reading/lecture notes taken by JMK ... The notes are in JMK's papers, then in the Marshall [Library] and now in King's [College Library]. JMK, according to Harrod (1951, p. 61) went to J.E. McTaggart's lectures on general philosophy during the 1902–3 academic year. Erdmann's philosophy is presumably J.E. Erdmann's *A History of Philosophy*, an English translation of which appeared in 1890.

12 It is in this longer-run context that I also interpret Keynes' statement in a May 1936 letter to Hubert Henderson (dealing with the latter's criticism of the *General Theory*): 'I should. I think, be prepared to argue that in a world ruled by uncertainty with an uncertain future linked to an actual present, *a final position of equilibrium*, such as one deals with in static economics, does not properly exist' (*JMK* XXIX: 222, italics added).

13 Here is another problematic aspect of Weintraub's interpretation: for this attributes to Keynes a 'theory of the price level' in terms of a 'wage-cost markup' (Weintraub 1978: 64). This may be the reason Weintraub prefaced his attribution with the comment that in doing so he was 'taking only mild liberties with Keynes'. Surely, however, there is a fundamental difference between the cost-markup theory of price and the marginal-cost theory of price, and it is the latter that Keynes consistently uses throughout the *General Theory* (see e.g. p. 55 (bottom), p. 283 (lines 4–5) and pp. 294–295).

For my present purposes, however, this is a secondary issue, my major point being that in any event the theory of price determination is a subsidiary concern of the *General Theory*.

14 I must admit to some inconsistency here: for the subtitle of Chick's book is 'A Reconsideration of the *General Theory*'. On the other hand, in the preface to her book (p. vii) she states:

> This is not a book in the history of economic doctrine as such, which is concerned with illuminating the author's point of view as brightly as possible on his own terms. I hope at several points to have done that, though I do not claim that this book reveals 'what Keynes really meant' ... it is a philosophical impossibility to *know* what someone else 'really meant'; what matters is to make coherent sense for oneself of what an author says and to evaluate its relevance to the problem at hand. (italics in original)

This last sentence clearly reflects an implicit acceptance of the deconstructionist approach to hermeneutics: see section I of this chapter.

I should also note that in what may in part have been Leijonhufvud's reaction to the criticisms of his interpretation of the *General Theory* presented in the review articles of his book by Grossman (1972) and Jackman (1974), Leijonhufvud (on pp. i–ii of his English foreword to the 1978 Japanese edition of his book) emphasized that his book was about 'theoretical problems that were current problems in the early or mid-sixties. . . . What Keynes might have meant, etc., was not one of the problems. Doctrine history was not what the book was about'.

15 See the references to these economists in the writings of such Post-Keynesians as Davidson (1972; 1981: 154–5) and Eichner (1979). Shackle's interpretation is also implicitly accepted by Joan Robinson in her paper on 'What Has Become of the Keynesian Revolution' (Robinson 1973: 3, n. 1, and text to which it is attached) and in her Foreword to Eichner (1979: xi). Though he does not refer explicitly to Shackle, Minsky (1975: 38) rejects the IS-LM interpretation of the *General Theory* on the same grounds that Shackle did. On Weintraub, see also the survey article by Eichner and Kregel (1975).

16 As is also its contention that Kalecki independently discovered the General Theory – a contention that I have examined in detail and rejected in Chapter 3 of my *Anticipations of the General Theory*? (Patinkin 1982).

17 On which, see Frank Knight's (1923) classic critique.

18 Another example of Milgate's approach to the interpretation of the *General Theory* is provided by his discussion of Keynes' criticism of the classical theory of interest in Chapter 14 of the book. Here Milgate (1982: 111) contends that this criticism 'has been progressively obscured by conventional interpretations'. And he then presents his alternative interpretation, which is based on his objection to the 'unqualified acceptance of the final text of Chapter 14' (ibid.: 122) and on his resort instead (ibid: 111–23) to his interpretation of the earlier draft of this chapter and the related Keynes–Harrod correspondence reproduced in *JMK* XIII.

19 On the same Shacklian grounds, Robinson could also have applied this epithet to the 45°-cross interpretation of the *General Theory* presented in Chapter 2 of her 1937 *Introduction to the Theory of Employment* (see note 6 above). In particular, Robinson concluded the exposition of this chapter with the following words:

> To sum up: . . . It is through changes in income that the equality of saving and investment is preserved. Thus the level of income is determined by the rate of investment and the desire to save; given the desire to save, the level of income that will rule is governed by the rate of investment. And given the rate of investment the level of income is determined by the desire to save.
> (1937: 16)

In a 1970 note on 'Quantity Theories Old and New', Robinson also objects to IS-LM on the grounds that it provided 'a mollifying version of his [Keynes'] system of ideas which turned it back once more into a variant of the quantity theory' (ibid.: 507)!

20 I Kings 14: 16. See Joan Robinson's (1977: 10) statement about 'the IS/LM model with which generations of students have been taught to misinterpret the *General Theory*'. Robinson's (1978) statement about Hicks' having 'repented' is quoted approvingly by Richard Kahn (1984: 160), who adds that Keynes' 1937 letter to Hicks left Hicks 'unrepentant'. This religious overtone is not unusual in Post-Keynesian writings. Thus Sidney Weintraub (1976) entitled his criticism of IS-LM 'Revision and Recantation in Hicksian Economics'. Similarly, Paul Davidson (1989: 23, n. 3) claimed that Axel Leijonhufvud 'recanted' on a certain point that he (Davidson) considered to be at variance with Post-Keynesian teachings.

21 For another instance of disregarding 'retroactive intent' – even when it is that of God Himself – see the wonderful Talmudic story cited at the beginning of my 'In Defense of IS-LM' (1990).

22 In a 1943 letter to Josiah Wedgwood, Keynes also said that 'it would be in the interests of the standards of life in the long run if we increased our capital quite materially' (*JMK* XXVII: 350).

23 This would also seem to be the conclusion that Dimsdale (1987: 224) draws from his study of Keynes' wartime memoranda: 'His [Keynes'] views on the design of counter-cyclical policy were a development of the ideas which he had put to the Committee on Economic Information from 1935 onwards. He favoured the use of fiscal measures, based on variations in public and semi-public investment, to offset the trade cycle'.

24 Namely, the comment in which he advocated preparing

> a regular survey and analysis of the relationship between sources of savings and different types of investment and a balance sheet showing how they have been brought into equality for the past year, and a forecast of the same for the year to come. If aggregate demand gave signs of being deficient, the analysis would indicate a deflationary gap exactly corresponding to the inflationary gap which we have so often discussed during the war. This survey and balance sheet ... would give an annual opportunity for examining whether the state of demand during the ensuing year looked like being adequate to maintain employment and national income at the desirable level and for the Government to explain to Parliament what steps it had in view to remedy a prospective disequilibrium in either direction.
>
> (*JMK* XXVII: 368–9)

25 In the sentence before the one that Meltzer quotes from Keynes' aforementioned letter to Meade, Keynes said that 'it is quite true that a fluctuating volume of public works at short notice is a clumsy form of cure and not likely to be completely successful' (*JMK* XXVII: 326). And I think that Keynes was here making a distinction between public works carried out 'at short notice' and those that would be carried out in accordance with the 'long-term programme' that he advocated in the following sentence of the letter.

26 The financing by borrowing of the public-works, expenditures that he advocated for dealing with depressions was a consistent feature of Keynes' policy thinking. Thus see his statement in a 1933 letter to *The Times* that 'I contemplate that public works would be paid for out of loans' (*JMK* XXI: 200), as well as his description of the financing of the government 'programme of domestic investment' that (under certain conditions) he advocated in the *Treatise* (II: 337–8). Indeed, in his prewar writings Keynes frequently referred to such public-works expenditures as 'loan expenditures': see e.g. the 1929 *Can Lloyd George Do It?* (*JMK* IX: esp. 115–21; written together with Hubert Henderson), the 1933 *Means to Prosperity* (*JMK* IX: 346–50, 354–5, 364–6), the *General Theory* (p. 128, n. 1), and the 1937 'How to Avoid a Slump' (*JMK* XXI: 390). The discussion in *Means to Prosperity* (*JMK* IX: bottom of p. 347) also makes it clear that when Keynes speaks of 'balancing the budget', he is not including 'loan expenditures' in the budget.

27 This is an obvious oversimplification of what was actually a complex sequence of events. For details, see Patinkin (1982: ch. 8) and references there cited. In early 1931, Keynes also recommended the imposition of tariffs, and dropped this recommendation after the devaluation a few months later.

28 Note that this fact in itself constitutes a refutation of Meltzer's contention (1988: 8) that 'from the [1923] *Tract [on Monetary Reform]* through his subsequent major works', Keynes 'favored principal reliance on rules, with strict limits on discretionary action and policy surprises'.

29 Joan Robinson and others had discussed the *General Theory* with Lerner before the latter wrote his review of the book (*JMK* XIV: 148, esp. n. 1). Robinson (1978: xiv–xv) and Kahn (1984: 182–3) have also described a weekend meeting in August 1933 with Meade (who, together with them, had been a member of the 1931 'Cambridge Circus') and Lerner which was devoted to clarifying various aspects of Keynes' thinking up to that point. Meade was also in close contact in other contexts with his Oxford colleague, Roy Harrod, as well as with Kahn (see Young 1989: 52–6, 70–3, *et passim*), and it is reasonable to assume that in this way he continued to receive some information about the development of the *General Theory*. There was also some minimal contact between Hicks and Keynes (Hicks 1973: 7–8).

30 For different approaches to *The Politics of Interpretation*, see the 1983 collection of papers and related discussions under that title, edited by WJT. Mitchell.

31 In the opening footnote of this chapter, Weintraub notes that 'with some minor changes', it is reproduced from his 1957 *Economic Journal* article on 'The Micro-Foundations of Aggregate Demand and Supply'. Though it is most unlikely that this was one of the 'minor changes' that he had in mind, it does seem to me that the connection he makes in this chapter between his aggregate supply curve and that of the *General Theory* is somewhat stronger than the connection he made in his 1957 article. Specifically, the opening paragraph of that article consists of the following declaration:

> This article attempts to construct an aggregate supply function without reference to what Keynes 'really' meant. Unlike recent contributions to the *Economic Journal* (and here a footnote provides references to the same articles and notes that were later listed in the footnote at the beginning of Chapter 2 of his 1958 book, just referred to in the text), it foregoes the attempt to link the concept, in detail and with supporting references, to Keynes. While discretion replaces valour, it remains beyond dispute that the very discussion must acknowledge the *General Theory* as the source and inspiration.

REFERENCES

Reprinted works are cited in the text by year of original publication; the page references to such works in the text are, however, to the pages of the reprint in question.

Barr, Nicholas (1988) 'The Phillips machine', *LSE Quarterly* 2, 305–37.

Brown, Arthur (1988) 'A worm's eye view of the Keynesian revolution', in John Hillard (ed.) *J.M. Keynes in Retrospect: The Legacy of the Keynesian Revolution* (Edward Elgar, Hants, England) 18–44.

Brunner, Karl and Allan H. Meltzer (1983) 'Strategies and tactics for monetary control', *Carnegie-Rochester Conference Series on Public Policy* 18, 59–103.

Bryce, Robert B. (1935) 'An introduction to a monetary theory of employment', in Patinkin and Leith (1977: 128–45). Also reproduced in JMK XXIX, 132–50.

Champernowne, D.G. (1936) 'Unemployment, basic and monetary: The classical analysis and the Keynesian', *Review of Economic Studies* 3, 201–16. As reprinted in Lekachman (1964: 153–73).

Chick, Victoria (1983) *Macroeconomics after Keynes: A Reconsideration of the General Theory* (Philip Allan, Oxford).

Coddington. Alan (1976) 'Keynesian economics: The search for first principles', *Journal of Economic Literature* 14, 1258–73.

Coddington, Alan (1979) 'Hicks's contribution to Keynesian economics', *Journal of Economic Literature* 17, 970–88.

Coddington, Alan (1983) *Keynesian Economics: The Search for First Principles* (George Allen & Unwin, London).

Davidson, Paul (1972) *Money and the Real World* (Macmillan, London).

Davidson, Paul (1981) 'Post Keynesian economics: solving the crisis in economic theory', in Daniel Bell and Irving Kristol (eds) *The Crisis in Economic Theory* (Basic Books, New York) 151–73.

Davidson, Paul (1989) 'Keynes and money', in Roger Hill (ed.) *Keynes, Money and Monetarism* (Macmillan, London) 2–26.

Dimsdale, N.H. (1987) 'Keynes on British budgetary policy 1914–1946', in Michael J. Boskin, John S. Flemming, and Stefano Gorini (eds) *Private Saving and Public Debt* (Basil Blackwell, Oxford) 208–33.

Eichner, Alfred S. (ed.) (1979) *A Guide to Post-Keynesian Economics* (M.E. Sharpe, White Plains, NY).

Eichner, Alfred S. and J.A. Kregel (1975) 'An essay on post-Keynesian theory: a new paradigm in economics', *Journal of Economic Literature* 13, 1293–314.

Fish, Stanley (1980) *Is There a Text in this Class? The Authority of Interpretive Communities* (Harvard University Press, Cambridge, MA).

Fisher, Irving (1892) 'Mathematical investigations in the theory of value and prices', *Transactions of the Connecticut Academy* 9, July. Reprinted with a new preface (Yale University Press, New Haven, CT, 1925). Reprinted (Kelley, New York, 1901).

Fisher, Irving (1930) *The Theory of Interest* (Macmillan, New York). Reprinted (Kelley and Millman, New York, 1954).

Friedman, Milton (1953) *Essays in Positive Economics* (University of Chicago Press, Chicago, IL).

Grossman, Herschel I. (1972) 'Was Keynes a "Keynesian"? A review article', *Journal of Economic Literature* 10, 26–30.

Hansen, Alvin H. (1936) 'Mr. Keynes on underemployment equilibrium', *Journal of Political Economy*, 44, 667–86.

Hansen, Alvin H. (1953) *A Guide to Keynes* (McGraw-Hill, New York).

Harcourt, G.C. (1980) 'A post-Keynesian development of the "Keynesian" model', in Edward J. Nell (ed.) *Growth, Profits, and Property: Essays in the Revival of Political Economy* (Cambridge University Press, Cambridge) 151–64.

Harcourt, G.C. (1987) 'Post-Keynesian economics', in John Eatwell, Murray Milgate, and Peter Newman (eds) *The New Palgrave: A Dictionary of Economics*, vol. 3 (Macmillan, London) 924–8.

Harrod, R.F. (1937) 'Mr. Keynes and traditional theory', *Econometrica* 5, 74–86. As reprinted in Lekachman (1964: 124–52).

Harrod, R.F. (1951) *The Life of John Maynard Keynes* (Macmillan, London).

Hart, A.G. (1947) 'Keynes' analysis of expectations and uncertainty', in S.E. Harris (ed.) *The New Economics: Keynes' Influence on Theory and Economic Policy* (Knopf, New York) 415–24.

Hicks, J.R. (1936) 'Mr. Keynes' theory of employment', *Economic Journal* 46, 238–53. As reprinted in Hicks (1982: 83–99).

Hicks, J.R. (1937) 'Mr. Keynes and the "Classics": a suggested interpretation', *Econometrica* 5, 147–59. As reprinted in Hicks (1982: 100–15).

Hicks, J.R. (1939) *Value and Capital* (Clarendon Press, Oxford).

Hicks, J.R. (1973) 'Recollections and documents', *Economica* 40, 2–11.

Hicks, J.R. (1974) *The Crisis in Keynesian Economics* (Basil Blackwell, Oxford).

Hicks, J.R. (1976) 'Time in economics', in A.M. Tang *et al.* (eds) *Evolution, Welfare and Time in Economics: Essays in Honor of Nicholas Georgescu-Roegen*. As reprinted in Hicks (1982: 282–300).

Hicks, J.R. (1979) 'On Coddington's interpretation: a reply', *Journal of Economic Literature* 17, 989–95.

Hicks, J.R. (1981) 'IS-LM: an explanation', *Journal of Post Keynesian Economics* 3, 139–54. As reprinted in Hicks (1982: 318–31).

Hicks, J.R. (1982) *Money, Interest and Wages: Collected Essays on Economic Theory*, vol. II (Basil Blackwell, Oxford).

Hirsch, E.D. Jr (1967) *Validity in Interpretation* (Yale University Press, New Haven, CT).

Hirsch, E.D. Jr (1976) *The Aims of Interpretation* (University of Chicago Press, Chicago, IL).

Jackman, Richard (1974) *Keynes and Leijonhufvud*, Oxford Economic Papers 26, 259–72.

Johnson, Harry G. (1961) *The General Theory after Twenty-Five Years*, American Economic Association Papers and Proceedings 51, 1–17.

Kahn, Richard F. (1984) *The Making of Keynes' General Theory* (Cambridge University Press, Cambridge).

Keynes, John Maynard (1923) *A Tract on Monetary Reform*. As reprinted in Keynes, *Collected Writings*, Vol. IV.

Keynes, John Maynard (1925) *The Economic Consequences of Mr. Churchill*. As reprinted in Keynes, *Collected Writings*, Vol. IX, 207–30.

Keynes, John Maynard (1930) *A Treatise on Money, Vol. I: The Pure Theory of Money*. As reprinted in Keynes, *Collected Writings*, Vol. V.

Keynes, John Maynard (1930) *A Treatise on Money, Vol. II: The Applied Theory of Money*. As reprinted in Keynes, *Collected Writings*, Vol. VI.

Keynes, John Maynard (1933) *The Means to Prosperity*. As reprinted in Keynes, *Collected Writings*, Vol. IX, 335–66.

Keynes, John Maynard (1936) *The General Theory of Employment Interest and Money*. As reprinted in Keynes, *Collected Writings*, Vol. VII.

Keynes, John Maynard (1937a) 'Alternative theories of the rate of interest', *Economic Journal* 47, 241–52. As reprinted in Keynes, *Collected Writings*, Vol. XIV, 201–215.

Keynes, John Maynard (1937b) 'The general theory of employment', *Quarterly Journal of Economics* 51, 209–23. As reprinted in Keynes, *Collected Writings*, Vol. XIV, 109–23.

Keynes, John Maynard (1937c) *How to Avoid a Slump*. As reprinted in Keynes, *Collected Writings*, Vol. XXI, 384–95.

Keynes, John Maynard (1938) 'Comment on D.H. Robertson, "Mr. Keynes and 'Finance'"', *Economic Journal* 48, 318–22. As reprinted in Keynes, *Collected Writings*, Vol. XIV, 229–233.

Keynes, John Maynard (1940) *How to Pay for the War*. As reprinted in Keynes, *Collected Writings*, Vol. IX, 367–439.

Keynes, John Maynard, *The General Theory and After: Part I, Preparation*, edited by Donald Moggridge, Vol. XIII of Keynes, *Collected Writings*.

Keynes, John Maynard, *The General Theory and After: Part II, Defense and Development*, edited by Donald Moggridge, Vol. XIV of Keynes, *Collected Writings*.

Keynes, John Maynard, *Activities 1931–1939: World Crises and Policies in Britain and America*, edited by Donald Moggridge, Vol. XXI of Keynes, *Collected Writings*.

Keynes, John Maynard, *Activities 1940–1946: Shaping the Post-war World: Employment and Commodities*, edited by Donald Moggridge, Vol. XXVII of Keynes, *Collected Writings*.

Keynes, John Maynard, *The General Theory and After: A Supplement*, edited by Donald Moggridge, Vol. XXIX of Keynes, *Collected Writings*.

Keynes, John Maynard, *Collected Writings*, Vols I–VI (1971), Vols VII–VIII (1973), Vols IX–X (1972), Vols XI–XII (1983), Vols XIII–XIV (1973), Vols XV–XVI

(1971), Vols XVII–XVIII (1978), Vols XIX–XX (1981), Vol. XXI (1982), Vol. XXII (1978), Vols XXIII–XXIV (1979), Vols XXV–XXVII (1980), Vol. XXVIII (1982), Vol. XXIX (1979), Vol. XXX (bibliography and index, 1989) (Macmillan, for the Royal Economic Society, London).

Keynes, John Maynard and Hubert Henderson (1929) *Can Lloyd George do it? An Examination of the Liberal Pledge.* As reprinted in Keynes, *Collected Writings,* Vol. IX, 86–125.

Klein, Lawrence (1947) *The Keynesian Revolution* (Macmillan, New York).

Knight, Frank H. (1921) *Risk, Uncertainty and Profit* (Houghton Mifflin, New York).

Knight, Frank H. (1923) 'The ethics of competition', *Quarterly Journal of Economics* 37, 579–624. As reprinted in Knight, *The Ethics of Competition and Other Essays* (Harper & Bros., New York, 1935) 41–75.

Kuhn, Thomas S. (1970) *The Structure of Scientific Revolutions*, 2nd enlarged edn (University of Chicago Press, Chicago, IL).

Lange, Oskar (1938) 'The rate of interest and the optimum propensity to consume', *Economica* 5, 12–32. As reprinted in *Readings in Business Cycle Theory, Selected by a Committee of the American Economic Association* (Blakiston, for the American Economic Association, Philadelphia, PA, 1944) 169–92.

Leijonhufvud, Axel (1968) *On Keynesian Economics and the Economics of Keynes: A Study in Monetary Theory* (Oxford University Press, New York).

Leijonhufvud, Axel (1978) Foreword to the Japanese edition of Leijonhufvud (1968) (Toyo Keizai Shinposha, Tokyo).

Lekachman, Robert (ed.) (1964) *Keynes' General Theory: Reports of Three Decades* (St Martin's Press, New York).

Leontief, Wassily (1936) 'The fundamental assumption of Mr. Keynes' monetary theory of unemployment', *Quarterly Journal of Economics* 51, 192–7.

Lerner, Abba P. (1936) 'The general theory', *International Labour Review* 34, 435–54. As reprinted in Lekachman (1964: 203–22).

Matthews, R.C.O. (1984) 'Animal spirits', *Proceedings of the British Academy* 70, 209–29.

Meade, J.E. (1937) 'A simplified model of Mr. Keynes' system', *Review of Economic Studies* 4, 98–107.

Meade, J.E. (1990) *The Cabinet Office Diary: 1944–46*, edited by Susan Howson and Donald Moggridge, Vol. IV of *The Collected Papers of James Meade* (Unwin Hyman, London).

Meltzer, Allan H. (1981) 'Keynes's General Theory: a different perspective', *Journal of Economic Literature* 29, 34–64.

Meltzer, Allan H. (1983) 'Monetary reform in an uncertain environment', *Cato Journal* 3, 93–112.

Meltzer, Allan H. (1987) 'Limits of short-run stabilization policy', *Economic Inquiry* 25, 1–13.

Meltzer, Allan H. (1988) *Keynes's Monetary Theory: A Different Interpretation* (Cambridge University Press, Cambridge).

Merton, Robert K. (1957) 'Priorities in scientific discovery', *American Sociological Review* 22, 635–59. As reprinted in Merton, *The Sociology of Science: Theoretical and Empirical Investigations*, edited by Norman W. Storer (University of Chicago Press, Chicago, IL, 1973) 286–324.

Milgate, Murray (1982) *Capital and Employment: A Study of Keynes's Economics* (Academic Press, London).

Minsky, Hyman P. (1975) *John Maynard Keynes* (Columbia University Press, New York).

Mitchell, W.J.T. (ed.) (1983) *The Politics of Interpretation* (University of Chicago Press, Chicago, IL).

Moggridge, D.E. (1986) 'Keynes and the international monetary system 1909–46', in Jon S. Cohen and G.C. Harcourt (eds) *International Monetary Problems and Supply-side Economics: Essays in Honour of Lorie Tarshis* (Macmillan, London) 56–83.

Modigliani, Franco (1944) 'Liquidity preference and the theory of interest and money', *Econometrica* 12, 45–88. As reprinted in *Readings in Monetary Theory, Selected by a Committee of the American Economic Association* (Blakiston, for the American Economic Association, Philadelphia, PA, 1951) 186–240.

Pasinetti, Luigi L. (1974) *Growth and Income Distribution: Essays in Economic Theory* (Cambridge University Press, Cambridge).

Patinkin, Don (1956) *Money, Interest and Prices: An Integration of Monetary and Value Theory* (Row, Peterson, Evanston, IL).

Patinkin, Don (1965) *Money, Interest and Prices: An Integration of Monetary and Value Theory*, 2nd edn (Harper and Row, New York).

Patinkin, Don (1976) *Keynes' Monetary Thought: A Study of its Development* (Duke University Press, Durham, NC).

Patinkin, Don (1982) *Anticipations of the General Theory? And Other Essays on Keynes* (University of Chicago Press, Chicago, IL).

Patinkin, Don (1983) 'New perspectives or old pitfalls? Some comments on Allan Meltzer's interpretation of the General Theory', *Journal of Economic Literature* 21, 47–51.

Patinkin, Don (1989) *Money, Interest, and Prices: An Integration of Monetary and Value Theory*, 2nd abridged edn with a new introduction (MIT Press, Cambridge, MA).

Patinkin, Don (1990) 'In defense of IS-LM', *Banca Nazionale del Lavoro: Quarterly Review* 172, 119–34.

Patinkin, Don, and J. Clark Leith (eds) (1977) *Keynes, Cambridge and the General Theory: The Process of Criticism and Discussion Connected with the Development of the General Theory* (Macmillan, London).

Phelps Brown, E.H. (1937) 'Report of the Oxford meeting, September 25–29, 1936', *Econometrica* 5, 361–83.

Phillips, A.W. (1950) 'Mechanical models in economic dynamics', *Economica* NS 17, 283–305.

Reddaway, W.B. (1936) 'The general theory of employment, interest and money', *Economic Record* 12, June. As reprinted in Lekachman (1964, 99–107).

Robertson, D.H. (1936) 'Some notes on Mr. Keynes' general theory of employment', *Quarterly Journal of Economics* 51, 168–91.

Robinson, Austin (1977) 'Keynes and his Cambridge colleagues', in Patinkin and Leith (1977: 25–38).

Robinson, Joan (1937) *Introduction to the Theory of Employment* (Macmillan, London).

Robinson, Joan (1962a) *Essays in the Theory of Economic Growth* (Macmillan, London).

Robinson, Joan (1962b) Review of 'Money, trade and economic growth' by Harry G. Johnson, *Economic Journal* 72, 690–2. As reprinted in part in Robinson, *Collected Economic Papers*, Vol. III (Basil Blackwell, Oxford, 1975) 100–2.

Robinson, Joan (1962c) *Economic Philosophy* (Aldine, Chicago, IL).

Robinson, Joan (1970) 'Quantity theories old and new', *Journal of Money, Credit and Banking* 2, 504–12.

Robinson, Joan (1973) 'What has become of the Keynesian revolution?', in Joan Robinson (ed.) *After Keynes* (Basil Blackwell, Oxford).

Robinson, Joan (1977) 'What are the questions?', *Journal of Economic Literature* 15, 1318–39. As reprinted in Robinson, *Collected Economic Papers*, Vol. V (Basil Blackwell, Oxford, 1980) 1–31.

Robinson, Joan (1978) *Contributions to Modern Economics* (Basil Blackwell, Oxford).

Robinson, Joan (1979) Foreword to Eichner (1979, xi–xxi).

Rymes, Thomas K. (ed.) (1989) *Keynes's Lectures, 1932–35: Notes of a Representative Student* (Macmillan, London).

Samuelson, Paul A. (1946) 'Lord Keynes and the General Theory', *Econometrica* 14, 187–200. As reprinted in Lekachman (1964: 315–31).

Samuelson, Paul A. (1947) *Foundations of Economic Analysis* (Harvard University Press, Cambridge, MA).

Schlesinger, James R. (1956) 'After twenty years: The General Theory', *Quarterly Journal of Economics* 70, 581–602.

Shackle, G.L.S. (1938) *Expectations, Investment and Income* (Oxford University Press, Oxford).

Shackle, G.L.S. (1949) *Expectation in Economics* (Cambridge University Press, Cambridge).

Shackle, G.L.S. (1953) 'A chart of economic theory', *Metroeconomica* 5, 1–10. As reprinted in Shackle, *Uncertainty in Economics: And Other Reflections* (Cambridge University Press, Cambridge, 1955) 217–26.

Shackle, G.L.S. (1961) 'Recent theories concerning the nature and role of interest', *Economic Journal* 71, 209–254. As reprinted in Shackle, *The Nature of Economic Thought: Selected Papers 1955–1964* (Cambridge University Press, Cambridge, 1966) 225–81.

Shackle, G.L.S. (1967) *The Years of High Theory: Invention and Tradition in Economic Thought, 1926–1939* (Cambridge University Press, Cambridge).

Shackle, G.L.S. (1973) 'Keynes and today's establishment in economic theory: a view', *Journal of Economic Literature* 11, 516–19.

Shackle, G.L.S. (1982) 'Sir John Hicks' "IS-LM: An explanation": a comment', *Journal of Post Keynesian Economics* 4, 435–8.

Simons, Henry (1936) 'Rules versus authorities in monetary policy', *Journal of Political Economy* 44, 1–30. As reprinted in Simons, *Economic Policy for a Free Society* (University of Chicago Press, Chicago, IL, 1948) 160–83.

Skinner, Quentin (1969) 'Meaning and understanding in the history of ideas', *History and Theory* 8, 3–53. As reprinted in Tully (1988: 29–78).

Skinner, Quentin (1976) 'Motives, intentions and the interpretation of texts', in D. Newton de Molina (ed.) *On Literary Intention* (Edinburgh University Press, Edinburgh) 210–21. As reprinted in Tully (1988: 68–78).

Taussig, F.W. (1936) 'Employment and the national dividend', *Quarterly Journal of Economics* 51, 198–203.

Tully, James (ed.) (1988) *Meaning and Context: Quentin Skinner and his Critics* (Polity Press, Cambridge).

Viner, Jacob (1936) 'Mr. Keynes on the causes of unemployment', *Quarterly Journal of Economics* 51, 147–67. As reprinted in Lekachman (1964: 235–53).

Weintraub, Sidney (1957) 'The micro-foundations of aggregate demand and supply', *Economic Journal* 67, 455–70.

Weintraub, Sidney (1958) *An Approach to the Theory of Income Distribution* (Chilton, Philadelphia, PA).

Weintraub, Sidney (1959) *A General Theory of the Price Level, Output, Income Distribution, and Economic Growth* (Chilton, Philadelphia, PA).

Weintraub, Sidney (1960) 'The Keynesian theory of inflation: the two faces of Janus?', *International Economic Review* 1, 143–55.

Weintraub, Sidney (1961) *Classical Keynesianism, Monetary Theory, and the Price Level* (Chilton, Philadelphia, PA).

Weintraub, Sidney (1976) 'Revision and recantation in Hicksian economics: a review article', *Journal of Economic Issues* 10, 618–27. As reprinted in Weintraub *et al.* (1978, 113–23).

Weintraub, S. *et al.* (1978) *Keynes, Keynesians and Monetarists* (University of Pennsylvania Press, Philadelphia, PA).

Young, Warren (1987) *Interpreting Mr. Keynes: The IS-LM Enigma* (Polity Press, Cambridge).

Young, Warren (1989) *Harrod and his Trade Cycle Group: The Origins and Development of the Growth Research Programme* (Macmillan, London).

Government publications

Great Britain (1944) *Employment Policy*, Parliamentary papers, Cmd 6527 (HMSO, London).

Postscript to note 8

In reply to my query about the conjectures of Howson and Brown, Shackle wrote me: 'I can say that my use of the term "hydraulic" was not influenced by the Phillips machine, unless quite unconsciously. I cannot say whether Coddington may have had this term suggested to him by *The Years of High Theory*.'

4 Keynes's *General Theory*

Interpreting the interpretations

Bill Gerrard

Economic Journal (1991) 101, March, pp. 276–87

Keynes's *General Theory* has given rise to a variety of Keynesian research programmes. The development of these different Keynesian research programmes is well documented (see e.g. Coddington 1976; Gerrard 1988; Hamouda and Harcourt 1988 for surveys of Keynesian and post-Keynesian economics). However, less attention has been paid to explaining a striking feature of this Keynesian diversity, namely, the stress placed on discovering the real meaning of Keynes's *General Theory*. The legitimacy of any particular Keynesian research programme has been judged with regard to the authenticity of its implied interpretation of Keynes. Inevitably this concern for authenticity has generated much controversy, enveloping Keynesian economics in a 'doctrinal fog' (Blaug 1980: 221). This chapter attempts to pierce that Keynesian doctrinal fog. The central thesis is that the causes of the controversy surrounding Keynes's *General Theory* lie, in part, in the different presuppositions made about the nature of interpretation. It is argued that much light can be shed on the Keynesian debate by drawing on the study of hermeneutics.

The structure of the chapter is as follows. The first section discusses the atomistic view of interpretation which is implicitly presupposed by most contributors to the Keynesian debate. Two variants of the atomistic view are considered: the objectivist/essentialist approach and the relativist approach. The second section provides an alternative presupposition, the organicist view of interpretation, as exemplified by Ricoeur's dialectical approach in hermeneutics. The chapter concludes with a re-examination of the Keynesian debate in the light of the organicist view of interpretation.

THE ATOMISTIC VIEW OF INTERPRETATION

A principal aim of Keynesian economics has been to give a definitive answer to the question 'What does Keynes's *General Theory* really mean?' Much of the resulting controversy arises from the nature of the question itself. In asking the question an atomistic view of interpretation is presupposed. The author, the text and the reader are treated as individual atomistic entities which are interrelated in a purely external manner: the author produces the text which the reader interprets. There are two variants of the atomistic view of interpretation: the objectivist/essentialist approach and the relativist approach.

The objectivist/essentialist approach

From the perspective of the objectivist/essentialist approach, the aim of interpretation is the rational reconstruction of the text in order to recover the author's original meaning. Interpretation is seen to be problematic because the author's meaning is hidden. The latency of the original meaning creates confusion and generates the possibility of multiple interpretations. The task of the interpreter is to resolve this confusion by discovering the 'true' meaning of a text. This presupposes that the true meaning is knowable.

Within the objectivist/essentialist approach, Keynes's *General Theory* is viewed as containing a single essential meaning which is hidden as the result of the confusion created either by Keynes himself or by the economics profession in its reading of Keynes. The belief that Keynes's *General Theory* contains a single essential meaning is shared by most interpreters of Keynes. Leijonhufvud (1968) claims to have found the 'economics of Keynes' as opposed to 'Keynesian economics', while Shackle (1967: ch. 12) seeks Keynes's 'ultimate meaning'. Fender (1981: 1–2) sets out to find the 'exact nature of the theoretical contribution of Keynes'; similarly, Chick (1983: v) attempts to remedy the fact that the 'macroeconomics that has been developed after Keynes, though claiming inspirations from the *General Theory*, in my view has not, with some outstanding exceptions, been macro-economics after the manner of Keynes – with the method and perspective and insight of Keynes'.

From the objectivist/essentialist perspective, it is necessary to explain why the essential meaning of the *General Theory* is hidden. There are three broad types of explanations.

The confusion is author-generated

A number of writers have suggested that Keynes himself is the cause of the confusion. There are a number of variants of this 'author-generated confusion' thesis.

(i) Technical incompetence

It is often argued that Keynes had limited analytical abilities. For example, Hahn (1982: x, xi) writes that 'I consider that Keynes had no real grasp of formal economic theorising (and also disliked it), and that he consequently left many gaping holes in his theory.' This follows a famous remark by Shove that 'Maynard had never spent the twenty minutes necessary to understand the theory of value' (quoted in Robinson 1964: 79).

(ii) The 'vision' thesis

Confusion arises as the inevitable consequences of the difficulties which Keynes faced in trying to formulate his underlying vision in a precise analytical manner. It is a line of argument originating with Schumpeter (1946: 501) who distinguishes between Keynes's vision, that is, his 'view about the basic features of society, about what is and what is not important' and Keynes's technique, that is, the 'apparatus by which he conceptualises his vision and which turns the latter into concrete propositions or theories'. According to Schumpeter the *General Theory* is the final result of a long struggle by Keynes to make his vision analytically operative. Leijonhufvud (1968: 10, 11) adopts Schumpeter's distinction, arguing that Keynes was not entirely successful in translating his vision into a logically watertight model.

(iii) Stylistic difficulties

Keynes is often accused of a lack of clarity. This is suggested by O'Donnell (1989a: 6) as a reason for the difficulties in the interpretation of Keynes. O'Donnell approvingly quotes Wittgenstein's maxim that if 'anything can be said, it can be said clearly'. Leijonhufvud (1968: 10, 11) goes as far as to say that the *General Theory* is 'a badly written book' and that the need for 'repairs' has led to confusion because different writers have corrected Keynes's model in inappropriate ways. It is also argued that Keynes's style is too loose and vague. This echoes Whitehead's criticism of Keynes's dissertation on probability as using the style of literature, not the style of logic and philosophy.

(iv) Inconsistencies

Some writers have suggested that Keynes did not have a coherent and consistent vision. It is an argument used by Leijonhufvud but also by Robinson (1973: 3) in her well-known comment that 'there were moments when we had some trouble in getting Maynard to see what the point of his revolution really was'.

(v) The 'grand mistake' thesis

An extreme example of the 'author-generated confusion' thesis is the neo-Ricardian argument that Keynes made a mistake in retaining the neoclassical concept of the marginal efficiency of capital (Milgate 1982). This created the possibility that, if the rate of interest is sufficiently low, there will be sufficient investment to maintain full employment. According to Milgate this undermined the principle of effective demand, the essence of the *General Theory*. Furthermore it forced Keynes to develop explanations of interest rate maladjustment; hence Keynes's misguided emphasis on expectations and liquidity preference.

The confusion is reader-generated

An alternative explanation of the confusion surrounding the *General Theory* is to focus on the actions of the audience. Again there are a number of variants of this explanation.

(i) Inappropriate framing

Readers have interpreted Keynes relative to an inappropriate frame of reference. This results in the development of a variety of 'subjective' interpretations based on personal beliefs and ideological and normative biases. In the process the 'objective' meaning of Keynes becomes lost. This line of argument is epitomised by Leijonhufvud's distinction between 'Keynesian economics' and the 'economics of Keynes'. It is an argument repeated by Fitzgibbons (1988: 1–5) when he points towards the problem of 'systematically biased interpretation'.

(ii) Selective reading

A closely related variant to the inappropriate framing argument is the problem created by readers considering only parts of the text. Thus O'Donnell (1989a: 4) sees the main reason for the multiple interpretations of Keynes as the 'tendency to base interpretations on selected parts, rather than the whole of his relevant writings'.

(iii) Reliance on secondary sources

The tendency towards multiple interpretations of Keynes has been exacerbated by the tendency to read about Keynes rather than to read Keynes himself.

The confusion is generated by differences in the composition of the stock of relevant textual evidence

Different interpretations may arise because of differences between interpreters with regard to the definition of the text to be analysed. There are two variants of this explanation.

(i) Which text?

With an author as productive as Keynes, an inevitable problem is whether to interpret the target text in isolation or in the context of the author's other related writings. This can lead to multiple interpretations if readers find inconsistencies between different texts. The definition of 'other relevant writings' may vary between interpreters, particularly with regard to the relative weights to be attached to earlier and later writings as well as to formal writings and more informal sources such as speeches, unpublished papers and private correspondence. Thus, for example, the recent emergence of the 'new' Keynesian fundamentalism associated with Carabelli (1988), Fitzgibbons (1988) and O'Donnell (1989a) amongst others, represents a shift of weight in favour of Keynes's early philosophical papers, a source largely ignored by previous interpreters.

(ii) Changes in availability

Not only can there be 'subjective' differences about the definition of the text, there may also be 'objective' differences over time as the stock of documents available for interpretation changes. Such changes have been particularly important in the interpretation of Keynes's *General Theory*. The publication of the *Collected Writings*, especially volumes XIII and XIV, shed considerable light on the development of Keynes's thought immediately before and after the publication of the *General Theory*. The stock of documents expanded subsequently with the publication of volume XXIX as the result of the discovery of a laundry basket of previously unknown papers by Keynes. These included early drafts of the *General Theory* focusing on the concept of a monetary production economy.

These various sources of confusion create the possibility of multiple interpretations. Convergence towards the correct interpretation is usually presumed to be ensured by the use of consistency with the textual evidence as the criterion of choice between competing interpretations (for example, Leijonhufvud 1968: 8). Interpretation is viewed, therefore, as a scientific problem. The scientific nature of interpretation has been highlighted by Stigler (1965) with particular reference to the problem of multiple interpretations of Ricardo. Stigler argues that hand-picked quotations are insufficient to validate any particular interpretation. He proposes instead the use of two different principles of interpretation: the principle of scientific exegesis and the principle of personal exegesis. Scientific exegesis is interpretation which aims to maximise the value of a text to the science. In this case the text of an interpretation is its consistency with the main analytical conclusions of the author. This type of interpretation is concerned with the 'strong' form of the text, that is, an amended form of the text which removes 'blemishes' such as logical errors and tautologies. Personal exegesis, on the other hand, aims to discover what the author really believed and thus the test of an interpretation becomes consistency with the author's style, that is, what the author actually wrote. According to Stigler this latter form of interpretation is of no direct relevance to scientific progress.

Stigler's separation of scientific and personal exegesis has been the subject of criticism by Aksoy (1989) and Hollander (1989). Both question whether scientific exegesis can really be considered as interpretation when it denies any significance to what the author really believed. Hollander criticises scientific exegesis for leading to the distortion of an author's writings since it justifies disregarding those parts of an author's writings deemed by the interpreter to be 'blemishes'. Hollander describes this as a 'lazy man's procedure' and argues for the need to explain the 'residuals', that is, the differences between the 'strong' form of the text and what the author actually wrote.

The controversy surrounding Stigler's scientific approach to interpretation is suggestive of an important, but often overlooked, characteristic of interpretation. 'Consistency with the textual evidence' is inadequate as an objective criterion for assessing competing interpretations. The definition of both 'consistency' and 'textual evidence' is open to debate. The textual evidence may be defined as the single target text only or it may include other relevant texts. Likewise 'consistency' is open to multiple interpretation. Stigler suggests two alternative definitions: consistency with the author's beliefs (i.e. personal exegesis). O'Donnell (1989b) has proposed a three stage consistency test for any interpretation of Keynes. According to O'Donnell, interpretations should be: (i) internally consistent; (ii) consistent with quotations taken in context; and (iii) consistent with all of an author's writings. This definition of consistency appears to be unnecessarily restrictive in at least two ways. First, it seems to impose on an author's writings a degree of integration and continuity over time which may be unwarranted. Second, it seems to exclude evidence drawn from sources other than the author's own writings.

Thus the choice between competing interpretations cannot be purely objective. Such choices must always be made on the basis of certain presuppositions. Any particular interpretation has a conventional foundation, a set of presuppositions which are treated as beyond doubt. This conventional foundation includes presuppositions about the aims of interpretation, the consistency criterion and the relevant evidence. Different writers may base their interpretations on different conventional foundations. Furthermore the very presupposition that the author's meaning is hidden provides the means by which any particular interpretation can be rendered consistent with the text. Any apparent inconsistency between an interpretation and the text can be explained away as the result of author-generated confusion. The objectivist/essentialist approach has a built-in immunising stratagem with which to protect the validity of any particular interpretation. The parallel with recent developments in the philosophy of science is clear. The Duhem–Quine thesis on the underdeterminacy of empirical testing has led to the recognition that science consists of theoretical structures with conventional foundations as exemplified by Kuhn's theory of paradigms and Lakatos's notion of scientific research programmes with hard cores.

The relativist approach

The contradictions within the objectivist/essentialist approach to interpretation have led some to adopt the relativist approach. Rather than viewing interpretation as the discovery of the author's meaning hidden within the text, the relativist approach treats interpretation as the product of the reader imposed on the text. Thus the analysis of interpretation moves from being text-centred to being reader-centred. There is no single essential meaning within a text, only a variety of reader-determined meanings. Interpretations are always relative to the frame of reference within which the reader is operating. This implies that there is no objective standard for a rational evaluation of alternative interpretations. The choice of interpretation is made by the individual reader on the basis of a subjectively determined frame of reference. Any interpretation can only ever be treated as consistent with its own underlying frame of reference. In this sense, one interpretation is as good as another.

From the relativist perspective, to ask the question 'What does Keynes's *General Theory* really mean?' is really to ask 'What does Keynes's *General Theory* mean to me, given my frame of reference?' Readers choose that interpretation which makes sense within their own world-view. For example, since the neo-Keynesians adopt the choice-theoretic and market-theoretic perspective of mainstream economic theory, it follows that they interpret Keynes's *General Theory* to be dealing with the effects of imperfections such as non-atomistic market structures or imperfect information which prevent the price mechanism from operating effectively.

The relativist approach, however, also suffers from self-contradictions. To adopt the relativist approach is to accept that the interpretive process is indeterminate. Relativism implies that 'anything goes'; consistency with the text is always relative to a subjectively determined frame of reference. This brings the validity of the process of interpretation itself into question. The relativist approach denies that interpretation can be the pursuit of understanding beyond that which is relative to the individual's own frame of reference. But this runs counter to the explicitly stated aims of those who engage in interpretation. Interpretations are advanced on the basis of intellectual and cognitive properties which are deemed to transcend subjectivist concerns. In order to justify the public presentation of an interpretation, interpreters adopt an objectivist/essentialist approach when advocating their own particular interpretations. Relativism cannot be followed consistently since it would deny the intellectual properties which interpreters always claim for their own interpretations. Relativism is a position that can be entertained but never occupied. The relativist approach, through the force of its own logic, becomes self-contradictory. Relativism always reverts to a form of 'back-door' objectivism in which writers use the relativist approach to criticise the interpretations of others but claim authenticity for their own interpretations. Practised in this form, relativism is but a variant of the 'reader-generated confusion' thesis.

To summarise: much of the confusion surrounding the interpretation of Keynes's *General Theory* arises from the presupposed atomistic view of interpretation. The atomistic view, in both its objectivist/essentialist and relativist forms, is self-contradictory. These contradictions have been carried over into the interpretation of Keynes. Thus the task of piercing the Keynesian doctrinal fog requires, as a first step, moving beyond the atomistic view of interpretation.

THE HERMENEUTIC APPROACH TO INTERPRETATION

An alternative view of interpretation is the organicist view which stresses the importance of context. The writing and reading of texts are processes which are socially and historically contingent. The author, the text and the reader are not atomistic entities but form a dynamic whole in which the nature of any part is defined by its interrelationship with the other parts. It is a general vision of the process of interpretation which finds its expression primarily in the study of hermeneutics.

Hermeneutics is the study of interpretation. It originated as the study of the principles of biblical exegesis, deriving its name from Hermes, the messenger of the Gods. Gradually hermeneutics extended its scope beyond the confines of biblical exegesis, becoming the study of textual interpretation in general. It was systematised in the nineteenth century in the writings of Schleiermacher who set out the basic principles of hermeneutics. Schleiermacher stressed the importance of context, arguing that the historical conditions of the author must be taken into account in recovering the original meaning of the text. In particular, it was crucial to understand the original audience to whom the text was directed. Following Schleiermacher, hermeneutics became closely associated with the German historicist school, especially Dilthey, who came to regard the hermeneutic approach as a general methodology for the human sciences. During the twentieth century hermeneutics has undergone at least two marked changes in orientation. In the writings of Heidegger and Gadamer, hermeneutics emerged as a general philosophical position, becoming an integral part of the work of the Frankfurt School. Later hermeneutics took a more linguistic turn, becoming synonymous with the structuralist approach to the study of language and symbols.

The ever-changing nature of hermeneutics means that there is no single coherent set of hermeneutic principles. Instead there are different conflicting traditions. Hirsch (1976) identifies three such traditions:

1 *The biblical/intuitionist tradition*, in which the concern is for the 'spirit' of the text. Meaning is seen as not fully expressible in words, implying that the understanding of a text requires getting behind the text. Schumpeter's

notion of vision is suggestive of the intuitionist tradition. Interpretation is more than logical deduction. It requires intuition in order to achieve 'communion' with the spirit of the text.

2 *The legal/positivist tradition*, in which the concern is for the 'letter of the law', that is, what is actually written. Meaning is seen as wholly contained within the text and recoverable by means of logical deduction. It is a tradition which has its origins in part in Jewish Talmudic scholarship. The latter is explicitly invoked by Patinkin (1978) in support of his contention that the students of Keynes's thought should concern themselves only with what Keynes actually said.

3 *The metaphysical tradition*, in which the original meaning of the text is seen as unrecoverable, and, hence, unknowable. Given the seemingly nihilistic implications of the metaphysical tradition for the interpretive process, it is a tradition that has little parallel in the Keynesian debate.

Given these very different traditions in hermeneutics it is important from the outset that hermeneutics should not be seen as a set of unquestionable principles which can settle the debates over Keynes's *General Theory* once and for all. Hermeneutics can be a double-edged sword.

A key concept in hermeneutics is the hermeneutic circle which arises from a general paradox within any organicist approach. To know the whole, one needs to know the parts. But the parts can be known only in the context of their interdependencies within the whole. Thus to know the whole requires that the whole be pre-known. This circularity has a 'narrow' and 'wider' sense. In the narrow sense the text itself is treated as a whole while in the wider sense the text is treated as part of the historical context.

Within hermeneutics, the hermeneutic circle has been subject to two very different interpretations (Hirsch 1976). The 'old' or 'romanticist' hermeneutics considers the aim of interpretation to be the recovery of the author's original meaning. The hermeneutic circle is the recognition of the need to understand the historical context of the text. In contrast, the 'new' hermeneutics considers the hermeneutic circle as the rejection of objectivity. Interpretation is always relative to the historical context of the reader. Thus, just as with the atomistic approach to interpretation, the hermeneutic approach is caught in an objectivist-versus-relativist controversy.

An attempt to transcend the objectivist–relativist duality in hermeneutics is to be found in the writings of Ricoeur (1976, 1981). Following Hirsch, Ricoeur views interpretation as a process of guess and validation in which interpreters marshall evidence to show a particular interpretation to be more or less probably true. Interpretation involves the logic of qualitative probability and uncertainty. However, unlike Hirsch, he does not view the aim of interpretation as the recovery of the author's original meaning which he considers to be 'a lost psychical event'. But the denial of this objective standard does not entail that anything goes in interpretation. The text contains potential meaning to be actualised by readers but it constrains the possibilities of that actualisation. For Ricoeur interpretation is the appropriation of the reference power of a text, that is, the actualisation of a text's ability to disclose possible ways of looking at the world. Interpretation involves what Gadamer termed the 'fusion of horizons'. The world horizon of the reader becomes fused with the world horizon of the author with the text acting as the mediating link. The resultant interpretation is not the function of the text or the reader alone. Rather it is the outcome of a dialectical process.

From the writings of Ricoeur and others it is possible to develop a hermeneutic framework for the analysis of interpretation using the following definitions:

- *understanding*: the construction of a text's meaning in its own terms
- *explanation*: the presentation of the understood meaning in terms accessible to a particular audience
- *interpretation*: the process of dynamic interaction between understanding and explanation
- *meaning*: the outcome of the process of interpretation
- *judgement*: the construction of a relation between the text and something external to it
- *criticism*: the explanation and evaluation of the judgement
- *application*: the process of dynamic interaction between judgement and criticism
- *significance*: the outcome of the process of application.

For Ricoeur these concepts are abstract poles within a concrete whole. Interpretation is a dialectic of understanding and explanation in which the understanding of a text affects its explanation and vice versa. Likewise application is a dialectic of judgement and criticism. At a higher level there is also a dialectical interaction between interpretation and application.

The dialectical approach of Ricoeur and other related organicist analyses of interpretation are able to provide an alternative set of presuppositions about the nature of interpretation to that associated with the atomistic view. This alternative set of presuppositions can be formulated in terms of four propositions.

Proposition 1 Interpretation is a multi-dimensional process with multiple objectives

Interpretation involves understanding and explanation as well as judgement and criticism. It aims not only to provide meaning to a text but also to evaluate the significance of the text. The complexity of interpretation needs to be recognised by writers in order to overcome the confusion. This conclusion is drawn by Aksoy (1989: 744) in his application of the hermeneutic perspective to the debates surrounding the interpretation of Ricardo: 'there is a great deal of confusion about the meaning and the purpose of the act of interpretation. In most cases, interpreters are found to be careless and inconsistent about the differences between interpretation, judgement, evaluation and application.'

Proposition 2 Interpretation is not an objective process but this does not imply that anything goes

There is no objective criterion of consistency with the textual evidence on which to base the rational evaluation of alternative interpretations. But anything does not go. The interpretive process is historically and socially contingent. Fish (1980) argues that interpreters are social beings, constrained by the set of characteristic beliefs of the particular interpretive community to which the interpreters belong. The interpretive community acts as the intellectual arbiter, setting the cognitive standards by which new interpretations are judged. The acceptance of a new interpretation involves both demonstration and persuasion. The interpretive community must be persuaded to change its paradigm, that is, the conventional foundations underlying the currently-accepted interpretation. It is only after the interpretive community has been persuaded to change its paradigm that the explanatory power of the new interpretation can be demonstrated.

Proposition 3 The significance of an interpretation is not determined by correspondence with the author's original meaning

The significance of an interpretation is something external to the text. It depends on the successful application of the insights gained from the text. In the case of an economics text, its significance can be seen as its ability to explain economic behaviour. The question of whether or not this is what the author really meant is largely irrelevant in this context. From this perspective, Stigler's distinction between personal and scientific exegesis can be justified to the extent that it represents the hermeneutic distinction between meaning and significance.

Proposition 4 The existence of multiple interpretations is not a problem

Multiple interpretations of a single text arise partly because of the inescapable vagueness of the written word. It is this vagueness which gives the text its reference power, its ability to disclose different possible ways of looking at the world. The text constrains the range of potential meanings but cannot determine the actualisation of any specific meaning by the reader. The continued existence of multiple interpretations need not, therefore, be treated as a problem to the extent that it is indicative of the high reference power of the text and the heterogeneity of the readership. It only becomes a problem if interpreted as such from an objectivist/essentialist perspective.

CONCLUSION: HOW TO PIERCE THE KEYNESIAN DOCTRINAL FOG

Much of the doctrinal fog surrounding the interpretation of Keynes has been generated by the confusion of interpretation and application. Interpreting Keynes's *General Theory* has involved two questions, the question of interpretation, 'What does Keynes's *General Theory* mean?', and the question of application 'What is the significance of Keynes's *General Theory* for explaining how the economy actually works?' The two questions are interdependent but they have tended to become interwoven in a very confusing manner. For example, Leijonhufvud (1968: 1) differentiates between what he calls the 'doctrinal-historical' question of understanding Keynes's *General Theory* and the task of discovering fresh perspectives with which to understand the economy and with which to assess economic theory. Leijonhufvud considers the latter to be the primary objective, the doctrinal-historical question being 'strictly secondary'. Yet the validity of the fresh perspective discovered by Leijonhufvud is assessed on the basis of it having 'a much firmer foundation in Keynes's writing than can be claimed for the [income-expenditure] interpretation' (p. 11). Thus Leijonhufvud considers his interpretation as the 'economics of Keynes'. Leijonhufvud does not assess his interpretation with regard to its relevancy to the understanding of the economy and economic theory but in terms of its authenticity as an exegesis of the real meaning of Keynes's *General Theory*.

Piercing the Keynesian doctrinal fog requires disentangling the question of interpretation and the question of application. The significance of Keynesian economics depends on its ability to provide an understanding of how the economy actually works. The significance of Keynesian economics does not depend on being the economics of Keynes. What Keynes himself believed is a question for the historians of economic thought, not for macroeconomists. This is not to say that interpretation is unimportant; quite the opposite. Rather the point is that the usefulness of an interpretation depends on its ability to generate a better understanding of economic behaviour. The interpretation of Keynes's *General Theory* has relevance for macroeconomics if and only if it can provide access to new understandings of the macro economy. Distinguishing between meaning as the aim of interpretation and significance as the aim of application will do much to overcome the confusion surrounding Keynes's *General Theory*.

The continuing achievement of Keynes's *General Theory* is its ability to generate a diversity of research programmes. This diversity has resulted from the fusion of Keynes's horizon as expressed in the *General Theory* with a series of very different horizons due to his interpreters and is evidence of the high reference power of Keynes's *General Theory*. It is a text which continues to disclose a number of different possible ways of looking at the macro economy. The recognition of this will clear the Keynesian doctrinal fog. The multiple interpretations of Keynes's *General Theory* need no longer be interpreted as a problem yet to be solved.

This conclusion that the economics profession should stop worrying about the multiple interpretations of Keynes's *General Theory* is an example of the therapeutic role that hermeneutics can have in economics. Hermeneutics can help economists become more self-aware about some of the causes of controversies in the subject-field, thereby helping to resolve these controversies. This is the pragmatic justification for introducing hermeneutics into economics. But hermeneutics can be a double-edged sword. Hermeneutics provides an attitude of mind, not a set of ready-made answers. Hermeneutic understanding can only emerge through a dialectical process of application to specific problems, the interpretation of Keynes's *General Theory* being one such application. If hermeneutics is introduced into economics as an abstract methodology, it will generate more heat than light. Hermeneutics is a study *of* controversy but it is also a study *in* controversy. The emergence of the rhetorical approach in economics exemplifies the possible dangers of replaying the old controversies of other subject-fields. Hermeneutics can be an effective medicine but should be marked 'handle with care'.

ACKNOWLEDGEMENTS

This chapter represents a development of themes contained in Gerrard (1989). I should like to thank Paul Anand, Roger Backhouse, John Brothwell, Meghnad Desai, Athol Fitzgibbons, John Hillard, Brian Hillier and the participants at the RES conference as well as the *Economic Journal* editors and an anonymous referee for much in the way of helpful criticism. The usual disclaimer applies.

REFERENCES

Aksoy, E. G. (1989) 'Problems of interpretation: hermeneutic circle, objectivity and validity in the interpretations of Ricardo', *Proceedings of the 16th Annual Meeting of the History of Economics Society, Richmond, VA*, 2, 725–47.
Blaug, M. (1980) *The Methodology of Economics: Or How Economists Explain*, Cambridge: Cambridge University Press.
Carabelli, A. (1988) *On Keynes's Method*, London: Macmillan.
Chick, V. (1983) *Macroeconomics after Keynes: A Reconsideration of the General Theory*, Oxford: Philip Allan.
Coddington, A. (1976) 'Keynesian economics: the search for first principles', *Journal of Economic Literature* 14, 1258–73.
Fender, J. (1981) *Understanding Keynes*, Brighton: Wheatsheaf.
Fish, S. (1980) *Is There a Text in This Class? The Authority of Interpretive Communities*, Cambridge, MA: Harvard University Press.
Fitzgibbons, A. (1988) *Keynes's Vision*, Oxford: Clarendon Press.
Gerrard, B. (1988) 'Keynesian economics: the road to nowhere?', in J. V. Hillard (ed.) *J. M. Keynes in Retrospect: The Legacy of the Keynesian Revolution*, Aldershot: Edward Elgar.

Gerrard, B. (1989) 'Some notes on interpreting Keynes' General Theory', IRISS, University of York Discussion Paper 140.

Hahn, F. H. (1982) *Money and Inflation*, Oxford: Basil Blackwell.

Hamouda, O. F. and Harcourt, G. C. (1988) 'Post-Keynesianism: from criticism to coherence?', *Bulletin of Economic Research* 40, 1–33.

Hirsch, E. D. (1976) *The Aims of Interpretation*, Chicago: Chicago University Press.

Hollander, S. (1989) 'Principles of textual interpretation: illustrated by Ricardian growth theory', *Proceedings of the 16th Annual Meeting of the History of Economics Society, Richmond, VA*, 2, 763–74.

Leijonhufvud, A. (1968) *On Keynesian Economics and the Economics of Keynes*, Oxford: Oxford University Press.

Milgate, M. (1982) *Capital and Employment*, London: Academic Press.

O'Donnell, R. (1989a) *Keynes: Philosophy, Economics and Politics*, London: Macmillan.

—— (1989b) 'Keynes on probability, expectations and uncertainty', paper presented at the 9th Keynes Seminar, University of Kent, Canterbury.

Patinkin, D. (1978) 'Keynes' aggregate supply function: a plea for common sense', *History of Political Economy* 10, 577–96.

Ricoeur, P. (1976) *Interpretation Theory: Discourse and the Surplus of Meaning*, Forth Worth, TX: Texas Christian University Press.

—— (1981) *Hermeneutics and the Human Sciences*, Cambridge: Cambridge University Press.

Robinson, J. (1964) *Economic Philosophy*, Harmondsworth: Penguin.

—— (1973) 'What has become of the Keynesian revolution?' In *After Keynes*, Oxford: Basil Blackwell.

Schumpeter, J. A. (1946) 'John Maynard Keynes 1883–1946', *American Economic Review* 36, 495–518.

Shackle, G. L. S. (1967) *The Years of High Theory*, Cambridge: Cambridge University Press.

Stigler, G. (1965) 'Textual exegesis as a scientific problem,' *Economica* 32, 447–50.

5 The fall and rise of Keynesian economics

Alan S. Blinder
Economic Record (1988) December, pp. 278–94

Keynesian economics came under much criticism in the 1970s. This chapter argues that the decline in Keynesian economics and the rise in, notably, new classical economics in this period related to their respective theoretical appeal rather than their ability to explain developments in the macroeconomy. As this has become increasingly recognized, and with the development of sound microeconomic foundations, Keynesian economics has again been on the rise.

1 INTRODUCTION

According to T. S. Kuhn's *The Structure of Scientific Revolutions* (1962), progress in 'normal science' requires an agreed-upon theoretical framework or 'paradigm' within which researchers work to solve puzzles. The stage is set for a paradigm change when anomalies are discovered and documented. After a period of turmoil and extensive questioning of old assumptions, a new theory may emerge which explains not only the anomalies but also the phenomena encompassed by the old theory. If so, the scientific revolution succeeds; although the new theory may itself be subsequently supplanted by a still newer one. Implicitly, a progressive science rarely, if ever, goes back to a previously discarded theory, for that theory was rejected for good reasons.

For a period of roughly 35 years, Keynesian theory provided a central paradigm for macroeconomists, and considerable progress was made on several empirical fronts. It was widely recognized that some of the ingredients of Keynesian economics (e.g. money illusion and/or nominal wage rigidity) rested on slender to non-existent microtheoretic foundations; and there were always dissenters. But, thought of as a collection of empirical regularities that fit together into a coherent whole, the theory worked tolerably well.

In the 1970s, however, the Keynesian paradigm was rejected by a great many academic economists, especially in the United States, in favour of what we now call new classical economics. By about 1980, it was hard to find an American academic macroeconomist under the age of 40 who professed to be a Keynesian. That was an astonishing intellectual turnabout in less than a decade, an intellectual revolution for sure.

Scientists from another discipline might naturally surmise that the data of the 1970s had delivered a stunning and unequivocal rejection of the Keynesian paradigm. They would look for some decisive observation or experiment that did to Keynes what the orbit of Mercury did to Newton. But they would look in vain.[1] I argue in Section 3 that there was no anomaly, that the ascendancy of new classicism in academia was instead a triumph of *a priori* theorizing over empiricism, of intellectual aesthetics over observation and, in some measure, of conservative ideology over liberalism. It was not, in a word, a Kuhnian scientific revolution.

If this is so, it helps explain a phenomenon that a Kuhnian would find puzzling: macroeconomics is already in the midst of another revolution which amounts to a return to Keynesianism – but with a much more rigorous theoretical flavour. The first stages of the Keynesian counter-revolution – which is still in progress – are summarized and evaluated in Section 4. But before doing this, I must define precisely what I mean by Keynesianism. This I do in Section 2.

2 WHAT IT MEANS TO BE A KEYNESIAN

The word 'Keynesian' means many things to many people. Decades ago, it was a carelessly applied label for economic liberals and interventionists in general. For a while in the late.1970s and early 1980s it became a pejorative term more or less synonymous with old-fashioned. No two people have precisely the same definition of Keynesian economics. But, as one of the few American economists of my generation who never shunned the label, I feel entitled to my own definition. To me, the heart of Keynesianism consists of six principal tenets.

First and foremost, Keynesian economics is a theory of aggregate demand and of the effects of aggregate demand on real output and inflation. The first three tenets follow from this.

1 A Keynesian believes that aggregate demand is influenced by a host of economic decisions, both private and public, and sometimes behaves erratically. Some decades ago, there were active, impassioned debates over the propositions that (a) monetary policy is powerless because money demand is infinitely elastic, or (b) fiscal policy is powerless because money demand is totally inelastic. But both of these are dead issues now. *Essentially all Keynesians and most monetarists now believe that both fiscal and monetary policy affect aggregate demand.*[2] Many new classicals, however, believe in debt neutrality – the doctrine that substitutions of debt for taxes have no effects on total demand.

2 *According to Keynesian theory, changes in aggregate demand, whether anticipated or unanticipated, have their greatest short-run impact on real output and employment, not on prices*, and the short run lasts long enough

to worry about.[3] In textbook expositions, this idea is conveyed by a short-run aggregate supply curve that is upward sloping, and probably quite flat except at high levels of capacity utilization, so that changes in aggregate demand are normally not dissipated in higher prices. In macroeconometric models, the same idea is captured by treating output and employment as demand-determined in the short run and letting an inertial Phillips curve determine inflation.

For a theoretical model to produce real effects from anticipated monetary policy, it is usually necessary to have some sort of nominal rigidity in the model; otherwise, an injection of money is like a currency reform which changes all prices equiproportionately.[4] So Keynesian models generally either assume or try to rationalize nominal rigidities. Because supply and demand curves derived from standard neoclassical maximizing principles are always homogeneous of degree zero in nominal quantities, this is not an easy task. Real effects of government purchases, however, are readily explained on strictly neoclassical grounds.[5]

Since prices do not absorb all shocks to demand, fluctuations in any component of spending will cause sympathetic movements in output. In most Keynesian models, the latter are larger than the former because of the multiplier; but a multiplier greater than one is not central to Keynesian analysis. A positive real multiplier is.

Although real effects from demand fluctuations are often called 'Keynesian effects', most monetarists accept the idea as well – at least as it pertains to monetary policy. So this tenet does not really divide those two schools of thought. However, at least some new classicals insist that changes in money affect real output only if they are unanticipated.

3 *Keynesians believe that goods markets and, especially, labour markets respond only sluggishly to shocks, i.e. that prices and wages do not move quickly to clear markets.* This issue, once again, divides Keynesians more from new classicals than from monetarists – although monetarists probably place more faith in the economy's natural servomechanism than Keynesians do. Milton Friedman (1968: 13), for example, has written that 'Under any conceivable institutional arrangements, and certainly those that now prevail in the United States, there is only a limited amount of flexibility in prices and wages.' In current parlance, that would certainly be called a 'Keynesian' position.

The next three tenets have to do directly with policy; and here Friedman and other monetarists part company with most Keynesians.

4 To a Keynesian, the actual levels of employment and unemployment have no special claim to optimality – partly because unemployment is subject to the caprice of aggregate demand, and partly because they believe that markets clear only gradually. In fact, *Keynesians typically see unemployment as both too high on average and too variable*, although they know that rigorous theoretical justification for these positions is hard to come by. Keynesians also feel certain that periods of recession or depression are

economic maladies, not Pareto-optimal responses to unattractive technological opportunities. All this is summarized in the term 'involuntary unemployment', which Keynesians deplore even though it has proved notoriously difficult to define.[6] On this tenet, new classicals differ sharply from Keynesians, with monetarists somewhere in between.

5 *Many, but not all, Keynesians advocate activist stabilization policy to reduce the amplitude of business cycles*, which they rank among the most important of all economic problems. Here monetarists generally join new classicals, as well as some conservative Keynesians, in doubting both the efficacy of stabilization policy and the wisdom of attempting it. Some new classicals go even further and question whether business cycles are a serious problem at all.[7]

The argument that economic knowledge is not secure enough to support what used to be called fine tuning is by now widely accepted, even by most Keynesians. Yet many Keynesians believe that more modest goals for stabilization policy – coarse tuning, if you will – are not only defensible but sensible. For example, an economist need not have detailed quantitative knowledge of lag structures to prescribe a dose of expansionary monetary policy when the unemployment rate is 10 per cent or more – as it has been in many countries in the 1980s. Furthermore, and this may be the most important point, the nature of government seems to abhor a vacuum of economic advice. If economists with admittedly limited knowledge refuse to offer their expert (if uncertain) counsel, assorted quacks with no knowledge at all will surely rush in to fill the void.

6 Finally, and even less unanimously, *many Keynesians are more concerned about combating unemployment than about conquering inflation.*[8] However, there are plenty of anti-inflation Keynesians; most of the world's current and past central bankers, for example, merit this title whether they like it or not. Needless to say, relative attitudes toward unemployment and inflation heavily influence the policy advice that economists give and that policy-makers accept. As a broad generalization, I think it safe to say that Keynesians are typically more aggressive about expanding aggregate demand than are non-Keynesians.

My six tenets divide naturally into two equal groups: the first three are clearly assertions about *positive* economics while the last three are mostly *normative*. The division of Keynesian economics into positive and normative components is central to understanding both the academic debate and its relevance to policy.

Positive Keynesianism is a matter of scientific judgement. A positive Keynesian believes that both monetary and fiscal policy can change aggregate demand, that fluctuations in aggregate demand have real effects, and that prices and wages do not move rapidly to clear markets. No policy prescriptions follow from these beliefs alone. And, as I have indicated, many economists who do not call themselves Keynesian would nevertheless accept the entire list.

Normative Keynesians add both value judgements and political judgements to the preceding list. A normative Keynesian believes that government should use its leverage over aggregate demand to reduce the amplitude of business cycles. He or she is probably also far more interested in filling in cyclical troughs than in shaving off peaks. These normative propositions are based on judgements that (a) macroeconomic fluctuations significantly reduce social welfare, (b) the government is knowledgeable and capable enough to improve upon free-market outcomes, and (c) unemployment is a more important problem than inflation.[9]

The long, and to some extent continuing, battle between Keynesians and monetarists, you will note, has been primarily fought over the *normative issues* – particularly (b) and (c).[10] Thus, by my definitions, most monetarists are positive Keynesians but not normative Keynesians. So are other conservatives who shun the label Keynesian. Protagonists in these debates agree on most positive issues but make different value judgements and seat-of-the-pants political judgements, and so reach different conclusions about policy. Their disagreements in many ways mirror disagreements among policy-makers.

The briefer, but more intense, debate between Keynesians and new classicals had, by contrast, been fought primarily over the tenets of *positive* Keynesianism. New classicals argue that anticipated changes in money do not affect real output; that markets, including the labour market, clear quickly by price;[11] and that business cycles may be Pareto optimal. Here 'objective' scientific evidence can be brought to bear and, in my judgement, the evidence on all three issues points strongly in the Keynesian direction.[12] But rather than try to summarize that evidence now, I want to make only one point: that arguments over the positive aspects of Keynesian economics are potentially resolvable by the accumulation of scientific evidence in a way that disputes over normative issues are not.

Before leaving the realm of definition, let me underscore several glaring and intentional omissions.

First, I have said nothing about *rational expectations*. Many Keynesians are doubtful about the validity of rational expectations as a behavioral hypothesis, as was Keynes himself.[13] Others are willing to accept it. But, when it comes to the large issues with which I have concerned myself so far, nothing much rides on whether or not expectations are rational. In particular, rational expectations models with sticky prices – like those of Fischer (1977) and Taylor (1980), for example – are thoroughly Keynesian by my definition. Details of model construction and quantitative answers to specific questions do, of course, depend on how expectations are modelled. And, for some issues, the expectational mechanism is crucial.[14] But, for the most part, these are not central to the debate between new classical and Keynesian economists.[15]

The second omission is the natural rate hypothesis. Pre-1970 Keynesianism included a Phillips curve that was negatively sloped even in the long run. This idea was rejected theoretically by Milton Friedman (1968), a monetarist, and Edmund Phelps (1968), a Keynesian, and shortly thereafter was also rejected in econometric studies by Keynesians like Robert Gordon (1972). Since about 1972, a Phillips curve that is vertical in the long run has been an integral part of Keynesian economics. So the natural rate hypothesis played essentially no role in the intellectual ferment of the 1972–85 period. Ironically, however, questions about its validity are now playing a role in the Keynesian renaissance. Specifically, models with hysteresis have reopened the theoretical and empirical debate over the natural rate hypothesis, especially for Europe. (More on this below.)

Third, I have ignored the choice between monetary and fiscal policy as the preferred instrument of stabilization policy. People differ along this dimension and occasionally change sides. By my definition, however, it is perfectly possible to be a Keynesian and still believe either that responsibility for stabilization policy should in principle be ceded to the monetary authority or that it is in practice so ceded.

3 THE FALL OF KEYNESIAN ECONOMICS

To start with, let me first dispose of the view, promoted in some quarters, that the demise of Keynesian economics was due to the doctrine's poor empirical predictions. Robert Lucas (1981: 559) wrote that 'Keynesian orthodoxy is in deep trouble, the deepest kind of trouble in which an applied body of theory can find itself: It appears to be giving seriously wrong answers to the most basic questions of macroeconomic policy'. He was talking about the collapse of the Phillips curve in the US during the 1970s, which he and Thomas Sargent had characterized as 'econometric failure on a grand scale' (Lucas and Sargent 1978: 57).

It is, of course, true that pre-1972 Phillips curves were ill-equipped to handle the food and energy shocks that dominated the period from 1972 to 1981 and, in consequence, badly underestimated inflation. But it is also true that Keynesians quickly added supply-side variables (like oil or import prices) to what had up to then been an entirely demand-oriented theory.[16] Soon thereafter supply shocks were also appended to empirical Phillips curves.[17] By the early 1980s, numerous studies had documented the fact that a conventional Phillips curve equation with a supply-shock variable (any one of several will do) fits the US data of the 1970s and 1980s extremely well.[18] The charge that empirical Keynesian models were, in Lucas and Sargent's (1978) words, 'wildly incorrect' is, well, wildly incorrect.

One objection frequently raised by supporters of new classical economics is that saving the Phillips curve after the fact by adding supply variables is like saving Ptolemaic astronomy by adding a new epicycle. I disagree. Any economic model is fundamentally a set of statements about the behaviour underlying supply and demand and the nature of the shocks impinging on each. For example, an empirical model of the market for wheat consists of a negatively sloped demand curve, a positively sloped supply curve, and some assumptions about the shocks hitting each. Analogously, a macroeconomic model must specify not only aggregate demand and supply behaviour but also the nature of the shocks that buffet the economy.

The empirical correlations implied by either sort of model depend on both the model's structure and the shocks that predominate during a particular historic period. For example, the same structural model of the wheat market will predict that price and quantity are negatively correlated if most of the shocks emanate from the supply side but positively correlated if most of the shocks come from the demand side. Analogously, pre-1973 Keynesian theory produced a negatively sloped statistical Phillips curve because of an unstated assumption that macroeconomic shocks come solely from the demand side – an assumption proved wrong by the events of the 1970s and 1980s. The very same model generates a positively sloped Phillips curve if the shocks come from the supply side, which is just what the econometric evidence says happened in the 1973–81 period.

If you don't trust econometrics, the following back-of-the envelope calculation should help drive home the point. Keynesian economists in the US in the 1960s and early 1970s developed what I used to call the Brookings Rule of Thumb: that each point-year of unemployment above the natural rate reduces the rate of inflation by 0.4–0.5 of a percentage point. Using a 5.6 per cent natural rate, the US experienced about 15 point-years of extra unemployment between 1980 and 1985 and, during those years, the inflation rate declined about 6–7 percentage points. Once you see how well the rule of thumb worked, you understand why conventional Phillips curves fit data from the 1980s so well.

Why, then, was the alleged demise of the Phillips curve trumpeted so loudly and so widely? I think the reason was the conjunction of two events – one historical, the other intellectual.

First, when supply shocks came to dominate the data in the 1970s, the familiar negative correlation between inflation and unemployment – which is clearly visible on a scatter diagram of data for the 1950s and 1960s – disappeared. The Phillips curve could no longer be depicted in two dimensions. To those too unsophisticated to distinguish between a simple correlation and a multivariate relationship, that seemed equivalent to the death of the Phillips curve.

Second, Lucas's (1976) insightful critiques of econometric policy evaluation provided an elegant *a priori* argument for why an empirical Phillips curve might collapse under the weight of a more inflationary policy.[19] Briefly, the argument went like this. A prototypical empirical Phillips curve explains inflation by lagged inflation and unemployment:

$$\dot{p}_t = a(L)\dot{p}_{t-1} + f(U_t) + e_t, \tag{1}$$

but is meant to signify a theory in which inflation really depends on expected inflation and unemployment:

$$\dot{p}_t = E_{t-1}(\dot{p}_t) + f(U_t) + e_t \tag{2}$$

It thus embodies an auxiliary hypothesis that the distributed lag $a(L)\dot{p}_{t-1}$ is a good statistical proxy for expected inflation. Lucas pointed out, correctly, that (1) will continue to fit the data well only as long as $a(L)\dot{p}_{t-1}$ remains the best predictor (i.e. the rational expectation) of inflation. If policy changes, the best forecasts of future inflation might also change, making (1) break down even if (2) is stable.

Academic readers of Lucas put two and two together and jumped like lemmings to the wrong conclusion. The facts were (a) that inflation rose and (b) that the correlation between inflation and unemployment changed. The (untested) assertion was that the Lucas critique explained why (b) followed from (a): the government had adopted a more inflationary policy, which in turn had changed $a(L)$.

It was remarkable how uncritically the Lucas critique was accepted. Had governments really decided to 'ride up' the Phillips curve toward higher inflation, as Lucas claimed, or had they simply encountered bad luck from the supply side? The former was assumed even though the latter seems clearly to have been the dominant factor quantitatively.[20] Did the more inflationary environment shift the distributed lag $a(L)$? Rather than seek evidence on this point, partisans of the Lucas critique became econometric nihilists. Theory, not data, was supposed to answer such questions; and theory allegedly said yes.

But, in fact, a rise in inflation need not mean that the univariate autoregressive representation of inflation must change (other than its constant). Whether or not the lag coefficients $a(L)$ actually shifted in the early 1970s is an empirical question. To investigate whether or not such a shift took place, I estimated simple autoregressions for US inflation over the period 1955:2 to 1987:4 subperiods. As a way of guarding against the danger of choosing among competing regressions on the basis of prior beliefs, the lag length (four quarters) and the price index (the GNP deflator) were specified *a priori* and never changed. I tested for statistically significant breaks in the autoregression at the ends of 1970, 1971, 1972 and 1973. The resulting *F* statistics were as follows:

break period	*F* statistic
1970:4/1971:1	0.92
1971:4/1972:1	0.85
1972:4/1973:1	0.77
1973:4/1974:1	0.21

None of these *F* statistics is remotely close to conventional significance levels. Thus, there is no evidence for a shift in the lag coefficients $a(L)$. And that, in turn, suggests that the breakdown of the old-fashioned Phillips curve cannot be attributed to the reason emphasized by Lucas. The strongest evidence for a break emerges if the sample is split 1955:2–1970:4 vs. 1971:1–1987:4. In that case, the $a(L)$ coefficients sum to 0.73 in the first period and 0.88 in the second, which is an increase, though not a dramatic one.

I have already noted that, once supply variables are added, contemporary Phillips curves look much like their ancestors of 1973. Supply shocks not only provide a more parsimonious explanation for both the rise of inflation and the fall of the Phillips curve, but one that can be substantiated empirically. Yet academic economists, at least American academic economists, opted *en masse* for Lucas's explanation, deserting Keynesianism in the process. Why? The rest of this section gives my personal answers. They are rooted in the sociology of science, in attachment to theory, and in ideology – not in empiricism. I take up the three factors in turn.

The sociology of economics

Many people have observed that economics has become a highly technical subject in recent decades, more so in the US than elsewhere. And technicians, of whatever discipline, prize technique; it's how the young cut their teeth. The rational expectations revolution was a godsend for aspiring young technicians. It not only pushed macroeconomic theory in more abstract and mathematical directions, but brought in its wake a new style of econometrics that was far more technically demanding than the old methods it sought to replace.[21]

The tools needed to carry out the new brands of theory and econometrics could not be found in the kit bags of the older economists, which gave the young a heavy competitive edge. Not only were they better trained mathematically and, being younger, more flexible of mind, but also they were less distracted by other pursuits and hence more willing and able to absorb the new techniques. As an extra bonanza, the Lucas critique provided a reason to shun the previously accumulated stock of econometric results as unreliable. Thus freed of any need to absorb the knowledge of the past, newly minted Ph.D. economists could concentrate on developing what they saw as the wave of the future.

It was a recipe for generational conflict within the discipline and, sure enough, the young were recruited disproportionately into the new classical ranks while few older economists converted.[22] Traditional Keynesian tools like IS-LM and large-scale macroeconometric models came to be viewed as relics of the past and, in a strange kind of guilt by association, Keynesian ideas like those discussed in Section 2 also came to be seen as outmoded. By 1980 or so, the adage 'there are no Keynesians under the age of 40' was part of the folklore of the (American) economics profession.

The saying, of course, was meant to encompass only *academic* economists and, indeed, only those in the elite institutions. In fact, virtually no non-academic economists converted to new classicism. Why the sharp bifurcation between professors on the one hand and business and government economists on the other? Part of the answer is that scholars are naturally the producers of new ideas while practitioners are the consumers. Fundamental debates over theory and statistical method belong in the academy, where the protagonists are better equipped to deal with them and have the luxury of a long time horizon. That, I suppose, is what ivory towers are for.

But another part of the explanation lies in the different market tests the two groups must meet. In academia, as in fashion, it is more important to be fresh and creative than to be correct. Cute models, after all, make snappy papers; the real world can be left to less original minds. I have heard it said that the surest route to academic success is to devise a clever proof of an absurd proposition. And dazzling displays of technical fireworks, perhaps accompanied by some impenetrable prose, regularly impress referees and editors of scholarly journals.

Incentives are quite different in business or government, where the important thing is to produce the right answer – or, rather, to *appear* to produce the right answer. Methodological innovation and purity count for little, cuteness for nothing, and technical virtuosity is unappreciated. A professional forecaster seeks accuracy, not scholarly kudos. A policy analyst wants to communicate with policy makers, not to dazzle them with technique.

That new classical ideas failed to migrate from the academy to the worlds of business and government – as Keynesian ideas had done 40 years earlier – suggests that they failed to meet the non-academic market test: they did not produce useful results. But that is getting ahead of my story.

The nature of economic theory

The triumph of new classical ideas in academia was also rooted in the nature of economic theory and in economists' fierce loyalty to it. We economists proudly distinguish ourselves from the lower social sciences by pointing to our illustrious theoretical heritage. In the economist's world, rational and self-interested people optimize subject to constraints. The resulting decision rules equating 'marginal this' to 'marginal that' lead to supplies and demands, which interact in markets to determine prices. These prices, in turn, guide the allocation of resources and the distribution of income. If not interfered with, markets tend to be highly competitive and have a strong tendency to clear by price. (Here the consensus begins to fray a bit.)

These are the canons of our faith. They are what gives economics the unity and cohesion that, say, sociology lacks. Rightly or wrongly, they also imbue economists with an imperialistic attitude toward the other social sciences – rather like Kipling's attitude toward India. We have a tight theory; they don't. We should treat the heathen kindly, if condescendingly, while we firmly propagate the faith.

Notice, however, that the central economic paradigm is entirely *microeconomic*. Keynesian macroeconomics coexists with it uneasily at best. In at least some Keynesian models, workers are less than rational. (For example, they may harbour money illusions.) Relative wages and notions of fairness probably matter in labour markets. Decision-makers frequently bump into corners, so that optimal decisions are no longer described by neoclassical marginal conditions. Markets may not clear, and in fact may display surpluses for long periods of time; so trading takes place at 'false prices'. In all these respects and others, Keynesians have long been infidels in the neoclassical temple.

The strength of neoclassical fundamentalism has ebbed and flowed over the decades. The worldwide depression of the 1920s and 1930s undermined it severely, thus paving the way for the Keynesian revolution. The prosperity of the 1960s and early 1970s probably helped restore it. New classical economics was quite explicitly a revival of neoclassical orthodoxy, a return to what Lucas (1987), echoing Marshall, called 'the only engine for the discovery of truth'.

Keynesians had long felt an agonizing tension between the macroeconomics they taught on Mondays and Wednesdays and the microeconomics they taught on Tuesdays and Thursdays. New classicals explicitly sought to end this tension by making macroeconomics more like microeconomics. All supply and demand decisions were to be derived rigorously from neoclassical 'first principles'. Aggregate demand and supply schedules were to be viewed as blow-ups of interior solutions to individual optimization problems. Markets were to be viewed as perfectly competitive and clearing. If necessary, bothersome empirical phenomena like involuntary unemployment were to be ignored, defined out of existence, or ingeniously rationalized by convoluted theoretical arguments.

Methodological purity has a seductive attraction to mathematically minded technicians – which helps explain why rational expectations came to be so intimately tied up in the debate. Modelling expectations as rational – that is, as optimal subject to informational constraints – is the analogue of modelling consumers as maximizing utility and producers as maximizing profits. Rational expectations was therefore a natural accompaniment – and, indeed, a major impetus – to the 'back to basics' movement. It was no accident, then, that those who favoured frictionless, optimizing, market-clearing models were immediately attracted to rational expectations as a behavioural hypothesis without bothering to look for evidence. Linking rational expectations to new classicism (thus leaving 'irrational' expectations to the Keynesians) helped the new theory win converts in the same way that celebrity endorsements help sell products. Theoretically minded economists were predisposed to believe in rational expectations and, at first, took the new classical baggage along with it.

The role of conservative ideology

There were also ideological overtones in the neoclassical revival which I have yet to mention, but which played an important role.

The basic neoclassical paradigm is profoundly conservative, as other social scientists – and, sometimes, our own students – remind us. Those who take it seriously as a description of the economy tend toward the Panglossian view of private economic transactions and look askance at government intervention. When this world view is transported from microeconomics to macroeconomics, it leads to theoretical models in which business cycles are benign, unimportant, or inevitable – perhaps all three. And it leads, as usual, to *laissez-faire* policy recommendations. For example, Edward Prescott (1986) asserts that 'costly efforts at stabilization are likely to be counterproductive' because the free-market business cycle is Pareto optimal.

Keynesians, as I indicated in Section 2, do not buy any of this. They argue that the very existence of macroeconomics as a subdiscipline owes to the massive market failures that we observe during recessions but which the neoclassical paradigm rules out. They believe that recessions are important, malign, and ameliorable, and so are ready to support government interventions designed to stabilize aggregate economic activity. As James Tobin once remarked, they worry more about Okun gaps than Harberger triangles.

The relative strengths of conservative and liberal ideology obviously vary both over time and through space. My argument is that new classical theory could have attracted a large following only in a country and at a time when right-wing ideology was on the ascendancy, as was true in the United States in the 1970s and 1980s.[23] Though we academics live in ivory towers, the social winds blow there, too.

Many observers have noticed that the new classical revolution was mainly restricted to the United States; it never really caught on in Europe. That was no coincidence, I think, for right-wing ideology has long found more adherents in the US than in Europe. The timing was also no accident; new classicism took root just when the political balance in the US was shifting toward the right. I don't believe such ideas would have sold in American academia during the 1960s.

What I have just said about the theoretical and ideological roots of new classical economics could equally well have been said about old classical economics. But the 1970s did not witness a revival of Pigou, or even of Friedman. It saw, instead, a movement towards the high-tech economic theory of Lucas and the high-tech econometrics of Sargent. The secret to the success of the new classical economics is that it managed to be at once ideologically backward looking and technologically forward looking. Given the temper of the times, that was a winning formula.

Or, rather, it was a winning formula in academia. Outside the academy, the emphasis on theoretical purity (at the possible expense of empirical validity) and technical wizardry were liabilities, not assets. In addition, the leaders of the new school, particularly Lucas and Sargent, were disinclined to press their views on policy-makers because they deemed macroeconomic science insufficiently developed to support such advice. Finally, as we shall see in the next section, the empirical implications of new classical theory were wide of the mark. For all these reasons, the theory that swept academia made hardly a ripple in the world of policy.

4 THE RISE OF KEYNESIAN ECONOMICS

I have argued that empirical evidence played little or no role in the fall of Keynesian economics in academia, which I have attributed instead to the theory's weak microeconomic underpinnings, to the curious sociology of our discipline, and to the rise of right-wing ideology.[24] The story behind the recent resurgence of Keynesianism is quite different, for here the empirical failures of new classical economics are central. In addition, however, new strains of theory are beginning to resolve the tension between microeconomics and macroeconomics in a fascinating way. Whereas new classical economists sought to remake macroeconomics in the image of neoclassical microeconomics, recent developments in economic theory may eventually lead to a reformulation of micro theory that resembles Keynesian economics. I will discuss each of these in turn, beginning with empirics.

Empirical evidence against the new classical paradigm

In view of the normally strong interplay between events and ideas, it is somewhat astounding that new classical economics caught on during the second half of the 1970s – a time when most of the world's industrial economies were struggling to emerge, often unsuccessfully, from deep and long recessions.

True to its classical roots, new classical theory emphasized the ability of a competitive price-auction economy to cure recessions by wage-price deflation. Its early forms attributed downturns to misperceptions about relative prices (such as real wages) that arise when people do not know the current price level, and implied that unemployment should vibrate randomly around its natural rate. But such misperceptions surely cannot be large in societies in which price indexes are published monthly and the typical monthly inflation rate is under 1 per cent; and they cannot be persistent if expectations are rational. Yet economic fluctuations in the late 1970s and 1980s were both large and persistent.

Later versions of new classical theory replaced monetary misperceptions with changes in perceived intertemporal terms of trade and added several features which produced persistent movements in employment and output.[25] But empirical research has never been able to find large intertemporal substitution effects. And theories that generate employment fluctuations from the supply side of the labour market stumble over the facts that labour supply looks to be quite inelastic (at least in the US) and real wages are nearly constant over the business cycle. They also have a hard time making the jump from persistent changes in *employment* to persistent – not to mention involuntary – *unemployment*. In stark contrast, the Keynesian model may be theoretically untidy; but it is certainly a model of persistent, involuntary unemployment.

So the events of the late 1970s seemed to support the incumbent theory and undermine the challenger. Yet the challenger prevailed. Curious.

Next came the 1980s, which were ushered in by another oil shock but were dominated by the Reagan–Volcker fiscal and monetary policy shocks and the European depression. I think it fair to say that new classical economics shed little light on any of these events. The events, however, cast deep shadows across the theory.

First according to new classical theory, a correctly perceived deceleration of money growth affects real output only via its effects on anticipated inflation and real interest rates. Virtually no one thinks real interest rate effects are very large, which is why simple models often ignore them. Yet when the Federal Reserve and the Bank of England announced that monetary policy would be tightened to fight inflation, and then made good on their promises, severe recessions followed in each country.[26] Could it have been that the tightening was unanticipated? Perhaps in part. The Fed did seem to get carried away, and perhaps both central banks lacked credibility at first. But surely the broad contours of the restrictive policies were anticipated, or at least correctly perceived as they unfolded.[27]

Old-fashioned Keynesian theory, which says that *any* monetary restriction is contractionary because firms and individuals are locked into nominal contracts, seems more consistent with actual events, even though it doesn't explain why nominal contracts exist. Strike one against the new theory.

Second, an offshoot of new classical theory due to Barro (1974) argued that debt-financed tax reductions should have neither real nor nominal effects because rational agents, correctly perceiving their future tax liabilities or those of their heirs, would act to offset them. The only observable consequence of such a policy, on this view, should be a rise in private saving to offset the government dissaving.

Naive Keynesian analysis, by contrast, sees the same event as an outward shift of the IS curve. If the LM curve is unchanged, real interest rates, real output, and the price level should all rise. If, as happened in the US, the stimulus to demand is snuffed out by contractionary monetary policy, real interest rates should rise even more. There is no reason to expect the private saving rate to rise.

Econometric studies of the Barro hypothesis have yielded highly inconclusive results. The answer seems to depend on who asks the question.[28] Observation of the real world seems to deliver a stronger verdict, however. Taxes were cut massively in the US between 1981 and 1984. Given the thin economic rationale for the policy, the Reagan tax cuts come as close to a truly exogenous fiscal experiment as we are ever likely to get – just the sort of thing that helps scholars discriminate among competing theories. What happened? The private saving rate did not rise. Real interest rates soared, even though a surprisingly large part of the shock was absorbed in exchange rates rather than in interest rates (so that net exports were crowded out rather than domestic investment). Real GNP growth seems not to have been affected; it grew at about the same rate as it had in the recent past.

It would be unfair to say that neoclassical theory offers no explanation for these events. A sudden rise in the productivity of capital in the US would be expected to raise domestic interest rates (and rates of return), draw in capital from abroad (thus causing a current account deficit), and appreciate the currency. The only trouble with this explanation is that the alleged jump in the productivity of capital is unobservable and unexplained. Why, for example, did it not also happen in other countries?[29] Why did measured productivity growth not accelerate? Furthermore, neither private saving nor investment really rose much as a share of US GNP. The neoclassical explanation does successfully explain the puzzling rise in the US stock market. But, if the productivity of capital soared only in the US, why did stock markets boom all over the world? And if the rise in capital's productivity was global, why did capital come pouring into the United States? Strike two against new classical theory.

Third, we then have the nasty matter of the European depression which, in some countries, has been as long and as deep as the depression of the 1920s and 1930s and which, at this writing, is still in progress. The Keynesian explanation is straightforward. Governments, led by the British and German central banks, decided to fight inflation by highly restrictive monetary and fiscal policies. The anti-inflationary crusade was facilitated by the European Monetary System which, in effect, spread the stern German monetary policy all over Europe. If Keynesian theory has any trouble explaining these events, it is because modern versions which incorporate the natural rate hypothesis are not Keynesian enough. (More on this below.)

The new classical explanation of the European depression is ... well, frankly, I am not sure there is one. Proponents of new classicism, and conservative economists in general, point to microeconomic interferences in labour markets. But most of these policies (like generous unemployment insurance) were in place in 1973 when unemployment was extremely low. In my country, three strikes and you are out. It is therefore not surprising that new classical economics began to lose supporters.

Even this recent history might not have been decisive, given the insular attitudes of academic economists. But there was more scholarly evidence as well.

First, new classical economists had made the Phillips curve a test case and interpreted it in their favour. But, as I have already related, a succession of econometric studies in the 1980s all concluded that the empirical Phillips curve was alive and well once you allowed for supply shocks, at least in the US. Gordon (1987) argues much the same for Europe.

Second, the newly developed technology for estimating models with rational expectations began to be applied; and the results were almost uniformly unfavourable to the new classical view.[30] Normally, the trio of hypotheses that (a) expectations are rational, (b) decision rules are first-order conditions to well-defined optimization problems, and (c) markets clear had to be tested jointly. And almost always the joint hypothesis was resoundingly rejected. Which was the weak leg of the tripod? Most economists, instinctively attracted by rational expectations, thought it was market clearing. But it really didn't matter, for the new classical edifice required the entire lot.

Finally, the validity of the rational expectations hypothesis itself was called into question. Directly observed expectational data were used to test for rationality. Mostly, these were tests of the *weak* forms of rationality: unbiasedness and/or efficiency. They did not, and could not, test for the much stronger form of rational expectations required by new classical theory: that people's subjective expectations match the mathematical expectations implied by the model. None the less, most of these tests rejected rational expectations.[31]

So by 1983 or 1984, academic macroeconomics was in the following somewhat embarrassing position. Keynesian economics had been maligned on the grounds that its theoretical foundations were prosaic at best, non-existent at worst, and certainly inelegant. Its heir apparent, new classical economics, boasted an elegant and technically sweet theory which passed internal consistency checks with flying colours, but which failed miserably when it came to consistency with observation. In the shorthand that was used both then and now, Keynesian economics was 'bad theory' which none the less seemed consistent with the facts while new classical economics was 'good theory' which, unfortunately, did not describe the way the world works.

This is, it seems to me, a curious usage of the terms 'good' and 'bad' – one which reflects the academic economist's preoccupation with elegance and mathematical structure over relevance and empirical accuracy. By these criteria, the 'good theory' is not the one that explains the data best, but rather the one that is truest to neoclassical orthodoxy – which sees people as self-interested and maximizing individuals, who calculate well, have no money illusion, and don't leave unexploited profit opportunities. That is the attitude of a mathematician who deals in logical constructs, not of a scientist who deals in facts. If real people are social beings who care not just about their own well-being but also about their relative position in society, who are not very good at doing calculations or deflating by a price index, and who have other things to do besides maximizing all the time, then Keynesian theory may be the 'good' theory after all – even if it is contaminated by ideas from other social sciences.

Of course, a theory can be judged good or bad only relative to some competitor. There are several senses in which Keynesian theory was and is not good enough. One is that empirical problems continue to beset macroeconometric models built in the Keynesian tradition. The collapse of the

LM curve is just the most obvious of these empirical failures, not the only one. Another problem is that the Keynesian model has such a weak micro-theoretic structure that it is hard – some would say impossible – to do welfare economics with it. While most Keynesians believe that successful stabilization policies improve social welfare, the theory itself does not really justify that belief.

In any case, the view in academia was then (and in some circles still is) that economists had to choose between a tight theory with severe empirical problems and a sloppy theory that none the less worked better empirically. There were two ways to proceed. Either efforts could be made to make Keynesian economics more theoretically respectable, or energy could be devoted to bringing new classical economics into closer contact with reality. Research is proceeding in both directions. In my judgement, the work that is being done along the first route is much the more interesting and promising, so I will dwell on that.

New theoretical foundations for Keynesian economics

Four new developments in economic theory, all of them still in progress, seem to me not only to shore up the theoretical foundations of Keynesianism, but actually to push micro theory in a Keynesian direction. None of them puts sticky nominal wages at centre stage.

Monopolistic competition

The first idea is to build a macro structure on the foundations of monopolistic, rather than perfect, competition. This helps produce a Keynesian environment in two respects. First, it leads to theoretical models in which firms always want to sell more at current prices because price exceeds marginal cost. Second, output levels in monopolistic equilibria are generally below the social optima, which echoes the Keynesian idea that employment is typically too low. The knotty intellectual problem was always that monopolistic competition theory pertains strictly to *relative* prices while nominal magnitudes matter in Keynesian macroeconomics.

Mankiw (1985) and Akerlof and Yellen (1985) solved this problem at more or less the same time by adding fixed costs of changing nominal prices to the model.[32] Suppose the money supply (M) falls by a small amount. Fixed costs of changing prices will deter some firms from cutting their nominal prices even though their first-bet nominal prices in a frictionless world would be proportional to M. In consequence, the price level will fall less than proportionately to M and real balances, and hence aggregate demand, will decline. More than likely, so will social welfare. On the up side, a small enough rise in M will induce only some firms to pay the fixed costs of raising their prices. So real balances, aggregate demand, and social welfare will all rise.

Mankiw and Akerlof and Yellen pointed to a kind of externality later made more precise by Blanchard and Kiyotaki (1987). This idea is important because economists like to rest the case for government intervention on externalities.

The argument goes as follows. Since each firm sits at the top of its profit hill, a small deviation from its first-best relative price has only a small effect on its profits. But because the pre-existing (monopoly) distortion causes output to be below the socially optimal level, the loss in social welfare is greater than the drop in profits. Although the firm loses little from its deviation from optimality, society loses much.

The so-called aggregate demand externality arises in the following way – which should sound familiar to Keynesians. In equilibrium, individual firms do not find it profitable to reduce their prices. Yet, if all firms would cut their prices simultaneously, real balances would rise, aggregate demand would expand, and all firms' profits (and social welfare) would rise. In a decentralized economy, there is no way to achieve such coordinated price cutting. But a sufficiently large rise in the money stock can accomplish the same thing – just as Keynes suggested more than 50 years ago.

This new strain of theorizing is appealing because it relies on just three seemingly realistic assumptions: (a) that demand curves for individual firms slope down: (b) that firms maximize profits; and (c) that lumpy transactions costs are incurred whenever a nominal price is changed. However, it does not provide a complete theoretical justification for Keynesian economics for several reasons.

The first is a technical point to which I will return. In a dynamic economy, fixed costs of price adjustment should lead firms to allow their relative prices to drift away from their first-best profit-maximizing levels most of the time. In that case, firms are not atop their profit hills, so a small change in a relative price (caused, say, by inflation) may have a large effect on profits – not the small effect envisioned by the theory.

Furthermore, while the theoretical results of monopolistic competition models are consistent with Keynesian insights, they lack certain important Keynesian features. For one thing, the main finding is that output is normally *too low*, not that it is *too variable*. Hence the obvious policy intervention is an output subsidy, not macro stabilization policy. Using this class of model to justify the Keynesian belief that output is too variable turns out to be quite tricky.[33] For another, the models do not produce any natural notion of involuntary unemployment which, as I noted earlier, plays a central role in the Keynesian tradition.

Efficiency wages

The next group of theories I will consider addresses itself directly to the involuntary unemployment question. Several microeconomic theories of the labour market based on imperfect, and usually asymmetric, information show that the market can be in equilibrium – in the sense that there are no unexploited profit opportunities – with supply unequal to demand. The simplest, and to me the most appealing, of these is the efficiency wage model. It also seems to accord best with common sense.

Here is a simple example that makes the point starkly.[34] Suppose output, $f(eL)$, depends on labour input in efficiency units, where L is physical labour input and e indicates effort. Suppose further, and this is the efficiency wage hypothesis, that e rises when the real wage, w, rises. Then profits:

$$f(e(w)L) - wL,$$

will be maximized when two conditions hold. First, the marginal product of labour must equal the wage per efficiency unit, $w/e(w)$. Second, the wage must be set at the point (if there is one!) at which the function $e(w)$ has unit elasticity.[35] The second condition fixes the equilibrium wage, call it w^*, on purely technological grounds. Given w^*, the first condition then determines optimal employment, L^*, as long as labour supply at w^* is at least as great as L^*.

An equilibrium with unemployment arises if L^* happens to fall below labour supply at w^*. It is a true equilibrium, not just a long-lasting dis-equilibrium, because profit-maximizing firms have no interest in reducing wages. It has involuntary unemployment that persists for an indefinite period of time because, at wage w^*, labour supply exceeds labour demand. All this sounds very Keynesian. But there is a hitch. Like the monopolistic competition models, efficiency wage theories are fundamentally models of *relative* prices and *real* wages. They have nothing to say about nominal magnitudes, and hence allow no role for nominal money, until they are altered to include fixed costs of changing nominal wages or prices.[36] Nor, in their current state of development, do they have much to say about *fluctuations* in employment.

Efficiency wage models do, however, have at least one more Keynesian aspect that I think important: they focus attention on relative wages.[37] Ask yourself why higher wages enhance productivity. Theorists have provided many possible answers, but the most plausible for advanced, industrial nations (where malnutrition is not the issue) is that workers who are paid well are inclined to perform better for their employers. Such behaviour can be rationalized if workers care about relative wages, as Keynes believed.

Fixed costs and inertia

A third important recent development in micro theory is the revision of the standard theory of optimization to include fixed costs of changing a deci-sion variable. This idea was mentioned earlier in the context of pricing decisions, where it helps impart inertia to the price level. But it also has obvious applications to inventory behaviour (where the idea originated), to the demands for both consumer and producer durables, to the demand for money, and to portfolio choice more generally.[38] Though the mathematics can get complicated quite quickly, the basic idea is completely intuitive and easy to grasp. I illustrate it in the case of a consumer durable, but the same idea applies in other contexts.

Suppose a consumer must pay a fixed transactions cost whenever she purchases a durable good, such as a car. Then, each time one of the basic determinants of demand for automobiles (such as income, interest rates, or relative price) changes, she is faced with the following choice. If she switches to the new first-best optimal car, she must pay a fixed cost. If she does not, she suffers an implicit utility cost from having a suboptimal car. Obviously, it does not pay her to adjust her car purchases continuously, for that would entail exorbitant transactions costs. Rather, optimal behaviour leads to a decision rule something like the so-called (S, s) rule of inventory theory: when the quality of the car deteriorates to some lower bound, s, purchase a new car of quality S; otherwise, do nothing. The parameters S and s are chosen optimally in view of transactions costs, income, and other pertinent information.

Once you think about continuous reoptimization and (S, s) as alternative models of behaviour, even for a little while, two things become clear. First, (S, s) is almost certainly more descriptive of the way people and businesses actually behave; they do nothing for long periods of time and then make large changes in their behaviour. Second, (S, s) behaviour is almost certainly a more sensible theoretical model on *a priori* grounds than continuous reoptimization.

Obviously, (S, s)-type reasoning provides different microfoundations for the traditional aggregative behavioural equations (consumption, investment, money demand, etc.) that constitute macroeconomic models. But what does it have to do with Keynesian versus new classical economics? Three things, principally. First, in a world with important fixed costs, optimizing agents are typically *not* at neoclassical tangencies where marginal this equals marginal that. Instead, behaviour displays a substantial amount of inertia. In the case of price setting, that is a characteristic Keynesian position, as I noted earlier.[39] Second, it leads us to expect to see occasional large adjustments to what appear to be small economy-wide shocks as a substantial number of decision-makers trip their (S, s) boundaries simultaneously. Third, the (S, s) view of the world suggests that a more volatile economic environment imposes real costs on individuals and businesses by making them trip their (S, s) barriers more frequently.[40] Though I have not seen the argument worked out formally, this would seem to support the traditional Keynesian advocacy of stabilization policy.

Hysteresis

Finally, it is important to mention the development of modern models of 'hysteresis', that is, models in which the economy's equilibrium state depends on the path we follow to get there, for these bring Keynesian economics back with a vengeance.

Old-fashioned Keynesian models assumed such hysteresis, without thinking much about it, and without using the fancy name. For example, the simplest Keynesian cross model, if taken literally, asserts that equilibrium can occur at *any* level of output, if aggregate demand is high enough. Similarly, the original Phillips curve implied that the economy could achieve equilibrium at a wide variety of (permanent) unemployment rates, each with its own unique (permanent) inflation rate. Both of these ideas were swept away by the natural rate revolution in the late 1960s and early 1970s and came to be thought of as muddled thinking. Economists, Keynesian or otherwise, came to believe that the long-run Phillips curve was vertical; no matter what happened to the economy in the interim, it could come to rest only at a unique 'natural' rate of unemployment determined by microeconomic factors.

Spurred on, I think, by observing what has happened in Europe, modern theorists are now constructing models that do not have the natural rate property. In these super-Keynesian models, expansionary demand management policies can raise employment permanently. In a neat reversal of Say's Law, demand here creates its own supply. Why might this be so? One simple and obvious mechanism is based on human capital. Suppose workers who are more experienced are also more productive, perhaps due to learning by doing on the job, and that, conversely, human capital deteriorates when not in use. Then a demand-induced boom will build human capital and hence raise potential GNP for the future; so output can be permanently raised. Conversely, a recession which idles workers will deplete the human capital stock and hence lead to lower potential GNP in the future. There is, then, no 'natural' level of employment. The equilibrium level depends on what came before.

The most popular and best developed hysteresis models nowadays are based not on human capital, but rather on the conflict between insiders and outsiders.[41] Suppose unions decide on wages, mindful of the fact that higher wages lead to lower employment but caring only about its members (the insiders). Suppose further that only employed workers are union's members; outsiders have no voice in the union's decisions. Now let a recession lead to lay-offs. The union's membership shrinks and, hence, the union begins to give more weight to higher wages and less weight to higher employment. That is, its optimal wage rises and its optimal employment level falls. The outsiders who lack jobs object to this decision, but have no way to change it; they are disenfranchised. The lower employment level brought about by the recession therefore becomes permanent. In the other direction, of course, this vicious circle becomes a virtuous circle. If a demand-induced boom leads to new hiring, some outsiders are transformed into insiders and the protected level of employment rises.[42]

5 IN CONCLUSION

The empirical evidence does not yet dictate that we adopt these four theoretical innovations. Most industries seem monopolistically rather than perfectly competitive; but no one has yet established that the major costs of price adjustments (and other adjustments) are fixed rather than variable. Nor is the evidence on the efficiency wage hypothesis overwhelming. And hysteresis seems to characterize some economies some of the time, not all economies all the time. But at least these hypotheses have not been refuted by the data.

If we put all four of these theoretical features together – an act of extreme *chutzpah*, to be sure – a thoroughly Keynesian world emerges. Decision variables, including nominal prices and wages, are inertial. Markets often equilibrate with excess supply. So, in particular, involuntary unemployment is common and firms have chronic excess capacity. At least within some range, the economy's equilibrium can be changed by demand management policies because there is no natural rate. Again within some range, welfare can be improved by expanding aggregate demand and by reducing the amplitude of cyclical fluctuations.

This world is different in every particular from the world envisioned by the new classical economics. But its theoretical foundations are no less strong, and perhaps stronger, which is why Keynesian economics now seems to be on the ascendancy in academia. More importantly, it sounds more like the world we live in, which is why some of us find new Keynesian theorizing so hopeful.

ACKNOWLEDGEMENTS

I am grateful to Ben Bernanke, John Campbell, Stephen Goldfeld, John Seater, Steven Sheffrin and Robert Trevor for helpful comments on an earlier draft.

NOTES

1 See Blinder (1979; 1987a: Ch. 3).
2 That does not, however, preclude the possibility that, for example, monetary policy might cancel the macro effects of fiscal policy by controlling nominal GNP.
3 That belief need not preclude the possibility that, for example, the division of any given change in nominal GNP into real effects and price effects might depend on whether or not the change is anticipated.
4 By monetary policy I mean, for example, an increase in base money paid out in lump-sum transfers. Open-market swaps of money for bonds are often (not always) non-neutral because they change interest rates. Monetary non-neutrality can also be rationalized by distribution effects; but these are typically considered unimportant and are rarely the focus of the debate.
5 See, for example, Barro (1981b).

6 For this reason, I have proposed that we rename involuntary unemployment as 'pornographic unemployment' (Blinder 1988).

7 See Lucas (1987) for an example. For a rebuttal, see Blinder (1987b).

8 I include myself here (see Blinder 1987a: Ch. 2; 1988).

9 I would not want to place the last of these beyond the realm of positive economics. There is a huge literature on the social costs of unemployment and inflation, and many Keynesians like myself have concluded from this evidence that the costs of low inflation are both small and readily avoidable. None the less, value judgements are still involved in the trade-off between unemployment and inflation.

10 The one prominent exception was mentioned above: the old debate over whether or not the LM curve is vertical. This has long been a dead issue.

11 The 'price' may be multifaceted. Complicated contractual agreements are allowed within the new classical approach.

12 I do not intend to join the philosophical debate over whether there is such a thing as objective scientific evidence.

13 See, for example, Blinder (1987b) and Lovell (1986).

14 One example is the effects of anticipated future changes in policy.

15 It should be noted that some new classicals disagree and see rational expectations as much more fundamental to the debate.

16 For the rudimentary theory, see Phelps (1978) and Gordon (1975). Phelps' ideas on the subject were first presented at an American Enterprise Institute meeting in April 1974; Gordon's were first offered at a meeting of the Savings and Loan Association that same month. Already in January 1974, Princeton graduate students were being asked (by me!) to analyse supply shocks in Keynesian models in examinations.

17 See Gordon (1977).

18 Some examples are Ando and Kennickell (1985), B. Friedman (1983), Gordon (1985) and Perry (1983). There are others.

19 Though Lucas's paper was published only in 1976, it had been given at a Carnegie-Rochester conference in April 1973 and was well known in academic circles years before it was published.

20 Blinder (1979; 1982) traces the relevant history for the US and supports the statement, which holds even though the world-wide boom of 1972–3 was surely demand-induced.

21 Thomas Sargent and Lars Hansen led in developing the new econometric methods. Sargent always referred to it as 'a technology'.

22 Regretfully, I have no data to support this quantitative assertion. Lucas, Sargent, Barro and Wallace are, of course, 'older economists' in this context. But they were the founders of the new school of thought.

23 Symmetrically, a conservative might argue that Keynesian ideas could only have caught on in a milieu (like that of the Great Depression) in which left-wing ideology was ascendant. Neither statement says anything about the validity of either doctrine.

24 That does not mean that Keynesianism encountered no empirical problems. The most prominent one was probably the collapse of the money-demand equation in the US, Canada, and many other countries. While this is commonly, and correctly, considered a disaster for monetarism, it also poses a serious problem for the Keynesian LM curve.

25 For a review, see Barro (1981a).

26 The story is even worse than this because money growth did not actually decelerate, except fleetingly, in either country. But that has to do with financial innovation and the collapse of the money-demand equation, which is as much a problem for Keynesian theory as for new classical theory.

27 In the case of the 1973–5 recession, Blinder (1981) points out that 'unanticipated money', as defined empirically by Barro and Rush (1980), does not come close to explaining the recession. I know of no similar calculation for the 1980s, but it would also not come close since it was declining velocity growth, not declining money growth, that made money tight in 1981–2.

28 For a comprehensive review of the evidence, see Brunner (1986).

29 The US corporate tax cuts enacted in 1981 have been suggested as an explanation. But there is controversy about this. See Blanchard and Summers (1984), Niskanen (1988) and Bosworth (1985).

30 See, for example, Rotemberg (1984).

31 Lovell (1986) offers a convenient summary of many studies, one of them by Muth (1985)!

32 Actually, Akerlof and Yellen (1985) appealed to 'near rationality' rather than to fixed costs. But the two amount to essentially the same thing. Also, the costs of changing prices do not have to be exclusively fixed to make the theory work.

33 See Ball and Romer (1987). However, DeLong and Summers (1988) argue that Keynesians ought to be more concerned with output being too low and less concerned with it being too variable.

34 For much greater detail, including applications to markets other than that for labour, see Greenwald and Stiglitz (1987a; 1987b).

35 The proof is straightforward. Maximizing profits with respect to w gives the first-order condition $f'(eL)e'(w) = 1$, while maximizing with respect to L gives $f'(eL) = w/e(w)$. Putting the two together implies $we'(w)/e = 1$.

36 That is what Akerlof and Yellen (1985) do.

37 I have elaborated on this theme at greater length in Blinder (1988).

38 On inventories, see Blinder (1981a). On consumer durables, see Bar-Ilan and Blinder (1988). On investment, see Dixit (1988). On the demand for money, see Bar-Ilan (1987). On portfolio choice, see Grossman and Laroque (1987).

39 This need not always be true. Caplin and Spulber (1987) show that price-level inertia may be absent in certain cases. But these are very special steady state cases.

40 However, the (S, s) range can (and presumably will) be widened if volatility increases.

41 See Lindbeck and Snower (1986), Blanchard and Summers (1986) and Drazen and Gottfries (1987).

42 Acceptance of this model does not necessarily lead to advocacy of expansionary demand-management policies. It might lead, instead, to policies that weaken the power of insiders.

REFERENCES

Akerlof, George and Yellen, Janet L. (1985) 'Can Small Deviations from Rationality Make Significant Differences to Economic Equilibria?', *American Economic Review* 75, 4, September, 708–20.

Ando, Albert F. and Kennickell, Arthur (1985) ' "Failure" of Keynesian Economics and "Direct" Effects of Money Supply: A Fact or a Fiction', University of Pennsylvania, mimeo.

Ball, Laurence and Romer, David (1987) 'Are Prices Too Sticky?' National Bureau of Economic Research working paper 2171, February.

Bar-Ilan, Avner (1987) 'Stochastic Analysis of Money Demand Using Impulse Control', Dartmouth College, mimeo.

Bar-Ilan, Avner and Blinder, Alan (1988) 'Consumer Durables and the Optimality of Usually Doing Nothing', January, mimeo.

Barro, Robert J. (1981a) 'The Equilibrium Approach to Business Cycles', in his *Money, Expectations, and Business Cycles*, Academic Press, New York, 41–78.

—— (1981b) 'Output Effects of Government Purchases', *Journal of Political Economy* 89, 6, December, 1086–121.

—— (1974) 'Are Government Bonds Net Wealth?', *Journal of Political Economy* **82**, November/December, 1095–117.

Barro, Robert J. and Mark Rush (1980) 'Unanticipated Money and Economic Activity', in Stanley Fischer (ed.) *Rational Expectations and Economic Policy*, University of Chicago Press, Chicago, 23–48.

Blanchard, Olivier and Kiyotaki, Nobuhiro (1987) 'Monopolistic Competition and the Effects of Aggregate Demand', *American Economic Review* 77, 4, September, 647–66.

Blanchard, Olivier and Summers, Lawrence (1984) 'Perspectives on High World Real Interest Rates', *Brookings Papers on Economic Activity* **2**, 273–324.

—— (1986) 'Hysteresis and the European Unemployment Problem', *NBER Macroeconomics Annual 1986*, 15–78.

Blinder, Alan S. (1988) 'The Challenge of High Unemployment', *American Economic Review* **78**, May, 1–15.

—— (1987a) *Hard Heads, Soft Hearts: Tough-Minded Economics for a Just Society*, Addison-Wesley.

—— (1987b) 'Keynes, Lucas and Scientific Progress', *American Economic Review* **78**, May, 130–6.

—— (1982) 'The Anatomy of Double Digit Inflation in the 1970s', in R.E. Hall (ed.) *Inflation: Causes and Effects*, University of Chicago Press, Chicago, 261–82.

—— (1981a) 'Retail Inventory Behaviour and Business Fluctuation', *Brookings Papers on Economic Activity* **2**, 443–505.

—— (1981b) 'Supply-Shock Inflation: Money, Expectations, and Accommodation', in M.J. Flanders and A. Razin (eds) *Development in an Inflationary World*, Academic Press, 61–101.

—— (1979) *Economic Policy and the Great Stagflation*, Academic Press.

Bosworth, Barry P. (1985) 'Taxes and the Investment Recovery', *Brookings Papers on Economic Activity* **1**, 1–45.

Brunner, Karl (1986) 'Fiscal Policy in Macro Theory: A Survey and Evaluation', in R.W. Hafer (ed.) *The Monetary versus Fiscal Policy Debate*, Rowman & Allanheld, 33–116.

Caplin, Andrew and Spulber, D. (1987) 'Menu Costs and the Neutrality of Money', *Quarterly Journal of Economics*, November.

DeLong, Bradford and Summers, Lawrence (1988) paper in preparation for Brookings Panel, September.

Dixit, Avinash (1988) 'Entry and Exit Decisions Under Uncertainty', Princeton University, May, mimeo.

Drazen, Allan and Gottfries, Nils (1987) 'Seniority Rules and the Persistence of Unemployment in a Dynamic Optimizing Model', mimeo.

Fischer, Stanley (1977) 'Long-Term Contracts, Rational Expectations, and the Optimal Money Supply Rule', *Journal of Political Economy* **85**, 191–205.

Friedman, Benjamin (1983) 'Recent Perspectives In and On Macroeconomics', National Bureau of Economic Research, working paper 1208.

Friedman, Milton (1968) 'The Role of Monetary Policy', *American Economic Review* **58**, 1–17.

Gordon, Robert J. (1987) 'Wage Gaps vs. Output Gaps: Is There A Common Story for All of Europe?', National Bureau of Economic Research working paper 2454, December.

—— (1985) 'Understanding Inflation in the 1980s', *Brookings Papers on Economic Activity*, 263–99.

Gordon, Robert J. (1977) 'Can the Inflation of the 1970s Be Explained?', *Brookings Papers on Economic Activity*, 253–77.

—— (1975) 'Alternative Responses of Policy to External Supply Shocks', *Brookings Papers on Economic Activity* 1, 183–206.

—— (1972) 'Wage-Price Controls and the Shifting Phillips Curve', *Brookings Papers on Economic Activity*, 385–421.

Greenwald, Bruce and Joseph E. Stiglitz (1987a) 'Keynesian, New Keynesian and New Classical Economics', *Oxford Economic Papers* **39**, 119–32.

—— (1987b) 'Imperfect Information, Credit Markets and Unemployment', *European Economic Review* **31**, 444–56.

Grossman, Sanford and Laroque, Guy (1987) 'The Demand for Durables and Portfolio Choice under Uncertainty', Princeton University, June, mimeo.

Kuhn, Thomas S. (1962) *The Structure of Scientific Revolutions*, University of Chicago Press, Chicago.

Lindbeck, Assar and Snower, Dennis (1986) 'Wage Setting, Unemployment, and Insider–Outsider Relations', *American Economic Review* **76**, May, 235–39.

Lovell, Michael E. (1986) 'Tests of the Rational Expectations Hypothesis', *American Economic Review* 76, 1, March, 110–24.

Lucas, Robert E. Jr (1987) *Models of Business Cycles*, Basil Blackwell.

—— (1981) 'Tobin and Monetarism: A Review Article', *Journal of Economic Literature* **XIX**, June, 558–67.

—— (1976) 'Econometric Policy Evaluation: A Critique', in Karl Brunner and Allan H. Meltzer (eds) *The Phillips Curve and Labor Markets*, Carnegie-Rochester Conferences on Public Policy, vol. 1, North-Holland Publishing Company, Amsterdam.

Lucas, Robert E. Jr and Sargent, Thomas (1978) 'After Keynesian Macroeconomics', in *After the Phillips Curve; Persistence of High Inflation and High Unemployment*, Conference Series 19, Federal Reserve Bank of Boston.

Mankiw, N. Gregory (1985) 'Small Menu Costs and Large Business Cycles: A Macroeconomic Model of Monopoly', *Quarterly Journal of Economics* **100**, May, 529–39.

Muth, John F. (1985) 'Short Run Forecasts of Business Activity', Indiana University, March, mimeo.

Niskanen, William A. (1988) *Reaganomics: An Insider's Account of the Policies and the People*, Oxford University Press, Oxford.

Perry, George L. (1983) 'What Have We Learned About Disinflation?', *Brookings Papers on Economic Activity*, 587–602.

Phelps, Edmund S. (1978) 'Commodity-Supply Shock and Full-Employment Monetary Policy', *Journal of Money, Credit and Banking* X, 2, May, 206–21.

—— (1968) 'Money-Wage Dynamics and Labor Market Equilibrium', *Journal of Political Economy* **78**, 678–711.

Prescott, Edward (1986) 'Theory Ahead of Business Cycle Measurement', Federal Reserve Bank of Minneapolis Research Department Staff Report 102, February.

Rotemberg, Julio J. (1984) 'Interpreting Some Statistical Failures of Some Rational Expectations Macroeconomic Models', *American Economic Review* **74**, 188–93.

Taylor, John B. (1980) 'Aggregate Dynamics and Staggered Contracts', *Journal of Political Economy* **88**, 1–23.

6 Price flexibility and output stability

An old Keynesian view

James Tobin
Journal of Economic Perspectives (1993) 7, Winter, pp. 45–65

In this symposium I shall play the role in which I was cast, the unreconstructed old Keynesian. Time was when I resisted labels and schools, naively hoping that our fledgling science was outgrowing them. I had, to be sure, been drawn into economics when the *General Theory* was an exciting revelation for students hungry for explanation and remedy of the Great Depression. At the same time, I was uncomfortable with several aspects of Keynes' theory, and I sought to improve what would now be called the microfoundations of his macroeconomic relations.

The synthesis of neoclassical and Keynesian analysis achieved in the 1950s and 1960s promised a reconciliation of the two traditions, or at least an understanding of the different contexts to which each applies. The hope and the promise were premature, to say the least. Since 1973 the dominant trend in macroeconomics has dismissed Keynesian theory. Nevertheless, Keynesian models continue to prove useful in empirical applications, forecasting and policy analysis. Macro-econometric models are mostly built on Keynesian frameworks. The gulfs between doctrine and observation, between theory and practice, are chronic sources of malaise in our discipline.

I have benefitted from Gregory Mankiw's 'refresher course' in modern macroeconomics (1990). He writes that recent developments – methodological, new classical, and new Keynesian – are to old macroeconomics as Copernicus was to Ptolemy. It just takes time before Copernican truths can outdo Ptolemaic approximations in practical applications.

Considering the alternatives, I do not mind being billed as a Keynesian, an old Keynesian at that. But old Keynesians come in several varieties, and I speak for no one but myself. Nor do I defend the literal text of the *General Theory*. Several generations of economists have criticized, amended, and elaborated that seminal work. I shall argue for the validity of the major propositions that distinguish Keynesian macroeconomics from old or new classical macroeconomics.

SUMMARY OF THE KEYNESIAN CASE

The central proposition of Keynesian economics is commonly described as follows: 'According to the Keynesian view, fluctuations in output arise largely from fluctuations in nominal aggregate demand. These fluctuations have real effects because nominal wages and prices are rigid' (Ball *et al.* 1988: 1). On the contrary, I shall argue that Keynesian macroeconomics neither asserts nor requires nominal wage and/or price rigidity. It does assert and require that markets not be instantaneously and continuously cleared by prices. That is a much less restrictive assumption, and much less controversial. It leaves plenty of room for flexibility in any commonsense meaning of the word.

Keynesian models were said to be vulnerable to the charge that 'the crucial nominal rigidities were assumed rather than explained', although 'it was clearly in the interests of agents to eliminate the rigidities they were assumed to create.... Thus the 1970s and 1980s saw many economists turn away from Keynesian theories and toward new classical models with flexible wages and prices' (Ball *et al.* 1988: 2). Those market-clearing models have not just flexible prices but *perfectly* and *instantaneously* flexible prices, an assumption that is surely more extreme, more arbitrary, and more devoid of foundations in individual rational behavior than the imperfect flexibility of Keynesian models.

The central Keynesian proposition is not nominal price rigidity but the principle of effective demand (Keynes 1936: ch. 3). In the absence of instantaneous and complete market clearing, output and employment are frequently constrained by aggregate demand. In these excess-supply regimes, agents' demands are limited by their inability to sell as much as they would like at prevailing prices. Any failure of price adjustments to keep markets cleared opens the door for quantities to determine quantities, for example real national income to determine consumption demand, as described in Keynes' multiplier calculus.

For this reason, Keynesian macroeconomics alleges that capitalist societies are vulnerable to very costly economy-wide market failures. Individuals would be willing to supply more labor and other resources in return for the goods and services the employment of those resources would enable them to consume now or in the future, but they cannot implement this willingness in market transactions. As the quotation from Ball *et al.* (1988) suggests, many contemporary theorists cannot believe any theory that implies socially irrational market failures. They suspect that individual irrationalities are lurking somewhere in the theory. In continuously price-cleared competitive markets, they know, individually rational behaviour implies collectively rational outcomes. But this theorem does not apply if markets and price-setting institutions do not produce perfectly flexible competitive prices. Individual rationality does not necessarily create the institutions that would guarantee 'invisible hand' results. Keynes was not questioning the rationality of individual economic agents; he was arguing that their behavior would yield optimal results if and only if they as citizens organized the necessary collective institutions and government policies. In the same spirit though in different contexts, some modern theoretical research has shown that welfare-improving policies may be designed even when asymmetries of information and incompleteness of markets prevent the achievement of global optima.

Ball, Mankiw, Romer and others style themselves as New Keynesians. Their program is to develop improved microeconomic foundations for imperfectly flexible prices. In the process, they hope to illuminate the paradox that individually rational or near-rational behavior can result in significant collective market failures. These are certainly laudable objectives. In the end, I suspect, the program will not change the essential substance of Keynesian macroeconomics. But it will make Keynes more palatable to theorists.

In Keynesian business cycle theory, the shocks generating fluctuations are generally shifts in *real* aggregate demand for goods and services, notably in capital investment. Keynes would be appalled to see his cycle model described as one in which 'fluctuations in output arise largely from fluctuations in nominal aggregate demand' (Ball *et al.* 1988: 2). The difference is important. The impact on real purchases of a one-time 1 percent shock to aggregate nominal spending will be eroded if and as nominal prices increase in response, and eliminated once prices have risen by the same 1 percent as nominal spending did. But suppose it is real demand that initially rises 1 per cent. At the prevailing prices nominal spending will rise 1 percent too. But if and as prices rise in response the 1 percent real demand shock becomes an ever larger amount of nominal spending. Its impact is not mechanically eroded by the price response; if it is absorbed, the process is subtle and indirect.

The big issue between Keynes and his 'old classical' opponents was the efficacy of the economy's natural market adjustment mechanisms in restoring full employment equilibrium, once a negative real demand shock had pushed the economy off that equilibrium. Keynes and Keynesians said those mechanisms were weak, possibly nonexistent or perverse, and needed help from government policy. That is still the major question of macroeconomic theory and policy, even though new classical economists finesse it by assuming that the economy can never be pushed out of equilibrium even for a moment. Keynes' classical contemporaries and predecessors would never have drawn real-world lessons from theories based on such an assumption. Their successors strain credulity when their models imply that markets are cleared and joblessness is voluntary when measured unemployment is 10 percent as truly as when it is 5 percent.

Keynesian theory of nominal wage stickiness does not deserve the disdain with which it is commonly regarded. It is not dependent on 'money illusion'. But Keynes certainly would have done better to assume imperfect or monopolistic competition throughout the economy, in both product and labor markets. In markets of these kinds, nominal prices are decision variables for sellers or buyers or are determined by negotiations between them. They therefore move only at discrete intervals. Despite considerable effort over the years to give macroeconomics improved microfoundations along these lines, there is plenty of scope for the 'New Keynesian' program of theoretical and empirical research on this topic.

In the absence of perfect flexibility, does greater flexibility of nominal prices strengthen the equilibrating mechanisms, or does it weaken them? Keynes doubted that the problems of involuntary unemployment and underutilized capacity would be mitigated by greater flexibility of nominal wages and prices. On the whole, he favored stable nominal wages. Critics of Keynesian macroeconomics forget this strand of the argument when they assume that without absolute 'rigidity' aggregate demand could never be deficient. Fortunately, this issue has been receiving greater attention in the last few years, with considerable support for Keynes' position.

MACROECONOMICS WITH EFFECTIVE DEMAND CONSTRAINED

The empirical relevance of Keynesian economics is based on its assertion that situations of pervasive excess supply often occur. An advanced capitalist industrial economy is frequently in a state in which most labor and product markets are not clearing at prevailing prices. As a result, workers are involuntarily unemployed and capital capacity is underutilized. The effective constraint on output is the aggregate demand for goods and services; likewise the effective constraint on employment is the amount of labor required to produce that output.

Keynesian unemployment must be differentiated from both frictional and classical unemployment. Frictional unemployment occurs because of microeconomic flux. Demands and supplies are continually shifting, bringing unemployment and excess capacity in some sectors and contemporaneous labor shortages and capacity bottlenecks elsewhere. The gross aggregates of these frictional excess supplies and excess demands vary together positively over time. In contrast, cyclical excess supplies and demands are negatively correlated; in economy-wide recessions and depressions, excess-supply markets and sectors predominate, while the reverse is true in inflationary booms. The amount of frictional unemployment depends on the strength of intersectoral shocks and on the mobility of factors of production in responding to them. Large and protracted shocks, for example in technology or in supplies and prices of key commodities like energy, convert frictional unemployment to *structural* unemployment. Neither is remediable by demand expansion alone.

A common species of classical unemployment occurs when jobs are limited because of excessive real wage rates imposed by governmental or trade union regulations. For individuals who would like to work at or below the wage floor, such unemployment is involuntary. For the workers collectively whose bargaining strength or political clout established the regulations, the unemployment could be regarded as the voluntary consequence of their exercise of monopoly power.

Identification of observed unemployment as classical or Keynesian is sometimes difficult. In either case unemployment might be observed to be associated with real wages above their full employment equilibrium values. In the Keynesian case, this could result from perfect competition among producing firms; they would be paying workers the high marginal products associated with low employment. The big difference between the two cases is that in the Keynesian case, but not in the classical case, real wages would decline on their own and output and employment would increase in response to expanded demand. In the classical case removal of the regulations would be essential.

There are several variations on the classical unemployment theme. One case is queuing for a high-wage job. An artificially high wage in a particular sector could draw workers from employment elsewhere to wait and hope. This model was originally designed to explain the heavy unemployment in the urban centers of developing countries, where the queuing requires living near the scarce jobs, far from alternative means of subsistence in traditional agriculture. It fits less well in advanced economies, where workers can search and apply for better jobs while employed. Another source of voluntary unemployment may be unemployment insurance benefits and other transfers that increase the reservation prices of persons without jobs. However, in the United States, where unemployment is measured by large household surveys conducted monthly by the Census, persons without jobs will be counted not as unemployed but as 'not in labor force' unless they report they have been actively searching. Although some misreporting doubtless occurs, it is small, not always in the same direction, and cannot begin to account for the cyclical variability of unemployment rates.

Agents who are unable to sell as much as they would like at prevailing prices restrict demands in other markets. Unemployed workers cut their consumption. Demand-constrained firms restrict their hiring of labor and their purchases of other inputs. Keynes' insight that quantities actually sold, if smaller than sales desired at existing prices, will keep demands in other markets below equilibrium values, was rediscovered and elaborated by self-styled 'disequilibrium theorists' 30 years later (Barro and Grossman 1971). In old Keynesian economics, multiplier theory formalized the determination of quantities by quantities. It did not and does not, however, preclude the relevance of other determinants of demand, notably prices and interest rates. In this respect it is more general than most of its latter-day extensions in 'disequilibrium theory'. In demand-constrained regimes, any agent's increase in demand – for example, more investment spending by a business firm – has positive externalities. It will increase the attainable consumption of third parties. In some modern literature, this idea of Keynes is revived and elaborated under the label 'strategic complementarity' (Cooper and John 1988).

Liquidity constraints are an important but extreme form of effective demand constraint. Some wage earners, no doubt, depend on each week's wages to buy the goods for that week's consumption. But Keynes' principle does not depend on such short horizons for consumption-smoothing. Expectations of future spells of unemployment, enhanced by present and recent experience, can limit the current consumption and durables purchases even of long-horizon households. Liquidity constraints and prospective effective demand constraints can also limit business investment. Common observation suggests that households and businesses, and governments too, differ widely in their horizons, i.e. the length of the future period over which expected resources are regarded as potentially available for spending today. These horizons, moreover, doubtless change over time with circumstances and behavior.

The multipliers relating change in aggregate demand to demand shocks, from policies or other events, are not as large as they were thought to be when the concept was first introduced and estimated in the 1930s. One reason is a substantial structural change in democratic capitalist economies. Governments are much larger relative to private sectors than before World War II, and their fiscal institutions are 'built-in stabilizers'. Their expenditures are quite unresponsive to current business conditions, while their revenues (net of transfers to the private sector) are cyclically sensitive and thus moderate swings in private incomes. A second reason is that economists have come to recognize that, thanks to accommodating capital markets as well as to their own foresight, most economic agents have horizons longer than one year.

While this consideration implies that multipliers of transient shocks are lower than for permanent changes, it by no means implies that they are zero. Both consumption and investment appear to be sensitive to contemporaneous and recent incomes. For most agents capital markets are far from perfect; in particular future and current labor incomes are not fungible. Moreover, expectations of economic futures, individual, national, and global, are influenced by current events, perhaps to an irrational extent.

As Keynes explicitly observed, his theory refers to economies with incomplete markets. In his day futures markets were rare, and contingent futures markets even rarer. They are still scarce. As Keynes explained, decisions not to spend now are not coupled with any definite orders for future or contingent deliveries. Typically they result in accumulations of assets that can be spent on anything at any future time. The multiplier effects of lower current spending propensities are not offset by specific and firm expectations of higher future demands.

BUSINESS CYCLES AS DEMAND FLUCTUATIONS

According to Keynesian macroeconomics, business cycles are fluctuations in aggregate effective demand, carrying output and employment in their wake. They do not reflect movements in market-clearing supply–equals–demand equilibria.

Supplies of labor and other factors of production move fairly smoothly from year to year and from cycle to cycle. So does economy-wide factor productivity, largely reflecting technological progress. Equilibrium output and employment cannot be as variable as actual cyclical observations. In the neoclassical neo-Keynesian synthesis, trend growth is supply-determined; markets are cleared; supply truly creates its own demand. In cyclical departures from trend, demand evokes its own supply. Keynesian short-run macroeconomics does not pretend to apply to problems of long-run growth and development.

Equilibrium cycle theories (Plosser 1989) are unconvincing. They rely on incredible volatility in technology, retrogressive as well as progressive. They rely on extreme intertemporal substitutions among work, leisure, and consumption. Or they contrive informational asymmetries and misperceptions that seem easy to correct. For example, a few years ago a popular theory attributed business cycles to confusions by suppliers of products and labor between increases in their own real prices, on the one hand, and economy-wide inflation, on the other. Evidently businesses and households were assumed to ignore the flood of current statistics on prices and money supplies.

I am using the word equilibrium to mean Walrasian market-clearing by prices, as is the current usage of both new classical macroeconomists and disequilibrium theorists. Keynes used it otherwise, to refer to a position of rest. That is why he referred to outcomes with involuntary unemployment as equilibria on a par with full employment, and why he termed his theory 'general' in the title of his book. The basic issue is not semantic. It is whether situations of general excess supply can and do exist for significant periods of time, whether or not they are called equilibria.

Some passages of the *General Theory* can be read to assert that involuntary unemployment is much more than a temporary cyclical phenomenon, that it is in the absence of remedial policies a chronic defect of capitalism. This was a natural enough view in the 1930s. In Alvin Hansen's American Keynesianism (e.g. Hansen 1938) secular stagnation was a central proposition. Formally, however, the analysis of the *General Theory* is limited to a time period short enough that the changes in capital stock resulting from non-zero investment can be ignored.

Postwar Keynesians, for the most part, have not regarded protracted depression as a likely outcome.[1] Chronic inflationary gaps could also occur, and alternations between excess-supply and excess-demand regimes were highly probable. Keynesian macroeconomics is two-sided. Deviations on both sides of Walrasian market-clearing can occur, though not necessarily with symmetrical symptoms. Excess demand in aggregate is mainly an 'inflationary gap', generating unfilled orders and repressed or open inflation, rather than significant extra output and employment. Macroeconomic stabilization requires two-sided countercyclical demand management.

In any case, habitual application of Keynesian remedies reinforces whatever natural mechanisms tend to return the economy to its full employment growth path. Expectations that those remedies will be used contribute to the stability of that equilibrium path.

THE EFFICACY OF CLASSICAL ADJUSTMENT MECHANISMS: INTEREST RATES

Suppose that shocks to current real demands for goods and services create, at existing prices and wages, excess supplies of labor and capital services. What are the variables whose changes would avert or eliminate macroeconomic disequilibrium? The leading candidates are current prices, which include both wages of labor as well as prices of products, and interest rates, which involve future as well as current prices. In what follows, I shall set forth Keynesian skepticism regarding the efficacy of these classical adjustment mechanisms.

If these mechanisms respond instantaneously to shocks, no actual discrepancy between demand and supply will occur or be observed. The shocks will be wholly absorbed in the market-clearing variables. This is the assumption of equilibrium business cycle theory and of the 'real business cycles' approach. It is this assumption that, among other things, enables new classical macroeconomists to dismiss out of hand real aggregate demand shocks and to react with incredulity when Keynesians mention them. However, if these adjustments do not occur instantaneously but take real time, then Keynesian situations of excess supply do occur. They occur even if prices and interest rates are falling at the same time. The consequence is that the quantity adjustments of the multiplier process start working counter to the possible equilibrating effects of interest rate and price reductions.

In standard Walrasian/Arrow-Debreu theory, perfect flexibility of all wages and prices, present and future, would maintain full employment equilibrium. Short of that, an old question of macroeconomic theory is whether, given current nominal wages and prices, changes in future money wages and prices – that is, in nominal interest rates – could do the job.

In old classical macroeconomics, interest rates are the equilibrators of both capital markets and goods markets. Their adjustment is crucial to the Say's Law story, which dismisses as vulgar superficiality notions that an economy could suffer from shortfalls in demand for commodities in aggregate. Market interest rates keep investment equal to saving at their full-employment levels – and therefore keep aggregate demand equal to full employment output – even if nominal product prices and wages stay put. Indeed classical doctrine is that the real equilibrium of the economy is independent of nominal prices, as if it were the outcome of moneyless frictionless multilateral Walrasian barter.[2]

Can interest rates do the job? The Keynesian insight is that the institutionally fixed nominal interest rate on currency, generally zero, limits the adjustment of nominal interest rates on non-money assets and imparts to them some stickiness even when they are above zero. As a result, after an aggregate demand shock they may not fall automatically to levels low enough to induce sufficient investment to absorb full employment saving. As a result, aggregate demand – consumption plus investment – will fall short of full employment supply.

The case for significant non-zero interest elasticity of money demand is simply that the opportunity costs of holding money fall as the interest rates available on non-money substitutes decline. As those rates approach the interest paid on money itself, zero at the lowest, the opportunity costs vanish. The interest rate on money sets the floor for other nominal market interest rates. The familiar specific money demand models – transactions costs, risk aversion, regressive interest rate expectations – all depend on the fixed nominal interest floor.

The interest-elasticity of money demand is a key parameter in macro-economic theory. Three cases can be distinguished. One is a classical extreme, often associated with the quantity theory of money: the elasticity is zero. At the other extreme is the Keynesian liquidity trap: market interest rates are so close to the floor that people are on the margin indifferent between money and other assets. In between is the vast middle ground, where the interest-elasticity of money demand is somewhere between zero and negative infinity. Undergraduate students of macroeconomics know, or used to know, that in standard models monetary policy can effectively alter spending in the classical and intermediate cases but not at the liquidity trap extreme. They also know, or used to know, that fiscal policy is effective in the liquidity trap and intermediate cases but not at the classical, monetarist extreme.

My focus here is somewhat different. The question is the efficacy of market interest rates as automatic stabilizers in the face of real demand shocks, when monetary quantities, fiscal parameters, and other policy instruments are fixed. The answer is not in dispute for the two extremes: they work in the classical case and not in the liquidity trap. Who owns the middle ground? Quantity theorists used to contend that classical proposi-tions obtain everywhere outside the liquidity trap. But the middle ground belongs to the Keynesians. Real demand shocks will move aggregate income despite their effects on interest rates, for the same reason that fiscal policies will do so. Unless the real supply of money is increased by monetary policy or by price reduction, the interest rate will not fall enough after a negative aggregate demand shock (the same thing as a negative investment-minus-saving shock) to maintain investment–equals–saving equality at full employment. The interest rate that would do that job would also require additional money supply – unless money demand is perfectly inelastic with respect to market interest rates.

Recent structural changes have made the monetary system more mon-etarist, more like what the quantity theorists said it always was. Bank deposit interest rates, even on the checkable deposits used for most transactions, now are market-determined and move up and down along with rates on non-money assets. The differential between them, the opportunity cost important in cash management, is less systematically related to the general level of interest rates than it used to be. This development has undoubtedly made the demand for deposits less elastic with respect to the interest rates that matter for demands for goods and services (on these developments see Tobin 1983).

However, the zero floor on nominal interest rates is still there. The monetary base, currency held outside banks plus bank reserves, remains interest-free. The money market in which the demand for and supply of bank reserves are equated is the fulcrum of the banking system and of the entire structure of interest rates. States of nature in which equilibrium would require negative real interest rates still have positive probability. Since nominal rates cannot be negative, full employment would not be possible in those contingencies unless expected inflation made real rates negative. The possibility of these states will influence the portfolio and investment decisions of rational agents.

Money demand is not the whole story. Keynes also stressed liquidity preference in a different form, sticky long-term interest rates. Because traditional expectations of future long rates persist in slumps, current long rates do not automatically follow short rates down far enough to induce the spurts in investment needed for recovery.

Classical and new classical theories assert that capital markets generate equilibrium real rates independently of what is happening to nominal interest rates and commodity prices. But the evidence is that nominal interest rates do matter. Changes in them are usually changes in real rates. Likewise changes in inflation expectations are not fully offset by changes in nominal rates. The 'Fisher equation' asserts that real interest rates are independent of nominal rates and inflation expectations, but Irving Fisher himself concluded from his empirical investigations that the proposition held if at all only in very long runs. Modern research has confirmed his findings.

THE EFFICACY OF CLASSICAL ADJUSTMENT MECHANISMS: NOMINAL WAGES AND PRICES

If interest rate adjustments cannot suffice, no matter how rapidly asset markets clear, the job falls to nominal prices. If it is a crime not to accept the instantaneous clearing by prices of product and labor markets as the foundation of macroeconomics, then Keynes and Keynesians are certainly guilty. But it is a caricature of Keynesian economics, no less false because it is widely believed, to attribute to Keynesians the assumption that nominal prices are perfectly rigid, for the entire time period over which the analysis is intended to apply. In fact Keynes himself did not contend that nominal prices and product prices are fixed independently of amounts of excess supply or demand, and neither do most Keynesians today.

The 'fixprice' method used in many textbooks was a convenient device for expounding the Keynesian calculus of adjustments of quantities to quantities and to interest rates. It was carried to extreme in modern formal 'disequilibrium theory'. The method is misleading when it conveys the impression that Keynesian economics assumes price rigidities and indeed is defined by that assumption. It is especially misleading if it gives the idea that such an assumption is necessary. This impression of Keynesian theory, whether the result of caricatures by its enemies or careless expositions by its friends, appears to be the source of the defection of many economists.

Consider a spectrum of the degree of nominal price flexibility from complete flexibility at one extreme to complete rigidity at the other. Complete flexibility means instantaneous adjustment, so that prices are always clearing markets, jumping sufficiently to absorb all demand or supply shocks. Complete rigidity means that nominal prices do not change at all during the period of analysis. In between are various speeds of price adjustment, various lengths of time during which markets are not clearing. Here again, as in the case of interest rate effects and despite common beliefs to the contrary, Keynesians own the middle ground. It is not true that only the arbitrary and gratuitous assumption of complete rigidity converts nominal demand shocks into real demand shocks and brings multipliers and IS-LM processes into play. Any degree of stickiness that prevents complete price adjustment at once has the same qualitative implications, and can even be treated by the fixprice method on an 'as if' basis.

Keynes argued that nominal wages would not fall rapidly in response to excess supplies of labor. At the same time, he asserted that real wages could fall if product prices rose as necessary to induce firms to expand employment. This asymmetry led many critics to suppose that Keynes was attributing 'money illusion' to workers and to dismiss Keynesian theory out of hand. Why would workers accept a cut in *real* wages achieved by an increase in the price of wage goods but resist cuts in money wages? Keynes' reason for this asymmetry is both empirically realistic and theoretically impeccable. Workers are concerned primarily with relative wages, with how their pay compares with the pay of those to whom they regard themselves at least equal in merit. Those concerns do not depend on money illusion, they are certainly not irrational, and there is a great deal of empirical evidence of their importance.

Labor markets are disaggregated and desynchronized. To any single worker or local group, a nominal wage cut appears to be a loss in relative wages; there is no assurance that others will also take cuts. On the other hand, an increase in the cost of living is the same for everybody. Workers may be perfectly prepared to receive lower real wages with unchanged relative wages, but labor market institutions give them no way to communicate this willingness.

The hole in this story is that it does not explain how the relative-wage concerns of employed workers prevail when there are unemployed workers willing to work for less pay – real, nominal, and relative. The power of insiders *vis-à-vis* employers and outsiders evidently derives from the costs of turnover among members of an interdependent working team. Insider power has lately been the subject of considerable theoretical and empirical inquiry, notably by Assar Lindbeck and his colleagues (Lindbeck and Snower 1990). Labor economists have long observed that queues of job-seekers outside the factory gate have little effect on the wages paid to employees inside. Hard times do bring wage cuts, but usually by so damaging the financial and competitive positions of employers that they can credibly threaten layoffs of senior workers and even plant closings and bank-ruptcies.

All Keynesian macroeconomics really requires is that product prices and money wages are not perfectly flexible, whatever may be the rationale for their behavior. After all, the Walrasian auctioneer of classical macroeco-nomics is itself not an implication of optimizing behavior. It is a fictitious institution with no presumptive priority over alternative institutional assumptions.

Seeking to win the game on his opponents' home field, Keynes pretended to be assuming pure competition in all markets. But his insights regarding labor markets implicitly recognized that wages are administered or nego-tiated prices, and for that reason alone are not perfectly flexible, not prices set in impersonal auction markets. His product markets, however, remained Marshallian. Given money wages and given the overall aggregate demand constraint, competition equated product prices to marginal cost. Thus real wages were equal to marginal productivity. But, as the existence of excess supply would imply, those wages exceeded the wages necessary to induce workers to supply the actual volume of employment.

Marginal productivity theory implies that real wages and employment or output would be negatively correlated in business cycles. But this implica-tion has been repeatedly refuted by empirical observations. This is not a blow to Keynesian policy recommendations, quite the contrary. If it is possible to expand demand and increase output and employment without lowering real wages, so much the better – there is less reason to worry that observed unemployment may be classical.

Clearly product markets, as well as labor markets, should be modeled as imperfectly competitive. There too prices are decision variables, a fact that at the very least suggests that they don't change every hour. When the economy is in a Keynesian excess-supply regime, dynamics of adjustment determine the paths of wages, markups, and product prices. The path of real wages lies between the classical labor demand the supply curves, and could be either pro-cyclical or counter-cyclical. Likewise, the paths of out-put and employment typically diverge from production functions. In the past 50 years a great deal of empirical work has been done on these relationships. Phillips curves and Okun's law are among the best known examples.

In addition, more formal models of nominal price inertia have been developed. Arthur Okun (1981) provided a theory of 'invisible handshakes', in which price adjustments are moderated in the interest of maintaining long-run customer–supplier relationships. Stanley Fischer (1977) and John Taylor (1980) formalized wage stickiness in models of overlapping staggered contracts. These models can apply even to non-union shops where wages are administered rather than negotiated; employers with large work forces change announced wage scales periodically. In a monograph that has attracted too little attention, Katsuhito Iwai (1981) gave Keynesian macroeconomics rigorous microfoundations in a model of monopolistic competition. A microeconomic world of imperfect competition is a Keynesian macroeconomic world, where nominal prices are imperfectly flexible.

Keynes' explanation of money-wage stickiness is the usual focus of discussion and criticism. It is to the second strand of his argument, commonly ignored, that I wish to direct major attention. Even if money wages and prices were more flexible, even if excess supplies of labor were to lead more rapidly to cuts in money wages, this greater flexibility would not prevent or cure unemployment. Given a contractionary shock in aggregate demand, deflation of money wages and prices would not restore real demand to its full employment value. This classical market-clearing adjustment mechanism was, in Keynes' view, much too frail to bear the weight of macroeconomic stabilization. In fact, Keynes recommended stability rather than flexibility in money wages.

Keynes did not challenge the efficacy of price adjustment mechanisms in clearing particular markets in the Marshallian partial equilibrium theory on which he had been reared. He did challenge the mindless application of those mechanisms to economy-wide markets. Founding what came to be known as macroeconomics, he was modeling a whole economy as a closed system. He knew he could not use the Marshallian assumption that the clearing of one market could be safely described on the assumption that the rest of the economy was unaffected.

Consider the difference between a local market for a particular kind of worker and the national market for all labor. Excess supply in the local printing trades, for example, would in a competitive market cause printers' wages to fall. Declining nominal wages would be declining real wages; both would be falling relative to the rest of the economy. The adjustments themselves would not have any noticeable effects on local printing firms' schedules of demand for printers or on workers' supply schedules. But suppose there is an economy-wide excess supply of labor. How is the conventional adjustment apparatus to be deployed?

The orthodox instinct is to think of the price in this market as the real wage. It is in terms of the real wage that the employers' downward sloping demand schedule, following the law of diminishing marginal productivity, is expressed. In the same terms are expressed workers' marginal choices between the consumption rewards of paid employment and the utilities of other uses of time. The orthodox expectation and prescription is that real wages fall to eliminate unemployment.

But, Keynes asks, how do workers and employers engineer an economy-wide reduction in real wages? The unemployment is nation-wide, but the markets where wages are set are decentralized. In every local market it is the money wage, not the real wage, that is determined. If money wage rates fall in all these excess-supply local labor markets, will real wages in fact fall?

It is certainly far from obvious. The relevant labor demand curves are the nominal values of marginal products. These values will fall, the demand curves shift down, if and as product prices fall. Product prices will fall because nominal labor incomes decline along with wage rates; as a result, workers' money demands for the products they produce will decline too. Here, then, is a case in which demand and supply schedules do not stay put while the price adjustment to excess supply takes place. It is illegitimate to appeal to the intuition that seems so credible for single markets. Instead, the question is whether proportionate deflation of all nominal prices will or will not increase aggregate effective real demand.[3]

Two issues in this debate need to be distinguished. The first concerns the relation of real aggregate demand to the *price level*. The second concerns its relation to the expected *rate of change* of prices. In discussing them, I shall not distinguish between money wages and nominal product prices or between their rates of change, but rather follow the assumption, conventional in this debate, that they move together. I remind you that the theoretical argument refers to a closed economy – maybe the United States in years gone by, or post-1992 Europe, or the whole OECD area.

Keynes in Book I of the *General Theory* denied that real aggregate demand was related at all to the price and money wage level. In effect, he turned the classical neutrality proposition against the classicals. If all money wages and prices are lowered in the same proportion, how can real quantities demanded be any different? Thus, if a real shock makes real demand deficient, how can a purely nominal price adjustment undo the damage?

Actually Keynes himself provided an answer in Chapter 19. If the nominal quantity of money remains the same, its real quantity increases, interest rates fall, and real demand increases. This scenario is often called the 'Keynes effect'. This mechanism would fail if demand for money became perfectly elastic with respect to interest rates – as in the liquidity trap discussed above – or if demand for goods for consumption and investment were perfectly inelastic.

Pigou (1943, 1947), Patinkin (1948, 1956 [1965]), and other authors provided another scenario, the 'Pigou effect' or 'real balance effect', which alleges a direct effect of increased wealth, in the case at hand taking the form of the increased real value of base money, on real consumption demand (possibly also on investment demand as wealth-owners seek to maintain portfolio balance between real and nominal assets). This effect does not depend on reduction of interest rates.

To an astonishing degree, the theoretical fraternity has taken the real balance effect to be a conclusive refutation of Keynes. Perhaps it does refute his claim to have found underemployment *equilibria*. If involuntary unemployment and excess capacity are pushing nominal wages and prices down, the economy is not in equilibrium in any sense. It is not in a position of rest, markets are not clearing, and expectations are not being realized. Equilibrium requires wages and prices so low that the purchasing power of net monetary wealth is so great that aggregate real demand creates jobs for all willing workers. In principle, as Leontief observed, prices could be low enough to enable you to buy the whole GNP for one thin dime.

Nevertheless the real balance effect is of dubious strength, and even of uncertain sign. Most nominal assets in a modern economy are 'inside' assets, that is the debts of private agents to other private agents. They wash out in accounting aggregation, leaving only the government's nominal debt to the private sector as net wealth. Some, though probably not all, of that debt is internalized by taxpayers. The base of the real balance effect is therefore quite small relative to the economy – in the United States the monetary base is currently only 6 percent of GNP. A 10 percent increase in the value of money would increase net wealth by 0.6 percent of GNP and, if the marginal propensity to spend from wealth were generously estimated at 0.10, would increase spending by 0.06 percent of GNP.

While Don Patinkin (1948) stressed the theoretical importance of the real balance effect, he disclaimed belief in its practical significance. In the Great Depression, he pointed out, the real value of net private balances rose 46 percent from 1929 to 1932, but real national income *fell* 40 percent.

That inside assets and debts wash out in accounting aggregation does not mean that the consequences of price changes on their real values wash out. Price declines make creditors better off and debtors poorer. Their marginal propensities to spend from wealth need not be the same. Common sense suggests that debtors have the higher spending propensities – that is why they are in debt! Even a small differential could easily swamp the Pigou effect – gross inside dollar-denominated assets are 200 percent of United States GNP.

Irving Fisher (1933) emphasized the increased burden of debt resulting from unanticipated deflation as a major factor in depressions in general and in the Great Depression in particular. Therefore, I like to call the reverse Pigou–Patinkin effect the Fisher wealth redistribution effect (not to be confused with other Fisher effects). It is quite possible that this Fisher effect is stronger than the Pigou and Keynes effects combined, particularly when output and employment are low relative to capacity.[4]

AGGREGATE DEMAND AND THE RATE OF CHANGE OF PRICES

The previous argument refers to *levels* of nominal wages and prices. An even more important argument refers to *rates of change*. The Keynes and Pigou effects compare high prices and low as if they were timeless alternatives, without worrying about the process of change from high to low in real time. Economists of their day argued in this way quite consciously, as dictated by the rules of the comparative statics games they were playing.

The process of change works on aggregate demand in just the wrong direction. Greater expected deflation, or expected disinflation, is an increase in the real rate of interest, necessarily so when nominal interest rates are constrained by the zero floor of the interest on money. Here is another Fisher effect, another factor Fisher stressed in his explanation of the Great Depression. Keynes stressed it too, as a pragmatic dynamic reinforcement of the lesson of his static general theory.

The problematic stability of price adjustment is evident in Figure 6.1. Here the horizontal axis represents expected price deflation or inflation, x. The vertical axis represents p the log of the price level. An upward sloping curve like E_1^* plots combinations (x, p) of expected price change and price level that generate the same aggregate real demand E. The slope reflects the assumptions that demand is related negatively to the price level and positively to its expected rate of change. In given circumstances, a higher curve refers to a lower demand E and a lower curve to higher demand. The curvature of the E^* loci reflects the assumption that the 'Keynes effect' of increases in real money balances in lowering interest rates declines as those balances increase and interest rates fall.

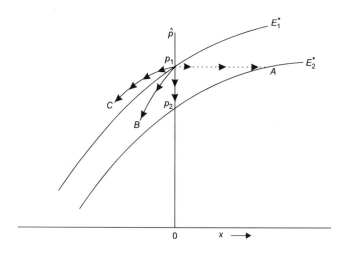

Figure 6.1 The problematic stability of price adjustment

Suppose that initially the 'isoquant' E_1^* makes demand equal to full employment equilibrium output Y^*, here taken to be constant. Points above or left of that isoquant are positions where E is lower than Y^*, characterized by Keynesian unemployment. Points below or right of E_1^* are positions of macroeconomic excess demand. In Figure 6.1, the equilibrium inflation rate (expected and actual) and price are $(0, p_1)$. Suppose now that a discrete one-time negative shock to real demand shifts the isoquant for $E = Y^*$ down to E_2^* so that the new equilibrium inflation rate and price are $(0, p_2)$. The old isoquant E_1^* now implies an E lower than Y^*. To restore equilibrium the price level must fall from p_1 to p_2. How is the price decline to be accomplished? One scenario is the Walrasian miracle, an instantaneous precipitous vertical descent, so that there is no time interval during which actual or expected price changes are other than zero. If jumps of that kind in p are excluded, there is no path of actual price changes and rationally expected prices that avoids departure from $E = Y^*$ during the transition. It would take a burst of positive inflation, actual and expected, to offset the negative demand shock, as at point A. But this would move the price level in the wrong direction.

The likely scenario is a path like B or C in Figure 6.1: the excess supply that now characterizes the initial equilibrium point $(0, p_1)$ and the first isoquant starts prices declining, and the anticipation of their decline is bad for aggregate demand. Along B the real balance effect is strong enough to overcome the negative effects of the deflation; aggregate demand E is increasing as the path hits lower isoquants. The new equilibrium may be attained, though probably by a damped cyclical process. Along C, however, the price level effect is too weak to win out, and the gap of E and Y below Y^* is increasing.

Fisher and Keynes were right. In Tobin (1975), I exhibited a simple formal macroeconomic system, classical in the sense that it has only one equilibrium, which is characterized by full employment, indeed by a 'natural' rate of unemployment. Given a zero natural real growth rate and a constant nominal monetary base, the price level is constant in that equilibrium.

Several specifications of the short-run dynamics of this model are possible. One is a Keynesian specification, as follows: (1) Production increases when desired purchases exceed actual current output, but not by the full amount of the gap. This adjustment can be thought of as response to undesired changes in inventories or unfilled orders. (2) Nominal prices follow expectations plus or minus a 'Phillips curve' adjustment to the difference between actual and full employment output. (3) Price change expectations adapt to the difference between actual and expected inflation or deflation.

Alternatively, the price change expectations could be regarded as rational expectations of the Phillips curve price adjustment mechanisms. That is, the impossibility of instantaneous jumps to the new equilibrium would be as intrinsic to the structure of the system as the system's static equations themselves.

The stability of this system requires, first, that the dynamics of output at constant prices, involving marginal propensities to spend and adjustments to excess or deficient inventories and other manifestations of demand/output gaps, is stable. Assuming this condition is met, stability depends on the relative strengths of the price level effects on demand – both 'Keynes' and 'Pigou' as modified by 'Fisher wealth redistribution' – and the real interest effect – another 'Fisher' – of expected deflation (or disinflation). The latter is the product of two coefficients, the response of price change expectations to actual change (equal to one if expectations are rational) and the response of real demand to expected price change. The real interest effect may well dominate if the real balance effect is weak, especially if the Fisher wealth redistribution effect overshadows it, and if the demand for money is highly sensitive to interest rates. The equilibrium is then unstable. Moreover, because of the curvature of the E^* loci, the system could be stable locally but unstable for large displacements.

I have experimented with simulations of a discrete-time approximation to this model, subjecting it to stochastic shocks to real aggregate demand. One extreme case is 'Walrasian': prices vary from period to period as necessary to keep goods markets always cleared, prices are always anticipated to equal their expected value corresponding to zero shock, and both output and aggregate demand always equal equilibrium full employment output. An opposite extreme is 'rigid-price Keynesian': prices are constant at their expected equilibrium value and expectations of price change are constant at zero. In between the extremes, nominal prices adjust with some inertia to excess real demand or supply, and expectations of price change adapt, more or less speedily, to observed changes.

In these simulations the underlying 'fixprice' dynamics are stable, and its parameters are the same in all cases. 'Greater price flexibility' can mean two things: (1) a larger Phillips curve coefficient relating price change to excess real demand or supply; (2) if expectations are taken to be adaptive, a larger coefficient of adaptation of price change expectations to actual price changes.

The issue is whether greater price flexibility increases or decreases the ratio between the standard deviation of the actual output gap and the standard deviation of the stochastic real demand shock. That ratio is zero in the Walrasian case, where the shock is always wholly absorbed in prices. It is of course positive for the rigid-price case. What happens in the intermediate cases? Not surprisingly, the results depend mainly on the same condition that determines stability or instability with respect to a single unrepeated shock. Greater flexibility in sense (1), a faster 'Phillips' adjustment, diminishes the test ratio when the stability condition is met – that is, the price level effect on demand is negative and bigger than the price change effect – and raises it otherwise. Greater flexibility in sense (2), faster adjustment of price expectations, always raises the test ratio.[5]

POLICIES, EXPECTATIONS AND STABILITY

Keynes stressed the central role of long-term expectations. He had in mind in particular expectations of real variables – effective demands and real returns on investments. They might be either stabilizing or destabilizing. If business managers believe that recessions will be quickly reversed, their actions will help to bring about recoveries. If they expect business activity to continue to be subnormal or to fall further, their pessimism may turn recession into depression. That is why policies and policy expectations are very important. After World War II, widespread perception that government fiscal and monetary policies would keep recessions short and shallow helped to keep them short and shallow. In these circumstances, the economy would work well if, as Keynes advocated, employers and workers kept average money wage rates stable, so that actual and expected price and wage changes were not a source of instability.

In the 1930s both Fisher and Keynes saw deflation as a cause of depression in production and employment, and advocated monetary and gold policies of reflation for recovery. Today, however, unexpectedly high prices are regarded as bearish economic news, and unexpectedly low prices as bullish. Is this a paradox? Does it mean that price flexibility is stabilizing after all? Again, policies and policy expectations are crucial. Today the public understands the high priorities central banks attach to inflation control. If prices are above the path to which the central bank is committed, it will take measures to contract demand. The faster private agents respond by lowering prices and wages, the sooner the monetary authorities will reflate. In this sense, price flexibility is stabilizing.

In contrast, extrapolative expectations are destabilizing. Policies – policy rules if you like – that create and sustain regressive expectations of output and price departures from equilibrium are stabilizing. Those facts are wholly consistent with the contentions of Fisher and Keynes, and of this paper, that in the absence of activist 'feedback' policies, monetary and fiscal, flexibility may well be destabilizing, both to prices and to real macro variables. Governments and central banks should not expect disinflation or deflation alone to maintain or restore full employment.

ACKNOWLEDGEMENT

I would like to express my gratitude for the faithful and valuable research assistance of Mitchell Tobin, Yale College 1992 (no relation).

NOTES

1 In Tobin (1955), stagnation is one possibility, the stable solution of a non-linear model whose unstable solution is a repetitive cycle.
2 Dudley Dillard (1988) calls this the 'barter illusion' of classical economics.

3 In formal general equilibrium theory the stability of markets determining relative prices cannot be guaranteed without special assumptions. This is *a fortiori* true if money is introduced and markets determine nominal prices. See the survey by Franklin Fisher (1987).

4 I have exhibited a dominant Fisher effect and examined its macroeconomic consequences in an IS-LM model that also has a Keynes effect, in Tobin (1980: ch. 1). See also Caskey and Fazzari (1987).

5 At long last the question whether price flexibility (in any sense short of the Walrasian auctioneer fairy tale) is stabilizing has begun to receive considerable attention. De Long and Summers (1986) have investigated this question using the Fischer–Taylor staggered-contract model (Fischer 1977; Taylor 1980), amended to allow both price-level and price-change effects on demand. Their most interesting simulation has the intuitively desirable property that close to the limit of perfect price flexibility greater price flexibility means greater real stability, while farther away from it the reverse is true. Similar results are obtained by Caskey and Fazzari (1988) and Chadha (1989).

REFERENCES

Ball, Lawrence, N. Gregory Mankiw, and David Romer, 'The New Keynesian Economics and the Output-Inflation Tradeoff', *Brookings Papers on Economic Activity* 1988 *1*, 1–65.

Barro, Robert, and Herschel Grossman, 'A General Disequilibrium Model of Income and Employment', *American Economic Review* March 1971, *61*, 82–93.

Caskey, John, and Steve Fazzari, 'Aggregate Demand Contractions with Nominal Debt Commitments', *Economic Inquiry* October 1987, *25*, 583–97.

Caskey, John, and Steven Fazzari, 'Price Flexibility and Macroeconomic Stability: An Empirical Simulation Analysis', Washington University Department of Economics, working paper 118, January 1988.

Chadha, Binky, 'Is Increased Price Inflexibility Stabilizing?', *Journal of Money, Credit and Banking* November 1989, *21*, 481–97.

Cooper, Russell, and Andrew John, 'Coordinating Coordination Failures in Keynesian Models', *Quarterly Journal of Economics* August 1988, *100*, 441–63.

De Long, J. Bradford, and Lawrence H. Summers, 'Is Increasing Price Flexibility Stabilizing?' *American Economic Review* December 1986, *76*, 1031–44.

Dillard, Dudley, 'The Barter Illusion in Classical and Neoclassical Economics', *Eastern Economic Journal* October–December 1988, *14*, 299–318.

Fischer, Stanley, 'Long-term Contracts, Rational Expectations, and the Optimal Money Supply Rule', *Journal of Political Economy* February 1977, *85*: 1, 191–205.

Fisher, Franklin, M., 'Adjustment Processes and Stability', in John Eatwell, Murray Milgate, and Peter Newman (eds) *The New Palgrave: A Dictionary of Economics*, London: Macmillan, 1987, 26–9.

Fisher, Irving, 'The Debt-Deflation Theory of Great Depressions', *Econometrica* October 1933, *1*, 337–57.

Hansen, Alvin H., *Full Recovery or Stagnation*, New York: W. W. Norton, 1938.

Iwai, Katsuhito, *Disequilibrium Dynamics* (Cowles Foundation Monograph 27), New Haven, CT: Yale University Press, 1981.

Keynes, John Maynard, *The General Theory of Employment, Interest, and Money*, New York: Harcourt Brace, 1936.

Lindbeck, Assar, and Dennis J. Snower, *The Insider-Outsider Theory of Employment and Unemployment*, Cambridge, MA: MIT Press, 1990.

Mankiw, N. Gregory, 'A Quick Refresher Course in Macroeconomics', *Journal of Economic Literature* December 1990, *28*, 1645–60.

Okun, Arthur M., *Prices and Quantities: A Macroeconomic Analysis,* Washington, DC: Brookings Institution, 1981.

Patinkin, Don, 'Price Flexibility and Full Employment', *American Economic Review* September 1948, *38*, 543–64.

Patinkin, Don, *Money, Interest, and Prices,* New York: Harper and Row, 1956, 2nd edn, 1965.

Pigou, Arthur Cecil, 'The Classical Stationary State', *Economic Journal* December 1943, *53*, 313–51.

Pigou, Arthur Cecil, 'Economic Progress in a Stable Environment', *Economica* August 1947, *14*, 180–90.

Plosser, Charles I., 'Understanding Real Business Cycles', *Journal of Economic Perspectives* Summer 1989, *3*:3, 51–77.

Taylor, John, 'Aggregate Dynamics and Staggered Contracts', *Journal of Political Economy* February 1980, *88*, 1–23.

Tobin, James, 'A Dynamic Aggregative Model', *Journal of Political Economy* April 1955, *63*, 103–15.

Tobin, James, 'Keynesian Models of Recession and Depression', *American Economic Review (Papers and Proceedings)*, May 1975, *55*, 195–202.

Tobin, James, *Asset Accumulation and Economic Activity,* Oxford: Basil Blackwell, 1980.

Tobin, James, 'Financial Structure and Monetary Rules', *Kredit und Kapital* 1983, *16*, 155–71.

Part II

The monetarist counter-revolution

Introduction

'Monetarism', a term first introduced by Karl Brunner (1968), refers to a school of economic thought which initially evolved in the United States to attack the orthodox Keynesian analysis and associated policy-activism of the 1950s and 1960s. The historical development of the orthodox monetarist school can be traced in three main stages (see Snowdon *et al.* 1994). The first main stage, from the mid-1950s to the mid-1960s, involved an attempt, by Professor Milton Friedman and his associates, to re-establish the quantity theory of money approach to macroeconomic analysis. In this approach changes in the money supply are regarded as the predominant, though not the only, factor explaining changes in money income. Friedman's (1956) seminal article on 'The Quantity Theory of Money: A Restatement' in which he asserted that the demand for money (and by implication velocity) is a stable function of a limited number of variables lies at the heart of the modern quantity theory approach. However, it was the breadth and depth of empirical evidence cited in Friedman and Schwartz's (1963) book on *A Monetary History of the United States, 1867–1960* which was particularly influential in reviving interest in the potency of money in generating cyclical fluctuations. Their analysis of the US historical record provided strong support for the view that *independent* movements of the stock of money played a significant role in causing macroeconomic instability. According to Lucas (1994) this book played 'an important – perhaps even decisive – role in the 1960s' debates over stabilization policy between Keynesians and monetarists'.

The second main stage in the development of orthodox monetarism involved the expectations-augmented Phillips curve analysis which was absorbed into monetarist analysis after the mid-to-late 1960s. Central to this phase is Friedman's 1967 Presidential Address to the American Economic Association, subsequently published in 1968 in the *American Economic Review* as 'The Role of Monetary Policy'. In this article (reprinted on pp. 164–79) Friedman denies the existence of a permanent/long-run trade-off between inflation and unemployment and introduces the natural rate of unemployment hypothesis. The essence of this hypothesis is a reaffirmation of the classical view that in the long run nominal magnitudes cannot determine real magnitudes such as employment and output. According to

Friedman monetary policy cannot, other than for very limited periods, achieve some target unemployment rate and any attempt to maintain unemployment below the natural rate will produce accelerating inflation; a prediction subsequently borne out by the experience of many western economies during the 1970s (see Snowdon and Vane 1997). In the conduct of monetary policy he prescribes that the authorities pursue a 'stable' rate of monetary growth in line with the trend /long-run growth rate of the economy to ensure long-run price stability. Friedman argues that the natural rate of unemployment can be reduced only by appropriate supply-side micro-orientated policies which improve the operation of the labour market. In 1981 Robert Gordon described Friedman's 1968 paper as probably the most influential article written in macroeconomics in the previous twenty years. More recently James Tobin (1995), one of Friedman's most eloquent, effective and long-standing critics, has described the paper as 'very likely the most influential article *ever* published in an economics journal' (emphasis added).

The third main stage in the development of orthodox monetarism came in the 1970s with the incorporation of the monetary approach to balance of payments theory and exchange rate determination into monetarist analysis. This made monetarist analysis which, up to that time, had been implicitly developed in the relatively closed economy context of the US economy under the Bretton Woods system, relevant to open economies such as the UK. It also provided an explanation of the international transmission of inflation in the late 1960s (see Frenkel and Johnson 1976).

While it is possible to outline the historical development of orthodox monetarism in these three main stages, it is far more problematic to specify a set of characteristics to which all monetarists would subscribe. Within the monetarist school there have been, and continue to be, differences of opinion and emphasis and it is impossible to produce a definitive list of characteristics of the monetarist viewpoint which would be universally accepted. Over the years there have been a number of papers which have sought to summarize the central distinguishing beliefs within the orthodox monetarist school of thought (see for example Brunner 1970; Friedman 1970; Purvis 1980). In his 1975 *Kredit und Kapital* article (reprinted on pp. 180–215) on 'The Structure of Monetarism', Thomas Mayer discusses twelve beliefs of varying significance which at that time were in his view generally held by monetarists in the United States. In Part I of his article Mayer discusses six propositions relating to theory and techniques of analysis, and in Part II six policy-orientated propositions. While he demonstrates the connections between the complete set of monetarist propositions identified, Mayer argues that economists can accept some of these propositions while rejecting others. Another attempt to specify monetarism's key characteristics is David Laidler's 1981 *Economic Journal* article entitled 'Monetarism: An Interpretation and an Assessment'. This article (reprinted on pp. 216–46) was initially prepared for presentation at a Conference on 'Monetarism – An Appraisal' organized by the Royal Economic Society (RES) in

London in July 1980. The March 1981 issue of the *Economic Journal* also includes an article by James Tobin appraising the monetarist counter-revolution, together with comments on both Laidler's and Tobin's articles by R. C. O. Matthews and James E. Meade, presented at the RES Conference. As the reader will discover, Laidler's article provides both an exposition and appraisal of monetarism in terms of four key characteristics, namely a quantity theory approach to macroeconomic analysis, an analysis of the division of money income fluctuations between the price level and real income, a monetary approach to balance-of-payments and exchange-rate theory, and an antipathy to activist stabilization policy and support for long-run monetary policy 'rules'.

However monetarism is defined, one characteristic which all monetarists agree upon is the emphasis given to controlling the money stock and prior to the 1980s 'velocity puzzle' a majority of monetarists supported a monetary growth rule or target, in order to both attain and maintain long-run price stability. The case for Friedman's 'stable' monetary growth rule is inextricably linked to empirical evidence of a stable demand for money function (and associated trend in velocity) for the post-war period up to the 1970s, both in the US and other economies. Evidence of money demand instability (and a shift in the trend of velocity, with velocity becoming more erratic) especially since 1981 in the United States and elsewhere has undermined the case for a fixed monetary growth rule. Franco Modigliani's 1988 *Contemporary Policy Issues* article (reprinted on pp. 247–61) entitled 'The Monetarist Controversy Revisited' examines two proposed 'feedback' monetary growth rules, and the case for stabilization policy, in the light of US experience during the 1980s.

Although within academia monetarism is no longer the influential force it was in the late 1960s and early 1970s, its apparent demise can in large part be attributed to the fact that a number of its insights have been absorbed into mainstream macroeconomics (see Mayer 1997). Most notably the expectations-augmented Phillips curve analysis, the view that the long-run Phillips curve is vertical and that money is neutral in the long run are all now widely accepted and form part of mainstream macroeconomics. Furthermore a majority of economists and central banks emphasize the rate of growth of the money supply when it comes to explaining and combating inflation over the long run. But perhaps the most important and lasting contribution of monetarism has been to persuade many economists to accept the idea that the potential of *activist discretionary* fiscal and monetary *policy* is much more limited than conceived prior to the monetarist counter-revolution.

REFERENCES

*Titles marked with an asterisk are particularly recommended for additional reading.
Brunner, K. (1968) 'The Role of Money and Monetary Policy', *Federal Reserve Bank of St Louis Review* 50, July, pp. 9–24.

*Brunner, K. (1970) 'The Monetarist Revolution in Monetary Theory', *Weltwirtschaftliches Archiv* 105, March, pp. 1–30.

Frenkel, J. A. and H. G. Johnson (eds) (1976) *The Monetary Approach to the Balance of Payments*, London: Allen and Unwin.

Friedman, M. (1956) 'The Quantity Theory of Money: A Restatement', in M. Friedman (ed.) *Studies in the Quantity Theory of Money*, Chicago: University of Chicago Press.

*Friedman, M. (1970) *The Counter-Revolution in Monetary Theory*, IEA Occasional Paper no. 33, London: Institute of Economic Affairs.

*Friedman, M. (1975) *Unemployment versus Inflation? An Evaluation of the Phillips Curve*, IEA Occasional Paper no. 44, London: Institute of Economic Affairs.

*Friedman, M. (1977) 'Nobel Lecture: Inflation and Unemployment', *Journal of Political Economy* 85, June, pp. 451–72.

Friedman, M. and A. J. Schwartz (1963) *A Monetary History of the United States, 1867–1960*, Princeton, NJ: Princeton University Press.

*Froyen, R. T. (1996) *Macroeconomics: Theories and Policies*, 5th edn, Chapters 9 and 10, London: Prentice-Hall.

Gordon, R. J. (1981) 'Output Fluctuations and Gradual Price Adjustment', *Journal of Economic Literature* 19, June, pp. 493–530.

*Hoover, K. D. (1984) 'Two Types of Monetarism', *Journal of Economic Literature* 22, March, pp. 58–76.

Hoover, K. D. and S. M. Sheffrin (eds) (1995) *Monetarism and the Methodology of Economics: Essays in Honour of Thomas Mayer*, Aldershot: Edward Elgar.

*Jansen, D. W., C. D. Delorme and R. B. Ekelund, Jr (1994) *Intermediate Macroeconomics*, Chapter 8, New York: West.

*Johnson, H. G. (1971) 'The Keynesian Revolution and the Monetarist Counter-Revolution', *American Economic Review* 61, May, pp. 1–14.

Lucas, R. E. Jr (1994) 'Review of Milton Friedman and Anna J. Schwartz's "A Monetary History of the United States, 1867–1960"', *Journal of Monetary Economics* 34, August, pp. 5–16.

*Mayer, T. (1990) *Monetarism and Macroeconomic Policy*, Aldershot: Edward Elgar.

*Mayer, T. (1997) 'What Remains of the Monetarist Counter-Revolution', in B. Snowdon and H. R. Vane (eds) *Reflections on the Development of Modern Macroeconomics*, Aldershot: Edward Elgar.

Purvis, D. D. (1980) 'Monetarism: A Review', *Canadian Journal of Economics* 1, February, pp. 96–121.

Snowdon, B. and H. R. Vane (1997) 'Modern Macroeconomics and its Evolution from a Monetarist Perspective: An Interview with Professor Milton Friedman', *Journal of Economic Studies* 24.

*Snowdon, B., H. R. Vane and P. Wynarczyk (1994) *A Modern Guide to Macroeconomics: An Introduction to Competing Schools of Thought*, Chapter 4, Aldershot: Edward Elgar.

*Tobin, J. (1981) 'The Monetarist Counter-Revolution Today: An Appraisal', *Economic Journal* 91, March, pp. 29–42.

Tobin, J. (1995) 'The Natural Rate as New Classical Economics', in R. Cross (ed.) *The Natural Rate of Unemployment: Reflections on 25 Years of the Hypothesis*, Cambridge: Cambridge University Press.

QUESTIONS

1 Compare and contrast the traditional quantity theory of money with its modern restatement.

2 What do you understand by the term 'monetarism'? In what ways does the monetarist approach to macroeconomics differ from the orthodox Keynesian approach?

3 'Monetarist analysis seeks to explain the short-run non-neutrality of money whilst preserving the classical view of long-run neutrality'. Explain and discuss.

4 How do fluctuations in the quantity of money influence real variables according to monetarist analysis?

5 What are the policy implications of Friedman's analysis of the expectations-augmented Phillips curve?

6 'The case for or against monetarism is fundamentally empirical, not theoretical'. Discuss.

7 What were the major factors which contributed to the rise of monetarism in academia and policy circles during the 1970s?

8 Critically examine the monetarist arguments against policy activism and assess the case for a monetary rule.

9 What remains of the 'monetarist counter-revolution'?

10 To what extent has Milton Friedman proved to be the most influential macroeconomist since Keynes?

7 The role of monetary policy

Milton Friedman
American Economic Review (1968) 58, March, pp. 1–17

There is wide agreement about the major goals of economic policy: high employment, stable prices, and rapid growth. There is less agreement that these goals are mutually compatible or, among those who regard them as incompatible, about the terms at which they can and should be substituted for one another. There is least agreement about the role that various instruments of policy can and should play in achieving the several goals.

My topic for tonight is the role of one such instrument – monetary policy. What can it contribute? And how should it be conducted to contribute the most? Opinion on these questions has fluctuated widely. In the first flush of enthusiasm about the newly created Federal Reserve System, many observers attributed the relative stability of the 1920s to the System's capacity for fine tuning – to apply an apt modern term. It came to be widely believed that a new era had arrived in which business cycles had been rendered obsolete by advances in monetary technology. This opinion was shared by economist and layman alike, though, of course, there were some dissonant voices. The Great Contraction destroyed this naive attitude. Opinion swung to the other extreme. Monetary policy was a string. You could pull on it to stop inflation but you could not push on it to halt recession. You could lead a horse to water but you could not make him drink. Such theory by aphorism was soon replaced by Keynes' rigorous and sophisticated analysis.

Keynes offered simultaneously an explanation for the presumed impotence of monetary policy to stem the depression, a nonmonetary interpretation of the depression, and an alternative to monetary policy for meeting the depression and his offering was avidly accepted. If liquidity preference is absolute or nearly so – as Keynes believed likely in times of heavy unemployment – interest rates cannot be lowered by monetary measures. If investment and consumption are little affected by interest rates – as Hansen and many of Keynes' other American disciples came to believe – lower interest rates, even if they could be achieved, would do little good. Monetary policy is twice damned. The contraction, set in train, on this view, by a collapse of investment or by a shortage of investment opportunities or by stubborn thriftiness, could not, it was argued, have been stopped by monetary measures. But there was available an alternative – fiscal policy. Government spending could make up for insufficient private investment. Tax reductions could undermine stubborn thriftiness.

The wide acceptance of these views in the economics profession meant that for some two decades monetary policy was believed by all but a few reactionary souls to have been rendered obsolete by new economic knowledge. Money did not matter. Its only role was the minor one of keeping interest rates low, in order to hold down interest payments in the government budget, contribute to the 'euthanasia of the rentier', and maybe, stimulate investment a bit to assist government spending in maintaining a high level of aggregate demand.

These views produced a widespread adoption of cheap money policies after the war. And they received a rude shock when these policies failed in country after country, when central bank after central bank was forced to give up the pretense that it could indefinitely keep 'the' rate of interest at a low level. In the United States, the public denouement came with the Federal Reserve–Treasury Accord in 1951, although the policy of pegging government bond prices was not formally abandoned until 1953. Inflation, stimulated by cheap money policies, not the widely heralded postwar depression, turned out to be the order of the day. The result was the beginning of a revival of belief in the potency of monetary policy.

This revival was strongly fostered among economists by the theoretical developments initiated by Haberler but named for Pigou that pointed out a channel – namely, changes in wealth – whereby changes in the real quantity of money can affect aggregate demand even if they do not alter interest rates. These theoretical developments did not undermine Keynes' argument against the potency of orthodox monetary measures when liquidity preference is absolute since under such circumstances the usual monetary operations involve simply substituting money for other assets without changing total wealth. But they did show how changes in the quantity of money produced in other ways could affect total spending even under such circumstances. And, more fundamentally, they did undermine Keynes' key theoretical proposition, namely, that even in a world of flexible prices, a position of equilibrium at full employment might not exist. Henceforth, unemployment had again to be explained by rigidities or imperfections, not as the natural outcome of a fully operative market process.

The revival of belief in the potency of monetary policy was fostered also by a re-evaluation of the role money played from 1929 to 1933. Keynes and most other economists of the time believed that the Great Contraction in the United States occurred despite aggressive expansionary policies by the monetary authorities – that they did their best but their best was not good enough.[1] Recent studies have demonstrated that the facts are precisely the reverse: the US monetary authorities followed highly deflationary policies. The quantity of money in the United States fell by one-third in the course of the contraction. And it fell not because there were no willing borrowers – not because the horse would not drink. It fell because the Federal Reserve

System forced or permitted a sharp reduction in the monetary base, because it failed to exercise the responsibilities assigned to it in the Federal Reserve Act to provide liquidity to the banking system. The Great Contraction is tragic testimony to the power of monetary policy – not, as Keynes and so many of his contemporaries believed, evidence of its impotence.

In the United States the revival of belief in the potency of monetary policy was strengthened also by increasing disillusionment with fiscal policy, not so much with its potential to affect aggregate demand as with the practical and political feasibility of so using it. Expenditures turned out to respond sluggishly and with long lags to attempts to adjust them to the course of economic activity, so emphasis shifted to taxes. But here political factors entered with a vengeance to prevent prompt adjustment to presumed need, as has been so graphically illustrated in the months since I wrote the first draft of this talk. 'Fine tuning' is a marvelously evocative phrase in this electronic age, but it has little resemblance to what is possible in practice – not, I might add, an unmixed evil.

It is hard to realize how radical has been the change in professional opinion on the role of money. Hardly an economist today accepts views that were the common coin some two decades ago. Let me cite a few examples.

In a talk published in 1945, E. A. Goldenweiser, then Director of the Research Division of the Federal Reserve Board, described the primary objective of monetary policy as being to 'maintain the value of Government bonds.... This country' he wrote, 'will have to adjust to a 2 1/2 per cent interest rate as the return on safe, long-time money, because the time has come when returns on pioneering capital can no longer be unlimited as they were in the past' [4, p. 117].

In a book on *Financing American Prosperity*, edited by Paul Homan and Fritz Machlup and published in 1945, Alvin Hansen devotes nine pages of text to the 'savings-investment problem' without finding any need to use the words 'interest rate' or any close facsimile thereto [5, pp. 218–27]. In his contribution to this volume, Fritz Machlup wrote, 'Questions regarding the rate of interest, in particular regarding its variation or its stability, may not be among the most vital problems of the postwar economy, but they are certainly among the perplexing ones' [5, p. 466]. In his contribution, John H. Williams – not only professor at Harvard but also a long-time adviser to the New York Federal Reserve Bank – wrote, 'I can see no prospect of revival of a general monetary control in the postwar period' [5, p. 383].

Another of the volumes dealing with postwar policy that appeared at this time, *Planning and Paying for Full Employment*, was edited by Abba P. Lerner and Frank D. Graham [6] and had contributors of all shades of professional opinion – from Henry Simons and Frank Graham to Abba Lerner and Hans Neisser. Yet Albert Halasi, in his excellent summary of the papers, was able to say, 'Our contributors do not discuss the question of money supply.... The contributors make no special mention of credit policy to remedy actual depressions.... Inflation ... might be fought more effectively by raising interest rates.... But... other anti-inflationary measures ...are preferable' [6, pp. 23–4]. *A Survey of Contemporary Economics*, edited by Howard Ellis and published in 1948, was an 'official' attempt to codify the state of economic thought of the time. In his contribution, Arthur Smithies wrote, 'In the field of compensatory action, I believe fiscal policy must shoulder most of the load. Its chief rival, monetary policy, seems to be disqualified on institutional grounds. This country appears to be committed to something like the present low level of interest rates on a long-term basis' [1, p. 208].

These quotations suggest the flavor of professional thought some two decades ago. If you wish to go further in this humbling inquiry, I recommend that you compare the sections on money – when you can find them – in the Principles texts of the early postwar years with the lengthy sections in the current crop even, or especially, when the early and recent Principles are different editions of the same work.

The pendulum has swung far since then, if not all the way to the position of the late 1920s, at least much closer to that position than to the position of 1945. There are of course many differences between then and now, less in the potency attributed to monetary policy than in the roles assigned to it and the criteria by which the profession believes monetary policy should be guided. Then, the chief roles assigned monetary policy were to promote price stability and to preserve the gold standard; the chief criteria of monetary policy were the state of the 'money market', the extent of 'speculation' and the movement of gold. Today, primacy is assigned to the promotion of full employment, with the prevention of inflation a continuing but definitely secondary objective. And there is major disagreement about criteria of policy, varying from emphasis on money market conditions, interest rates, and the quantity of money to the belief that the state of employment itself should be the proximate criterion of policy.

I stress nonetheless the similarity between the views that prevailed in the late 1920s and those that prevail today because I fear that, now as then, the pendulum may well have swung too far, that, now as then, we are in danger of assigning to monetary policy a larger role than it can perform, in danger of asking it to accomplish tasks that it cannot achieve, and, as a result, in danger of preventing it from making the contribution that it is capable of making.

Unaccustomed as I am to denigrating the importance of money, I therefore shall, as my first task, stress what monetary policy cannot do. I shall then try to outline what it can do and how it can best make its contribution, in the present state of our knowledge – or ignorance.

WHAT MONETARY POLICY CANNOT DO

From the infinite world of negation, I have selected two limitations of monetary policy to discuss: (1) it cannot peg interest rates for more than very limited periods; (2) it cannot peg the rate of unemployment for more than very limited periods. I select these because the contrary has been or is widely believed, because they correspond to the two main unattainable tasks that are at all likely to be assigned to monetary policy, and because essentially the same theoretical analysis covers both.

Pegging of interest rates

History has already persuaded many of you about the first limitation. As noted earlier, the failure of cheap money policies was a major source of the reaction against simple-minded Keynesianism. In the United States, this reaction involved widespread recognition that the wartime and postwar pegging of bond prices was a mistake, that the abandonment of this policy was a desirable and inevitable step, and that it had none of the disturbing and disastrous consequences that were so freely predicted at the time.

The limitation derives from a much misunderstood feature of the relation between money and interest rates. Let the Fed set out to keep interest rates down. How will it try to do so? By buying securities. This raises their prices and lowers their yields. In the process, it also increases the quantity of reserves available to banks, hence the amount of bank credit, and, ulti- mately the total quantity of money. That is why central bankers in parti- cular, and the financial community more broadly, generally believe that an increase in the quantity of money tends to lower interest rates. Academic economists accept the same conclusion, but for different reasons. They see, in their mind's eye, a negatively sloping liquidity preference schedule. How can people be induced to hold a larger quantity of money? Only by bidding down interest rates.

Both are right, up to a point. The *initial* impact of increasing the quantity of money at a faster rate than it has been increasing is to make interest rates lower for a time than they would otherwise have been. But this is only the beginning of the process not the end. The more rapid rate of monetary growth will stimulate spending, both through the impact on investment of lower market interest rates and through the impact on other spending and thereby relative prices of higher cash balances than are desired. But one man's spending is another man's income. Rising income will raise the liquidity preference schedule and the demand for loans; it may also raise prices, which would reduce the real quantity of money. These three effects will reverse the initial downward pressure on interest rates fairly promptly, say, in something less than a year. Together they will tend, after a somewhat longer interval, say, a year or two, to return interest rates to the level they would otherwise have had. Indeed, given the tendency for the economy to overreact, they are highly likely to raise interest rates temporarily beyond that level, setting in motion a cyclical adjustment process.

A fourth effect, when and if it becomes operative, will go even farther, and definitely mean that a higher rate of monetary expansion will correspond to a higher, not lower, level of interest rates than would otherwise have prevailed. Let the higher rate of monetary growth produce rising prices, and let the public come to expect that prices will continue to rise. Borrowers will then be willing to pay and lenders will then demand higher interest rates – as Irving Fisher pointed out decades ago. This price expectation effect is slow to develop and also slow to disappear. Fisher estimated that it took several decades for a full adjustment and more recent work is consistent with his estimates.

These subsequent effects explain why every attempt to keep interest rates at a low level has forced the monetary authority to engage in successively larger and larger open market purchases. They explain why, historically, high and rising nominal interest rates have been associated with rapid growth in the quantity of money, as in Brazil or Chile or in the United States in recent years, and why low and falling interest rates have been associated with slow growth in the quantity of money, as in Switzerland now or in the United States from 1929 to 1933. As an empirical matter, low interest rates are a sign that monetary policy *has been* tight – in the sense that the quantity of money has grown slowly; high interest rates are a sign that monetary policy *has been* easy – in the sense that the quantity of money has grown rapidly. The broadest facts of experience run in precisely the opposite direction from that which the financial community and academic economists have all generally taken for granted.

Paradoxically, the monetary authority could assure low nominal rates of interest – but to do so it would have to start out in what seems like the opposite direction, by engaging in a deflationary monetary policy. Similarly, it could assure high nominal interest rates by engaging in an inflationary policy and accepting a temporary movement in interest rates in the opposite direction.

These considerations not only explain why monetary policy cannot peg interest rates; they also explain why interest rates are such a misleading indicator of whether monetary policy is 'tight' or 'easy'. For that, it is far better to look at the rate of change of the quantity of money.[2]

Employment as a criterion of policy

The second limitation I wish to discuss goes more against the grain of current thinking. Monetary growth, it is widely held, will tend to stimulate employment; monetary contraction, to retard employment. Why, then, cannot the monetary authority adopt a target for employment or unemployment – say, 3 percent unemployment; be tight when unemployment is less than the target; be easy when unemployment is higher than the target; and in this way peg unemployment at, say, 3 percent? The reason it cannot is precisely the same as for interest rates – the difference between the immediate and the delayed consequences of such a policy.

Thanks to Wicksell, we are all acquainted with the concept of a 'natural' rate of interest and the possibility of a discrepancy between the 'natural' and the 'market' rate. The preceding analysis of interest rates can be translated fairly directly into Wicksellian terms. The monetary authority can make the market rate less than the natural rate only by inflation. It can make the market rate higher than the natural rate only by deflation. We have added only one wrinkle to Wicksell – the Irving Fisher distinction between the nominal and the real rate of interest. Let the monetary authority keep the nominal market rate for a time below the natural rate by inflation. That in turn will raise the nominal natural rate itself, once anticipations of inflation become widespread, thus requiring still more rapid inflation to hold down the market rate. Similarly, because of the Fisher effect, it will require not merely deflation but more and more rapid deflation to hold the market rate above the initial 'natural' rate.

This analysis has its close counterpart in the employment market. At any moment of time, there is some level of unemployment which has the property that it is consistent with equilibrium in the structure of *real* wage rates. At that level of unemployment, real wage rates are tending on the average to rise at a 'normal' secular rate, i.e. at a rate that can be indefinitely maintained so long as capital formation, technological improvements, etc., remain on their long-run trends. A lower level of unemployment is an indication that there is an excess demand for labor that will produce upward pressure on real wage rates. A higher level of unemployment is an indication that there is an excess supply of labor that will produce downward pressure on real wage rates. The 'natural rate of unemployment', in other words, is the level that would be ground out by the Walrasian system of general equilibrium equations, provided there is imbedded in them the actual structural characteristics of the labor and commodity markets, including market imperfections, stochastic variability in demands and supplies, the cost of gathering information about job vacancies and labor availabilities, the costs of mobility, and so on.[3]

You will recognize the close similarity between this statement and the celebrated Phillips Curve. The similarity is not coincidental. Phillips' analysis of the relation between unemployment and wage change is deservedly celebrated as an important and original contribution. But, unfortunately, it contains a basic defect – the failure to distinguish between *nominal* wages and *real* wages – just as Wicksell's analysis failed to distinguish between *nominal* interest rates and *real* interest rates. Implicitly, Phillips wrote his article for a world in which everyone anticipated that nominal prices would be stable and in which that anticipation remained unshaken and immutable whatever happened to actual prices and wages. Suppose, by contrast, that everyone anticipates that prices will rise at a rate of more than 75 per cent a year – as, for example, Brazilians did a few years ago. Then wages must rise at that rate simply to keep real wages unchanged. An excess supply of labor will be reflected in a less rapid rise in nominal wages than in anticipated prices,[4] not in an absolute decline in wages. When Brazil embarked on a policy to bring down the rate of price rise, and succeeded in bringing the price rise down to about 45 percent a year, there was a sharp initial rise in unemployment because under the influence of earlier anticipations, wages kept rising at a pace that was higher than the new rate of price rise, though lower than earlier. This is the result experienced, and to be expected, of all attempts to reduce the rate of inflation below that widely anticipated.[5]

To avoid misunderstanding, let me emphasize that by using the term 'natural' rate of unemployment, I do not mean to suggest that it is immutable and unchangeable. On the contrary, many of the market characteristics that determine its level are man-made and policy-made. In the United States, for example, legal minimum wage rates, the Walsh-Healy and Davis-Bacon Acts, and the strength of labor unions all make the natural rate of unemployment higher than it would otherwise be. Improvements in employment exchanges, in availability of information about job vacancies and labor supply, and so on, would tend to lower the natural rate of unemployment. I use the term 'natural' for the same reason Wicksell did – to try to separate the real forces from monetary forces.

Let us assume that the monetary authority tries to peg the 'market' rate of unemployment at a level below the 'natural' rate. For definiteness, suppose that it takes 3 percent as the target rate and that the 'natural' rate is higher than 3 percent. Suppose also that we start out at a time when prices have been stable and when unemployment is higher than 3 percent. Accordingly, the authority increases the rate of monetary growth. This will be expansionary. By making nominal cash balances higher than people desire, it will tend initially to lower interest rates and in this and other ways to stimulate spending. Income and spending will start to rise.

To begin with, much or most of the rise in income will take the form of an increase in output and employment rather than in prices. People have been expecting prices to be stable, and prices and wages have been set for some time in the future on that basis. It takes time for people to adjust to a new state of demand. Producers will tend to react to the initial expansion in aggregate demand by increasing output, employees by working longer hours, and the unemployed, by taking jobs now offered at former nominal wages. This much is pretty standard doctrine.

But it describes only the initial effects. Because selling prices of products typically respond to an unanticipated rise in nominal demand faster than prices of factors of production, real wages received have gone down – though real wages anticipated by employees went up, since employees implicitly evaluated the wages offered at the earlier price level. Indeed, the simultaneous fall *ex post* in real wages to employers and rise *ex ante* in real wages to employees is what enabled employment to increase. But the decline *ex post* in real wages will soon come to affect anticipations. Employees will start to reckon on rising prices of the things they buy and to demand higher nominal wages for the future. 'Market' unemployment is below the 'natural' level. There is an excess demand for labor so real wages will tend to rise toward their initial level.

Even though the higher rate of monetary growth continues, the rise in real wages will reverse the decline in unemployment, and then lead to a rise, which will tend to return unemployment to its former level. In order to keep unemployment at its target level of 3 per cent, the monetary authority would have to raise monetary growth still more. As in the interest rate case, the 'market' rate can be kept below the 'natural' rate only by inflation. And, as in the interest rate case, too, only by accelerating inflation. Conversely, let the monetary authority choose a target rate of unemployment that is above the natural rate, and they will be led to produce a deflation, and an accelerating deflation at that.

What if the monetary authority chose the 'natural' rate – either of interest or unemployment – as its target? One problem is that it cannot know what the 'natural' rate is. Unfortunately, we have as yet devised no method to estimate accurately and readily the natural rate of either interest or unemployment. And the 'natural' rate will itself change from time to time. But the basic problem is that even if the monetary authority knew the 'natural' rate, and attempted to peg the market rate at that level, it would not be led to a determinate policy. The 'market' rate will vary from the natural rate for all sorts of reasons other than monetary policy. If the monetary authority responds to these variations, it will set in train longer-term effects that will make any monetary growth path it follows ultimately consistent with the rule of policy. The actual course of monetary growth will be analogous to a random walk, buffeted this way and that by the forces that produce temporary departures of the market rate from the natural rate.

To state this conclusion differently, there is always a temporary trade-off between inflation and unemployment; there is no permanent trade-off. The temporary trade-off comes not from inflation *per se*, but from unanticipated inflation, which generally means, from a rising rate of inflation. The widespread belief that there is a permanent trade-off is a sophisticated version of the confusion between 'high' and 'rising' that we all recognize in simpler forms. A rising rate of inflation may reduce unemployment, a high rate will not.

But how long, you will say, is 'temporary'? For interest rates, we have some systematic evidence on how long each of the several effects takes to work itself out. For unemployment, we do not. I can at most venture a personal judgement, based on some examination of the historical evidence, that the initial effects of a higher and unanticipated rate of inflation last for something like two to five years; that this initial effect then begins to be reversed; and that a full adjustment to the new rate of inflation takes about as long for employment as for interest rates, say, a couple of decades. For both interest rates and employment, let me add a qualification. These estimates are for changes in the rate of inflation of the order of magnitude that has been experienced in the United States. For much more sizeable changes, such as those experienced in South American countries, the whole adjustment process is greatly speeded up.

To state the general conclusion still differently, the monetary authority controls nominal quantities – directly, the quantity of its own liabilities. In principle, it can use this control to peg a nominal quantity – an exchange rate, the price level, the nominal level of national income, the quantity of money by one or another definition – or to peg the rate of change in a nominal quantity – the rate of inflation or deflation, the rate of growth or decline in nominal national income, the rate of growth of the quantity of money. It cannot use its control over nominal quantities to peg a real quantity – the real rate of interest, the rate of unemployment, the level of real national income, the real quantity of money, the rate of growth of real national income, or the rate of growth of the real quantity of money.

WHAT MONETARY POLICY CAN DO

Monetary policy cannot peg these real magnitudes at predetermined levels. But monetary policy can and does have important effects on these real magnitudes. The one is in no way inconsistent with the other.

My own studies of monetary history have made me extremely sympathetic to the oft-quoted, much reviled, and as widely misunderstood, comment by John Stuart Mill. 'There cannot . . .,' he wrote, 'be intrinsically a more insignificant thing, in the economy of society, than money; except in the character of a contrivance for sparing time and labour. It is a machine for doing quickly and commodiously, what would be done, though less quickly and commodiously, without it: and like many other kinds of machinery, it only exerts a distinct and independent influence of its own when it gets out of order' [7, p. 488].

True, money is only a machine, but it is an extraordinarily efficient machine. Without it, we could not have begun to attain the astounding growth in output and level of living we have experienced in the past two centuries – any more than we could have done so without those other marvelous machines that dot our countryside and enable us, for the most part, simply to do more efficiently what could be done without them at much greater cost in labor.

But money has one feature that these other machines do not share. Because it is so pervasive, when it gets out of order, it throws a monkey wrench into the operation of all the other machines. The Great Contraction is the most dramatic example but not the only one. Every other major contraction in the United States has been either produced by monetary disorder or greatly exacerbated by monetary disorder. Every major inflation has been produced by monetary expansion – mostly to meet the overriding demands of war which have forced the creation of money to supplement explicit taxation.

The first and most important lesson that history teaches about what monetary policy can do – and it is a lesson of the most profound importance – is that monetary policy can prevent money itself from being a major source of economic disturbance. This sounds like a negative proposition: avoid major mistakes. In part it is. The Great Contraction might not have occurred at all, and if it had, it would have been far less severe, if the monetary authority had avoided mistakes, or if the monetary arrangements had been those of an earlier time when there was no central authority with the power to make the kinds of mistakes that the Federal Reserve System made. The past few years, to come closer to home, would have been steadier and more productive of economic well-being if the Federal Reserve had avoided drastic and erratic changes of direction, first expanding the money supply at an unduly rapid pace, then, in early 1966, stepping on the brake too hard, then, at the end of 1966, reversing itself and resuming expansion until at least November, 1967, at a more rapid pace than can long be maintained without appreciable inflation.

Even if the proposition that monetary policy can prevent money itself from being a major source of economic disturbance were a wholly negative proposition, it would be none the less important for that. As it happens, however, it is not a wholly negative proposition. The monetary machine has gotten out of order even when there has been no central authority with anything like the power now possessed by the Fed. In the United States, the 1907 episode and earlier banking panics are examples of how the monetary machine can get out of order largely on its own. There is therefore a positive and important task for the monetary authority – to suggest improvements in the machine that will reduce the chances that it will get out of order, and to use its own powers so as to keep the machine in good working order.

A second thing monetary policy can do is provide a stable background for the economy – keep the machine well oiled, to continue Mill's analogy. Accomplishing the first task will contribute to this objective, but there is more to it than that. Our economic system will work best when producers and consumers, employers and employees, can proceed with full confidence that the average level of prices will behave in a known way in the future – preferably that it will be highly stable. Under any conceivable institutional arrangements, and certainly under those that now prevail in the United States, there is only a limited amount of flexibility in prices and wages. We need to conserve this flexibility to achieve changes in relative prices and wages that are required to adjust to dynamic changes in tastes and technology. We should not dissipate it simply to achieve changes in the absolute level of prices that serve no economic function.

In an earlier era, the gold standard was relied on to provide confidence in future monetary stability. In its heyday it served that function reasonably well. It clearly no longer does, since there is scarce a country in the world that is prepared to let the gold standard reign unchecked – and there are persuasive reasons why countries should not do so. The monetary authority could operate as a surrogate for the gold standard, if it pegged exchange rates and did so exclusively by altering the quantity of money in response to balance of payment flows without 'sterilizing' surpluses or deficits and without resorting to open or concealed exchange control or to changes in tariffs and quotas. But again, though many central bankers talk this way, few are in fact willing to follow this course – and again there are persuasive reasons why they should not do so. Such a policy would submit each country to the vagaries not of an impersonal and automatic gold standard but of the policies – deliberate or accidental – of other monetary authorities.

In today's world, if monetary policy is to provide a stable background for the economy it must do so by deliberately employing its powers to that end. I shall come later to how it can do so.

Finally, monetary policy can contribute to offsetting major disturbances in the economic system arising from other sources. If there is an independent secular exhilaration – as the postwar expansion was described by the proponents of secular stagnation – monetary policy can in principle help to hold it in check by a slower rate of monetary growth than would otherwise be desirable. If, as now, an explosive federal budget threatens unprecedented deficits, monetary policy can hold any inflationary dangers in check by a slower rate of monetary growth than would otherwise be desirable. This will temporarily mean higher interest rates than would otherwise prevail – to enable the government to borrow the sums needed to finance the deficit – but by preventing the speeding up of inflation, it may well mean both lower prices and lower nominal interest rates for the long pull. If the end of a substantial war offers the country an opportunity to shift resources from wartime to peacetime production, monetary policy can ease the transition by a higher rate of monetary growth than would otherwise be desirable – though experience is not very encouraging that it can do so without going too far.

I have put this point last, and stated it in qualified terms – as referring to major disturbances – because I believe that the potentiality of monetary policy in offsetting other forces making for instability is far more limited than is commonly believed. We simply do not know enough to be able to recognize minor disturbances when they occur or to be able to predict either what their effects will be with any precision or what monetary policy is required to offset their effects. We do not know enough to be able to achieve stated objectives by delicate, or even fairly coarse, changes in the mix of monetary and fiscal policy. In this area particularly the best is likely to be the enemy of the good. Experience suggests that the path of wisdom is to use monetary policy explicitly to offset other disturbances only when they offer a 'clear and present danger'.

HOW SHOULD MONETARY POLICY BE CONDUCTED?

How should monetary policy be conducted to make the contribution to our goals that it is capable of making? This is clearly not the occasion for presenting a detailed 'Program for Monetary Stability' – to use the title of a book in which I tried to do so [3]. I shall restrict myself here to two major requirements for monetary policy that follow fairly directly from the preceding discussion.

The first requirement is that the monetary authority should guide itself by magnitudes that it can control, not by ones that it cannot control. If, as the authority has often done, it takes interest rates or the current unemployment percentage as the immediate criterion of policy, it will be like a space vehicle that has taken a fix on the wrong star. No matter how sensitive and sophisticated its guiding apparatus, the space vehicle will go astray. And so will the monetary authority. Of the various alternative magnitudes that it can control, the most appealing guides for policy are exchange rates, the price level as defined by some index, and the quantity of a monetary total – currency plus adjusted demand deposits, or this total plus commercial bank time deposits, or a still broader total.

For the United States in particular, exchange rates are an undesirable guide. It might be worth requiring the bulk of the economy to adjust to the tiny percentage consisting of foreign trade if that would guarantee freedom from monetary irresponsibility – as it might under a real gold standard. But it is hardly worth doing so simply to adapt to the average of whatever policies monetary authorities in the rest of the world adopt. Far better to let the market, through floating exchange rates, adjust to world conditions the 5 per cent or so of our resources devoted to international trade while reserving monetary policy to promote the effective use of the 95 per cent.

Of the three guides listed, the price level is clearly the most important in its own right. Other things the same, it would be much the best of the alternatives – as so many distinguished economists have urged in the past. But other things are not the same. The link between the policy actions of the monetary authority and the price level, while unquestionably present, is more indirect than the link between the policy actions of the authority and any of the several monetary totals. Moreover, monetary action takes a longer time to affect the price level than to affect the monetary totals and both the time lag and the magnitude of effect vary with circumstances. As a result, we cannot predict at all accurately just what effect a particular monetary action will have on the price level and, equally important, just when it will have that effect. Attempting to control directly the price level is therefore likely to make monetary policy itself a source of economic disturbance because of false stops and starts. Perhaps, as our understanding of monetary phenomena advances, the situation will change. But at the present stage of our understanding, the long way around seems the surer way to our objective. Accordingly, I believe that a monetary total is the best currently available immediate guide or criterion for monetary policy – and I believe that it matters much less which particular total is chosen than that one be chosen.

A second requirement for monetary policy is that the monetary authority avoid sharp swings in policy. In the past, monetary authorities have on occasion moved in the wrong direction – as in the episode of the Great Contraction that I have stressed. More frequently, they have moved in the right direction, albeit often too late, but have erred by moving too far. Too late and too much has been the general practice. For example, in early 1966, it was the right policy for the Federal Reserve to move in a less expansionary direction – though it should have done so at least a year earlier. But when it moved, it went too far, producing the sharpest change in the rate of monetary growth of the postwar era. Again, having gone too far, it was the right policy for the Fed to reverse course at the end of 1966. But again it went too far, not only restoring but exceeding the earlier excessive rate of monetary growth. And this episode is no exception. Time and again this has been the course followed – as in 1919 and 1920, in 1937 and 1938, in 1953 and 1954, in 1959 and 1960.

The reason for the propensity to overreact seems clear: the failure of monetary authorities to allow for the delay between their actions and the subsequent effects on the economy. They tend to determine their actions by today's conditions – but their actions will affect the economy only six or nine or twelve or fifteen months later. Hence they feel impelled to step on the brake, or the accelerator, as the case may be, too hard.

My own prescription is still that the monetary authority go all the way in avoiding such swings by adopting publicly the policy of achieving a steady rate of growth in a specified monetary total. The precise rate of growth, like the precise monetary total, is less important than the adoption of some stated and known rate. I myself have argued for a rate that would on the average achieve rough stability in the level of prices of final products, which I have estimated would call for something like a 3 to 5 percent per year rate of growth in currency plus all commercial bank deposits or a slightly lower rate of growth in currency plus demand deposits only.[6] But it would be better to have a fixed rate that would on the average produce moderate inflation or moderate deflation, provided it was steady, than to suffer the wide and erratic perturbations we have experienced.

Short of the adoption of such a publicly stated policy of a steady rate of monetary growth, it would constitute a major improvement if the monetary authority followed the self-denying ordinance of avoiding wide swings. It is a matter of record that periods of relative stability in the rate of monetary growth have also been periods of relative stability in economic activity, both in the United States and other countries. Periods of wide swings in the rate of monetary growth have also been periods of wide swings in economic activity.

By setting itself a steady course and keeping to it, the monetary authority could make a major contribution to promoting economic stability. By making that course one of steady but moderate growth in the quantity of money, it would make a major contribution to avoidance of either inflation or deflation of prices. Other forces would still affect the economy, require change and adjustment, and disturb the even tenor of our ways. But steady monetary growth would provide a monetary climate favorable to the effective operation of those basic forces of enterprise, ingenuity, invention, hard work, and thrift that are the true springs of economic growth. That is the most that we can ask from monetary policy at our present stage of knowledge. But that much – and it is a great deal – is clearly within our reach.

ACKNOWLEDGEMENTS

This chapter was the presidential address delivered at the Eightieth Annual Meeting of the American Economic Association, Washington, DC, 29 December 1967.

I am indebted for helpful criticisms of earlier drafts to Armen Alchian, Gary Becker, Martin Bronfenbrenner, Arthur F. Burns, Phillip Cagan, David D. Friedman, Lawrence Harris, Harry G. Johnson, Homer Jones, Jerry Jordan, David Meiselman, Allan H. Meltzer, Theodore W. Schultz, Anna J. Schwartz, Herbert Stein, George J. Stigler and James Tobin.

NOTES

1 In [2], I have argued that Henry Simons shared this view with Keynes, and that it accounts for the policy changes that he recommended.

2 This is partly an empirical not theoretical judgment. In principle, 'tightness' or 'ease' depends on the rate of change of the quantity of money supplied compared to the rate of change of the quantity demanded excluding effects on demand from monetary policy itself. However, empirically demand is highly stable, if we exclude the effect of monetary policy, so it is generally sufficient to look at supply alone.

3 It is perhaps worth noting that this 'natural' rate need not correspond to equality between the number unemployed and the number of job vacancies. For any given structure of the labor market, there will be some equilibrium relation between these two magnitudes, but there is no reason why it should be one of equality.

4 Strictly speaking, the rise in nominal wages will be less rapid than the rise in anticipated nominal wages to make allowance for any secular changes in real wages.

5 Stated in terms of the rate of change of nominal wages, the Phillips Curve can be expected to be reasonably stable and well defined for any period for which the *average* rate of change of prices, and hence the anticipated rate, has been relatively stable. For such periods, nominal wages and 'real' wages move together. Curves computed for different periods or different countries for each of which this condition has been satisfied will differ in level, the level of the curve depending on what the average rate of price change was. The higher the average rate of price change, the higher will tend to be the level of the curve. For periods or countries for which the rate of change of prices varies considerably, the Phillips Curve will not be well defined. My impression is that these statements accord reasonably well with the experience of the economists who have explored empirical Phillips Curves.

Restate Phillips' analysis in terms of the rate of change of real wages – and even more precisely, anticipated real wages – and it all falls into place. That is why students of empirical Phillips Curves have found that it helps to include the rate of change of the price level as an independent variable.

6 In an article on 'The Optimum Quantity of Money', I conclude that a still lower rate of growth, something like 2 percent for the broader definition, might be better yet in order to eliminate or reduce the difference between private and total costs of adding to real balances. [Article was published in Friedman (1969) *The Optimum Quantity of Money and Other Essays*, Chicago: Aldine.]

REFERENCES

1 H. S. Ellis (ed.) (1948) *A Survey of Contemporary Economics*, Philadelphia, PA.
2 Milton Friedman (1967) 'The Monetary Theory and Policy of Henry Simons', *Journal of Law and Economics* Oct., *10*: 1–13.
3 —— (1959) *A Program for Monetary Stability*, New York.
4 E. A. Goldenweiser (1945) 'Postwar Problems and Policies', *Federal Reserve Bulletin* Feb., *31*: 112–21.
5 P. T. Homan and Fritz Machlup (eds) (1945) *Financing American Prosperity*, New York.
6 A. P. Lerner and F. D. Graham (eds) (1946) *Planning and Paying for Full Employment*, Princeton, NJ.
7 J. S. Mill (1929) *Principles of Political Economy*, Bk III, Ashley ed., New York.

8   The structure of monetarism

Thomas Mayer
Kredit und Kapital (1975) 8, pp. 191–215, 292–313

In recent years the term 'monetarism' has come into vogue.[1] Defined in a very narrow sense it is the view that changes in the money stock are the predominate factor explaining changes in money income, and hence is merely a new term for 'quantity theory'. But used in a broader sense the term 'monetarism' encompasses a number of other propositions apart from the quantity theory of money. Unfortunately, this whole set of views is commonly judged as a single unit. This contributes to an unfortunate division of economists into monetarists and Keynesian schools with a resulting polarization. It is my impression that the Keynesians have a predisposition to reject all monetarist propositions on the basis of their 'guilt by association' with other monetarist propositions, while monetarists have the opposite tendency. I will therefore try to do two things in this chapter. One is to show the interrelations between the various monetarist propositions, and to illustrate that they do indeed form a coherent whole. The other is to show that despite this, the connection between various monetarist propositions is loose enough so that one can judge each one on its own merits rather than having to accept or reject monetarist doctrine as a whole. However, I will not try to judge the validity of monetarism.

To do this it is necessary as a first step to define the set of propositions which characterize monetarists and distinguish them from Keynesians. Unfortunately there is no single place where one can find a listing of all monetarist propositions, and I have therefore had to construct my own list.[2] In doing so I have tried to err on the side of inclusiveness rather than exclusiveness, and I am dealing therefore with monetarism in the broad sense of a *Weltanschauung*. Any such listing is, of course, quite arbitrary and the reader may want to add or to delete items from the following list.[3]

1 The quantity theory of money, in the sense of the predominance of the impact of monetary factors on nominal income.
2 The monetarist model of the transmission process.
3 Belief in the inherent stability of the private sector.
4 Irrelevance of allocative detail for the explanation of short-run changes in money income, and belief in a fluid capital market.

5 Focus on the price level as a whole rather than on individual prices.
6 Reliance on small rather than large econometric models.
7 Use of the reserve base or similar measure as the indicator of monetary policy.
8 Use of the money stock as the proper target of monetary policy.
9 Acceptance of a monetary growth rule.
10 Rejection of an unemployment-inflation trade-off in favor of a real Phillips-curve.
11 A relatively greater concern about inflation than about unemployment compared to other economists.
12 Dislike of government intervention.

The first four of these items are ones listed by Karl Brunner in his description of monetarism,[4] while items 2 and 7–9 can be found in David Fand's survey of monetarism.[5] On the other side of the debate James Tobin has characterized it by items 1, 7, 8, 9 and 10 in the above list.[6] Item 5, the focus on the price level as a whole, while usually not explicit, is implicit in typical monetarist discussion of inflation, particularly in their rejection of cost-push inflation. Item 6, the preference for small models, while certainly not a basic part of monetarist doctrine, is something which most monetarists seem to have in common. Item 10, the real Phillips curve, is listed by Leonall Andersen.[7] Item 11, concern about inflation, is admittedly a rather questionable item, based only on my general impression of monetarist writings and verbal tradition.[8] The final item, dislike of government regulation, is a view that seems to be generally shared by monetarists, at least in the United States.

These twelve items are, of course, not all equally significant. The first four are the basic ones and can be used to define monetarism. A monetarist need not accept any of the other eight.[9] But monetarists do tend to accept these other eight propositions too. And my purpose here is to describe a set of beliefs which are shared by economists who call themselves monetarists (and to a much lesser extent by other economists) rather than to set out a set of beliefs which are the sufficient and necessary conditions for an economist to be called a monetarist.[10]

The way I will now proceed is to start with the quantity theory, and then take up each of the other components in the order listed, and see to what extent they are dependent or independent of the previously discussed components. In the first part of this chapter I will deal with the first six propositions. In the second part, I will deal with propositions 7–12 and will summarize the results obtained in both parts.

I THE QUANTITY THEORY

The quantity theory is the most basic component of monetarism. By the quantity theory I mean the proposition that changes in the money stock are the dominant determinant of changes in money income.[11] This is a very general version which does not commit one to a specific theory of the transmission process, a process treated separately in the next section. A very important aspect of the quantity theory–Keynesian dispute involves the speed of adaption of the economy.[12] Keynesians would not – or at least should not – deny that in the long run changes in nominal income are dominated by changes in the money stock.

The above definition of the quantity theory clearly fits both the Friedmanian and the *Brunner–Meltzer* versions. It is not at all clear, however, that it also fits the *Patinkin* version. This is due to two characteristics of *Patinkin's* model. First, while changes in the stock of money ultimately bring about equivalent changes in the price level we are not told how long this process takes. Hence someone may completely accept the *Patinkin* model, and yet, in forecasting next year's money income might not pay very much attention to recent changes in the money stock because these changes will have their effects only in some far-off equilibrium.[13] Second, while *Patinkin's* model tells us that changes in the money supply have proportional effects on money income, this does not necessarily deny that changes in other variables also affect money income. And if changes in these other variables have important effects on income, then the essential monetarist proposition that variations in money income are explained mainly by changes in the money stock need no longer hold. Thus a Patinkian might well use a Keynesian model for ordinary forecasting purposes instead of a quantity theory model.

This is not to deny that *Patinkin's* model is a quantity theory model, but it is a quantity theory model in a different sense from the way I am defining the quantity theory here. His model has, to a large extent, a quantity theorist's 'engine of analysis',[14] but the conclusions he reaches are not necessarily those of the quantity theory in the short run as distinct from the long run.[15] Since monetarism is a policy-oriented doctrine, concerned very much with the short run, *Patinkin's* version of the quantity theory can be excluded from it.

II THE TRANSMISSION PROCESS

The monetarist's version of the transmission process by which changes in the money stock affect income follows naturally from his research strategy which is to focus on the supply and demand for real money balances.[16] If the public finds itself with excess balances it will reduce them by increasing expenditures, presumably on both goods and bonds. By contrast, the Keynesian focuses on relative yields, and therefore phrases the story differently. If the public has excess money balances this must mean that the yield on its money balances is less than the yield it can obtain on other assets, and hence it buys other assets. Such a portfolio realignment to bring yields (adjusted for risk, etc.) into equality is likely to involve primarily assets which are similar to money, that is securities rather than goods. Hence, monetarists and Keynesians typically have a different range of assets in mind when they think of the transmission process. This difference is illustrated by the Keynesian calling the price of money the interest rate since he thinks of money as a fund which can be either held as money or lent, while the monetarist thinks of the price of money as the inverse of the price level, since money is used to buy goods.[17]

Unfortunately, this genuine dispute, as well as disputes relating to the measurement problem discussed below, are often obscured by a spurious dispute about whether money affects income 'directly' or only 'indirectly'. This difference is terminological; one can reformulate the monetarist story in terms of the interest rate and the Keynesian story in a way that omits the interest rate. An increase in the real stock of money lowers the imputed real interest rate on money balances. Hence, a monetarist, instead of saying that the public has more money than it wants to hold, and thus increases expenditures, can say that the public's imputed interest rate on money holdings has fallen while the yield on other assets is constant. Thus, directly to equalize marginal yields, and indirectly because of the increase in the money stock, the public increases expenditures. Conversely, the Keynesian can use his liquidity preference diagram to show that an increase in the public's money stock means that the public is now holding more than its optimal stock of money, and hence, to equalize rates of return on the margin, buys securities. Essentially the point here is the following: given a demand curve, whether for a commodity such as apples, or for the holding of money, we can described any change either in terms of price (the interest rate) or in terms of quantities (the stock of money). As long as we have a given demand curve it does not matter; we must get the same answer regardless of which axis of the diagram we look at. Hence, on a level of formal theory where one can ignore measurement problems, it is unimportant whether one formulates the analysis in terms of the money stock or in terms of the interest rate.[18] This dispute is spurious. It is therefore not surprising that Y. C. *Park* in his careful survey of the transmission process concluded that 'at the level of general description there appear to be no significant differences in the transmission process of monetary influences among a variety of monetary economists'.[19]

A genuine aspect of the dispute, however, relates to the stability of the demand for money which is part of the previously discussed hypothesis that nominal income changes are dominated by changes in the money stock. If the demand for money is unstable (in a numerical sense), perhaps because of shifts in the marginal efficiency of investment, then knowledge that the supply of money has increased no longer allows us to predict with any degree of confidence that expenditures will actually increase. This is so regardless of whether one phrases the process in Keynesian or monetarist terms. The real difference between the two schools is that the Keynesian tends to take the possibility of an unstable demand for money much more seriously than does the monetarist, in part because he has a different theory of the interest rate.[20] Hence, in predicting expenditures the Keynesian prefers to look at what is happening to the rate of interest, thus taking account of changes in both the demand for, and the supply of, money. The monetarist, on the other hand, though he would agree in principle that changes in the money supply may give a misleading answer because of changes in money demand, does not treat this danger as seriously as does the Keynesian.

However, one must beware of exaggerating this difference. Although in the *General Theory Keynes* did give the impression that the demand for money is highly unstable, modern Keynesians no longer seem to believe this, and instead treat the demand for money as fairly stable. On the other hand, *Friedman* has stated that the quantity theorist looks upon the demand for money as being a stable function of other variables, rather than as necessarily being stable in a numerical sense.[21]

Since changes in the interest rate register demand as well as supply shifts, they clearly have more information content than changes in the money supply. One might, therefore, ask why anyone would look at the money supply rather than at the rate of interest. This question brings us to the second substantive issue, the measurement problem. The above discussion has assumed implicitly that both 'the' interest rate and 'the' money stock can be measured without error, or that they are measured with equivalent errors. But this is questionable. Monetarists prefer to use the money stock rather than the rate of interest because they believe that the money stock can be measured much better. The term 'the rate of interest' as used in formal theory is a theoretical term, and for any empirical work with it it is necessary to find an accurately measurable counterpart. The monetarist typically believes that this creates insuperable difficulties. One difficulty is that 'the' rate of interest is an amalgam of a vast number of specific long-term and short-term rates, and that there is no clear way in which these rates can all be combined into a single measure. Term structure theory is not a completely reliable guide. The second difficulty is that by no means all the rates which should be combined into 'the' interest rate can be observed in the market. Imputed rates used internally by households and firms should be included, and due allowance should also be made for borrowing costs other than the measured interest rate, for example the cost of deteriorating balance sheet ratios. Third, what is relevant for economic decisions is the expected real rate of interest, which cannot be observed in the market, and cannot be approximated reliably by econometric techniques. Since changes in the inflation rate are frequently large relative to changes in the real interest rate, changes in the nominal rate may be a very poor guide to changes in the expected real rate. Hence, monetarists argue, in practice the money stock is a much better measuring rod than is the interest rate.

It is, of course, open for Keynesians to reply that the money stock is also measured badly. Again the problem is that the theoretical term, 'money', as used in the quantity theory does not have a clear-cut empirical counterpart. Should it be approximated by M_1 or M_2? This is an issue on which monetarists disagree among themselves.[22] Presumably, the proper counterpart is some weighted mean, but there exists no reliable way of estimating it.[23] Furthermore, as in the case of the interest rate one should make some adjustment for the anticipated inflation rate. Surely, it does affect how the public feels about the adequacy of its cash balances. Hence, it is open to the Keynesian to argue that despite the difficulties of measuring 'the' rate of interest, it can be measured more accurately than 'the' money stock.

Problems of measuring the money stock are likely to seem more serious to a Keynesian than to a quantity theorist because someone who believes that the money stock cannot be measured accurately is likely to be skeptical of the empirical evidence claiming to show that changes in the money stock explain changes in money income. But it does not necessarily follow from this that a Keynesian need be more worried about the difficulty of measuring the money supply than about measuring the interest rate. He may well take the position that, while neither variable can be measured accurately, the interest rate is measured with a greater error than is the money stock. There is certainly nothing in Keynesian theory to deny this. The exposition of the argument in terms of the interest rate rather than the money stock, both in the *General Theory* and the subsequent Keynesian literature, can often be explained by the argument being on a high level of abstraction where measurement problems can be ignored. Thus, while it is hard to see why a quantity theorist would prefer to use the interest rate in his description of the transmission process, it is not hard to see why a Keynesian may agree with a quantity theorist in looking at the money stock rather than the rate of interest.

A third substantive difference between the Keynesian and monetarist transmission processes relates to the range of assets considered. The monetarist looks at an increase in the money supply as having raised the public's money holdings relative to its holdings of securities and all types of real assets. Hence, to bring marginal yields into equilibrium the public now spends these excess balances to acquire securities, capital goods and consumer goods. The Keynesian, however, typically treats the increase in the money stock as affecting only investment, and not consumption.[24] There are two reasons for this. First, by looking at the interest rate the Keynesian adopts a borrowing-cost interpretation; an increase in the money stock lowers interest rates, and this lower cost of borrowing stimulates demand for goods which are bought with credit; that is, it stimulates business investment, residential construction, and perhaps investment in consumer durables.[25] Demand for nondurables is not directly affected because they are usually not bought on credit. A second reason is that the Keynesian often makes the simplifying assumption that the propensity to consume is not directly affected by the interest rate, so that an increase in the money stock affects only investment.[26]

How does this difference in the range of assets relate to the magnitude of the impact of changes in the money stock, and hence to the question whether changes in money income are dominated by changes in the money stock? On a level of rather causal empiricism there is a direct relationship. If monetary changes affect consumption as well as investment then money probably has a much great effect on income than is the case if it can affect only 'investment' including perhaps consumer durables.[27] But this reasoning while suggestive is hardly conclusive. Someone might accept the Keynesian transmission process, believing that changes in the money stock operate only via investment, and yet he might think that, due to a high interest elasticity of investment, this effect is very powerful. On the other hand, someone might believe that changes in the stock of money affect both consumption and investment, but that this total effect is quite weak.

Another substantive difference is newer. Karl *Brunner* and Allan *Meltzer* have developed a new version of the monetarist transmission process.[28] They argue that the Friedmanian version, which is really what was discussed above, is essentially Keynesian in its underlying theory, and they have set out a theoretical critique of this Keynesian transmission process. It focuses on a relative price process and stock effects which tend to bring the system towards a classical rather than a Keynesian equilibrium.[29]

Thus there are four links between the hypothesis of the primacy of changes in the quantity of money and the monetarist – as opposed to the Keynesian – version of the transmission process. One is the stability of the demand for money, the second is the relative measurability of money and interest rates, the third is the range of assets considered, and the fourth concerns the relative price effects and stock effects discussed by *Brunner* and *Meltzer*.

Are these links compelling in the sense that someone who accepts the monetarist story on one must also accept it on the other? The answer is, no. Clearly, one can accept the Keynesian version of the transmission process and yet believe that monetary factors dominate money income. All one has to do is to believe that the interest elasticity is high for investment and low for the liquidity preference function. Conversely, one can accept the monetarist transmission process, and yet reject the quantity theory as an explanation of most observed changes in income. Thus, while the demand for money may be relatively stable (compared to the seriousness of the errors introduced by the measurement problem), the stock of money may be even more stable. And while someone who believes in the primacy of the monetary impulse is likely to believe that money can be measured fairly well, he could also believe that the interest rate can be measured just as well or better. Moreover, changes in the quantity of money could exert all their (strong) effects on income through investment. Finally, someone may consider the *Brunner–Meltzer* analysis of the relative price and stock effects to be valid, but might believe that in the short run and intermediate run these effects are relatively minor. In other words, one cannot logically infer how money affects income from the strength of the monetary impulse and vice versa.

III STABILITY OF THE PRIVATE SECTOR

Monetarists generally believe that the private sector is inherently stable if left to its own devices and not disturbed by an erratic monetary growth rate. Many, probably most, Keynesians deny this. The nature of this dispute is complex. Keynesians typically do not deny that the private sector is stable in the sense that it is damped rather than explosive. As Lawrence *Klein* has pointed out, some leading Keynesian econometric models show the economy to be stable in its response to stochastic shocks.[30] However, Keynesians look upon the private sector as being unstable in another sense. This is that it is inherently subject to erratic shocks, primarily due to changes in the marginal efficiency of investment. To a Keynesian many factors can, and do, cause substantial changes in aggregate demand, changes which may then lead to damped oscillations.

By contrast, monetarists treat aggregate demand as the resultant of a stable demand for money and an unstable supply of money. They look upon the private sector as stable because its demand for money is stable, and attribute most, though certainly not all, the actually observed instability to fluctuations in the money supply induced by the monetary authorities.[31] Thus, this dispute about the stability of the private sector is tied directly into the basic dispute about the quantity theory, the extent to which changes in aggregate demand are explained primarily by changes in the money supply rather than by changes in the marginal efficiency of investment, etc.[32]

But even so, the tie between the quantity theory and the stability of the private sector is not complete; someone can reject the quantity theory, and yet believe in the inherent stability of the private sector. For example, a Keynesian who believes that fiscal policy is so badly timed that it is destabilizing, and that monetary policy has also not been a net stabilizer, would have to believe that the private sector is stabler than is indicated by the actually observed fluctuations in GNP. Yet there is nothing about such a view which is contrary to Keynesian theory, or which requires the quantity theory as its foundation. Thus one can be a Keynesian in one's basic theory, and, at the same time, accept the monetarist proposition that the private sector is inherently stable or at least stabler than the private and government sectors combined. Admittedly, it is much harder to see how a quantity theorist could believe in the instability of the private sector.

IV IRRELEVANCE OF ALLOCATIVE DETAIL AND BELIEF IN THE FLUIDITY OF CAPITAL MARKETS

One of the points of distinction between the monetarists and the Keynesians is that in trying to determine short-run changes in income the Keynesian, unlike the monetarist, typically focuses on what happens in particular sectors of the economy. With unstable private sectors (in the sense defined above) fluctuations can start in various sectors, or be conditioned by the particular characteristics of a sector. For example, a rise in the interest rate may have different effects on residential construction, and hence on total output, at a time when mortgage lending institutions are already short of liquidity than at a time when they have a large liquidity buffer. More fundamentally, Keynesians predict, or explain, income by looking at expenditure motives in each sector. Hence, they have to analyze each sector.

The monetarists, by contrast, look upon expenditures as determined by the excess supply of, or demand for, real balances. They therefore have to look at the behavior of only a single market, the market for real balances.[33]

The Keynesian's concern with allocative detail, that is the behavior of different sectors, is reinforced by a frequent tendency among Keynesians to treat the capital market as imperfect so that capital rationing can occur. Hence, in estimating aggregate demand Keynesians are not satisfied with knowing the total amount of liquidity in the economy. They also want to know the liquidity of specific sectors, such as financial institutions serving the mortgage market.[34] This emphasis on imperfect capital markets and credit rationing is also connected with the common Keynesian emphasis on borrowing conditions as the only channel through which monetary policy operates.[35] Hence, they want to know a great deal about various interest rates and financial markets in assessing the influence of monetary factors on money income. And their belief that capital markets are imperfect explains why Keynesians seem much more interested in flow of funds analysis than are most monetarists, despite the fact that the flow of funds deals with the monetarist's item of central concern, money.

Another reason for the Keynesian emphasis on sectorial detail is probably the tendency of many Keynesians to favor government intervention. Efficient government intervention obviously requires detailed knowledge of many sectors since the intervention is likely to focus on specific 'troubles' in particular sectors. Finally, as will be discussed in the next section, many Keynesians look upon inflation as sometimes being due, at least in part, to developments in particular sectors rather than as due to the monetarist's single pervasive factor.

By contrast, in explaining short-run changes in income, monetarists usually express little interest in allocative detail.[36] They make a sharp distinction between relative prices which are affected by the fortunes of various sectors, and the general price level which is affected by the quantity of money. They do not build up their estimate of national income by adding up incomes in various sectors as Keynesians do, but rather, they work 'from the top down'. Using changes in the money stock they estimate total expenditures, and then, if they happen to be interested in it, they might investigate the allocation of this fixed expenditure total among various sectors. Their assumption of a fluid capital market fortifies monetarists in their belief that a given increase in the money stock will have more or less the same effect on aggregate incomes, though not of course, on the relative incomes of various sectors, regardless of where it is injected.[37] And their belief in the stability of the private sector and in the absence of a need for government intervention gives monetarists little incentive to focus their attention on developments in various sectors.[38] This is reinforced by the fact that the monetarist, unlike the Keynesian, does not typically try to specify the channels through which monetary factors operate, and hence does not try to gauge the impact of monetary factors by looking at their impact on different sectors.

Hence, monetarists' disregard of allocative detail in explaining short-run income changes is a natural outgrowth of their basic position. It results from their belief in the quantity theory, i.e. in the primacy of money supply changes in explaining income. It is also connected with their view of the transmission process, in which expenditure motives and the peculiarities of individual sectors are unimportant and the borrowing cost approach to gauging the influence of monetary factors is rejected. But this does not mean that monetarists must necessarily de-emphasize allocative detail in their prediction of income fluctuations. Someone might accept all the other basic and characteristic monetarist positions, and yet believe that the capital market is highly imperfect, that capital rationing is important, and that the flow of funds between various sectors therefore plays some role in determining income.[39] Similarly, monetarists might favor government intervention either because they are skeptical of the stability of the private sector, or because they favor government intervention for some other reason; in principle one could certainly be a monetarist and also a socialist.

At the same time, a Keynesian need not believe in the imperfection of the capital market and the importance of capital rationing. Neither of these ideas plays a role in the *General Theory*. More significantly, one can accept the general framework of Keynesian analysis without believing in the instability of the private sector, and in the advisability of government intervention, and hence not be concerned with allocative problems on these grounds. It is only the Keynesian focus on expenditure motives that provided a basic reason for the Keynesian's interest in allocative detail.

V THE PRICE LEVEL VERSUS INDIVIDUAL PRICES

One major distinction between monetarists and most Keynesians is the way of looking at the price level.[40] This is a subtle distinction that is seldom, if ever, made explicit. Basically there are two ways of approaching the price level. One is to treat it as an aggregate phenomenon, determined by the interaction of only two factors, aggregate demand and aggregate output. This view draws a sharp distinction between the price level as a whole and relative prices. Specific events in particular industries, such as an increase in the degree of monopoly, union pressure, or bad harvests obviously affect relative prices. But they affect the price level only to the extent that they also affect either aggregate demand or output. Thus if prices rise in industry A without raising aggregate demand, this rise in the price of A has to be matched either by a reduction of output, or by a decline in the average of all other prices.

The alternative way of treating the price level is to approach it as the weighted sum of individual prices. These prices are then explained by the interaction of supply and demand in individual industries with the pricing policies of various industries. Changes in aggregate demand are certainly not ignored in this framework since they affect the demand curve faced by each industry, but there is considerable emphasis on the particular behavior of individual industries.

Both of these ways of looking at the price level are formally correct. While, they must therefore yield the same answers to someone who possesses all the required information, they do lead to different research strategies, and are therefore likely in practice to provide different answers.

Monetarists clearly use the aggregative approach to the price level. They look at changes in the quantity of money to determine changes in aggregate demand, and then allocate changes in aggregate demand between changes in prices and changes in output.[41] In this approach, at least in its simple version, the pricing decisions made by any particular industry have no effect on the overall price level, but affect only relative prices.[42] Hence, the monetarist typically rejects cost-push explanations of inflation.

It might be worth noting in passing that this rejection of all cost-push phenomena may well be unwarrented even within the monetarist framework. If industry A (with an inelastic demand) raises its prices, and thus reduces the aggregate demand that is available for other industries, these industries may respond, at least in part, not by cutting prices, but by cutting output. Insofar as this occurs, the general price level is raised by the behavior of industry A, and not just the relative price of commodity A. The extent to which this happens is an empirical question, and is likely to depend upon the degree of inflation in the economy. If prices in general are rising then, as industry A raises its prices other industries can adjust their prices for this merely by not raising them by as much as they otherwise would. On the other hand, at a time when prices are generally stable they would have to lower their prices absolutely in order to offset the rise in the price of commodity A, and there is considerable evidence that prices are sticky downward.

The monetarist's macroeconomic, rather than microeconomic, approach to the price level fits in well with two of the previously discussed characteristics of monetarism. First, insofar as the rise in the price of one particular industry results in a price decline in other industries the economic system is inherently stable, at least as far as cost-push inflation is concerned. Second, if the price behavior of individual industries has no effect on the general price level, then this is one more reason for ignoring allocative detail. However, it should be noted, that while monetarists' approach to the price level therefore goes along well with their belief in the stability of the private sector and the irrelevance of allocative detail, in neither case is the relationship one of logical entailment. One can accept the monetarist hypotheses about the irrelevance of allocative detail, and the stability of the private sector, and yet, at the same time, accept the Keynesian approach to the price level.[43]

The typical Keynesian's view of the price level is quite different from the monetarist view. To be sure, in the Keynesian model the price level is also determined by aggregate demand and supply, but to Keynesians this formulation is not useful because they cannot take aggregate demand as given.[44] The monetarist, by contrast, can do this; if industry A raises its price, this does not change aggregate demand which depends upon the money stock.[45] But to the Keynesian the money stock is only one of several factors determining aggregate demand. Thus while the rise in the price of commodity A lowers the real money stock, it may also raise the marginal efficiency of investment, particularly in industry A. In other words, while to the monetarist aggregate demand, as determined by the quantity of money, functions as a budget constraint, in the Keynesian system it is a variable. Hence, to the Keynesian it is at least possible that a rise in the price of commodity A raises aggregate demand enough so that other prices (and outputs) will not have to fall, and might even rise.

Since the aggregate demand effects of a rise in the price of commodity A are uncertain, the Keynesian is tempted to ignore them. And this temptation is frequently not resisted. A typical example is a study by Otto *Eckstein* and Gary *Fromm* in which they investigated the effect on the wholesale price index of the rise in the price of steel. They considered both the direct effect as well as the indirect effect of the steel price increase being passed forward by steel users, and concluded that 'if steel prices had behaved like other industrial prices, the total wholesale price index would have risen by 40 percent less over the last decade'.[46] To a monetarist such a statement gives us only an arithmetic relationship which has no economic meaning because it ignores aggregate demand, and hence other prices.[47] And, indeed, it is hard to see how a Keynesian can really justify ignoring the indirect repercussions.

But the roots of this oversimplification can already be found in the *General Theory* since *Keynes* looked upon prices as determined by the wage rate and the marginal physical product of labor. Indeed *Keynes* specifically tried to bring the theory of the price level into contact with microeconomic factors such as marginal cost, and to eliminate the dichotomy between the determination of individual prices by marginal cost etc., and of the price level by macroeconomic factors such as the quantity of money and its velocity. Thus he wrote in Chapter 21 of the *General Theory*: 'One of the objects of the foregoing chapters has been to escape from this double life and bring the theory of price as a whole back to close contact with the theory of value.'[48]

This Keynesian tendency to look at the price level as determined by costs in various industries has been furthered in recent years by an extensive empirical literature which estimates prices more on the basis of shifts in costs than on the basis of shifts in demand.[49] (However, this evidence is not always easy to interpret because changes in costs may be the result of changes in demand.)[50] In addition, it has probably gained in acceptability from the use, as a first approximation or as an elementary teaching tool, of the Keynesian supply curve dichotomized at full employment. If changes in aggregate demand affect only output and not prices until full employment is reached, then if one is trying to explain the price level under conditions of less than full employment, the fact that a price rise in industry A changes the demand experienced in other industries can be ignored.

But while many – perhaps most – Keynesians treat the price level in the way just described, this way of looking at the price level is far from being a necessary implication of the Keynesian model. A Keynesian could focus on the overall price level rather than on its individual component prices to the same extent as a monetarist does without abandoning any basic part of Keynesian theory. As pointed out above, the only way a Keynesian can ignore the effects of the rise in the price of commodity A on the demand left over for other commodities is to assume that this rise in the price of commodity A generates an exactly offsetting increase in demand. But there is nothing in Keynesian theory that requires this to occur. The increase in the price of commodity A reduces real balances thus lowering demand. To be sure, this may be offset by an increase in the marginal efficiency of capital, but this need not happen. The effect of the increase in the price of commodity A on the marginal efficiency of investment may even be negative, or if it is positive, it need not be great enough to offset all the effect of the decline in real balances. Keynesian theory is silent on this. Strange as it may seem, there appears to be virtually no Keynesian literature on the effect of a rise in a particular price on income.[51] It is, of course, true that a change in demand for other commodities could affect the output of other commodities rather than their prices, but whether this happens or not depends upon where we are along the aggregate supply curve.[52]

Thus, this dispute about the determinants of the price level is not so much a dispute between monetarism and Keynesianism as it is a dispute between monetarism and a particular specification of Keynesianism. And while this specification is a popular one, and is perhaps accepted by most Keynesians, it represents only one line of development of the basic Keynesian model.

Moreover, monetarists too need not accept the typically monetarist position discussed above. They may argue that while a rise in the price of commodity A will eventually lower the prices of other commodities, in the short run it will lower their outputs rather than their prices. Hence, a Keynesian can accept the typically monetarist view on this issue, and a monetarist can adopt the typically Keynesian view, without either one abandoning the fundamental Keynesian or monetarist position.[53]

VI   LARGE VERSUS SMALL MODELS

While Keynesians usually prefer large-scale structural models, monetarists prefer small reduced-form models.[54] This dispute on model size involves many issues which are extraneous to the monetarist debate. To a large extent it is an issue in theoretical econometrics concerned with the validity of the single equation approach, rather than an issue in monetary economics. Moreover, as *Friedman* has pointed out, it involves also the question of whether we know enough to be able to represent complex reality by the greatly simplified systems used even by large models.[55] Hence, *Friedman* considers the debate about large versus small models to be 'almost entirely independent of the monetarist versus Keynesian point of view'.[56]

But even so, there are several ways in which the use of a reduced form model goes along well with monetarist hypotheses. One way relates to the transmission process. If changes in the money stock affect income through a limited number of channels then it is tempting to cover each of these channels, and thus to use a structural model. But if monetary changes affect the economy in a very large number of ways, as the monetarist claims, then even a large structural model is not likely to pick up all of them. Hence a reduced-form approach is likely to be more reliable.

Second, one of the great advantages of large structural models is that they provide detailed information on various economic sectors. This makes large structural models attractive to Keynesians, who are interested in allocative detail, but does little to recommend them to monetarists who are not interested in allocative detail. Furthermore, by focusing on expenditure motives, and looking upon people as being consumers, investors in inventories, etc., the Keynesian is naturally concerned with many sectors. The monetarist, on the other hand, is concerned with people only as money holders, and hence is interested in only one sector, the supply of and demand for money. Third, someone who is concerned about the instability of the private sector in the sense that erratic shifts in expenditure incentives cause serious fluctuations, is likely to believe that to predict income one needs a large model which allows for the impact of these erratic factors on various sectors.

The relationship between the quantity theory *per se* and the choice of structural models versus reduced-form models is much less clear. *Ex ante*, there is little, if any, reason why someone who believes in the strength of the monetary impulse, should necessarily believe in the desirability of reduced-form models. But there is an *ex post* relationship due to the fact that the most famous of all reduced form models, the *Andersen–Jordan* model, yields monetarist conclusions while structural models generally yield Keynesian conclusions. But the relationship between model size and the results obtained from the model are far from firm. Edward *Gramlich* has shown that *Andersen–Jordan* type models can generate not only monetarist results, but also Keynesian, or inbetween, results depending on the monetary variables used.[57]

Thus there are many links between various monetarist propositions and a preference for reduced form models. But as indicated above this linkage is not strong. A monetarist might well reject the use of reduced form models, while a Keynesian might prefer such models since the dispute is largely a matter of choice of estimation technique.

This concludes the discussion of the six monetarist propositions which relate to theory and techniques of analysis. In the second part I will discuss the remaining six policy-oriented propositions.

In the first part I selected twelve propositions characterizing the monetarist outlook, and discussed six of them. I will now discuss the remainder, and then summarize both parts. Three of these propositions relate to monetary policy. They are the choice of an indicator, the choice of a target, and the use of a monetary growth rule.[58]

VII   MONETARY INDICATORS

A monetary policy indicator is a variable that measures the thrust, that is the direction and magnitude, of monetary policy. It should therefore be a variable which is closely controlled by the central bank rather than being endogenous to the economy. Accurate data on it should be available without delay, and they should have a very high correlation with the target, or goal, variables. These requirements rule out both the money stock and the long-term interest rate as monetary indicators. To be sure, to a monetarist the stock of money is the ultimate indicator of monetary policy in a different sense, because changes in the money stock foretell changes in income. But, at least in the United States, accurate data on the money stock are not available quickly, and besides, the money stock is partly endogenous, being some distance removed from central bank actions. Hence, it cannot be used as an indicator as the term is defined in this context. Similarly, for the Keynesian the long-term interest rate is not an adequate indicator because it is not under the close control of the central bank. Thus, neither monetarists nor Keynesians can use as their indicators those variables which would fit best into their models. Both of them have to select other indicators which are closer to the tools used by the central bank.

Monetarists favor some measure of total reserves such as the reserve base adjusted for changes in reserve requirements or else unborrowed reserves. These are clearly under the control of the central bank, they are measured accurately without delay, and they have a powerful effect on the money stock, the monetarists' target variable. Keynesians, on the other hand, probably use the short-term interest rate as their favored indicator.[59] The short-term rate can then be related to one of their target variables, the long-term interest rate, via term structure theory. And in addition, the short-term rate is a target in its own right to Keynesians since it affects flows into depository institutions, and hence residential construction. But this does not make it an indicator.

But it is important to note that the choice of a monetary policy indicator is to a considerable extent isolated from the rest of the Keynesian–monetarist dispute. Monetarists choose a monetary base measure for two reasons. One is that their analysis of the money supply process tells them that this is the variable which best reflects monetary policy actions. The second is that they believe the monetary base (adjusted for reserve requirement changes) to be the best indicator of future changes in the money stock. As far as the first of these reasons is concerned this involves little dispute with Keynesians if only because few Keynesians have bothered to formulate a money supply hypothesis.

Turning to the second reason, the predictive power of a base measure, it is certainly true that one can predict the money stock fairly well in this way. But suppose that it were shown that changes in the short-term interest rate are an even better indicator of changes in the money stock. In this case, monetarists should use the short-term interest rate as their indicator to predict the money stock. And the possibility that the short-term interest rate is a better predictor of the money stock than are various reserve measures is by no means farfetched.[60] Furthermore, if it were somehow shown that monetary policy changes are reflected better by the Federal Funds rate than by a reserve base measure, monetarists could abandon their money supply hypothesis without thereby weakening their belief in any of the other monetarist propositions.

Conversely, Keynesians could select total reserves as their policy indicator, and use this variable, rather than the short-term rate, to predict long-term interest rates. The unsettled state of term structure theory hardly provides us with much confidence in trying to predict the long-term rate on the basis of the short-term rate. Empirically, David *Fand* has shown that while there is a fairly high correlation between long-term and short-term rates, 'in a cyclical context, the long rate is relatively independent of the short-run movements in the short rates'.[61]

In addition to its use in gauging policy, a monetary indicator can also be used to measure the thrust of the monetary impulse regardless of whether this arises in the private or public sector. For this a monetarist may want to use the money stock, while a Keynesian may want to use a short-term interest rate. Thus, if the money stock is growing at, say, a 10 percent rate, while the Federal Funds rate is 12 percent, a monetarist would call this a situation of monetary ease, while a Keynesian would call it tight money.

This distinction has some superficial relation to the dispute about the transmission mechanism because the Keynesian is looking at an interest rate while the monetarist is using the money stock. But, as discussed above, this dispute is, in part, a matter of terminology rather than a genuine dispute. (And, as will be shown below, in part it is the result of many Keynesians not being faithful to their Wicksellian tradition.)

Another connection is that to the Keynesian the short-term interest rate is a valid partial indicator because it affects the flow of funds into financial intermediaries, and hence residential mortgage lending and construction. (This is a channel stressed strongly in the FMP-model.)

Thus, here we have a component of monetarism which has only a limited relationship to the other components. The dispute about the proper indicator is to a considerable extent an isolated technical issue. Its intrusion into the monetarist–Keynesian debate can perhaps be explained as an historical accident. In the past the Federal Reserve has used short-term interest rates and money market conditions as its indicator in a different sense from the way the indicator concept is defined here. Instead of treating short-term rates and money market conditions as an intermediate step on the way to long-term interest rates or to the money stock, it looked at short-term rates and money market conditions as an immediate guide to how its policy is affecting income. In this way – which does not allow the money stock to be a recognized part of the process – the use of short-term rates and money market conditions is, of course, contrary to monetarism. But as a result of the insights which monetarists have brought to this debate indicators are no longer thought of in this way.

VIII   MONETARY POLICY TARGETS

Obviously monetarists want to use the money stock as the target of monetary policy. Keynesians, on the other hand, prefer to use long-term interest rates or, in some cases, bank credit or total credit. The extent to which each of these targets fits into the underlying theories of both schools can be seen best by considering the arguments for each of these targets.

To start with a comparison of the interest rate target and the money stock target there is again the measurement problem previously discussed in connection with the transmission process.

But with respect to the problem of chosing a target, the Keynesian is less worried about the difficulties of measuring the interest rate. This is so because one important Keynesian channel for the impact of monetary policy operates through the flows of funds into depository institutions. And since such flows depend upon a comparison of interest rates of depository institutions with open market rates, the problem of infering the expected real rate from the nominal interest rate does not arise. (And the problem of combining various observed and imputed rates into 'the interest rate' is also less serious.) Furthermore, another channel is the effect of interest rates on the market value of the households' stock of securities, and hence on consumption. Here too, the problem of measuring the interest rate is not serious. However, for the traditional 'cost of capital' effect of interest rates on investment, the measurement problem still exists.

Apart from the measurement problem the choice of a target involves another issue which arises from our inability to predict precisely changes in the liquidity preference schedule and in expenditure incentives.[62] If we would know very accurately the liquidity preference curve as well as expenditure incentives, then the central bank could easily select the interest rate which would optimize its objectives. Since with a known liquidity preference curve we can infer a particular quantity of money for each rate of interest and vice versa, leaving aside the above discussed measurement problem, it would be a matter of complete indifference whether the central bank picks a particular interest rate target or a money stock target.

But in actuality the central bank does not know the liquidity preference schedule and the strength of the expenditure incentives accurately. Suppose that the liquidity preference curve shifts outward unexpectedly. All the central bank observes is a rise in the interest rate. If it uses an interest rate target it responds to this rise in the interest rate by increasing the quantity of money sufficiently to lower it back to its previous level.[63] What it does is to satisfy the increased demand for money, or in terms of the cash balance equation, it offsets the rise in the Cambridge 'k' by raising 'M', thus keeping 'PT' constant. If it had used a money stock target instead of its interest rate target, it would have kept the money stock constant and allowed the interest rate to rise. This increase in the interest rate would then have reduced income below its previous (presumably optimal) level.

On the other hand, suppose that the liquidity preference curve is predictable, but that expenditure incentives increase unexpectedly.[64] This too raises the rate of interest. If the central bank has an interest rate target and counteracts this rise in the interest rate, it allows income to rise in an unintended way. In other words, if expenditure incentives increase the interest rate should also increase, thus acting as an automatic stabilizer. Hence, if it is expenditure motives rather than the liquidity preference function which changes in an unpredicted way, then an interest rate target does harm, and a money stock target is preferable. But if it is the liquidity preference function which is the unpredictable one, then an interest rate target is superior.[65]

On both of these issues a monetarist prefers a money stock target. Regarding the measurement problem, someone who accepts the monetarist transmission process believes that the money stock can be measured more accurately than can the interest rate. On the relative predictability of the liquidity preference function and the expenditure functions a quantity theorist considers the liquidity preference function (i.e. the demand for money) to be the stabler of the two.[66] Hence, the monetarist's preference for a money stock target over an interest rate target can be seen as an implication of the quantity theory and its transmission mechanism.

Apart from the money stock and the long-term interest rate there is a third major potential target for monetary policy. This is a credit measure, such as bank credit or total credit. Here too, the quantity theory and the monetarist's version of the transmission process decide the issue for the monetarist. As a quantity theorist, the monetarist believes that the effect of changes in the money stock on income is more important than the effect of changes in bank credit, for otherwise he or she would hold a quantity theory of bank credit rather than a quantity theory of money. Moreover, in the analysis of the transmission process the monetarist rejects a credit and borrowing cost interpretation.[67]

The matter is more complex for Keynesians. As indicated above, the problem of measuring the interest rate is of serious concern to them only with respect to the cost of capital channel. Since different Keynesians attach different weights to this channel, it is hard to say how significant the measurement problem is for the Keynesian's choice of a target. Furthermore, a Keynesian may – or may not – be concerned about the difficulties of measuring the money stock.

With regard to the second issue, the relative predictability of the liquidity preference and expenditure functions, *Keynes* originally considered both the liquidity preference function and the investment function to be erratic without indicating which was the more unstable. Modern Keynesians, on the other hand, have de-emphasized the speculative motive for liquidity preference which for *Keynes* was the source of its instability, and appear to believe that the liquidity preference function is fairly stable and predictable. On the other hand, Keynesians also believe that investment and consumption, while unstable, are predictable. It is therefore not really clear whether Keynesians typically consider the liquidity preference function or the expenditure functions to be the more predictable. Perhaps there is a presumption that, on the whole, they consider the demand for money to be the more predictable variable which should make them prefer a money stock target.

Moreover, insofar as they are the intellectual heirs of the Wicksellian tradition, Keynesians should prefer a money stock target to an interest rate target. It was *Wicksell* who taught us the dangers of keeping the money rate of interest fixed (as happens with an interest rate target) when the natural rate of interest changes. All in all, Keynesian theory is more or less neutral on the issue of the money stock versus the interest rate as the target.

The third potential target is the volume of bank credit, or total credit. Some Keynesians have accepted such targets and they, of course, differ sharply from the monetarists. But one can be a good Keynesian while rejecting the reasoning of the *Radcliffe* Report.

IX   THE MONETARY GROWTH RULE

The next component of monetarism is the constant money growth rule. Such a rule fits well into the monetarist framework on several counts. First, it is closely related to the quantity theory. If the demand for money is indeed constant when adjusted for trend, then a constant growth rate of the supply of money would result in income too growing at a constant rate.[68] Hence, someone who accepts the quantity theory of money is much more likely to favor constant money growth than is someone who believes either that the demand for money is unstable, or that fluctuations in income are largely due to nonmonetary factors, factors which the central bank can offset.[69] Second, a belief in constant money growth also fits in with the monetarist's belief that the private sector is inherently stable. If this is the case there is at best a limited amount of good that could be accomplished by variations in the money growth rate. Third, belief in a constant money growth rate requires acceptance of a money stock target, for the monetary growth rule is really only a special version of the use of a monetary target; it merely sets a specific, unvarying target.

In addition, the constant money growth rule also has some connection, albeit a looser connection, with two other components of monetarism, the disinterest in allocative detail, and the monetarist view of the price level. Someone who is interested in allocative detail is likely to be concerned, from time to time, with the impact of financial stringency on a particular sector, such as residential construction. He is therefore likely to feel, at least occasionally, that the monetary growth rate should be changed to protect a particular sector. A monetarist who believes that allocative detail is outside the purview of macroeconomic stabilization policy is much less likely to feel this way. The monetarist view of the price level reinforces the case for a monetary rule by implying that one of the factors which might cause someone to favor variations in the monetary growth rate, cost-push inflation, does not occur.

Having seen how the monetary growth rule fits into the rest of monetarism let us see to what extent it conflicts with Keynesian theory. It does conflict in one way because Keynesians look upon velocity as being variable; a belief connected with their view that the private sector is unstable, and with their emphasis on the interest elasticity of the demand for money. Hence, to the Keynesians a constant rate of monetary growth would not result in an acceptable degree of income stability. However, Keynesians may well accept some of the other arguments mentioned above which cause monetarists to favor a constant growth rate. Thus, Keynesians need not consider it desirable to change the money growth rate to accommodate particular sectors of the economy. And similarly, they need not accept the likelihood of cost-push inflation, or they may feel that while cost-push inflation is a serious possibility it should be resisted by not creating the additional money stock demand at higher prices. Moreover, as pointed out above, Keynesians may well accept the use of a money stock target.

Despite the fact that the monetary growth rule fits in so well with a large number of monetarist propositions, it is in a very important way a separate issue, independent of the validity of all other monetarist propositions. This is so because the main arguments for a constant monetary rule are essentially quite different from what has been discussed so far. They are that monetary policy affects the economy with long and unpredictable lags, or that the central bank is likely to be inefficient and follow goals other than income stabilization.[70] These hypotheses are not derivable from other monetarist propositions, nor do they conflict in any important way with Keynesian propositions. Yet while, strictly speaking, these two hypotheses are neither necessary nor sufficient conditions for the desirability of a monetary rule, they are close to it.[71] Thus, if it were shown conclusively that the lags of monetary policy are so long and variable that discretionary monetary policy is likely to be destabilizing, or that the central bank is too inefficient to operate a successful stabilization policy, then many – probably most – Keynesians would support a monetary rule. And concern that a discretionary stabilization policy may be destabilizing is far from being a monetarist monopoly. In fact, a classic article warning of this danger was written by a Keynesian, A. W. *Phillips*.[72]

Conversely, if it were shown conclusively that discretionary policy can stabilize the economy, then probably most monetarists would reject the monetary growth rule. To be sure, a monetarist with beliefs in a stable demand for money, and in the inherent stability of the private sector, is likely to expect that even a successful stabilization policy will do relatively little good, but it could still do some good. Hence, it is not surprising that belief in a stable monetary growth rule is not a component of *Friedman's* definition of monetarism.[73] Thus, the debate about a monetary growth rule transcends the issue of monetarism versus Keynesianism.[74]

X   ABSENCE OF AN INFLATION-UNEMPLOYMENT TRADE-OFF

Having looked at the basic theory of the monetarists, their choice of estimation procedures, and their views on monetary policy there remain three monetarist propositions having to do with economic policy in general. One of these is the monetarists' belief that, except in the short run, the *Phillips* curve is in real terms, so that, at most, there exists a very limited trade-off between inflation and unemployment.

The real *Phillips* curve is related to three of the previously discussed monetarist propositions, the quantity theory, the stability of the private sector, and the stable monetary growth rate. If the *Phillips* curve (over the time span relevant for analysis) is in real terms, then an increase in the quantity of money does not affect real income, but affects only prices since it merely changes the wage unit. Moreover changes in Keynesian variables such as fiscal policy then have no lasting effect on real income.[75]

But a Keynesian could accept the real *Phillips* curve and still claim that changes in the marginal efficiency of investment are more important than changes in the monetary growth rate in explaining short run fluctuations in real income. This is so because, with a belief in the instability of the private sector, a Keynesian believes that much of the time the economy is in a situation where the marginal efficiency of investment has changed, and the nominal wage has not yet adapted to this change, so that real income is affected.

The stable money growth rate rule too has a connection with the real *Phillips* curve. One objection to it is that it would not allow the central bank to intervene when unemployment becomes too high. But if there exists only a very short-run trade-off between unemployment and inflation such intervention would do little good, and hence a monetary growth rate rule becomes more acceptable.[76]

Having seen that the real *Phillips* curve fits into the monetarist framework, to what extent is it inconsistent with the Keynesian framework? One obvious inconsistency arises in an historical context. In the *General Theory* *Keynes* sharply rejected *Pigou's* assumption that workers bargain for a real wage (which is what the real *Phillips* curve says), and argued instead that workers bargain for a certain money wage.

A second inconsistency relates to the current Keynesian, or neo-Keynesian, model. In this model the *Phillips* curve fixed in nominal terms is used to determine the price level. If a real *Phillips* curve is substituted for the nominal *Phillips* curve a Keynesian has no way of determining the equilibrium price level.[77] In this way, the acceptance of the real *Phillips* curve would weaken Keynesian theory.

But despite this, the debate about the real or nominal nature of the *Phillips* curve is to a considerable extent independent of the Keynesian–monetarist debate. It is essentially an empirical issue which has to be resolved by detailed studies of the labor market, rather than by settling the monetarist–Keynesian debate in some other way, and then deducing the nature of the *Phillips* curve from the result reached in the monetarist–Keynesian debate. If empirical studies were to show conclusively that the *Phillips* curve is in real terms a Keynesian could surely accept this result without abandoning Keynesian theory in favor of monetarism. Conversely, if the empirical evidence were to show that the *Phillips* curve is fixed in nominal terms, a monetarist could easily live with this conclusion.

XI CONCERN ABOUT INFLATION

Monetarists appear to be more concerned than are Keynesians about the disadvantages of unanticipated inflation, and to be relatively less concerned about the disadvantages of unemployment.[78] This choice between these two evils can be related to several of the foregoing characteristics of monetarists. One is that the quantity theorist pays much more attention to the likelihood of price changes than does the Keynesian. Indeed, one of the standard criticisms which monetarists make of Keynesians is to accuse them of assuming that the price level is constant.[79] And someone who considers price level changes to be a serious possibility will obviously be concerned much more about potential inflation than someone who more frequently takes the price level as constant.

Second, there is the belief in the inherent stability of the private sector at an acceptable rate of unemployment. While modern Keynesians may readily concede that underemployment cannot be an equilibrium, they still stress that serious underemployment may occur frequently, and continue for a very long time. The monetarist, by contrast, has a stronger belief in the corrective forces that bring the private sector close to full employment if it is left undisturbed by government policy. Hence, the monetarist worries less about unemployment than the Keynesian does.

Third, there is the monetary growth rule. A stable monetary growth rule would limit the potential inflation rate by denying the economy the additional liquidity needed during an inflation. Hence, someone who is very concerned about inflation, and the inflationary bias of the political process, might be led by this to favor the monetary growth rule.[80] On the other hand, if velocity falls or productivity increases to an extent unanticipated when the monetary rule is instituted, substantial unemployment might result. Hence a Keynesian who is very concerned about unemployment may, for this reason, reject a stable money growth rule.

A fourth, rather tenuous, connection is that, by accepting a real *Phillips* curve monetarists abandon any hope of being able, except in the short run, to lower unemployment at the cost of inflation. And while this may not make monetarists more concerned about inflation, it causes them to oppose as essentially useless inflationary policies which aim at raising employment.

But again, the issue under discussion is far removed from the main area of monetarist–Keynesian contention. For example, if we had conclusive evidence on the validity of the quantity theory and the monetarist transmission process, it would probably do little to change our relative degree of concern about inflation and unemployment. This depends much more on other issues, such as the effects of inflation on income distribution, and on fundamentally ethical judgments.

XII DISLIKE OF GOVERNMENT INTERVENTION

The final characteristic of monetarists, at least in the United States, is a dislike of government intervention. This is not limited to macroeconomics; in general monetarists appear to be much more satisfied with the outcome of market processes than most Keynesians are. There is, of course, no way of proving that this attitude should be considered a component of monetarism, rather than a characteristic which those economists who are monetarists happen to have for extraneous reasons. However, a dislike of government regulations fits very well with most of the previously discussed components of monetarism. Thus, a belief in the quantity theory implies that there should be no countercyclical fiscal policy. Moreover, a countercyclical fiscal policy might result in the government sector expanding in a recession more than it shrinks in the expansion, so that it grows secularly.[81] In any case, if the private sector is inherently stable no countercyclical policy may be needed or be desirable. Someone who objects to government regulations is less likely to be interested in allocative detail than someone who has to have information about various sectors to plan government policy. And conversely, if the behavior of various sectors does not matter for macroeconomic policy, some government regulations should be abolished. Furthermore, if the behavior of the price level is essentially independent of the pricing policies and wage policies followed in 'strategic industries' then this is another reason why some government regulations are unnecessary.

Using the money stock rather than interest rates or bank credit as the target of monetary policy means that the government can leave the determination of interest rates and bank credit to free market, and can confine its attention to the stock of money, something just about always considered outside the domain of the private market. A monetary growth rule obviously reduces the need for discretionary policy. And if the *Phillips* curve is such that one cannot successfully trade off unemployment and inflation then here is another task the government should not attempt.

Finally, there are several links between a concern about inflation and concern about the growth of government. One is that inflation can easily lead to political pressures for the imposition of wage and price controls. A second is that, given a progressive tax system, inflation raises the share of the government sector with the resulting temptation to increase government expenditures. A third link is that since one way that government expenditures have risen is through inflationary finance, prevention of inflation may indirectly limit government expenditures. Fourth, deficit expenditures when financed by newly created money, as is so often the case, tend to be inflationary.

A critic of monetarism might therefore be tempted to claim that monetarism is basically an 'ideological' doctrine; that it consists of finding seemingly technical reasons to hide a basic commitment in favor of unfettered capitalism. But this temptation to play amateur psychoanalyst should be firmly resisted. A monetarist can reply to it very easily by reversing the argument, and claiming that the ideological element in the debate rests with the Keynesians; that it is their ideological commitment to government regulations and the growth of bureaucracy that makes them reject the monetarist's sound arguments on various technical issues of monetary economics.

On a more worthwhile level than such name-calling it should be noted that while opposition to government regulations fits in well with monetarism, it is still a very loose connection in one important sense.[82] One can be a radical and yet accept all the other monetarist propositions discussed above. Thus, radicals might even accept the constant monetary growth rule on the basis that this is the best one can do under capitalism.[83] In fact, a planner in an almost totally controlled economy, such as China, should find the quantity theory more useful than the Keynesian theory.[84] Conversely, one can be a right-wing extremist without being a monetarist.

XIII SOME OTHER DIFFERENCES

If one wants to look for a common thread connecting various monetarist propositions one need not confine oneself to an ideological consideration since there is a methodological element available.

We live in a world too complex for our intellectual apparatus. We must therefore do either of two things. One is to take account of a great many factors at the cost of being able to see their interrelations only in a vague, clouded way. The other is to simplify drastically, and to look at only a few factors. Along these lines one can classify economists into 'cloud makers' and into 'oversimplifiers', to use two derogatory terms. Using this dichotomy the Keynesian is a cloud maker while the monetarist is an oversimplifer.[85] Thus the quantity theory is simpler than the Keynesian theory in the sense of taking account of fewer variables.[86] The picture is less obvious as far as the monetarist transmission process is concerned. The monetarist view of this process is certainly more cloudy and less clear than the Keynesian one, since monetarists believe that it works through a large number of channels, some of which they cannot specify. However, a vague transmission process, when combined with *Friedman's* methodological views results in a simple, rather than a complex, view of the world. *Friedman* finds a close relationship between changes in money and in nominal income, and presumably does not feel greatly worried by the fact that it is difficult to specify the transmission process.[87] He stresses predictive power rather than descriptive realism.[88]

The monetarist's hypothesis that the private sector is inherently stable also helps to simplify the analysis, since, if true, this means that we do not have to concern ourselves in macroeconomics with fluctuations in expenditure motives. Hence, one can dispense with the detailed Keynesian analyses of consumption and investment, as well as many complex business cycle theories. Monetarists' disinterest in allocative detail obviously also simplifies macroeconomics. The same is true for their use of small, rather than large, econometric models, and for their focus on the overall price level rather than on the prices charged in individual industries.

Using total reserves rather than a combination of short-term interest rates and money market conditions as an indicator of monetary policy helps to simplify the analysis of monetary policy. Indeed, monetarists have criticized the use of money market conditions because of the complexity and vagueness it introduces.[89] The use of a stable money growth rate also obviously simplifies the conduct of monetary policy. Indeed, one of the leading monetarist arguments for it is that we do not have the required information, such as knowledge of lags, to do better with discretionary policy than a simple growth rate rule does. And a *Phillips* curve that does not allow for any unemployment–inflation trade-off simplifies macroeconomics by removing one very difficult question, selection of the optimal trade-off. Only two components of monetarism, the use of a money stock target, and the concern about inflation do not fit the picture of monetarism as simplification.

There exists also another element that links six monetarist propositions. This is the monetarist's skepticism about how much we really know about the short-run workings of the economy. Monetarists generally seem to be less optimistic about this than are Keynesians. If we really do know little about the short-run behavior of the economy, then the monetarist transmission process is less subject to the criticism that it does not try to spell out the channels of monetary influence in any detail. Any attempt to do this could then be considered presumptuous. Second, if our knowledge of short-run economic behavior is limited, then we may not have an adequate framework for using information about allocative detail. Third, we then do not know enough to build useful large-scale econometric models. Fourth, the less our knowledge, the weaker is the case for 'fine tuning', and the stronger is the case for a monetary rule,[90] and hence the use of a money stock target. Finally, the less we know about the economy the less likely are government regulations to improve it.

XIV   CONCLUSION

This chapter has dealt with various propositions that make up monetarism, broadly defined, and showed that they form a coherent whole. With one exception (the use of a total reserve measure as the indicator of monetary policy) they fit together in the sense that definitive proof of the validity of one of the more basic propositions would increase the plausibility of some of the other propositions. Figure 8.1 shows relations which have been traced here between the various propositions.

But this does not mean that monetarism is a paradigm which must be accepted or rejected as a whole. As pointed out above, with the exception of the quantity theory itself, and perhaps its transmission process, every single proposition of monetarism is one which Keynesians could accept while rejecting others, and still maintain their adherence to basic Keynesian theory. In particular, the policy propositions are readily detachable from the theoretical propositions of monetarism, and can be accepted without qualms by a Keynesian. Conversely, someone who accepts some of the monetarist propositions, including the two most basic ones (the quantity theory and the monetarist version of the transmission process) need not therefore accept all the others.

Hence, a good case can be made for abolishing the term 'monetarism' altogether, and for treating each proposition independently. This would reduce the unfortunate polarization of economists into monetarists and anti-monetarists, with the accompanying tendency to accept or reject various propositions on a basis other than the empirical evidence bearing on them.[91] Admittedly, this may well be the counsel of perfection since the term 'monetarism' is now so well established and convenient. But eclecticism is fully justified.[92]

ACKNOWLEDGEMENTS

I am indebted for helpful comments to Karl *Brunner*, Thomas *Cargill*, H. *Cheng*, Benjamin *Friedman*, Milton *Friedman*, Michael *Hamburger*, Michael

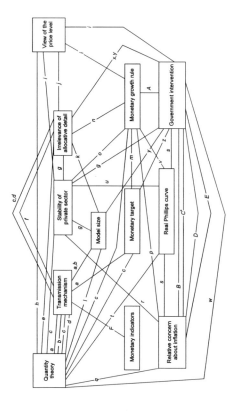

Figure 8.1 Interrelation of monetarist propositions

Notes:

a measurement problems
b range of assets considered
c stability of demand for money
d relative price and stock effects
e disinterest in expenditure motives
f unimportance of expenditure motives and of peculiarities of sectors
g little concern about instability
h aggregate demand determined by quantity of money
i immunity to cost-push inflation
j irrelevance of price behavior in individual industries
k disinterest in particular sectors
l results reached by models
m growth rule as special type of monetary target
n no need to help particular sectors
o little need to offset fluctuations
p prevent unanticipated inflation
q focus on price flexibility

r natural rate of unemployment
s absence of unemployment-inflation trade-off
t adaptive expectations and emphasis on distinction between real and nominal magnitudes
u real variables unaffected by inflation
v absence of trade-off ameliorates potential loss from monetary rule
w ineffectiveness of fiscal policy
x information on sectors not needed
y intervention in sectors not needed for macroeconomic policy
z no interference with interest rates or credit volume
A no discretionary monetary policy
B less danger of wage and price controls
C inflationary impact of government expenditures financed by new money creation
D inflation raises government receipts
E inflationary finance facilitates additional expenditures
F focus on the money stock rather than on interest rate and disregard of the financial intermediation-residential construction channel

Keran, Allan *Meltzer*, Franco *Modigliani*, Manfred J. M. *Neumann*, Roger *Spencer*, Edward *Shaw*, Daniel *Vencill*, and to members of workshops and seminars at the Board of Governors, Federal Reserve System, the San Francisco Federal Reserve Bank, and MIT, none of whom are responsible for any remaining errors.

NOTES

1 The term 'monetarism' was originated by Karl *Brunner* ('The Role of Money and Monetary Policy', *Federal Reserve Bank of St Louis Review* 50, July 1968, pp. 8–24), and was popularized by David *Fand*; see for instance his 'Monetarism and Fiscalism', *Banca Nazionale del Lavoro Quarterly Review* 94, September 1970, pp. 3–34 and 'Ein monetaristisches Modell des Geldwirkungsprozesses', *Kredit und Kapital* 3 (1970), pp. 361–85.

2 Similarly, there is no authoritative listing of Keynesian propositions. I have interpreted Keynesian theory as a theory represented by the views of such economists as James Duesenberry, Franco Modigliani, Paul Samuelson and James Tobin rather than by the more extreme views which can be found in the writings of economists such as Alvin Hansen. Hence, what I am calling 'Keynesian theory' is to some extent a synthetic theory which has probably been influenced by monetarism.

3 Throughout my discussion deals only with monetarist school as it exists in the United States.

4 *Brunner*, 'The "Monetarist Revolution" in Monetary Theory', *Weltwirtschaftliches Archiv* 105, no. 1, 1970, pp. 1–30.

5 *Fand* also mentions another item, the monetarist's belief in long and variable lags. But at present many Keynesians also believe that monetary policy has long lags. David *Fand*, 'Monetarism and Fiscalism', loc. cit.

6 James *Tobin, The New Economics One Decade Older* (Princeton, NJ, pp. 58–9). Actually, as far as item 7 is concerned *Tobin* refers to the money stock rather than total reserves, but this is a minor difference. Also, item 8 is implicit, rather than explicit in *Tobins's* list. Paul *Samuelson* ('Reflections on the Merits and Demerits of Monetarism' in James *Diamond* (ed.) *Issues in Fiscal and Monetary Policy*, Chicago, IL, 1971, pp. 7–21) lists the quantity theory and the monetary growth rate rule as the two basic propositions of monetarism. To these he adds the belief in wage and price flexibility, and in the response of the interest rate to inflation (two propositions which can be treated as part of the quantity theory) and a belief in the real nature of the Phillips curve with the associated belief in a natural rate of unemployment. He then stated (p. 20) that 'there is no reason why monetarists should believe this except that all of these notions happen to be believed by one man, Professor *Friedman*'. (For a similar statement see James *Tobin*, op. cit., p. 62.) This not only ignores the work of *Brunner* and *Meltzer*, but also ignores the various linkages discussed below.

7 'The State of the Monetarist Debate', *Federal Reserve Bank of St Louis Review* 56, September 1973, pp. 5–6. Although *Andersen* states that it is also accepted by 'many other economists' it is frequently rejected by Keynesians.

8 For a typical example see James *Tobin's* criticisms of the policy recommendations made by the, mainly monetarist, 'Shadow Open Market Committee' (James *Tobin*, 'Monetary Policy in 1974 and Beyond', *Brookings Papers on Economic Activity* 1974: 1, pp. 219–32.

9 Thus Allan *Meltzer* wrote (private communication) 'I do not accept any but points 1 to 4 as part of monetarism. The other points are, for me, propositions

that I accept to varying degrees. Many are unrelated to monetarism. For example, your point 5 is a Hicksian proposition about composite goods. It should be accepted by all economists.' It is certainly true that item 5 can be considered as a theorem about composite goods, but there is still a decision to be made as a matter of research strategy, rather than as a matter of formal theory, whether one analyzes the general price level as a single unit or by looking at individual prices.

10 However, I have omitted the international aspect of monetarism, the proposition that with fixed exchange rates a country's money stock and price level depend not on its own monetary policy, but on the whole world's monetary policy. At least in the United States, this proposition has not played much of a role in monetarist discussions. But adding it to my list would not change my conclusions because, as Harry *Johnson* has pointed out, 'a properly understood Keynesian approach to the system as a whole would produce the same conclusion' (H. G. *Johnson* and A. R. *Nobay* (eds) *Issues in Monetary Economics*, London, Oxford University Press, 1974, p. 50.) Besides, it is essentially part of the first proposition, the quantity theory. I have also omitted an item mentioned by *Brunner* ('The Role of Money and Monetary Policy', op. cit., p. 9), the belief that the monetary authorities can control the stock of money. This is now accepted by many Keynesians as well, though admittedly, Keynesians tend to qualify it more than monetarists do.

The various hypotheses I describe as monetarist do, of course, predate the development of the term 'monetarism'. The quantity theory, together with its transmission process, has an ancient history, as do, though perhaps to a lesser extent, the next three items. Items 6, 7 and 10 are newer because the problems they present are newer. A hundred years ago nobody was worried about the proper size of an econometric model, or about the correct monetary indicator. Debate about items 8 and 9 can, to some extent, be traced back to the banking school–currency school debate. The final two items again, do have a long history. What is new about monetarism is therefore primarily its combination of hypotheses into a single doctrine.

11 The modern Keynesian theory differs from the quantity theory in denying that changes in the money stock dominate changes in income, but it does not claim that changes in the money stock are unimportant. According to J. R. *Hicks* (*The Crisis in Keynesian Economics*, Oxford, 1974, pp. 31–2) *Keynes* himself 'must surely in some sense, perhaps a very weak sense, have been a monetarist. He has nevertheless been read to imply that there is nothing to be done with money.'

12 Thus the growing literature on search costs is relevant to the monetarist–Keynesian debate and monetarists attach more importance to search costs than do Keynesians.

13 To be sure, if there are long lags in the effects of money on income then one might predict next years's income by changes in the money stock in previous years, but if the lags are highly variable, even this would not work.

14 *Patinkin's* model uses the quantity theory's analytic procedures insofar as it focuses on the gap between desired and actual real balances. However, it is Keynesian in its use of capital theory since, as *Patinkin* has argued, the Cambridge school did not use capital theory in its monetary analysis to any significant extent. (See Don *Patinkin*, 'Keynesian Monetary Theory and the Cambridge School', in H. G. *Johnson* and A. R. *Nobay*, op. cit., pp. 3–30.)

15 This difference between looking at the quantity theory as an engine of analysis and looking at it as the conclusion that money matters a great deal is at the heart of a dispute between *Friedman* and *Patinkin*. *Patinkin*, focusing on the fact that *Friedman* – like *Keynes*, but unlike pre-Keynesian quantity theorists – uses capital theory in his monetary analysis, has argued that *Friedman's* theory is

more a Keynesian than a quantity theory. (Don *Patinkin,* 'The Chicago Tradition, the Quantity Theory and *Friedman*', *Journal of Money, Credit and Banking* I, Feb. 1969, pp. 46–70, and '*Friedman* on the Quantity Theory and Keynesian Economics', *Journal of Political Economy* 80, September/October 1972, pp. 883–905.) *Friedman's* reply was to object to *Patinkin's* 'propensity to take the "quantity theory" to mean one thing, and one thing only, namely the long-run proposition that money is neutral, even though he fully recognizes, indeed insists, that quantity theorists (myself included) were concerned mostly with short-run fluctuations'. ('Comments on the Critics', *Journal of Political Economy* 80, September/October 1972, p. 932.) Perhaps the point should be stated differently by saying that *Friedman* classifies theories on the basis of the conclusions they reach, while *Patinkin* classifies them on the basis of the analytic method used.

16 I will not describe the monetarist transmission processes here in any detail. *Friedman's* variant stresses substitution effects, and the influence of changes in the money stock on the nominal interest rate while the *Brunner–Meltzer* variant stresses relative price and stock effects. Both variants attach much importance to the distinction between nominal and real rates of interest, and more generally, pay greater attention to price changes than Keynesians typically do.

I am discussing only the transmission process for changes in the quantity of money, and not for fiscal policy, etc. The monetarist argument that fiscal policy changes result in counteracting changes, such as 'crowding out', which offset them after some time, is really part of the previously discussed monetarist proposition, that changes in money income are explained largely by changes in the money stock.

17 Thus in commenting on a draft of this chapter Milton *Friedman* wrote (private communication): 'I believe an important distinction between Keynesian and monetarist views is one that I have not myself stressed sufficiently but that comes out in the course of some of your comments. This is the distinction between money and credit and most particularly in what one regards as the price of money. The Keynesian approach invariably regards the interest rate as the price of money whereas the quantity theory approach regards the interest rate as the price of credit and the inverse of the price level as the price of money. This is exremely important in connection with the way in which the demand curve for money is used.'

18 Cf. Milton *Friedman*, 'A Theoretical Framework for Monetary Analysis', National Bureau of Economic Research, Occasional Paper 112 (New York, 1971), p. 28.

19 Y. C. *Park*, 'Some Current Issues on the Transmission Process of Monetary Policy', International Monetary Fund, Staff Papers, March 1972, p. 38.

20 Many monetarists believe that if the quantity of money is increased the nominal interest rate declines only very temporarily. It soon rises back to its previous level, and, due to the *Fisher* effect, even exceeds it. The monetarist therefore looks upon the expected real interest rate as fairly stable. Hence, one of the factors which can cause fluctuations in the quantity of money demanded, changes in the expected real interest rate, seems much less important to the monetarist than to the Keynesian. Another important reason why monetarists take the demand for money as stable is that, as discussed below, the monetarist treats expenditure incentives as much more stable than the Keynesian does, and hence considers the expected real rate of interest, and therefore the demand for money, to be stabler than Keynesians do.

21 'The Quantity Theory of Money: A Restatement', reprinted in Milton *Friedman, The Optimum Quantity of Money* (Chicago, 1969) ch. 2.

22 In the United States the growth rates of M_1 and M_2 have diverged widely, presumably in large part due to restrictions on interest payments on deposits.

For example, between December 1972 and December 1973 M_1 grew at a 6.1 percent rate while M_2 (excluding large certificates of deposit) grew at an 8.9 percent rate, that is at a 69 percent greater rate.

23 Some attempts have been made to settle this issue by seeing whether M_1 or M_2 have a closer correlation with income. But these attempts founder on the fact that the 'reverse causation' bias may be greater for one measure than for the other.

24 To be sure, in the mainly Keynesian Federal Reserve–MIT–Penn model the interest rate has a strong effect on consumption. But this is not true for the more typically Keynesian models.

25 According to Karl *Brunner* ('The Monetarist Revolution in Monetary Theory', op.cit., p. 3) the borrowing-cost interpretation is post-Keynesian rather than part of *Keynes'* own thought.

26 *Keynes'* evidence for the interest inelasticity of consumption is extremely casual (*The General Theory*, London, 1936, pp. 93–4), but this rather arbitrary judgment allowed him to make a great simplification. This is to dichotomize his model into decisions made about the disposition of income (to save it or consume it) and decisions made about asset composition (to hold money or bonds). He did not have to consider the feedback effect of asset decisions on consumption through changes in the propensity to consume as the interest rate changes.

27 Although this is no more than a surmise I suspect that the debate about the channels of monetary influence received some of its impetus from the fact that at one time empirical studies of business investment behavior showed the interest rate as playing, at best, a very small role. Hence, monetarists had a strong reason to argue that changes in the money stock do not operate just through business investment, while Keynesians had an incentive to treat business investment as the only link between changes in the money stock and income.

28 Karl *Brunner* and Allan *Meltzer*, 'Money, Debt and Economic Activity', *Journal of Political Economy* 80, September/October 1972, pp. 951–77; Karl *Brunner*, 'A Survey of Selected Issues in Monetary Theory', *Schweizerische Zeitschrift für Volkswirtschaft und Statistik* 107, 1971, pp. 1–146.

29 Y. C. *Park* (op. cit., p. 31) has argued that '*Brunner* and *Meltzer* – contrary to their claim – accept the Keynesian view of the nature of the transmission process; what they seem to reject is the heuristic simplification of reality with regard to the range of assets considered in the Keynesian income/expenditure theory.' This statement is very much open to question if one treats as 'Keynesian' not every single factor mentioned in the *General Theory* and post-Keynesian writings, but only those which are stressed.

30 'The State of the Monetarist Debate: Comment', *Federal Reserve Bank of St Louis Monthly Review* 55, September 1973, p. 11.

31 An approach which looks at expenditure incentives is likely to come up with different results than one which focuses on the demand for money. The latter – on an intuitive level at least – seems stable, while – again on an intuitive level – expenditure incentives seem highly variable. Obviously, these two intuitions are in conflict due to *Walras'* Law. Perhaps the resolution of this conflict is that while the incentives for particular expenditures looked at one at a time seem unstable, much of this instability averages out in the sense that one sector may be depressed while another is in a boom.

32 Leonall *Andersen* ('The State of the Monetarist Debate', *Federal Reserve Bank of St Louis Monthly Review* 55, September 1973, pp. 2–8) has pointed to another factor as the difference between Keynesian and monetarist views on the stability of the private sector, the length of time it takes to return to the neighborhood of equilibrium when the economy is subjected to a shock.

33 This does not mean that monetarists can ignore all institutional detail. They have to consider numerous institutional factors (which differ among countries) in their analysis of the money supply process. But this is different from concern with allocative detail.

34 Thus in the, mainly Keynesian, Federal Reserve–MIT–Penn model, one of the major channels by which monetary changes affect income is credit rationing.

35 Obviously, a large sophisticated model, like the above mentioned one, can have several channels, and is not confined to borrowing costs. But for most Keynesian expositions borrowing costs are the channel.

36 This does not mean that monetarists are uninterested in allocative detail *per se*. They are often strongly interested in it because they look upon government interference with financial markets as creating very serious problems. Thus they oppose the suppression of financial deepening. In the United States monetarists are much more critical of Regulation Q (the limitation of interest payments on bank deposits) than are Keynesians. It is only with respect to the use of allocative detail as a predictor of short-run changes in income that monetarists have shown less interest in it than Keynesians.

37 But to the extent that the velocity of money differs in various sectors the monetarist has an incentive to analyze the distribution of money between various sectors. For a notable example see Richard *Selden*, 'The Postwar Rise in the Velocity of Money', *Journal of Finance* 16, December 1961, pp. 483–545.

38 This statement is subject to one qualification. The monetarist is likely to pay a great deal of attention to the efficiency of one sector, the financial sector, and to point out the distortions created in this sector by government regulations.

39 Admittedly, capital rationing tends to make the demand for money less stable.

40 One way of determining whether someone is a Keynesian or a monetarist is to ask for a quick and intuitive answer to the following question: 'Suppose the price of petroleum rises. What will this do to the average of other prices?'

41 See, for example, Keith *Carson*, 'A Monetarist Model for Economic Stabilization', *Federal Reserve Bank of St Louis Review* 52, April 1970, pp. 7–25.

42 This is subject to the caveat that the central bank might raise the money stock to maintain output when some prominent industries raise their wages and prices, or when unemployment develops.

43 The private sector may be stable even in the sense of being immune to cost-push inflation even if individual price increases do not result in corresponding price decreases in other sectors. This is so if, and only if, the forces making for cost-push are weak. Similarly, erratic shifts in expenditure motives could destabilize the private sector even if the monetarist's approach to the price level is correct. And allocative detail would then be important.

44 Cf. Sidney *Weintraub*, *Keynes and the Monetarists* (New Brunswick, NJ, 1973) ch. 7.

45 Admittedly, this reasoning is only a first approximation, for it ignores the fact that an increase in the price level, by raising the interest rate, raises velocity. However, monetarists may feel justified in ignoring this effect as minor because they may believe that the interest elasticity of the demand for money is low.

46 Otto *Eckstein* and Gary *Fromm*, 'Steel and the Postwar Inflation', Study Paper 2, US Congress, Joint Economic Committee, 86th Congress, 1st Session, Washington, DC, 1959, p. 34.

47 See Denis *Karnosky*, 'A Primer on the Consumer Price Index', *Federal Reserve Bank of St Louis Review* 56, July 1974, p. 7.

48 *General Theory*, op. cit., p. 293.

49 See William *Nordhaus*, 'Recent Developments in Price Dynamics', in Board of Governors, Federal Reserve System, *The Econometrics of Price Determination*,

Conference (Washington, DC 1972). See also W. *Godley* and W. *Nordhaus*, 'Pricing in the Trade Cycle', *Economic Journal* 82, September 1972, pp. 853–82. Perhaps this tendency of Keynesians to treat prices as cost determined represents a partial fusion of the Keynesian and institutionalist schools.

50 A leading monetarist, Phillip *Cagan*, has suggested that the dependence of price changes on changes in costs can be explained as a short run phenomenon resulting from the difficulties which firms have in coordinating their price changes (Phillip *Cagan*, *Inflation: The Hydra-Headed Monster*, Washington, DC, 1974, pp. 21–4.)

51 The only serious Keynesian discussion of this issue I know of is Abraham *Bergson's* 'Price Flexibility and the Level of Income', *Review of Economics and Statistics* XXV, February 1943, pp. 2–5.

52 It is not clear whether a Keynesian is more likely than a monetarist to believe that the change will be in output rather than in prices. On the one hand, a Keynesian is more likely to stress price inflexibility and situations of under-employment. On the other hand, many monetarists stress expectational effects, and anticipatory pricing in inflation. Insofar as prices are set in anticipation of inflation, a decline in demands is likely to affect output rather than prices even during an inflation when downward price flexibility is not a problem.

53 And while monetarists frequently consider prices to be fairly flexible, one can be a monetarist without this belief.

54 However, a number of fairly small Keynesian models do exist. It may be worth noting that if one is trying to evaluate the Keynesian–monetarist debate by comparing the predictive powers of monetarist and Keynesian models one should compare the monetarist model (i.e. the *Andersen–Jordan* model), not with large Keynesian models such as the *Wharton* model, as is sometimes done, but with small Keynesian models. Thus, the finding that the *Andersen–Jordan* model does well compared to the *Wharton* and OBE models (cf. Yoel *Haitovsky* and George *Treyz*, 'Forecasts with Quarterly Macroeconomic Models, Equation Adjustment and Benchmark Predictions: The U.S. Experience', *Review of Economics and Statistics* LIV, August 1972, pp. 317–25) is not as important for the Keynesian–monetarist dispute as is the finding that the *Andersen–Jordan* model's performance is not outstanding when compared to that of small Keynesian models. (See S.K. *McKnees*, 'A Comparison of the GNP Forecasting Accuracy of the Fair and St. Louis Econometric Models', in *Federal Reserve Bank of Boston, New England Economic Review*, September/October 1973, pp. 29–34, and J. W. *Elliot*, 'A Direct Comparison of Short-Run GNP Forecasting Models', *Journal of Business* 46, January 1973, pp. 33–60). The trouble with the *Wharton* or OBE model may be its structural, rather than its Keynesian, characteristics.

55 See Milton *Friedman*, 'Comment', in Universities-National Bureau Committee for Economic Research, Conference on Business Cycles (New York, 1951), pp. 112–14.

56 Private communication.

57 'The Usefulness of Monetary and Fiscal Policy as Discretionary Stabilization Tools', *Journal of Money, Credit and Banking* III, May 1971, Part 2, pp. 506–32.

58 The indicators–targets dichotomy has been challenged by Benjamin *Friedman* ('Targets, Instruments and Indicators of Monetary Policy', *Journal of Monetary Economics* 1, October 1975). However, since I am dealing here with the dispute between monetarists and Keynesians both of whom generally use this dichotomy, I am accepting it without questioning its validity.

59 I have phrased this statement in such a tentative way because I am far from certain that most Keynesians really prefer the short-term rate as their indicator. Unlike the monetarists, Keynesians have not written much on this topic.

60 See Richard *Davis* and Frederick *Schadrack*, 'Forecasting the Monetary Aggregates with Reduced Form Equations', in Federal Reserve Bank of New York, *Monetary Aggregates and Monetary Policy* (New York, 1974), pp. 60–71. See also Fred J. *Levine*, 'Examination of the Money-Stock Control Approach of *Burger, Kalish*, and *Babb*', *Journal of Money, Credit and Banking* V, November 1973, pp. 924–38; and James *Pierce*, and Thomas *Thomson*, 'Some Issues in Controlling the Stock of Money', in Federal Reserve Bank of Boston, *Controlling Monetary Aggregates II: The Implementation* (Boston n.d.), pp. 115–36.

61 David *Fand*, 'A Time Series Analysis of the "Bills-Only" Theory of Interest Rates', *Review of Economics and Statistics* XLVIII, November 1966, p. 369.

62 For a detailed exposition of this argument see William *Poole*, 'Optimal Choice of Monetary Policy Instruments in a Simple Stochastic Macro Model', *Quarterly Journal of Economics* 84, May 1970, pp. 197–216; and 'Rules of Thumb for Guiding Monetary Policy' in Board of Governors, Federal Reserve System, *Open Market Policies and Operating Procedures*, Staff Studies, Washington, DC, pp. 135–89.

63 The assumption that the money growth rate and the interest rate are negatively correlated is justified by the analysis being only very short run.

64 It is worth noting that what is relevant is not the stability of either the IS or LM curve, but its predictability since the central bank can readily offset predictable fluctuations.

65 A third aspect of the choice between a money stock target and an interest rate target relates to the problem of lags in the effects of monetary policy. Since many types of expenditures respond only slowly to a change in the interest rate the effects of monetary policy tend to be delayed. But this delay can be offset if interest rates initially overshoot their new level. (See Donald *Tucker*, 'Dynamic Income Adjustments to Money Supply Changes', *American Economic Review* LVI, June 1966, pp. 433–49.) Insofar as the central bank follows a money stock target such an overshoot occurs automatically. But with an interest rate target, the central bank may fail to allow for the required overshoot. And even if it aims for an overshoot, it does not know how large it should be.

66 The monetarists look upon expenditure motives as stable too, unless disturbed by variations in the money growth rate, since they treat the private sector as stable, but even so, they take the demand for money as the stabler one.

67 A fourth potential target, and money market conditions, is hardly taken seriously anymore, at least in the United States.

68 A monetary growth rule is supposed to provide a growth rate of money income which is stable, though this may be a stable rate of inflation or deflation.

69 This conclusion is subject to the caveat that in their formal theory monetarists consider the demand for money to be stable only in a functional sense. Hence, if many of the variables in the money demand functions fluctuate, the demand for money, and therefore income, would also fluctuate under a constant money supply rule. But according to *Friedman*, and perhaps to most monetarists, this distinction between the functional stability and the constancy of the demand for money does not create a serious problem. Insofar as the demand for money is a function of permanent income or wealth it is likely to grow at a steady rate. To be sure, it is also a function of the nominal rate of interest. But fluctuations in the nominal interest rate are largely the result of previous fluctuations in the money growth rate and prices. Hence, given a constant money growth rule, velocity would tend to be fairly stable in a numerical, as well as a functional, sense.

70 Another reason sometimes given for a monetary growth rule is that it reduces arbitrary government interference, substituting as it does the rule of law for the rule of humans.

71 They are not really necessary conditions, because someone might advocate the monetary growth rule solely on the basis that it curbs arbitrary government power. They are also not really sufficient conditions because some might reject the rule, even though it would stabilize income, because they believe that monetary policy should be used to stabilize particular sectors of the economy, to help government finance, or to obtain balance of payments equilibrium, etc.

The belief that stabilization policies are actually destabilizing may appear to conflict with one Keynesian proposition, the instability of the private sector. If the government sector has been a net contributor to instability it would seem that the private sector must be relatively stable. But this reasoning is questionable. At least in the United States, discretionary fiscal policy has frequently not behaved countercyclically; government expenditures have frequently risen at times of high activity. Similarly, if one accepts a money stock measure of monetary policy it also has usually not been countercyclical in the post-war period.

72 'Some Notes on the Estimation of Time-Forms of Reactions in Interdependent Dynamic Systems', *Economica* 23, May 1956, pp. 99–113.

73 *The Counter-Revolution in Monetary Theory* (London 1970), p. 26.

74 In any case, the debate about stable money growth versus discretionary policy is in the process of becoming technologically obsolete. Recent work suggests that an intermediate position, a stable central bank reaction function to changes in income, may well be superior to both a fixed money growth rule and to ad hoc discretionary policy. (See J. Phillip *Cooper, Development of the Monetary Sector, Prediction and Policy Analysis in the FRB-MIT-Penn Model*, Lexington, MA, 1974.)

75 Cf. Jerome *Stein*, 'Unemployment, Inflation and Monetarism', *American Economic Review* LXIV, December 1974, pp. 867–87. Two other ways in which the real *Phillips* curve fits in well with the quantity theory are the quantity theory's emphasis on the distinction between real and nominal magnitudes, and the use of adaptive expectations in both the modern quantity theory and the real *Phillips* curve analysis.

76 The direction of the connection between the real *Phillips* curve and the monetary growth rule is from the real *Phillips* curve to the growth rate rule rather than vice versa.

77 Insofar as prices are changing, Keynesians could use an expectational adjustment model to derive a modified *Phillips* curve which would then allow them to determine the price level. But if the inflation rate stays constant long enough for expectations to have fully adapted, Keynesians could predict neither the price level nor the unemployment rate unless they have independent information on what the natural rate of unemployment is. However, the same is true for monetarists. They also need a specialist in labor markets to tell them the natural rate of unemployment.

78 And there are monetarist objections even to fully anticipated inflation. As *Friedman* has pointed out (*The Optimum Quantity of Money*, op. cit., ch. 1) the price level should be falling to induce the public to hold the optimum quantity of money.

79 See, for example, Milton *Friedman*, 'Comments on the Critics', op. cit., pp. 917–18.

80 Admittedly, a constant monetary growth rate, if set at too high a level, might result in inflation. But this would be a fully anticipated inflation.

81 See James *Tobin*, op. cit., p. 63. However, *Tobin* also points out a negative relationship; insofar as fiscal policy has little, or no, effect on income, inflation cannot be used as an excuse for cutting the budget.

82 See ibid., p. 63.

83 Radicals, unless they are Marxist, need not reject the monetarist's belief in the inherent stability of the private sector since their objection to capitalism could be founded on grounds other than instability.

84 The Keynesian's marginal efficiency of investment and the multiplier play little, or no, role in determining income in a controlled economy. On the other hand, since the public has freedom to adjust its money holdings the quantity theory is relevant.

85 This does not imply that the quantity theorist thinks we live in a simple world. One may want to use simple models precisely because the world is so complex that no complex, but still manageable, model can do it justice. This can be seen readily on an empirical level. If we try to forecast a variable which has determinants of only moderate complexity we tend to use a standard 'explanatory' regression. But if we try to forecast a variable with extremely complex determinants we are more likely to use a naive model or some other autoregressive scheme.

86 The *Brunner-Meltzer* version of the quantity theory gives the impression of being more complex than the Keynesian theory since it criticizes Keynesian theory for ignoring some important effects. But this appearance is due, in part, to the fact that when *Brunner* and *Meltzer* criticize the Keynesian model they focus on the greatly oversimplified IS–LM diagram which does not give the full Keynesian story. Although they introduce some additional variables, they omit some of the Keynesian variables.

87 To be sure, *Friedman* believes that the mere correlation of money and income is not enough to establish the quantity theory, that a plausible transmission process is needed. (See Milton *Friedman* and Anna *Schwartz*, 'Money and Business Cycles', *Review of Economics and Statistics* XLV, February 1963, Supplement, p. 59.) However, a vague, generalized sketch of the transmission process may suffice for this.

88 Karl *Brunner*, too, has rejected the type of descriptive realism that tests theories by evaluating the validity of their assumptions. (See his 'Assumptions and the Cognitive Quality of Theories', *Synthese* 20, 1969, pp. 501–25.

89 See Karl *Brunner* and Allan *Meltzer*, *Some General Features of the Federal Reserve's Approach to Policy*, US Congress, House, Committee on Banking and Currency, Subcommittee on Domestic Finance, 88th Congress, 2nd Session (Washington, DC 1964).

90 This statement is subject to the objection that a great deal of knowledge is required to decide on the correct long run growth rate rule. But monetarists believe that the economy can adapt itself to any monetary growth rate as long as this rate is stable.

91 As Cyrus *Gordon* (*Riddles in History*, New York, 1974, p. 156) has put it, 'all schools of thought are in reality "schools of un-thought" to the extent that they prevent us from going to where the facts should lead us'.

92 Thus Karl *Brunner* has argued that: 'the four major issues [in the monetarist debate] allow a variety of combinations.... The evolution of such a spectrum with a "middle ground" should enrich our future research activities. Such activities should yield substantive results over the years to the extent that economists successfully avoid the "media propensity" of equating all issues with ideological positions', "Commentary on "The State of the Monetarist Debate"', *Federal Reserve Bank of St Louis Review* 55, September 1973, p. 14.

9   Monetarism

An interpretation and an assessment

David Laidler
Economic Journal (1981) 91, March, pp. 1–28

Like beauty, 'monetarism' tends to lie in the eye of the beholder, and before it can be assessed it must be defined. Though there have been several valuable attempts over the years to specify monetarism's key characteristics,[1] I shall not rely upon them in this chapter. Each of them has been heavily conditioned by its time and place of writing, and monetarism has evolved over the years in response to changing circumstances, and in different ways in different places, as new hypotheses have either been developed or absorbed. Thus, I will begin this chapter with my own characterisation of monetarism. In my view, the key characteristics of monetarism are as follows:

1 A 'quantity theory' approach to macroeconomic analysis in two distinct senses: (*a*) that used by Milton Friedman (1956) to describe a theory of the demand for money, and (*b*) the more traditional sense of a view that fluctuations in the quantity of money are the dominant cause of fluctuations in money income.
2 The analysis of the division of money income fluctuations between the price level and real income in terms of an expectations-augmented Phillips curve whose structure rules out an economically significant long-run inverse trade-off between the variables.
3 A monetary approach to balance-of-payments and exchange-rate theory.
4 (*a*) Antipathy to activist stabilisation policy, either monetary or fiscal, and to wage and price controls, and (*b*) support for long-run monetary policy 'rules' or at least prestated 'targets', cast in terms of the behaviour of some monetary aggregate rather than of the level of interest rates.

The first characteristic categorises the theoretical core of monetarism as it developed in the 1950s and 1960s, the second and third represent theory developed or absorbed by monetarists since the mid-1960s, while the fourth summarises a view of macroeconomic policy issues which, even though it is neither logically implicit in their positive analysis, nor their exclusive property, has remained reasonably constant among monetarists since the mid-1950s.

Before discussing these characteristics of monetarism in detail, let me deal briefly with two propositions that some might feel should be included in the above list. First, on the one hand, monetarists have frequently been accused of failing to give any account of the transmission mechanism of monetary policy, and have had attributed to them a belief in some mysterious 'direct' influence of money on expenditure; on the other hand they have themselves sometimes referred to a characteristically 'monetarist model' of that same transmission mechanism cast in terms of portfolio substitution among a wide variety of assets including reproducible capital, and even perhaps non-durable consumption goods. I believe that this is and always has been a non-issue. The claim that monetarists have failed to specify their transmission mechanism has been untrue from the very outset (see, for example, Brunner 1961; Friedman and David Meiselman 1963; Friedman and Anna Schwartz 1963*b*), and although the mechanism propounded in those papers is a good deal more sophisticated and better grounded in relative price theory than that embodied in the textbook macroeconomic models of the 1950s, or in the econometric models of that vintage, there is no essential difference between it and that analysed for example by James Tobin and his associates.[2]

Second, monetarists are often said to prefer 'small' to 'big' econometric models, and their views about the importance of the quantity of money for the determination of the general price level have undoubtedly led them to take highly aggregated systems seriously. Moreover, early large-scale econometric models were not constructed so as to highlight any strong effects of money on economic activity. Monetarists criticised them, as much for being Keynesian, as for being 'big'. Even so, subsequent developments have clearly shown that 'big' models can easily take on some very monetarist characteristics, while the Albert Ando and Franco Modigliani (1965) and Michael De Prano and Mayer (1965) papers demonstrate that single equation reduced form techniques can as well produce 'Keynesian' as 'monetarist' results.[3] Empirical analysis of all sorts has been used by both sides in the monetarist controversy, and if there is a method of empirical research more frequently associated with monetarist work than Keynesian, it is not small model or single equation econometrics, but National Bureau techniques of business cycle analysis.[4] Thus though empirical techniques have, in specific instances, provided something to argue about, there seems to me to be no clear dividing line between the statistical methodology of monetarists and their opponents about which one can usefully generalise.

I THE QUANTITY THEORY OF MONEY

It has often been said that Friedman's celebrated essay on the Quantity Theory could just as well have been called 'The Theory of Liquidity Preference – a Restatement'. Harry Johnson (1962) argued that Friedman's work on the demand for money should be viewed as a development of a fundamentally Keynesian capital theoretic approach to monetary theory and Don Patinkin (1969) later documented that it was indeed just that. However, I would stress the word *development* here, for 'Keynesian' though Friedman's model is, it is no more *Keynes'* model than Keynes' 'Marshallian' theory of income determination is Marshall's theory; and it differed from other developments of Keynes' theory of liquidity preference that appeared at about the same time in a number of ways.

First, it abstracted from any specific characteristics that money might have because it is a financial asset; Friedman treated money instead 'as if' a service-yielding consumer durable to which the permanent income hypothesis of consumption could be applied, just as Margaret Reid (1962) applied it to housing, or the contributors to Arnold Harberger (1960) did to a variety of other durable goods. In this respect Friedman's approach stands in sharp contrast to the analyses of William Baumol (1952) and Tobin (1956; 1958) as it does in its claim to be a theory of the total demand for money in the macroeconomy rather than of some component of that demand. Second, Friedman explicitly recognised inflation as an own rate of return on money and postulated a well-determined functional relationship between the expected inflation rate and the demand for money, a relationship whose existence Maynard Keynes (and some of his disciples) explicitly denied (see Roy Harrod 1971).

Finally, and so obviously that the matter is usually overlooked, Friedman asserted that the demand for money was, *as an empirical matter*, a stable function of a few measurable arguments. Keynes did not believe that – his empirically stable relationship was the consumption function – and nor did (or perhaps do) many of his British followers.[5] Moreover, pre-Keynesian monetary theorists did not believe in an empirically stable demand for money function either. Though they often enough assumed a constant velocity of circulation that is by no means the same thing, and in any event, they typically did so in order to make their analytic points with the maximum of clarity, and not with the intention of stating a belief about the nature of the real world. It is only with the publication of Friedman's essay that statements to the effect that the velocity of circulation is, *as a practical matter*, a stable function of a few arguments become central to debates about monetary economics. Its stress on this hypothesis makes monetarism a very different doctrine from classical and neoclassical economics, no matter what other similarities there may be, though it should be noted explicitly that the econometricians among American Keynesians have not found it necessary to adopt a monetarist label as a result of contemplating the possibility of the empirical stability of the relationship.[6]

In 1971 it was possible to argue that this characteristic monetarist belief in a stable demand for money function was well supported by empirical evidence as I did in Laidler (1971). However, the 1970s have produced a good deal of evidence to suggest that the relationship has shifted in an unpredicted way in a number of countries. There is not space to go into details here, but I would be willing to defend the following assertions.[7]

First, the instability in question is often presented, particularly in the United States, as a matter of a cumulative deterioration in the ability of the function to track data. This cumulative deterioration is largely an illusion stemming from the use of dynamic simulations of relationships containing a lagged dependent variable. A *one-time shift* of such a function will, as a matter of arithmetic, lead to a *cumulative deterioration* of its dynamic simulation goodness of fit that should not be read as implying a *continuous* tendency of the relationship to shift. On the other hand, I do not believe we can safely conclude that such one-time shifts in the demand for money function have not occurred, despite the fact, again particularly in the United States, that some formulations of the relationship turn out to deteriorate significantly less than others during the 1970s. When important issues like the stability of the demand for money function begin to depend, for example, on just which interest rate or rates one uses to proxy the opportunity cost of holding money, I believe that the correct conclusion is not that the variable which provides the best fit this time around is the 'right' one, but that our knowledge of the details of the relationship is more fragile than we thought. Finally, arguments to the effect that the demand for money function has not 'really' shifted, that we can restore its stability by taking note of institutional change and redefining 'money' so as to take account of its effects, need to be handled carefully. They are relevant to the interpretation of economic history, but the successful conduct of policy requires that specific actions be taken *vis-à-vis* precisely defined aggregates in order to achieve particular policy goals. To say, after the event, that our policy did not work because new assets evolved whose existence affected the outcome of our policies in a way that we could have forecast had we only been able to foresee their invention, may be true, but it is not very helpful in enabling us to do better next time, unless the evolution in question was, as it sometimes can be, the predictable outcome of some policy action or other.

Shifts in the demand measured for money function are not a new phenomenon. Evidence drawn from more than one country shows that the demand for money function shifted as the institutional framework evolved long before 1974. To cite but four examples: the income elasticities of demand for money seem to have fallen significantly in both the United States and Britain in the twentieth century (see Laidler 1971), the abolition of interest payments on demand deposits in the United States in 1933 was associated with a change in the nature of the demand function for narrow money (see Charles Lieberman 1980), as was the growth of Savings and Loan Associations in the 1940s (see Cagan and Schwartz 1975), or in Britain, the introduction of 'Competition and Credit Control' in 1971. Such shifts in the demand for money function are not new, then, but they are important. Though two of the above examples were the result of policy changes and might have been predicted *ex ante*, two were not. In any event these effects of institutional change on the demand for money function have important implications for our views on the proper conduct of monetary policy, as I shall argue in Section 4.

In the traditional vocabulary of economics, the phrase 'quantity theory of money' referred to a theory of (or better an approach to the analysis of) the relationship between the supply of money and the general price level. The characteristic monetarist belief that variations in the supply of money are the 'dominant impulse' (to borrow Brunner's phrase) causing fluctuations in money income is clearly related to this traditional version of the quantity theory, but modern monetarists are more clearcut in their attribution of a dominant causative role to the money supply than were quantity theorists of earlier vintages.[8] The difference here is surely attributable to monetarists' belief in a stable demand for money function, because earlier quantity theorists spent much of their time contemplating the empirical possibility of autonomous shifts in velocity. However, it takes more than a belief in a stable demand for money function to yield the monetarist view of these matters.

Setting aside the important complications that arise in the open economy, there are two ways in which a conventional analytic model of the IS-LM variety can be made to produce 'monetarist' results. First in its under-employment form, if, relative to expenditure, the demand for money is insensitive to interest rates then the quantity of money comes to dominate the determination of the level of real income. Now obviously a monetarist must deny that the interest elasticity of demand for money is infinite, and this has been done often and explicitly, but it is mainly in Britain that such a denial has been thought to amount to a distinctively monetarist statement. A number of textbook writers (including myself) have gone to the other extreme and used the assumption of a zero interest elasticity of demand for money to generate monetarist propositions from an under-employment IS-LM model. However, Friedman's (1959) study of the United States function is a notable exception to the general tendency of demand for money studies – including those of such monetarists as Brunner and Meltzer (e.g. 1963) – to find a significant interest elasticity of demand for money, and his inability to find a relationship turned out to be the result of faulty statistical method (see Laidler 1966; Friedman 1966). Thus, the existence or non-existence of a statistically significant interest elasticity of demand for money has not been a serious issue between monetarists and their opponents for at least fifteen years. If it had been, it is hard to see how monetarists, not least Friedman could have contributed to the analysis of the welfare costs of inflation, or how Friedman and Meiselman could have accepted their own evidence of the importance of autonomous expenditure as an influence on money income during the depression years with such equanimity.[9]

If we rule out the vertical LM curve, we can still get an IS-LM model to produce monetarist results if we assume full employment, and then postulate that the major source of disturbance is variations in the level – or rate of change of – the nominal money supply. With the determinants of velocity, except the expected rate of inflation, thus pinned down at full employment, and with fluctuations in money income thus reduced to fluctuations in the price level, the characteristics of the demand for money function – other than its stability and homogeneity in the general price level and its sensitivity to fluctuations in the expected inflation rate – become quite irrelevant to the relationship between the quantity of money and money income. A Keynesian of course would agree, as an analytic matter, with this proposition, but would probably deny what the monetarist would claim: namely that, if the IS-LM model is to be used as a framework for discussion at all – and there are some monetarists, notably Brunner and Meltzer, who would not want to use it at any price – then this full employment version of it is frequently the empirically relevant one.

To put matters this way is, in effect, to say that monetarists' belief in the quantity theory as a theory of money income boils down to the view that sustained inflation is caused by an expanding money supply. This is not too far from the mark, and much of the spread of monetarism since the mid-1960s stems from its ability to provide a readily comprehensible explanation of inflation along these lines. However, to cast the monetarist approach to the analysis of inflation in terms of a 'full employment' IS-LM model is difficult to justify except as a very first approximation. Though monetarists are among those who have written at considerable length about the interaction of the quantity of money and the price level in models where 'full employment' is the rule, the models in question have been long-run equilibrium growth models, not versions of short-run IS-LM analysis; in any event the 'money and growth' literature and, to a lesser extent, that dealing with 'money and welfare', even though it builds on Friedman's formulation of the relationship between the demand for real balances and the expected rate of inflation as a well-defined inverse function, is properly viewed, not as an offshoot of monetarism, but as an extension of Patinkin's (1956) theoretical analysis of the classical dichotomy and the neutrality of money to deal with the *long-run* properties of a *growing* economy, in the presence of variations in the *rate of change* of the nominal money supply.[10] In dealing with the interaction of the quantity of money, money income, and prices, the essential monetarist contribution has been to postulate the existence of stable relationships among these variables as an *empirical* matter, and to draw *practical* conclusions about the proper conduct of *short-run* stabilisation policy from studying their nature, and the 'money, growth and welfare' literature has next to nothing to say about these matters.

When it comes to empirical propositions about the relationship between money and money income, what was once monetarist heresy is now close to being received orthodoxy. In this respect monetarism has made an important positive contribution to macroeconomics. In the United States it seems now to be widely accepted that the correlation between the quantity of money and money income that long runs of time series data display is not just the result of coincidence, but does in fact constitute evidence for the existence of a causative relationship that has run primarily from money to money income rather than vice versa. The weight of the evidence produced by Friedman and his various collaborators (not to mention predecessors) and the persuasiveness of their arguments, has changed enough minds to warrant the conclusion that, in an important sense, 'we are all monetarists' now. Elsewhere in the world, not least in Britain, there has been a similar movement of opinion. Certainly one no longer hears much about velocity being variable 'almost without limit'. However, one does hear more about 'reverse causation' in Britain as an explanation of the correlation between money and money income than one does in the United States (I shall take this matter up below).

Even so, monetarist doctrine asserts not just that variations in the quantity of money lead to systematic variations in money income, but also, that those variations are primarily in prices rather than real income. Although, as I have already noted, much of monetarism's popular appeal stems from its claim to provide an easily comprehensible theory of inflation, that theory of inflation is by no means universally accepted. The view that the influence of money on money income falls on its real income component and not on prices has constituted a 'Keynesian' alternative to the monetarist position on these matters and the 'expectations-augmented Phillips Curve' has provided a focus for debate about them.[11] That is why a particular set of beliefs about its nature is a vital ingredient of monetarist doctrine.

II   THE EXPECTATIONS AUGMENTED PHILLIPS CURVE

The notion of a trade-off between inflation and unemployment was widely prevalent in Keynesian literature even before Arthur Brown (1955), William Phillips (1958) and Richard Lipsey (1960) formalised it in terms of what seemed to be an empirically stable functional relationship. Monetarists have long doubted its existence, instead asserting a belief in the 'inherent stability' of the private sector in the absence of policy-induced monetary disturbances, by which they have usually meant nothing more complex than that the system tends in and of itself to operate at or near 'full employment', regardless of the inflation rate, if policy-makers do not upset matters. The papers of Edmund Phelps (1967) and Friedman (1968) provided a framework in terms of which differences of opinion about these matters could be stated sharply enough to be confronted with empirical evidence. Although some commentators (e.g. Helmut Frisch 1977) treat the Phillips curve as providing an alternative theory of inflation to the monetarist approach, this is surely a mistake. In its expectations-augmented form, it emerged at the turn of the decade to provide what Friedman (1970) called 'the missing equation' in the monetarist model of inflation.

It is possible to derive this 'missing equation' from two very different theoretical bases, and disagreements here are of quite fundamental importance for macroeconomics, but the first round in the debate about the expectations augmented Phillips curve, and the one that was crucially relevant to monetarism, paid little attention to these matters. It was almost entirely empirical because the relationship in question enabled alternative viewpoints about important and pressing policy issues to be formulated and investigated in an easily manageable way. With Δp the inflation rate, Δp^e the expected inflation rate, and y some measure, either direct or indirect, of the deviation of output from its 'full employment' level, and v a 'catchall' vector of other influences, systematic as well as random, the general form of the relationship may be written as follows:

$$\Delta p = gy + b\Delta p^e + v. \tag{1}$$

A whole spectrum of beliefs about the nature of inflation may be expressed in terms of this simple equation, depending upon the values assigned to its parameters. Thus, the extreme 'sociological' view of the determination of the price level, that was widely prevalent in Britain in the early 1970s, would predict that the parameters g and b were essentially equal to zero, implying that monetary policies, if they had any effect on money income, would influence real income alone.[12] The behaviour of prices, in this view, was determined by exogenous factors that would all go into the catchall vector v. At the other extreme, typical monetarists of the early 1970s would argue that g was positive, so that inflation would, relative to expectations, be low in a depressed economy, and high in an over-expanded one. They would also argue that the coefficient b on expected inflation would be equal to unity, and would supplement equation (1) with some formula for the formation of expectations, typically based on the error learning hypothesis, that ensured that, eventually, any constant actual inflation rate would come to be fully anticipated. For them, therefore, any trade-off between inflation and deviations of output from full employment was a temporary one which vanished in the long run. The typical 'American Keynesians' of the same vintage would agree with the monetarists about the parameter g, and about the reasonableness of assuming that expectations would eventually catch up with experience, but would assign a value of less than unity to the parameter b, thus ensuring that though the price in terms of inflation of increasing output was higher in the long run than in the short run, it did not, as the monetarists asserted, ever become infinitely high.[13] They might also argue that equation (1) omitted to mention explicitly many factors that in particular times and places might have an important influence on the inflation rate, and which it will suffice here to think of as being captured in v.

There is not space here to survey the extensive empirical literature that these issues generated, but its upshot may be summarised easily enough. The evidence that, other things equal, inflation varies with the level of aggregate demand is overwhelming. To the extent that differences of opinion here ever set monetarism apart from other points of view – and I think they probably did in Britain, though not in North America – then surely we have here another case of 'we are all monetarists now'.[14] There has also been a swing towards the typically monetarist belief that in the long run there is no economically significant inflation–output trade-off. The more rapid inflation of the 1970s and the more sophisticated methods of modelling expectations developed over the same period have provided empirical evidence of a type that we did not have in 1971 to support this belief. There is still substantial disagreement though on the question of how fast the economy converges on the long-run solution. Finally there is more of a consensus about the importance of the influence of 'other' factors on the inflation rate than there was. Monetarists are willing to agree that factors such as the activities of OPEC, unexpected real shocks, or sudden changes in the level of indirect taxes, can affect the behaviour of the price level 'temporarily' against the background of long-run trends determined by monetary factors; Keynesians, particularly American ones, in their turn are now willing to agree that the long-run trend of inflation may well be determined by monetary factors while continuing to stress the importance of special factors for the short run. However, as we shall now see, there is much less of a consensus about the theoretical basis of the Phillips curve than there is about its empirical properties.

As originally analysed by Lipsey, the Phillips curve dealt with the reaction of the money wage to the existence of a general condition of excess demand for labour in the economy, and therefore of the general price level to the excess demand for goods. Excess demand was conceived of, not as a purely *ex ante* notion such as we meet in theoretical analyses of Walrasian tâtonnement, but as a realised quantity such as appears in models of economies made up of markets characterised by sticky prices. In their original critiques of the Phillips curve, Friedman (1968) and Phelps (1967) both concentrated on the point that disequilibrium in the labour market might be expected to bring pressure to bear on real wages rather than on money wages *per se*, and that what would happen to the latter would therefore be critically influenced by what was thought to be happening to the general price level. Each of them, though Phelps more explicitly so than Friedman, treated unemployment as a quantity signal that conveyed to economic agents the desirability of varying prices, and hence seemed to be providing a crucial correction to what remained a fundamentally Keynesian approach to the analysis of wage and price stickiness.[15]

On the other hand, most of the contributors to the well-known Phelps (1969) volume started from a very different theoretical basis to provide an explanation of the interaction of output and prices, though the similarity of their conclusions to those stated by Phelps and Friedman at first distracted attention from what in retrospect was the much more important theoretical matter of different premises.[16] According to this alternative approach, which was anticipated by Irving Fisher (1911), the expectations-augmented Phillips curve is in fact an aggregate supply curve. Equation (1) is derived from

$$y = (1/g)(p - p^e) \tag{2}$$

combined with the following definition of the expected rate of inflation

$$\Delta p^e \equiv p^e - p_{-1} \tag{3}$$

Brunner and Meltzer were quick to adopt this interpretation of the expectations augmented Phillips curve. They had already developed a view of the transmission of monetary impulses in asset markets that stressed the role of relative prices as signalling devices, and found it easy enough to extend that line of reasoning to the markets for output and labour services as well (see Meltzer 1969).[17] By now there can be no doubt that this aggregate supply curve interpretation of inflation employment interaction is the dominant one among monetarists. However, not all monetarists have accepted it (see, for example, Cagan 1979), and as I shall now argue, it raises issues that go well beyond the traditional subject matter of the monetarist debate.

To say that the Phillips curve is an aggregate supply curve is to say that fluctuations in output and employment in response to price level variations represent the voluntary choices of individuals operating in markets which are continually clearing. Since voluntary choices made on the basis of erroneous expectations are by no means the same thing as choices that lead to the outcome which agents would have desired, this is not to deny that deviations of output and unemployment from the 'natural' levels they would attain if expectations were fulfilled represent a serious problem.[18] However, it is to locate the cause of unemployment, not in the failure of markets to bring together all willing buyers and sellers in *ex ante* mutually satisfactory trades, but rather in a failure of markets (and other social institutions as well perhaps) to convey sufficient information to enable the expectations upon which those trades are based to be formed accurately in an economy subjected to stochastic shocks.

If fluctuations in output and employment about their natural rates are the result of the failure of expectations to be realised, the manner in which expectations are formed must play a vital role in their analysis. That is why the 'rational expectations' hypothesis is a natural supplement to the aggregate supply curve interpretation of the Phillips curve. If agents suffer losses in utility as a result of making expectational errors, they have an incentive to use all available information in forming their expectations up to the point at which the marginal benefit from improving their accuracy equals the marginal cost of doing so. The rational expectations hypothesis does *not* say that every agent's expectations are always as accurate (i.e. have as small a variance) as they would be if agents were equipped with a 'true' econometric model of the economy in which they operate (though it is sometimes convenient to formulate it that way in analytic and empirical exercises), but it does say that their expectations will not be wrong *systematically* over time and to that extent will resemble those generated by such a 'true' model in being unbiased and serially uncorrelated. Agents who form expectations in a manner that leads to systematic error will find themselves persistently making the wrong choices; hence in the very course of their market activities, they will be provided *gratis* with the information necessary to eliminate that systematic error.

If each individual makes only random errors in forming expectations, two questions naturally arise: how does it happen that at a particular moment the expectations of a predominant number of agents in the economy should be in error in one particular direction so that aggregate output and employment come to deviate from their 'natural rates', and how does it happen that the fluctuations in output and employment which are observed in any actual economy come to display that pattern of serial correlation summarised in the term 'business cycle'? The answer to the first question given by Lucas (1972) is by now well known. If individuals have more up-to-date information about the money prices that rule in the markets in which they operate as sellers than about others, then in order to assess the pattern of relative prices upon which their quantity decisions rest, they must form expectations about the behaviour of other money prices. An unforeseen shock affecting the whole economy which leads to a change in the general price level will influence individual money prices, and will have its consequences everywhere misread as reflecting relative price changes. Hence quantities supplied will everywhere change.

If that was all there was to it, output and employment fluctuations would be random over time. However, if there are time delays in getting information to agents, if there are costs of adjusting output decisions once taken, or if some of the goods over-produced in error in the face of a positive unexpected shock to the price level are durable, then the effects of that shock will persist over time.[19] By the time its effects on output have petered out there will be too many durable goods in the economy – capital will be 'too deep' – and the marginal productivity of labour in terms of consumption in industries producing durable goods will fall. If workers prefer to take extra leisure when their marginal productivity is low, and if the price system operates so as to inform them of when that is the case, there will be a voluntary fall in the level of employment that will persist until the structure of the economy's capital stock is restored. The objection to this explanation of the cycle, that it predicts more wage variability than we observe in the real world, can be countered by arguments to the effect that firms and households find it mutually beneficial to enter into wage contracts under which wages do not instantaneously fluctuate in tune with the marginal productivity of labour, but under which firms are permitted to lay off workers in such a way that the latter still take more leisure at times when their marginal productivity is unusually low, even though the behaviour of wages no longer signals the fact.

Readers will find the last paragraph reminiscent of the Austrian business cycle theory of the 1920s and 1930s, and that is no accident. It is the Austrians, and not, as Solow (1980) has suggested, Pigou, who are the predecessors of Lucas, Sargent and their associates. Like Ludwig von Mises and Friedrich von Hayek, they have set themselves the task of producing a theory of the business cycle that is firmly based on the notion that all market phenomena represent the harmonious outcome of the voluntary choices of maximising individuals. However these neo-Austrians have gone beyond their predecessors to produce a theory in which output and employment as well as prices fluctuate as a result of such voluntary choices. Whatever we may think of the empirical relevance of that theory, and its proponents show an admirable, and un-Austrian, willingness to submit their ideas to empirical tests,[20] we must surely agree that its very construction represents an intellectual achievement of the highest order.

One can admire a theory without agreeing with it, and there are many including myself who would challenge the basic assumption upon which the analysis just discussed is based, namely that it is legitimate to model the economy 'as if' markets always clear. It is one thing to agree that commodity and asset markets dominated by specialist traders ought, and indeed do, display the characteristics associated with continuous clearing and rational expectations, and quite another to attribute similar character-istics to the markets for many components of final output, and above all to the labour market. One may follow Hicks (1974) in distinguish-ing between 'flexprice' and 'fixprice' markets, assign the labour market to the latter category, and argue that the interaction of inflation and unem-ployment is best analysed on the premise that the Phillips curve represents the disequilibrium response of prices to a mismatching of supply and demand.

Of course the 'neo-Austrians' are well aware that there is no Walrasian auctioneer to set prices, and no recontracting to ensure that trade takes place only at market clearing prices; but they do assert that individual agents – or their representatives – are acute enough in their bargaining to ensure that money wages and prices universally behave 'as if' markets operated along such Walrasian lines, that they perceive the possibility of realising mutual gains by adjusting wages downward when excess supply turns up in the market in which they are operating, and act upon that perception.[21] However one can have no difficulty accepting the proposition that, even in labour markets, if it is mutually beneficial to lower money wages (or their rate of change), agents will discover this and will agree to do so, but still find it hard to understand how the relevant information is conveyed to the agents in question without the intervention of quantity signals. In a Walrasian market, the auctioneer can discover that the price is too high by adding up notional supplies and finding out that they exceed notional demands, to use Robert Clower's (1965) terms, but how can participants in any actual labour market find out that money wages there are too high without some of them discovering first that they are unable to sell all the services that they would like at the going rate?

If adjustments in the level (or rate of change) of money wages and prices to aggregate demand shocks are anything other than instantaneous, then markets fail to clear, trade takes place at false prices, and quantity signals, perhaps amplified by multiplier effects, become an integral part of the mechanism whereby monetary changes are transmitted to the behaviour of the price level. This line of analysis is as 'Keynesian' in spirit as the clearing market approach is 'Austrian', and its existence permits one to subscribe to the expectations-augmented Phillips curve without also being committed to a clearing market rational expectations approach to the analysis of economic fluctuations. Moreover, the approach in question does *not* differ from the clearing market view in denying that individuals perceive and then engage in all available mutually beneficial trades. It simply denies that they do so infinitely rapidly. I do not see why, as for example Barro (1979) has suggested, to postulate an infinite speed of price adjustment in the face of excess demand or supply is to conform to sound microeconomic principles, and to postulate anything significantly slower is to propose an '*ad hoc* non-theory'.

The non-clearing market approach to analysing inflation employment interaction is not obviously incompatible with the notion of rational expectations. If output fluctuations convey information about the appropriate behaviour concerning price setting as this approach suggests, they can be regarded as constituting one of the ingredients of the expectations upon which such behaviour is based. In that case the term Δp^e in equation (1) can be thought of as summarising influences upon expectations *other than quantity signals*.[22] To say this begs the question of what those 'other influences' on expectations might be, but leaves open the possibility that the same type of information to which the rational expectations hypothesis draws our attention could be incorporated without difficulty into models based on the non-clearing market approach. Observations on the past behaviour of the money supply, for example, might well provide agents with information about the appropriate way to set prices, and might be included among those 'other' influences, as might, in an open economy, variations in prices ruling elsewhere in the world economy, variations in exchange rates, and so on.[23]

The non clearing-market interpretation of the Phillips curve needs to be reconciled with the basic facts of the business cycle. Once given, why do output signals not result in an immediate adjustment of prices to a market clearing level? The answer here is straightforward – a quantity signal will lead to a response in price behaviour only to the extent that agents believe that the shock which gave rise to it will persist into the future. Inability to disentangle short-term from persistent shocks will lead to a tendency to underreact to quantity signals, and hence to cause them to be drawn out over time. I would conjecture that the Austrian-style arguments about the role of errors made with respect to the production of durable goods in the business cycle can be superimposed upon this fundamentally Keynesian explanation of the persistence of output fluctuations should anyone wish to do so.[24]

Although theoretical analysis of the interaction of output, employment and prices in terms of an expectations-augmented Phillips curve can thus proceed along two very different lines, it is a mistake to treat debate about these issues as simply the latest round in the monetarist controversy. Though monetarists and Keynesians are in much closer agreement than they were about the empirical stability of the demand for money function, and about the empirical nature of output–inflation interaction, they still take the same diametrically opposed views on the proper conduct of macro-economic policy that they did in the mid-1950s, and divisions of opinion here do not, as I shall argue below, depend upon differences of views about the theoretical basis of price–output interaction. Since the policy debate is undoubtedly a continuation of the monetarist controversy, and since disputes about the theoretical basis of the Phillips curve clearly deal with a new set of issues, it seems to me to be misleading to treat what I have here termed the neo-Austrian view as synonymous with monetarism, as for example Frank Hahn (1980) does. I shall discuss the policy aspects of the monetarist controversy in Section 4, but before I do so, it will be convenient to discuss the place of the monetary approach to balance of payments and exchange rate theory in monetarist doctrine.

III THE MONETARY APPROACH TO BALANCE OF PAYMENTS AND EXCHANGE RATE ANALYSIS

The monetary approach to balance of payments and exchange rate analysis represents in some respects a revival of the English classical approach to these problem areas. However, the monetary approach differs in important ways from classical analysis, and the very characteristics that thus distinguish it are borrowed from closed economy monetarism.[25] Most important, advocates of the monetary approach postulate the existence of a stable demand for money function, not just as a working simplification, but as an empirical hypothesis; it is this hypothesis that transforms the approach from an accounting framework into a body of substantive theory. Furthermore, in early statements of the doctrine, its proponents tied down the real income argument of that function by assuming full employment but they soon learned how to replace this assumption with an expectations-augmented Phillips curve approach to price-output interaction.[26] In effect the monetary approach to balance of payments and exchange rate analysis provided the means whereby these characteristically monetarist hypotheses were made relevant to economies other than the United States which, under the Bretton Woods system, was about as close an approximation to a closed economy that was also a separate political entity as the world has ever seen.

Monetarism thus came to be important only outside the United States, not least in Britain, in alliance with the monetary approach to balance of payments and exchange rate analysis.

Until 1971 the world was on a system of fixed exchange rates against the United States dollar. Under such a system the existence of a stable demand for money function, whose arguments are beyond the direct control of the domestic authorities, implies that the money supply is an endogenous variable that must adjust to demand. Given this insight, evidence that suggests, for example in the United Kingdom in the 1950s and 1960s, that causation seems to have run predominantly from money income to money, rather than vice versa, is no embarrassment to monetarists provided that they are also willing to attribute most of the variation in money income to causative factors originating abroad. Moreover, although the expectations-augmented Phillips curve tells us that in general we should expect to find no stable inverse trade-off between inflation and unemployment, post-war United Kingdom data do display just such a well determined relationship down to 1967, and this fact needs explaining. The monetary approach to balance of payments analysis suggests two complementary reasons why this should be the case. First it notes that, so long as a fixed exchange rate is to be maintained, the prices of tradable goods sold domestically are going to be determined in the long run, not domestically, but on world markets, and from this it follows that the domestic price level's long-run behaviour is going to be constrained by the behaviour of prices in the world at large. Economic agents do not have to be more than merely sensible to perceive this fact and to incorporate it into their expectations. If world prices are relatively stable, and they were until the late 1960s, then so are inflation expectations, and our expectations-augmented Phillips curve, equation (1), no matter how we interpret its microeconomic origins, will predict that the data will generate a stable inflation–unemployment trade-off.

This explanation of the existence of a stable inflation–unemployment trade-off in post-war Britain is an important component of what may fairly be called monetarist hypotheses, about the nature of the stop-go cycle in the 1950s and 1960s and about the degeneration of that economy's performance in the 1970s, which contrast strongly with conventional 'Keynesian' accounts of the same phenomena. The latter begin from the proposition that Britain has a peculiarly high marginal propensity to import, so that, under the Bretton Woods system, attempts to run the economy at a high degree of capacity utilisation, though they produced only a small and on the whole acceptable amount of inflation, were frustrated by balance of payments pressure which forced a reversal of policy. The monetarist hypothesis about stop-go, on the other hand, has it that high levels of demand were associated with high rates of domestic credit expansion which, under fixed exchange rates, generated balance of payments problems in large measure as an *alternative* to domestic inflationary pressure. The conventional view seemed to imply that Britain's economic performance could be improved by adopting exchange rate flexibility and allowing a depreciating currency to offset the balance of payments effects of a high propensity to import. With a flexible exchange rate, the economy could be run at a higher level of capacity utilisation and could grow more rapidly without interference from a balance of payments 'constraint'. According to this view a series of exogenous shocks and the autonomous activities of trade unions undermined a basically well-founded strategy when it was adopted in the 1970s. The monetarist view, on the other hand, argues that the adoption of exchange rate flexibility replaced a balance of payments problem with a domestic inflation problem when expansionary policies were pursued, and did nothing to influence the economy's ability to sustain either a higher level or rate of growth of real income. For the monetarist, therefore, the deterioration of British economic performance after 1972 was the predictable (and predicted) consequence of a policy of expanding aggregate demand against a background of exchange rate flexibility.[27]

Now the monetary approach to balance of payments analysis does far more than make monetarist analysis relevant to Britain. It also permits the explanation of the international spread of inflation in the late 1960s in terms of the repercussions in the world economy of United States monetary expansion, and it treats the breakdown of the Bretton Woods system as the culmination of this process. However, it is only fair to note that such analysis performs less well in the face of the behaviour displayed by the international monetary system since exchange rates began to float in the early 1970s. The prediction that the behaviour of exchange rates can be analysed fruitfully as if determined in efficient asset markets does seem to be supported by the data. However, a basic postulate of the monetary approach is that the equilibrium value of the exchange rate between any two currencies reflects purchasing power parity. Just as data generated under fixed rates show that the price levels of particular economies can display considerable autonomy for substantial periods of time, so under flexible exchange rates systematic and persistent deviations of exchange rates from purchasing power parity do seem to be possible. Though purchasing power parity considerations underlie the behaviour of long period averages of data, implying that, ultimately the terms of trade between countries are independent of monetary factors, there seems to be ample room for short-run deviations from the long-run pattern. Just why this should be the case, and what explains the patterns of such deviations as we observe, are important and, at the moment, open questions.[28]

Be all that as it may, the present regime of flexible exchange rates came into being because the authorities in various countries learned that they could not control such politically important variables as domestic inflation and unemployment while continuing to adhere to the Bretton Woods arrangements. The diversity of inflation rates among countries since 1971 supports the view that the adoption of flexible rates allows such variables to have their behaviour predominantly determined at home; and long before the 1970s, monetarists, not least of course Friedman, argued that the adoption of exchange rate flexibility was a necessary prerequisite to the pursuit of monetarist policies in individual countries. In the 1970s we have seen the emergence of conditions under which individual countries could implement independent monetary policies, and as I have suggested above, it is mainly on the matter of policy prescriptions that sharp differences between monetarists and their opponents persist. I shall therefore devote the penultimate section of this chapter to a discussion of these matters.

IV POLICY ISSUES

As we have seen, when it comes to propositions about the demand for money function, the relationship between money and money income, and output inflation interaction, there is a real sense in which 'we are all monetarists now'. The issues that nowadays distinguish monetarists from their opponents concern the conduct of economic policy. As he did in the 1950s the monetarist still wants fiscal policy to stick mainly to its traditional tasks of influencing resource allocation and the distribution of income and wealth, and monetary policy to adhere to some simple rule under which the monetary aggregates do not react to short-run fluctuations either in real output or prices; the Keynesian on the other hand is still a proponent of activist stabilisation policy.

These policy issues are not independent of the theoretical questions that we have discussed earlier, and indeed, much of the current popularity among monetarists of the neo-Austrian approach to the analysis of price–output interaction stems from the erroneous belief that it provides the only sound basis for scepticism about the effectiveness of activist stabilisation policies. Many Keynesians focus their attacks on that same piece of analysis in the belief, just as erroneous, that if they succeed in refuting it, they also succeed in restoring the case for activist stabilisation policy. Now the approach in question does indeed imply that output and employment can be influenced by policy only to the extent that it causes prices to vary in a way that agents in the private sector do not foresee, while the rational expectations hypothesis tells us that if such effects were systematic, the private sector would discover the fact, adapt to it, and thereby render policy ineffective. It follows at once that the only macroeconomic policy that can influence income and employment is a purely random one, and no supporter of 'fine tuning' could possibly recommend that.

The argument just sketched out is logically watertight. So is this counter-argument: if inflation–output interaction reflects the role of quantity signals in the mechanism whereby various shocks, including those imparted by policy, have their effects transmitted to prices, the way is opened for monetary and fiscal policy to exert a systematic influence upon output and employment. However, there is much more than this to be said about the feasibility and desirability of activist policies. If there was not, how could it be that Friedman (1960) was able systematically to state his views on policy more than a decade before Lucas (1976) and Sargent and Neil Wallace (1975) developed the theoretical arguments that are now so widely regarded as the only logical underpinning of those views? The Lucas–Sargent–Wallace analysis certainly provides a *sufficient* basis for monetarist policy prescriptions, but it is not a *necessary* basis for them: it is one thing to say that the world is so structured that policy can systematically influence output and employment in the short run, and another thing altogether to say that policy makers have enough knowledge to use that ability in a way that will be beneficial.

If it is agreed that in the long run the Phillips curve is essentially vertical – or perhaps even positively sloped if allowance is made for super-non-neutralities – then that certainly does not rule out the possibility of the economy slipping below its natural rate of output in a short run that may be of considerable duration, or the possibility that there exists an appropriate menu of monetary and fiscal policies that might hasten its return to that natural rate without generating any serious costs during the transition. As a first step to exploiting this possibility though, those in charge of policy would need to know what the natural rates of output and employment actually are. As a second step, they would need accurate information upon where the economy actually is, and where it would move in the absence of a policy change, not to mention at what pace. Armed with this not inconsiderable amount of information, policy makers would know that they were in a position where it might be useful to deploy some policy measure or other. To design the policy would of course require them to know about the size and time path of the economy's response to the measures they might take, factors which even the loosest application of the rational expectations idea tells us are likely to be influenced by the policy measures themselves.

Now I will readily agree that we have the mathematical and statistical tools available for tackling the design of stabilisation policy along the foregoing lines, and I also agree that our econometric models contain answers to all the quantitative questions that I have just raised. However the conclusion that I draw from all this is that we are probably rather good at fine tuning econometric models.[29] One can rest the monetarist case against activist policy on the proposition that markets always clear and that expectations are rational, but one can also rest it on the much more down-to-earth proposition that we are too ignorant of the structure of the economies we live in and of the manner in which that structure is changing to be able safely to implement activist stabilisation policy in the present environment, or in the foreseeable future.

Among the penalties for making errors in fine tuning that concern monetarists are those that come in the form of uncomfortably high and perhaps accelerating inflation that would result from setting over-optimistic targets for employment and output. Thus, if there is something in the policy environment that weakens the ability of the inflation rate to accelerate, the penalties for such errors are milder, and the case against fine tuning developed above can be softened a little. In the 1950s and 1960s, there can be little doubt that the British authorities did succeed in fine tuning income and employment variables within the rather narrow bounds laid down by what then appeared to be balance of payments constraints. The monetarist interpretation of that period implies that the background of monetary stability implicit in the commitment to a fixed exchange rate was the real constraint on how far fine-tuning policy could be pushed and also that it provided the necessary conditions for its limited success. However the fact remains that the experience in question does show that a limited degree of fine tuning is feasible if only a background of long-run price stability is assured, and is seen to be assured.

It is hard for a monetarist to see how one could avoid assigning to monetary policy the role of providing that necessary assurance.[30] A fixed exchange rate regime is one way of tying down monetary policy, and the adoption of some sort of a money supply growth rule would be an alternative. But this means that fine tuning would have to be by fiscal policy. Such a conclusion will be of little consolation to American Keynesians who are forced by the inability of American institutions to deliver rapid changes reliably in fiscal variables to assign to monetary variables a far more important role in stabilisation policy than their British counterparts ever did. However it may do a little to cheer up the British, for whom a return to the days of 'never had it so good' might be a welcome relief from the consequences of 'going for growth'.

As should be apparent from the last few paragraphs, I regard the question of whether governments should or should not indulge in a limited amount of fiscal fine tuning as a secondary issue for monetarists.[31] Related questions concerning public sector borrowing and the share of the public sector in National Income are even more peripheral to the monetarist debate. No matter what the public perception of these matters might be, I insist that monetarist doctrine tells one that there are severe limits to the extent to which public sector borrowing can be financed by money creation, and beyond that has nothing to say about whether a 'high' or 'low' level of such borrowing is in and of itself desirable. Similarly monetarism offers no guidance as to how big the public sector of any economy ought to be. It is a macroeconomic doctrine and the issues at stake in debates about the size of the public sector, the welfare state, and so on are fundamentally microeconomic in nature.

Monetarism however has had a good deal to say about wage and price control policies. It has opposed them, not just for ideological reasons, but for the much more down to earth reason that they have not been expected to work.[32] This position has been mainly and justifiably defended on the basis of empirical evidence: in the post-Korean war period it is hard indeed to find any wage-price control scheme that has not produced disappointing results over any period longer than a few months. However monetarists have also sometimes opposed controls on theoretical grounds, particularly in the context of open economies. They have noted that under fixed exchange rates the behaviour of world prices and hence the domestic prices of traded goods cannot be controlled by domestic regulations, any more than can the money supply. They have also pointed out that under flexible rates, though the money supply is under control, neither the exchange rate nor world prices can be regulated separately. In either case in an open economy wage and price controls inevitably impinge upon 'the domestic component' of the price level and are hence policies towards relative prices. For that reason, they cannot for long influence the behaviour of the general price level, unless they are accompanied by a battery of quantitative restrictions, not least on foreign trade, that very few of their advocates have been willing to contemplate.

In the 1960s wage and price controls came to be regarded as an alternative to monetary policy in the control of inflation, and in the early 1970s serious attempts were made in both Britain and the United States to use them as such. In both cases the attempts failed sufficiently dramatically that the proponents of controls now regard them at best as supplementary devices to be deployed in harmony with more traditional demand side policies rather than as a serious alternative to such measures. Though such a viewpoint stops short of the blanket opposition to controls that, along with other monetarists, I would still be willing to defend, it does represent a substantial move in a monetarist direction from positions taken in the early 1970s. Here, as in other instances, much of the heat has gone out of the monetarist controversy.[33]

There is more to practical monetarism than scepticism about fiscal fine tuning and opposition to wage and price controls. Its key positive tenet is that monetary weapons should be assigned to the attainment and maintenance of long-run price stability, and hence that those same monetary weapons not be used for fine-tuning purposes. In this respect, as with the other components of the doctrine which we considered earlier, there has been a considerable growth in the acceptance of monetarism. Propositions about the desirability of setting rules and targets for the growth of monetary aggregates are now commonplace in the statements of central banks. If monetarists complain – and they do – about the failure of Keynesian policies since the mid-1960s, then simple fairness requires them to say something about the lessons that they have learned about the viability of their own policy proposals from what many observers believe to have been widespread and sustained efforts to apply them during the 1970s.

The first thing to be said on this score is that the case for monetary growth-rate rules, as initially stated by Friedman (and Edward Shaw) was put in terms of the capacity of such a policy to *maintain* stability in an already stable economy – it was a policy prescription for *staying out* of trouble. However, it has been only since our economies have found themselves deeply *in trouble* that monetarist policy proposals have attracted the attention of policy makers. There is much less unanimity among monetarists about how to tackle the problem of restoring stability than there is about how to maintain it. Though all monetarists would agree that a return to a modest growth rate of some monetary aggregate or other is the long-run goal, the neo-Austrians would favour a rapid return to such a rule, while those of us who take a more traditional view of the nature of the Phillips trade-off have advocated 'gradualism'.

Unless we take the cynical view that the rhetoric of central bankers bears no relationship to their intentions, we must conclude that in a number of places attempts have been made to implement gradualist policies. There are two questions to be asked about those attempts: first, is it the case that those attempts have resulted in a systematic and gradual reduction in the rate of growth of any monetary aggregate? Second, if such attempts have anywhere been successful, did that success lead to a reduction in the inflation rate? As is well known, policy has in the main failed on the first count. Only in Canada, to the best of my knowledge, have the authorities set, and on the whole succeeded in achieving, pre-stated monetary growth targets over an extended period. It is equally well known that the single most important reason for this failure, at least in the United States and Britain, has been the unwillingness of those in charge of monetary policy to give up setting interest rate targets when they adopted targets for the money supply, combined with a proclivity to stick with the interest rate target when the two came into conflict, as they inevitably had to sooner or later. This has not been universally the case, however. Germany and Switzerland have had difficulty sticking to money supply targets because of concern with the behaviour of the exchange rates rather than interest rates, as Sumner (1980) has noted, while political concern over the exchange rate and interest rates during the winter of 1979–80 posed a serious threat to the continuation of the Canadian experiment.

It would be easy enough to argue in the light of all this that recent experience offers essentially no test of monetarist gradualism, but that seems to be going too far. Monetarists have usually treated questions of income distribution and resource allocation as separate and distinct from those of monetary policy. This dichotomy is a useful one when the problem for monetary policy is to *maintain* already existing stability, but can all too easily lead one to neglect the way in which monetary policy interacts with allocation and distribution when its implementation requires sharp (albeit temporary) increases in interest rates. A key factor here is of course the political importance of the housing market, and of the behaviour of mortgage interest rates. In retrospect, it is clear that monetarists did not do a very good job of educating policy makers – both elected and otherwise – about the problems that adopting monetarist policies would generate in this area. Some of us did raise these matters, but apparently not loudly enough.[34] High interest rates have turned out to be more difficult for politicians to face up to than high unemployment rates, and that was not foreseen.

There are also technical problems with implementing monetarist policies. The manipulation of interest rates as the centrepiece of monetary policy long antedates the Keynesian revolution, and was quite appropriate in economies whose monetary rule was to maintain convertibility into gold or some other currency at a fixed price. However the day-to-day operating procedures of central banks, the very organisation of their decision-making processes, not to mention the structure of the private markets in which they operate are all geared by force of tradition to making and implementing decisions about interest rates. Although monetarists have done a great deal of work on the basic economics of the money supply process under different policy regimes, and though some of them, notably Brunner and Meltzer, have frequently scolded their colleagues for neglect of these issues, hindsight suggests that they did not recognise the extent to which the problem of implementing a different monetary policy might require a basic overhaul of institutions if it was to be solved, an overhaul that might involve a considerable break with traditional practices, and hence be hard to implement, or that, if they did, they were unable to convince policy makers to undertake that overhaul at the same time as they adopted monetarist rhetoric.

If central banks, apart from the Bank of Canada, have not in fact succeeded in smoothly slowing down monetary expansion rates in a sustained way, a number of them have nevertheless managed to create contractions in monetary growth rates that have been sharp and persistent enough to bite. Associated with these contractions have been the 'shifts' of the demand for money function that I discussed earlier in this chapter. As the reader will recall, I argued that these shifts were, in all probability, real phenomena, and not statistical artefacts, that such shifts were nothing new, and that they were probably to be explained, at least in part, by institutional changes which themselves might plausibly be interpreted as a response to monetary policy. I believe that these shifts of the demand for money function, relatively small though they have been, force us to reassess a fundamental tenet of practical monetarism, namely the injunction to fix *ex ante* a growth rate rule for the money supply, and then ensure adherence to it by taking away from the monetary authorities the discretion to do otherwise.

Objections to such a proposal have frequently been cast in terms of the question 'How are you going to define the money supply for purposes of implementing this policy?' The answer typically given has been that it does not much matter, because if the rate of growth of one monetary aggregate is pinned down, all the others will end up behaving consistently, at least on average over the kind of time periods for which stability in monetary policy is really important. That answer is surely valid if one is dealing with an economy in which there is no institutional change in the private sector, but that does not make it as adequate a response to the question as I once thought it did. Suppose we agreed to set a rule for the growth rate of M1 and that initially we could agree on what assets to include in that aggregate.

What if after the rule had been implemented some new asset, for example a new kind of chequing account, evolved? Perhaps the demand function for M1 as initially defined would then shift, but if *ex post* we included the new asset in our definition of M1 we might still be able to show that the demand for narrow money had not 'really' shifted, after all.

Such problems would not arise if we were not too specific in laying down the precise definition of money that was to bind policy makers in the future. However, to do that would leave it open to the discretion of someone at some time in the future to decide just how to define the monetary aggregate whose rate of growth was tied down with a rule, and that amounts to giving them the discretion to ignore the rule in question. It is hard to resist the implication that it does not seem to be possible, let alone desirable, to eliminate all scope for discretionary policy in a world in which the monetary system is in a state of evolution. I hasten to add that this does not imply that attempts to implement short-run fine tuning of the economy by way of manipulating interest rates are all of a sudden alright, or that it is fruitless to require central banks to announce target ranges for monetary expansion over, say, one or two year time horizons. However it does imply that it is as a practical matter impossible to prevent policy makers doing the wrong things if they so wish by tying them down to a monetary growth-rate rule. Unless we can accurately foresee the path that innovations in the financial sector are going to take, someone somewhere is going to have to be granted the discretion to deal with them when they arise. The monetarist injunction not to use monetary policy for fine tuning is not affected by these considerations, but the proposal that the once and for all enactment of a simple rule can lead to that injunction being implemented is undermined. That seems to me to be a rather severe criticism of monetarist policy doctrine.

V CONCLUDING COMMENTS

As the reader will by now have seen, it is my view that the core of monetarism has consisted of a series of empirical propositions and policy prescriptions, all of which are quite consistent with mainstream economic theory. One can approach the analysis of social questions in terms of the maximising behaviour of individual agents without believing in a stable demand for money function, or a vertical long-run Phillips curve, but evidence that such relationships exist need in no way disturb one's theoretical preconceptions. Although there have been episodes in the monetarist debate where the relevance of mainstream economics to the analysis of such social questions as inflation and unemployment has been vigorously questioned, particularly in Britain, it has mainly been about questions amenable to being settled with reference to empirical evidence, as Mayer (1978) has also argued.

Viewed in this light, I would suggest that, in all but one aspect, the monetarist debate is as close to being over as an economic controversy ever is. The demand for money function does seem to be more stable over time than the early critics of monetarism suggested, while shifts in it have been neither new phenomena, nor of sufficient magnitude seriously to undermine long-run relationships between money and money income. Puzzles about 'reverse causation' in the data for countries such as Britain cease to be puzzles when the openness of the economy and the nature of the exchange-rate regime are taken account of. There is now much less disagreement about the empirical nature of the interaction of real income and inflation: there is a short-run trade-off between inflation and unemployment and it does seem to vanish in the long run. Though we should not underrate the importance of the consensus that has been achieved on the foregoing issues – or neglect to mention explicitly that the consensus in question is not universal – this does not mean that there is now no controversy in macroeconomics. As we have seen two areas remain contentious.

First, one aspect of the monetarist debate remains alive, and that concerns the proper conduct of monetary policy. I doubt that my own view, that the case for governing monetary policy by rules is impossible to sustain in the face of careful consideration of the influence of institutional change on the behaviour over time of the demand for money function, will find a great deal of support among monetarists at present, while I would be surprised to find it regarded as sufficient of a concession to 'fine tuning', and it really is no such thing, to satisfy the Keynesians. Thus, I would expect debates about this matter to keep the monetarist controversy alive for a while yet.

The other, and in my view far more important, issue has to do with the market-theoretic foundations of macroeconomics. The issues raised by Lucas and his collaborators are not the issues that have traditionally concerned participants in the monetarist debate and it is misleading to approach them as if they were. The debate about the assumptions of clearing markets and rational expectations as a basis for macroeconomics is a new one, and as Brian Kantor (1979) has suggested is really about whether Keynes' *General Theory* carried economics forward or took it on a fruitless detour. Though it has very little to do with monetarism, it nevertheless concerns issues of fundamental theoretical importance for macroeconomics. Let us hope that this new controversy proves to be as fruitful as the monetarist controversy has been.

ACKNOWLEDGEMENTS

I have benefited greatly from the extensive comments of John Foster, Milton Friedman, John Helliwell, Geoffrey Kingston, Clark Leith, Thomas Mayer, Ronald Shearer and George Zis, none of whom is to be held responsible for the views that I espouse. The financial support of the Social Science and Humanities Research Council of Canada is gratefully acknowledged.

NOTES

1 See, for example, James Boughton (1977), Karl Brunner (1970), Nicholas Kaldor (1970), Harry Johnson (1972), Thomas Mayer (1978), Franco Modigliani (1977), Douglas Purvis (1980). This list is far from exhaustive.

2 This is the judgement of Johnson (1962) and Brunner (1970), among others.

3 Consider, for example, the London Business School model of the UK economy (see Jim Ball and Terry Burns 1976). The Canadian RDX2 model also seems to me to fall into this category.

4 See, for example, Friedman and Schwartz (1963a) and Philip Cagan (1979). Note that such monetarists as Brunner and Meltzer, however, do not use National Bureau techniques. They are mainly associated with the Chicago branch of monetarism.

5 The Radcliffe Report (1959) is based on the proposition that the demand for money function is essentially nonexistent as a stable relationship. For a later statement of the same point of view see Kaldor (1970) or Joan Robinson (1970).

6 Note in particular that the Keynesian James Tobin was the author of a pioneering econometric study of the demand for money function (see Tobin 1947). See also his review of Friedman and Schwartz (1963a), where further econometric estimates of the demand for money function are presented (Tobin 1965).

7 I have dealt with the matters taken up here in much greater length in Laidler (1980).

8 But as with all such blanket judgements as this there are important exceptions. Irving Fisher's empirical work on the relationship between money and prices presented in *The Purchasing Power of Money* (1911) is not so far removed from modern monetarism.

9 But this of course is not to say that Friedman has always paid as much attention to the interest elasticity of the demand for money as his critics might have wished. See for example the various reviews of the monetary history of the United States, but note that the monetarist Allan Meltzer (1965) was as critical on this score as any other reviewer. What we are here dealing with is a characteristic of some of the work of one, albeit the most important, monetarist rather than of monetarism in general.

10 Mayer (1978) argues, correctly I believe, that Patinkin should not be regarded as a monetarist. This of course is not to deny the important influence that Patinkin's work had on subsequent monetary analysis. See, for example, Jonson (1976b).

11 There seems to have been a systematic shift in British opinion from the Radcliffe view that money does not matter at all, to the view that money matters for real income but not for prices. To trace this development is beyond the scope of this paper. However, the work of Richard Kahn shows clearly that it has taken place. Compare his evidence to the Radcliffe Committee with, for example, Kahn (1976).

12 See Peter Wiles (1973) for a particularly extreme version of the sociological approach to inflation.

13 I have in mind here, in particular, the work of Robert Solow (1968) and James Tobin (1972).

14 See Anthony Santomero and John Seater (1978) for a well-balanced survey of the evidence on these matters.

15 Notice that in some of his subsequent writings on inflation-unemployment interaction Friedman adopts an aggregate supply curve interpretation of the Phillips curve (see, for example, Friedman 1975).

16 See the papers by Armen Alchian, Robert E. Lucas and Leonard Rapping, Donald Gordon and Alan Hynes, and Dale Mortensen, all in the Phelps (1969) volume.

17 In later work carried out by Brunner and Meltzer and their associates, a version appears of the aggregate supply curve in which the rate of change of output rather than the level of output affects the rate of inflation. This form of the relationship appears to stem from their tendency to treat the expected inflation rate as synonymous with the rate of change of the expected price level. See Brunner and Meltzer (1978) and particularly the comments there by Bennett McCallum.

18 Thus, though I agree with much of what Willem Buiter (1980) has to say about this theory of employment, I cannot accept his characterisation of it as 'The Macroeconomics of Dr. Pangloss'. It might be noted that in the aggregate supply curve interpretation of the Phillips curve, the natural unemployment rate becomes a long-run equilibrium concept. In the price reaction function interpretation of the relationship it seems to me to be synonymous with the Keynesian concept of the minimum feasible unemployment rate. For a perceptive discussion of some of the issues involved here see Thomas Wilson (1976).

19 I base the following arguments on the papers of Lucas (1975), Thomas Sargent (1976) and Lucas (1977). The first two of these papers are extremely technical and I am by no means sure that I am doing justice to them in the discussion that follows. Milton Friedman has pointed out to me that one can say that errors are random or systematic only if one is also specific about both the *time at* which expectations are formed, and the *period for* which they are formed. If one is now planning for, say a five-year horizon, then the rational expectations hypothesis permits the actual value of any variable to deviate systematically from its *ex ante* expected value over any interval of less than five years. This matter is clearly related to questions raised by adjustment lags, the durability of certain goods, and so on, since the horizon over which a decision taken now is likely to be binding is also presumably the horizon over which a rational agent would seek to form expectations about relevant variables. To the best of my knowledge, the published literature has not recognised this point explicitly, and it deserves much more attention than I have space to give it here.

20 To comment on the empirical work in question, notably that of Robert J. Barro (1978), would take us beyond the scope of this chapter.

21 Robert J. Barro (1979) presents a particularly forceful and clearcut statement of what I am calling the 'neo-Austrian' view on these matters. Robert Solow (1979) might be regarded as providing a traditional Keynesian rebuttal of this line of argument. Note that questions of the relevant time horizon, raised in note 19, are again relevant here.

22 Alternatively, as Michael Wickens has suggested to me, we may think of Δp^e as being a rational expectation of inflation conditional upon information available at an earlier time than that at which the quantity signal is received.

23 I base the foregoing discussion on conversations and correspondence that I have had with Marcus Miller and Peter Jonson on various occasions. See also Clements and Jonson (1979).

24 A more extensive account of these matters is given in Laidler (1975: ch. I). Note that Brunner, Alex Cuckeirman and Meltzer (1979) provide an analysis of persistent shocks within an aggregate supply curve framework. Note also that Peter Howitt (1979) argues that, once explicit attention is paid to the role of inventories in the price setting process, the contrast between clearing-market and non-clearing-market approaches to economic modelling becomes blurred, and to some extent semantic rather than substantive in nature.

25 The locus classicus for pioneering work on the monetary approach to balance of payments analysis is, of course, Frenkel and Johnson (1976).

26 See, for example, Laidler (1975: ch. 9) and Jonson (1976 *a*).

27   It is worth pointing out that I set out much of the foregoing argument in my 1972 Lister Lecture. See Laidler (1975: ch. 10), where the lecture is reprinted. The argument is developed in further detail in Laidler (1976 *a*).

28   Frenkel (1980) provides a useful and accessible overview of the issues involved here and the evidence on them.

29   John Helliwell has suggested to me that the application of policy optimisation techniques to such models is better regarded as a test of their validity than as a preliminary to actual policy making.

30   It is worth noting that the Radcliffe Committee (1959) regarded the task of monetary policy to be the achievement of background stability for the economy. Their view differed from the monetarist approach to the same issue in putting interest rates at the centre of the policy making process rather than any monetary aggregate. In the kind of sociological theorising about inflation that was particularly popular in Britain in the early 1970s incomes policy was to be assigned the task of stabilising prices and expectations.

31   I would emphasise that this is not a new position on my part. It is one that I have consistently taken. Of course the questions about the effectiveness of fiscal policy are important ones for macroeconomists, and the Brown University Conference on Monetarism (see Jerome Stein 1976) dealt almost exclusively with such issues. I accept Purvis' (1980) judgement that the outcome of that conference was to show beyond a reasonable doubt that 'fiscal policy matters' but also his judgement that in retrospect the debate about the effectiveness of fiscal policy has not been the most important one in the monetarist debate, however important an issue it might be in its own right for macroeconomics.

Finally note that the foregoing discussion ignores the question as to whether, even if we had enough knowledge to ensure that fine tuning could be used beneficially, the political process would permit it to be used in that way. This question, as Milton Friedman has pointed out to me, is a vital one in any practical debate about activist policies.

32   Of course there has been a considerable ideological content to the monetarist debate and I would not deny that for a moment. Nor would I take the position that there is anything reprehensible about ideological debates *per se*. I play these issues down in this chapter not because, from a broader perspective I would regard them as unimportant, but because my expertise as an economist does not put me in a position to say anything very useful about them.

33   Michael Parkin, Michael Sumner and Robert Jones (1972) is still an admirable source of information about wage and price controls in the British economy. Michael Walker (1976) contains much useful information on other countries. Note that the views that I state here about the importance of using wage and price controls, if they are to be used, in conjunction with monetary and fiscal policy, rather than instead of such policies, are those of the McCracken Committee. See McCracken *et al.* (1977).

34   See Laidler (1976*b*), particularly Chapters 7 and 9, for an earlier statement of my own views on the role of the housing market and its interaction with monetary policy and inflation. I readily acknowledge that the source is an obscure one.

REFERENCES

Ando, A. and Modigliani, F. (1965) 'The relative stability of monetary velocity and the investment multiplier', *American Economic Review* 55 (September), pp. 693–728.

Ball, R. J. and Burns, T. (1976) 'The inflationary mechanism in the U.K. economy', *American Economic Review* 66 (September), pp. 478–84.

Barro, R. J. (1978) 'Unanticipated money, output and the price level in the United States', *Journal of Political Economy* 86 (August), pp. 549–81.

——(1979) 'Second thoughts on Keynesian economics', *American Economic Review* 69 (May), papers and proceedings, pp. 54–9.

Baumol, W. J. (1952) 'The transactions demand for cash: an inventory theoretic approach', *Quarterly Journal of Economics* 66 (November), pp. 545–56.

Boughton, James M. (1977) 'Does Monetarism Matter', in Elmus Wicker (ed.) *Lilley Conference on Recent Developments in Economics April 21–23*. Bloomington, IN, Indiana University.

Brown, Arthur J. (1955) *The Great Inflation 1939–1951*, London: Oxford University Press.

Brunner, K. (1961) 'The report of the Commission on money and credit', *Journal of Political Economy* 69 (December), pp. 605–20.

——(1970) 'The monetarist revolution in monetary theory', *Weltwirtschaftliches Archiv* 105, pp. 1–30.

——(1978) 'Issues of post-Keynesian monetary analysis', in Thomas Mayer (1978).

Brunner, K., and Meltzer, A. H. (1963) 'Predicting velocity: implications for theory and policy', *Journal of Finance* 18 (May), pp. 319–54.

——(eds) (1978) *The Inflation Problem*. Carnegie–Rochester Public Policy Conference Series, Amsterdam: North-Holland.

Brunner, K., Cukierman, A. and Meltzer, A. H. (1979) 'Stagflation, persistent unemployment and the permanence of economic shocks', Carnegie–Mellon University (mimeo).

Buiter, W. H. (1980) 'The macroeconomics of Dr. Pangloss: a critical survey of the New Classical Macroeconomics', *Economic Journal* 90 (March), pp. 34–50.

Cagan, P. (1978) 'Monetarism in historical perspective'. In Thomas Mayer (1978).

——(1979) *Persistent Inflation*, New York: Columbia University Press.

Cagan, P. and Schwartz, A. J. (1975) 'Has the growth of money substitutes hindered monetary policy?' *Journal of Money, Credit and Banking* 7 (May), pp. 137–60.

Clements, K. W. and Jonson, P. D. (1979) 'Unanticipated money, disequilibrium modelling and rational expectations', *Economic Letters* 2, pp. 303–8.

Clower, R. W. (1965) 'The Keynesian counterrevolution: a theoretical appraisal', *The Theory of Interest Rates* (ed. F. H. Hahn and F. P. R. Brechling), London: Macmillan.

De Prano, M. and Mayer, T. (1965) 'Tests of the relative importance of autonomous expenditure and money', *American Economic Review* 55 (September), pp. 729–52.

Fisher, I. (1911) *The Purchasing Power of Money*, New York.

Frenkel, J. (1980) 'Flexible Exchange Rates in the 1970s', in Laurence H. Meyer (ed.) *Stabilisation Policies Lessons from the 70s and Implications for the 80s*, St Louis, Washington University and Federal Reserve Bank of St Louis.

Frenkel, J. and Johnson, H. G. (1976) *The Monetary Approach to Balance of Payments Theory*, London: George Allen and Unwin.

Friedman, M. (1956) 'The quantity theory of money: a restatement', in *Studies in the Quantity Theory of Money* (ed. M. Friedman), Chicago: University of Chicago Press.

——(1959) 'The demand for money: some theoretical and empirical results', *Journal of Political Economy* 67 (June), pp. 327–51.

——(1960) *A Program for Monetary Stability*, New York: Fordham University Press.

——(1966) 'Interest rates and the demand for money', *Journal of Law and Economics* 9 (October).

——(1968) 'The role of monetary policy', *American Economic Review* 58 (March), pp. 1–17.

Friedman, M. (1970) 'A theoretical framework for monetary analysis', *Journal of Political Economy* 78 (March–April), pp. 193–238.

——(1975) *Unemployment Versus Inflation*, London: Institute of Economic Affairs.

Friedman, M. and Meiselman, D. (1963) 'The relative stability of monetary velocity and the investment multiplier in the United States, 1898–1958. Commission on Money and Credit', *Stabilization Policies*, Englewood Cliffs, NJ: Prentice-Hall.

Friedman, M. and Schwartz, A. J. (1963a) *A Monetary History of the United States, 1867–1960*, Princeton, NJ: Princeton University Press for the NBER.

——(1963b) 'Money and business cycles', *Review of Economics and Statistics* 45 (February), supplement, pp. 32–64.

Frisch, H. (1977) 'Inflation theory 1963–1975: a second generation survey', *Journal of Economic Literature* 15 (December), pp. 1289–317.

Hahn, F. H. (1980) 'Monetarism and Economic Theory', *Economica* NS 47 (February), pp. 1–18.

Harberger, A. C. (ed.) (1960) *The Demand for Durable Goods*, Chicago: University of Chicago Press.

Harrod, R. F. (1971) 'Discussion paper', in *Monetary Theory and Monetary Policy in the 1970's* (ed. G. Clayton, J. C. Gilbert and R. Sedgewick), London: Oxford University Press.

Hicks, J. R. (1974) *The Crisis in Keynesian Economics*, Oxford: Basil Blackwell.

Howitt, P. W. (1979) 'Evaluating the non-market-clearing approach', *American Economic Review* 69 (May), Papers and Proceedings, pp. 60–4.

Johnson, H. G. (1962) 'Monetary theory and policy', *American Economic Review* 52 (June), pp. 335–84.

——(1972) *Inflation and the Monetarist Controversy*, De Vries Lectures, 1971. Amsterdam: North Holland.

Jonson, P. D. (1976a) 'Money and economic activity in the open economy, the United Kingdom 1880–1970', *Journal of Political Economy* 84 (October), pp. 979–1012.

——(1976b) 'Money, prices and output: an integrative essay', *Kredit und Kapital* 9, pp. 499–518.

Kahn, R. F. (1976) 'Inflation: a Keynesian view', *Scottish Journal of Political Economy* 23 (February), pp. 11–15.

Kaldor, N. (1970) 'The new monetarism', *Lloyd's Bank Review* (July), pp. 1–18.

Kantor, B. (1979) 'Rational expectations and economic thought', *Journal of Economic Literature* 17 (December), pp. 1422–75.

Laidler, D. (1966) 'The rate of interest and the demand for money: some empirical evidence', *Journal of Political Economy* 74 (December), pp. 545–55.

——(1971) 'The influence of money on economic activity: a survey of some current problems', in *Monetary Theory and Monetary Policy in the 1970's* (ed. G. Clayton, J. C. Gilbert and R. Sedgewick), London: Oxford University Press.

——(1975) *Essays on Money and Inflation*, Manchester: University of Manchester Press; Chicago: University of Chicago Press.

——(1976a) 'Inflation in Britain: a monetarist analysis', *American Economic Review* 76 (September), pp. 485–500.

——(et al.) (1976b) *Study on the Possible Part Played by Certain Primary Non-employment Incomes in the Inflationary Process in the United Kingdom*, Commission of the European Communities, Brussels.

——(1980) 'The demand for money in the United States: yet again' (ed. K. Brunner and A. H. Meltzer), Carnegie-Rochester Conference Series, *The State of Macroeconomics*, Amsterdam: North Holland.

Lieberman, C. (1980) 'The long-run and short-run demand for money revisited', *Journal of Money, Credit and Banking*.

Lipsey, R. G. (1960) 'The relationship between unemployment and the rate of change of money wage rates in the United Kingdom, 1862–1957', *Economica* 27, pp. 1–31.

Lucas, R. E., Jr (1972) 'Expectations and the neutrality of money', *Journal of Economic Theory* 4, pp. 103–24.

—— (1975) 'An equilibrium model of the business cycle', *Journal of Political Economy* 83 (November–December), pp. 1113–44.

—— (1976) 'Econometric policy evaluation: a critique', *The Phillips Curve and Labour Markets* (ed. K. Brunner and A. H. Meltzer), Carnegie-Rochester Conference Series, Amsterdam: North Holland.

—— (1977) 'Understanding business cycles', in *Stabilization of the Domestic and International Economy* (ed. K. Brunner and A. H. Meltzer), Carnegie-Rochester Conference Series, Amsterdam: North Holland.

McCracken, P. *et al.* (1977) *Towards Full Employment and Price Stability* (McCracken Report), Paris: OECD.

Mayer, T. (1978) *The Structure of Monetarism*, New York: W. W. Norton.

Meltzer, A. H. (1965) 'Monetary theory and monetary history', *Schweizerische Zeitschrift Volkswirtschaft und Statistik* (Spring), pp. 409–22.

—— (1969) 'Money intermediation and growth', *Journal of Economic Literature* 7 (March), pp. 27–56.

Modigliani, F. (1977) 'The monetarist controversy, or should we forsake stabilization policies?', *American Economic Review* 67 (March), pp. 1–19.

Parkin, J. M., Sumner, M. T. and Jones, R. A. (1972) 'A survey of the econometric evidence on the effects of incomes policy on the rate of inflation', in *Incomes Policy and Inflation* (ed. J. M. Parkin and M. T. Sumner), Manchester: University of Manchester Press.

Patinkin, D. (1965) *Money, Interest and Prices*, 2nd edn, originally published 1956, New York: Harper Rowe.

—— (1969) 'The Chicago tradition the quantity theory and Friedman', *Journal of Money, Credit and Banking* 1 (February), pp. 46–70.

Phelps, E. (1967) 'Phillips curves expectations of inflation and optimal unemployment over time', *Economica* NS 34 (August), pp. 254–81.

—— (*et al.*) (1969) *Microeconomic Foundations of Employment and Inflation Theory*, New York: W. W. Norton.

Phillips, A. W. (1958) 'The relation between unemployment and the rate of change of money wage rates in the United Kingdom, 1861–1957', *Economica* NS 25 (November), pp. 283–99.

Purvis, D. D. (1980) 'Monetarism – a review', *Canadian Journal of Economics* 1 (February), pp. 96–121.

Radcliffe Committee (Committee on the Working of the Monetary System) (1959) *Report*, London: HMSO.

Reid, M. (1962) *Housing and Income*, Chicago: University of Chicago Press.

Robinson, J. (1970) 'Quantity theories old and new', *Journal of Money, Credit and Banking* 2 (November), pp. 504–12.

Santomero, A. M. and Seater, J. J. (1978) 'The inflation–unemployment trade-off: a critique of the literature', *Journal of Economic Literature* 16 (June), pp. 499–544.

Sargent, T. J. (1976) 'A classical macroeconomic model for the United States', *Journal of Political Economy* 84 (April), pp. 207–38.

Sargent, T. J. and Wallace, N. (1975) 'Rational expectations, the optimal monetary instrument and the optimal money supply rule', *Journal of Political Economy* 83 (April), pp. 241–54.

Solow, R. M. (1968) 'Recent controversies on the theory of inflation: an eclectic view', in *Symposium on Inflation – Its Causes, Consequences and Control* (ed. S. Rousseas), New York: Calvin K. Kazanjian Economics Foundation.

Solow, R. M. (1979) 'Alternative approaches to macroeconomic theory: a partial view', *Canadian Journal of Economics* 12 (August), pp. 339–54.

——(1980) 'On theories of unemployment', *American Economic Review* 70 (March), pp. 1–11.

Stein, J. (1976) *Monetarism*, Amsterdam: North-Holland.

Sumner, M. T. (1980) 'The operation of monetary targets', in K. Brunner and A. H. Meltzer (eds) *Monetary Institutions and the Policy Process*, Carnegie-Rochester Public Policy Conference Series, Amsterdam: North-Holland.

Tobin, J. (1947) 'Liquidity preference and monetary policy', *Review of Economics and Statistics* 29 (May), pp. 124–31.

——(1956) 'The interest elasticity of transactions demand for cash', *Review of Economics and Statistics* 38 (August), pp. 241–7.

——(1958) 'Liquidity preference as behaviour towards risk', *Review of Economic Studies* 25 (February), pp. 65–86.

——(1965) 'The monetary interpretation of history', *American Economic Review* 55 (June), pp. 464–85.

——(1972) 'Inflation and unemployment', *American Economic Review* 62 (March), pp. 1–18.

Walker, M. (ed.) (1976) *The Illusion of Wage and Price Control*, Vancouver, BC: Fraser Institute.

Wiles, P. (1973) 'Cost inflation and the state of economic theory', *Economic Journal* 83, pp. 377–98.

Wilson, T. (1976) 'The natural rate of unemployment', *Scottish Journal of Political Economy* 23 (February), pp. 99–107.

10 The monetarist controversy revisited

Franco Modigliani
Contemporary Policy Issues (1988) 6, October, pp. 3–18

I am delighted with the success of this conference honoring Michael Hamburger, and I am impressed by both the attendance and the outpouring of love, respect, and admiration for his work. I wish I could claim some credit for this success since, after all, he was a student of mine. Unfortunately, I cannot do so in good conscience. One reason for his coming to the Carnegie Institute of Technology for his graduate work was to study with me. But because I left soon after he arrived, he was my student for only a short time – a year or so. Since leaving Carnegie, I often have felt a bit guilty for abandoning Mike just a year after he arrived.

My topic for today actually was inspired by the last letter that Michael wrote to me – a letter of congratulations on the Nobel award, dated Oct. 15, 1985. It was a very warm letter in which he first gave me undeserved credit by asserting that 'you probably had more influence on my career than anyone else.' He proceeded to say that 'to keep you up-to-date on my activities, I am enclosing two of my latest reports. I believe that you will approve of the evolution of my thinking.'

I must confess that because we were buried under a deluge of wonderful moving messages, I was unable to read the enclosures at that time. It was only when I heard the heartbreaking news of his death that I suddenly remembered I had not quite finished reading his message. I finally managed to do so.

CHARACTERISTICS OF MONETARISM

The enclosures were two issues of his monthly publication, *Economic Insights*. I found their content – especially that of August 1985, entitled 'Money Growth Is Not Excessive' – quite extraordinary and gratifying. That report showed, without a shadow of a doubt, that Michael had abandoned 'Monetarism' with a capital 'M', as defined in my American Economic Association presidential address (1977). He had rejoined the ranks of monetarists with a small 'm' – those like me and countless others concerned with the role of money in our economy.

As I suggested in that paper, the difference between a true Monetarist and the rest of us has little to do with views regarding the workings of the economy. By now, no significant disagreements – at least between Keynesians and Monetarists – exist over the proposition that money counts. To be sure, Monetarists sometimes attribute to Keynesians the view that Keynesian monetary theory rests on the liquidity trap. That mechanism may be of notable logical significance, but hardly anyone would claim that it is of practical significance under *present* circumstances. Nor can there be differences of principle regarding fiscal policy. Monetarists, including Milton Friedman, presumably now accept the view that the demand for money depends on interest rates. Therefore, they must also agree with others that fiscal policy – at least government expenditure – has some real effects. Nor is there any difference in accepting the view that money is neutral in the long run. The vertical Phillips curve is generally accepted now, and I would say that it was widely adopted within just a few years of the time the hypothesis was formulated.

Instead, to determine what really distinguishes the M's from the rest, we must search along very different lines. First, how stable is the economy in the absence of stabilization policies? For the Monetarists, the economy is stable enough so that stabilization policies are not needed. For the non-Monetarists, the economy suffers from enough instability so as to benefit, in principle, from active stabilization. Second, how effective are stabilization policies? According to non-Monetarists, stabilization policies can contribute to stability not only in principle but also in practice. For Monetarists, discretionary stabilization destabilizes the economy as a result of long and variable lags, and because those charged with carrying out the policy are ineffective. And finally, true Monetarists will argue that even if stabilization were both needed and feasible, we still should not trust the government with the necessary power since the bureaucracy has the propensity to act in its own self-interest. Non-Monetarists like myself recognize that public servants are not infallible saints and that, under some circumstances, they may make mistakes and/or be influenced by self-interest. By no means, however, do these dangers justify depriving ourselves of all discretion, at least where it matters – to wit, in well-administered countries where government actions are open to public scrutiny.

Given these fundamental beliefs, Monetarists conclude that one must forsake stabilization policies. This implies, in particular, forsaking the use of monetary policy as a stabilization device and instead requiring money to grow mechanically at a rate fixed once and for all. I have come to appreciate how Monetarists view the holiness of this principle by watching Friedman advising on the appropriate monetary policy in diverse complex situations and each time coming up, unfailingly, with the same practical answer: 3 percent.

Accordingly, I conclude that the essential characteristics distinguishing Monetarists from others is their insistence on a steady growth of money – fixed for a long time, if not forever, and in any event not responsive to developing circumstances. The only exception that they have made to their principles of constant growth has occurred when the economy, for whatever reason, has reached a high level of inflation. Then they have recommended a money growth path beginning with a rate close to that of inflation and declining gradually until the growth coincides with the real growth trend of the economy and, they hope, inflation has been squeezed out of the economy. But even in this case, the path is fixed in advance.

Michael's article in *Economic Insights* (August 1985) to which he called my attention showed that he had both the honesty and the flexibility to give up the Monetarist position he had long held by expressing his approval of the course that the Fed pursued in 1985. This course involved abandoning the growth target, set at the beginning of the year as part of a program of gradual re-entry from inflation, and accepting a much higher growth of money. The purpose of the higher growth was to track the initial GNP target in the face of a rise in money demand or, equivalently, of a large decline in velocity, amounting to 5 percent, for the first half of the year. Not only was he abandoning Monetarism, he was quite open about it: 'I believe you will approve of the evolution of my thinking.' By mid-1986, he not only was approving of the unprecedented high growth rate of M1 to offset the continuing velocity decline, but even was complaining because the Fed failed to take into account the prospective velocity decline by announcing an insufficiently high target. This caused a large discrepancy between realization and target which, in his view, disturbed the financial markets (see *Economic Insights* June 1986). In short, Michael had concluded that it was wrong to enforce, at all costs, a constant or transiently declining growth of money. Instead, the time had come to target income and to adjust money growth and money targets as necessary so as to achieve the income target in light of changing velocity.

One must recognize that Hamburger was not the first to defect from Monetarism. Already in 1983, the Council of Economic Advisers gave up its earlier prescription of 'a gradual reduction in the rate of growth of the money stock until the rate is consistent with price stability' (*Economic Report of the President, 1983*, p. 23). Influenced by the 1982 experience, and especially by the sharp fall in velocity, the Council acknowledged the need 'to balance the principle of stable money growth with the need to take account of changing asset preferences that may alter the velocity of money ... One possible way [to do so] is to use the observed behavior of nominal GNP to guide a gradual recalibration of the monetary growth targets ... Basing the recalibration of monetary targets on nominal GNP is consistent with the basic principle of pursuing a stable monetary policy' (*Economic Report of the President, 1983*, pp. 23–4).

But probably the first to abandon the Monetarist bandwagon was the Federal Reserve itself. It did so as early as 1982 by responding to the large decline in velocity with an unusually high infusion of money. Actually, some question exists as to whether the Fed abandoned Monetarism in

1982 or instead had never really embraced it. We know that around 1979, in the face of continuing and rising inflation, the Fed had adopted a policy of renewed emphasis on monetary growth targets announced in advance – in place of interest rate targets. However, favoring money growth targets is a necessary but by no means sufficient condition to being admitted to the ranks of true Monetarists.

MONETARISM AND THE FED

The main reason to question the seriousness of the Fed's commitment to Monetarism is that despite its announcement of targets during these early years, the growth of money supply appeared extremely jagged – periods of very rapid growth followed by periods of stagnation or even decline – and hence was a far cry from a constant growth rate. However, economists generally agree that so long as the variability of money is merely short run, it should not be of much consequence. On the other hand, the behavior over longer periods – such as four-quarter changes – does not appear inconsistent with Monetarists' prescriptions.

One may begin by looking at the target's behavior for the four-quarter change. Table 10.1 reports target and actual four-quarter changes for all monetary aggregates. The table also reports the Fed's so-called 'economic projections' and actual four-quarter changes for its monetary policy objectives – namely GNP, real GNP, the GNP deflator, and unemployment.

One can see from the first row, which relates to M1, that up until 1982 the M1 target declines year after year. This is true whether we rely on the midpoint or on the upper limit of the target range. (The target rises from 1979 to 1980, but one may attribute this to the fact that the 1979 target related to a somewhat different aggregate, M1A.) The decline is not large, but the path traced certainly is broadly consistent with the Monetarists' prescription. Similarly, the actual growth of M1 tended to decline through 1981 up until the third quarter of 1982, even if the behavior of the actual growth was less steady than that of the target.

But several other aspects of the Fed's behavior appear quite inconsistent with Monetarism. One conspicuous example is the rather broad target range that the Fed announced for M1 and the other aggregates: for the period 1979–82, typically 3 percentage points and not less than $2\frac{1}{2}$. Monetarists holding that 3 percent growth is the only acceptable target must regard this much room as a devious way to reintroduce discretion.

Another highly suspicious practice is that throughout this period, the Fed announced targets for a substantial array of aggregates – generally four, though not always the same four. These targets generally could be expected to prove inconsistent with each other *ex post*. Thus, the only effect of this practice was to give the Fed extra leeway regarding any one target, in particular M1, by giving the Fed the option regarding the target to which it would adhere.

One more highly revealing aspect of the Fed's behavior is that throughout the years 1979–82, the actual growth of M1 exceeded the targeted growth except in 1981. Nor could one attribute this excess to the pursuit of a different target or targets since during this period, the actual growth of M2 and M3 also was on the high side of the corresponding targets without exception. To be sure, the excess for M1 and the other targets was not very large if compared with the upper limit of the target range. But when one considers the very large range announced and the extra potential leeway resulting from the multiple targets, one must conclude that – contrary to Monetarist tenets – the Fed felt no strong obligation to stick to the targets whenever doing so seemed to interfere with the pursuit of other non-Monetarist goals.

This evidence suggests rather convincingly that the Federal Open Market Committee (FOMC) never really embraced Monetarism. The reason that the FOMC shifted to an emphasis on aggregates was not a Monetarist conversion but rather a matter of convenience. First, it had difficulty selecting appropriate interest rate targets in the presence of significant and variable inflation. With inflation, the usual difficulty of determining appropriate interest rates is compounded by that of assessing price expectations and the pervasive effects of taxation. Second, the Fed was very conscious of the need for a tough anti-inflationary policy at the cost of very high interest rates, but it was concerned about the antagonism that such a policy surely would engender and that, in the end, might even interfere with the Fed's ability to carry out the task. In addition, the FOMC might also tend to procrastinate when circumstances call for enforcing unusually high interest rates. Adoption of Monetarist-like growth targets could reduce this potential hostility and procrastination, since doing so would make unnecessary the explicit targeting of unpopular sky-high interest rates and since part of the blame could be shifted to the Monetarists, who were then riding high.

The variable that the Fed seemed especially concerned with and endeavored to track was not the growth of M1 (or any other monetary aggregate) but that of nominal GNP – specifically, its real implications. The main evidence supporting this proposition is that throughout the years 1979 to 1981, GNP was uniformly within the projected range and was generally close to the middle while the monetary aggregates were missed and systematically exceeded. Note also that the GNP path – both projected and achieved – was characterized by a slow but steady decline in the growth rate. This suggests a courageous choice of final targets and a very skilled execution. The Fed had no illusion that a sudden burst of 'rational expectations' would make it possible to slow down money and nominal GNP growth without adverse consequences for output and employment. Quite the contrary, the chosen path of nominal GNP was seen as leading to painful consequences. Thus, in 1980, the targeted real growth range fell almost entirely on the negative side and the actual growth was negative. In

Table 10.1 Federal Reserve 'targets' and actual changes in monetary aggregates and 'projections' and actual changes in other variables

	1979 Target	1979 Actual	1980 Target	1980 Actual	1981 Target	1981 Actual	1982 Target	1982 Actual
M1[a]	1.5–4.5	5.5	4.0–6.5	7.3	3.5–6.0	5.1	2.5–5.5	8.6
M2[b]	5.0–8.0	8.2	6.0–9.0	8.9	5.0–9.0	9.2	6.0–9.0	9.1
M3[b]	6.0–9.0	10.4	6.5–9.5	9.6	5.5–9.5	12.3	6.5–9.5	9.9
Total domestic nonfinancial debt[c]	7.5–10.5	12.3	6.0–9.0	7.9	6.0–9.0	8.8	6.9	9.5
GNP	9.75	9.9	7.5–11.0	9.5	9.0–12.0	9.3	8.0–10.5	3.25
(revised value)	(8.0–10.0)		(5.0–7.5)		(10.0–11.5)		(5.5–7.5)	
GNP central tendency								
(revised value)								
GNP implicit price deflator		9.0	9.0–11.0	9.8	9.0–10.5	8.6	6.5–7.75	4.5
(revised value)	(8.5–10.5)		(9.0–10.0)		(7.5–9.0)		(4.75–6.0)	
Real GNP	2.2	1.0	–2.5–0.5	–0.3	–1.5–1.5	–0.9	1.5–3.0	–0.87
(revised value)			(–2.5––0.5)		(1.0–3.5)		(0.5–1.5)	
Real GNP central tendency								
(revised value)								
Unemployment rate	6.2	5.9	6.75–8.0	7.5	8.0–8.5	8.3	8.25–9.5	10.8
(revised value)			(8.5–9.75)		(7.5–8.25)		(9.0–9.75)	

Notes:
[a] For 1979, the values are for M1A. For 1981, the values are adjusted for the NOW account shift.
[b] Definition changes after 1982 (and also seasonal and benchmark adjustments). See *Federal Reserve Bulletin*, February 1984. p. 84.
[c] For the years 1979 to 1982, the series shown refer to bank credit.

Table 10.1 (continued)

	1983		1984		1985		1986	
	Target	Actual	Target	Actual	Target	Actual	Target	Actual
M1	4.0–8.0	10.2	4.0–8.0	5.4	4.0–7.0	12.1	3.0–8.0	15.2
M2	7.0–10.0	12.1	6.0–9.0	7.9	6.0–9.0	8.8	6.0–9.0	8.9
M3	6.5–9.5	9.8	6.0–9.0	10.7	6.0–9.5	7.7	6.0–9.0	8.8
Total domestic nonfinancial debt	8.5–11.5	11.5	8.0–11.0	13.9	9.0–12.0	13.5	8.0–11.0	12.9
GNP	7.5–11.5	10.5	8.0–10.5	9.7	7.0–8.5	5.4	5.0–8.5	5.2
(revised value)	(9.25–10.75)		(9.5–11.5)		(6.25–7.75)		(2.75–6.5)	
GNP central tendency	8.0–9.0		9.0–10.0		7.5–8.0		6.5–7.25	
(revised value)	(9.75–10.0)		(10.5–11.0)		(6.5–7.0)		(4.75–5.75)	
GNP implicit price deflator	3.5–5.5	4.1	4.0–6.0	3.6	3.0–4.75	3.1	2.5–4.5	2.1
(revised value)	(4.0–5.25)		(3.25–4.5)		(3.25–4.25)		(1.5–3.75)	
Real GNP	3.0–5.5	6.06	3.5–5.0	5.8	3.5–4.25	2.25	2.75–4.25	2.5
(revised value)	(4.75–6.0)		(6.0–7.0)		(2.25–3.25)		(2.25–3.5)	
Real GNP central tendency	3.5–4.5		4.0–4.75		3.5–4.0		3.0–3.5	
(revised value)	(5.0–5.75)		(6.25–6.75)		(2.75–3.0)		(2.5–3.0)	
Unemployment rate	9.5–10.5	8.4	7.25–8.0	7.2	6.5–7.25	7.0	6.25–6.75	6.7
(revised value)	(9.0–9.75)		(6.5–7.25)		(6.75–7.25)			

Note: Data are rates of change, fourth quarter to fourth quarter. For unemployment, data are the rates in each fourth quarter.
Sources: Federal Reserve Bulletin, various issues. Targets are from 'Monetary Policy Report to the Congress' (MPRC), published in February of the given year or afterward. Revisions are from MPRC, published in July or afterward. Actual values of monetary and credit aggregates are from *Monetary Policy Objectives for 1987*, Summary Report of the Federal Reserve Board, 10, Feb. 1987, p. 11. Actual values of other variables for various years are from the following sources: 1979–1982, MPRC, published in February following the given year; 1979–1985, Statistical Annex of the *Federal Reserve Bulletin*, published in April following the given year; 1986, *Economic Indicators*, February 1987, p. 3.

1981, the projection centered on zero and the outcome also was close to zero. The observed behavior of target setting and realizations during the period prior to 1983 indicates that the Fed was concerned primarily with tracking final targets, essentially GNP. Even though monetary targets were announced regularly, presumably they represented not a true commitment but rather the best guess as to how much monetary growth would be required so as to achieve the final target, perhaps shaved down to placate the Monetarists. If the announced target ever proved to be inconsistent with achieving the final target, then the monetary targets would be set aside – as happened repeatedly between 1979 and 1982. But up until 1981, the inconsistencies were reasonably small.

As a result, during these early years, the actual behavior of M1 had a Monetarist quality. One must explain this by the circumstance that up until 1982, no serious perceived discrepancy existed between Monetarist prescriptions and a desirable course for GNP. However, beginning with the sharp decline in velocity in 1982, the inconsistencies became glaring. The Fed finally was forced to choose between either staying close to the money growth target or tracking GNP and giving up the pretense of Monetarism. Unfortunately, this realization had occurred too late to prevent a serious contraction which, following years of no growth or even declines, played havoc with the world economy.

Since 1982, the relationship between the choice of targets and the realizations of monetary and final targets is similar to that prevailing during the earlier period, but it is even less coherent with Monetarist behavior. In 1983, the monetary targets mostly were increased but nonetheless the realizations exceeded the targets – some by large margins – while GNP growth again fell within the target ranges. In 1984, the monetary aggregates – including M1 – were mostly on track, but then so was GNP. Hence, one cannot tell whether the Fed truly was concerned with tracking GNP or with tracking M1. During 1985 and 1986, on the other hand, the Table 10.1 data leave little doubt that the Fed again endeavored to track GNP and, to this end, was prepared to let M1 grow at a rate much higher than targets as well as Monetarist standards. Unfortunately, the M1 growth proved neither large enough nor timely enough to achieve the GNP targets, particularly the real ones.

On the whole, the evidence suggests that during this second period also, the Fed was continuing to behave in a non-Monetarist fashion by focusing on tracking the GNP targets while disregarding the monetary growth targets.

What can one learn from this rich experience of the years since 1979 about the controversy surrounding stabilization policies? I find this experience quite instructive in providing strong support for the proposition stated in my earlier paper (Modigliani 1977): '[A] private enterprise economy using an intangible money *needs* to be stabilized, *can* be stabilized and therefore *should* be stabilized.'

CASE FOR STABILIZATION POLICY

The proposition that the economy must be stabilized is amply supported by the dramatic variability of M1 velocity, especially since 1981. The implications of such variability are as follows. Suppose that the Fed had followed a strict Monetarist policy of increasing M1 at a constant rate. For this particular period, suppose that the Fed chose a rate around 5 percent – a figure mentioned frequently in Policy Statements of the Shadow Open Market Committee. Then the growth of M1 would have been lower than the actual by 2.3 percentage points in 1980, 3.6 percentage points in 1982, 5.2 percentage points in 1983, 7.1 percentage points in 1985, and 10.2 percentage points in 1986. The discrepancies in the money stock are even more enlightening. In 1980, it would have fallen short of the actual by 2.1 percent of the actual and the gap would have risen to 9.9 percent by 1983, to nearly 16.0 percent by 1985, and to 23.4 percent by 1986. This enormous shortfall of money clearly would have played havoc with the economy. How much would nominal GNP have declined? If the velocity were little affected by the money supply – a viewpoint that Monetarists occasionally embrace – then one would have to conclude that nominal GNP would have been one-fourth, or roughly $1 trillion, lower than it actually was by the end of 1986. At the same time, the GNP contraction presumably would have led to a price level somewhat below the current one. Hence, the contraction in real output and employment would have been somewhat smaller than one-fourth.

In addition, the assumption that velocity would remain constant in the face of a large contraction in the money supply is not tenable. First, much evidence – including the Hamburger demand for money equation – indicates that the demand for money adjusts slowly to its final determinant. According to the Hamburger estimate, the adjustment speed could be placed at about 11 percent a quarter, or roughly 40 percent a year. This slow adjustment implies that in the face of a contraction in the money supply, the velocity would decline initially or, equivalently, the GNP would tend to contract by a percentage appreciably larger than the change in money supply. At the same time, the rise in interest accompanying the contraction of M1 could be expected to raise the velocity. By relying on the standard Hicksian IS-LM paradigm, one can readily establish that the elasticity of GNP with respect to a change in money depends on three elasticities: that of saving with respect to income and that of investment and money demand with respect to the interest rate. If, as a rough approximation, we put the elasticity of saving at unity, the short-run elasticity of investment at 0.5, and use Hamburger's parameter estimates (speed of adjustment, 40 percent a year; elasticity of money demand with respect to interest rates in first year of 20 percent), we find that the short-run elasticity of GNP with respect to a change in the money supply is somewhere around 0.7, though one might expect it to decline substantially as the system gradually adjusts to the change. This is true if wages are rigid, though one might expect them to adjust in the longer run.

But even with these qualifications, the impact of the money shortfall under a Monetarist policy of constant and relatively low money growth would have been devastating. This experience demonstrates clearly that at least some circumstances exist in which Monetarists' constant money growth policy with no discretion would prove disastrous. In other words, the system needs a stabilizing monetary policy.

My next proposition is that an effective stabilization policy is feasible. The experiment since the late 1970s illustrates this point well. During the period 1979 to 1986, actual GNP fell squarely within the projected range in six of these years. During the remaining two years, 1982 and 1985, GNP fell short of target and the discrepancies were substantial. But one point to note about these two years is that the actual growth of money was well above the M1 growth target set for the year which, in turn, was above the Monetarists' target. This means that the Fed used discretion in deviating from the money targets so as to approach the GNP target without overshooting it.

I conclude, therefore, that using discretion to track GNP paid off handsomely during this period in terms of a smooth re-entry from inflation. Of course, as all neo-Keynesians knew, we could not achieve that re-entry without substantial unemployment – especially following the second oil shock. But the Fed had the courage to stick to the path, though it may have tried to disinflate too quickly in 1982. And since that year, the Fed has produced a path with both declining inflation (at least until 1987) and rising output and employment.

POLICY RULES

The recent experience with unstable velocity has led to a string of defections from Monetarism besides those of the Fed, the Council of Economic Advisers, and Michael Hamburger. Among those who have given up Monetarism (i.e. a money growth rate either constant or fixed long in advance) are previously hard-line Monetarists such as Allan Meltzer, Bennett McCallum, William Poole, and Thomas Mayer. All have been forced to recognize that the original formulation of Monetarism cannot be viable after the experience since the late 1970s. Thus, they have endeavored to find a solution that, in keeping with the spirit of Monetarism, avoids giving the monetary authority any discretionary powers. This has led them to propose replacing the original constant growth rule with some other kind of rule – one that will adjust money growth so as to allow it to reflect variation in velocity. Ideally, one would want to adjust the change in money growth for the current-period velocity change. But, of course, the current velocity is not known. One could draw some inferences about it from a model of the economy, but a Monetarist could never recommend this since it would violate the principle of no discretion. These considerations have led both

Meltzer (1984) and Mayer (1987) to propose a 'rule' according to which one year's growth of some stated aggregate will equal a constant that is related to the desirable long-run growth trend of nominal income, less the percentage increase in velocity over some recent past year. The only difference between these two authors' proposals is that Mayer suggests applying the rule to M1 whereas Meltzer recommends applying it to the base. McCallum (1984) also has proposed a rule that would add to the constant trend a correction 'increasing the rate [of money growth] if nominal GNP is below its target and vice versa.' But one can show that this rule reduces to the Meltzer–Mayer rule so long as the 'correction' of money growth during each period *equals* the previous year's deviation of GNP from target.

The rule has intuitive appeal, at least if one supposes that velocity can be described by a random walk with moderate variance. Under these conditions, the proposed rule could well represent a substantial improvement over the Monetarist rule. But then, as we have just seen, the latter rule would have performed so miserably that outperforming it would be no great achievement. The relevant question is how it would have performed in terms of income variability, both absolutely and relative to the actual performance of the Fed, especially over the recent difficult period of erratic velocity behavior.

One can endeavor to answer this question by simulating the results of the Meltzer *et al.* rule.[1] To this end, recall that the proposed money supply rule can be written as

$$\hat{m}(t) = a - v(t - 1). \tag{1}$$

Here, $\hat{m}(t)$ is the current-period money growth called for by the rule, a is the long-term growth trend, and $v(t - 1)$ is the change in velocity over the recent past, which we shall identify operationally with the previous year. In addition, we have the relationship

$$\hat{y}(t) = \hat{m}(t) + \hat{v}(t) \tag{2}$$

where $\hat{v}(t)$ is the change in velocity that actually would occur during period t if $m(t)$ were equal to $\hat{m}(t)$. Unfortunately, $\hat{v}(t)$ is not directly observable. To get around this difficulty, let us first assume, that $\hat{v}(t)$ can be approximated with $v(t)$ – the change actually *observed* during the period – even though generally the change in money supply under the rule, $\hat{m}(t)$, would differ from the actual, $m(t)$. With this assumption, we can substitute for $\hat{m}(t)$ from equation (1) into equation (2):

$$\hat{y}(t) = a + v(t) - v(t - 1) = y(t) + \hat{m}(t) - m(t). \tag{3}$$

This can readily be used to compute $\hat{y}$. Column (1) of Table 10.2 shows the resulting value of $\hat{y}$ for the years 1980 to 1986, assuming for a the value of 5 percent.[2] Column (2) shows the corresponding money growth called for by rule (1). For comparison, columns (3) and (4) show the *actual* growth in GNP and money supply.

Table 10.2 Simulations of Mayer *et al.* Money Supply Rule

	$\hat{y}$ (1)	$\hat{m}$ (2)	y (3)	m (4)	y^* (5)
1978			14.8	8.2	
1979			9.9	5.5	
1980	2.8	0.6	9.5	7.3	7.5
1981	7.0	2.8	9.3	5.1	10.7
1982	−4.6	0.8	3.2	8.6	−2.2
1983	10.7	10.4	10.5	10.2	14.6
1984	9.0	4.7	9.7	5.4	9.0
1985	−6.0	0.7	5.4	12.1	−3.8
1986	1.7	11.7	5.2	15.2	8.0
Mean value (1980–6)	2.9	4.5	7.5	9.1	6.3
Range (1980–6)	16.7	11.1	7.3	10.1	18.4

Notes:
Column (1): From equation (3) and data in columns (2), (3), and (4) of this table.
Column (2): From equation (1) and the relevant data in Table 10.1. For the purpose of computation, $a = 5.0$ and the growth rate of velocity, $v(t - 1)$, is approximated by the percentage change in nominal GNP less the percentage change in M1, in the previous year, as given in columns (3) and (4) of this table.
Column (3): From Table 10.1, row indicating actual nominal GNP growth.
Column (4): From Table 10.1, row indicating actual M1 growth.
Column (5): From equation (4) and columns (2), (3), and (4) of this table.

The table indicates that letting the money supply be determined according to the latest rule the new Monetarism favors would have produced rather devastating and destabilizing results, at least under the assumption of $\hat{v}(t) = v(t)$. From column (1), we observe that despite the correction for growth, the rise of money supply would have been on average rather inadequate. The actual money growth was a hefty 9.1 percent which, judging from the *ex post* result, could not be deemed significantly excessive. By contrast, the money growth pursuant to the rule hardly matched the long-run trend of 5 percent. This may seem surprising given the velocity fall during much of this period, but the *lagged* velocity actually rose slightly. To be sure, the average growth rate may not be too relevant since it depends on the somewhat arbitrary choice of a in equation (1). More revealing is that the money supply growth according to the rule is even more variable than is the actual growth – even if by a small margin, or a range of about 11 versus 10 percent.

However, what matters most is not the growth of money but the behavior of income. Given the unstable growth of the money supply, one should not be surprised that the behavior of nominal income growth under the rule is also quite unsatisfactory. The average growth of nominal income turns out to be only 2.9 percent as compared with the actual growth of 7.5 percent.

Clearly, growth under the rule is inadequate by a wide margin. But again, the most damaging characteristic of the rule's performance is the great instability in the path of income. The variations in actual income growth stay within a range of 7 percentage points, which reduces to 5 if one omits 1982. But for the path generated by the rule, the range becomes 16.7 percentage points (from –6.0 percent in 1985 to 10.7 percent in 1983) and does not decline by omitting 1982. The greater instability of income under the rule reflects the rule's calling for money supply growth substantially lower than the actual precisely during those years when the income growth already was inadequate – such as 1982, 1985, and 1986 – or when the actual growth did not seem excessive, such as 1980. Similarly, the only year in which the rule calls for money growth larger than the actual is 1983, when the historical growth already was the largest. During two of these years, 1982 and 1985, the rule would have resulted in actual contraction in nominal income whereas the actual path shows none. During the two remaining years, 1980 and 1986, the nominal growth is so small as to imply a decline in real income.

Altogether, in no single year does the rule call for a growth rate clearly more appropriate than the historical one. In fact, one can verify that with the single exception of 1984, such performance is distinctly inferior to even a mechanical 5 percent growth rate.

However, these results must be qualified in that many may question our assumption that the velocity under the rule can be equated with that observed historically. We should expect instead that a faster (or a slower) money growth should affect velocity in two ways: (i) through the gradual adjustment of money demand and (ii) through the effect of money on interest rates and thereby on aggregate demand. Therefore, we have attempted to estimate the extent to which velocity, under the rule, would differ from the observed one. To this end, we recall that in the short run, an increase in money above that observed should tend to be accompanied by a fall in velocity. In fact, we suggested that this fall could be placed at 0.2, implying a short-run elasticity of income with respect to money of about 0.7. Allowing also for the slow adjustment of money demand on which Hamburger reported, we estimated the change in income resulting from the Mayer *et al.* rule but with adjusted velocity, y^*, as

$$y^* - y = 0.83(\hat{m} - m) - 0.5[\hat{m}(t-1) - m(t-1)] \qquad (4)$$

where the last term reflects the slow adjustment of money demand. The growth of income, y^*, estimated with this alternative procedure is reported in column (5) of Table 10.2, while $\hat{m}$ is unchanged and is given in column (2).

Column (5) indicates that allowing for a variable velocity may, on the whole, improve somewhat the performance of the money rule – see e.g. the smaller contraction during 1982 and 1985 and the larger growth during 1980 and 1986. The outcome of the rule still remains quite poor compared with the historical behavior: y^* still is appreciably smaller than y when y

already was too small (1982 and 1985) and appreciably larger when y already was quite large (1981 and 1983). As a result, the variability of y^* remains quite large. The range of more than 18 percentage points far exceeds that of y or even $\hat{y}$ – or even a 5 percent rule. Thus, whether or not we allow for a velocity response, the tests seemingly lead to the same negative conclusion and suggest that the main source of instability from applying the rule arises from the sharp acceleration and deceleration of velocity such as those occurring during 1982, 1983, and 1985. The discretionary policy of the Fed weathered the storm much better than did the proposed rule, as evaluated in column (1) or column (5).

The conclusion that one should draw from this experiment seems clear enough: the new Monetarist rule of Mayer *et al.* is entirely unacceptable since in some circumstances, such as the recent episode, it would lead to instability of major proportions.[3] To be sure, our simulations are not exhaustive. In particular, one could experiment with somewhat different lags on which to base the velocity correction. But such experiments could not radically change our conclusions. Indeed, the attraction of Monetarists' rules has been that they were mechanical and did not require fine tuning: so long as money grew at a constant rate, the rate itself was a mere detail. But rules that depend critically on the specification of the lags would only reinforce mistrust of monetary management by rule.

This, in turn, leads me to formulate two suggestions. In the first place, those proposing the new rule should go back to the drawing board and experiment with less naive rules by taking into account the earlier control literature.[4] Second, if this exercise leads to a truly promising rule, then room for a compromise could exist between Monetarists who insist on a rule and everybody else who is unwilling to trust major decisions to any mechanical preprogrammed rule. I suggest a setup under which the rule normally would be used to determine the growth of money. However, the monetary authority would have the option of making a discretionary departure from the rule if it provided an explicit justification for the departure, under appropriate procedure. Reasons for such a departure would have to include impending macro policy changes, such as major changes in expenditures or taxes and in net exports. Under the proposed eclectic arrangement, the rule would serve as a check on discretion while discretion would serve as a check on the rule. This check is vital since, as Table 10.2 indicates, the risks of instability and disastrous outcomes are much too great to justify placing ourselves entirely at the mercy of any mechanical rule.

NOTES

1 The test that follows has some similarity to that presented in my 1964 article. Of course, the money supply rule tested is a different one. Furthermore, at least in the variant described below, the simulation allows for the feedback of the money path on velocity, including the effect of lags.

2 The percentage change in velocity is approximated as the difference between the percentage change in GNP and that in M1, which can be calculated from columns (3) and (4) of Table 10.2.

3 Poole (1986) has proposed a different rule in which the change in money supply is given by a constant (or a declining trend) plus a fraction of the change in interest rates. This clearly is an improvement if the velocity change comes mostly from interest rates, though not if they come from other sources. Poole provides a graph comparing the money supply according to his rule with the actual for the period 1915–85. Unfortunately, this graph is not very enlightening for several reasons: (i) the scale is very small; (ii) the graph does not show the rates of *change*; and (iii) in the simulation, he uses the simultaneous interest rate which clearly would be unavailable in practice.

I have tried to replicate Poole's simulation for the period 1980–6 by using annual data and a one-quarter lag for interest rates. The results indicate that Poole's rule is a definite improvement over the Mayer *et al.* rule, notably in 1982, but still must be rated as unreliable. For example, during two years, the M1 growth that his rule calls for is only about half as large as the actual while real GNP is below target.

4 The literature is quite voluminous and extends over several decades. The following selection is purely indicative: Phillips (1954, 1957), Cooper and Fischer (1974), Chow (1975), Craine *et al.* (1976), Tinsley and von zur Muehlen (1981).

REFERENCES

Chow, G. C. (1975) *Analysis and Control of Dynamic Economic Systems*, New York: Wiley.

Cooper, J. P. and S. Fischer (1974) 'A Method for Stochastic Control of Non-linear Econometric Models and an Application', *Annals of Economic and Social Measurement* January.

Craine, R., A. Havenner and P. Tinsley (1976) 'Optimal Macro Economic Control Policies', *Annals of Economic and Social Measurement* May.

McCallum, B. T. (1984) 'Monetarist Rules in the Light of Recent Experience', *American Economic Review, Papers and Proceedings* May.

Mayer, T. (1987) 'Replacing the FOMC by a PC', *Contemporary Policy Issues* April, pp. 31–43.

Meltzer, A. (1984) 'Overview', in *Price Stability and Public Policy*, Federal Reserve Bank of Kansas City.

Modigliani, F. (1964) 'Some Empirical Tests of Monetary Management and of Rules vs. Discretion', *Journal of Political Economy* June.

——(1977) 'The Monetarist Controversy or, Should We Forsake Stabilization Policies?' *American Economic Review* March.

Phillips, A. W. (1954) 'Stabilization Policy in a Closed Economy', *Economic Journal* June.

——(1957) 'Stabilization Policy and the Time-Forms of Lagged Responses', *Economic Journal* June.

Poole, W. (1986) 'Is Monetarism Dead?', *Business Economics* October.

Tinsley, P. and P. von zur Muehlen (1981) 'A Maximum Probability Approach to Short-Run Policy', *Journal of Econometrics* January.

Part III

The challenge of rational expectations and new classical macroeconomics

Introduction

During the 1970s (at least as far as the United States was concerned) the new classical research programme replaced monetarism as the main counter-revolutionary theory to Keynesianism. The primary objective of early new classical theorists was to build macroeconomic models based on firm microeconomic foundations involving continuous market clearing and optimization by economic agents. The leading US exponents of, and/or contributors to, the first phase of this research programme include Robert Lucas Jr, Thomas Sargent, Robert Barro, Edward Prescott and Neil Wallace. In their 1978 paper entitled 'After Keynesian Macroeconomics' (reprinted on pp. 270–94), Robert Lucas and Thomas Sargent argue that Keynesian models in the 1960s were fatally flawed as they lacked sound microfoundations and incorporated an adaptive expectations hypothesis which is inconsistent with maximizing behaviour. In addition to these theoretical failings they also argue that in the 1970s Keynesian macroeconometric models experienced 'econometric failure on a grand scale' and that being subject to the Lucas critique could not be used to guide policy. In their place Lucas and Sargent advocate 'equilibrium' new classical models (in which markets always clear and 'rational' agents optimize) suggesting that equilibrium models can account for the main features of the business cycle with economic fluctuations being triggered by unanticipated (monetary) shocks. In the final section of their paper they respond to four lines of criticism which have been raised against equilibrium new classical models relating to the assumption of continuous market clearing, the observed persistence of cyclical movements in output and employment, linearity, and the neglect of learning. For a discussion of the rhetoric surrounding this article see Backhouse (1997).

New classical models are based on the (highly controversial) assumption of continuous market clearing, together with the rational expectations and aggregate supply hypotheses. In these models fluctuations in output and employment reflect the voluntary response of rational economic agents who misperceive money price changes for relative price changes due to incomplete information. Rodney Maddock and Michael Carter's 1982 *Journal of Economic Literature* article (reprinted on pp. 295–313) entitled 'A Child's

Guide to Rational Expectations' examines a number of key issues surrounding the structure and policy implications of new classical models. The article is entertainingly couched in the form of a play involving a conversation between two students, one Keynesian in orientation and the other more disposed to monetarism. In a series of scenes set in a student's union, first over coffee and later over a beer, the two students discuss the basic ideas underlying rational expectations; the implications for stabilization policy of combining the rational expectations hypothesis with a new classical aggregate supply hypothesis (most notably surrounding the policy impotence or ineffectiveness proposition); criticisms of the new classical approach; and finally evidence on, and the significance of, 'new classical' rational expectations models.

The structure of new classical models leads to a number of controversial policy implications which, in addition to the policy ineffectiveness proposition, feed into the debate over the role and conduct of stabilization policy. One of the most debated policy implications that result from the new classical approach concerns the 'Ricardian equivalence theorem', a term first introduced by James Buchanan (1976). The theorem is also sometimes known as the 'Ricardo-Barro equivalence theorem' as it was developed in its modern form by Robert Barro (1974) but was first articulated by the famous nineteenth-century English economist David Ricardo, who ironically expressed doubts about its validity. In essence this theorem states that the effects of an increase in government expenditure on the economy will be the same whether it is financed by increased taxation or borrowing from the private sector. In the latter case it is claimed that the private sector will merely react to a bond-financed increase in government expenditure by saving more in the present period in order to meet future tax liabilities. In this approach changes in the government budget deficit caused by tax changes have no effect on aggregate demand. In his 1989 *Journal of Economic Perspectives* article (reprinted on pp. 314–33) on 'The Ricardian Approach to Budget Deficits', Robert Barro discusses five major theoretical objections which have been put forward in the literature to Ricardian equivalence, and the empirical evidence on the effects of budget deficits on interest rates, saving and the current account balance.

The final contribution is David Laidler's 1986 *Banca Nazionale Del Lavoro Quarterly Review* article entitled 'The New-Classical Contribution to Macroeconomics' (reprinted on pp. 334–58). Laidler critically assesses the basic premises underlying new classical macroeconomics and considers what contributions of lasting importance the new classical school has made to macroeconomics since the early 1970s. After examining the relationship between monetarism and new classical macroeconomics, Laidler considers the relative explanatory power of these two doctrines with respect to the empirical evidence and the new classical claim that their approach incorporates a superior analytical method. He concludes by suggesting that the application of certain basic ideas which underlie the new classical approach to macroeconomics has been unnecessarily restrictive. In particular, he questions that the maximizing behaviour of agents should always be analysed in the context of continuously clearing markets, and that agents' rational expectations accord with those that would be generated with knowledge of the 'true' model of the economy. However, Laidler also accepts that the insistence on equilibrium modelling of individuals as the basis for macroeconomic modelling has been both valuable and beneficial.

Although the early 1980s witnessed the demise of the mark I (monetary surprise) version of the new classical approach (not least due to the implausibility of supposed information gaps relating to aggregate price level and money supply data, and the failure of empirical tests to provide strong support for the policy ineffectiveness proposition) it set down the seeds for the development of a mark II version, commonly referred to as the real business cycle approach, in which real supply-side factors rather than monetary impulses are emphasized in explaining economic fluctuations. Before turning to four articles which consider various aspects of the real business cycle approach in Part IV, it would be useful to summarize the contribution that the first phase of this new classical revolution has made to macroeconomics. That contribution can be seen in four main directions. First, it has led to the widespread practice of applying equilibrium modelling to macroeconomic analysis. Second, it has accelerated the movement towards the now much more widely accepted view that any satisfactory macroeconomic analysis needs to be based on firm microfoundations. Third, it has led to the widespread adoption of the rational expectations hypothesis in macroeconomics. Finally, the insights provided by the incorporation of the rational expectations hypothesis into macroeconomic models, together with the literature on time-inconsistency and the Lucas critique, have led economists to critically reappraise the traditional approaches to policy-making and evaluation.

REFERENCES

*Titles marked with an asterisk are particularly recommended for additional reading.
*Abel, A. B. and B. S. Bernanke (1995) *Macroeconomics*, 2nd edn, Chapter 11, New York: Addison Wesley.
*Backhouse, R. E. (1997) 'The Rhetoric and Methodology of Modern Macroeconomics', in B. Snowdon and H. R. Vane (eds) *Reflections on the Development of Modern Macroeconomics*, Aldershot: Edward Elgar.
Barro, R. J. (1974) 'Are Government Bonds Net Wealth?', *Journal of Political Economy* 82, November/December, pp. 1095–117.
Barro, R. J. (1984) 'What Survives of the Rational Expectations Revolution? Rational Expectations and Macroeconomics in 1984', *American Economic Review* 74, May, pp. 179–82.
*Barro, R. J. (1989) 'New Classical and Keynesians, or the Good Guys and Bad Guys', *Schwiez Zeitschrift für Volkswirtschaft und Statistik* 3, pp. 263–73.
*Barro, R. J. and V. Grilli (1994) *European Macroeconomics*, Chapter 20, London: Macmillan.

Buchanan, J. M. (1976) 'Barro on the Ricardian Equivalence Theorem', *Journal of Political Economy* 84, April, pp. 337–42.

*Carter, M. and R. Maddock (1984) *Rational Expectations: Macroeconomics for the 1980s?*, London: Macmillan.

*Dornbusch, R. and S. Fischer (1994) *Macroeconomics*, 6th edn, Chapter 9, New York: McGraw-Hill.

*Froyen, R. T. (1996) *Macroeconomics: Theories and Policies*, 5th edn, Chapter 11, London: Prentice-Hall.

*Gordon, R. J. (1993) *Macroeconomics*, 6th edn, Chapter 7, New York: HarperCollins.

*Hall, R. E. and J. B. Taylor (1993) *Macroeconomics*, 4th edn, Chapter 15, New York: W. W. Norton.

*Hoover, K. D. (1992) 'The Rational Expectations Revolution: An Assessment', *Cato Journal* Spring/Summer, pp. 81–96.

*Jansen, D. W., C. D. Delorme and R. B. Ekelund, Jr (1994) *Intermediate Macroeconomics*, Chapter 9, New York: West.

Kantor, B. (1979) 'Rational Expectations and Economic Thought', *Journal of Economic Literature* 17, December, pp. 1422–41.

Klamer, A. (1984) 'Levels of Discourse in New Classical Economics', *History of Political Economy* 16, Summer, pp. 263–90.

*Klamer, A. (1984) *The New Classical Macroeconomics: Conversations with New Classical Economists and their Opponents*, Brighton: Wheatsheaf.

*Lucas, R. E. Jr (1977) 'Understanding Business Cycles', in K. Brunner and A. H. Meltzer (eds) *Stabilization of the Domestic and International Economy*, Amsterdam: North Holland.

Maddock, R. (1984) 'Rational Expectations Macrotheory: A Lakatosian Case Study in Programme Adjustment', *History of Political Economy* 16, Summer, pp. 291–310.

*Mankiw, N. G. (1994) *Macroeconomics*, 2nd edn, Chapters 11 and 16, New York: Worth.

Minford, P. (1997) 'Macroeconomics: Before and After Rational Expectations', in B. Snowdon and H. R. Vane (eds) *Reflections on the Development of Modern Macroeconomics*, Aldershot: Edward Elgar.

*Shaw, G. K. (1984) *Rational Expectations: An Elementary Exposition*, Brighton: Wheatsheaf.

*Sheffrin, S. M. (1996) *Rational Expectations*, 2nd edn, Cambridge: Cambridge University Press.

*Snowdon, B. and H. R. Vane (1996) 'The Development of Modern Macroeconomics: Reflections in the Light of Johnson's Analysis after Twenty-Five Years', *Journal of Macroeconomics* 18, Summer, pp. 381–401.

*Snowdon, B., H. R. Vane and P. Wynarczyk (1994) *A Modern Guide to Macroeconomics: An Introduction to Competing Schools of Thought*, Chapter 5, Aldershot: Edward Elgar.

*Tobin, J. (1980) 'Are New Classical Models Plausible Enough to Guide Policy?', *Journal of Money, Credit and Banking* 12, November, pp. 788–99.

QUESTIONS

1 'Orthodox monetarism and early new classical models represent two types of monetarism'. Critically examine this view.

2 Explain why in the new classical market clearing model the Phillips curve emerges as a result of imperfect information about the aggregate price level.

3 Critically assess the importance of the rational expectations hypothesis within the new classical approach to macroeconomics. What are the implications for stabilization policy?

4 'The crucial assumption in new classical analysis is market clearing not rational expectations'. Do you agree?

5 In new classical models only unanticipated monetary shocks can affect real output and employment. How plausible is this theory as an explanation of economic fluctuations?

6 Assess the significance of the Lucas critique with respect to the construction of macroeconomic models.

7 Compare and contrast the traditional and Ricardian approaches to the impact of budget deficits.

8 Outline the dynamic time inconsistency argument in favour of a monetary rule. Does this analysis point towards the desirability of having an independent central bank?

9 To what extent do the real output and employment effects of disinflation depend on the credibility and reputation of the policy-maker?

10 Evaluate the contribution made to macroeconomic analysis by new classical theorists in the period 1972–82. What remains of the first phase of the new classical revolution?

11 After Keynesian macroeconomics

Robert E. Lucas and Thomas J. Sargent
After the Phillips Curve: Persistence of High Inflation and High Unemployment (1978) Boston, MA: Federal Reserve Bank of Boston, pp. 49–72.

INTRODUCTION

For the applied economist, the confident and apparently successful application of Keynesian principles to economic policy which occurred in the United States in the 1960s was an event of incomparable significance and satisfaction. These principles led to a set of simple, quantitative relationships between fiscal policy and economic activity generally, the basic logic of which could be (and was) explained to the general public, and which could be applied to yield improvements in economic performance benefiting *everyone*. It seemed an economics as free of ideological difficulties as, say, applied chemistry or physics, promising a straightforward expansion in economic possibilities. One might argue about how this windfall should be distributed, but it seemed a simple lapse of logic to oppose the windfall itself. Understandably and correctly, this promise was met at first with skepticism by non-economists; the smoothly growing prosperity of the Kennedy–Johnson years did much to diminish these doubts.

We dwell on these halcyon days of Keynesian economics because, without conscious effort, they are difficult to recall today. In the 1970s, the US economy has undergone its first major depression since the 1930s, to the accompaniment of inflation rates in excess of 10 percent per annum. These events have been transmitted (by consent of the governments involved) to other advanced countries and in many cases have been amplified. These events did not arise from a reactionary reversion to outmoded, 'classical' principles of tight money and balanced budgets. On the contrary, they were accompanied by massive governmental budget deficits and high rates of monetary expansion: policies which, although bearing an admitted risk of inflation, promised according to modern Keynesian doctrine rapid real growth and low rates of unemployment.

That these predictions were wildly incorrect, and that the doctrine on which they were based is fundamentally flawed, are now simple matters of fact, involving no novelties in economic theory. The task which faces contemporary students of the business cycle is that of sorting through the wreckage, determining which features of that remarkable intellectual event called the Keynesian Revolution can be salvaged and put to good use, and which others must be discarded. Though it is far from clear what the outcome of this process will be, it is already evident that it will necessarily involve the reopening of basic issues in monetary economics which have been viewed since the 1930s as 'closed', and the re-evaluation of every aspect of the institutional framework within which monetary and fiscal policy is formulated in the advanced countries.

This chapter is in the nature of an early progress report on this process of re-evaluation and reconstruction. We begin by reviewing the econometric framework by means of which Keynesian theory evolved from discon- nected, qualitative 'talk' about economic activity into a system of equations which could be compared to data in a systematic way, and provide an operational guide in the necessarily quantitative task of formulating monet- ary and fiscal policy. Next, we identify those aspects of this framework which were central to its failure in the 1970s. In so doing, our intent will be to establish that the difficulties are *fatal:* that modern macroeconomic models are of *no* value in guiding policy, and that this condition will not be remedied by modifications along any line which is currently being pursued.

This diagnosis, if successful, will suggest certain principles which a useful theory of business cycles must possess. In the latter part of this chapter we shall review some recent research which is consistent with these principles.

MACROECONOMETRIC MODELS

The Keynesian Revolution was, in the form in which it succeeded in the United States, a revolution in *method*. This was not Keynes's [13] intent, nor is it the view of all of his most eminent followers. Yet if one does not view the revolution in this way, it is impossible to account for some of its most important features: the evolution of macroeconomics into a quantitative, *scientific* discipline, the development of explicit statistical descriptions of economic behavior, the increasing reliance of government officials on tech- nical economic expertise, and the introduction of the use of mathematical control theory to manage an economy. It is the fact that Keynesian theory lent itself so readily to the formulation of explicit econometric models which accounts for the dominant scientific position it attained by the 1960s.

As a consequence of this, there is no hope of understanding either the success of the Keynesian Revolution or its eventual failure at the purely verbal level at which Keynes himself wrote. It will be necessary to know something of the way macroeconometric models are constructed and the features they must have in order to 'work' as aids in forecasting and policy evaluation. To discuss these issues, we introduce some notation.

An econometric model is a system of equations involving a number of endogenous variables (variables that are determined by the model), exogen- ous variables (variables which affect the system but are not affected by it), and stochastic or random shocks. The idea is to use historical data to estimate the model, and then to utilize the estimated version to obtain estimates of the consequences of alternative policies. For practical reasons, it is usual to use a standard linear model, taking the structural form.[1]

$$A_0 y_t + A_1 y_{t-1} + \ldots + A_m y_{t-m} = B_0 x_t + B_1 x_{t-1} + \ldots + B_n x_{t-n} + \varepsilon_t \quad (1)$$

$$R_0 \varepsilon_t + R_1 \varepsilon_{t-1} + \ldots + R_r \varepsilon_{t-r} = u_t, R_0 \equiv I. \quad (2)$$

Here y_t is an (Lx1) vector of endogenous variables, x_t is a (Kx1) vector of exogenous variables, and ε_t and u_t are each (Lx1) vectors of random disturbances. The matrices A_j are each (LxL); the B_j's are (LxK), and the R_j's are each (LxL). The (Lx1) disturbance process u_t is assumed to be a serially uncorrelated process with $Eu_t = 0$ and with contemporaneous covariance matrix $Eu_t u_t' = \sum$ and $Eu_t u_s' = 0$ for all $t \neq s$. The defining characteristic of the exogenous variables x_t is that they are uncorrelated with the ε's at all lags so that $Eu_t x_s'$ is an (LxK) matrix of zeroes for all t and s.

Equations (1) are L equations in the L current values y_t of the endogenous variables. Each of these structural equations is a behavioral relationship, identity, or market clearing condition, and each in principle can involve a number of endogenous variables. The structural equations are usually not 'regression equations',[2] because the ε_t's are in general, by the logic of the model, supposed to be correlated with more than one component of the vector y_t and very possibly one or more components of the vectors $y_{t-1}, \cdots y_{t-m}$.

The structural model (1) and (2) can be solved for y_t in terms of past y's and x's and past shocks. This 'reduced form' system is

$$y_t = -P_1 y_{t-1} - \ldots - P_{r+m} y_{t-r-m} + Q_0 x_t + \ldots + Q_{r+n} x_{t-n-r} + A_0^{-1} u_t \quad (3)$$

where[3]

$$P_s = A_0^{-1} \sum_{j=-\infty}^{\infty} R_j A_{s-j}$$

$$Q_s = A_0^{-1} \sum_{j=-\infty}^{\infty} R_j B_{s-j}.$$

The reduced form equations are 'regression equations', that is, the disturbance vector $A_0^{-1} u_t$ is orthogonal to $y_{t-1}, \ldots, y_{t-r-m}, x_t, \ldots, x_{t-n-r}$. This follows from the assumptions that the x's are exogenous and that the u's are serially uncorrelated. Therefore, under general conditions the reduced form can be estimated consistently by the method of least squares. The population parameters of the reduced form (3) together with the parameters of a vector autoregression for x_t,

$$x_t = C_1 x_{t-1} + \ldots + C_p x_{t-p} + a_t \quad (4)$$

where $Ea_t = 0$ and $Ea_t \cdot x_{t-j} = 0$ for $j \geqslant 1$ completely describe all of the first and second moments of the (y_t, x_t) process. Given long enough time series, good estimates of the reduced form parameters – the P_j's and Q_j's – can be obtained by the method of least squares. Reliable estimates of those parameters is all that examination of the data by themselves can deliver.

It is not in general possible to work backwards from estimates of the P's and Q's alone to derive unique estimates of the structural parameters, the A_j's, B_j's, and R_j's. In general, infinite numbers of A, B, and R's are compatible with a single set of P's and Q's. This is the 'identification problem' of econometrics. In order to derive a set of estimated structural parameters, it is necessary to know a great deal about them in advance. If enough prior information is imposed, it is possible to extract estimates of the (A_j, B_j, R_j)'s implied by the data in combination with the prior information.

For purposes of *ex ante* forecasting, or the unconditional prediction of the vector $y_{t+1}, y_{t+2}, \cdots$ given observation of y_s and $x_s, s \leqslant t$, the estimated reduced form (3), together with (4), is sufficient. This is simply an exercise in a sophisticated kind of extrapolation, requiring no understanding of the structural parameters or, that is to say, of the *economics* of the model.

For purposes of *conditional* forecasting, or the prediction of the future behavior of some components of y_t and x_t *conditional* on particular values of other components, selected by policy, one needs to know the structural parameters. This is so because a change in policy *necessarily* alters some of the structural parameters (for example, those describing the past behavior of the policy variables themselves) and therefore affects the reduced form parameters in highly complex fashion (see the equations defining P_s and Q_s, below (3)). Without knowledge as to which structural parameters remain invariant as policy changes, and which change (and how), an econometric model is of *no* value in assessing alternative policies. It should be clear that this is true *regardless* of how well (3) and (4) fit historical data, or how well they perform in unconditional forecasting.

Our discussion to this point has been at a high level of generality, and the formal considerations we have reviewed are not in any way specific to *Keynesian* models. The problem of identifying a structural model from a collection of economic time series is one that must be solved by anyone who claims the ability to give quantitative economic advice. The simplest Keynesian models are attempted solutions to this problem, as are the large-scale versions currently in use. So, too, are the monetarist models which imply the desirability of fixed monetary growth rules. So, for that matter, is the armchair advice given by economists who claim to be outside the econometric tradition, though in this case the implicit, underlying structure is not exposed to professional criticism. *Any* procedure which leads from the study of observed economic behavior to the quantitative assessment of alternative economic policies involves the steps, executed poorly or well, explicitly or implicitly, which we have outlined above.

KEYNESIAN MACROECONOMETRICS

In Keynesian macroeconometric models structural parameters are identified by the imposition of several types of *a priori* restrictions on the A_j's, B_j's, and R_j's. These restrictions usually fall into one of the following categories:[4]

(a) *A priori* setting of many of the elements of the A_j's and B_j's to zero.
(b) Restrictions on the orders of serial correlation and the extent of the cross serial correlation of the disturbance vector ε_t, restrictions which amount to *a priori* setting many elements of the R_j's to zero.
(c) *A priori* categorization of variables into 'exogenous' and 'endogenous'. A relative abundance of exogenous variables aids identification.

Existing large Keynesian macroeconometric models are open to serious challenge for the way they have introduced each category of restriction.

Keynes's *General Theory* was rich in suggestions for restrictions of type (a). It proposed a theory of national income determination built up from several simple relationships, each involving a few variables only. One of these, for example, was the 'fundamental law' relating consumption expenditures to income. This suggested one 'row' in equations (1) involving current consumption, current income, and *no other* variables, thereby imposing many zero-restrictions on the A_i and B_j. Similarly, the liquidity preference relation expressed the demand for money as a function of income and an interest rate *only*. By translating the building blocks of the Keynesian theoretical system into explicit equations, models of the form (1) and (2) were constructed with many theoretical restrictions of type (a).

Restrictions on the coefficients R_i governing the behavior of the 'error terms' in (1) are harder to motivate theoretically, the 'errors' being by definition movements in the variables which the *economic* theory cannot account for. The early econometricians took 'standard' assumptions from statistical textbooks, restrictions which had proved useful in the agricultural experimenting which provided the main impetus to the development of modern statistics. Again, these restrictions, well-motivated or not, involve setting many elements in the R_i's equal to zero, aiding identification of the model's structure.

The classification of variables into 'exogenous' and 'endogenous' was also done on the basis of prior considerations. In general, variables were classed as 'endogenous' which were, as a matter of institutional fact, determined largely by the actions of private agents (like consumption or private investment expenditures). Exogenous variables were those under governmental control (like tax rates, or the supply of money). This division was intended to reflect the ordinary meaning of the word 'endogenous' to mean 'determined by the [economic] system' and 'exogenous' to mean 'affecting the [economic] system but not affected by it'.

By the mid-1950s, econometric models had been constructed which fit time series data well, in the sense that their reduced forms (3) tracked past data closely and proved useful in short-term forecasting. Moreover, by means of restrictions of the three types reviewed above, it was possible to identify their structural parameters A_i, B_j, R_k. Using this estimated structure, it was possible to simulate the models to obtain estimates of the consequences of different government economic policies, such as tax rates, expenditures or monetary policy.

This Keynesian solution to the problem of identifying a structural model has become increasingly suspect as a result of developments of both a theoretical and statistical nature. Many of these developments are due to efforts to researchers sympathetic to the Keynesian tradition, and many were well advanced well before the spectacular failure of the Keynesian models in the 1970s.[5]

Since its inception, macroeconomics has been criticized for its lack of 'foundations in microeconomic and general equilibrium theory'. As astute commentators like Leontief [14] (disapprovingly) and Tobin [37] (approvingly) recognized early on, the creation of a distinct branch of theory with its own distinct postulates was Keynes's conscious aim. Yet a main theme of theoretical work since the *General Theory* has been the attempt to use microeconomic theory based on the classical postulate that agents act in their own interests to suggest a list of variables that belong on the right side of a given behavioral schedule, say, a demand schedule for a factor of production or a consumption schedule.[6] But from the point of view of identification of a given structural equation by means of restrictions of type (a), one needs reliable prior information that certain variables should be *excluded* from the right-hand side. Modern probabilistic microeconomic theory almost never implies either the exclusion restrictions that were suggested by Keynes or those that are imposed by macroeconometric models.

To take one example that has extremely dire implications for the identification of existing macro models, expectations about the future prices, tax rates, and income levels play a critical role in many demand and supply schedules in those models. For example, in the best models, investment demand typically is supposed to respond to businessmen's expectations of future tax credits, tax rates, and factor costs. The supply of labor typically is supposed to depend on the rate of inflation that workers expect in the future. Such structural equations are usually identified by the assumption that, for example, the expectation about the factor price or rate of inflation attributed to agents is a function *only* of a few lagged values of the variable itself which the agent is supposed to be forecasting. However, the macro models themselves contain complicated dynamic interactions among endogenous variables, including factor prices and the rate of inflation, and generally imply that a wise agent would use current and many lagged values of many and usually most endogenous and exogenous variables in the model in order to form expectations about any one variable. Thus, virtually any version of the hypothesis that agents behave in their own interests will contradict the identification restrictions imposed on expectations formation. Further, the restrictions on expectations that have been used to achieve identification are entirely arbitrary and have not been derived from any deeper assumption reflecting first principles about economic behavior. No general first principle has ever been set down which would imply that, say, the expected rate of inflation should be modeled as a linear function of lagged rates of inflation alone with weights that add up to unity, yet this hypothesis is used as an identifying restriction in almost all existing models. The casual treatment of expectations is not a peripheral problem in these models, for the role of expectations is pervasive in the models and exerts a massive influence on their dynamic properties (a point Keynes himself insisted on). The failure of existing models to derive restrictions on expectations from any first principles grounded in economic theory is a symptom of a somewhat deeper and more general failure to derive behavioral relationships from any consistently posed dynamic optimization problems.

As for the second category, restrictions of type (b), existing Keynesian macro models make severe *a priori* restrictions on the R_j's. Typically, the R_j's are supposed to be diagonal so that cross equation lagged serial correlation is ignored and also the order of the ε_t process is assumed to be short so that only low-order serial correlation is allowed. There are at present no theoretical grounds for introducing these restrictions, and for good reasons there is little prospect that economic theory will soon provide any such grounds. In principle, identification can be achieved without imposing any such restrictions. Foregoing the use of category (b) restrictions would increase the category (a) and (c) restrictions needed. In any event, existing macro models do heavily restrict the R's.

Turning to the third category, all existing large models adopt an *a priori* classification of variables into the categories of strictly endogenous variables, the y_t's, and strictly exogenous variables, the x_t's. Increasingly, it is being recognized that the classification of a variable as 'exogenous' on the basis of the observation that it *could* be set without reference to the current and past values of other variables has nothing to do with the econometrically relevant question of how this variable has *in fact* been related to others over a given historical period. Moreover, in light of recent developments in time series econometrics, we know that this arbitrary classification procedure is not necessary. Christopher Sims [34] has shown that in a time series context the hypothesis of econometric exogeneity can be tested. That is, Sims showed that the hypothesis that x_t is strictly econometrically exogenous in (1) necessarily implies certain restrictions that can be tested given time series on the y's and x's. Tests along the lines of Sims's ought to be used as a matter of course in checking out categorizations into exogenous and endogenous sets of variables. To date they have not been. Prominent builders of large econometric models have even denied the usefulness of such tests.[7]

FAILURE OF KEYNESIAN MACROECONOMETRICS

Our discussion in the preceding section raised a number of theoretical reasons for believing that the parameters identified as structural by the methods which are in current use in macroeconomics are not structural in fact. That is, there is no reason, in our opinion, to believe that these models have isolated structures which will remain invariant across the class of interventions that figure in contemporary discussions of economic policy. Yet the question of whether a particular model is structural is an empirical, not a theoretical, one. If the macroeconometric models had compiled a record of parameter stability, particularly in the face of breaks in the stochastic behavior of the exogenous variables and disturbances, one would be skeptical as to the importance of prior theoretical objections of the sort we have raised.

In fact, however, the track record of the major econometric models is, on any dimension other than very short-term unconditional forecasting, very poor. Formal statistical tests for parameter instability, conducted by sub-dividing past series into periods and checking for parameter stability across time, invariably reveal major shifts (for one example, see [23]). Moreover, this difficulty is implicitly acknowledged by model-builders themselves, who routinely employ an elaborate system of add-factors in forecasting, in an attempt to offset the continuing 'drift' of the model away from the actual series.

Though not, of course, designed as such by anyone, macroeconometric models were subjected in the 1970s to a decisive test. A key element in all Keynesian models is a 'trade-off' between inflation and real output: the higher is the inflation rate; the higher is output (or equivalently, the lower is the rate of unemployment). For example, the models of the late 1960s predicted a sustained unemployment rate in the United States of 4 percent as consistent with a 4 percent annual rate of inflation. Many economists at that time urged a deliberate policy of inflation on the basis of this prediction. Certainly the erratic 'fits and starts' character of actual US policy in the 1970s cannot be attributed to recommendations based on Keynesian models, but the inflationary bias *on average* of monetary and fiscal policy in this period should, according to all of these models, have produced the lowest average unemployment rates for any decade since the 1940s. In fact, as we know, they produced the highest unemployment since the 1930s. This was econometric failure on a grand scale.

This failure has not led to widespread conversions of Keynesian economists to other faiths, nor should it have been expected to. In economics, as in other sciences, a theoretical framework is always broader and more flexible than any particular set of equations, and there is always the hope that, if a particular specific model fails, one can find a more successful one based on 'roughly' the same ideas. It has, however, already had some important consequences, with serious implications both for economic policy-making and for the practice of economic science.

For policy, the central fact is that Keynesian policy recommendations have no sounder basis, in a scientific sense, than recommendations of non-Keynesian economists or, for that matter, non-economists. To note one consequence of the wide recognition of this, the current wave of protectionist sentiment directed at 'saving jobs' would have been answered, in the late 1960s, with the Keynesian counter-argument that fiscal policy can achieve the same end, but more efficiently. In the late 1970s, of course, no one would take this response seriously, so it is not offered. Indeed, economists who in the late 1960s championed Keynesian fiscal policy as an *alternative* to inefficient direct controls increasingly favor the latter as 'supplements' to Keynesian policy. The idea seems to be that if people refuse to obey the equations we have fit to their past behavior, we can pass laws to *make* them do so.

Scientifically, the Keynesian failure of the 1970s has resulted in a new openness. Fewer and fewer economists are involved in monitoring and refining the major econometric models; more and more are developing alternative theories of the business cycle, based on different theoretical principles. In addition, increased attention and respect are accorded to the theoretical casualties of the Keynesian Revolution, to the ideas of Keynes's contemporaries and of earlier economists whose thinking has been regarded for years as outmoded.

At the present time, it is impossible to foresee where these developments will lead. Some, of course, continue to believe that the problems of existing Keynesian models can be resolved within the existing framework, that these models can be adequately refined by changing a few structural equations, by adding or subtracting a few variables here and there, or perhaps by disaggregating various blocks of equations. We have couched our preceding criticisms in such general terms precisely to emphasize their generic character and hence the futility of pursuing minor variations within this general framework.

A second response to the failure of Keynesian analytical methods is to renounce analytical methods entirely, returning to 'judgmental' methods. The first of these responses identifies the quantitative, scientific goals of the Keynesian Revolution with the details of the particular models so far developed. The second renounces both these models and the objectives they were designed to attain. There is, we believe, an intermediate course, to which we now turn.

EQUILIBRIUM BUSINESS CYCLE THEORY

Economists prior to the 1930s did not recognize a need for a special branch of economics, with its own special postulates, designed to explain the business cycle. Keynes founded that subdiscipline, called *macroeconomics*, because he thought that it was impossible to explain the characteristics of business cycles within the discipline imposed by classical economic theory, a discipline imposed by its insistence on adherence to the two postulates (a) that markets be assumed to clear, and (b) that agents be assumed to act in their own self-interest. The outstanding fact that seemed impossible to reconcile with these two postulates was the length and severity of business depressions and the large-scale unemployment which they entailed. A related observation is that measures of aggregate demand and prices are positively correlated with measures of real output and employment, in apparent contradiction to the classical result that changes in a purely nominal magnitude like the general price level were pure 'unit changes' which should not alter real behavior. After freeing himself of the strait-jacket (or discipline) imposed by the classical postulates, Keynes described a model in which rules of thumb, such as the consumption function and liquidity preference schedule, took the place of decision functions that a classical economist would insist be derived from the theory of choice. And rather than require that wages and prices be determined by the postulate that markets clear – which for the labor market seemed patently contradicted by the severity of business depressions – Keynes took as an unexamined postulate that money wages are 'sticky', meaning that they are set at a level or by a process that could be taken as uninfluenced by the macroeconomic forces he proposed to analyze.

When Keynes wrote, the terms 'equilibrium' and 'classical' carried certain positive and normative connotations which seemed to rule out either modifier being applied to business cycle theory. The term 'equilibrium' was thought to refer to a system 'at rest', and both 'equilibrium' and 'classical' were used interchangeably, by some, with 'ideal'. Thus an economy in classical equilibrium would be both unchanging and unimprovable by policy interventions. Using terms in this way, it is no wonder that few economists regarded equilibrium theory as a promising starting point for the understanding of business cycles, and for the design of policies to mitigate or eliminate them.

In recent years, the meaning of the term 'equilibrium' has undergone such dramatic development that a theorist of the 1930s would not recognize it. It is now routine to describe an economy following a multivariate stochastic process as being 'in equilibrium', by which is meant nothing more than that at each point in time, postulates (a) and (b) above are satisfied. This development, which stemmed mainly from work by K. J. Arrow [2] and G. Debreu [6], implies that simply to look at any economic time series and conclude that it is a 'disequilibrium phenomenon' is a meaningless observation. Indeed, a more likely conjecture, on the basis of work by Hugo Sonnenschein [36], is that the general hypothesis that a collection of time series describes an economy in competitive equilibrium is *without content*.[8]

The research line being pursued by a number of us involves the attempt to discover a particular, econometrically testable equilibrium theory of the business cycle, one that can serve as the foundation for quantitative analysis of macroeconomic policy. There is no denying that this approach is 'counter-revolutionary', for it presupposes that Keynes and his followers were wrong to give up on the possibility that an equilibrium theory could account for the business cycle. As of now, no successful equilibrium macro-econometric model at the level of detail of, say, the FMP model, has been constructed. But small theoretical equilibrium models have been constructed that show potential for explaining some key features of the business cycle long thought to be inexplicable within the confines of classical postulates. The equilibrium models also provide reasons for understanding why estimated Keynesian models fail to hold up outside of the sample over which they have been estimated. We now turn to describing some of the key facts about business cycles and the way the new classical models confront them.

For a long time most of the economics profession has, with some reason, followed Keynes in rejecting classical macroeconomic models because they seemed incapable of explaining some important characteristics of time series measuring important economic aggregates. Perhaps the most important failure of the classical model seemed to be its inability to explain the positive correlation in the time series between prices and/or wages, on the one hand, and measures of aggregate output or employment, on the other hand. A second and related failure was its inability to explain the positive correlations between measures of aggregate demand, like the money stock, and aggregate output or employment. Static analysis of classical macroeconomic models typically implied that the levels of output and employment were determined independently of both the absolute level of prices and of aggregate demand. The pervasive presence of the above mentioned positive correlations in the time series seems consistent with causal connections flowing from aggregate demand and inflation to output and employment, contrary to the classical 'neutrality' propositions. Keynesian macroeconometric models do imply such causal connections.

We now have rigorous theoretical models which illustrate how these correlations can emerge while retaining the classical postulates that markets clear and agents optimize.[9] The key step in obtaining such models has been to relax the ancillary postulate used in much classical economic analysis that agents have perfect information. The new classical models continue to assume that markets always clear and that agents optimize. The postulate that agents optimize means that their supply and demand decisions must be functions of real variables, including perceived relative prices. Each agent is assumed to have limited information and to receive information about some prices more often than other prices. On the basis of their limited information – the lists that they have of current and past absolute prices of various goods – agents are assumed to make the best possible estimate of all of the *relative* prices that influence their supply and demand decisions. Because they do not have all of the information that would enable them to compute perfectly the relative prices they care about, agents make errors in estimating the pertinent relative prices, errors that are unavoidable given their limited information. In particular, under certain conditions, agents will tend temporarily to mistake a general increase in all absolute prices as an increase in the *relative* price of the good that they are selling, leading them to increase their supply of that good over what they had previously planned. Since everyone is, on average, making the same mistake, aggregate output will rise above what it would have been. This increase of output will rise above what it would have been. This increase of output above what it would have been will occur whenever this period's average economy-wide price level is above what agents had expected this period's average economy-wide price level to be on the basis of previous information. Symmetrically, average output will be decreased whenever the aggregate price turns out to be lower than agents had expected. The hypothesis of 'rational expectations' is being imposed here because agents are supposed to make the best possible use of the limited information they have and are assumed to know the pertinent objective probability distributions. This hypothesis is imposed by way of adhering to the tenets of equilibrium theory.

In the preceding theory, disturbances to aggregate demand lead to a positive correlation between unexpected changes in the aggregate price level and revisions in aggregate output from its previously planned level. Further, it is an easy step to show that the theory implies correlations between revisions to aggregate output and unexpected changes in any variables that help determine aggregate demand. In most macroeconomic models, the money supply is one determinant of aggregate demand. The preceding theory easily can account for positive correlations between revisions to aggregate output and unexpected increases in the money supply.

While such a theory predicts positive correlations between the inflation rate or money supply, on the one hand, and the level of output on the other, it also asserts that those correlations do not depict 'trade-offs' that can be exploited by a policy authority. That is, the theory predicts that there is no way that the monetary authority can follow a systematic activist policy and achieve a rate of output that is on average higher over the business cycle than what would occur if it simply adopted a no-feedback, X-percent rule of the kind Friedman [8] and Simons [32] recommended. For the theory predicts that aggregate output is a function of current and past unexpected changes in the money supply. Output will be high only when the money supply is and has been higher than it had been expected to be, i.e. higher than average. There is simply no way that on average over the whole business cycle the money supply can be higher than average. Thus, while the preceding theory is capable of explaining some of the correlations long thought to invalidate classical macroeconomic theory, the theory is classical both in its adherence to the classical theoretical postulates and in the 'nonactivist' flavor of its implications for monetary policy.

Small-scale econometric models in the sense of the second section of this chapter have been constructed which capture some of the main features of the equilibrium models described above.[10] In particular, these models incorporate the hypothesis that expectations are rational, or that all available information is utilized by agents. To a degree, these models achieve econometric identification by invoking restrictions in each of the three categories (a), (b) and (c). However, a distinguishing feature of these 'classical' models is that they also heavily rely on an important fourth category of identifying restrictions. This category (d) consists of a set of restrictions that are derived from probabilistic economic theory, but play no role in the Keynesian framework. These restrictions in general do not take the form of zero restrictions of the type (a). Instead, the restrictions from theory typically take the form of *cross-equation* restrictions among the A_j, B_j, C_j parameters. The source of these restrictions is the implication from economic theory that current decisions depend on agents' forecasts of future variables, combined with the implication that these forecasts are formed optimally, given the behavior of past variables. These restrictions do not have as simple a mathematical expression as simply setting a number of parameters equal to zero, but their economic motivation is easy to understand. Ways of utilizing these restrictions in econometric estimation and testing are being rapidly developed.

Another key characteristic of recent work on equilibrium macroeconometric models is that the reliance on entirely *a priori* categorizations (c) of variables as strictly exogenous and endogenous has been markedly reduced, although not entirely eliminated. This development stems jointly from the fact that the models assign important roles to agents' optimal forecasts of future variables, and from Christopher Sims's demonstration that there is a close connection between the concept of strict econometric exogeneity and the forms of the optimal predictors for a vector of time series. Building a model with rational expectations necessarily forces one to consider which set of other variables helps forecast a given variable, say income or the inflation rate. If variable y helps predict variable x, then Sims's theorems imply that x cannot be regarded as exogenous with respect to y. The result of this connection between predictability and exogeneity has been that in equilibrium macroeconometric models the distinction between endogenous and exogenous variables has not been drawn on an entirely *a priori* basis. Furthermore, special cases of the theoretical models, which often involve side restrictions on the R_j's not themselves drawn from economic theory, have strong *testable* predictions as to exogeneity relations among variables.

A key characteristic of equilibrium macroeconometric models is that as a result of the restrictions across the A_j, B_j, and C_j's, the models predict that in general the parameters in *many* of the equations will change if there is a policy intervention that takes the form of a change in one equation that describes how some policy variable is being set. Since they ignore these cross-equation restrictions, Keynesian models in general assume that all other equations remain unchanged when an equation describing a policy variable is changed. Our view is that this is one important reason that Keynesian models have broken down when there have occurred important changes in the equations governing policy variables or exogenous variables. Our hope is that the methods we have described will give us the capability to predict the consequences for all of the equations of changes in the rules governing policy variables. Having that capability is necessary before we can claim to have a scientific basis for making quantitative statements about macroeconomic policy.

At the present time, these new theoretical and econometric developments have not been fully integrated, although it is clear they are very close, both conceptually and operationally. Our preference would be to regard the best currently existing equilibrium models as prototypes of better, future models which will, we hope, prove of practical use in the formulation of policy. But we should not understate the econometric success already attained by equilibrium models. Early versions of these models have been estimated and subjected to some stringent econometric tests by McCallum [20], Barro [3], [4], and Sargent [27], with the result that they do seem capable of explaining some broad features of the business cycle. New and more sophisticated models involving more complicated cross-equation restrictions are in the works (Sargent [29]). Work to date has already shown that equilibrium models are capable of attaining within-sample fits about as good as those obtained by Keynesian models, thereby making concrete the point that the good fits of the Keynesian models provide no good reason for trusting policy recommendations derived from them.

CRITICISM OF EQUILIBRIUM THEORY

The central idea of the equilibrium explanations of business cycles as sketched above is that economic fluctuations arise as agents react to *unanticipated* changes in variables which impinge on their decisions. It is clear that *any* explanation of this general type must carry with it severe limitations on the ability of governmental policy to *offset* these initiating changes. First, governments must somehow have the ability to foresee shocks which are invisible to private agents but at the same time lack the ability to reveal this advance information (hence defusing the shocks). Though it is not difficult to write down theoretical models in which these two conditions are assumed to hold, it is difficult to imagine actual situations in which such models would apply. Second, the governmental countercyclical policy must *itself* be unanticipatable by private agents (certainly a frequently realized condition historically) while at the same time be systematically related to the state of the economy. Effectiveness then rests on the inability of private agents to recognize systematic patterns in monetary and fiscal policy.

To a large extent, criticism of equilibrium models is simply a reaction to these implications for policy. So wide is (or was) the consensus that *the* task of macroeconomics is the discovery of the particular monetary and fiscal policies which can eliminate fluctuations by reacting to private sector instability that the assertion that this task either should not, or cannot be performed is regarded as frivolous independently of whatever reasoning and evidence may support it. Certainly one must have some sympathy with this reaction: an unfounded faith in the curability of a particular ill has served often enough as a stimulus to the finding of genuine cures. Yet to confuse a possibly functional *faith* in the existence of efficacious, re-active monetary and fiscal policies with scientific evidence that such policies are known is clearly dangerous, and to use such faith as a criterion for judging the extent to which particular theories 'fit the facts' is worse still.

There are, of course, legitimate issues involving the ability of equilibrium theories to fit the facts of the business cycle. Indeed, this is the reason for our insistence on the preliminary and tentative character of the particular models we now have. Yet these tentative models share certain features which can be regarded as *essential*, so it is not unreasonable to speculate as to the likelihood that *any* model of this type can be successful, or to ask: what will equilibrium business cycle theorists have in ten years if we get lucky?

Four general reasons for pessimism which have been prominently advanced are (a) the fact that equilibrium models postulate cleared markets, (b) the assertion that these models cannot account for 'persistence' (serial correlation) of cyclical movements, (c) the fact that econometrically implemented models are linear (in logarithms), and (d) the fact that learning behavior has not been incorporated. We discuss each in turn in distinct subsections.

Cleared markets

One essential feature of equilibrium models is that all markets clear, or that all observed prices and quantities be explicable as outcomes of decisions taken by individual firms and households. In practice, this has meant a conventional, competitive supply-equals-demand assumption, though other kinds of equilibrium can easily be imagined (if not so easily analyzed). If, therefore, one takes as a basic 'fact' that labor markets do not clear one arrives immediately at a contradiction between theory and fact. The facts we actually have, however, are simply the available time series on employment and wage rates, plus the responses to our unemployment surveys. Cleared markets is simply a principle, not verifiable by direct observation, which may or may not be useful in constructing successful hypotheses about the behavior of these series. Alternative principles, such as the postulate of the existence of a third-party auctioneer inducing wage 'rigidity' and non-cleared markets, are similarly 'unrealistic', in the not especially important sense of not offering a good description of observed labor market institutions.

A refinement of the unexplained postulate of an uncleared labor market has been suggested by the indisputable fact that there exist long-term labor contracts with horizons of two or three years. Yet the length *per se* over which contracts run does not bear on the issue, for we know from Arrow and Debreu that if infinitely long-term contracts are determined so that prices and wages are contingent on the same information that is available under the assumption of period-by-period market clearing, then precisely the same price-quantity process will result with the long-term contract as would occur under period-by-period market clearing. Thus equilibrium theorizing provides a way, probably the only way we have, to construct a *model* of a long-term contract. The fact that long-term contracts exist, then, has *no* implications about the applicability of equilibrium theorizing. Rather, the real issue here is whether actual contracts can be adequately accounted for within an equilibrium model, that is, a model in which agents are proceeding in their own best interests. Stanley Fischer [7], Edmund Phelps and John Taylor [26], and Robert Hall [12] have shown that some of the 'non-activist' conclusions of the equilibrium models are modified if one substitutes for period-by-period market clearing the imposition of long-term contracts drawn contingent on restricted information sets that are exogenously imposed and that are assumed to be independent of monetary and fiscal regimes. Economic theory leads us to predict that costs of collecting and processing information will make it optimal for contracts to be made contingent on a small subset of the information that could possibly be collected at any date. But theory also suggests that the particular set of information upon which contracts will be made contingent is not immutable but depends on the structure of costs and benefits to collecting various kinds of information. This structure of costs and benefits will change with every change in the exogenous stochastic processes facing agents. This theoretical presumption is supported by an examination of the way labor contracts differ across high-inflation and low-inflation countries and the way they have evolved in the United States since the mid-1950s.

So the issue here is really the same fundamental one involved in the dispute between Keynes and the classical economists: is it adequate to regard certain superficial characteristics of existing wage contracts as given when analyzing the consequences of alternative monetary and fiscal regimes? Classical economic theory denies that those characteristics can be taken as given. To understand the implications of long-term contracts for monetary policy, one needs a model of the way those contracts are likely to respond to alternative monetary policy regimes. An extension of existing equilibrium models in this direction might well lead to interesting variations, but it seems to us unlikely that major modifications of the implications of these models for monetary and fiscal policy will follow from this.

Persistence

A second line of criticism stems from the correct observation that if agents' expectations are rational and if their information sets include lagged values of the variable being forecast, then agents' forecast errors must be a serially uncorrelated random process. That is, on average there must be no detectable relationships between this period's forecast error and any previous period's forecast error. This feature has led several critics to conclude that equilibrium models are incapable of accounting for more than an insignificant part of the highly serially correlated movements we observe in real output, employment, unemployment and other series. Tobin has put the argument succinctly in [38]:

> One currently popular explanation of variations in employment is temporary confusion of relative and absolute prices. Employers and workers are fooled into too many jobs by unexpected inflation, but only until they learn it affects other prices, not just the prices of what they sell. The reverse happens temporarily when inflation falls short of expectation. This model can scarcely explain more than transient disequilibrium in labor markets.
>
> So how can the faithful explain the slow cycles of unemployment we actually observe? Only by arguing that the natural rate itself fluctuates, that variations in unemployment rates are substantially changes in voluntary, frictional, or structural unemployment rather than in involuntary joblessness due to generally deficient demand.

The critics typically conclude that the theory attributes only a very minor role to aggregate demand fluctuations and necessarily depends on disturbances to aggregate supply to account for most of the fluctuations in real output over the business cycle. As Modigliani [21] characterized the implications of the theory: 'In other words, what happened to the United States in the 1930s was a severe attack of contagious laziness.'

This criticism is fallacious because it fails to distinguish properly between 'sources of impulses' and 'propagation mechanisms', a distinction stressed by Ragnar Frisch in a classic 1933 paper [9] that provided many of the technical foundations for Keynesian macroeconometric models. Even though the new classical theory implies that the forecast errors which are the aggregate demand 'impulses' are serially uncorrelated, it is certainly logically possible that 'propagation mechanisms' are at work that convert these impulses into serially correlated movements in real variables like output and employment. Indeed, two concrete propagation mechanisms have already been shown in detailed theoretical work to be capable of performing precisely that function. One mechanism stems from the presence of costs to firms of adjusting their stocks of capital and labor rapidly. The presence of these costs is known to make it optimal for firms to spread out over time their response to the relative price signals that they receive. In the present context, such a mechanism causes a firm to convert the serially uncorrelated forecast errors in predicting relative prices into serially correlated movements in factor demands and in output.

A second propagation mechanism is already present in the most classical of economic growth models. It is known that households' optimal accumulation plans for claims on physical capital and other assets will convert serially uncorrelated impulses into serially correlated demands for the accumulation of real assets. This happens because agents typically will want to divide any unexpected changes in the prices or income facing agents. Thus, the demand for assets next period depends on initial stocks and on unexpected changes in the prices or income facing agents. This dependence makes serially uncorrelated surprises lead to serially correlated movements in demands for physical assets. Lucas [16] showed how this propagation mechanism readily accepts errors in forecasting aggregate demand as an 'impulse' source.

A third likely propagation mechanism is identified by recent work in search theory.[11] Search theory provides an explanation for why workers who for some reason find themselves without jobs will find it rational not necessarily to take the first job offer that comes along but instead to remain unemployed for some period until a better offer materializes. Similarly, the theory provides reasons that a firm may find it optimal to wait until a more suitable job applicant appears so that vacancies will persist for some time. Unlike the first two propagation mechanisms mentioned, consistent theoretical models that permit that mechanism to accept errors in forecasting aggregate demand as an impulse have not yet been worked out for mainly technical reasons, but it seems likely that this mechanism will eventually play an important role in a successful model of the time series behavior of the unemployment rate.

In models where agents have imperfect information, either of the first two and most probably the third mechanism is capable of making serially correlated movements in real variables stem from the introduction of a serially uncorrelated sequence of forecasting errors. Thus, theoretical and econometric models have been constructed in which in principle the serially uncorrelated process of forecasting errors is capable of accounting for any proportion between zero and one of the steady-state variance of real output or employment. The argument that such models must necessarily attribute most of the variance in real output and employment to variations in aggregate supply is simply wrong logically.

Linearity

Most of the econometric work implementing equilibrium models has involved fitting statistical models that are linear in the variables (but often highly non-linear in the parameters). This feature is subject to criticism on the basis of the indisputable principle that there generally exist non-linear models that provide better approximations than linear models. More specifically, models that are linear in the variables provide no method of detecting and analyzing systematic effects of higher than first-order moments of the shocks and the exogenous variables on the first moments of the endogenous variables. Such systematic effects are generally present where the endogenous variables are set by risk-averse agents.

There is no *theoretical* reason that most applied work has used linear models, only compelling technical reasons given today's computer techno-logy. The predominant technical requirement of econometric work which imposes rational expectations is the ability to write down analytical expres-sions giving agents' decision rules as functions of the parameters of their objective functions and as functions of the parameters governing the exo-genous random processes that they face. Dynamic stochastic maximum problems with quadratic objectives, which give rise to linear decision rules, *do* meet this essential requirement, which is their virtue. Only a few other functional forms for agents' objective functions in dynamic stochastic optimum problems have this same necessary analytical tractability. Computer technology in the foreseeable future seems to require working with such a class of functions, and the class of linear decision rules has just seemed most convenient for most purposes. No issue of *principle* is involved in selecting one out of the very restricted class of functions available to us. *Theoretically*, we know how to calculate via expensive recursive methods the non-linear decision rules that would stem from a very wide class of objective functions; no new econometric principles would be involved in estimating their parameters, only a much higher computer bill. Further, as Frisch and Slutsky emphasized, linear stochastic difference equations seem a very flexible device for studying business cycles. It is an open question whether for explaining the central features of the business cycle there will be a big reward to fitting non-linear models.

Stationary models and the neglect of learning

Benjamin Friedman and others have criticized rational expectations models apparently on the grounds that much theoretical and almost all empirical work has assumed that agents have been operating for a long time in a stochastically stationary environment. As a consequence, typic-ally agents are assumed to have discovered the probability laws of the variables that they want to forecast. As Modigliani made the argument in [21]:

> At the logical level, Benjamin Friedman has called attention to the omission from [equilibrium macroeconomic models] of an explicit learn-ing mechanism, and has suggested that, as a result it can only be inter-preted as a description not of short-run but of long-run equilibrium in which no agent would wish to recontract. But then the implications of [equilibrium macroeconomic models] are clearly far from startling, and their policy relevance is almost nil (p. 6)

But it has been only a matter of analytical convenience and not of necessity that equilibrium models have used the assumption of stochastically stationary 'shocks' and the assumption that agents have already learned the probability distributions that they face. Both of these assumptions can be abandoned, albeit at a cost in terms of the simplicity of the model.[12] In fact, within the framework of quadratic objective functions, in which the 'separation principle' applies, one can apply the 'Kalman filtering formula' to derive optimum linear decision with time dependent coefficients. In this framework, the 'Kalman filter' permits a neat application of Bayesian learning to updating optimal forecasting rules from period to period as new information becomes available. The Kalman filter also permits the derivation of optimum decision rules for an interesting class of nonstationary exogenous processes assumed to face agents. Equilibrium theorizing in this context thus readily leads to a *model* of how process non-stationarity and Bayesian learning applied by agents to the exogenous variables leads to time-dependent coefficients in agents' decision rules.

While models incorporating Bayesian learning and stochastic non-stationarity are both technically feasible and consistent with the equilibrium modeling strategy, almost no successful applied work along these lines has come to light. One reason is probably that non-stationary time series models are cumbersome and come in so many varieties. Another is that the hypothesis of Bayesian learning is vacuous until one either arbitrarily imputes a prior distribution to agents or develops a method of estimating parameters of the prior from time series data. Determining a prior distribution from the data would involve estimating a number of initial conditions and would proliferate nuisance parameters in a very unpleasant way. It is an empirical matter whether these techniques will pay off in terms of explaining macroeconomic time series; it is not a matter distinguishing equilibrium from Keynesian macroeconometric models. In fact, no existing Keynesian macroeconometric model incorporates either an economic model of learning or an economic model in any way restricting the pattern of coefficient nonstationarities across equations.

The macroeconometric models criticized by Friedman and Modigliani, which assume agents have 'caught on' to the stationary random processes they face, give rise to systems of linear stochastic difference equations of the form (1), (2), and (4). As has been known for a long time, such stochastic difference equations generate series that 'look like' economic time series. Further, if viewed as *structural* (i.e. invariant with respect to policy interventions) the models have some of the implications for countercyclical policy that we have described above. Whether or not these policy implications are correct depends on whether or not the models are structural and not at all on whether the models can successfully be caricatured by terms such as 'long run' or 'short run'.

It is worth re-emphasizing that we do not wish our responses to these criticisms to be mistaken for a claim that existing equilibrium models can satisfactorily account for all the main features of the observed business cycle. Rather, we have argued that no sound reasons have yet been advanced which even suggest that these models are, as a class, *incapable* of providing a satisfactory business cycle theory.

SUMMARY AND CONCLUSIONS

Let us attempt to set out in compact form the main arguments advanced in this chapter. We will then comment briefly on the main implications of these arguments for the way we can usefully think about economic policy.

First, and most important, existing Keynesian macroeconometric models are incapable of providing reliable guidance in formulating monetary, fiscal and other types of policy. This conclusion is based in part on the spectacular recent failures of these models, and in part on their lack of a sound theoretical or econometric basis. Second, on the latter ground, there is no hope that minor or even major modification of these models will lead to significant improvement in their reliability.

Third, *equilibrium* models can be formulated which are free of these difficulties and which offer a different set of principles which can be used to identify structural econometric models. The key elements of these models are that agents are *rational*, reacting to policy changes in a manner which is in their best interests privately, and that the impulses which trigger business fluctuations are mainly unanticipated shocks.

Fourth, equilibrium models already developed account for the main qualitative features of the business cycle. These models are being subjected to continued criticism, especially by those engaged in developing them, but arguments to the effect that equilibrium theories are, in principle, incapable of accounting for a substantial part of observed fluctuations appear due mainly to simple misunderstandings.

The policy implications of equilibrium theories are sometimes caricatured, by friendly as well as unfriendly commentators, as the assertion that 'economic policy does not matter' or 'has no effect'.[13] This implication would certainly startle neoclassical economists who have successfully applied equilibrium theory to the study of innumerable problems involving important effects of fiscal policies on resource allocation and income distribution. Our intent is not to reject these accomplishments, but rather to try to *imitate* them, or to extend the equilibrium methods which have been applied to many economic problems to cover a phenomenon which has so far resisted their application: the business cycle.

Should this intellectual arbitrage prove successful, it will suggest important changes in the way we think about policy. Most fundamentally, it directs attention to the necessity of thinking of policy as the choice of stable 'rules of the game', well understood by economic agents. Only in such a setting will economic theory help us to predict the actions agents will choose to take. Second, this approach suggests that policies which affect behavior mainly because their consequences cannot be correctly diagnosed, such as monetary instability and deficit financing, have the capacity only to disrupt. The deliberate provision of misinformation cannot be used in a systematic way to improve the economic environment.

The *objectives* of equilibrium business cycle theory are taken, without modification, from the goal which motivated the construction of the Keynesian macroeconometric models: to provide a scientifically based means of assessing, quantitatively, the likely effects of alternative economic policies. Without the econometric successes achieved by the Keynesian models, this goal would be simply inconceivable. Unless the now evident limits of these models are also frankly acknowledged, and radically different new directions taken, the real accomplishments of the Keynesian Revolution will be lost as surely as those we now know to be illusory.

ACKNOWLEDGEMENTS

We wish to acknowledge the benefit of criticism of an earlier draft by William Poole and Benjamin Friedman.

NOTES

1 Linearity is a matter of convenience, not of principle. See pp. 287–88.
2 A 'regression equation' is an equation to which the application of ordinary least squares will yield consistent estimates.
3 In these expressions for P_s and Q_s, take matrices not previously defined (for example, any with negative subscripts) to be zero.
4 These three categories certainly do not exhaust the set of possible identifying restrictions, but in Keynesian macroeconometric models most identifying restrictions fall into one of these three categories. Other possible sorts of identifying restrictions include, for example, *a priori* knowledge about components of $\sum$, and cross-equation restrictions across elements of the A_j, B_j, and C_j's. Neither of these latter kinds of restrictions is extensively used in Keynesian macroeconometrics.
5 Criticisms of the Keynesian solutions of the identification problem along much the following lines have been made in Lucas [17], Sims [33], and Sargent and Sims [31].
6 [This note was added in revision, in part in response to Benjamin Friedman's comments.] Much of this work was done by economists operating well within the Keynesian tradition, often within the context of some Keynesian macroeconometric model. Sometimes a theory with optimizing agents was resorted to in order to resolve empirical paradoxes by finding variables that had been omitted from some of the earlier Keynesian econometric formulations. The works of Modigliani and Friedman on consumption are good examples of this line of work, a line whose econometric implications have been extended in important work by Robert Merton. The works of Tobin and Baumol on portfolio balance and of Jorgenson on investment are also in the tradition of applying optimizing microeconomic theories for generating macroeconomic behavior relations. Since the late 1940s, Keynesian econometric models have to a large extent developed along the line of trying to model agents' behavior as stemming from more and more sophisticated optimum problems. Our point here is certainly *not* to assert that Keynesian economists have completely foregone any use of optimizing

microeconomic theory as a guide. Rather, it is that, especially when explicitly stochastic and dynamic problems have been studied, it has become increasingly apparent that microeconomic theory has very damaging implications for the restrictions conventionally used to identify Keynesian macroeconometric models. Furthermore, as Tobin [37] emphasized long ago, there is a point beyond which Keynesian models must suspend the hypothesis either of cleared markets or of optimizing agents if they are to possess the operating characteristics and policy implications that are the hallmarks of Keynesian economics.

7 For example, see the comment by Albert Ando [35, esp. pp. 209–10], and the remarks of L. R. Klein [24].

8 For an example that illustrates the emptiness at a general level of the statement that 'employers are always operating along dynamic stochastic demands for factors', see the remarks on econometric identification in Sargent [29]. In applied problems that involve modeling agents' optimum decision rules, one is impressed at how generalizing the specification of agents' objective functions in plausible ways quickly leads to econometric under-identification. A somewhat different class of examples is seen in the difficulties in using time series observations to refute the view that 'agents only respond to unexpected changes in the money supply'. A distinguishing feature of the equilibrium macroeconometric models described below is that predictable changes in the money supply do not affect real GNP or total employment. In Keynesian models, predictable changes in the money supply do cause real GNP and employment to move. At a general level, it is impossible to discriminate between these two views by observing time series drawn from an economy described by a stationary vector random process (Sargent [28]).

9 See Edmund S. Phelps *et al.* [25] and Lucas [15], [16].

10 For example, Sargent [27]. Dissatisfaction with the Keynesian methods of achieving identification has also led to other lines of macroeconometric work. One line is the 'index models' described by Sargent and Sims [31] and Geweke [10]. These models amount to a statistically precise way of implementing Wesley Mitchell's notion that there is a small number of common influences that explain the covariation of a large number of economic aggregates over the business cycle. This 'low dimensionality' hypothesis is a potential device for restricting the number of parameters to be estimated in vector time series models. This line of work is *not* entirely a-theoretical (but see the comments of Ando and Klein in Sims [35]), though it is distinctly unKeynesian. As it happens, certain equilibrium models of the business cycle do seem to lead to low dimensional index models with an interesting pattern of variables' loadings on indexes. In general, modern Keynesian models do not so easily assume a low-index form. See the discussion in Sargent and Sims [31].

11 For example [19], [22] and [18].

12 For example, see Crawford [5] and Grossman [11].

13 A main source of this belief is probably Sargent and Wallace [30], in which it was shown that in the context of a fairly standard macroeconomic model, but with agents' expectations assumed rational, the choice of a reactive monetary rule is of *no* consequence for the behavior of real variables. The point of this example was to show that within *precisely* that model used to rationalize reactive monetary policies, such policies could be shown to be of no value. It hardly follows that *all* policy is ineffective in *all* contexts.

REFERENCES

1 Ando, Albert, 'A Comment', in [35].

2 Arrow, Kenneth J., 'The Role of Securities in the Optimal Allocation of Risk Bearing', *Review of Economic Studies* 31 (1964): 91–6.

3 Barro, Robert J., 'Unanticipated Money Growth and Unemployment in the United States', *American Economic Review* 67 (1977): 101–15.

4 —— 'Unanticipated Money, Output and the Price Level in the United States', *Journal of Political Economy* 86 (1978): 549–80.

5 Crawford, Robert, 'Implications of Learning for Economic Models of Uncertainty', Manuscript. Pittsburgh: Carnegie-Mellon University, 1971.

6 Debreu, Gerard, *The Theory of Value*, New York: Wiley, 1959.

7 Fischer, Stanley, 'Long-term Contracts, Rational Expectations, and the Optimal Money Supply Rule', *Journal of Political Economy* 85 (1977): 191–206.

8 Friedman, Milton, 'A Monetary and Fiscal Framework for Economic Stability', *American Economic Review* 38 (1948): 245–64.

9 Frisch, Ragnar, 'Propagation Problems and Impulse Problems in Dynamic Economics', reprinted in *AEA Readings in Business Cycles*, edited by R. A. Gordon and L. R. Klein, vol. X, 1965.

10 Geweke, John, 'The Dynamic Factor Analysis of Economic Time Series', in *Latent Variables in Socio-Economic Models*, edited by D. Aigner and A. Goldberger, pp. 365–83. Amsterdam: North Holland, 1977.

11 Grossman, Sanford, 'Rational Expectations and the Econometric Modeling of Markets Subject to Uncertainty: A Bayesian Approach', *Journal of Econometrics* 3 (1975): 255–72.

12 Hall, Robert E., 'The Macroeconomic Impact of Changes in Income Taxes in the Short and Medium Runs', *Journal of Political Economy* 86 (1978): S71–S86.

13 Keynes, J. M., *The General Theory of Employment, Interest, and Money*, London: Macmillan, 1936.

14 Leontief, W., 'Postulates: Keynes' General Theory and the Classicists', in *The New Economics, Keynes' Influences on Theory and Public Policy*, edited by S. Harris, Clifton, NJ: Augustus Kelley, 1965.

15 Lucas, R. E. Jr, 'Expectations and the Neutrality of Money', *Journal of Economic Theory* 4, no. 2 (April 1972): 102–23.

16 —— 'An Equilibrium Model of the Business Cycle', *Journal of Political Economy* 83, no. 6 (December 1975): 1113–44.

17 —— 'Econometric Policy Evaluation: A Critique', in *The Phillips Curve and Labor Markets*, edited by K. Brunner and A. H. Meltzer, Carnegie-Rochester Conference Series on Public Policy, 1:19–46, Amsterdam: North Holland, 1976.

18 Lucas, R. E. Jr., and Prescott, Edward C. 'Equilibrium Search and Unemployment', *Journal of Economic Theory* 7 (1974): 188–209.

19 McCall, John, 'The Economics of Information and Optimal Stopping Rules', *Journal of Business* 38 (1965): 300–17.

20 McCallum, Bennett, 'Rational Expectations and the Natural Rate Hypothesis: Some Consistent Estimates', *Econometrica* 44 (1976): 43–52.

21 Modigliani, Franco, 'The Monetarist Controversy, or Should We Forsake Stabilization Policies?', *American Economic Review* (March 1977): 1–19.

22 Mortensen, Dale T., 'A Theory of Wage and Employment Dynamics', in [25].

23 Muench, T., Rolnick, A., Wallace, N., and Weiler, W. 'Tests for Structural Change and Prediction Intervals for the Reduced Forms of Two Structural Models of the U.S.: The FRB-MIT and Michigan Quarterly Models', *Annals of Economic and Social Measurement* 313 (1974).

24 Okun, Arthur, and Perry, George L. (eds) *Brookings Papers on Economic Activity*, 1973, vol. 3, remarks attributed to Lawrence Klein, p. 644.

25 Phelps, E. S. *et al.*, *Microeconomic Foundations of Employment and Inflation Theory*, New York: Norton, 1970.

26 Phelps, E. S. and Taylor, John, 'Stabilizing Powers of Monetary Policy under Rational Expectations', *Journal of Political Economy* 85 (1977): 163–90.

27 Sargent, T. J. 'A Classical Macroeconometric Model for the United States', *Journal of Political Economy* (1976).

28 —— 'The Observational Equivalence of Natural and Unnatural Rate Theories of Macroeconomics', *Journal of Political Economy* (June 1976).

29 —— 'Estimation of Dynamic Labor Demand Schedules Under Rational Expectations', *Journal of Political Economy* (December 1978).

30 Sargent, J. J. and Wallace, Neil, ' "Rational" Expectations, the Optimal Monetary Instrument, and the Optimal Money Supply Rule', *Journal of Political Economy* 83 (1975): 241–54.

31 Sargent, T. J., and Sims, C.A. 'Business Cycle Modeling Without Pretending to Have Too Much A Priori Economic Theory', in *New Methods in Business Cycle Research*, edited by C. Sims, Federal Reserve Bank of Minneapolis, 1977.

32 Simons, Henry C., 'Rules Versus Authorities in Monetary Policy', *Journal of Political Economy* 44 (1936): 1–30.

33 Sims, C. A., 'Macroeconomics and Reality', *Econometrica* 48 (1980): 1–48.

34 —— 'Money, Income, and Causality', *American Economic Review* (September 1972).

35 —— (ed.) *New Methods in Business Cycle Research: Proceedings from a Conference*, Federal Reserve Bank of Minneapolis, October, 1977.

36 Sonnenschein, Hugo, 'Do Walras' Identity and Continuity Characterize the Class of Community Excess Demand Functions?', *Journal of Economic Theory* 6 (1973): 345–54.

37 Tobin, James, 'Money Wage Rates and Employment', in *The New Economies*, edited by S. Harris, Clifton, NJ: Augustus Kelley, 1965.

38 —— 'How Dead is Keynes?', *Economic Inquiry* (October 1977) 15: 459–68.

12 A child's guide to rational expectations

Rodney Maddock and Michael Carter
Journal of Economic Literature (1982) 20, March, pp. 39–51

SCENE I

Prologue

(Two students sharing coffee in the union of an Australian university.)
Ernie: Did you read that ridiculous article in *Challenge* the other day?
Bert: Which?
Ernie: Somebody named Bennett McCallum was saying that rational expectations proved that the government could not stabilize the economy. Hang on, I've got it here: 'An accurate understanding of how expectations are formed leads to the conclusion that short-run stabilization policies are untenable' (McCallum 1980: 37). I don't know how they could develop theories like that. It's pretty obvious that government policy does affect the economy in the short run.
Bert: He didn't say they could not *affect* the economy in the short run or even in the long run. The key word is *stabilize*.[1] Just think about what's happened in the last few years – record inflation and record unemployment. You don't call that stabilization, do you?

Ernie: Well, maybe they've been stable at high levels but I take your point. There does seem to have been some breakdown of the ways in which the government can influence the macroeconomy. Do these rational expectations blokes think they have a model to explain stagflation?

Bert: Yes, they do. It's caused by misguided governments following Keynesian policies that haven't worked, don't work, and won't work in the future.[2]

Ernie: I suppose they advocate doing nothing and letting the 'free market' do its worst. Great! They sound just like Friedman and all those old-fashioned monetarists. They have always said inflation was just a monetary phenomenon and macro policy couldn't shift the economy to higher levels of employment.

Bert: Yes, that's right. Most economists now agree that the long-run Phillips curve is vertical.[3] That means that there exists a natural rate of unemployment.[4] Government policy can bring about a departure from that only in the short run and then only by fooling people. But you can't fool all the people all the time. Therefore, systematic policy is ineffective.[5]

Ernie: I'm not at all sure that the long-run Phillips curve is vertical.[6] We used to have about 1 per cent unemployment; now we seem to be stuck at about 8 per cent. How can you explain that with a vertical Phillips curve. 'The Phillips curve is vertical but moves around a lot' – hardly seems much of a theory.[7] Even if it is vertical and we can't get away from it except by fooling people, clearly the government can fool people. Every time it changes policy the people don't know about the new policy for a while so it takes time before they catch up.[8]

Bert: But that's just what rational expectations is all about! It suggests that people anticipate the effects of the new policy. If that's true, then the policies won't cause any increase in employment!

Ernie: How on earth are people supposed to anticipate the effects of policy? I just can't see it. Have they all got econometric models under the sink?[9]

Bert: (*Angrily*) Now you're just being silly. Have you read *any* of the basic literature – Lucas, Sargent, Wallace, and so on?

Ernie: I've looked at some but it just seems unreal – too many equations. They never define exactly how they think anybody forms these 'rational expectations'.

Bert: Look, I've got to go to my macro lecture. How about we meet again tomorrow, and I'll introduce you to the magnificent world of rational expectations. Same time?

SCENE II

The idea of rational expectations

(In the same place, next day.)

Bert: Well, are you ready to try to understand what rational expectations is about?

Ernie: Yes. Have you got it figured out yet?

Bert: I've been thinking about it. Let's go through it systematically. First, we can talk about just what rational expectations are. Then we can look at the way the policy impotence result is derived. By then we should have a pretty clear idea of what this line of research is all about so we can try to figure out how it relates to the Phillips curve, monetarism, econometric models, and all that. OK?

Ernie: Alright. What's the definition of rational expectations? What on earth might irrational expectations be?

Bert: First things first. Let's start with familiar ground. What would you say is the basic behavioral assumption of economic behavior?

Ernie: Utility maximization, I suppose.

Bert: More or less. I would say that the basic assumption about individual behavior is that economic agents do the best they can with what they have. This principle forms the basis of consumption theory, production theory, human capital theory and so on.

Ernie: So it's the basis of microeconomics.[10] But what's that got to do with expectations?

Bert: Everything. At its most fundamental, rational expectations theorists argue that the same principle should be applied to the formation of expectations. If you want a definition, how about: *rational expectations is the application of the principle of rational behavior to the acquisition and processing of information and to the formation of expectations.*[11]

Ernie: Am I to infer that my utility function and I sit down together and rationally decide how much information I should acquire in order to form the expectations that will help me maximize my utility? Incredible!

Bert: Yes, you can attack it that way if you like, but that's a more general criticism of utility theory which we can argue about some other time. All I'm saying here is that if one considers economic agents to be rational maximizers, then it's consistent[12] to consider information gathering and expectation formation as determined by the same procedure.

Ernie: OK. So you'd insist upon a rational expectations postulate that private economic agents gather and use information efficiently. That means you believe the marginal costs of gathering and using information are equated to their marginal benefits. McCallum doesn't agree with you. He says: 'Individual agents use *all* available and relevant information'[13] and it seems to me that Sargent and Lucas say the same. It almost seems as if they think information is a free good.[14]

Bert: That's a good point. Many theorists have ignored the costs of information used in the formation of expectations. That is one of my criticisms of the literature. But I think it is useful to distinguish between rational expectations as a principle of informational efficiency and rational expectations as it appears in some of the macroeconomic literature.[15]

Ernie: The term 'rational' is quite confusing in the context and you are right that the distinction between the two things is important. But what difference does rational expectations make to individuals? Can you give examples?

Bert: The example most often used in the literature involves the allocation of time between labor and leisure.[16] In deciding how many hours to work this period, an individual must take account of expected future wages and not just the present wage. For example, if you expect the real wage to be $10 per hour this week, and $1 next week, then it makes sense to work as much as possible this week, and have some time off next week. Therefore the number of hours worked in any period, that is, the labor supply, will depend not only on the current real wage but on expected future real wages. A rational expectation of real wages will take into account all available information, including the effects of government policy.

Ernie: But my old man works 40 hours every week – he doesn't have much choice.

Bert: But your old man's boss does. When he is deciding whether to hire more people or lay them off, he needs to take into account future prices and wages. His expectations should be based on all the available information. This includes, among other things, the impact of future government policy.

Ernie: OK. I see how the level of employment might depend upon expectations and how 'good' expectations are better than 'bad' ones. But I can't see why that means that there is no room for government policy.

Deriving the impotence result

Bert: Without realizing it you've just made a very important distinction. The relationship between the level of employment and expectations is logically quite separate from beliefs about how expectations are formed. The conclusion that there is no scope for government policy – the impotence result – depends crucially upon imposing a special assumption about expectations – rational expectations – upon a special type of macroeconomic model.

Ernie: Well I think I understand the meaning of rational expectations. What types of macro models do rational expectations theorists use?

Bert: (Drawing a diagram – Figure 12.1.) Most of them work with the idea that the levels of output and prices are determined by the intersection of an aggregate demand and aggregate supply function. The aggregate supply curve is taken to be vertical, so that output cannot deviate from Y_n as a direct result of any change in the level of demand. Thus government policies designed to change the level of aggregate demand are not likely to be effective. The level Y_n is the output associated with equilibrium in the labor market at the natural rate of unemployment so we can call Y_n the natural rate of output or income for the economy.[17]

Consider the possibility that the government takes action that may, at first blush, be supposed to increase output. For example, let it act to increase nominal income and aggregate money demand. Money wage

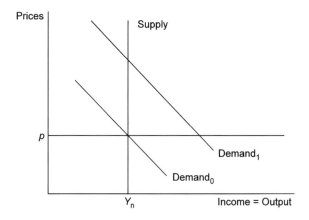

Figure 12.1

rates will tend to rise, and if workers regard this as equivalent to an increase in real wages, employment will increase and output will temporarily rise to a level higher than Y_n. But if production is carried on subject to diminishing returns to labor, prices will rise relative to nominal wages, and real wages will fall. When workers realize this, employment will fall back to its original position, and output will return to Y_n. At this point, nominal wage rates and prices are higher (the nominal demand curve crosses the vertical supply curve at a higher level), but output and employment are back where they started. Since the aggregate supply curve had not shifted, the possibility of increasing employment and output arises only as long as people confuse nominal changes in wages (for example) with real changes. This means that government policy will increase the level of income in real terms only if it is able to fool people into confusing nominal changes with real ones.[18]

Ernie: That's ridiculous! The 'natural' rate of unemployment depends intimately upon all sorts of government policies – for example tax laws, minimum wage laws, immigration policy, school-leaving age, etc., etc. Do you really mean that the government can't change aggregate supply by increasing the investment allowance? Or by going to war, for that matter?

Bert: You're right, you're right! I should have been more careful. Clearly government policy can alter the natural rate of unemployment or, if you like, the position of the aggregate curve. What I should have said is that the only way in which government policy can bring about *deviations* from the natural rate of unemployment is by inducing private agents to have mistaken expectations. Let's write down a simple model.

(Bert's scribbling is attached as Appendix B. For those who like mathematical descriptions it should make the discussion clearer but is not a necessary adjunct.)

Ernie: That makes your position clearer. The actual aggregate supply function implies that deviations of actual output from the natural rate are directly proportional to deviations of actual prices from expected prices. Since people with rational expectations never make mistakes about policy rules, policy will never fool them, and output will never deviate from its natural rate as a result of any policy rule.

Bert: That's the idea but you've put it too strongly. If government policies are random, they will be effective although not necessarily desirable. It's the systematic component of policy that the theory suggests will be ineffective.

Ernie: I'm not too sure about the neutrality-of-money proposition[19] generally but will let it ride for now. You explain the rest of the argument – then I'll put my objections one by one.

Bert: Now the point of rational expectations is that people won't be surprised by any systematic policy. Any government that relies upon a policy rule – one that has a fixed growth of the money supply, or one systematically related to income or unemployment – will never cause any deviation from the natural rate.[20] A random policy will affect real output. But any policy rule that is systematically related to economic conditions, for example one designed with stabilization in mind, will be perfectly anticipated, and therefore have no effect on output or employment. In other words, to have real effects, monetary policy must be completely unpredictable. Any systematic policy will be impotent.[21]

Ernie: Can we put it this way? Rational expectations are based on all available information. The available information set includes the government policy rule. Therefore, a rational expectation of inflation, for example, will include the anticipated effects of government policy so that the policy will have no effect on output.[22]

Bert: Yes, that pretty well sums it up.

Criticisms

Ernie: Now that I think I understand what you're on about, can I tell you what I think is wrong with the model?

Bert: OK.

Ernie: First, I don't like your supply curve. There are lots of criticisms one could make, but the most important in the context of the model is that you assume an extreme form of the neutrality of money.[23] Perfectly anticipated inflation has no real effects in your model. That's clearly wrong. Buiter (1980) put the standard argument in terms of the portfolio readjustments required because inflation changes the real rate of return on those financial assets which have a zero nominal return. Personally, I think the distortions introduced by the progressive tax structure in an inflationary situation are far more important empirically.

Bert: Yes, but all models are approximations.

Ernie: True, but not all approximations are good approximations! Here's another problem. If expectations are rational, then expectation errors should be randomly distributed over time. A straightforward implication of that for this model is that the level of output (or unemployment) is uncorrelated over time. Yet everybody knows that the GNP and unemployment series have a high degree of serial correlation.[24] We tend to go through a series of years in which unemployment is below the 'natural rate', and then a series of years in which it is above the 'natural rate'. It doesn't seem to be distributed very randomly. Compare the 1960s and 1970s in Australia – it's the old story of business cycle expansion and contraction.

Bert: I can't deny the serial correlation in the unemployment or income series. Most rational expectations models include lagged income or lagged unemployment as explanatory variables in the supply function.[25] This does make the models fit the data better, but there is no good theoretical justification for it. Lucas is the only one I know who really addresses the issue.[26] He relies on the well-known 'fact' that all people live on islands. At the end of each trading period people choose a new island at random. Since they don't know the history of their new island, they can't distinguish immediately between real and nominal effects.[27]

Ernie: These island models seem appropriate to a society in which the fastest form of communication is a floating coconut. Hasn't Lucas ever heard of radio and the telephone?[28]

Bert: I have to agree with you. I said that the explanations for persistence weren't very convincing, especially when the government regularly publishes lots of statistics. The newspapers carry stock exchange prices every day. The information seems to be essentially free.

There is another line of argument though. If prices change suddenly, firms can increase their production less than their sales by using up some of their inventories. If there is no price shock in the next period production would then be raised to build inventories back to their original level. Thus there would be an increase in production to meet the original stock and for as long thereafter as the restocking took.

Ernie: But that implies there should be a strong relationship between inventory cycles and output cycles and that's not really true, is it?

Bert: Well, the relation is far from perfect. I was really just suggesting that in an economy characterized by durable goods it shouldn't be too difficult to accept that adjustments of various sorts will have effects that persist.[29] We really don't have a good explanation for persistence (serial correlation). I willingly concede that point. What's next?

Ernie: OK. Even if all that information is freely available, you assume that all the agents know the correct model of the economy. How...

Bert: No, I don't. Well, not me really. I mean that rational-expectations people don't necessarily say that *everybody* knows the correct model of the economy. They suggest that some arbitrage process takes place whereby the people who have the correct model dominate the outcome.[30] If there are misapprehensions, then well-informed agents can make profits at the expense of the ill-informed. This will inevitably lead the system to converge to the rational expectations equilibrium. As your old mate, John Maynard Keynes, said:

> actions based on inaccurate anticipations will not long survive experiences of a contrary character, so that the facts will soon override anticipation except where they agree.

(Keynes 1930: 160)

Ernie: Granted there is a role for arbitrage. But how do we know that expectations of the experts will converge on the true value? Give me any rational expectations model and I think I can show you a reasonable adjustment process that will not converge to the rational expectations equilibrium.

Bert: And I can probably show you one that can. Unless the theorists specify an adjustment mechanism, we can't really argue about this point. Rational expectations theorists haven't addressed this problem.[31]

Ernie: That's a big gap in your theory. But let me read to you what Robert Shiller says:

> Even if a model does eventually converge on a rational expectations equilibrium, it may take such a long time to do so that, since the structure of the economy changes occasionally, the economy is never close to a rational expectations equilibrium.

(Shiller 1978: 39)

To recalculate a quarterly econometric model after a change in policy rule might take 20 quarters. To estimate the effect of policy based on the new estimates might take another 20 quarters. Thus, even if the process converges, each stage in the convergence to the new equilibrium could take five years – by which time we may all be dead!

Bert: But if the Government's objective is to stabilize the economy, then it wants to make sure that private expectations are rational, and hence it will inform the public of any new policy rule.[32]

Ernie: That doesn't get you out of hot water. First, the learning problem doesn't concern the policy rule alone. Agents also have to learn the structure of economy, which is subject to change. Econometric modellers don't have an outstanding record of success, do they? Second, why do you assume that the government's objective is to stabilize the economy? It seems to me that the government's real objective is to remain in power – you know, the political business cycle idea.[33] And if that is their objective it may be in their interest to hide information and fool the public. If that is the case the voters can hardly be expected to believe the signals the government is sending out and the whole macroeconomic process degenerates into a guessing game.

Bert: But you must agree that most macroeconomics does assume the objective of stabilization. This literature falls into that tradition which is concerned with government policy rules designed to achieve macroeconomic stabilization.[34]

Ernie: Let's go and get a beer.[35]

SCENE III

(In the union bar)

Testing

Bert: Now the testing is a bit tricky. It's a pretty young research program and there are no well-accepted testing procedures as yet. The principal difficulty is that we are really testing a joint hypothesis – the economic model and the expectations mechanism. That makes it difficult to decide just where the responsibility for failures of tests really lie.

Ernie: But why can't you just test the expectations mechanism directly? Ask people what they expect, and see if they are right?

Bert: Stephen Turnovsky (1970) and James Pesando (1975) and a couple of other people have done that, but the results have been inconclusive. Economists traditionally don't like surveys, anyway.

Ernie: Well, how have rational expectations protagonists tried to test the theory?

Bert: Basically they have taken two different approaches. Have a look at the supply function again. The natural rate hypothesis will allow non-random deviations only if there are expectations errors of some sort. Under the rational expectations hypothesis there are no expectations errors – or at most, only random ones. Thus, deviations from the natural rate of output must be random.[36] In particular, deviations cannot be systematically related to any other explanatory variable, for example the (lagged) money supply or the wage rate. And so the first type of test is essentially to see whether deviations from the natural rate are systematically related to any other variables. This test has been applied in a number of different ways especially by Sargent (1973; 1976). In those papers the joint hypothesis – natural rate and rational expectations – was rejected in a number of cases, jointly rejected because they were jointly tested. With slightly different specifications, they weren't. Sargent concludes that rational expectations is 'not obscenely at variance with the data.'[37]

Ernie: Remarkable resilience, eh!

Bert: Yes, what's more, his next paper was entitled 'The Observational Equivalence of Natural and Unnatural Rate Theories of Macroeconomics.'[38] This initiated the second approach to testing rational expectations. It was based on the idea that what rational expectations models *add*, compared with other models, is that price expectations take into account the policy rule the government is using. If that rule does not change, ordinary models and rational expectations models will fit any data set equally well, though probably with different parameters. What it means is that you can only distinguish between rational expectations macro models and ordinary ones if the policy rule has changed.[39] It seems a reasonable idea to me.

Ernie: Maybe.

Bert: Well, anyway, it gave Sargent and Salih Neftci (1978) an idea for a new type of test. First, they estimated the government's policy rule by regressing the money supply on past levels of income. They then analysed the results to see if there had been any significant changes in the relationship, that is, to see if the policy rule had changed.[40] They found changes in 1929 and 1964. They then looked at some ordinary macroeconomic models to see whether the parameters had changed at about the same time that the policy rule changed. In each case they found some evidence that it had.[41]

Ernie: Well, that seems like a reasonable sort of approach. Really it depends on the rational expectations idea – that people change their behavior as policy changes – rather than on the natural rate proposition. I'm inclined to agree that people take into account what the government is trying to do when they plan for the future but the extreme form of the natural rate of unemployment is an over-simplification of a complex world. Of course, the test is a bit tricky. It's not really clear to me that that's the way to estimate the government policy rule and then, even if it is, there are probably other non-rational expectations mechanisms which would suggest a change in the econometric structure as a result of a change in policy rule. There's no real alternative hypothesis involved in the test!

Bert: Everyone agrees it's not a very strong test; it's titled 'A Little Bit of Evidence . . .', but it is suggestive and does focus upon the relation between expectations and the policy rule and not upon the natural rate. It gets away from the dogmatic form of the natural rate, impotence of policy area, and focuses upon the positive contribution of the rational expectations idea.

Significance

Ernie: OK, we've covered the model and the evidence, such as it is. What's all the fuss about?

Bert: Well, it really nails the Phillips curve. Much post-war stabilization policy has been based on the idea that there is a trade-off between unemployment and inflation that the government can exploit by influencing aggregate demand – the so-called Phillips curve. Friedman largely undermined that with the natural rate idea. He said that policy worked only by fooling people and that in the long-run they could not be fooled. This still left the way open for effective short-run policy. If people have rational expectations they won't be fooled. If people have rational expectations they won't be fooled by *systematic* policy *even in the short run* so there is no scope for short-run policy either. This explains why the Phillips curve became unstable the moment policy-makers tried to exploit it.

Ernie: But the explanation depends really heavily, as you've already agreed, upon the particular macroeconomic model you have set up.[42] The monetarists have grabbed this idea[43] to support their traditional position that active government policy is not desirable.[44] It's largely been their baby until now. The reason is not hard to see. The impotence result strongly supports their ideological position that the government should keep its hands off the economy.[45]

Bert: That's rather harsh. Monetarists are no more ideological than other economists. What would be your 'un-ideological' view of rational expectations?

Ernie: I've been wondering how a future historian of thought might assess it. I think rational expectations theory will be seen as a very important development in economics, but *not* because of the impotence result. Rational expectations are important in any situation in which market behavior is influenced by expectations. Take the case of an aggregate demand deficiency in a Keynesian model. The usual argument is that monetary expansion will work through affecting interest rates so that gradually the economy shifts to a higher output level. With rational expectations the shift to the new level would be extremely rapid. If business people understand the economic implications of expansionary government policy, they can expand their output in anticipation of those effects rather than waiting for the rise in demand to be obvious in the market. In that case, far from policy being impotent, rational expectations may make policy *more* effective.

This example, by the way, illustrates the fact that most of the rational expectations literature has a particular economic model built in, one in which all markets clear instantaneously; unemployment is, therefore, voluntary, hence 'natural'; and money is necessarily neutral. But if that model is not applicable, policy need not be impotent, and, as said, rational expectations may make it more rapidly effective.

What's more rational expectations can be applied in microeconomic situations.[46] Cobweb models of dynamic behavior in commodity markets depend upon 'irrationality of expectations' – the idea that next year's prices will be the same as this year's or even a simple extrapolation of it. Clearly, producers can do better than that, and if they have rational expectations the market is likely to approach its equilibrium quite quickly.

Bert: You're right! The idea can be applied in a wide variety of models but what about your general conclusions about policy formation?

Ernie: Yes, I agree that there are important implications for policy design. Private economic agents are intelligent decision-makers and can be expected to take the effects of government policy changes into account in deciding their behavior. This means that the policy-maker must anticipate the effect of policy on private expectations and the consequent changes in behavior. In practical terms it means that we need to know a lot more about the availability and use of information by private decision-makers.[47] Thus, the focus of the theory of policy should be on expectations and information and on their role in determining behavior.

Bert: I think you can go further. People used to think that the only reason stabilization policy didn't work well was that policy-makers didn't have enough knowledge about the structure of the economy. Rational expectations has taught us that the problem may not be just one of the *absolute* knowledge of the authorities but rather of how much more or less they know than the public does – a problem of *relative* knowledge. If this is true, the problem will always be with us.

Conclusion

Ernie: Well, I started off inclined towards Robert A. Gordon's view that rational expectations is an example of a recent development in economics 'in which theory proceeds with impeccable logic from unrealistic assumptions to conclusions that contradict the historical record' (1976: 5). But now I see that that's a bit too harsh.

Most of the research on rational expectations has exhibited great technical competence, 'impeccable logic', and considerable ingenuity. This has contributed in no small measure to its apparent success, and to the confusion and uncertainty which rational expectations have aroused in the rest of the economics profession. The fundamental simplicity of the ideas involved has become obscured by overly rigorous development, and especially by the unconvincing resort to extraneous constructions, such as the 'islands' mentioned above.

Undoubtedly, it is the impotence of policy results that has aroused most attention. Yet these results depend very heavily on a particular type of macroeconomic model usually embodying a strong form of the natural rate hypothesis. If you start with 'classical' models in which policy can have no real effects, it is hardly surprising that you get results in which policy is impotent. Because of this the novelty of rational expectations has become bundled up with tired and worn notions of the way in which the world works. It is vitally important to unbundle these ideas.

The rational expectations hypothesis, in itself, should not be provocative to economists. It merely brings expectations within the scope of individual maximizing behavior. Expectations used to be handled within economic models on an ad hoc basis. Rational expectations provides a way of incorporating expectations which is consistent with the orthodox economic theorizing.

The development of rational expectations theory will make a more significant contribution to economics in the impetus it gives to research on the vital areas of learning and expectations formation. It brings to the fore questions about the availability and use of information. Instead of being the finale of the monetarist's case against policy intervention, it should be seen as the prologue for a revitalized theory of expectations, information and policy.

Bert: I guess you're right. Let's go and get another beer.

APPENDIX A: AGGREGATE SUPPLY

The underlying inspiration for rational expectations macro models is derived from the notion of general equilibrium. With price flexibility, for given endowments and skills, a condition of general equilibrium requires equilibrium in the labor markets. In such a world all unemployment is voluntary, everybody who wants a job has one. Every individual has labor hours and assets allocated according to some personal optimum. The remaining unemployment can be termed the 'natural' rate of unemployment and the level of output termed the 'natural' level of output.

Abstracting from inter-industry shifts in production, the only way output can change is through a change in employment. To increase or decrease the level of output government policy must alter the equilibrium in the labor markets. But if the natural rate of unemployment represents an optimal position for private actors, how can government policy affect it?

The models rational expectations theorists usually work with suggest that this is possible only if the government is able to fool people. If people confuse nominal wage changes for real ones, they might reallocate their portfolios and their hours of work, and thus increase output. While allowing for this possibility the models suggest that such a change would not be desirable for the worker (representing a suboptimal decision) and would be avoided if they had rational expectations. They suggest that the labor supply decision is made in *real* terms so that labor market equilibrium is independent of prices which, in turn, is taken to imply that output is independent of prices. This result is presented in a vertical aggregate supply curve.

Alternative macro-economic theories suggest that the optimal allocation decisions of private actors *will* be affected by changes in prices, but *not* just because people are fooled. If this were true, increases in aggregate demand could increase output and employment even with rational expectations. One argument for the proposition suggests that people don't hold money in their asset portfolios simply for transaction purposes. If prices go up, the desirability of holding such money goes down, changing people's private allocation decisions, and perhaps the rate of capital formation or number of hours worked. Thus it might be said that the rational expectations models assume that the only motive for holding money is the transactions motive.

APPENDIX B: ALGEBRA OF THE MODEL

$$\text{Supply} : y_t - \bar{y} = a(p_t - p_t^*) + u_t \tag{1}$$

$$\text{Demand} : y_t = -bp_t + cx_t \tag{2}$$

$$\text{Expectations} : p_t^* = E[p_t \mid I_{t-1}] \tag{3}$$

where y_t = income

$\bar{y}$ = income level corresponding to the natural rate of unemployment

p_t = prices

p_t^* = price expectations

x_t = government policy instrument, e.g. money supply

I_{t-1} = all information available at time $t - 1$

u_t = random error term; $Eu_t = 0$

E = expectations operator.

Equating demand and supply, we obtain the following reduced form equation:

$$p_t = \frac{1}{a+b}(ap_t^* + cx_t - \bar{y} - u_t) \tag{4}$$

Now, by the rational expectations assumption (3)

$$p_t^* = E[p_t \mid I_{t-1}]$$

$$\text{using [4]} \quad = E\left[\frac{1}{a+b}(ap_t^* + cx_t - \bar{y} - u_t)\right]$$

$$= \frac{1}{a+b}(aEp_t^* + cEx_t - E\bar{y} - Eu_t)$$

But $Ep_t^* = p_t^*, E\bar{y} = \bar{y}, Eu_t = 0$

$$\text{so} \quad p_t^* = \frac{1}{a+b}(ap_t^* + cEx_t - \bar{y}) \tag{5}$$

Subtracting (5) from (4)

$$p_t - p_t^* = \frac{1}{a+b}[c(x_t - Ex_t) - u_t] \tag{6}$$

Substituting (6) in equation (1)

$$\begin{aligned} y_t - \bar{y} &= \frac{a}{a+b}[c(x_t - Ex_t) - u_t] + u_t \\ &= \frac{ac}{a+b}(x_t - Ex_t) + \frac{b}{a+b}u_t \end{aligned} \tag{7}$$

That is, the deviation of output from the 'natural' level $\bar{y}$ depends only on the unsystematic component of government policy $(x - Ex_t)$. To see this, assume that the government uses the following policy rule:

$$x_t = kx_{t-1} + ly_{t-1} + mp_{t-1} - np_{t-2} + v_t \tag{8}$$

where v_t is a random variable, $Ev_t = 0$.

Then,

$$Ex_t = kx_{t-1} + ly_{t-1} + mp_{t-1} - np_{t-2} \tag{9}$$

Subtracting (9) from (8)

$$x_t - Ex_t = v_t$$

Putting this in (7)

$$y_t - \bar{y} = \frac{ac}{a+b} v_t + \frac{b}{a+b} u_t$$

$$= \frac{1}{a+b} (acv_t + bu_t)$$

Deviations of y_t from $\bar{y}$ are thus entirely random. This implies that systematic government policy is impotent *(in this model)*, since the systematic component of any policy will be incorporated in Ex_t, and therefore be cancelled out in forming $x_t - Ex_t$.

ACKNOWLEDGEMENTS

Our thanks to Neville Cain for his inspiration for this chapter and to our colleagues at ANU, notably Malcolm Gray, Adrian Pagan and Jim Trevithick, for their comments. We are also grateful to Fred Gruen and to an anonymous referee and the editor of *Journal of Economic Literature* for their assistance. All faults, of course, remain ours.

NOTES

1 Usually defined as minimization of the variance around some fixed macroeconomic objectives (Gregory Chow 1970).
2 There is a clear ideological component to much rational-expectations work and opponents will be tempted to dismiss the theory on ideological grounds. Later we suggest that there are merits in the theory quite separate from its use to support particular propositions about the role of government.
3 See M. Friedman (1968) and Robert J. Gordon (1976) for views on this. Appendix A deals with the issue in some more detail.
4 'Natural' in the sense that everybody who wants a job at the going wage has one. This definition denies the possibility of unemployment arising from a failure of effective demand and hence from the 'Keynesian' problem (Edmond Malinvaud 1977). There is no necessary connection between vertical Phillips curves and a natural rate of employment.
5 This is Friedman's proposition that in the long run anticipated and actual economic values must be equal so that policies that work through illusions, or systematically wrong anticipations, will be ineffective in that long run.
6 Gordon (1976) considers a number of possibilities mainly relying on different forms of sluggish price adjustment.
7 Robert Hall (1975) makes this criticism. As he interpreted the evidence, most of the variation in output came from changes in the natural rate, provoking questions about the importance of a theory which only explained deviations from the natural rate. It would be a useful theory if it explained the movements in the rate itself.
8 John Taylor (1975) explores the possibilities for policy while people learn the new rule. Benjamin Friedman (1979) addresses the same question.

9 John Muth (1961: 317) in outlining what he meant by rational expectations anticipated this criticism.

10 There is clearly some tension in macroeconomics between its empirical behavioral aspects (e.g. the consumption function) and its derivation of insights from a microeconomic basis (e.g. permanent income hypothesis). The micro foundations of macroeconomics literature, for example Geoffrey Harcourt (1977) attempts to resolve this conflict but, so far, not very successfully.

11 This is *not* the approach usually adopted by rational expectations theorists (n. 15). It is, however, closer to the usual economic methodology and seems preferable.

12 That is, consistent with the methodological approach of explaining all behavior in terms of utility maximization.

13 McCallum (1980: 38). In fact, Ernie has quoted McCallum out of context. He goes on to admit that information costs are neglected for simplicity.

14 Edgar Feige and Douglas Pierce (1976) consider the implications of costly information for rational expectations.

15 The distinction seems important for clarifying ideas within macroeconomics. The all-information approach adopted by Sargent *et al.* should ideally be given another name, for example 'Muth expectations', since the adjective 'rational' is normally reserved in economics to describe the outcome of a utility maximization process. J. J. Sijben writes: 'Muth's view implies that economic agents build up their expectations as if they are fully informed of the process which ultimately generates the real outcome of the variable concerned' (1980: 66). Pushed further, McCallum follows the line that all models are 'unrealistic', which seems to lead him to the position that theories stand or fall on their predictions.

16 Rational expectations in labor supply decisions have fairly obvious corollaries on capital investment decisions (Robert Lucas, 1975, for example).

17 Appendix A deals with the problems of the vertical aggregate supply curve in more detail. It should be noted that the models are usually expressed in logarithms so that the real debate concerns rates of change rather than levels. The distinction is neglected here.

18 As Thomas Sargent and Neil Wallace suggest 'it must somehow trick the public' (1976: 177). The argument is more complex with capital in the model as may be clear from Appendix A.

19 The idea that changes in money supply do not influence people's preferred hours of work, portfolio holdings, etc. Again, this is considered in Appendix A.

20 Sargent and Wallace (1976: 177–8), put this argument in almost the same form. Expectations can be wrong but not systematically wrong (i.e. biased), hence there is no scope for systematic policy.

21 Gordon (1976) makes this clear. See especially pp. 200–1.

22 This follows the usual solution method followed by rational expectations models. See Lucas (1973) for an example.

23 Some criticisms are discussed in Appendix A.

24 This was Hall's criticism (1975), and is also put by Gordon to Sargent (1973: 478).

25 Lucas (1973) introduced the lagged term with a footnote explaining that not all deviation from the natural rate of unemployment could be accounted for by the error in expectations terms.

26 Lucas (1975) attempts a systematic explanation for the serial correlation in terms of information lags. See Rodney Maddock (1979) for a discussion of the importance of persistence for the rational expectation program.

27 'The idea behind this island abstraction is not, of course, to gain insight into maritime affairs, or to comment on the aimlessness of life. It is intended simply to capture in a tractable way the fact that economic activity offers agents a

succession of ambiguous, unanticipated opportunities which cannot be expected to stay fixed while more information is collected. It seems safe and, for my purposes, sensible to abstract here from the fact that in reality this situation can be slightly mitigated by the purchase of additional information' (Lucas 1975: 1120).

28 Lucas does actually mention the problem in the quotation in note 27, but makes nothing of it.

29 These issues are raised in a penetrating discussion of the problem of persistence by Gordon (1981).

30 For example, Muth (1961) argued that economists could sell the information profitably if expectations were not rational. Since he wrote, many have done so. This suggests that market forces would tend to drive decisions to those rationally based.

31 Shiller (1978: 38) focuses upon the issue of convergence. There seem to be two separate issues involved. Since rational expectations for this period depend upon estimates about the future while the future depends in part upon present expectations, there need be no unique rational expectation for the current period. In many models, methods of adjusting expectations (i.e. forecasts) of the future will either converge on a rational-expectations solution or explode. The implicit argument of protagonists seems to be that since we do not observe prices exploding off to infinity we need only consider converging cases. This type of counter-factual reasoning is somewhat dubious. The dynamics of expectation formation might still be explosive but some other fact or – e.g. policy action – act to constrain the explosive tendency.

32 Sargent and Wallace (1976: 181–3) argue this point.

33 The nature of the problem when the government's objectives vary over time does not seem to have been well explored. Clearly, rational expectations forces economists to think more about the precise nature of learning.

34 Following the tradition of Dutch economists Jan Tinbergen (1952) and Henri Theil (1958).

35 Following a sound Australian tradition.

36 Actually, some allowance in the tests is made for persistence by the inclusion of lagged values of the dependent variable.

37 The theory suggests that no extra information would significantly contribute to the prediction. The evidence would thus appear to falsify the theory. Sargent (1976a), instead, went on to try an alternative type of test. See especially p. 233.

38 Sargent (1976b) and Sargent and Wallace (1975) start to develop this idea.

39 Since expectations are usually unobservable they are eliminated from econometric models to be estimated by introducing an equation about their relation to known variables. The parameters of this equation then become embedded in the actual reduced form equations which are estimated. An 'equation' for rational expectations incorporates the parameters of the policy rule being used by the government. Under the assumption of rational expectations these parameters of the policy rule become embedded in the reduced form (i.e. estimating) equations of the economy. Thus they suggest that structure of the economy, as measured by usual econometric models, will appear to change whenever the policy rule changes.

40 Using M1 there was a policy change, but with M2 none appeared to have taken place.

41 The tests were non-parametric.

42 Alan Preston and Adrian Pagan (1982: ch. 10) explore the way in which the impotence result depends on particular specifications of the macroeconomic model being considered. They develop a more general model that includes the usual rational expectations models as particular cases.

43 Lucas and Leonard A. Rapping used adaptive expectations (1969a), then rational distributed lag expectations (1969b) before Lucas first introduced rational expectations (1972). Where adaptive expectations assumed that people just simply adapted to past errors, rational distributed lag expectations were the very best econometrically predicted estimates of prices derived from analysis of all past price information.

44 Any stable understandable rule would have no effect if people were exactly able to predict it. By that test a 'discretionary' rule and a fixed money growth rate rule would be equally impotent. If stochastic effects of discretionary rules are allowed for however, these cannot be predicted and would introduce fluctuations into the system. See Sargent and Wallace (1976) for a discussion of the issues.

45 McCallum's (1980) popularization of their position carries the inference that the results are quite robust, but that does not appear to be the case. See Preston and Pagan (1982).

46 The seminal article by Muth (1961) deals with microeconomic market situations.

47 Sargent and Wallace (1975: 251) provide a start in this direction by modelling a case where government has an information advantage over private actors.

REFERENCES

Buiter, Willem, 'The Macroeconomics of Dr. Pangloss: A Critical Survey of the New Classical Macroeconomics', *Economic Journal* March 1980, *90*(1), pp. 34–50.

Chow, Gregory, 'Optimal Stochastic Control of Linear Economic Systems', *Journal of Money, Credit and Banking* Aug. 1970, *2*(3), pp. 291–302.

Decanio, Stephen, 'Rational Expectations and Learning from Experience', *Quarterly Journal of Economics* 1979, *93*(1), pp. 47–57.

Feige, Edgar, and Pearce, Douglas, 'Economically Rational Price Expectations', *Journal of Political Economy* 1976, *84*(3), pp. 499–522.

Friedman, Benjamin, 'Optimal Expectations and the Extreme Information Assumptions of "Rational Expectations" Macromodels', *Journal of Monetary Economics* Jan. 1979, *5*(1), pp. 23–41.

Friedman, Milton, 'The Role of Monetary Policy', *American Economic Revolution* March 1968, *58*(1), pp. 1–17.

Gordon, Robert A., 'Rigor and Relevance in a Changing Institutional Setting', *American Economic Review* 1976, *66*(1), pp. 1–14.

Gordon, Robert J., 'Recent Developments in the Theory of Inflation and Unemployment', *Journal of Monetary Economics* April 1976, *2*(2), pp. 185–220.

—— 'Output Fluctuations and Gradual Price Adjustment', *Journal of Economic Literature* June 1981, pp. 493–530.

Hall, Robert E., 'The Rigidity of Wages and the Persistence of Unemployment', *Brookings Papers on Economic Activity* 1975, *2*, pp. 301–49.

Harcourt, Geoffrey (ed.) *The Microeconomic Foundations of Macroeconomics*, London: Macmillan, 1977.

Keynes, John, *A Treatise on Money*, vols I and II, New York: Harcourt Brace, 1930.

Lucas, Robert E. Jr, 'Testing the Natural Rate Hypothesis', in *The Econometrics of Price Determination, Conference*, edited by Otto Eckstein, Washington, DC: Federal Reserve Board, 1972, pp. 50–9.

—— 'Some International Evidence on Output–Inflation Tradeoffs', *American Economic Review* June 1973, *63*(3), pp. 326–34.

—— 'An Equilibrium Model of the Business Cycle', *Journal of Political Economy* Dec. 1975, *83*(6), pp. 1113–44.

—— 'Econometric Policy Evaluation: A Critique', *Journal of Monetary Economics* Supplementary Series 1976, *1*, pp. 19–46.

Lucas, Robert E. Jr and Rapping, Leonard A., 'Price Expectations and the Phillips Curve', *American Economic Review* June 1969a, *59*(3), pp. 342–50.

—— 'Real Wages, Employment and Inflation', *Journal Political Economy* Sept./Oct. 1969b, *77*(5), pp. 721–54.

Maddock, Rodney, 'Rational Expectations, Political Business Cycles and the Course of Macroeconomic Theory', Unpublished Ph.D thesis, Duke University, 1979.

Malinvaud, Edmond, *The Theory of Unemployment Reconsidered*, New York: Wiley; Oxford: Blackwell, 1977.

McCallum, Bennett T., 'The Significance of Rational Expectations Theory', *Challenge* Jan./Feb. 1980, pp. 37–43.

Muth, John, 'Rational Expectations and the Theory of Price Movements', *Econometrica* July 1961, *29*(3), pp. 315–35.

Neftci, Salih and Sargent, Thomas, 'A Little Bit of Evidence on the Natural Rate Hypothesis from the U.S.', *Journal of Monetary Economics* 1978, *4*(1), pp. 315–19.

Pesando, James, 'A Note on the Rationality of the Livingston Price Expectations', *Journal of Political Economy* Aug. 1975, *83*(4), pp. 849–58.

Preston, Alan and Pagan, Adrian, *The Theory of Economic Policy: Statics and Dynamics*, New York: Cambridge University Press, 1982.

Sargent, Thomas, 'Rational Expectations, the Real Rate of Interest, and the Natural Rate of Unemployment', *Brookings Papers on Economic Act*, 1973, *2*, pp. 429–72.

—— 'A Classical Macroeconomic Model for the United States', *Journal of Political Economy* April 1976a, *84*(2), pp. 207–37.

—— 'The Observational Equivalence of Natural and Unnatural Rate Theories of Macroeconomics', *Journal of Political Economy* June 1976b, *84*(3), pp. 631–40.

Sargent, Thomas, and Wallace, Neil, ' "Rational" Expectations, the Optimal Monetary Instrument and the Optimal Money Supply Rule', *Journal of Political Economy* 1975, *83*(2), pp. 241–55.

—— 'Rational Expectations and the Theory of Economic Policy', *Journal of Monetary Economics* April 1976, *2*(2), pp. 169–83.

Shiller, Robert J., 'Rational Expectations and the Dynamic Structure of Macroeconomic Models: A Critical Review', *Journal of Monetary Economics* Jan. 1978, *4*(1), pp. 1–44.

Sijben, J.J., *Rational Expectations and Monetary Policy*, Alphen aan den Rijn, The Netherlands: Sijthoff and Noordhoff, 1980.

Taylor, John, 'Monetary Policy during the Transition to Rational Expectations', *Journal of Political Economy* 1975, *83*(5), pp. 1009–21.

Theil, Henri, *Economic Forecasts and Policy*, Amsterdam: North-Holland, 1958.

Tinbergen, Jan, *On the Theory of Economic Policy*, Amsterdam: North-Holland, 1952.

Turnovsky, Stephen J., 'Empirical Evidence on the Formation of Price Expectations', *Journal American Statistical Association* Dec. 1970, *65*(332), pp. 1441–54.

13 The Ricardian approach to budget deficits

Robert J. Barro
Journal of Economic Perspectives (1989) 3, Spring, pp. 37–54

In recent years there has been a lot of discussion about US budget deficits. Many economists and other observers have viewed these deficits as harmful to the US and world economies. The supposed harmful effects include high real interest rates, low saving, low rates of economic growth, large current-account deficits in the United States and other countries with large budget deficits, and either a high or low dollar (depending apparently on the time period). This crisis scenario has been hard to maintain along with the robust performance of the US economy since late 1982. This performance features high average growth rates of real GNP, declining unemployment, much lower inflation, a sharp decrease in nominal interest rates and some decline in expected real interest rates, high values of real investment expenditures, and (until October 1987) a dramatic boom in the stock market.

Persistent budget deficits have increased economists' interest in theories and evidence about fiscal policy. At the same time, the conflict between standard predictions and actual outcomes in the US economy has, I think, increased economists' willingness to consider approaches that depart from the standard paradigm. In this paper I will focus on the alternative theory that is associated with the name of David Ricardo.

THE STANDARD MODEL OF BUDGET DEFICITS

Before developing the Ricardian approach, I will sketch the standard model. The starting point is the assumption that the substitution of a budget deficit for current taxation leads to an expansion of aggregate consumer demand. In other words, desired private saving rises by less than the tax cut, so that desired national saving declines. It follows for a closed economy that the expected real interest rate would have to rise to restore equality between desired national saving and investment demand. The higher real interest rate crowds out investment, which shows up in the long run as a smaller stock of productive capital. Therefore, in the language of Franco Modigliani (1961), the public debt is an intergenerational burden in that it leads to a smaller stock of capital for future generations. Similar reasoning applies to pay-as-you-go social security programs, as has been stressed by Martin Feldstein (1974). An increase in the scope of these programs raises the aggregate demand for goods, and thereby leads to a higher real interest rate and a smaller stock of productive capital.

In an open economy, a small country's budget deficits or social security programs would have negligible effects on the real interest rate in international capital markets. Therefore, in the standard analysis, the home country's decision to substitute a budget deficit for current taxes leads mainly to increased borrowing from abroad, rather than to a higher real interest rate. That is, budget deficits lead to current-account deficits. Expected real interest rates rise for the home country only if it is large enough to influence world markets, or if the increased national debt induces foreign lenders to demand higher expected returns on this country's obligations. In any event, there is a weaker tendency for a country's budget deficits to crowd out its domestic investment in the short run and its stock of capital in the long run. However, the current-account deficits show up in the long run as a lower stock of national wealth – and correspondingly higher claims by foreigners.

If the whole world runs budget deficits or expands the scale of its social insurance programs, real interest rates rise on international capital markets, and crowding-out of investment occurs in each country. Correspondingly, the world's stock of capital is lower in the long run. These effects for the world parallel those for a single closed economy, as discussed before.

THE RICARDIAN ALTERNATIVE

The Ricardian modification to the standard analysis begins with the observation that, for a given path of government spending, a deficit-financed cut in current taxes leads to higher future taxes that have the same present value as the initial cut. This result follows from the government's budget constraint, which equates total expenditures for each period (including interest payments) to revenues from taxation or other sources and the net issue of interest-bearing public debt. Abstracting from chain-letter cases where the public debt can grow forever at the rate of interest or higher, the present value of taxes (and other revenues) cannot change unless the government changes the present value of its expenditures. This point amounts to economists' standard notion of the absence of a free lunch – government spending must be paid for now or later, with the total present value of receipts fixed by the total present value of spending. Hence, holding fixed the path of government expenditures and non-tax revenues, a cut in today's taxes must be matched by a corresponding increase in the present value of future taxes.[1]

Suppose now that households' demands for goods depend on the expected present value of taxes – that is, each household subtracts its share of this present value from the expected present value of income to determine a net wealth position. Then fiscal policy would affect aggregate consumer demand only if it altered the expected present value of taxes. But the preceding argument was that the present value of taxes would not change as long as the present value of spending did not change. Therefore, the substitution of a budget deficit for current taxes (or any other rearrangement of the timing of taxes) has no impact on the aggregate demand for goods. In this sense, budget deficits and taxation have equivalent effects on the economy – hence the term, 'Ricardian equivalence theorem'.[2] To put the equivalence result another way, a decrease in the government's saving (that is, a current budget deficit) leads to an offsetting increase in desired private saving, and hence to no change in desired national saving.

Since desired national saving does not change, the real interest rate does not have to rise in a closed economy to maintain balance between desired national saving and investment demand. Hence, there is no effect on investment, and no burden of the public debt or social security in the sense of Modigliani (1961) and Feldstein (1974). In a setting of an open economy there would also be no effect on the current-account balance because desired private saving rises by enough to avoid having to borrow from abroad. Therefore, budget deficits would not cause current-account deficits.

THEORETICAL OBJECTIONS TO RICARDIAN EQUIVALENCE

I shall discuss five major theoretical objections that have been raised against the Ricardian conclusions. The first is that people do not live forever, and hence do not care about taxes that are levied after their death. The second is that private capital markets are 'imperfect', with the typical person's real discount rate exceeding that of the government. The third is that future taxes and incomes are uncertain. The fourth is that taxes are not lump sum, since they depend typically on income, spending, wealth, and so on. The fifth is that the Ricardian result hinges on full employment. I assume throughout that the path of government spending is given. The Ricardian analysis applies to shifts in budget deficits and taxes for a given pattern of government expenditures; in particular, the approach is consistent with real effects from changes in the level or timing of government purchases and public services.

In many cases it turns out that budget deficits matter, and are in that sense non-Ricardian. It is important, however, to consider not only whether the Ricardian view remains intact, but also what alternative conclusions emerge. Many economists raise points that invalidate strict Ricardian equivalence, and then simply assume that the points support a specific alternative; usually the standard view that a budget deficit lowers desired national saving and thereby drives up real interest rates or leads to a current-account deficit. Many criticisms of the Ricardian position are also inconsistent with this standard view.

Finite horizons and related issues

The idea of finite horizons, motivated by the finiteness of life, is central to life-cycle models – see, for example, Franco Modigliani and Richard Brumberg (1954) and Albert Ando and Franco Modigliani (1963). In these models individuals capitalize only the taxes that they expect to face before dying. Consider a deficit-financed tax cut, and assume that the higher future taxes occur partly during the typical person's expected lifetime and partly thereafter. Then the present value of the first portion must fall short of the initial tax cut, since a full balance results only if the second portion is included. Hence the net wealth of persons currently alive rises, and households react by increasing consumption demand. Thus, as in the standard approach sketched above, desired private saving does not rise by enough to offset fully the decline in government saving.

A finite horizon seems to generate the standard result that a budget deficit reduces desired national saving. The argument works, however, only if the typical person feels better off when the government shifts a tax burden to his or her dependants. The argument fails if the typical person is already giving to his or her children out of altruism. In this case people react to the government's imposed intergenerational transfers, which are implied by budget deficits or social security, with a compensating increase in voluntary transfers (Barro 1974). For example, parents adjust their bequests or the amounts given to children while the parents are still living. Alternatively, if children provide support to aged parents, the amounts given can respond (negatively) to budget deficits or social security.

The main idea is that a network of intergenerational transfers makes the typical person a part of an extended family that goes on indefinitely. In this setting, households capitalize the entire array of expected future taxes, and thereby plan effectively with an infinite horizon. In other words, the Ricardian results, which seemed to depend on infinite horizons, can remain valid in a model with finite lifetimes.

Two important points should be stressed. First, intergenerational transfers do not have to be 'large'; what is necessary is that transfers based on altruism be operative at the margin for most people.[3] Specifically, most people must be away from the corner solution of zero transfers, where they would, if permitted, opt for negative payments to their children. (The results also go through, however, if children typically support their aged parents.) Second, the transfers do not have to show up as bequests at death. Other forms of intergenerational transfers, such as *inter vivos* gifts to children, support of children's education, and so on, can work in a similar manner. Therefore, the Ricardian results can hold even if many persons leave little in the way of formal bequests.

One objection to Ricardian equivalence is that some persons, such as those without children, are not connected to future generations (see James Tobin and Willem Buiter 1980: 86 ff.). Persons in this situation tend to be made wealthier when the government substitutes a budget deficit for taxes. At least this conclusion obtains to the extent that the interest and principal payments on the extra public debt are not financed by higher taxes during the remaining lifetimes of people currently alive. However, the quantitative effects on consumption tend to be small. For example, if the typical person has 30 years of remaining life and consumes at a constant rate, a one-time budget deficit of $100 per person would increase each person's real consumption demand by $1.50 per year if the annual real interest rate is 5 percent, and by $2.10 per year if the real interest rate is 3 percent.[4]

The aggregate effect from the existence of childless persons is even smaller because people with more than the average number of descendants experience a decrease in wealth when taxes are replaced by budget deficits. (In effect, although some people have no children, all children must have parents.) In a world of different family sizes, the presumption for a net effect of budget deficits on aggregate consumer demand depends on different propensities to consume out of wealth for people with and without children. Since the propensity for those without children tends to be larger (because of the shorter horizon), a positive net effect on aggregate consumer demand would be predicted. However, the quantitative effect is likely to be trivial. Making the same assumptions as in the previous example, a budget deficit of $100 per capita would raise real consumption demand per capita by 30 cents per year if the real interest rate is 5 percent, and by 90 cents if the real interest rate is 3 percent.

A variety of evidence supports the proposition that intergenerational transfers – defined broadly to go beyond formal bequests – are operative for most people. Michael Darby (1979: ch. 3) and Laurence Kotlikoff and Lawrence Summers (1981) calculate that the accumulation of households' assets in the United States for the purpose of intergenerational transfers is far more important than that associated with the life cycle. This observation suggests that most people give or receive intergenerational transfers – a conclusion that supports the Ricardian position. Franco Modigliani (1988) contests this conclusion, but Laurence Kotlikoff (1988) shows that Modigliani's findings derive from an extremely narrow view of intergenerational transfers. Modigliani focuses on bequests at death, and he also does not treat interest earnings on prior bequests as income attributable to intergenerational transfers.

Some authors accept the idea that intergenerational transfers are important, but argue that the motivation for the transfers matters for the results. Douglas Bernheim, Andrei Shleifer and Lawrence Summers (1985) consider the possibility that bequests, instead of being driven by altruism, are a strategic device whereby parents induce their children to behave properly. Some imaginative evidence is presented (involving how often children visit and communicate with their parents) to document the importance of strategic bequests. In this strategic model, if the government redistributes income from young to old (by running a deficit or raising social security benefits), the old have no reason to raise transfers to offset fully the government's actions. Instead, the old end up better off at the expense of the young, and aggregate consumer demand rises. Then, as in the standard approach, real interest rates increase or domestic residents borrow more from abroad.

One shortcoming of this approach is that it treats the interaction between parents and children as equivalent to the purchases of services on markets. In this setting parents would tend to pay wages to children, rather than using bequests or other forms of intergenerational transfers. These features – as well as the observation that most parents seem to care about their children's welfare – can be better explained by introducing altruism along with a desire to influence children's behavior. In this case Ricardian equivalence may or may not obtain. Consider the utility that a parent would allocate to his or her child if there were no difficulty in motivating the child to perform properly. Suppose that the parent can design a credible threat involving bequests that entails the loss of some part of this utility for the child. (Note that if no threats are credible, the whole basis for strategic bequests disappears.) If the threat is already large enough to induce the behavior that the parent desires, Ricardian equivalence still holds. For example, if the government runs a budget deficit, the parent provides off-setting transfers to the child, and thereby preserves the child's level of utility, as well as the behavior sought by the parent. On the other hand, the parent may have to allow excess utility to the child to secure a sufficient threat against bad performance. Then a budget deficit enables the parent to reduce the child's utility (as desired), while maintaining or even enhancing the threat that influences behavior. In this case Ricardian equivalence would not hold.

Other economists argue that the uncertainty of the time of death makes many bequests unintended, and that such bequests would not respond very much to budget deficits. The imperfection of private annuity markets is usually mentioned to explain why unintended bequests are significant. But this reasoning is backwards, since annuities do not entail greater adverse selection problems than many other types of insurance. The small amount of private annuities outstanding, other than the substantial amount in the form of pensions, reflects primarily a lack of demand, which itself is an indication that people desire to make the most of the bequests that occur. In any event, since the Ricardian results involve a broad concept of intergenerational transfers, rather than especially bequests at death, a focus on formal bequests is misplaced.

Imperfect loan markets

Many economists argue that the imperfection of private credit markets is central to an analysis of the public debt; see, for example, Robert Mundell (1971). To consider this argument, assume that a closed economy consists of two types of infinite-lived economic agents; those of group A who have the same discount rate, r, as the government (and are therefore willing to hold the government's debt), and those of group B who have the higher discount rate, $\tilde{r} > r$. The constituents of group A would include large businesses, pension funds, and some individuals. The members of group B, such as small businesses and many households, possess poor collateral; therefore, loans to these people imply large costs of evaluation and enforcement. It follows that the members of group B face higher borrowing rates (even after an allowance for default risk) than the government. Whether or not they are actually borrowing, the high discount rate $\tilde{r}$ for group B corresponds to a high rate of time preference for consumption and a high marginal return on investment.

Suppose that the government cuts current taxes and runs a budget deficit. Further, assume that the division of the tax cut between groups A and B – say fifty-fifty – is the same as the division of the higher future taxes needed to service the extra debt. Since those from group A experience no net change in wealth, they willingly hold their share of the extra public debt. For group B, where the discount rate $\tilde{r}$ exceeds r, the present value of the extra future taxes falls short of the tax cut. The members of this group are better off because the tax cut effectively enables them to borrow at the lower interest rate, r. This cut in the effective borrowing rate motivates the members of group B to raise current consumption and investment.

In the aggregate a budget deficit now raises aggregate demand, or equivalently, the aggregate of desired private saving increases by less than one-to-one with the government's deficit. It follows that the real interest rate r, which applies to group A and the government, must rise to induce people to hold the extra public debt. Hence there is crowding out of consumption and investment by members of group A. For group B, the opportunity to raise current consumption and investment means that the rate of time preference for consumption and the marginal return to investment would decline. That is, the discount rate $\tilde{r}$ falls. Thus, the main effects are a narrowing of the spread between the two discount rates, r and $\tilde{r}$, and a diversion of current expenditures from group A to group B. In the aggregate investment may either rise or fall, and the long-term effect on the capital stock is uncertain. The major change, however, is a better channeling of resources to their ultimate uses. Namely the persons from group B – who have relatively high values for rates of time preference and for marginal returns to investment – command a greater share of current output. In any event the outcomes are non-neutral, and in that sense non-Ricardian.

The important finding from the inclusion of imperfect loan markets is that the government's issue of public debt can amount to a useful form of financial intermediation. The government induces people with good access to credit markets (group A) to hold more than their share of the extra public debt. Those with poor access (group B) hold less than their share, and thereby effectively receive loans from the first group. This process works because the government implicitly guarantees the repayment of loans through its tax collections and debt payments. Thus loans between

A and B take place even though such loans were not viable (because of 'transaction costs') on the imperfect private credit market.

This much of the argument may be valid, although it credits the government with a lot of skill in the collection of taxes from people with poor collateral (which is the underlying source of the problem for private lenders). Even if the government possesses this skill, the conclusions do not resemble those from the standard analysis. As discussed before, budget deficits can amount to more financial intermediation, and are in that sense equivalent to a technological advance that improves the functioning of loan markets. From this perspective it is reasonable to find a reduced spread between various discount rates and an improvement in the allocation of resources. If the government really is better at the process of intermediating, more of this activity – that is, more public debt – raises perceived wealth because it actually improves the workings of the economy.

In the preceding analysis, the imperfection of credit markets reflected costs of enforcing the collection of loans. A different approach, followed by Toshiki Yotsuzuka (1987) in his extension of the models of Mervyn King (1986) and Fumio Hayashi (1987), allows for adverse selection among borrowers with different risk characteristics. Individuals know their probabilities of default, but the lenders' only possibility for learning these probabilities comes from observing the chosen levels of borrowing at going interest rates. In this setting the government's borrowing amounts to a loan to a group that pools the various risk classes. Such borrowing matters if the private equilibrium does not involve similar pooling. However, by considering the incentives of lenders to exchange or not exchange information about their customers, Yotsuzuka argues that the private equilibrium typically involves a pooled loan of limited quantity at a relatively low interest rate. Then the high-risk types may borrow additional amounts at a high interest rate. (The assumption is that this additional borrowing is not observable by other lenders.) In this case the government's borrowing replaces the private pooled lending, and leads to no real effects. That is, Ricardian equivalence holds despite the imperfect private loan market where high-risk people face high marginal borrowing rates. The general lesson again is that Ricardian equivalence fails because of imperfect credit markets only if the government does things in the loan market that are different from, and perhaps better than, those carried out privately.

Uncertainty about future taxes and incomes

Some economists argue that the uncertainty about individuals' future taxes – or the complexity in estimating them – implies a high rate of discount in capitalizing these future liabilities (Martin Bailey 1971: 157–8; James Buchanan and Richard Wagner 1977: 17, 101, 130; Martin Feldstein 1976: 335). In this case, a substitution of a budget deficit for current taxes raises net wealth because the present value of the higher expected future taxes falls short of the current tax cut. It then follows that budget deficits raise aggregate consumer demand and reduce desired national saving.

A proper treatment of uncertainty leads to different conclusions. Louis Chan (1983) first considers the case of lump-sum taxes that have a known distribution across households. However, the aggregate of future taxes and the real value of future payments on public debt are subject to uncertainty. In this case a deficit-financed tax cut has no real effects. Individuals hold their share of the extra debt because the debt is a perfect hedge against the uncertainty of the future taxes. (This analysis assumes that private credit markets have no 'imperfections' of the sort discussed earlier.)

Suppose now that future taxes are still lump sum but have an uncertain incidence across individuals. Furthermore, assume that there are no insurance markets for relative tax risks. Then a budget deficit tends to increase the uncertainty about each individual's future disposable income. Chan (1983: 363) shows for the 'usual case' (of non-increasing absolute risk aversion) that people react by reducing current consumption and hence, by raising current private saving by more than the tax cut. Consequently, the effects on real interest rates, investment, the current account, and so on are the opposites of the standard ones.

The results are different for an income tax (Chan 1983: 364–6; Robert Barsky, Gregory Mankiw and Stephen Zeldes 1986). Suppose that each person pays the tax τy_i, where y_i is the person's uncertain future income. Suppose that there are no insurance markets for individual income risks, and that τ is known. (The analysis thus abstracts from uncertainties in relative tax rates across individuals.) In this case a budget deficit raises the future value of τ and thereby reduces the uncertainty about each individual's future disposable income. In effect, the government shares the risks about individual disposable income to a greater extent. It follows that the results are opposite to those found before; namely, a budget deficit tends to raise current consumption and hence, to raise private saving by less than the tax cut.

Overall, the conclusions depend on the net effect of higher mean future tax collections on the uncertainty associated with individuals' future disposable incomes. Desired national saving tends to rise with a budget deficit if this uncertainty increases, and vice versa.

The timing of taxes

Departures from Ricardian equivalence arise also if taxes are not lump sum; for example, with an income tax. In this situation, budget deficits change the timing of income taxes, and thereby affect people's incentives to work and produce in different periods. It follows that variations in deficits are non-neutral, although the results tend also to be inconsistent with the standard view.

Suppose, for example, that the current tax rate on labor income, τ_1, declines, and the expected rate for the next period, τ_2, rises. To simplify matters, assume that today's budget deficit is matched by enough of a surplus next period so that the public debt does not change in later periods. Because the tax rate applies to labor income, households are motivated to work more than usual in period 1 and less than usual in period 2. Since the tax rate does not apply to expenditures (and since wealth effects are negligible here), desired national saving rises in period 1 and falls in period 2. Therefore, in a closed economy, after-tax real interest rates tend to be relatively low in period 1 – along with the budget deficit – and relatively high in period 2 – along with the surplus. In an open economy, a current-account surplus accompanies the budget deficit, and vice versa. Hence the results are non-Ricardian, but also counter to the standard view. (Temporary variations in consumption taxes tend to generate the standard pattern where real interest rates, current-account deficits, and budget deficits are positively correlated.)

Unlike in the Ricardian case where debt and deficits do not matter, it is possible in a world of distorting taxes to determine the optimal path of the budget deficit, which corresponds to the optimal time pattern of taxes. In effect, the theory of debt management becomes a branch of public finance; specifically, an application of the theory of optimal taxation.

One result is that budget deficits can be used to smooth tax rates over time, despite fluctuations in government expenditures and the tax base.[5] For example, if time periods are identical except for the quantity of government purchases – which are assumed not to interact directly with labor supply decisions – optimality dictates uniform taxation of labor income over time. This constancy of tax rates requires budget deficits when government spending is unusually high, such as in wartime, and surpluses when spending is unusually low.

Constant tax rates over time will not be optimal in general; for example, optimal tax rates on labor income may vary over the business cycle. To the extent that some smoothing is called for, budget deficits would occur in recessions, and surpluses in booms. If optimal tax rates are lower than normal in recessions and higher than normal in booms, the countercyclical pattern of budget deficits is even more vigorous. The well-known concept of the full-employment deficit, as discussed in E. Cary Brown (1956) and Council of Economic Advisers (1962: 78–82), adjusts for this cyclical behavior of budget deficits.

The tax-smoothing view has implications for the interaction between inflation and budget deficits if the public debt is denominated in nominal terms. Basically, the fiscal authority's objective involves the path of tax rates and other real variables. Therefore, other things equal, a higher rate of expected inflation (presumably reflecting a higher rate of monetary growth) motivates a correspondingly higher growth rate of the nominal, interest-bearing debt. This response keeps the planned path of the real public debt invariant with expected inflation. This behavior means that differences in expected rates of inflation can account for substantial variations in budget deficits if deficits are measured in the conventional way to correspond to the change in the government's nominal liabilities. This element is, however, less important for an inflation-adjusted budget deficit, which corresponds to the change in the government's real obligations (Jeremy Siegel 1979; Robert Eisner and Paul Pieper 1984).

With perfect foresight, the strict tax-smoothing model implies constant tax rates. More realistically, new information about the path of government spending, national income, and so on, would lead to revisions of tax rates. However, the sign of these revisions would not be predictable. Thus, in the presence of uncertainty, tax smoothing implies that tax rates would behave roughly like random walks.

It is possible to use the tax-smoothing approach as a positive theory of how the government operates, rather than as a normative model of how it should act.[6] Barro (1979; 1986) shows that this framework explains much of the behavior of US federal deficits from 1916 to 1983, although the deficits since 1984 turn out to be substantially higher than predicted. Over the full sample, the major departures from the theory are an excessive reaction of budget deficits to the business cycle (so that tax rates fall below 'normal' during recessions) and an insufficient reaction to temporary military spending (so that tax rates rise above normal during wars). These departures are found also by Chaipat Sahasakul (1986), who looks directly at the behavior of average marginal tax rates. Barro (1987: section 3) finds for the British data from the early 1700s through 1918 that temporary military spending is the major determinant of budget deficits. Also, unlike the US case, the results indicate a one-to-one response of budget deficits to temporary spending.

Full employment and Keynesian models

A common argument is that the Ricardian results depend on 'full employment', and surely do not hold in Keynesian models. In standard Keynesian analysis (which still appears in many textbooks), if everyone thinks that a budget deficit makes them wealthier, the resulting expansion of aggregate demand raises output and employment, and thereby actually makes people wealthier. (This result holds if the economy begins in a state of 'involuntary unemployment'.) There may even be multiple, rational expectations equilibria, where the change in actual wealth coincides with the change in perceived wealth.

This result does not mean that budget deficits increase aggregate demand and wealth in Keynesian models. If we had conjectured that budget deficits made people feel poorer, the resulting contractions in output and employment would have made them poorer. Similarly, if we had started with the Ricardian notion that budget deficits did not affect wealth, the Keynesian results would have verified that conjecture. The odd feature of the standard Keynesian model is that *anything* that makes people feel wealthier actually makes them wealthier (although the perception and actuality need not correspond quantitatively). This observation raises doubts about the formulation of Keynesian models, but says little about the effect of budget deficits. Moreover, in equilibrium models that include unemployment (such as models with incomplete information and search), there is no clear interplay between the presence of unemployment and the validity of the Ricardian approach.

EMPIRICAL EVIDENCE ON THE ECONOMIC EFFECTS OF BUDGET DEFICITS

It is easy on theoretical grounds to raise points that invalidate strict Ricardian equivalence. Nevertheless, it may still be that the Ricardian view provides a useful framework for assessing the first-order effects of fiscal policy. Furthermore, it is unclear that the standard analysis offers a more accurate guide. For these reasons it is especially important to examine empirical evidence.

The Ricardian and standard views have different predictions about the effects of fiscal policy on a number of economic variables. The next three sections summarize the empirical evidence on interest rates, saving, and the current-account balance.

Interest rates

The Ricardian view predicts no effect of budget deficits on real interest rates, whereas the standard view predicts a positive effect, at least in the context of a closed economy. Many economists have tested these propositions empirically (for a summary, see US Treasury Department 1984). Typical results show little relationship between budget deficits and interest rates. For example, Charles Plosser (1982: 339) finds for quarterly US data from 1954 to 1978 that unexpected movements in privately held federal debt do not raise the nominal yield on government securities of various maturities. In fact, there is a weak tendency for yields to decline with innovations in federal debt. Plosser's (1987: Tables VIII and XI) later study, which includes data through 1985, reaches similar conclusions for nominal and expected real yields. Paul Evans (1987b) obtains similar results for nominal yields with quarterly data from 1974 to 1985 for Canada, France, Germany, Japan, the United Kingdom, and the United States.

Evans (1987a: Tables 4–6) finds for annual US data from 1931 to 1979 that current and past real federal deficits have no significant association with nominal interest rates on commercial paper or corporate bonds, or with realized real interest rates on commercial paper. Over the longer period from 1908 to 1984, using monthly data, there is some indication of a negative relation between deficits and nominal or real interest rates (Evans 1987a: Tables 1–3). Evans also explores the effects of expected future budget deficits or surpluses. He assumes that people would have expected future deficits in advance of tax cuts, such as in 1981, and future surpluses in advance of tax hikes. But interest rates turn out typically not to rise in advance of tax cuts and not to fall in advance of tax hikes.

Overall, the empirical results on interest rates support the Ricardian view. Given these findings it is remarkable that most macroeconomists remain confident that budget deficits raise interest rates.

Consumption and saving

Many empirical studies have searched for effects of budget deficits or social security on consumption and saving. Most of these studies – exemplified by Levis Kochin (1974) and the papers surveyed in Louis Esposito (1978) – rely on estimates of coefficients in consumption functions. Basically, the results are all over the map, with some favoring Ricardian equivalence, and others not.

The inconclusive nature of these results probably reflects well-known identification problems. The analysis does not deal satisfactorily with the simultaneity between consumption and income, and also has problems with the endogeneity of budget deficits. For example, deficits and saving (or investment) have strong cyclical elements, and it is difficult to sort out the causation in these patterns. Because of these problems, I regard as more reliable some results that exploit situations that look more like natural experiments.

One such study, a comparison of saving in Canada and the United States was carried out by Chris Carroll and Lawrence Summers (1987). They note that the private saving rates in the two countries were similar until the early 1970s, but have since diverged; for 1983–5 the Canadian rate was higher by about six percentage points. After holding fixed some macroeconomic variables and aspects of the tax systems that influence saving, the authors isolate a roughly one-to-one, positive effect of government budget deficits on private saving. That is, the rise in the private saving rate in Canada, relative to that in the United States, reflected the greater increase in the Canadian budget deficit as a ratio to GNP. Thus, as implied by the Ricardian view, the relative values of the net national saving rates in the two countries appeared to be invariant with the relative values of the budget deficits. These results are particularly interesting because the focus on relative performance in Canada and the United States holds constant the many forces that have common influences on the two countries. It may be that this procedure lessens the problems of identification that hamper most studies of consumption functions.

Recent fiscal policy in Israel comes close to a natural experiment for studying the interplay between budget deficits and saving.[7] In 1983 the gross national saving rate of 13 percent corresponded to a private saving rate of 17 percent and a public saving rate of −4 percent. In 1984 the dramatic rise in the budget deficit led to a public saving rate of −11 percent. (A principal reason for the deficit was the adverse effect of the increase in the inflation rate on the collection of real tax revenues.) For present purposes, the interesting observation is that the private saving rate rose from 17 percent to 26 percent, so that the national saving rate changed little; actually rising from 13 percent to 15 percent. Then the stabilization program in 1985 eliminated the budget deficit, along with most of the inflation, so that the public saving rate increased from −11 percent in 1984 to 0 in 1985–6 and −2 percent in 1987. The private saving rate decreased dramatically at the same time – from 26 percent in 1984 to 19 percent in 1985 and 14 percent in 1986–7. Therefore, the national saving rates were relatively stable, going from 15 percent in 1984 to 18 percent in 1985, 14 percent in 1986, and 12 percent in 1987. The main point is that this evidence reveals the roughly one-to-one offset between public and private saving that the Ricardian view predicts.

Finally, I should note the 'Reagan experiment', which featured large US budget deficits from 1984 to 1987 during a peacetime boom. (While an interesting experiment – applauded on scientific grounds even by opponents of Reagan – the magnitudes are much less dramatic than those in Israel.) Unfortunately, the effects of recent US budget deficits on US investment and saving are controversial, especially because it is unclear whether recent investment and saving rates are high or low.

National accounts measures of rates of net investment and net national saving are low, and have often been cited. But the ratio of real gross investment (broadly defined to include purchases of consumer durables) to real GNP averaged 27.9 percent from 1984 to 1987, as compared to an average of 23.8 percent from 1947 to 1987. In fact, the recent investment ratios represent a post-World War II high. If saving is measured (as I would argue is appropriate) by the change in the real market value of assets, recent saving rates have not been low. For example, the change in real household net worth as a ratio to real GNP averaged 11.2 percent from 1984 to 1987, as compared to a mean of 10.1 percent from 1949 to 1987.[8] Thus, while a good portion of recent US budget deficits may qualify as exogenous, it is not yet clear how these deficits affected US investment and saving.

Current-account deficits

Popular opinion attributes the large current-account deficits in the United States since 1983 to the effects of budget deficits. Figure 13.1 shows the values since 1948 of the ratio of the total government budget surplus (national accounts' version) to GNP (solid line) and the ratio of net foreign investment to GNP (dotted line).[9] Through 1982 there is no association between these two variables (correlation = −0.02). However, including the

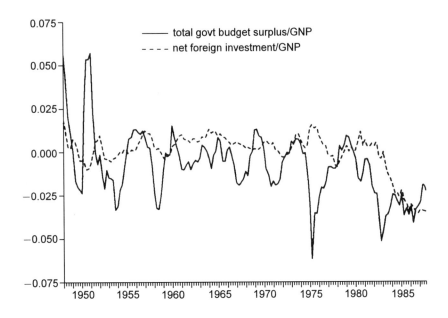

Figure 13.1 US budget and current-account surpluses, 1948–87
Note: Data are seasonally adjusted, quarterly values from Citibase

data since 1983 raises the correlation to 0.37. In effect, the US data since World War II reveal a single incident – the period since 1983 – when budget and current-account deficits have been high at the same time. While this co-movement is interesting, it does not by itself provide strong support for the view that budget deficits cause current account deficits.

Evans (1988: Tables 1–5) carried out a cross-country empirical investigation of the relation between budget and current account deficits. He looked first at annual, post-World War II data for Canada, with the United States used as a proxy for the rest of the world. (In a model where budget deficits matter, the current account deficit responds to the home country's budget deficit relative to the budget deficit in the rest of the world.) Then he looked at quarterly data since 1973 on the United States, Canada, France, Germany, and the United Kingdom, with the aggregate of the major industrialized countries (other than the country under study) used to represent the rest of the world. Evans's overall finding is that the results are consistent with the Ricardian hypothesis that current-account balances are independent of budget deficits. (Only the estimates for Germany suggest a positive relation between budget and current account deficits, but the results in this case are not statistically significant.) Evans reacts to his findings with the question, 'If large U.S. budget deficits did not produce the large U.S. current-account deficits of the 1980s, what did?' and concludes that this question is an interesting topic for future research (Evans 1988: 31).

CONCLUDING OBSERVATIONS

The Ricardian approach to budget deficits amounts to the statement that the government's fiscal impact is summarized by the present value of its expenditures. Given this present value, rearrangements of the timing of taxes – as implied by budget deficits – have no first-order effect on the economy. Second-order effects arise for various reasons, which include the distorting effects of taxes, the uncertainties about individual incomes and tax obligations, the imperfections of credit markets, and the finiteness of life. To say that these effects are second order is not to say that they are uninteresting; in fact, the analysis of differential taxation in the theory of public finance is second order in the same sense. However, careful analysis of these effects tends to deliver predictions about budget deficits that differ from those of standard macroeconomic models.

I have argued that empirical findings on interest rates, consumption and saving, and the current-account balance tend mainly to support the Ricardian viewpoint. However, this empirical analysis involves substantial problems about data and identification, and the results are sometimes inconclusive. It would be useful to assemble additional evidence, especially in an international context.

Although the majority of economists still lean toward standard macroeconomic models of fiscal policy, it is remarkable how respectable the Ricardian approach has become in the last decade. Most macroeconomists now feel obligated to state the Ricardian position, even if they then go on to argue that it is either theoretically or empirically in error. I predict that this trend will continue and that the Ricardian approach will become the benchmark model for assessing fiscal policy.

There is a parallel between the Ricardian equivalence theorem on intertemporal government finance and the Modigliani-Miller (1958) theorem on corporate finance. Everyone knows that the Modigliani-Miller theorem is literally incorrect in saying that the structure of corporate finance does not matter. But the theorem rules out numerous sloppy reasons for why this structure might have mattered, and thereby forces theoretical and empirical analyses into a disciplined, productive mode. Similarly, I would not predict that most analysts will embrace Ricardian equivalence in the sense of concluding that fiscal policy is irrelevant. But satisfactory analyses will feature explicit modeling of elements that lead to departures from Ricardian equivalence, and the predicted consequences of fiscal policies will flow directly from these elements.

ACKNOWLEDGEMENTS

I am grateful for support of research from the National Science Foundation. Also, I appreciate the high quality comments provided by the editors of *Journal of Economic Perspectives*.

NOTES

1 The calculations use the government's interest rate in each period to calculate present values, and assume perfect foresight with respect to future government expenditures and taxes. For further discussion see Ben McCallum (1984) and Robert Barro (1989).

2 The term, Ricardian equivalence theorem, was introduced to macroeconomists by James Buchanan (1976). After Gerald O'Driscoll (1977) documented Ricardo's reservations about this result, some economists have referred to the equivalence finding as being non-Ricardian. But, as far as I have been able to discover, David Ricardo (1951) was the first to articulate this theory. Therefore, the attribution of the equivalence theorem to Ricardo is appropriate even if he had doubts about some of the theorem's assumptions. As to whether the presence of this idea in Ricardo's writings is important for scientific progress, I would refer to Nathan Rosenberg's (1976: 79) general views on innovations in the social sciences: 'what often happens in economics is that, as concern mounts over a particular problem ... an increasing number of professionals commit their time and energies to it. We then eventually realize that there were all sorts of treatments of the subject in the earlier literature.... We then proceed to read much of our more sophisticated present-day understanding back into the work of earlier writers whose analysis was inevitably more fragmentary and incomplete than the later achievement. It was this retrospective view which doubtless inspired Whitehead to say somewhere that everything of importance has been said before – but by someone who did not discover it.' (This last point relates to 'Stigler's Law', which states that nothing is named after the person who discovered it.)

3 Philippe Weil (1987) and Miles Kimball (1987) analyze conditions that ensure an interior solution for intergenerational transfers. Douglas Bernheim and Kyle Bagwell (1988) argue that difficulties arise if altruistic transfers are pervasive. See Barro (1989) for a discussion of their analysis.

4 The assumption is the real debt remains permanently higher by the amount of the initial deficit. For some related calculations, see Merton Miller and Charles Upton (1974: ch. 8) and James Poterba and Lawrence Summers (1987: section I).

5 For discussions of the tax-smoothing model of budget deficits, see A. C. Pigou (1928: ch. 6) and Robert Barro (1979; 1986).

6 A colleague of mine argues that a 'normative' model should be defined as a model that fits the data badly.

7 I am grateful to Ed Offenbacher for calling my attention to the Israeli experience. The data, all expressed in US dollars, are from Bank of Israel (1987).

8 Household net worth comes from Board of Governors of the Federal Reserve System (1988). The nominal year-end figures were divided by the fourth-quarter GNP deflator. The Federal Reserve numbers include stocks, housing, and consumer durables at estimated market value, but bonds at par value. I made no adjustments for households' liabilities for future taxes associated with the government's debt net of assets. There is a conceptual problem here because some of this liability is already reflected in the market values of households' stocks, housing, and so on. Also, the Federal Reserve's measures of government liabilities and assets are not well developed.

9 The data are quarterly, seasonally adjusted values from Citibase. The results are similar if the federal surplus is used instead of the total government surplus.

REFERENCES

Ando, Albert, and Franco Modigliani, 'The "Life Cycle" Hypothesis of Saving: Aggregate Implications and Tests', *American Economic Review* March 1963, *53*, 55–84.

Bailey, Martin J., *National Income and the Price Level*, 2nd edn, New York: McGraw Hill, 1971.

Bank of Israel, *Annual Report*, Jerusalem, 1987.

Barro, Robert J., 'Are Government Bonds Net Wealth?', *Journal of Political Economy* November/December 1974, *82*, 1095–117.

Barro, Robert J., 'On the Determination of the Public Debt', *Journal of Political Economy* October 1979, *87*, 940–71.

Barro, Robert J., 'U.S. Deficits since World War I', *Scandinavian Journal of Economics* 1986, *88*, no. 1, 195–222.

Barro, Robert J., 'Government Spending, Interest Rates, Prices, and Budget Deficits in the United Kingdom, 1701–1918', *Journal of Monetary Economics* September 1987, *20*, 221–47.

Barro, Robert J., 'The Neoclassical Approach to Fiscal Policy', in Robert J. Barro (ed.) *Modern Business Cycle Theory*, Cambridge, MA: Harvard University Press, 1989.

Barsky, Robert B., N. Gregory Mankiw, and Stephen P. Zeldes, 'Ricardian Consumers with Keynesian Propensities', *American Economic Review* September 1986, *76*, 676–91.

Bernheim, B. Douglas, Andrei Shleifer, and Lawrence H. Summers, 'The Strategic Bequest Motive', *Journal of Political Economy* December 1985, *93*, 1045–76.

Bernheim, B. Douglas and Kyle Bagwell, 'Is Everything Neutral?', *Journal of Political Economy* April 1988, *96*, 308–38.

Board of Governors of the Federal Reserve System, *Balance Sheets for the U.S. Economy, 1948–87*, Washington, DC, October 1988.

Brown, E. Cary, 'Fiscal Policy in the' Thirties: a Reappraisal', *Journal of Political Economy* December 1956, *46*, 857–79.

Buchanan, James M., 'Barro on the Ricardian Equivalence Theorem', *Journal of Political Economy* April 1976, *84*, 337–42.

Buchanan, James M. and Richard E. Wagner, *Democracy in Deficit*, New York: Academic Press, 1977.

Carroll, Chris and Lawrence H. Summers, 'Why Have Private Savings Rates in the United States and Canada Diverged?', *Journal of Monetary Economics* September 1987, *20*, 249–79.

Chan, Louis K. C., 'Uncertainty and the Neutrality of Government Financing Policy', *Journal of Monetary Economics* May 1983, *11*, 351–72.

Council of Economic Advisers, *Annual Report*, Washington, DC: US Government Printing Office, 1962.

Darby, Michael, R., *The Effects of Social Security on Income and the Capital Stock*, Washington, DC: American Enterprise Institute, 1979.

Eisner, Robert and Paul Pieper, 'A New View of the Federal Debt and Budget Deficits', *American Economic Review* March 1984, *74*, 11–29.

Esposito, Louis, 'Effect of Social Security on Saving: Review of Studies Using U.S. Time-Series Data', *Social Security Bulletin* May 1978, *41*, 9–17.

Evans, Paul, 'Interest Rates and Expected Future Budget Deficits in the United States', *Journal of Political Economy* February 1987a, *95*, 34–58.

Evans, Paul, 'Do Budget Deficits Raise Nominal Interest Rates? Evidence from Six Industrial Countries', *Journal of Monetary Economics* September 1987b, *20*, 281–300.

Evans, Paul, 'Do Budget Deficits Affect the Current Account?', unpublished, Ohio State University, August 1988.

Feldstein, Martin S., 'Social Security, Induced Retirement, and Aggregate Capital Accumulation', *Journal of Political Economy* September/October 1974, *82*, 905–926.

Feldstein, Martin S., 'Perceived Wealth in Bonds and Social Security: a Comment', *Journal of Political Economy* April 1976, *84*, 331–6.

Hayashi, Fumio, 'Tests for Liquidity Constraints: a Critical Survey and some New Observations', in Truman F. Bewley (ed.) *Advances in Econometrics, Fifth World Congress*, Cambridge: Cambridge University Press, 1987.

Kimball, Miles S., 'Making Sense of Two-Sided Altruism', *Journal of Monetary Economics* September 1987, *20*, 301–26.

King, Mervyn A., 'Tax Policy and Consumption Smoothing', unpublished, London School of Economics, April 1986.

Kochin, Levis A., 'Are Future Taxes Anticipated by Consumers?', *Journal of Money, Credit and Banking* August 1974, *6*, 385–394.

Kotlikoff, Laurence J., 'Intergenerational Transfers and Savings', *Journal of Economic Perspectives* Spring 1988, *2*, 41–58.

Kotlikoff, Laurence J. and Lawrence H. Summers, 'The Role of Intergenerational Transfers in Aggregate Capital Accumulation', *Journal of Political Economy* August 1981, *89*, 706–732.

McCallum, Ben T., 'Are Bond-financed Deficits Inflationary? A Ricardian Analysis', *Journal of Political Economy* February 1984, *92*, 123–35.

Miller, Merton H. and Charles W. Upton, *Macroeconomics, a Neoclassical Introduction*, Homewood, IL: Irwin, 1974.

Modigliani, Franco, 'Long-run Implications of Alternative Fiscal Policies and the Burden of the National Debt', *Economic Journal* December 1961, *71*, 730–55.

Modigliani, Franco, 'The Role of Intergenerational Transfers and Life Cycle Saving in the Accumulation of Wealth', *Journal of Economic Perspectives* Spring 1988, *2*, 15–40.

Modigliani, Franco and Richard Brumberg, 'Utility Analysis and the Consumption Function: an Interpretation of Cross-Section Data', in K. K. Kurihara (ed.) *Post-Keynesian Economics*, New Brunswick, NJ: Rutgers University Press, 1954.

Modigliani, Franco and Merton H. Miller, 'The Cost of Capital, Corporation Finance and the Theory of Investment', *American Economic Review* June 1958, *48*, 261–97.

Mundell, Robert A., 'Money, Debt, and the Rate of Interest', in R. A. Mundell, *Monetary Theory*, Pacific Palisades, CA: Goodyear, 1971.

O'Driscoll, Gerald P., 'The Ricardian Nonequivalence Theorem', *Journal of Political Economy* February 1977, *85*, 207–10.

Pigou, A. C., *A Study in Public Finance*, London: Macmillan, 1928.

Plosser, Charles I., 'Government Financing Decisions and Asset Returns', *Journal of Monetary Economics* May 1982, *9*, 325–52.

Plosser, Charles I., 'Further Evidence on the Relation between Fiscal Policy and the Term Structure', *Journal of Monetary Economics* September 1987, *20*, 343–67.

Poterba, James M. and Lawrence H. Summers, 'Finite Lifetimes and the Savings Effects of Budget Deficits', *Journal of Monetary Economics* September 1987, *20*, 369–91.

Ricardo, David, 'Funding System', in Piero Sraffa (ed.) *The Works and Correspondence of David Ricardo, volume IV, Pamphlets and Papers, 1815–1823*, Cambridge: Cambridge University Press, 1951.

Rosenberg, Nathan, *Perspectives on Technology*, Cambridge: Cambridge University Press, 1976.

Sahasakul, Chaipat, 'The U.S. Evidence on Optimal Taxation over Time', *Journal of Monetary Economics* November 1986, *18*, 251–75.

Siegel, Jeremy J., 'Inflation-Induced Distortions in Government and Private Saving Statistics', *Review of Economics and Statistics* April 1979, *61*, 83–90.

Tobin, James and Willem Buiter, 'Fiscal and Monetary Policies, Capital Formation, and Economic Activity', in George M. von Furstenberg (ed.) *The Government and Capital Formation*, Cambridge: Ballinger, 1980.

US Treasury Department, *The Effect of Deficits on Prices of Financial Assets: Theory and Evidence*, Washington, DC: US Government Printing Office, 1984.

Weil, Philippe, 'Love Thy Children: Reflections on the Barro Debt Neutrality Theorem', *Journal of Monetary Economics* May 1987, *19*, 377–91.

Yotsuzuka, Toshiki, 'Ricardian Equivalence in the Presence of Capital Market Imperfections', *Journal of Monetary Economics* September 1987, *20*, 411–36.

14 The new-classical contribution to macroeconomics

David Laidler
Banca Nazionale Del Lavoro Quarterly Review (1986) March,
pp. 27–55

INTRODUCTION

Macroeconomics is prone to 'revolutions' – intellectual upheaval in which some new idea or ideas claiming to establish fresh and valid insights into the workings of the economic system sweep away a prevailing orthodoxy. Since the mid-1930s the 'Keynesian revolution' has overwhelmed 'classical economics' so-called, to be succeeded in turn by a 'monetarist revolution' which seemed to overthrow 'Keynesian' economics. Since the early 1970s 'monetarism' has in turn yielded to a 'new-classical revolution' which self-consciously, and much more thoroughly than monetarism, has sought to re-establish macroeconomics on foundations that bear a close resemblance to those of certain strands in pre-Keynesian economics.[1] In every case, the superiority of the 'new' approach has undoubtedly been oversold by its adherents, but, at the same time, insights and tools of lasting value have also been added to the corpus of economic knowledge.

This chapter is devoted to assessing new-classical ideas, and to asking what of lasting importance this school of macroeconomics has contributed since the early 1970s. It deals in turn with the relationship between new-classical economics and monetarism, the relative explanatory power of these two bodies of doctrine over empirical evidence, and the claims of new-classical economics to embody a superior analytic method. It argues that, although the particular ways in which new-classical macroeconomics has applied its basic ideas, notably in its insistence that the interaction of the maximizing behaviour of individuals be analysed in the context of continuously clearing markets, and that agents' expectations be represented by the predictions of the true model of the economy in which they operate, are unnecessarily restrictive, its stress on equilibrium behaviour conditioned by the state of individual agents' expectations as a basis for macro modelling is nevertheless valuable, and has been salutary for the discipline.

MONETARISM AND NEW-CLASSICAL MACROECONOMICS

New-classical macroeconomics was initially a response to the inflation of the 1960s and 1970s, and to monetarist analysis of that inflation. Indeed, in its earliest manifestations, it appeared to be nothing more than an attempt to restate monetarist analysis with greater rigour than its pioneers – notably Milton Friedman – had achieved.[2] In order to put matters in perspective it will be helpful to recall the nature of the intellectual problem which that inflation created for most macroeconomists. Quite simply the empirical evidence it generated proved to be utterly inconsistent with then prevailing Keynesian views about how the economy worked, and about how policy could be used to improve its performance. Expansionary demand side policies, predominantly fiscal, could, according to that orthodoxy, generate lasting reductions in unemployment at the cost of somewhat higher, but nevertheless stable, inflation. When the Keynesian experiment occurred, it failed.[3] Gains in output and employment, where they materialized at all, proved to be temporary, and inflation, instead of shifting once to a new higher level, rose continuously.

Monetarist macroeconomics (whose components were available before the event, be it noted) explained these facts by arguing: first that Keynesian orthodoxy had underestimated the role of the quantity of money as an influence on aggregate demand in general and the behaviour of prices in particular; and second that the idea of a stable inflation–unemployment trade-off – the Phillips curve – was based on an implicit assumption that the private sector of the economy suffered from perpetual money illusion. To the pressure of aggregate demand as a proximate influence on the inflation rate, Friedman (1968) – not to mention Phelps (1967) – added the expected rate of inflation. Furthermore, because Friedman viewed inflation expectations as deriving from past experience, and as being formed in such a way that expectations would in fact come to catch up with experience eventually, he argued that any attempt to reduce the unemployment rate below that determined by the normal frictions inherent in the labour market would lead, in the long run, not to higher, but to rising, inflation.

From the point of view of policy prescriptions and empirical judgements about the reliability of particular functional relationships in the economy, monetarism presented a clear alternative to Keynesian orthodoxy, but constituted no radical theoretical challenge to it. Keynesian models already contained a demand for money function, and if monetarism was correct in arguing that this relationship was more stable than had in the past been believed, such a modification could easily enough be accommodated.[4] If expected inflation belonged as an extra variable in the Phillips curve, and depended upon the past behaviour of inflation, that would alter one's view of what demand management policy could accomplish, but it did not require any fundamental change in economists' vision of how the economy worked. There is no stronger evidence in favour of the latter judgement than the fact that the first explicit monetarist analytic models were recognizable extensions of the IS-LM model.[5] Moreover large-scale Keynesian econometric systems proved easily able to absorb monetarist ideas as well.

The difficulty here was that the new version of the Phillips curve was hardly more satisfactory than the old one from an analytic point of view. Though the proposition that money wages and prices tend, given expectations, to rise faster the higher the level of aggregate demand in the economy, might be a plausible enough empirical generalization, it does not constitute an explanation of the phenomenon which relates it to the purposeful maximizing behaviour of individual economic agents. The monetarist 'expectations-augmented Phillips curve' was an empirical observation in need of an explanation, not a well grounded structural relationship in its own right. In attempting to provide an explanation of it, new-classical economists, and in particular Robert E. Lucas Jr (1972), set in motion the 'New-Classical Revolution', based upon two analytic devices, namely the aggregate supply curve and the rational expectations hypothesis.[6] Though the rational expectations idea has probably attracted more attention, it is its use of a particular version of the aggregate supply curve which constitutes the most fundamental innovation of new-classical economics. Keynesian macro-economics (including its monetarist variation) can accommodate rational expectations, but it cannot be reconciled with the universal existence of the continuously clearing flexible price competitive markets which are a *sine qua non* of the 'aggregate supply curve' explanation of the Phillips curve.

Sticky prices lie at the very heart of Keynesian macroeconomics, and it explains quantity fluctuations in goods and labour markets as equilibrating movements arising because prices do not immediately change when aggregate demand shifts. The postulate of price flexibility lies at the centre of new-classical economics. It has it that prices always move to equilibrate markets when demand shifts, but that individual agents, who are not fully informed about the behaviour of all money prices in the economy, mistake money price changes in the markets for the goods they sell for relative price changes. Hence they respond by changing the quantities of goods they supply. In the aggregate, an unperceived demand increase which raises the general price level therefore causes an expansion of output along an aggregate supply curve, and a fall of demand causes a contraction. Output and employment fluctuation such as we observe in the real world are, according to new-classical economics, voluntary responses to misperceived price signals. They occur because prices change. Keynesian economics (including its monetarist variant) explains quantity changes as occurring because prices do not change fast enough to keep markets cleared. In this vital matter the contrast between the two approaches could not be more stark.[7]

Now the clearing markets hypothesis of new-classical economics is logically compatible with the idea that expectations are naively extrapolated from past experience, but the use of the two ideas in conjunction certainly strains credulity. If agents are in no way tied down by sticky prices, and make costly errors in quantity decisions because of faulty expectations about the behaviour of prices in markets other than those in which they are currently active as sellers, they have every incentive to make their expectations as accurate as possible, and to use all available information in order to do so. Maximizing agents should be presumed to form expectations, as Sargent and Wallace (1973: 328) put it, so that they 'depend, in a proper way, on the same things that economic theory says actually determine that variable'. Hence, though the literature of the 1960s and early 1970s does contain examples of models which combine clearing markets with adaptive expectations, such hybrids soon vanished to be replaced by a substantial body of new-classical theory, based upon the twin hypotheses of clearing markets and rational expectations.[8]

THE CASE FOR NEW-CLASSICAL MACROECONOMICS

Economists have no clearly agreed criteria for deciding among competing bodies of theory, but certain factors are widely accepted as being relevant. The ability to explain past events, or (even better) to forecast future ones, is highly valued, as is the closely related capacity to yield insights into the nature of policy options available, and into the likely outcome of whichever option is chosen. Also important are matters of logical coherence, and intellectual compatibility with other available and accepted doctrines. Proponents of new-classical macroeconomics have, at various times, claimed it to be superior to Keynesian and monetarist alternatives on all three criteria.[9]

As will already be apparent, I quite agree that the western world's experience with inflation and unemployment of the 1970s constitutes a massive refutation of 'Keynesian economics' as the term was understood in the mid-1960s. Nor would I deny that the new-classical macroeconomics of the late 1970s, emphasizing as it did the role of the quantity of money in generating inflation, and the crucial role played by expectations in the inflationary process, provided a superior explanation of that experience. If we were forced to make a choice between these two alternatives alone, we would have to accept the claims of Lucas and Sargent (1978) that their brand of macroeconomics is the only respectable one available. However, we are not forced to make this choice.[10]

Before the inflation of the 1970s was dreamed of, monetarists, such as Friedman (*e.g.* 1959) and Brunner and Meltzer (*e.g.* 1963) had been attacking Keynesian orthodoxy for underestimating the importance of the quantity of money. Furthermore, Friedman and Phelps (surely no monetarist) had, as we have seen, criticized the idea of a permanent inflation–unemployment trade-off in the mid-1960s on the grounds that the behaviour of inflation expectations, themselves endogenous to the structure of the economy, would render any such trade-off temporary. As we have also noted, however, these ideas could be, and eventually were, easily incorporated into otherwise orthodox Keynesian models, but Keynesian models *so modified* do very well indeed in explaining the 1970s.[11] A system in which prices are sticky (though not rigid), in which quantities change to absorb demand side shocks in the short run, and in which inflation expectations though mainly backward looking, are endogenous, can account for the 1970s experience at least as well as any new-classical system based on price flexibility, clearing markets and rational expectations. To put it in terms of labels, the empirical experience of the 1970s does not force one to reject the 'monetarist' variation on the 'Keynesian' model and embrace 'new-classical macroeconomics'.

The methodological criteria proposed by new-classical economists in defence of their work have much in common with those sketched above, and implicitly or explicitly adopted by economists in general. If they did not, it would be hard to explain why their arguments have proved so widely persuasive. However, though claims to superior predictive power, and to deeper insights into the nature of economic policy processes, have certainly been made from time to time on behalf of new-classical macroeconomics, it has also, from the very outset, been presented as the product of a major advance in the application of analytical methods; and, with the passage of time, its proponents have come to place increasing emphasis on this last factor, claiming that their macroeconomics is more logically coherent and more closely related to micro theory than anything which went before it. It is certainly true, as we shall now see, that these are the strongest arguments in favour of new-classical economics.

To begin with, and uncontroversially, new-classical economists tell us that an important purpose of macroeconomic models is to deduce predictions about the behaviour of an economy when subjected to various shocks. Equally uncontroversially, they argue that key components of such a model should be logically coherent and well tested propositions about the behaviour of individual agents. That these propositions about individual agents should in turn be derived from analysis of rationally purposeful utility maximizing behaviour might be less universally accepted, but I do not wish to quarrel about this particular principle.[12] Reasons for controversy begin to arise only when we seek an institutional framework in terms of which it is possible to derive coherent predictions about the behaviour of the economy as a whole from knowledge of individual behaviour, and I shall argue in due course that the particular choice made at this point by the new-classicals is not the only respectable one available to us.

Be that as it may, new-classical economists propose that we model agents as operating in an environment of perfect competition, in which markets costlessly adjust to maintain the supply and demand for every good and service, not least labour, in constant equilibrium. Their competitive model differs from traditional treatments of perfectly competitive economies inasmuch as agents in it do not have full information about the structure of relative prices when they engage in trade. The demand and supply schedules which determine the equilibrium structure of market prices in a new-classical model are conditional, not upon full and accurate information about that same structure of market prices, but upon agents' perceptions (expectations is the more commonly used word) of that structure. Because agents are supposed to be purposeful rational maximizers, they form their expectations so that they differ from the actual values of the variables in question only to the extent of a serially uncorrelated random error. For agents to operate on the basis of any other kind of expectations would result in them encountering unnecessary losses, and hence in violating the purposeful utility maximization assumption.

The 'rational' approach to modelling expectations formation has been translated by new-classical economists into the postulate that agents form expectations 'as if' they were fully informed about the structure of the economy in which they operate, and make mistakes only to the extent that the economy is subjected to random exogenous shocks, either in the form of 'policy surprise' – any systematic component of policy behaviour being, and being perceived to be, part of the economy's structure, – or in more recent literature, random fluctuations in technology, 'real shocks' as they are called. In such a framework, given currently (and only rather recently) available analytic techniques, it is possible to derive predictions about the aggregate behaviour of the economy directly from premises concerning individual behaviour. More to the point, these predictions in certain important ways mimic the behaviour of real world economies, specifically in the matter of co-movements of money wages and prices and quantities of employment and output over the course of the business cycle, and indeed the very fact that new-classical macroeconomics involves the exploitation of these new analytic techniques is sometimes advanced as an argument in its favour.[13]

The really critical point, however, as far as the proponents of new-classical economics are concerned, is that the above-mentioned analytic techniques, in their current state of development, can be used to derive macro-predictions with empirical content from nothing but well specified micro-premises only on the assumptions of representative agents operating in competitive markets cleared by flexible prices. A model which postulates some form of wage or price stickiness inevitably involves the use of some (allegedly) *ad hoc* element in forming the link between micro-postulates and macro-predictions. This is not because there do not exist models of individual maximizing behaviour that explain price stickiness, because there obviously do, but because our current analytic capacity does not permit us except in exceptionally simple examples (*e.g.* Howitt 1981) to embed such behaviour in a model of the economy as a whole, to allow for the way in which such behaviour might influence expectations, and then explicitly to derive macro predictions.

As a result, those who wish both to postulate phenomena such as price stickiness and to build models with empirical content, are led to introduce qualitative empirical 'laws' into them and to permit the data to find quantitative values for the parameters which characterize these 'laws'. One way of looking at the issues at stake here is in terms of alternative strategies for evading that perennial barrier to truly rigorous macroeconomics, the aggregation problem. The new-classical assumptions of representative agents plus perfect competition certainly permit clearly defined links to be established between individual and market experiments without recourse to empirical laws, but those links are only as defensible as the assumptions that permit them to be forged.

Even so, if we regard the presence of 'free parameters', as Lucas (1980) calls them, in a model to be a fatal drawback, then new-classical macroeconomics, with its assumptions of universal competition among representative agents, perfect price flexibility, and rational expectations, has no rivals. If it is objected that perhaps empirical evidence might nevertheless have a role to play in such a judgement, the answer offered by the proponents of new-classical economics, notably Lucas (1980), is that, since their basic model uses no 'free parameters', a model which fits the facts better, or at least as well, can always be constructed by adding one (or more) such parameter to a basic new-classical system. Economic models are not supposed to be descriptions of all elements of reality (whatever that might be); and to show that greater descriptive accuracy may be achieved by the addition of free parameters is said to be neither surprising nor compelling as an argument against new-classical economics. I shall now turn to an examination of this argument.

EMPIRICAL EVIDENCE AND 'FREE PARAMETERS'

I remarked earlier that there is no completely agreed set of methodological criteria for judging economic models. As a matter of simple logic, it cannot be denied that, if rigorous connections between maximizing premises and ultimate conclusions is regarded as the be all and end all of economic analysis, then new-classical macroeconomics is indeed the only game worth playing. The most that individuals who deny this viewpoint can do is explain why they think that other criteria are relevant, show how the criteria support their position, and hope that their reasoning will be taken seriously. Such is my purpose here.

My starting point is that the ultimate aim of economic theory is to explain observations, in the sense of deducing statements which describe such observations from more general premises. Moreover, and quite crucially, such premises should also yield other statements whose truth is not contradicted by the facts. The more general the predictive power of a set of premises (and the more propositions about purposeful maximizing behaviour, and the fewer theoretically unsupported generalizations relying upon 'free parameters' there are among them) the better. An economics which can deduce true predictions about all the phenomena that might interest us from nothing but premises about maximizing behaviour is presumably the ideal towards which we are all striving. That we are unlikely to achieve this ideal is not the point, though. Rather it is that, even if we did stumble upon it, we could never know this. The most we can ever be sure of about our models is that they have not been contradicted by evidence gathered to date. In the very nature of things we can never know that they are true in the sense that they never will be contradicted.

As a practical matter we must always be more concerned with criteria for choosing among less than ideal theories than with laying down unattainable and non-operational standards of theoretical perfection. For this rather humdrum task, primacy must be accorded to empirical evidence, because it is surely uncontroversial that a theory which makes systematically false predictions about some phenomenon is itself false, and in need of modification, no matter how closely it satisfies other criteria.[14] Even so we must be careful when we advance this last proposition not also to demand that a theory's predictions be 'descriptively accurate'. A theory may abstract from all manner of phenomena, have nothing to say about them, and hence be 'descriptively inaccurate' (or incomplete), but that does not make it false. The question of falsity only arises when a theory yields definite predictions about some phenomenon which turn out to be untrue. Descriptive inaccuracy is an inherent quality of any abstract model; but falsity is not. To use a standard platitude of the elementary logic class as an illustration, the reason why the proposition 'all swans are white' is false is not that this statement fails to mention feathers, and into the bargain has nothing to say about ducks; rather it is that some black swans do exist.

My reason for denying the inherent superiority of new-classical macroeconomics is not, therefore, that there might be interesting facts from which it abstracts and about which it has nothing to say; rather it is that it makes false predictions about the very phenomena with which it purports to deal, and that if it is to be rescued, parameters every bit as 'free' as those utilized in the Keynesian (or monetarist) alternative seem to be required. The original task which new-classical economics set itself was to provide a foundation in qualitative microeconomic reasoning for Friedman's propositions about the temporary nature of the inflation–unemployment trade-off. The fact that it succeeded in doing so is, however, not an empirical argument in its favour. That statements describing a set of already known facts may be deduced from a model is evidence, not of its truth, but of the logical skills of the person who constructed it. An empirical test arises only when conclusions yielded by the same model about facts not used to discipline its construction, and better still, initially unsuspected, are compared with those facts.[15] Here, new-classical economics finds itself in trouble.

To begin with, it gets rid of the free parameter linking money wage and price changes to 'excess demand' by postulating that the Phillips trade-off reflects, among other parameters of the system, the elasticity of the supply of labour with respect to real wages. In doing so it yields a testable prediction about the quantitative relationship between inflation and employment fluctuations. Empirical evidence shows that the relative amplitudes of those fluctuations do not square up with what we think we know from micro-studies about this supply elasticity. Aggregate employment fluctuations seem to be systematically much too large relative to inflation fluctuations to be treated as movements along a supply curve of labour when the labour force misperceives nominal wage changes as reflecting real wage changes, and hence to be accounted for along new-classical lines. Closely related, the nature of the interaction of employment and real wages over the business cycle is hard to reconcile with the new-classical postulate that the real wage is always equal to the marginal product of labour and that employment fluctuations involve movements along a downward sloping marginal product schedule.[16]

In a new-classical world, quantities change because prices fluctuate. Output and employment should therefore vary at least simultaneously with (or perhaps lag behind) the price level; but it is a stylized fact of real world business cycles that quantity changes seem to precede associated price level changes. Moreover, if the price level is free to move to keep the supply and demand for money in equilibrium, the economy should always be on its long-run demand for money function; but empirical observations suggest that the economy is often and systematically 'off' this relationship for extensive periods of time.[17] In the early 1980s, predictions about all of these phenomena were put to the test in one real world experiment which was surely just as damaging to the new-classical economics of the 1970s as the experience of the 1970s was to the Keynesian orthodoxy of the 1960s. Then, in a number of countries, sudden, but nevertheless well publicized, monetary contractions were followed by unusually low real balances (relative to the values of the variables determining their demand), rapid and severe output and employment contractions, and only later by price and money wage responses; according to new-classical economics they should have generated price changes on the spot, and, being well publicized, only a rather mild quantity response.[18]

The new-classical economist does of course have answers to all of these questions. To begin with, monetary contraction will only have its major effect on prices if it is expected that the authorities will persist with such a policy. The policy must, that is to say, be credible if it is to influence behaviour by way of its effects on expectations. In a new-classical model the less credible is a policy, the more will the price level changes it generates be misread for relative price changes, and the larger will be the quantity responses. Perhaps policy was not, despite the publicity, credible in the early 1980s. As to the arrival of quantity changes before price level responses this could have been the result either of our observations of the price level being unreliable, because they are based upon posted prices rather than those at which trade 'really' took place, or because the downturn in question did not stem from monetary contraction after all, but from some exogenous contractionary shift on the supply side of the economy. Why were economies apparently 'off' their demand for money functions? Perhaps these functions were estimated using data that only imperfectly measure the true variables upon which the demand for money depends. In this case, an apparent departure of the economy from its demand for money function might be an illusion created by measurement error.[19]

It may, of course, be that all of these propositions have some truth to them, but it is also the case that they offer to the new-classical economist a rich array of free parameters with which to rescue his model from empirical evidence. How fast, and by what mechanisms does any policy become credible? How can we test propositions about measurement error when they result from our inability to observe the true variables? How are we to allocate responsibility for a particular cyclical turning point between demand side and unobservable supply side factors without referring to the timing and amplitudes of price and quantity fluctuations? The point of all this is not to suggest that new-classical macroeconomics is unique in relying upon *ex post ad hoc* postulates about the values of free parameters to reconcile it with empirical evidence. The criticisms which its adherents advanced of alternative approaches for using free parameters were not without merit. The point is rather that new-classical economics appears to be in the same trouble as these alternative approaches, because it can avoid recourse to free parameters for just so long as it avoids confrontation with empirical evidence, and no longer. That can hardly be comfortable for proponents of an approach whose major claim to superiority lies in a claim that it avoids such problems.

Perhaps the new-classical economist would answer the foregoing argument with a 'so what?' After all, Lucas (1980) did tell us that the addition of free parameters to a new-classical model would indeed improve its predictive performance. This answer will not quite do, however. A Keynesian (or monetarist) model, to the extent that it relies on expectations, must also face up to problems concerning the credibility of policy and hence is no improvement upon a new-classical system in this respect. However, it can dispense with conjectures about unobservable supply side shocks, measurement error, and such, when confronted with the data. If we add the postulate of price stickiness to an ordinary full information Walrasian general equilibrium framework, we may model the occurrence of quantity movements in advance of price changes in the face of demand side shocks to the economy as an equilibrating mechanism, and we have no difficulties in generating persistence over time in fluctuations in real variables, including real balances. Nor do we have to puzzle over the relative magnitudes of price-quantity fluctuations. The empirical puzzles which require new-classical economics to add free parameters do not, that is to say, arise in the Keynesian framework it seeks to supplant, once a free parameter characterizing price stickiness is allowed to do its work.[20]

The choice here is between two models, one of which (the new-classical model) happens to yield predictions about output fluctuations without resort to free parameters, and one of which (the monetarist version of the Keynesian alternative) does not; and it would be an easy one to make if other predictions yielded by the new-classical model were empirically supported, but, as we have seen, they are not. The choice between new-classical and Keynesian economics is thus a choice about which free parameters to use and at what stage in the analysis to deploy them when modifying a standard full information Walrasian model. It is not about whether to do without them or not.

THE PRICE STICKINESS POSTULATE

In the light of the preceding discussion, the monetarist variant of the traditional Keynesian model begins to look attractive. Moreover as I shall now argue, its attractiveness is further enhanced by the fact that the free parameters it utilizes are rather harmless, linking as they do rates of change of money wages and prices to the levels of 'excess' demand and supply in particular markets.[21] To begin with, though Keynesian theory does not tie down the parameters in question to any particular quantitive value, they are nevertheless *not* left to take on whatever value might be needed to reconcile a model with any data it might encounter. These parameters are at least required to take a non-negative sign, thus ruling out a rather wide variety of logically possible observations whose real world occurrence would therefore refute the Keynesian model.

More important, the price stickiness postulate amounts to a good deal more than an unfounded *ex post* and *ad hoc* rationalization of otherwise inexplicable observations about the interaction of quantities and prices over time. It is, at the very least, a descriptively accurate empirical generalization whose truth is quite independent of any macreoconomic observations. In the real world, pricing in many branches of the labour market *is* characterized by contracts which set terms for money wages and endure for rather long time periods; similar long term contracts, also negotiated in terms of money, *do* characterize many final output markets as well; the contracts in question *are not* all negotiated at the same time, and they *do* overlap; it *does* follow from these facts that, in the aggregate, money wage and price levels *will* display just the kind of stickiness with respect to demand changes that Keynesian macroeconomics postulates; and it also follows that quantities *will* indeed fluctuate, as Keynesian economics says they will, instead of prices. That *is* what the work of Fischer (1977), Phelps and Taylor (1977) and Okun (1981), among others, is all about.

Moreover, the micro-economics literature *does* enable us to explain wage and price stickiness in terms of maximizing behaviour. Barro (1972) and Kawasaki *et al.* (1983), among others, invoke costs of changing prices as a reason for the phenomenon. There exists a literature, surveyed by Hall (1980), which explains wage stickiness as the outcome of contracts designed to share the risks inherent in demand fluctuations between firms and their employees. Mancur Olson (1984) has argued that the existence of rent-seeking coalitions in the market sector of the economy is likely to be associated with wage and price stickiness, for the simple reason that such coalitions find it easier to monitor the pricing behaviour of their members than to enforce agreements about quantities.

What then is the difficulty about accepting wage and price stickiness? The problem is that, though it is easy enough to explain the existence of sticky wages and prices at the level of the individual experiment, it has not, thus far, proved possible to explain why the stickiness in question should characterize *money* wages and prices as opposed to *relative* wages and prices. Thus Barro (1977b) purported to show that optimal contracts should be concerned with relative prices, and argued that models dealing with them cannot therefore be used to explain money wage and money price stickiness. Since contracts set in money terms do exist in the real world, the correct inference to draw here is that there must be something missing from the particular maximizing models that deny their occurrence. Incredibly, new-classical economists seem to have concluded that the maximizing models must be correct, that the facts about contracts cannot be what they patently are, and that they therefore must not be used as a basis for an empirical generalization which, when inserted into macro-economic model, helps it to yield useful predictions about the world.[22]

Now, if the claim of new-classical economics to be able to deduce everything with which it deals from nothing other than fundamental premises about tastes and technology were true, the reluctance of its proponents to use an unexplained empirical generalization about contracts being set in terms of money would be understandable. However, quite apart from its need for 'free' parameters already discussed, new-classical economics also requires us to accept important unsupported assertions about institutional arrangements. Consider: in every new-classical model agents trade, but the existence of trade presupposes a system of property rights and legal arrangements permitting their exchange; and new-classical models are frequently used to analyse policy problems of one sort or another, but the existence of policy presupposes both that a government of some description exists, and that this institution has a capacity for purposeful behaviour.

We might prefer it if we could explain the existence of these social institutions as the outcome of the maximizing behaviour of the individuals who inhabit the economy. However, we do have to start somewhere, and our inability to explain social institutions as the consequences of individual tastes and technology should not prevent us from getting on with our economics.[23] Precisely: but what is monetary exchange, including the practice of contracting in money terms, if not a social institution on the same level as property rights, markets, and government? And why should our inability to explain it prevent us assuming it as a starting point for certain pieces of economic analysis? However, if we do treat monetary exchange as such a starting point, we can of course explain money wage and price stickiness in terms of the analysis invoked above.

To sum up, the assumption of price stickiness used in conventional Keynesian macroeconomics does permit a degree of freedom in the determination of certain parameter values that is larger than ideal. Moreover, we do not, in the current state of knowledge, have a full understanding of the phenomenon. However, given the institution of monetary exchange, money wage and price stickiness can be explained as the result of maximizing behaviour; they do exist at the micro level, and they do have certain implications for macroeconomic phenomena that appear to conform to the facts. Given the choice, therefore, between a macroeconomics which recognizes the existence of price stickiness and one which refuses to do so, there does not seem to be very much harm done if we opt for the former, particularly since the alternative approach also seems to rely on a good share of free parameters and unexplained institutional assumptions to get results with non-falsified predictive content.

RATIONAL EXPECTATIONS

The notion that the world may, and indeed ought, to be modelled as if the activities of individual agents were co-ordinated in continuously clearing flexible price competitive markets is one foundation of new-classical economics. The other is the rational expectations hypothesis. The idea that expectations about the future behaviour of prices must be important determinants of current market behaviour is an old one, as is the closely related proposition that, only if such expectations are fulfilled, can the economy be said to be in full equilibrium.[24] In extending these notions by arguing, first, that we should think of expectations as being the output of an economic model, knowledge of whose structure is attributed to agents, and second, that for full equilibrium to rule, the model in question must be the 'true' one of the economy under analysis, new-classical economics has made a contribution of immense importance to our understanding of these matters. Economic theory has been permanently changed by these insights, and for the better.[25] That being said, I am not enthusiastic about the way in which new-classical economists have *applied* these insights. Two issues in particular are worth considering, the first having to do with the choice of the 'model' of the economy which one attributes to agents in analysing their behaviour, and the second having to do with interaction between policy authorities and the private sector, and specifically the way in which the question of 'credibility' is handled.

For analytic exercises designed to reveal the long run equilibrium properties of economic models, it is of course quite appropriate to attribute to agents within the model knowledge of that same model. Any other basis for expectations formation would, under some condition or other, lead agents into systematic error, causing them to revise their method of forming expectations. Hence, it could not be a component of a full equilibrium structure. To say this, however, is not to say that this same procedure is appropriate as a foundation for applied work on any particular historical episode.[26] If it is true that expectations should 'depend, in a proper way, on the same things that economic theory says actually determine that variable', then surely, when trying to understand the behaviour of a particular economy at a particular time in its history, we should attribute to agents expectations based, not on what we now believe is the proper model of that economy, but rather on what the economic theory available and believed at that time and place said was a proper model.

We may illustrate this proposition with a concrete example. Among the seminal papers of new-classical economics are empirical studies, by Robert J. Barro (1977a; 1978), of the influence of money on unemployment, output and prices in the United States since the Second World War. It is the essential claim of these papers that only 'unanticipated' changes in the quantity of money affected employment and output (relative to trend) over this period; agents inhabiting the economy at that time are treated by Barro as believing in the equilibrium competitive model of new-classical economics, supplemented by a primitive version of the quantity theory of money, and as using this model for forming their expectations.[27] However, if, in the 1945–76 period agents really had held new-classical beliefs, there would have been no need for a new-classical revolution. As it is, we know very well that until the mid-1970s, firm beliefs in a certain kind of Keynesian economics, whose centrepiece was a permanent inflation unemployment trade-off, were the common property of US policy-makers and key private sector agents alike. Indeed the primary claim made by Lucas and Sargent (1978) to support the scientific importance of their work was that it had undermined just this Keynesian consensus. That being the case, logical consistency requires new-classical economics to model the economic history of the period in question by postulating that agents operating within the US economy used an erroneous Keynesian model to form their expectations. To do otherwise would be to wind up in a hopeless logical tangle.

The point illustrated here is of course quite general. New-classical economics argues, with great persuasiveness, that the nature of agents' information about the structure of the economy is itself an important component of that structure. If that information changes, then so does the economy's behaviour. If it is right so to argue, then the state of economic knowledge itself becomes a key ingredient of any economic model, and economic history cannot be studied without recourse to the history of economic thought. This latter insight is not new, of course. It is central to the kind of Austrian economics associated particularly with the later work of von Hayek, but he was led to this position from a starting point very similar to the stance of contemporary new-classical economists.[28] The fact that the latter insist that agents, living at any time or place, should be thought of as believing that the economy which they inhabit behaves 'as if' it was driven by the mechanisms highlighted by a theory first advocated by a particular group of American economists in the 1970s, certainly sets them apart from the later Austrians. The comparison here is hardly in favour of new-classical economists, however.

A similar type of unhistoric naïveté is to be found in the way in which new-classical economics approaches the problem of 'policy credibility'. It is undoubtedly true that, in a new-classical world, a well-publicized change in, say, monetary policy, will have its effects concentrated on prices only if the publicity is believed. Just as traditional Keynesians – though their ancestors here are Meade and Tinbergen, not Keynes – viewed the policy-maker's task as the maximization of a social utility function subject to a constraint given by the structure of the economy, so new-classical economists regard the typical private sector agent as maximizing a private utility function subject to a structure determined both by the activities of other private sector agents, and by the activities of policy-makers. Suppose that both policy-makers and private sector agents are aware of this: how do they interact? The answer, we are told, will be found by the application of 'differential game theory' in which policy-makers and private sector agents communicate and establish credibility with one another solely through observable behaviour.[29] Ultimately in such games an 'equilibrium' emerges in which each agent's maximizing behaviour imposes a constraint on the other which leads to that behaviour being sustained. Analysis of this type is intellectually challenging, but a little scepticism about its empirical relevance is surely in order.

'Policy-makers' in the real world are not entities who exist outside of their society and economy. They are endogenous self-interested maximizing agents. Moreover, they interact with the private sector in many more ways than by giving and receiving market signals to establish their credibility. In particular, they achieve the positions that they do, and maintain them, as the result of political processes in which private sector agents participate. A whole literature in the area of 'public choice' analysis is devoted to all of this, and I am not saying anything novel in drawing attention to these matters.[30] I am however suggesting that to rest one's analysis of macroeconomic policy making on 'differential game theory' is simply to ignore this critical dimension of the policy-making process. Perhaps political institutions have nothing to do with the way in which policy is made and changed; perhaps ideology has no influence here either; but I doubt it. Rather, I suspect that the new-classical approach to the analysis of policy-making, in ignoring these factors, threatens to lead us down a blind alley.

CONCLUDING COMMENTS

The bulk of this chapter has been critical of new-classical macroeconomics. This does not mean that such analysis has nothing of importance to say to us; quite the contrary. Though the 'new-classical revolution' has had exaggerated claims made on its behalf, and it is these exaggerated claims which I have been concerned to criticize in this chapter, it is also the case, as noted at the very outset of this chapter, that 'revolutions' in macroeconomics usually leave behind them contributions of lasting importance to be absorbed into the mainstream of the discipline. The new-classical revolution has certainly done this, as I shall now argue.

Consider first the new-classical insistence on equilibrium modelling. If it is desired to construct an economics with predictive content, then the postulate that agents formulate purposeful and consistent plans and that they are able to execute those plans is surely a useful starting point; but at the level of the individual, the execution of such plans is precisely what we mean when we speak of equilibrium behaviour. If assumptions about the nature of plans do not permit us to say anything about actions, as they can not if we entertain the possibility of 'disequilibrium' at the level of the individual agent, then an economics based on the analysis of the individual can have no predictive content. This idea is an old one, to be sure, having been a constant theme in Austrian economics from Menger (1871) onwards, but a glance at the macroeconomics literature of the 1960s will soon confirm that we had lost sight of it, and needed to be reminded of its importance. New-classical economics did just that.

The difficulty with new-classical economics lies not in the equilibrium postulate *per se*, but in its insistence that we model the economy as a whole as if the equilibrium strategies of individuals were formulated and executed in an institutional framework characterized by continuously clearing competitive markets. The fact that such a framework is the only one which, in the current state of analytic techniques, permits a seamless connection between the analysis of the microeconomic equilibrium of the individual and macro behaviour, is no reason for insisting that macro-predictions obtained by other less pristine methods are unworthy of consideration. That, though, is what new-classical macroeconomics have, quite unjustifiably, been doing. However, we ought not to let dissatisfaction with a particular application of a methodological precept lead us to underestimate its general importance.

Equilibrium modelling of individuals surely ought to be the basis of macroeconomic reasoning, and the fewer empirical generalizations about behaviour we need to make to get from such a basis to empirically robust predictions about the economy as a whole, the better.

Exactly parallel arguments to these may be advanced about the rational expectations idea. This is hardly surprising, since there is a real sense in which this hypothesis is simply a particular consequence of the purposeful maximizing postulate. The idea that the state of agents' knowledge, and the nature of their expectations about future events, form a key part of the economy's current structure, and help to determine the outcome of current maximizing behaviour, is hardly new. It was, as has been pointed out, a prominent ingredient of Austrian economics, but once more, a glance at the macroeconomic literature of the 1960s (replete as it is with exercises in which the consequences of alternative policy measures are derived from the same, allegedly structural, representation of the private sector of the economy) will show how badly we needed to be reminded of this insight.

As with the equilibrium idea, criticisms of the rational expectations notion advanced above have been of the particular and very special ways in which it has been applied, rather than of the basic idea itself. It is at best logically dubious to analyse historical episodes 'as if' agents involved in them possessed a vision of the economy which has been created only since the mid-1970s. When the very purpose of the analysis in question is to expose flaws in the economics which was commonly believed during the episode under analysis, perhaps stronger epithets are called for. Nevertheless it is important to formulate hypotheses about the way in which the state of knowledge influences the structure of the economy at particular times and places, and to investigate the way in which that structure changes in the light of actual experience and of changes in economic doctrines. That is the key implication of the rational expectations idea for empirical work.

Problems posed by the credibility of policy for the predictive content of macroeconomics are also real. To argue, as I have, that new-classical economists do not seem to be following the most fruitful path in investigating such matters (which probably lie in an analysis of the way in which private and public sector agents interact through political processes) does not alter the fact that it has been the new-classicals' initial insights which have compelled macroeconomists in general to recognize the importance of these questions. They have stressed that a positive theory of government behaviour must be an important factor conditioning private sector behaviour, and I have criticized them, not for advancing this view, but for failing even to attempt to incorporate currently available positive theories of government into their work.

It is worth pointing out explicitly that the problems with new-classical economics discussed in this chapter are, in a fundamental sense, different aspects of a single issue. At least since the first publication of Smith's *Wealth of Nations* (1776) economists have been arguing about the extent to which a society that organizes its economic activity on the basis of voluntary exchange of private property rights can be expected to achieve a coherent solution to problems of resource utilization and allocation (not to mention distribution). From their arguments has emerged an increasingly clear understanding that analysis of the institutional framework within which, and the processes whereby, the decisions of agents are co-ordinated, and the information upon which those decisions are based is disseminated, must lie at the heart of any attempt to come to grips with these issues.

New-classical economists insist that we assume agents to possess, as common knowledge, almost all systematic information about the structure of the economy relevant to their welfare before we model their decision-making. They also insist that, in analysing the interaction of agents, we must assume that their behaviour is co-ordinated by a price mechanism that never permits their plans to be incompatible for long enough to have observable consequences. In short, new-classical economics requires that we treat certain (and extreme) propositions about a market economy's capacity for solving problems of disseminating information and co-ordinating decisions, not as hypotheses to be questioned and investigated, but as axiomatic assumptions. To adhere to the 'first principles' of analysis upon which new-classical economics is based requires that we give up questioning the coherence of economic activity co-ordinated by markets and confine our activities to describing the nature of a coherence that is presumed to exist. If the popularity of Keynesian economics in the years following the Depression was, as Lucas is said to have told *Newsweek* (14 February 1985: 60), 'based on political needs, not economic truth' then, so, surely, as Howitt (1986) has remarked, does the current popularity of new-classical economics reflect its compatibility with the ideology of the New Right.

And yet the pioneers of new-classical economics are no more ideologues than was Keynes. Disinterested seriousness about following the logic of an argument wherever it might lead is surely the hallmark of the writings of Lucas and Sargent, and let it be said explicitly, that, in this chapter I intend to accuse them of no worse an offence than permitting this very seriousness of purpose to lead them into carrying good ideas too far and sometimes in the wrong direction. If this characterization of the 'new-classical revolution' is accepted, it has not, of course, in this respect been different from other periods of advance in economic knowledge. The Keynesian revolution and the monetarist revolution were both in their own ways equally open to criticism on such grounds in their respective days. More to the point, in rejecting the extremes to which new-classical economics has taken them, we should not lose sight of the fact that the ideas in question are, after all, good ones. When, as I hope it will, the main thrust of macroeconomics research returns to addressing problems of *Information and Co-ordination*, to borrow yet another phrase from Leijonhufvud (1982) it surely will do so with a much clearer understanding of the role of purposeful maximizing individual behaviour in the solution of these problems than could have been possible had the new-classical revolution never occurred.

ACKNOWLEDGEMENTS

I am grateful to Dieter Helm, Peter Howitt, Jurek Konieczny, Thomas Mayer and George Stadler for helpful conversations and correspondence about aspects of this chapter.

NOTES

1 For an account of the nature of 'revolutions' in economics, illustrated with reference to the Keynesianism and monetarism, see Johnson (1971). A number of commentators (*e.g.* Tobin 1981; Howitt 1986) treat new-classical economics as

a 'Mark 2' version of monetarism. For a contrary view, see Laidler (1982: ch. 1) where I argue that whereas, from the point of view of the analytic structure of the models it utilized, monetarism was a development of Keynesian theory, new-classical economics in important respects is a throwback to the Austrian economics of the 1920s and early 1930s. This theme also runs through much of this chapter but, because the adjective 'neo-Austrian' seems to upset some people, I have not used it here.

2 Lucas has made this point on a number of occasions (see *e.g.* 1980).

3 The choice of the word 'occurred' is not accidental. Though in some places (*e.g.* Britain) fiscal expansion in the mid-1960s and again in the early 1970s was deliberately used in an attempt to generate real 'growth', the experiment in the United States was less wholeheartedly and self-consciously 'Keynesian', but had a great deal to do with the politics of financing the Vietnam War. Note that, in this chapter, I am using the adjective 'Keynesian' to refer to the economics of what Lucas (*e.g.* 1980) referred to as the 'Neo-Classical Synthesis'. I am not talking about the 'Economics of Keynes', to borrow Leijonhufvud's (1968) phrase.

4 Harry Johnson as long ago as 1970 noted the effects of 'conditioned Keynesian reflexes' in preventing the idea of a stable demand for money function being incorporated into British Keynesian thought. American Keynesians, such as James Tobin (*e.g.* 1981) and Franco Modigliani (*e.g.* 1977) were much more open minded in this respect.

5 Thus Milton Friedman's early 1970s 'Monetary Framework' (1974) was explicitly cast in IS-LM terms, while Brunner and Meltzer (*e.g.* 1976a) used an extended IS-LM model to expound their important insights about the role of credit markets in the process of money creation. So strong were the IS-LM roots of Brunner and Meltzer's work at that time that at least one commentator, Dornbusch (1976), was misled into believing that their essential contribution could be grasped without any extension at all to the IS-LM framework. Dornbusch's misconception did at least have the productive consequence of provoking an exceptionally clear statement from Brunner and Meltzer (1976b) of where they saw their contribution as lying. This author too, in analysing inflation unemployment dynamics, used a vertical LM curve IS-LM model as a starting point (Laidler 1973).

6 The aggregate supply curve interpretation of the Phillips curve was not a component of early Monetarism though Friedman did accept it on at least one later occasion. In 1968 he said 'Phillips' analysis ... contains a basic defect – the failure to distinguish between *nominal* wages and *real* wages' (Friedman's italics). In 1975, (pp. 12–14), in a pamphlet explicitly dealing with the role of rational expectations and such in monetarist analysis, while continuing to point up this nominal–real confusion, he characterized taking 'the *rate of change of prices* as the independent variable' as 'the truth' and taking 'the level of *employment* to be the independent variable' as 'error' (Friedman's italics). Friedman's acceptance of the aggregate supply curve interpretation of the Phillips curve, quite clearcut in this 1975 pamphlet, was never thoroughgoing, however. Thus, the 'framework' of 1974 is used, without apology, as the theoretical starting point for the analysis contained in Friedman and Schwartz (1983) and is quite incompatible with new-classical style equilibrium macroeconomics.

7 I have discussed these issues in some detail in Laidler (1982) particularly chs 1, 3 and 4. It is this fundamental theoretical difference which leads me to treat new-classical macroeconomics as a distinct body of analysis, rather than as a simple extension of 'monetarism'.

8 Thus the paper by Lucas and Rapping, among others contained in the famous Phelps (1970) volume, was based on just such a hybrid.

9 There has been a considerable change of emphasis over time here. The claim to have a superior method of analysis looms much larger in more recent defences of their work by new-classicals, than in earlier ones. Compare for example Lucas and Sargent (1978) to their recorded comments in Klamer (1984) which led Kramer himself to argue that the new-classical revolution was a matter of method and rhetoric, rather than substance. Howitt (1986) rightly criticizes Klamer for this judgement.

10 As Lucas (1980) himself acknowledged. Not so Sargent. See Klamer (1984: 66–7).

11 Which is not to say that no differences remained between Keynesians and monetarists. For example, though there is little difference between this author's views on the way in which the economy works, and those expressed by say Modigliani (1977) or Lipsey (1981), I am much less optimistic than are they about the scope for stabilization policy. In general, there is considerable continuity between the policy views of monetarists and new-classicals, and it is this continuity that persuades Tobin (1981) and Howitt (1986) to take the work of the latter as an extension of that of the former. I regard theoretical differences as decisive in this matter of classification. See Laidler (1982) particularly chs 1 and 3.

12 The reader's attention is drawn to the use of the word 'purposeful' here. To adherents of revealed preference analysis, for whom consistent behaviour is logically *equivalent* to utility maximization, as opposed to being a *consequence* of it, the methodological case for new-classical macroeconomics, particularly as it relates to the rational expectations idea will not perhaps be as strong as I here present it. It might be noted, that in stressing the individualistic maximizing foundations of their model, as opposed to its empirical content, New-classicals are reverting to a weighting of methodological criteria used by Austrians in the 1920s and 1930s. See especially Robbins (1935).

13 Lucas (1980) comes close to arguing along such lines. I do not find this style of argument persuasive.

14 In his contributions to Klamer (1984) Sargent at one point appears to accept this view of the ultimate primacy of empirical evidence. See Klamer (1984: 68). However, the general thrust of his work, and that of other new-classicals seems to be to stress the importance of deriving results from what they take to be 'first principles'. For this indulgence in the 'Cartesian fallacy' they are, rightly in my view, taken to task by Brunner in his contribution to Klamer (1984: 191–5). The reader who is familiar with Brunner's methodological views on these issues will recognize the common debt that we both owe to Karl Popper.

15 The danger here is one that Sargent is aware of. See Klamer (1984: 75–6). We may illustrate it from an earlier episode in the development of macroeconomics. Their ability to deal with the conflict between time series and cross section evidence on the consumption income relationship did not constitute an empirical argument in favour of the Friedman (1957) and Modigliani and Brumberg (1954) theories of the consumption function, but only confirmed the logical powers of their authors. They knew about the evidence in question before they constructed their models and calibrated them to it. The important empirical content of their theories which rendered them testable lay in their ability to tell us about other empirical regularities, which either had not been observed, or were not regarded as being related to the theoretical foundations of consumer theory, until new theoretical insights were put to work.

16 On the matter of real wages and employment, see Geary and Kennan (1982).

17 See Laidler (1982: ch. 2) and Lane (1983) for discussion of this matter.

18 This is not to say that the 1980s experience was any more the outcome of a conscious attempt to implement new-classical policies than was the 1970s the

result of a conscious Keynesian experiment. Nevertheless, before the event, new-classical economists did make confident predictions about the outcome of pre-announced monetary contraction. Thus, Lucas is quoted by *Time* magazine, 27 Aug. 1979 p. 29 as having said 'Ideally we should announce a monetary expansion policy of 4% annually for the next seven years and then stick to it. People would respond, and inflation would be cured with a minimal risk of a deep recession'. The basis of such prediction as this was the Sargent and Wallace (1976) analysis of the effects of rational expectations on the ability of the monetary authorities to influence real variables. Nowadays it is claimed that this paper was taken more seriously and literally by its readers than by its authors. (See Sargent in Klamer 1984: 70–1.) Certainly, the opening of the paper in question suggests that the analysis which it contains is to be treated as a counterexample to a prevailing Keynesian view of policy, rather than as serious alternative, but its last two or three pages mount a strong case for treating it as just such an alternative.

19 A New-Classical economist should treat the 'credibility' alibi with care. Before the event, Sargent and Wallace (1976: 181) developed what they characterized as a 'telling argument' against its empirical relevance. On the matter of the demand for money, see Goodfriend (1985) and Kohn and Manchester (1985).

20 Laidler (1985) demonstrates that price stickiness is an *alternative* to new-classical assumptions in generating such results rather than a supplement to them, and does so in terms of a model in which agents are all 'in equilibrium' in the sense of being able to execute their *ex ante* plans, albeit not with the expected results *ex post*. The model in question is not of course an equilibrium framework in the sense that markets are cleared by flexible prices. Instead quantity fluctuations play an equilibrating role in some markets. Note that some new-classical economists (*e.g.* Barro 1977b) have argued that even with sticky wage and price contracts it is possible to model quantity fluctuations as taking place 'as if' they reflected appropriate market clearing responses to variations in agents' perceptions of the marginal product and marginal disutility of labour. This is true enough, but hard to take seriously as an empirical proposition, because it implies that agents have enough information to take market clearing decisions in the absence of price signals. For a discussion of this, see Laidler (1982: 90–2).

21 One must be careful here, because the phrase 'excess demand' has strong over-tones of 'disequilibrium' about it and there is much semantic confusion in the macroeconomics literature caused by contributors referring to any non-flexible-price-Walrasian system as a 'disequilibrium' one. Excess demand is here used to refer to the difference between the level of output at which markets currently clear, and that at which they would clear if prices were perfectly flexible and all expectations were completely fulfilled. The literature with which I am dealing here treats the latter as a unique level of output, determined by tastes, technology, and market institutions, but work by Diamond (1984) and Howitt (1985) on search equilibria suggests that we ought not to take such uniqueness for granted once we get away from an economy presided over by a Walrasian auctioneer. The work to which I refer here provides a complementary analysis of potentially great importance to short-run sticky price macroeconomic models.

22 Montgomery and Shaw (1985) have investigated the role of money wage sticki-ness in an otherwise new-classical framework, have conceded it to be a pervasive phenomenon, but have argued that it has little explanatory power over quantity fluctuations. The basis for this last conclusion appears to be the assumption that, wage contracts notwithstanding, money prices are perfectly flexible, and hence it misses the point of Keynesian analysis which models quantity fluctuations as an alternative equilibrating mechanism to price fluctuations, and not as a response to them.

23 However, see Rowe (1985) for a pioneering attempt to come to grips with problems of this sort.

24 The argument was well developed by Hayek (1928), and according to Hansson (1983) a slightly later version of it, developed initially by Gunnar Myrdal, was seminal to much Swedish dynamic economics in the 1930s. See also McCloughry (1984).

25 I have developed this argument at greater length in Laidler (1984). The interaction of expectations and the structure of the economy is most fully developed by Lucas (1976) in what I suspect will turn out to be the most durably important paper of the new-classical revolution.

26 Thus, I stand by the judgement offered by Laidler and Parkin (1975: 771) that 'The Rational Expectations hypothesis... is probably better suited to a characterization of expectations formation in the very long run.' I do not wish to imply that my co-author would still subscribe to this view, though.

27 The argument here abstracts from more down to earth issues such as whether the proposition that only 'unanticipated money' affects output is uniquely a prediction of new-classical macroeconomics (it isn't – see Laidler 1985), or whether the data actually do support Barro's analysis (they don't appear to – see Mishkin 1982).

28 Hayek paid increasing attention to problems of knowledge as a determinant of economic behaviour and became less and less inclined to ascribe empirical content to what we would now call a full rational expectations equilibrium, such as he described (1928), from the mid-1930s onwards. The turning point in his thought is perhaps to be found in Hayek (1937). On this matter see also McCloughry (1984).

29 Both Lucas and Sargent recommend differential game theory in their contributions to Klamer (1984: 55, 73). It is instructive to compare their discussion of this issue with Karl Brunner's contribution to the same volume (Klamer 1984: 185–6). Brunner has, of course, long been acutely aware of the role of political processes in forming policies and conditioning the private sector's responses to them.

30 The contribution of Mancur Olson (1982; 1984), and of James Buchanan and his associates (see *e.g.* Buchanan, Tollison and Tulloch 1980) to this literature are well known. It is surely no accident that two prominent monetarists who have refused to join the 'New-classical revolution', Karl Brunner and Allan Meltzer, have also worked in the public choice area. It should also be noted that Harry Johnson drew similar conclusions to those developed here about the interaction of expectations, policy, and political processes as long ago as 1972.

REFERENCES

Barro, R. J. (1972) 'A Theory of Monopolistic Price Adjustment', *Review of Economic Studies* 34, January, 17–26.

Barro, R. J. (1977a) 'Unanticipated Money Growth and Unemployment in the United States', *American Economic Review* 67, March, 101–15.

Barro, R. J. (1977b) 'Long-Term Contracting, Sticky Prices, and Monetary Policy', *Journal of Monetary Economics* 3, July, 305–16.

Barro, R. J. (1978) 'Unanticipated Money, Output and the Price Level in the United States', *Journal of Political Economy* 86, August, 549–81.

Brunner, K. and Meltzer, A. H. (1963) 'Predicting Velocity: Implications for Theory and Policy', *Journal of Finance* 18, May, 319–54.

Brunner, K. and Meltzer, A. H. (1976a) 'An Aggregative Theory for a Closed Economy', in J. Stein (ed.) *Monetarism*, Amsterdam: North-Holland.

Brunner, K. and Meltzer, A. H. (1976b) 'Reply', in J. Stein (ed.) *Monetarism*, Amsterdam: North-Holland.

Buchanan, J., Tollison, R. D. and Tulloch, G. (eds) (1980) *Towards a Theory of the Rent Seeking Society*, College Station: Texas A&M Press.

Diamond, P. A. (1984) *A Search Equilibrium Approach to the Microfoundations of Macroeconomics*, Cambridge, MA: MIT Press.

Dornbusch, R. (1976) 'Comments on Brunner and Meltzer', in J. Stein (ed.) *Monetarism*, Amsterdam: North-Holland.

Fischer, S. (1977) 'Long-Term Contracts, Rational Expectations and the Optimal Money Supply Rule', *Journal of Political Economy* 85, February, 191–206.

Friedman, M. (1957) *A Theory of the Consumption Function*, Princeton, NJ: Princeton University Press for the NBER.

Friedman, M. (1959) 'The Demand for Money – Some Theoretical and Empirical Results', *Journal of Political Economy* 67, June, 327–51.

Friedman, M. (1968) 'The Role of Monetary Policy', *American Economic Review* 58, March, 1–17.

Friedman, M. (1974) *Milton Friedman's Monetary Framework*, R. J. Gordon (ed.) ch. 1, Chicago: University of Chicago Press.

Friedman, M. (1975) *Unemployment Versus Inflation*, London: Institute of Economic Affairs.

Friedman, M. and Schwartz, A. J. (1983) *Monetary Trends in the United States and the United Kingdom*, Chicago: University of Chicago Press for the NBER.

Geary, P. and Kennan, J. (1982) 'The Employment Real Wage Relationship: An International Study', *Journal of Political Economy* 90, August, 854–71.

Goodfriend, M. (1985) 'Reinterpreting Money Demand Regressions', in K. Brunner and A. H. Meltzer (eds) *Understanding Monetary Regimes Carnegie-Rochester Conference Series*, vol. 22, Amsterdam: North-Holland.

Hall, R. (1980) 'Employment Fluctuations and Wage Rigidity', *Brookings Papers on Economic Activity* 1, 91–123.

Hansson, B. A. (1983) *The Stockholm School and the Development of Dynamic Method*, London: Croom Helm.

Hayek, F. A. von (1928) 'Intertemporal Price Equilibrium and Movements in the Value of Money', translated and reprinted (1984) in F.A. Hayek, *Money Capital and Fluctuations: Early Essays*, R. McCloughry (ed.), Chicago: University of Chicago Press.

Hayek, F. A. von (1937) 'Economics and Knowledge', *Economica* n.s. 4, February, 33–54.

Howitt, P. W. (1981) 'Activist Monetary Policy under Rational Expectations', *Journal of Political Economy* 89, April, 249–69.

Howitt, P. W. (1985) 'Transactions Costs in the Theory of Unemployment', *American Economic Review* 75, March, 88–100.

Howitt, P. W. (1986) 'Conversations with Economists – A Review Essay', *Journal of Monetary Economics* 18, July.

Johnson, H. G. (1970) 'Recent Developments in Monetary Theory – A Survey', in D. Croome and H. G. Johnson (eds) *Money in Britain*, London: Oxford University Press.

Johnson, H. G. (1971) 'The Keynesian Revolution and the Monetarist Counter-Revolution', *American Economic Review* 61, May, 9–22.

Johnson, H. G. (1972) *Inflation and the Monetarist Controversy*, Amsterdam: North-Holland.

Kawasaki, S., McMillan J. and Zimmerman, K. F. (1983) 'Inventories and Price Flexibility', *Econometrica* 51, May, 599–610.

Klamer, A. (1984) *Conversations with Economists*, Totowa, NJ: Roman and Allanheld.

Kohn, M. and Manchester, J. (1985) 'International Evidence on Misspecification of the Standard Money Demand Equation', *Journal of Monetary Economics* 16, March, 87–94.

Laidler, D. (1973) 'The Influence of Money on Real Income and Inflation – A Simple Model with Some Empirical Tests for the United States 1953–72', *Manchester School* 61, December.

Laidler, D. (1982) *Monetarist Perspectives*, Deddington: Philip Allan; Cambridge, MA: Harvard University Press.

Laidler, D. (1984) 'Did Macroeconomics Need the Rational Expectations Revolution?', in G. Mason (ed.) *Macroeconomics: Theory, Policy and Evidence*, Winnipeg, Manitoba: Institute for Social and Economic Research.

Laidler, D. (1985) 'Price Stickiness, Buffer-Stock Money, and Persistent Fluctuations in Output and Real Balances', UWO Department of Economics Research Report 8509 (mimeo).

Laidler, D. and Parkin, J. M. (1975) 'Inflation – A Survey', *Economic Journal* 75, December, 741–809.

Lane, T. (1983) 'Essays in monetary control', unpublished Ph.D dissertation, University of Western Ontario.

Leijonhufvud, A. (1982) *On Keynesian Economics and the Economics of Keynes*, London: Oxford University Press.

Leijonhufvud, A. (1968) *Information and Coordination*, London: Oxford University Press.

Lipsey, R. G. (1981) 'Presidential Address: The Understanding and Control of Inflation – Is There a Crisis in Macroeconomics?', *Canadian Journal of Economics* 14, November, 545–76.

Lucas, R. E. Jr (1972) 'Expectations and the Neutrality of Money', *Journal of Economic Theory* 4, 103–24.

Lucas, R. E. Jr (1976) 'Econometric Policy Evaluation', in K. Brunner and A.H. Meltzer (eds) *The Phillips Curve and the Labour Market, Carnegie-Rochester Conference Series*, vol. 1, Amsterdam: North-Holland.

Lucas, R. E. Jr (1980) 'Methods and Problems in Business Cycle Theory', *Journal of Money, Credit and Banking* 12, November, part II, 696–715.

Lucas, R. E. Jr and Rapping, L.A. (1970) 'Real Wages, Employment and Inflation', in E. Phelps *et al.*, *The Microeconomic Foundations of Employment and Inflation Theory*, New York: Norton.

Lucas, R. E. Jr and Sargent, T.J. (1978) 'After Keynesian Economics', in *After the Phillips Curve: Persistence of High Inflation and High Unemployment*, Boston, MA: Federal Reserve Bank of Boston.

McCloughry, R. (1984) 'Editor's Introduction', to F. A. Hayek, *Money Capital and Fluctuations: Early Essays*, R. McCloughry (ed.), Chicago: University of Chicago Press.

Menger, C. (1871) *Principles of Economics*, tr. and ed. J. Dingwall and B. Hoselitz (1950), Glencoe, IL: The Free Press.

Mishkin, F. (1982) 'Does Anticipated Monetary Policy Matter? An Econometric Investigation', *Journal of Political Economy* 90, February, 22–51.

Modigliani, F. (1977) 'The Monetarist Controversy, or Should We Forsake Stabilisation Policy', *American Economic Review* 67, March, 1–19.

Modigliani, F. and Brumberg, R. (1954) 'Utility Analysis and the Consumption Function: An Interpretation of the Cross-Section Data', in K.K. Kurihara (ed.) *Post Keynesian Economics*, New Brunswick, NJ: Rutgers University Press.

Montgomery, E. and Shaw, K. (1985) 'Long Term Contracts, Expectations and Wage Inertia', *Journal of Monetary Economics* 16, September, 209–26.

Okun, A. (1981) *Prices and Quantities: A Macroeconomic Analysis*, Washington, DC: Brookings Institution.

Olson, M. (1982) *The Rise and Decline of Nations*, New Haven, CT: Yale University Press.

Olson, M. (1984) 'Microeconomic Incentives and Macroeconomic Decline', *Weltwirtschaftliches Archiv* 120, 631–45.

Phelps, E. (1967) 'Phillips Curves, Expectations of Inflation and Optimal Unemployment Over Time', *Economica* NS 34, August, 254–81.

Phelps, E. *et al.* (1970) *Microeconomic Foundations of Employment and Inflation Theory*, New York: Norton.

Phelps, E. and Taylor, J. (1977) 'Stabilizing Powers of Monetary Policy under Rational Expectations', *Journal of Political Economy* 85, February, 163–90.

Robbins, L.C. (1935) *An Essay on the Nature and Significance of Economic Science*, London: Macmillan.

Rowe, N. (1985) 'Rules and institutions', unpublished Ph.D dissertation, University of Western Ontario.

Sargent, T. and Wallace, N. (1973) 'Rational Expectations and the Dynamics of Hyperinflation', *International Economic Review* 14, 328–50.

Sargent, T. and Wallace, N. (1976) 'Rational Expectations and the Theory of Economic Policy', *Journal of Monetary Economics* 2, May, 169–83.

Smith, A. (1776) *An Inquiry into the Nature and Causes of the Wealth of Nations*, London.

Tobin, J. (1981) 'The Monetarist Counter-Revolution Today – An Appraisal', *Economic Journal* 91, March, 29–42.

Part IV

The real business cycle approach to economic fluctuations

Introduction

The real business cycle school, a predominantly US school of thought, evolved out of the new classical school in the 1980s. The research programme associated with this second phase of equilibrium theorizing was initiated by Kydland and Prescott's (1982) seminal article and following Long and Plosser (1983) has come to be referred to as the real business cycle approach. In stark contrast to the earlier new classical models, proponents of real business theory reject the view that unanticipated monetary shocks generate fluctuations in output and employment. Instead the real business cycle school views business cycles as being predominantly caused by persistent *real* (or supply-side) shocks, rather than monetary (or demand-side) shocks to the economy (some models emphasize shocks to government expenditure: see Barro and Grilli 1994). These real shocks, the focus of which involve large random fluctuations in the rate of technological progress, cause the aggregate production function to shift. Rational economic agents are held to optimally respond to the resultant fluctuations in relative prices by altering their supply of labour and consumption. As such, fluctuations in output and employment are regarded as Pareto efficient responses to real technological shocks to the aggregate production function. Furthermore observed fluctuations in output are viewed as fluctuations in the natural (trend) rate of output, rather than deviations of output from a smooth deterministic trend, thereby resulting in the abandonment of the established convention of distinguishing between short-run cycles and long-run trend.

In his 1986 *Federal Reserve Bank of Minneapolis Quarterly Review* article (reprinted on pp. 366–88) on 'Theory Ahead of Business Cycle Measurement', Edward Prescott, a leading exponent of the real business cycle approach, maintains that the large fluctuations in output and employment displayed in the US economy are in accord with the predictions of standard economic theory, given the persistent nature of technological shocks and significant intertemporal substitution in labour supply and employment decisions. Prescott uses a model based on the orthodox neoclassical growth model and argues that the artificial economy he constructs displays fluctuations in aggregate time series with statistical properties which are close to those experienced by the US economy since the Korean War. In conclusion he controversially suggests that, as fluctuations in output and employment are the optimal responses to irregular technological shocks, 'costly efforts at stabilization are likely to be counterproductive'. Lawrence Summer's 1986 *Federal Reserve Bank of Minneapolis Quarterly Review* article (reprinted on pp. 389–95) entitled 'Some Skeptical Observations on Real Business Cycle Theory' examines four main criticisms of the type of real business cycle model put forward by Prescott. These criticisms, which concern the parameters used by Prescott in his model, evidence on technological shocks and intertemporal substitution in employment, price data, and breakdowns in the exchange mechanism, lead Summers to reject this radical approach as an explanation of aggregate instability.

Another leading exponent of the real business cycle approach is Charles Plosser. In his 1989 *Journal of Economic Perspectives* article (reprinted on pp. 396–424) entitled 'Understanding Real Business Cycles', Plosser provides a very accessible introduction to the real business cycle approach to business fluctuations, in which dynamic general equilibrium models are constructed to help understand the behaviour of aggregate economic variables following changes in the economic environment. Plosser demonstrates how the predicted annual growth rates of *real* output, consumption, investment, wage rate and hours worked, derived from the basic neoclassical model of capital accumulation, appear to mirror a significant portion of the actual behaviour of these five variables for the US economy between 1955 and 1985. While real business cycle models have typically focused on real technological shocks as the main source of economic fluctuations, Plosser also considers some potential areas for research to develop and extend the real business cycle approach, including shocks arising from changes in preferences and the quantity of money. In the final contribution, also reprinted from the 1989 Summer issue of the *Journal of Economic Perspectives*, Gregory Mankiw in his article entitled 'Real Business Cycles: A New Keynesian Perspective' acknowledges that 'while real business cycle theory has served the important function of stimulating and provoking scientific debate', he predicts that it will 'ultimately be discarded as an explanation of observed fluctuations'. Mankiw highlights what he regards as two fundamental weaknesses of the approach, namely the reliance given to large technological disturbances as the main source of economic fluctuations and the intertemporal substitution of leisure in explaining changes in employment.

The real business cycle approach, like the new classical approach from which it evolved, has proved to be highly controversial. Critics of the real business cycle research programme remain convinced that it has a number of serious deficiencies. Contrary to the 'strong' version (see McCallum 1989) in which monetary disturbances have negligible, if any, consequences for real variables, most economists believe that in the short run aggregate demand disturbances arising from changes in monetary policy can have significant real effects because of the nominal price and wage rigidities which characterize actual economies (see Part V). Furthermore many economists reject the view that stabilization policy has no role to play. Nevertheless real business cycle theorists have made two important and lasting contributions to macroeconomics. First, real business cycle theory has challenged the pre-1980 consensus that growth and fluctuations are distinct phenomena to be studied separately, requiring different analytical tools. By integrating the theory of growth and fluctuations, the direction of modern business cycle research has been irreversibly changed. Second, rather than attempting to provide models capable of conventional econometric testing, real business cycle theorists, inspired by the work of Kydland and Prescott (1982) have developed the calibration method. While calibration does not, to date, provide a method that allows one to judge between the performance of real and other business cycle models, it has provided an important new contribution to the methodology of macroeconomics research (see Hoover 1995; Wickens 1995). This new research methodology for macroeconomics, with its emphasis on the stylized facts of the business cycle (see Ryan and Mullineux 1997) to be explained and the construction of general equilibrium dynamic models which can replicate such stylized facts, has focused attention on, and stimulated renewed interest into, empirical knowledge of business cycle phenomena. In short the major contribution of the real business cycle approach has been to raise fundamental questions relating to the meaning, significance and characteristics of economic fluctuations.

REFERENCES

*Titles marked with an asterisk are particularly recommended for additional reading.
*Abel, A. B. and B. S. Bernanke (1995) *Macroeconomics*, 2nd edn, Chapters 9 and 11, New York: Addison Wesley.
*Barro, R. J. and V. Grilli (1994) *European Macroeconomics*, Chapter 12, London: Macmillan.
Danthine, J. P. and J. B. Donaldson (1993) 'Methodological and Empirical Issues in Real Business Cycle Theory', *European Economic Review* 37, January, pp. 1–35.
*Froyen, R. T. (1996) *Macroeconomics: Theories and Policies*, 5th edn, Chapter 12, London: Prentice-Hall.
*Gordon, R. J. (1993) *Macroeconomics*, 6th edn, Chapter 7, New York: HarperCollins.
*Hall, R. E. and J. B. Taylor (1993) *Macroeconomics*, 4th edn, Chapters 4 and 15, New York: W. W. Norton.
Hoover, K. D. (1995) 'Facts and Artifacts: Calibration and the Empirical Assessment of Real Business-Cycle Models', *Oxford Economic Papers* 47, pp. 24–44.
*Jansen, D. W., C. D. Delorme and R. B. Ekelund, Jr (1994) *Intermediate Macroeconomics*, Chapter 11, New York: West.
Kydland, F. E. and E. C. Prescott (1982) 'Time to Build and Aggregate Fluctuations', *Econometrica* 50, November, pp. 1345–70.
*Kydland, F. E. and E. C. Prescott (1990) 'Business Cycles: Real Facts and a Monetary Myth', *Federal Reserve Bank of Minneapolis Quarterly Review* 14, Spring, pp. 3–18.

Long, J. B. and C. I. Plosser (1983) 'Real Business Cycles', *Journal of Political Economy* 91, February, pp. 39–69.

*Lucas, R. E. Jr (1977) 'Understanding Business Cycles', in K. Brunner and A. H. Meltzer (eds) *Stabilization of the Domestic and International Economy*, Amsterdam: North Holland.

McCallum, B. T. (1989) 'Real Business Cycle Models', in R. J. Barro (ed.) *Modern Business Cycle Theory*, Cambridge, MA: Harvard University Press.

*Mankiw, N. G. (1994) *Macroeconomics*, 2nd edn, Chapter 14, New York: Worth.

*Mullineux, A. W. and D. G. Dickinson (1992) 'Equilibrium Business Cycles: Theory and Evidence', *Journal of Economic Surveys* 6, pp. 321–58.

*Plosser, C. I. (1994) 'Interview with Charles Plosser', in B. Snowdon, H. R. Vane and P. Wynarczyk, *A Modern Guide to Macroeconomics: An Introduction to Competing Schools of Thought*, Aldershot: Edward Elgar.

*Ryan, C. and A. W. Mullineux (1997) 'The Ups and Downs of Modern Business Cycle Theory', in B. Snowdon and H. R. Vane (eds) *Reflections on the Development of Modern Macroeconomics*, Aldershot: Edward Elgar.

*Snowdon, B. and H. R. Vane (1995) 'New Classical Macroeconomics Mark II: The Real Business Cycle Model', *Economics and Business Education* 3, Winter, pp. 153–6.

*Snowdon, B., H. R. Vane and P. Wynarczyk (1994) *A Modern Guide to Macroeconomics: An Introduction to Competing Schools of Thought*, Chapter 6, Aldershot: Edward Elgar.

*Stadler, G. W. (1994) 'Real Business Cycles', *Journal of Economic Literature* 32, December, pp. 1750–83.

Wickens, M. (1995) 'Real Business Cycle Analysis: A Needed Revolution in Macroeconometrics', *Economic Journal* 105, November, pp. 1637–48.

QUESTIONS

1 What are the main differences between the mark I new classical and real business cycle models?

2 How are fluctuations in employment explained in the real business cycle model?

3 What are the 'stylized facts' of the business cycle? Have business cycle theorists successfully explained these facts?

4 To what extent have economists succeeded in developing a satisfactory equilibrium model of the business cycle since the early 1970s?

5 Is there any role for stabilization policy in a real business model?

6 Compare and contrast the conventional approach to econometric testing with the calibration method advocated by real business cycle theorists.

7 'If these theories are correct, they imply that the macroeconomics developed in the wake of the Keynesian Revolution is well confined to the ashbin of history' (Summers 1986). Critically examine this view of real business cycle theories.

8 How do real business cycle theorists reconcile their view that variations in the quantity of money are unimportant for explaining economic fluctuations with the empirical evidence which appears to show a money-output link?

9 Is the calculation of the Solow residual a satisfactory and reliable method of identifying the variance of technology shocks?

10 'Real business cycle theory is not only a competitor to Keynesian macroeconomics but also represents a serious challenge to all monetarist models as well as early new classical explanations of aggregate instability'. Explain and discuss.

15 Theory ahead of business cycle measurement

Edward C. Prescott
Federal Reserve Bank of Minneapolis Quarterly Review (1986) Fall,
pp. 9–22

Economists have long been puzzled by the observations that during peace-time industrial market economies display recurrent, large fluctuations in output and employment over relatively short time periods. Not uncommon are changes as large as 10 percent within only a couple of years. These observations are considered puzzling because the associated movements in labor's marginal product are small.

These observations should not be puzzling, for they are what standard economic theory predicts. For the United States, in fact, given people's ability and willingness to intertemporally and intratemporally substitute consumption and leisure and given the nature of the changing production possibility set, it would be puzzling if the economy did not display these large fluctuations in output and employment with little associated fluctuations in the marginal product of labor. Moreover, standard theory also correctly predicts the amplitude of these fluctuations, their serial correlation properties, and the fact that the investment component of output is about six times as volatile as the consumption component.

This perhaps surprising conclusion is the principal finding of a research program initiated by Kydland and me (1982) and extended by Kydland and me (1984), Hansen (1985a) and Bain (1985). We have computed the competitive equilibrium stochastic process for variants of the constant elasticity, stochastic growth model. The elasticities of substitution and the share parameters of the production and utility functions are restricted to those that generate the growth observations. The process governing the technology parameter is selected to be consistent with the measured technology changes for the American economy since the Korean War. We ask whether these artificial economies display fluctuations with statistical properties similar to those which the American economy has displayed in that period. They do.[1]

I view the growth model as a paradigm for macro analysis – analogous to the supply and demand construct of price theory. The elasticities of substitution and the share parameters of the growth model are analogous to the price and income elasticities of price theory. Whether or not this paradigm dominates, as I expect it will, is still an open question. But the early results indicate its power to organize our knowledge. The finding that when uncertainty in the rate of technological change is incorporated into the growth model it displays the business cycle phenomena was both dramatic and unanticipated. I was sure that the model could not do this without some features of the payment and credit technologies.

The models constructed within this theoretical framework are necessarily highly abstract. Consequently, they are necessarily false, and statistical hypothesis testing will reject them. This does not imply, however, that nothing can be learned from such quantitative theoretical exercises. I think much has already been learned and confidently predict that much more will be learned as other features of the environment are introduced. Prime candidates for study are the effects of public finance elements, a foreign sector, and, of course, monetary factors. The research I review here is best viewed as a very promising beginning of a much larger research program.

THE BUSINESS CYCLE PHENOMENA

The use of the expression *business cycle* is unfortunate for two reasons. One is that it leads people to think in terms of a time series' business cycle component which is to be explained independently of a growth component; our research has, instead, one unifying theory of both of these. The other reason I do not like to use the expression is that it is not accurate; some systems of low-order linear stochastic difference equations with a nonoscillatory deterministic part, and therefore no cycle, display key business cycle features (see Slutzky 1927). I thus do not refer to business cycles, but rather to business cycle *phenomena*, which are nothing more nor less than a certain set of statistical properties of a certain set of important aggregate time series. The question that I and others have considered is, Do the stochastic difference equations that are the equilibrium laws of motion for the stochastic growth display the business cycle phenomena?

More specifically, we follow Lucas (1977: 9) in defining the business cycle phenomena as the recurrent fluctuations of output about trend and the co-movements among other aggregate time series. Fluctuations are by definition deviations from some slowly varying path. Since this slowly varying path increases monotonically over time, we adopt the common practice of labeling it *trend*. This trend is neither a measure nor an estimate of the unconditional mean of some stochastic process. It is, rather, defined by the computational procedure used to fit the smooth curve through the data.

If the business cycle facts were sensitive to the detrending procedure employed, there would be a problem. But the key facts are not sensitive to the procedure if the trend curve is smooth. Our curve-fitting method is to take the logarithms of variables and then select the trend path $\{\tau_t\}$ which minimizes the sum of the squared deviations from a given series $\{Y_t\}$ subject to the constraint that the sum of the squared second differences not be too large. This is

$$\min_{\{\tau_t\}_{t=1}^T} \sum_{t=1}^{T}(Y_t - \tau_t)^2$$

subject to

$$\sum_{t=2}^{T-1}[(\tau_{t+1} - \tau_t) - (\tau_t - \tau_{t-1})]^2 \leq \mu.$$

The smaller is μ, the smoother is the trend path. If $\mu = 0$, the least squares linear time trend results. For all series, μ is picked so that the Lagrange multiplier of the constraint is 1600. This produces the right degree of smoothness in the fitted trend when the observation period is a quarter of a year. Thus, the sequence $\{\tau_t\}$ minimizes

$$\sum_{t=1}^{T}(Y_t - \tau_t)^2 + 1600 \sum_{t=2}^{T-1}[(\tau_{t+1} - \tau_t) - (\tau_t - \tau_{t-1})]^2.$$

The first-order conditions of this minimization problem are linear in Y_t and τ_t, so for every series, $\tau = AY$, where A is the same $T \times T$ matrix. The deviations from trend, also by definition, are

$$Y_t^d = Y_t - \tau_t \text{ for } t = 1, \ldots, T.$$

Unless otherwise stated, these are the variables used in the computation of the statistics reported here for both the United States and the growth economies.

An alternative interpretation of the procedure is that it is a high pass linear filter. The facts reported here are essentially the same if, rather than defining the deviations by $Y^d = (I - A)Y$, we filtered the Y using a high pass band filter, eliminating all frequencies of 32 quarters or greater. An advantage of our procedure is that it deals better with the ends of the sample problem and does not require a stationary time series.

To compare the behaviors of a stochastic growth economy and an actual economy, only identical statistics for the two economies are used. By definition, a *statistic* is a real valued function of the raw time series. Consequently, if a comparison is made, say, between the standard deviations of the deviations, the date t deviation for the growth economy must be the same function of the data generated by that model as the date t deviation for the US economy is of that economy's data. Our definitions of the deviations satisfy this criterion.

Figure 15.1 plots the logs of actual and trend output for the US economy during 1947–82, and Figure 15.2 the corresponding percentage deviations from trend of output and hours of market employment. Output and hours clearly move up and down together with nearly the same amplitudes.

Table 15.1 contains the standard deviations and cross serial correlations of output and other aggregate time series for the US economy during 1954–82. Consumption appears less variable and investment more variable than

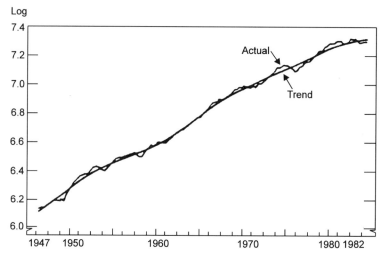

Figure 15.1 Actual and trend logs of US gross national product (Quarterly, 1947–82)
Source of basic data: Citicorp's Citibase data bank

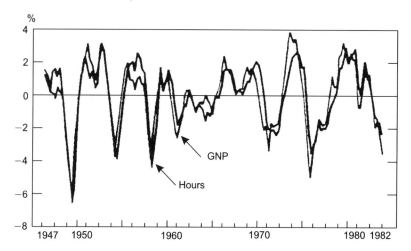

Figure 15.2 Deviations from trend of gross national product and nonfarm employee hours in the United States (Quarterly, 1947–82)
Source of basic data: Citicorp's Citibase data bank

output. Further, the average product of labor is procyclical but does not vary as much as output or hours.

THE GROWTH MODEL

This theory and its variants build on the neoclassical growth economy of Solow (1956) and Swan (1956). In the language of Lucas (1980: 696), the model is a 'fully articulated, artificial economic system' that can be used to

Table 15.1 Cyclical behavior of the US economy
(Deviations from trend of key variables, 1954:1–1982:4)

Variable x	Standard deviation	Cross correlation of GNP with		
		x(t-1)	x(t)	x(t+1)
Gross national product	1.8%	0.82	1.00	0.82
Personal consumption expenditures				
Services	0.6	0.66	0.72	0.61
Nondurable goods	1.2	0.71	0.76	0.59
Fixed investment expenditures	5.3	0.78	0.89	0.78
Nonresidential investment	5.2	0.54	0.79	0.86
Structures	4.6	0.42	0.62	0.70
Equipment	6.0	0.56	0.82	0.87
Capital stocks				
Total nonfarm inventories	1.7	0.15	0.48	0.68
Nonresidential structures	0.4	−0.20	−0.03	0.16
Nonresidential equipment	1.0	0.03	0.23	0.41
Labor input				
Nonfarm hours	1.7	0.57	0.85	0.89
Average weekly hours in mfg.	1.0	0.76	0.85	0.61
Productivity (GNP/hours)	1.0	0.51	0.34	−0.04

Source of basic data: Citicorp's Citibase data bank

generate economic time series of a set of important economic aggregates. The model assumes an aggregate production function with constant returns to scale, inputs labor n and capital k, and an output which can be allocated either to current consumption c or to investment x. If t denotes the date, $f : R^2 \to R$ the production function, and z_t, a technology parameter, then the production constraint is

$$x_t + c_t \leq z_t f(k_t, n_t)$$

where $x_t, c_t, k_t, n_t \geq 0$. The model further assumes that the services provided by a unit of capital decrease geometrically at a rate $0 < \delta < 1$:

$$k_{t+1} = (1 - \delta)k_t + x_t.$$

Solow completes the specification of his economy by hypothesizing that some fraction $0 < \sigma < 1$ of output is invested and the remaining fraction $1 - \sigma$ consumed and that n_t is a constant – say, $\bar{n}$ – for all t. For this economy, the law of motion of capital condition on z_t is

$$k_{t+1} = (1 - \delta)k_t + \sigma z_t f(k_t, \bar{n}).$$

Once the $\{z_t\}$ stochastic process is specified, the stochastic process governing capital and the other economic aggregates are determined and realizations of the stochastic process can be generated by a computer.

This structure is far from adequate for the study of the business cycle because in it neither employment nor the savings rate varies, when in fact they do. Being explicit about the economy, however, naturally leads to the question of what determines these variables, which are central to the cycle.

That leads to the introduction of a stand-in household with some explicit preferences. If we abstract from the labor supply decision and uncertainty (that is, $z_t = \bar{z}$ and $n_t = \bar{n}$), the standard form of the utility function is

$$\sum_{t=0}^{\infty} \beta^t u(c_t) \quad \text{for} \quad 0 < \beta < 1$$

where β is the subjective time discount factor. The function $u : R_+ \to R$ is twice differentiable and concave. The commodity space for the deterministic version of this model is l_∞, infinite sequences of uniformly bounded consumptions $\{c_t\}_{t=0}^{\infty}$.

The theorems of Bewley (1972) could be applied to establish existence of a competitive equilibrium for this l_∞ commodity-space economy. That existence argument, however, does not provide an algorithm for computing the equilibria. An alternative approach is to use the competitive welfare theorems of Debreu (1954). Given local nonsaturation and no externalities, competitive equilibria are Pareto optima and, with some additional conditions that are satisfied for this economy, any Pareto optimum can be supported as a competitive equilibrium. Given a single agent and the convexity, there is a unique optimum and that optimum is the unique competitive equilibrium allocation. The advantage of this approach is that algorithms for computing solutions to concave programming problems can be used to find the competitive equilibrium allocation for this economy.

Even with the savings decision endogenous, this economy has no fluctuations. As shown by Cass (1965) and Koopmans (1965), the competitive equilibrium path converges monotonically to a unique rest point or, if z_t is growing exponentially, to a balanced growth path. There are multisector variants of this model in which the equilibrium path oscillates (see Benhabib and Nishimura 1985; Marimon 1984). But I know of no multisector model which has been restricted to match observed factor shares by sector, which has a value for β consistent with observed interest rates, and which displays oscillations.

When uncertainty is introduced, the household's objective is its expected discounted utility:

$$E\left\{\sum_{t=0}^{\infty} \beta^t u(c_t)\right\}.$$

The commodity vector is now indexed by the history of shocks; that is, $\{c_t(z_1, \ldots, z_t)\}_{t=0}^{\infty}$ is the commodity point. As Brock and Mirman (1972) show, if the $\{z_t\}$ are identically distributed random variables, an optimum to the social planner's problem exists and the optimum is a stationary stochastic process with $k_{t+1} = g(k_t, z_t)$ and $c_t = c(k_t, z_t)$. As Lucas and Prescott (1971) show, for a class of economies that include this one, the social optimum is the unique competitive equilibrium allocation. They also show that for these homogeneous agent economies, the social optimum is also the unique sequence-of-markets equilibrium allocation. Consequently, there are equilibrium time-invariant functions for the wage $w_t = w(k_t, z_t)$ and the rental price of capital $r_t = r(k_t, z_t)$, where these prices are relative to the date t consumption good. Given these prices, the firm's period t problem is

$$\max\nolimits_{k_t, n_t \geq 0} \{y_t - r_t k_t - w_t n_t\}$$

subject to the output constraint

$$y_t \leq z_t f(k_t, n_t).$$

The household's problem is more complicated, for it must form expectations of future prices. If a_t is its capital stock, its problem is

$$\max E \sum_{t=0}^{\infty} \beta^t u(c_t)$$

subject to

$$c_t + x_t \leq w_t n + r_t a_t$$
$$a_{t+1} \leq (1 - \delta)a_t + x_t$$

and given $a_0 - k_0$. In forming expectations, a household knows the relation between the economy's state (k_t, z_t) and prices, $w_t = w(k_t, z_t)$ and $r_t = r(k_t, z_t)$. Further, it knows the process governing the evolution of the per capita capital stock, a variable which, like prices, is taken as given.

The elements needed to define a *sequence-of-markets equilibrium* are the firm's policy functions $y(k_t, z_t)$, $n(k_t, z_t)$, and $k(k_t, z_t)$; the household's policy functions $x(a_t, k_t, z_t)$ and $c(a_t, k_t, z_t)$; a law of motion of per capita capital $k_{t+1} = g(k_t, z_t)$; and pricing functions $w(k_t, z_t)$ and $r(k_t, z_t)$. For equilibrium, then,

- The firm's policy functions must be optimal given the pricing functions.
- The household's policy functions must be optimal given the pricing functions and the law of motion of per capita capital.
- Spot markets clear; that is, for all k_t and z_t

$$\bar{n} = n(k_t, z_t)$$
$$k_t = k(k_t, z_t)$$
$$x(k_t, k_t, z_t) + c(k_t, k_t, z_t) = y(k_t, z_t).$$

(Note that the goods market must clear only when the representative household is truly representative, that is, when $a_t = k_t$).
- Expectations are rational; that is,

$$g(k_t, z_t) = (1 - \delta)k_t + x(k_t, k_t, z_t).$$

This definition still holds if the household values productive time that is allocated to nonmarket activities. Such time will be called *leisure* and denoted l_t. The productive time endowment is normalized to 1, and the household faces the constraints

$$n_t + l_t \leq 1$$

for all t. In addition, leisure is introduced as an argument of the utility function, so the household's objective becomes the maximization of

$$E \sum_{t=0}^{\infty} \beta^t u(c_t, l_t).$$

Now leisure – and therefore employment – varies in equilibrium.

The model needs one more modification: a relaxation of the assumption that the technology shocks z_t are identically and independently distributed random variables. As will be documented, they are not so distributed. Rather, they display considerable serial correlation, with their first differences nearly serially uncorrelated. To introduce high persistence, we assume

$$z_{t+1} = \rho z_t + \epsilon_{t+1}$$

where the $\{\epsilon_{t+1}\}$ are identically and independently distributed and ρ is near 1. With this modification, the recursive sequence-of-markets equilibrium definition continues to apply.

USING DATA TO RESTRICT THE GROWTH MODEL

Without additional restrictions on preferences and technology, a wide variety of equilibrium processes are consistent with the growth model. The beauty of this model is that both growth and micro observations can be used to determine its production and utility functions. When they are so used, there are not many free parameters that are specific to explaining the business cycle phenomena and that cannot be measured independently of those phenomena. The key parameters of the growth model are the intertemporal and intratemporal elasticities of substitution. As Lucas (1980: 712) emphasizes, 'On these parameters, we have a wealth of inexpensively available data from census cohort information, from panel data describing the reactions of individual households to a variety of changing market conditions, and so forth.' To this list we add the secular growth observations which have the advantage of being experiments run by nature with large changes in relative prices and quantities and with idiosyncratic factors averaged out.[2] A fundamental thesis of this line of inquiry is that the measures obtained from aggregate series and those from individual panel data must be consistent. After all, the former are just the aggregates of the latter.

Secularly in the United States, capital and labor shares of output have been approximately constant, as has r, the rental price of capital. However, the nation's real wage has increased greatly – more than 100 percent since the Korean War. For these results to hold, the model's production function must be approximately Cobb-Douglas:

$$z_t f(k_t, n_t) = z_t k_t^{1-\theta} n_t^\theta.$$

The share parameter θ is equal to labor's share, which has been about 64 percent in the postwar period, so $\theta = 0.64$. This number is smaller than that usually obtained because we include services of consumer durables as part of output. This alternative accounting both reduces labor's share and makes it more nearly constant over the postwar period.

The artificial economy has but one type of capital, and it depreciates at rate δ. In fact, different types of capital depreciate at different rates, and the pattern of depreciation over the life of any physical asset is not constant. Kydland and I (1982, 1984) simply pick $\delta = 0.10$. With this value and an annual real interest rate of 4 percent, the steady-state capital–annual output ratio is about 2.6. That matches the ratio for the US economy and also implies a steady-state investment share of output near the historically observed average. Except for parameters determining the process on the technology shock, this completely specifies the technology of the simple growth model.

A key growth observation which restricts the utility function is that leisure per capita l_t has shown virtually no secular trend while, again, the real wage has increased steadily. This implies an elasticity of substitution between consumption c_t and leisure l_t near 1. Thus, the utility function restricted to display both constant intertemporal and unit intratemporal elasticities of substitution is

$$u(c_t, l_t) = ([c_t^{1-\phi} l_t^\phi]^{1-\gamma} - 1)/(1 - \gamma)$$

where $1/\gamma > 0$ is the elasticity of substituting between different date composite commodities $c_t^{1-\phi} l_t^\phi$. This leaves γ and the subjective time discount factor β [or, equivalently, the subjective time discount rate $(1/\beta) - 1$] to be determined.

The steady-state interest rate is

$$i = (1/\beta) - 1 + \gamma(\dot{c}/c).$$

As stated previously, the average annual real interest rate is about 4 percent, and the growth rate of per capita consumption $\dot{c}/c$ has averaged nearly 2 percent. The following studies help restrict γ. Tobin and Dolde (1971) find that a γ near 1.5 is needed to match the life cycle consumption patterns of individuals. Using individual portfolio observations, Friend and Blume (1975) estimate γ to be near 2. Using aggregate stock market and consumption data, Hansen and Singleton (1983) estimate γ to be near 1. Using international data, Kehoe (1984) also finds a modest curvature parameter γ. All these observations make a strong case that γ is not too far from 1. Since the nature of fluctuations of the artificial economy is not very sensitive to γ, we simply set γ equal to 1. Taking the limit as $\gamma \to 1$ yields

$$u(c_t, l_t) = (1 - \phi) \log c_t + \phi \log l_t.$$

This leaves β and ϕ still to be determined.

Hansen (1985b) has found that growing economies – that is, those with z_t having a multiplicative, geometrically growing factor $(1 + \lambda)^t$ with $\lambda > 0$ – fluctuate in essentially the same way as economies for which $\lambda = 0$. This justifies considering only the case $\lambda = 0$. If $\lambda = 0$, then the average interest rate approximately equals the subjective time discount rate.[3] Therefore, we set β equal to 0.96 per year or 0.99 per quarter.

The parameter ϕ is the leisure share parameter. Ghez and Becker (1975) find that the household allocates approximately one-third of its productive time to market activities and two-thirds to nonmarket activities. To be consistent with that, the model's parameter ϕ must be near two-thirds. This is the value assumed in our business cycle studies.

Eichenbaum *et al.* (1984) use aggregate data to estimate this share parameter ϕ, and they obtain a value near five-sixths. The difference between two-thirds and five-sixths is large in the business cycle context. With $\phi = 2/3$, the elasticity of labor supply with respect to a temporary change in the real wage is 2, while if $\phi = 5/6$, it is 5. This is because a 1 percent change in leisure implies a $\phi/(\phi - 1)$ percent change in hours of employment.

We do not follow the Eichenbaum-Hansen-Singleton approach and treat ϕ as a free parameter because it would violate the principle that parameters cannot be specific to the phenomena being studied. What sort of science would economics be if micro studies used one share parameter and aggregate studies another?

The nature of the technological change

One method of measuring technological change is to follow Solow (1956) and define it as the changes in output less the sum of the changes in labor's input times labor share and the changes in capital's input times capital share. Measuring variables in logs, this is the percentage change in the technology parameter of the Cobb-Douglas production function. For the US economy between the third quarter of 1955 and the first quarter of 1984, the standard deviation of this change is 1.2 percent.[4] The serial autocorrelations of these changes are $\rho_1 = -0.21, \rho_2 = -0.06, \rho_3 = 0.04, \rho_4 = 0.01$, and $\rho_5 = -0.05$. To a first approximation, the process on the percentage change in the technology process is a random walk with drift plus some serially uncorrelated measurement error. This error produces the negative first-order serial correlation of the differences.

Further evidence that the random walk model is not a bad approximation is based on yearly changes. For the quarterly random walk model, the standard deviation of this change is 6.63 times the standard deviation of the quarterly change. For the US data, the annual change is only 5.64 times as large as the quarterly change. This, along with the negative first-order serial correlation, suggests that the standard deviation of the persistent part of the quarterly change is closer to $5.64/6.63 = 0.85$ than to 1.2 percent. Some further evidence is the change over four-quarter periods – that is, the change from a given quarter of one year to the same quarter of the next year. For the random walk model, the standard deviation of these changes is 2 times the standard deviation of the quarterly change. A reason that the standard deviation of change might be better measured this way is that the measurement noise introduced by seasonal factors is minimized. The esti- mate obtained in this way is 0.95 percent. To summarize, Solow growth accounting finds that the process on the technology parameter is highly persistent with the standard deviation of change being about 0.90.[5]

The Solow estimate of the standard deviation of technological change is surely an overstatement of the variability of that parameter. There undoubt- edly are non-negligible errors in measuring the inputs. Since the capital input varies slowly and its share is small, the most serious measurement problem is with the labor input. Fortunately there are two independent measures of the aggregate labor input, one constructed from a survey of employers and the other from a survey of households. Under the assumption of orthogonality of their measurement errors, a reasonable estimate of the variance of the change in hours is the covariance between the changes in the two series. Since the household survey is not used to estimate aggregate output, I use the covariance between the changes in household hours and output as an esti- mate of the covariance between aggregate hours and output. Still using a share parameter of $\theta = 0.75$, my estimate of the standard deviation of the percentage change in z_t is the square root of var $(\Delta \hat{y}) - 2\theta\mathrm{cov}(\Delta \hat{h}_1, \Delta \hat{y}) + \theta^2\mathrm{cov}(\Delta \hat{h}_1, \Delta \hat{h}_2)$, where the caret (ˆ) denotes a measured value. For the sample period my estimate is 0.763 percent. This is probably a better estimate than the one which ignores measurement error.

Still, my estimate might under- or overstate the variance of technological change. For example, the measurement of output might include significant errors. Perhaps measurement procedures result in some smoothing of the series. This would reduce the variability of the change in output and might reduce the covariance between measured hours and output.

Another possibility is that changes in hours are associated with corres- ponding changes in capital's utilization rate. If so, the Solow approach is inappropriate for measuring the technology shocks. To check whether this is a problem, I varied θ and found that $\theta = 0.85$ yields the smallest estimate, 0.759, as opposed to 0.763 for $\theta = 0.75$. This suggests that my estimate is not at all sensitive to variations in capital utilization rates.

To summarize, there is overwhelming evidence that technological shocks are highly persistent. But tying down the standard deviation of the technology change shocks is difficult. I estimate it as 0.763. It could very well be larger or smaller, though, given the accuracy of the measure- ments.

THE STATISTICAL BEHAVIOR OF THE GROWTH MODELS

Theory provides an equilibrium stochastic process for the growth economy studied. Our approach has been to document the similarities and differences between the statistical properties of data generated by this stochastic process and the statistical properties of American time series data. An alternative approach is to compare the paths of the growth model if the technological parameters $\{z_t\}$ were those experienced by the US economy. We did not attempt this because theory's predictions of paths, unlike its predictions of the statistical properties, are sensitive to what Leamer (1983: 43) calls 'whimsical' modeling assumptions. Another nontrivial problem is that the errors in measuring the innovations in the z_t process are as large as the innovations themselves.

The basic growth model

With the standard deviation of the technology shock equal to 0.763, theory implies that the standard deviation of output will be 1.48 percent. In fact, it is 1.76 percent for the post-Korean War American economy. For the output of the artificial economy to be as variable as that, the variance of the shock must be 1.0, significantly larger than the estimate. The most important deviation from theory is the relative volatility of hours and output. Figure 15.3 plots a realization of the output and employment deviations from trend for the basic growth economy. A comparison of Figures 15.2 and 15.3 demonstrates clearly that, for the US economy, hours in fact vary much more than the basic growth model predicts. For the artificial economy, hours fluctuate 52 percent as much as output,

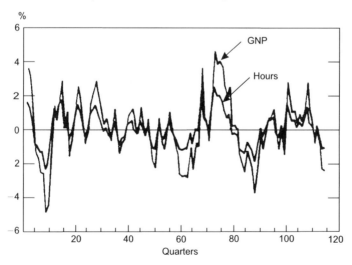

Figure 15.3 Deviations from trend of GNP and hours worked in the basic growth economy

whereas for the US economy, the ratio is 0.95. This difference appears too large to be a result of errors in measuring aggregate hours and output.

The Kydland-Prescott economy

Kydland and I (1982, 1984) have modified the growth model in two important respects. First, we assume that a distributed lag of leisure and the market-produced good combine to produce the composite commodity good valued by the household. In particular,

$$u(c_t, \sum_{i=0}^{\infty} \alpha_i l_{t-i}) = (1/3)\log c_t$$

$$+ (2/3)\log \sum_{i=0}^{\infty} \alpha_i l_{t-i}$$

where $\alpha_{i+1}/\alpha_i = 1 - \eta$ for $i = 1, 2, \ldots$ and $\sum_{i=0}^{\infty} \alpha_i = 1$.

Kydland (1983) provides justification for this preference ordering based on an unmeasured, household-specific capital stock that, like c_t and l_t, is an input in the production of the composite commodity. The economy studied has $\alpha_0 = 0.5$ and $\eta = 0.1$. This increases the variability of hours.

The second modification is to permit the workweek of capital to vary proportionally to the workweek of the household. For this economy, increases in hours do not reduce the marginal product of labor as much, so hours fluctuate more in response to technology shocks of a given size.

The statistical properties of the fluctuations for this economy are reported in Table 15.2. As is clear there, hours are now about 70 percent as variable as output. This eliminates much of the discrepancy between theory and measurement. If the standard deviation of the technology shock is 0.72 percent, then fluctuations in the output of this artificial economy are as large as those experienced in the US economy.

A comparison of Tables 15.1 and 15.2 shows that the Kydland-Prescott economy displays the business cycle phenomena. It does not quite demonstrate, however, that there would be a puzzle if the economy did not display the business cycle phenomena. That is because the parameters α_0 and η have not been well tied down by micro observations.[6] Better measures of these parameters could either increase or decrease significantly the amount of the fluctuations accounted for by the uncertainty in the technological change.

The Hansen indivisible labor economy

Labor economists have estimated labor supply elasticities and found them to be small for full-time prime-age males (see, for example, Ashenfelter 1984). Heckman (1984), however, finds that when movements between employment and nonemployment are considered and secondary workers

Table 15.2 Cyclical behavior of the Kydland-Prescott economy*

Variable x	Standard deviation	Cross correlation of GNP with		
		x(t-1)	x(t)	x(t+1)
Gross national product	1.79%	0.60	1.00	0.60
	(0.13)	(0.07)	(–)	(0.07)
Consumption	0.45	0.47	0.85	0.71
	(0.05)	(0.05)	(0.02)	(0.04)
Investment	5.49	0.52	0.88	0.78
	(0.41)	(0.09)	(0.03)	(0.03)
Inventory stock	2.20	0.14	0.60	0.52
	(0.37)	(0.14)	(0.08)	(0.05)
Capital stock	0.47	−0.05	0.02	0.25
	(0.07)	(0.07)	(0.06)	(0.07)
Hours	1.23	0.52	0.95	0.55
	(0.09)	(0.09)	(0.01)	(0.06)
Productivity (GNP/hours)	0.71	0.62	0.86	0.56
	(0.06)	(0.05)	(0.02)	(0.10)
Real interest rate (annual)	0.22	0.65	0.60	0.36
	(0.03)	(0.07)	(0.20)	(0.15)

Note: * These are the means of 20 simulations, each of which was 116 periods long; the numbers in parentheses are standard errors
Source: Kydland and Prescott (1984)

are included, elasticities of labor supply are much larger. He also finds that most of the variation in aggregate hours arises from variation in the number employed rather than in the hours worked per employed person.

These are the observations that led Hansen (1985a) to explore the implication of introducing labor indivisibilities into the growth model. As shown by Rogerson (1984), if the household's consumption possibility set has nonconvexities associated with the mapping from hours of market production activities to units of labor services, there will be variations in the number employed rather than in the hours of work per employed person. In addition, the aggregate elasticity of labor supply will be much larger than the elasticity of those whose behavior is being aggregated. In this case aggregation matters, and matters greatly.

There certainly are important nonconvexities in the mapping from hours of market activities to units of labor services provided. Probably the most important nonconvexity arises from the considerable amount of time required for commuting. Other features of the environment that would make full-time workers more than twice as productive as otherwise similar half-time workers are not hard to imagine. The fact that part-time workers typically are paid less per hour than full-time workers with similar human capital endowments is consistent with the existence of important nonconvexities.

Hansen (1985a) restricts each identical household to either work $\bar{h}$ hours or be unemployed. His relation is as depicted by the horizontal lines in

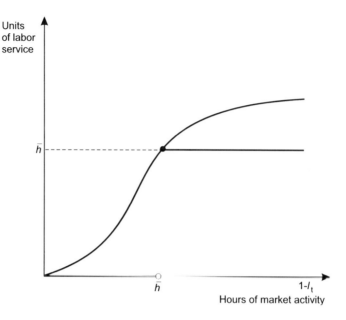

Figure 15.4 Relation between time allocated to market activity and labor service

Figure 15.4. This assumption is not as extreme as it appears. If the relation were as depicted by the curved line, the behavior of the economy would be the same. The key property is an initial convex region followed by a concave region in the mapping from hours of market activity to units of labor service.

With this modification, lotteries that specify the probability of employment are traded along with market-produced goods and capital services. As before, the utility function of each individual is

$$u(c, l) = (1/3) \log c + (2/3) \log l.$$

If an individual works, $l = 1 - \bar{h}$; otherwise, $l = 1$. Consequently, if π is the probability of employment, an individual's expected utility is

$$E\{u(c, l)\} = (1/3) \log c + (2/3) \pi \log (1 - \bar{h}).$$

Given that per capita consumption is $\bar{c}$ and per capita hours of employment $\bar{n}$, average utility over the population is maximized by setting $c = \bar{c}$ for all individuals. If $\bar{l}$, which equals $1 - \pi\bar{h}$, denotes per capita leisure, then maximum per capita utility is

$$U(\bar{c}, \bar{l}) = (1/3) \log \bar{c} + (2/3)[(1 - \bar{l})/\bar{h}] \log (1 - \bar{h}).$$

This is the utility function which rationalizes the per capita consumption and leisure choices if each person's leisure is constrained to be either $1 - \bar{h}$ or 1. The aggregate intertemporal elasticity of substitution between differ-

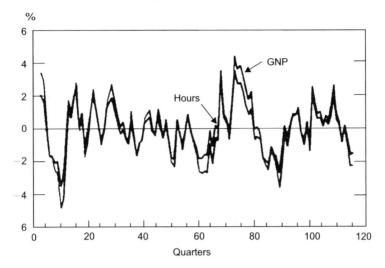

Figure 15.5 Deviations from trend GNP and hours worked in Hansen's indivisible labor economy
Source: Gary D. Hansen, Department of Economics, University of California, Santa Barbara

ent date leisures is infinity independent of the value of the elasticity for the individual (in the range where not all are employed).

Hansen (1985a) finds that if the technology shock standard deviation is 0.71, then fluctuations in output for his economy are as large as those for the US economy. Further, variability in hours is 77 percent as large as variability in output. Figure 15.5 shows that aggregate hours and output for his economy fluctuate together with nearly the same amplitude. These theoretical findings are the basis for my statement in the introduction that there would be a puzzle if the economy did not display the business cycle phenomena.

Empirical labor elasticity

One important empirical implication of a shock-to-technology theory of fluctuations is that the empirical labor elasticity of output is significantly larger than the true elasticity, which for the Cobb-Douglas production function is the labor share parameter. To see why, note that the capital stock varies little cyclically and is nearly uncorrelated with output. Consequently, the deviations almost satisfy

$$y_t = \theta h_t + z_t$$

where y_t is output, h_t hours, and z_t the technology shock. The empirical elasticity is

$$\eta = \text{cov}(h_t, y_t)/\text{var}(h_t)$$

which, because of the positive correlation between h_t and z_t, is considerably larger than the model's θ, which is 0.64. For the basic, Kydland-Prescott, and Hansen growth economies, the values of η are 1.9, 1.4, and 1.3, respectively.

Because of measurement errors, the empirical elasticity for the US economy is not well-estimated by simply computing the ratio of the covariance between hours and output and dividing by the variance of hours. The procedure I use is based on the following probability model:

$$\hat{y}_t = y_t + \epsilon_{1t}$$
$$\hat{h}_{1t} = h_t + \epsilon_{2t}$$
$$\hat{h}_{2t} = h_t + \epsilon_{3t}$$

where the cart (^) denotes a measured value. The ϵ_{it} are measurement errors. Here, the $\hat{h}_{1t}$ measure of hours uses the employer survey data while the $\hat{h}_{2t}$ measure uses the household survey data. Since these are independent measures, a maintained hypothesis is that ϵ_{2t} and ϵ_{3t} are orthogonal. With this assumption, a reasonable estimate of var (h_t) is the sample covariance between $\hat{h}_{1t}$ and $\hat{h}_{2t}$. Insofar as the measurement of output has small variance or ϵ_{1t} is uncorrelated with the hours measurement errors or both, the covariance between measured output and either measured hours series is a reasonable estimate of the covariance between output and hours. These two covariances are 2.231×10^{-4} and 2.244×10^{-4} for the sample period, and I take the average as my estimate of cov (h_t, y_t) for the US economy. My estimate of the empirical labor elasticity of output is

$$\hat{\eta} = \left[\text{cov}(\hat{h}_{1t}, \hat{y}_t) + \text{cov}(\hat{h}_{2t}, \hat{y}_t) \right] / 2\text{cov}(\hat{h}_{1t}, \hat{h}_{2t})$$
$$= 1.1.$$

This number is considerably greater than labor's share, which is about 0.70 when services of consumer durables are not included as part of output. This number strongly supports the importance of technological shocks in accounting for business cycle fluctuations. Nevertheless, the number is smaller than those for the Kydland-Prescott and Hansen growth economies.

One possible reason for the difference between the US economy and the growth model empirical labor elasticities of output is cyclical measurement errors in output. A sizeable part of the investment component of output is hard to measure and therefore not included in the US National Product Accounts measure of output, the gross national product (GNP). In particular, a firm's major maintenance expenditures, research and development expenditures, and investments in human capital are not included in GNP. In good times – namely, when output is above trend – firms may be more likely to undertake major repairs of a not fully depreciated asset, such as replacing the roof of a 30-year-old building which has a tax life of 35 years.

Such an expenditure is counted as maintenance and therefore not included in GNP even though the new roof will provide productive services for many years. The incentive for firms to do this is tax savings: by expensing an investment rather than capitalizing it, current tax liabilities are reduced. Before 1984, when a railroad replaced its 90-pound rails, the expenditure was treated as a maintenance expense rather than an investment expenditure. If these and other types of unmeasured investment fluctuate in percentage terms more than output, as do all the measured investment components, the volatility of GNP is larger than measured. We do know that investment in rails was highly procyclical and volatile in the postwar period. A careful study is needed to determine whether the correction for currently unmeasured investment is small or large.

Another reason to expect the American economy's labor elasticity to be less than the model's is that the model shocks are perfectly neutral with respect to the consumption and investment good transformation. Persistent shocks which alter the product transformation frontier between these goods would cause variation in output and employment but not in the productivity parameters. For fluctuations so induced, the empirical labor elasticity of output would be the true elasticity. Similarly, relatively permanent changes in the taxing of capital – such as altering depreciation rates, the corporate income tax rate, or the investment tax credit rate – would all result in fluctuations in output and employment but not in the productivity parameters.

A final reason for actual labor elasticity to be less than the model's is the way imports are measured. An increase in the price of imported oil, that is, an increase in the quantity of output that must be sacrificed for a given unit of that input, has no effect on measured productivity. From the point of view of the growth model, however, an oil price increase is a negative technology shock because it results in less output, net of the exports used to pay for the imported oil, available for domestic consumption and investment. Theory predicts that such shocks will induce variations in employment and output, even though they have no effect on the aggregate production function. Therefore, insofar as they are important, they reduce the empirical labor elasticity of output.

EXTENSIONS

The growth model has been extended to provide a better representation of the technology. Kydland and I (1982) have introduced a technology with more than one construction period for new production capacity.[7] We have also introduced inventory as a factor of production. This improves the match between the model's serial correlation properties and the US postwar data, but has little effect on the other statistics.

Kydland (1984) has introduced heterogeneity of labor and found that if there are transfers from high human capital people to low human capital people, theory implies that hours of the low fluctuate more than hours of the high. It also implies a lower empirical labor elasticity of output than the homogeneous household model.

Bain (1985) has studied an economy that is richer in sectoral detail. His model has manufacturing, retailing, and service-producing sectors. A key feature of the technology is that production and distribution occur sequentially. Thus there are two types of inventories – those of manufacturers' finished goods and those of final goods available for sale. With this richer detail, theory implies that different components of aggregate inventories behave in different ways, as seen in the data. It also implies that production is more volatile than final sales, an observation considered anomalous since inventories can be used to smooth production (see, for example, Blinder 1984).

Much has been done. But much more remains to be explored. For example, public finance considerations could be introduced and theory used to predict their implications. As mentioned above, factors which affect the rental price of capital affect employment and output, and the nature of the tax system affects the rental price of capital. Theory could be used to predict the effect of temporary increases in government expenditures such as those in the early 1950s when defense expenditures increased from less than 5 to more than 13 percent of GNP. Theory of this type could also be used to predict the effect of terms-of-trade shocks. An implication of such an exercise most likely will be that economies with persistent terms-of-trade shocks fluctuate differently than economies with transitory shocks. If so, this prediction can be tested against the observations.

Another interesting extension would be to explicitly model household production. This production often involves two people, with one specializing in market production and the other specializing in household production while having intermittent or part-time market employment. The fact that, cyclically, the employment of secondary wage earners is much more volatile than that of primary wage earners might be explained.

A final example of an interesting and not yet answered question is, how would the behavior of the Hansen indivisible labor economy change if agents did not have access to a technology to insure against random unemployment and instead had to self-insure against unemployment by holding liquid assets? In such an economy, unlike Hansen's, people would not be happy when unemployed. Their gain of more leisure would be more than offset by their loss as an insurer. Answering this question is not straightforward, because new tools for computing equilibria are needed.

SUMMARY AND POLICY IMPLICATIONS

Economic theory implies that, given the nature of the shocks to technology and people's willingness and ability to intertemporally and intratemporally substitute, the economy will display fluctuations like those the US economy displays. Theory predicts fluctuations in output of 5 percent and more from trend, with most of the fluctuation accounted for by variations in employment and virtually all the rest by the stochastic technology parameter. Theory predicts investment will be three or more times as volatile as output and consumption half as volatile. Theory predicts that deviations will display high serial correlation. In other words, theory predicts what is observed. Indeed, if the economy did not display the business cycle phenomena, there would be a puzzle.

The match between theory and observation is excellent, but far from perfect. The key deviation is that the empirical labor elasticity of output is less than predicted by theory. An important part of this deviation could very well disappear if the economic variables were measured more in conformity with theory. That is why I argue that theory is now ahead of business cycle measurement and theory should be used to obtain better measures of the key economic time series. Even with better measurement, there will likely be significant deviations from theory which can direct subsequent theoretical research. This feedback between theory and measurement is the way mature, quantitative sciences advance.

The policy implication of this research is that costly efforts at stabilization are likely to be counterproductive. Economic fluctuations are optimal responses to uncertainty in the rate of technological change. However, this does not imply that the amount of technological change is optimal or invariant to policy. The average rate of technological change varies much both over time within a country and across national economies. What is needed is an understanding of the factors that determine the average rate at which technology advances. Such a theory surely will depend on the institutional arrangements societies adopt. If policies adopted to stabilize the economy reduce the average rate of technological change, then stabilization policy is costly. To summarize, attention should be focused not on fluctuations in output but rather on determinants of the average rate of technological advance.

ACKNOWLEDGEMENTS

This paper was presented at a Carnegie-Rochester Conference on Public Policy and will appear in a volume of the conference proceedings. It appears here with the kind permission of Allan H. Meltzer, editor of that volume. The author thanks Finn E. Kydland for helpful discussions of the issues reviewed here, Gary D. Hansen for data series and some additional results for his growth economy, Lars G. M. Ljungqvist for expert research assistance, Bruce D. Smith and Allan H. Meltzer for comments on a preliminary draft, and the National Science Foundation and the Minneapolis Federal Reserve Bank for financial support. The views expressed herein are those of the author alone.

NOTES

1 Others (e.g. Barro 1981; Long and Plosser 1983) have argued that these fluctuations are not inconsistent with competitive theory that abstracts from monetary factors. Our finding is much stronger, standard theory predicts that the economy will display the business cycle phenomena.
2 See Solow (1970) for a nice summary of the growth observations.
3 Actually, the average interest rate is slightly lower because of risk premia. Given the value of γ and the amount of uncertainty, the average premium is only a fraction of a percent. See Mehra and Prescott (1985) for further details.
4 I use Hansen's (1984) human capital-weighted, household hour series. The capital stock and GNP series are from Citicorp's Citibase data bank.
5 The process $z_{t+1} = .9z_t + \epsilon_{t+1}$ is, like the random walk process, highly persistent. Kydland and I find that it and the random walk result in essentially the same fluctuations.
6 Hotz, *et al.* (1985) use annual panel data to estimate α_0 and η and obtain estimates near the Kydland-Prescott assumed values.
7 Altug (1983) has introduced two types of capital with different gestation periods. Using formal econometric methods, she finds evidence that the model's fit is improved if plant and equipment investment are not aggregated.

REFERENCES

Altug, S. (1983) 'Gestation lags and the business cycle', Working paper, Carnegie-Mellon University.
Ashenfelter, O. (1984) 'Macroeconomic analyses and microeconomic analyses of labor supply', in *Essays on Macroeconomic Implications of Financial and Labor Markets and Political Processes*, K. Brunner and A. H. Meltzer (eds), Carnegie-Rochester Conference Series on Public Policy 21: 117–55, Amsterdam: North-Holland.
Bain, I. R. M. (1985) 'A theory of the cyclical movements of inventory stocks', Ph.D. dissertation, University of Minnesota.
Barro, R. J. (1981) 'Intertemporal substitution and the business cycle', in *Supply Shocks, Incentives and National Wealth*, K. Brunner and A. H. Meltzer (eds), Carnegie-Rochester Conference Series on Public Policy 14: 237–68, Amsterdam: North-Holland.
Benhabib, J. and Nishimura, K. (1985) 'Competitive equilibrium cycles', *Journal of Economic Theory* 35: 284–306.
Bewley, T. F. (1972) 'Existence of equilibria in economies with infinitely many commodities', *Journal of Economic Theory* 4: 514–40.
Blinder, A. S. (1984) 'Can the production smoothing model of inventory behavior be saved', Working paper, Princeton University.
Brock, W. A. and Mirman, L. J. (1972) 'Optimal economic growth and uncertainty: the discounted case', *Journal of Economic Theory* 4: 479–513.
Cass, D. (1965) 'Optimum growth in an aggregative model of capital accumulation', *Review of Economic Studies* 32: 233–40.
Debreu, G. (1954) 'Valuation equilibrium and Pareto optimum', *Proceedings of the National Academy of Science* 70: 558–92.
Eichenbaum, M. S., Hansen, L. P., and Singleton, K. S. (1984) 'A time series analysis of representative agent models of consumption and leisure choice under uncertainty', Working paper, Carnegie-Mellon University.
Friend, I. and Blume, M. E. (1975) 'The demand for risky assets', *American Economic Review* 65: 900–22.

Ghez, G. R. and Becker, G. S. (1975) 'The allocation of time and goods over the life cycle', New York: National Bureau of Economic Research.

Hansen, G. D. (1984) 'Fluctuations in total hours worked: a study using efficiency units', Working paper, University of Minnesota.

——(1985a) 'Indivisible labor and the business cycle', *Journal of Monetary Economics* 16: 309–27.

——(1985b) 'Growth and fluctuations', Working paper, University of California, Santa Barbara.

Hansen, L. P. and Singleton, K. J. (1983) 'Stochastic consumption, risk aversion, and the temporal behavior of asset returns', *Journal of Political Economy* 91: 249–65.

Heckman, J. (1984) 'Comments on the Ashenfelter and Kydland papers', in *Essays on Macroeconomic Implications of Financial and Labor Markets and Political Processes*, K. Brunner and A. H. Meltzer (eds), Carnegie-Rochester Conference Series on Public Policy 21: 209–24, Amsterdam: North-Holland.

Hotz, V. S., Kydland, F. E. and Sedlacek, G. L. (1985) 'Intertemporal preferences and labor supply', Working paper, Carnegie-Mellon University.

Kehoe, P. J. (1984) 'Dynamics of the current account: theoretical and empirical analysis', Working paper, Harvard University.

Koopmans, T. C. (1965) 'On the concept of optimal economic growth', in *The Econometric Approach to Development Planning*, Chicago: Rand-McNally.

Kydland, F. E. (1983) 'Nonseparable utility and labor supply', Working paper, Hoover Institution.

——(1984) 'Labor-force heterogeneity and the business cycle', in *Essays on Macroeconomic Implications of Financial and Labor Markets and Political Processes*, K. Brunner and A. H. Meltzer (eds), Carnegie-Rochester Conference Series on Public Policy 21: 173–208, Amsterdam: North-Holland.

Kydland, F. E. and Prescott, E. C. (1982) 'Time to build and aggregate fluctuations', *Econometrica* 50–70.

——(1984) 'The workweek of capital and labor', Research Department Working Paper 267, Federal Reserve Bank of Minneapolis.

Leamer, E. E. (1983) 'Let's take the con out of econometrics', *American Economic Review* 73: 31–43.

Long, J. B. and Plosser, C. I. (1983) 'Real business cycles', *Journal of Political Economy* 91: 39–69.

Lucas, R. E. Jr (1977) 'Understanding business cycles', in *Stabilization of the Domestic and International Economy*, K. Brunner and A. H. Meltzer (eds), Carnegie-Rochester Conference Series on Public Policy 5: 7–29, Amsterdam: North-Holland.

——(1980) 'Methods and problems in business cycle theory' *Journal of Money, Credit and Banking* 12: 696–715. Reprinted in *Studies in Business-Cycle Theory*, pp. 271–96, Cambridge, MA: MIT Press, 1981.

Lucas, R. E. Jr and Prescott, E. C. (1971) 'Investment under uncertainty', *Econometrica* 39: 659–81.

Marimon, R. (1984) 'General equilibrium and growth under uncertainty: the turnpike property', Discussion Paper 624, Northwestern University, Center for Mathematical Studies in Economics and Management Science.

Mehra, R. and Prescott, E. C. (1985) 'The equity premium: a puzzle', *Journal of Monetary Economics* 15: 145–61.

Rogerson, R. D. (1984) 'Indivisible labor, lotteries and equilibrium', in *Topics in the Theory of Labor Markets*, ch. 1, Ph.D. dissertation, University of Minnesota.

Slutzky, E. (1927) 'The summation of random causes as the source of cyclic processes', in *Problems of Economic Conditions*, ed. Conjuncture Institute. Moskva (Moskow), vol. 3, no. 1, revised English version, 1937, in *Econometrica* 5: 105–46.

Solow, R. M. (1956) 'A contribution to the theory of economic growth', *Quarterly Journal of Economics* 70: 65–94.

—— (1970) *Growth Theory*, Oxford: Oxford University Press.

Swan, T. W. (1956) 'Economic growth and capital accumulation', *Economic Record* 32: 334–61.

Tobin, J. and Dolde W. (1971) 'Wealth, liquidity and consumption', in *Consumer Spending and Monetary Policy: The Linkages*, Monetary Conference Series 5: 99–146, Boston, MA: Federal Reserve Bank of Boston.

16 Some skeptical observations on real business cycle theory

Lawrence H. Summers
Federal Reserve Bank of Minneapolis Quarterly Review (1986) Fall,
pp. 23–7

The increasing ascendancy of real business cycle theories of various stripes, with their common view that the economy is best modeled as a floating Walrasian equilibrium, buffeted by productivity shocks, is indicative of the depths of the divisions separating academic macroeconomists. These theories deny propositions thought self-evident by many academic macroeconomists and all of those involved in forecasting and controlling the economy on a day-to-day basis. They assert that monetary policies have no effect on real activity, that fiscal policies influence the economy only through their incentive effects, and that economic fluctuations are caused entirely by supply rather than demand shocks.

If these theories are correct, they imply that the macroeconomics developed in the wake of the Keynesian Revolution is well confined to the ashbin of history. And they suggest that most of the work of contemporary macroeconomists is worth little more than that of those pursuing astrological science. According to the views espoused by enthusiastic proponents of real business cycle theories, astrology and Keynesian economics are in many ways similar: both lack scientific support, both are premised on the relevance of variables that are in fact irrelevant, both are built on a superstructure of nonoperational and ill-defined concepts, and both are harmless only when they are ineffectual.

The appearance of Ed Prescott's stimulating paper, 'Theory Ahead of Business Cycle Measurement', affords an opportunity to assess the current state of real business cycle theory and to consider its prospects as a foundation for macroeconomic analysis. Prescott's paper is brilliant in highlighting the appeal of real business cycle theories and making clear the assumptions they require. But he does not make much effort at caution in judging the potential of the real business cycle paradigm. He writes that 'if the economy did not display the business cycle phenomena, there would be a puzzle', characterizes without qualification economic fluctuations as 'optimal responses to uncertainty in the rate of technological change', and offers the policy advice that 'costly efforts at stabilization are likely to be counter productive'.

Prescott's interpretation of his title is revealing of his commitment to his theory. He does not interpret the phrase *theory ahead of measurement* to mean that we lack the data or measurements necessary to test his theory. Rather, he means that measurement techniques have not yet progressed to the point where they fully corroborate his theory. Thus, Prescott speaks of the key deviation of observation from theory as follows: 'An important part of this deviation could very well disappear if the economic variables were measured more in conformity with theory. That is why I argue that theory is now ahead of business cycle measurement'.

The claims of real business cycle theorists deserve serious assessment, especially given their source and their increasing influence within the economics profession. Let me follow Prescott in being blunt. My view is that real business cycle models of the type urged on us by Prescott have nothing to do with the business cycle phenomena observed in the United States or other capitalist economies. Nothing in Prescott's papers or those he references is convincing evidence to the contrary.

Before turning to the argument Prescott presents, let me offer one lesson from the history of science. Extremely bad theories can predict remarkably well. Ptolemaic astronomy guided ships and scheduled harvests for two centuries. It provided extremely accurate predictions regarding a host of celestial phenomena. And to those who developed it, the idea that the earth was at the center seemed an absolutely natural starting place for a theory. So, too, Lamarckian biology, with its emphasis on the inheritance of acquired characteristics, successfully predicted much of what was observed in studies of animals and plants. Many theories can approximately mimic any given set of facts; that one theory can does not mean that it is even close to right.

Prescott's argument takes the form of the construction of an artificial economy which mimics many of the properties of actual economies. The close coincidence of his model economy and the actual economy leads him to conclude that the model economy is a reasonable if abstract representation of the actual economy. This claim is bolstered by the argument that the model economy is not constructed to fit cyclical facts but is parameterized on the basis of microeconomic information and the economy's long-run properties. Prescott's argument is unpersuasive at four levels.

ARE THE PARAMETERS RIGHT?

First, Prescott's claim to have parameterized the model on the basis of well-established microeconomic and long-run information is not sustainable. As one example, consider a parameter which Prescott identifies as being important in determining the properties of the model, the share of household time devoted to market activities. He claims that is one-third. Data on its average value over the last century indicate, as Martin Eichenbaum, Lars Hansen, and Kenneth Singleton (1986) have noted, an average value of one-sixth since 1956. This seems right – a little more than half the adult population works, and those who work work about a quarter of the time.

I am unable to find evidence supporting Prescott's one-third figure in the cited book by Gilbert Ghez and Gary Becker (1975). To take another example, Prescott takes the average real interest rate to be 4 percent. Over the 30-year period he studies, it in fact averaged only about 1 percent. This list of model parameters chosen somewhat arbitrarily could be easily extended.

A more fundamental problem lies in Prescott's assumption about the intertemporal elasticity of substitution in labor supply. He cites no direct microeconomic evidence on this parameter, which is central to his model of cyclical fluctuations. Nor does he refer to any aggregate evidence on it. Rather, he relies on a rather selective reading of the evidence on the intertemporal elasticity of substitution in consumption in evaluating the labor supply elasticity. My own reading is that essentially all the available evidence suggests only a minimal response of labor to transitory wage changes. Many studies (including Altonji 1982; Mankiw *et al.* 1985; Eichenbaum *et al.* 1986) suggest that the intertemporal substitution model cannot account at either the micro or the macro level for fluctuations in labor supply.

Prescott is fond of parameterizing models based on long-run information. Japan has since the mid-1950s enjoyed real wage growth at a rate four times the US rate, close to 8 percent. His utility function would predict that such rapid real wage growth would lead to a much lower level of labor supply by the representative consumer. I am not aware that this pattern is observed in the data. Nor am I aware of data suggesting that age/hours profiles are steeper in professions like medicine or law, where salaries rise rapidly with age.

Prescott's growth model is not an inconceivable representation of reality. But to claim that its parameters are securely tied down by growth and micro observations seems to me a gross overstatement. The image of a big loose tent flapping in the wind comes to mind.

WHERE ARE THE SHOCKS?

My second fundamental objection to Prescott's model is the absence of any independent corroborating evidence for the existence of what he calls *technological shocks*. This point is obviously crucial since Prescott treats technological shocks as the only driving force behind cyclical fluctuations. Prescott interprets all movements in measured total factor productivity as being the result of technology shocks or to a small extent measurement error. He provides no discussion of the source or nature of these shocks, nor does he cite any microeconomic evidence for their importance. I suspect that the vast majority of what Prescott labels technology shocks are in fact the observable concomitants of labor hoarding and other behaviour which Prescott does not allow in his model.

Two observations support this judgment. First, it's hard to find direct evidence of the existence of large technological shocks. Consider the oil shocks, certainly the most widely noted and commented on shocks of the postwar period. How much might they have been expected to reduce total factor productivity? In one of the most careful studies of this issue, Ernst Berndt (1980: 85) concludes that 'energy price or quantity variations since 1973 do not appear to have had a significant direct role in the slowdown of aggregate labor productivity in U.S. manufacturing, 1973–77.' This is not to deny that energy shocks have important effects. But they have not accounted for large movements in measured total factor productivity.

Prescott assumes that technological changes are irregular, but is unable to suggest any specific technological shocks which presage the downturns that have actually taken place. A reasonable challenge to his model is to ask how it accounts for the 1982 recession, the most serious downturn of the postwar period. More generally, it seems to me that the finding that measured productivity frequently declines is difficult to account for technologically. What are the sources of technical regress? Between 1973 and 1977, for example, both mining and construction displayed negative rates of productivity growth. For smaller sectors of the economy, negative productivity growth is commonly observed.

A second observation casting doubt on Prescott's assumed driving force is that while technological shocks leading to changes in total factor productivity are hard to find, other explanations are easy to support. Jon Fay and James Medoff (1985) surveyed some 170 firms on their response to downturns in the demand for their output. The questions asked were phrased to make clear that it was exogenous downturns in their output that were being inquired about. Fay and Medoff (1985: 653) summarize their results by stating that 'the evidence indicates that a sizeable portion of the swings in productivity over the business cycle is, in fact, the result of firms' decisions to hold labor in excess of regular production requirements and to hoard labor.' According to their data, the typical plant in the US manufacturing sector paid for 8 percent more bluecollar hours than were needed for regular production work during the trough quarter of its most recent downturn. After taking account of the amount of other worthwhile work that was completed by blue-collar employees during the trough quarter, 4 percent of the blue-collar hours paid for were hoarded. Similar conclusions have been reached in every other examination of microeconomic data on productivity that I am aware of.

In Prescott's model, the central driving force behind cyclical fluctuations is technological shocks. The propagation mechanism is intertemporal substitution in employment. As I have argued so far, there is no independent evidence from any source for either of these phenomena.

WHAT ABOUT PRICES?...

My third fundamental objection to Prescott's argument is that he does price-free economic analysis. Imagine an analyst confronting the market for ketchup. Suppose she or he decided to ignore data on the price of ketchup. This would considerably increase the analyst's freedom in accounting for fluctuations in the quantity of ketchup purchased. Indeed, without looking at the price of ketchup, it would be impossible to distinguish supply shocks from demand shocks. It is difficult to believe that any explanation of fluctuations in ketchup sales that did not confront price data would be taken seriously, at least by hard-headed economists.

Yet Prescott offers us an exercise in price-free economics. While real wages, interest rates, and returns to capital are central variables in his model, he never looks at any data on them except for his misconstrual of the average real interest rate over the postwar period. Others have confronted models like Prescott's to data on prices with what I think can fairly be labeled dismal results. There is simply no evidence to support any of the price effects predicted by the model. Prescott's work does not resolve – or even mention – the empirical reality emphasized by Robert Barro and Robert King (1982) that consumption and leisure move in opposite directions over the business cycle with no apparent procyclicality of real wages. It is finessed by ignoring wage data. Prescott's own work with Rajnish Mehra (1985) indicates that the asset pricing implications of models like the one he considers here are decisively rejected by nearly 100 years of historical experience. I simply do not understand how an economic model can be said to have been tested without price data.

I believe that the preceding arguments demonstrate that real business cycle models of the type surveyed by Prescott do not provide a convincing account of cyclical fluctuations. Even if this strong proposition is not accepted, they suggest that there is room for factors other than productivity shocks as causal elements in cyclical fluctuations.

...AND EXCHANGE FAILURES?

A fourth fundamental objection to Prescott's work is that it ignores the fact that partial breakdowns in the exchange mechanism are almost surely dominant factors in cyclical fluctuations. Consider two examples. Between 1929 and 1933, the gross national product in the United States declined 50 percent, as employment fell sharply. In Europe in the mid-1980s, employment has not risen since 1970 and unemployment has risen more than fivefold in many countries. I submit that it defies credulity to account for movements on this scale by pointing to intertemporal substitution and productivity shocks. All the more given that total factor productivity has increased more than twice as rapidly in Europe as in the United States.

If some other force is responsible for the largest fluctuations that we observe, it seems quixotic methodologically to assume that it plays no role at all in other smaller fluctuations. Whatever mechanisms may have had something to do with the depression of the 1930s in the United States or the depression today in Europe presumably have at least some role in recent American cyclical fluctuations.

What are those mechanisms? We do not yet know. But it seems clear that a central aspect of depressions, and probably economic fluctuations more generally, is a breakdown of the exchange mechanism. Read any account of life during the Great Depression in the United States. Firms had output they wanted to sell. Workers wanted to exchange their labor for it. But the exchanges did not take place. To say the situation was constrained Pareto optimal given the technological decline that took place between 1929 and 1933 is simply absurd, even though total factor productivity did fall. What happened was a failure of the exchange mechanism. This is something that no model, no matter how elaborate, of a long-lived Robinson Crusoe dealing with his changing world is going to confront. A model that embodies exchange is a minimum prerequisite for a serious theory of economic downturns.

The traditional Keynesian approach is to postulate that the exchange mechanism fails because prices are in some sense rigid, so they do not attain market-clearing levels and thereby frustrate exchange. This is far from being a satisfactory story. Most plausible reasons why prices might not change also imply that agents should not continue to act along static demand and supply curves. But it hardly follows that ignoring exchange failures because we do not yet fully understand them is a plausible strategy.

Where should one look for failures of the exchange process? Convincing evidence of the types of mechanisms that can lead to breakdowns of the exchange mechanism comes from analyses of breakdowns in credit markets. These seem to have played a crucial role in each of the postwar recessions. Indeed, while it is hard to account for postwar business cycle history by pointing to technological shocks, the account offered by, for example, Otto Eckstein and Allen Sinai (1986) of how each of the major recessions was caused by a credit crunch in an effort to control inflation seems compelling to me.

CONCLUSION

Even at this late date, economists are much better at analyzing the optimal response of a single economic agent to changing conditions than they are at analyzing the equilibria that will result when diverse agents interact. This unfortunate truth helps to explain why macroeconomics has found the task of controlling, predicting, or even explaining economic fluctuations so difficult. Improvement in the track record of macroeconomics will require the development of theories that can explain why exchange sometimes works well and other times breaks down. Nothing could be more counterproductive in this regard than a lengthy professional detour into the analysis of stochastic Robinson Crusoes.

NOTE

An earlier version of these remarks was presented at the 25 July 1986 meeting of the National Bureau of Economic Research Economic Fluctuations Group.

REFERENCES

Altonji, Joseph G. (1982) 'The intertemporal substitution model of labour market fluctuations: an empirical analysis', *Review of Economic Studies* 49 (special issue): 783–824.

Barro, Robert J. and King, Robert G. (1982) 'Time-separable preferences and intertemporal-substitution models of business cycles', working paper 888, National Bureau of Economic Research.

Berndt, Ernst R. (1980) 'Energy price increases and the productivity slowdown in United States manufacturing', in *The Decline in Productivity Growth*, pp. 60–89, Conference Series 22, Boston, MA: Federal Reserve Bank of Boston.

Eckstein, Otto, and Sinai, Allen (1986) 'The mechanisms of the business cycle in the postwar era', in *The American Business Cycle: Continuity and Change*, ed. Robert J. Gordon, pp. 39–105. National Bureau of Economic Research Studies in Business Cycles, vol. 25, Chicago: University of Chicago Press.

Eichenbaum, Martin S., Hansen, Lars P., and Singleton, Kenneth J. (1986) 'A time series analysis of representative agent models of consumption and leisure choice under uncertainty', working paper 1981, National Bureau of Economic Research.

Fay, Jon A. and Medoff, James L. (1985) 'Labor and output over the business cycle: some direct evidence', *American Economic Review* 75 (September): 638–55.

Ghez, Gilbert R. and Becker, Gary S. (1975) *The Allocation of Time and Goods over the Life Cycle*, New York: National Bureau of Economic Research.

Mankiw, N. Gregory, Rotemberg, Julio J., and Summers, Lawrence H. (1985) 'Intertemporal substitution in macroeconomics', *Quarterly Journal of Economics* 100 (February): 225–51.

Mehra, Rajnish, and Prescott, Edward C. (1985) 'The equity premium: a puzzle', *Journal of Monetary Economics* 15 (March): 145–61.

17 Understanding real business cycles

Charles I. Plosser
Journal of Economic Perspectives (1989) 3, Summer, pp. 51–77

The 1960s were a time of great optimism for macroeconomists. Many economists viewed the business cycle as dead. The Keynesian model was the reigning paradigm and it provided all the necessary instructions for manipulating the levers of monetary and fiscal policy to control aggregate demand. Inflation occurred if aggregate demand was stimulated 'excessively' and unemployment arose if demand was 'insufficient'. The only dilemma faced by policymakers was determining the most desirable location along this inflation–unemployment tradeoff or Phillips curve. The remaining intellectual challenge was to establish coherent microeconomic foundations for the aggregate behavioral relations posited by the Keynesian framework, but this was broadly regarded as a detail that should not deter policymakers in their efforts to 'stabilize' the economy.

The return of the business cycle in the 1970s after almost a decade of economic expansion, and the accompanying high rates of inflation, came as a rude awakening for many economists. It became increasingly apparent that the basic Keynesian framework was not the appropriate vehicle for understanding what happens during a business cycle nor did it seem capable of providing the empirically correct answers to questions involving changes in the economic environment or changes in monetary or fiscal policy. The view that Keynesian economics was an empirical success even if it lacked sound theoretical foundations could no longer be taken seriously.

The essential flaw in the Keynesian interpretation of macroeconomic phenomenon was the absence of a consistent foundation based on the choice theoretic framework of microeconomics. Two important papers, one by Milton Friedman (1968) and the other by Robert Lucas (1976), forcefully demonstrated examples of this flaw in critical aspects of the Keynesian reasoning and set the stage for modern macroeconomics.

A central feature of the Keynesian system of the 1960s was the tradeoff between inflation and some measure of real output or unemployment. Friedman argued that basic microeconomic principles demanded that this long-run Phillips curve must be vertical. That is, general microeconomic principles implied that individuals (firms) maximizing their utility (profit) resulted in real demand (and supply) curves that are homogeneous of degree zero in nominal prices and money income. Thus sustained inflation was compatible with any level of real demand (or supply) of goods. A central Keynesian tenet was therefore in stark conflict with microeconomic principles.[1]

Lucas reinforced this point by arguing that microeconomic foundations frequently implied that the sorts of behavioral relations exploited by the Keynesian model builders were incapable of correctly evaluating changes in economic policy. Lucas's specific examples stressed that expectations about future policy will systematically influence current decisions and thus alter the behavioral relations exploited by empirical implementations of the Keynesian analysis. Moreover, Lucas argued, expectations could not be formulated or specified in an arbitrary manner and be consistent with individual maximization, but should be viewed as rational in the sense of Muth (1961).

The absence of an underlying choice theoretic framework also plagued the dynamic elements of Keynesian models. Business cycles have long been characterized in terms of how they evolve over time. In particular, discussions regarding how shocks to the economic system were propagated across time and across sectors in the economy were a central theme of Mitchell (1927) and other early students of the business cycle such as von Hayek (1932). The foundations of the Keynesian model, however, were static and focused on determining output at a point in time, while treating the capital stock as given. Dynamic elements were introduced through accelerator mechanisms (investment and inventories) and later in the form of price or wage adjustment equations and partial adjustment models of one form or another. These dynamic specifications, however, did not arise from any choice theoretic framework of maximization, but were simply behavioral rules that characterized either agents or, more frequently, markets in general. One economist's behavioral formulation for dynamic adjustment was as good as any other, and it was simply an empirical question which one seemed to fit the data best.

These problems are fundamental. They suggest that the underpinnings of our understanding of economic fluctuations are likely to be found somewhere other than a suitably modified version of the Keynesian model. Indeed, there is a growing body of research in macroeconomics that begins with the idea that in order to understand business cycles, it is important and necessary to understand the characteristics of a perfectly working dynamic economic system.[2] Hicks (1933: 32) makes this point quite clearly, arguing that the 'idealized state of dynamic equilibrium...give(s) us a way of assessing the extent or degree of disequilibrium.' In 1939, Hicks set out the basic elements and tools for determining the character of the 'idealized state' in more detail in *Value and Capital*. Progress towards understanding this idealized state is essential because it is logically impossible to attribute an important portion of fluctuations to market failure without an understanding of the sorts of fluctuations that would be observed in the absence of the hypothesized market failure. Keynesian models started out asserting market failures (like unexplained and unexploited gains from trade) and thus could offer no such understanding. Fortunately, since the late 1970s, economists have developed the analytical tools to follow through with the Hicks program.[3] The basic approach is to build on the earlier work in growth theory to construct small-scale dynamic general equilibrium models and attempt to understand how aggregate economic variables behave in response to changes in the economic environment, like changes in technology, tastes, or government policies.

Real business cycle models take the first necessary steps in evaluating and understanding Hicks' 'idealized state of dynamic equilibrium'. Consequently, these models must be at the core of any understanding economists will provide of business cycles. This brief chapter is intended to provide readers with an introduction to the real business cycle approach to business fluctuations.

THE BASIC REAL BUSINESS CYCLE FRAMEWORK

Real business cycle models view aggregate economic variables as the outcomes of the decisions made by many individual agents acting to maximize their utility subject to production possibilities and resource constraints. As such, the models have an explicit and firm foundation in microeconomics. More explicitly, real business cycle models ask the question: how do rational maximizing individuals respond over time to changes in the economic environment and what implications do those responses have for the equilibrium outcomes of aggregate variables?

To address these questions, it is necessary to specify the economic environment and how it evolves through time. It also requires specifying the criteria that economic agents use in choosing appropriate patterns of such variables as consumption, investment and work effort. It is important in developing a model of this sort to recognize that business cycles are fundamentally phenomena that are characterized by their behavior through time. For example, when we think of business cycles, we frequently think about notions of persistence or serial correlation in economic aggregates; comovement among economic activities; leading or lagging variables relative to output; and different amplitudes or volatilities of various series. The objective of any model of the business cycle is to generate a coherent understanding of how and why these characteristics arise. Thus a model of fluctuations must be dynamic at its most basic level and not a collection of anecdotal behavioral rules attached to an otherwise static framework.

The neoclassical model of capital accumulation

The most basic model of economic dynamics is the neoclassical model of capital accumulation. While many readers may be familiar with some versions of this framework as a model of optimal economic growth – following the work of Cass (1965), Koopmans (1965) and Solow (1956) – it is better viewed as framework for economic dynamics (see Hicks 1965: 4). As such it is natural to consider it as the benchmark model for our understanding of economic fluctuations as well as growth.[4] What is somewhat remarkable is that the implications for fluctuations of this neoclassical approach have not been seriously explored until recently.[5]

A simple economic environment to consider is an economy populated by many identical agents (households) that live forever. The utility of each agent is some function of the consumption and leisure they expect to enjoy over their (infinite) lifetimes. Each agent is also treated as having access to a constant returns to scale production technology for the single commodity in this economy. The production function requires both capital, which depreciates over time, and work effort. In addition, the production technology is assumed to be subject to temporary productivity shifts or technological changes which provide the underlying source of variation in the economic environment to which agents must respond. For simplicity, assume that these shifts, past and future, are known with certainty to all agents and thus agents have perfect foresight. The choices each consumer must make are how to allocate their hours between work and leisure, and how to allocate their supply of the single good between investment in future capital and current consumption. Of course, the model imposes resource constraints such that the sum of consumption and investment is less than or equal to output and the sum of time spent working and at leisure is less than or equal to some fixed amount of time in the period. Consumption, labor, leisure, capital and investment must also be nonnegative. The Appendix presents a mathematical summary of such a model.

This model is clearly simple and unrealistic, but for present purposes that is an advantage. After all, the model is not intended to capture a complex reality, but, at this point, only to provide a benchmark of the features of a dynamic market equilibrium. It is a purely real model, driven by technology or productivity disturbances and hence, following Long and Plosser (1983), it has been labeled a *real business cycle model*. But despite this model's simplicity, the equilibrium behavior of the model exhibits many important characteristics that are generally associated with business cycles.

Equilibrium outcomes

How does one think about the competitive equilibrium prices and quantities that are implied by this framework? The first step is to recognize that all individuals are alike, thus it is easy to imagine a representative agent, Robinson Crusoe, and ask how his optimal choices of consumption, work effort and investment evolve over time. Do these optimally chosen quantities correspond to the per capita quantities that would be produced by a competitive equilibrium involving many agents interacting in the markets for current and future goods and labor? The answer to this question is

400 Charles I. Plosser

provided to us by Debreu (1954) and Prescott and Lucas (1972) in the affirmative. In other words, we can interpret the utility maximizing choices of consumption, investment and work effort by Robinson Crusoe as the per capita outcomes of a competitive market economy.

Robinson Crusoe's choice problem is to maximize his lifetime utility subject to the production technology and a sequence of resource constraints, a problem that can be viewed in the familiar framework of constrained optimization. (See the Appendix for more detail.) Given specific functional forms for the utility function and the production function, some initial conditions and the sequence of productivity disturbances, one could, in principle, derive a set of decision rules that describe Robinson's optimal consumption, work, and investment decisions in terms of the current (predetermined) capital stock and the past *and* future productivity disturbances. These decisions, in turn, imply an amount of total output via the production function. The optimal quantities also imply market prices for labor (a real wage) and one-period loans (a real interest rate). Another important characteristic of these models is that in the absence of productivity disturbances, Robinson Crusoe's optimal choice of consumption, work effort, investment, and thus output will, under a broad set of conditions, converge to constant or steady state values.

Under most specifications of preferences and production functions, it is impossible to solve analytically this maximization problem for the optimal decision rules of Robinson Crusoe. Consequently, real business cycle researchers find it necessary to compute approximate solutions to Robinson Crusoe's choice problem in the neighborhood of the steady state. The approximate decision rules are linear functions of the predetermined capital stock and all productivity disturbances. The details of the procedures available to compute the approximately optimal quantities and competitive prices from this framework are beyond the scope of this chapter but the economic intuition underlying the resulting optimal decisions is relatively straightforward.[6]

Responses to productivity disturbances

Imagine Crusoe observes a temporarily high value of productivity. How will he respond? One option would be for him to consume the above normal output holding investment and work effort fixed. This is clearly a feasible outcome, but one that says shocks are totally absorbed within a period and thus have no implications for future decisions or outcomes. A moment's reflection, however, suggests that Crusoe values future consumption and leisure in addition to current consumption and, opportunities/technology permitting, would prefer to consume more output in the future as well as today. This intertemporal transfer can be accomplished in this setting because the production function permits Crusoe to invest in capital that will help produce output in subsequent periods. Thus investment should respond positively to the temporary shock. The effect on work effort is ambiguous. Current productivity is temporarily high which encourages intertemporal substitution of current for future work and intertemporal substitution of current consumption for leisure. Wealth, on the other hand, is higher and that acts to reduce current and future work effort. For plausible parameterizations of the model the substitution effect dominates so that current work effort rises. Thus the temporary shock is propagated forward and the effects of the shock show up in higher output, consumption and leisure in the future. This simple intuition illustrates why variables like output and consumption are likely to be serially correlated *even when shocks to the environment are uncorrelated and purely temporary.*

If the productivity shock observed by Robinson Crusoe is more long-lived or persistent, then his responses would be different. For example, a more persistent increase in productivity would tend to raise wealth more significantly by raising future output. Robinson Crusoe's incentive to increase investment would plausibly be reduced and his incentive to increase current consumption would be increased. There would also be less incentive to work harder today because the wealth effect is stronger and the intertemporal substitution effect is reduced. Quantitative results require a more specific formulation.[7]

Thus, a productivity disturbance results in a dynamic response by Robinson Crusoe that involves variations in output, work effort, consumption and investment over many periods. It is important to stress that there are no market failures in this economy, so Robinson Crusoe's response to the productivity shifts are optimal and the economy is Pareto efficient at all points in time. Put another way, any attempt by a social planner to force Crusoe to choose any allocation other than the ones indicated, such as working more than he currently chooses, or saving more than he currently chooses, are likely to be welfare reducing. Therefore, business cycle characteristics exhibited by this economy are chosen in preference to outcomes that exhibit no business cycles.

The decision rules summarize the solution to Robinson Crusoe's dynamic optimization problem. As stated above they depend explicitly on the current *and* future productivity disturbances. In richer models that include government (see below), these decision rules would also depend on current and future actions of the government. Consequently, these rules provide the basis for evaluating policy in a manner that is not subject to the criticism Lucas (1976) levied on models that possess simple behavioral relations among current and past economic variables that are assumed to be invariant with respect to changes in the actions of government.

Supply or demand

It is common to refer to these real business cycle models as models that are driven by aggregate 'supply shocks'.[8] While such a description seems approximately accurate for the model driven by productivity shifts, and thus innocuous enough, it is potentially misleading. In the first place trying to think about these dynamic general equilibrium models in terms of supply and demand is slippery. In these models shocks occur to either preferences, technologies/opportunities, or resources and endowments. Unfortunately, these shocks do not easily translate into either supply or demand disturbances. Each type of shock will generally affect both the supply and demand schedules in a particular market. For example, shifts in technology influence both the supply of goods for a given level of inputs (work effort in particular), and the demand for goods through its effect on wealth and the labor/leisure decision.

Second, while most of the analyses to date have focused on the version of the model where variations in technology are the source of changes in the environment, one could just as easily specify the changes as arising from variations in preferences or tastes. This would lead to a real business cycle model driven by what some would label as 'demand shocks'. In addition, the model can be expanded to include a government sector (discussed further below) that could also be considered a source of 'demand shocks'.[9] Thus there is nothing inherent in the real business model that limits it to the analysis of variations in technology or supply.

Stochastic models and uncertainty

The discussion, at several points, has noted the explicit dependence of Robinson Crusoe's decisions on the future path of productivity. It is natural to ask if the framework can be adapted to handle uncertainty, where the productivity disturbance is a random variable whose future values are uncertain. The answer to this question is yes and is based on the seminal work of Brock and Mirman (1972). As in the certainty case discussed above, however, analytical solutions for the decision rules under uncertainty are rare.[10] It has been common practice to rely on what is called certainty equivalence. This procedure takes the linear decision rules obtained as the approximate solution to the certainty model and replaces the future productivity disturbances with their conditional expected value given information available at time t.[11] The resulting set of time paths for consumption, work effort and capital are then a linear rational expectations equilibrium rather than a perfect foresight equilibrium.

ECONOMIC GROWTH AND BUSINESS CYCLES

The neoclassical model of capital accumulation outlined in the previous section predicts that per capita values of output, capital and consumption will, in the absence of disturbances to productivity, converge to constants or steady state values. The evidence, however, is that per capita values in the United States and most other industrialized countries grow continually over time. For example, from 1954 to 1985, per capita real GNP grew at an average annual rate of about 1.5 percent. The basic neoclassical model does not offer an explanation of this sustained growth in per capita values.

In a classic paper, Robert Solow (1957) argued that technical change, in addition to the capital per worker, was an important source of variation in output per capita.[12] Solow constructed estimates of US technological change using data from 1909 to 1949. He concluded that productivity grew at an average rate of 1.5 percent per year during the period. Output per capita, on the other hand, grew at an average annual rate of 1.7 percent. Solow then argued that these productivity changes were empirically uncorrelated with changes in capital per worker. He concluded that about 85 percent of the real per capita growth during this period was accounted for by technological change or productivity and only about 15 percent by increases in capital per worker. Thus, based on Solow's evidence, one would conclude that changes in productivity and technology are the major factors determining economic growth.

While technological progress has been recognized as an important factor determining economic growth, at least since Solow's seminal work, it has been common to think of economic growth as something that can be studied independently of economic fluctuations. Or to put the point another way, it is often presumed that the factors that influence growth have only second order implications for economic fluctuations. In fact the use of the phrase 'growth theory' was an intentional attempt to distinguish it from a theory of the business cycle. As stressed by Hicks (1965: 4), however, there is no compelling economic rationale underlying this view.

> The distinction between trend and fluctuation is a statistical distinction; it is an unquestionably useful device for statistical summarizing. Since economic theory is to be applied to statistics, which are arranged in this manner, a corresponding arrangement of theory will (no doubt) often be convenient. But this gives us no reason to suppose that there is anything corresponding to it on the economic side which is at all fundamental. We have no right to conclude, from the mere existence of the statistical device, that the economic forces making for trend and for fluctuation are any different, so that they have to be analyzed in different ways. It is inadvisable to start our economics from the statistical distinction, though it will have to come in at an appropriate point, as an instrument of application.

Nevertheless, it has been common to think of business cycle models as separate from models of economic growth and to characterize business cycles as the deviations from some smooth, usually deterministic, trend that proxies for growth. Theories of the business cycle are then constructed to explain these deviations. Thus, while rarely explicitly recognized, tests of these business cycle theories are actually joint tests of the model for growth (the trend) and the model for the cycle.

Nelson and Plosser (1982) argue that real per capita output, as well as many other economic time series, behave as if they have random walk components (much like the log of stock prices). Random walks have the important property that there is no tendency for the process to return to any particular level or trend line once displaced. Thus, unpredicted shocks to productivity permanently alter the level of productivity. Nelson and Plosser also argue that Solow's technology series also behaves like a random walk.

The observation that the log of productivity follows a random walk with drift (drift meaning the changes have a non-zero mean) has some important implications. First, a random walk is a nonstationary stochastic process, which means that it possesses no affinity for any particular mean. Random walks are also referred to as stochastic trends because while they may exhibit growth, they do not fluctuate about any particular deterministic path. If shocks to productivity are permanent, each one determines a new growth path. Therefore, detrending economic time series with a deterministic time trend and then assuming that the deviations from the trend will exhibit some tendency to return to the trend line would be econometrically incorrect and may be quite misleading.[13]

Second, the fact that productivity grows over time raises some additional complications for the neoclassical model described in the previous section. In particular, if productivity is growing then output, consumption and capital per capita will also tend to grow over time. If, for example, output and consumption grew at different rates, in the long run, then the consumption/output ratio would be driven to zero or one. To prevent this, it is usually required that these per capita values converge to constant, but equal growth rates, so that the model possesses steady state growth. In addition, work effort cannot grow in the steady state because available hours are bounded from above and below. For these restrictions to be satisfied additional requirements must be placed on the form of the production process and utility function. Of particular importance is the requirement that permanent technological progress must be expressible as labor augmenting or Harrod-neutral.[14]

Third, King *et al.* (1988b) and King *et al.* (1987) show that the neoclassical model with random walk technological progress implies that output, consumption and investment per capita will all contain a common random walk component or stochastic trend. This structure is consistent with the empirical observations of Nelson and Plosser discussed above. In addition, King *et al.* (1987) investigate the common stochastic trend implication for output, consumption and investment and conclude that it provides a reasonable representation of the data. As noted above, hours worked per capita will not contain a stochastic growth component since the number of available hours per time period is in fixed supply.

If these labor augmenting productivity shifts can be characterized as the engine of economic growth, what does the simple neoclassical model of optimal capital accumulation predict about the response of output, consumption, investment, work effort and wages to these technological shifts? The permanent change in productivity sets in motion a series of dynamic responses that move Robinson Crusoe and the economy towards a new growth path. For example, 1 percent permanent (once and for all) change in labor productivity in the long run leads to a one percent permanent increase in the level of capital stock, consumption, output and investment once the transitory dynamics have been dissipated. These transitory dynamics are important for understanding fluctuations. They are initiated by the requirement that the economy must move to a permanently higher capital stock. To get there requires substantial increases in investment in the near term that taper off to a new higher steady state level as the economy converges to the higher capital stock. There will also be gradual increases in consumption and output towards their respective higher steady state levels. Work effort will also be temporarily high along the transition path. While wealth has increased, which discourages current work effort, productivity is also higher which encourages work effort. Productivity is higher because the desired or steady capital stock has risen. Thus in the near term real interest rates rise, which induces intertemporal substitution of current for future work effort. The responses, and thus the fluctuations that are present in the model, are the result of the same factors that generate economic growth. The real business cycle model, therefore, provides an integrated approach to the theory of growth and fluctuations.

REAL BUSINESS CYCLES AND THE 1954–85 US ECONOMY

The simple neoclassical model described earlier is clearly an incomplete model of the US economy. Nevertheless, useful insights into the properties of the model can be obtained by providing a more quantitative assessment of the model's explanatory power. The strategy is to choose explicit functional forms for Robinson Crusoe's utility function and production function and then to compute the approximate equilibrium behavior of output, consumption, investment, work effort and wages implied by the model when the technology shifts are computed following Solow. These predicted series can then be compared to the actual performance of the US economy.

The first step is to specify explicit functions for the production technology and preferences. A natural choice for the production function that also satisfies the restrictions necessary for steady state growth is the Cobb-Douglas formulation. There is some latitude in the choice of Robinson Crusoe's preferences. King *et al.* (1988a) derive the class of admissible preference functions if the economy is to possess steady state growth. One admissible utility function is logarithmic preferences. Based on these specifications of preferences and technology and the random walk properties of the technology shifts, approximate optimal decisions of Robinson Crusoe can be obtained and used to calculate how he will respond to the Solow technology shifts.[15]

Summary statistics for the US economy

Table 17.1 highlights some of the statistical properties of postwar business fluctuations. The period begins in 1954 in order to avoid potential complications raised by the very high levels of government spending during the Korean War. Output Y is real nonfarm business product per capita and hours N is the average fraction of the week spent working by nongovernment employees per capita. The remaining empirical counterparts to the variables in the model are: consumption, C, the sum of real consumption of nondurables and services per capita; investment, I, the sum of real nonresidential fixed investment and real consumption of consumer durables; and the real wage rate, w, the real average hourly earnings of all production workers.

There are, of course, a number of ways of summarizing these types of data. I have chosen the typical practice of using sample moments to describe the central characteristics. Growth rates are chosen because the model predicts that log levels will possess stochastic trends (or random walk components) so that population moments do not exist. While virtually all empirical investigations of business cycles start by detrending the data, the real business cycle model I have described here integrates growth and fluctuations and provides the detrending instructions to obtain variables that possess well-defined distributions.

The moments presented in Table 17.1 are the sample means, standard deviations, serial correlation (autocorrelation) coefficients and correlations with output. The mean growth rate of output and consumption is about

Table 17.1 Summary statistics 1954–85

Variable	Mean	Standard deviation	Autocorrelation[a] ρ_1	ρ_2	ρ_3	Correlation with output	Correlation with actual
			Panel A: Actual				
$\Delta\log(Y)$	1.55	2.71	0.13	−0.17	−0.16	1.00	1.00
$\Delta\log(C)$	1.56	1.27	0.39	0.08	0.05	0.78	1.00
$\Delta\log(I)$	2.59	6.09	0.14	−0.28	−0.19	0.92	1.00
$\Delta\log(N)$	−0.09	2.18	0.17	−0.32	−0.24	0.81	1.00
$\Delta\log(w)$	0.98	1.80	0.44	−0.16	−0.08	0.59	1.00
			Panel B: Predicted				
$\Delta\log(Y)$	1.56	2.48	0.30	0.18	0.14	1.00	0.87
$\Delta\log(C)$	1.65	1.68	0.55	0.44	0.37	0.96	0.76
$\Delta\log(I)$	1.37	4.65	0.14	0.00	−0.02	0.97	0.72
$\Delta\log(N)$	−0.08	0.89	0.07	−0.09	−0.12	0.87	0.52
$\Delta\log(w)$	1.64	1.76	0.51	0.40	0.33	0.97	0.65

*Note:*a The approximate standard error of the estimated autocorrelations is 0.18

1.5 percent per year. Wage growth is less and investment growth is somewhat more. Hours, on the other hand, exhibit no growth at all and actually fall by about 0.1 percent per year. Standard deviations provide information on the relative volatility of the different series. Investment growth is the most volatile followed by output, hours, wages and consumption respectively. Autocorrelations measure the amount of persistence of the series from one year to the next. For example, the correlation coefficient between the growth in consumption in one year is about 0.4 with the previous year's growth in consumption. Only real wages and consumption show much evidence of persistence in growth rates. Finally, all the series are highly correlated with output and thus are procyclical. The lowest correlation with output is exhibited by real wage growth with a correlation coefficient of 0.59 and the highest is investment with a correlation coefficient of 0.92.

Productivity shifts

In order to see more quantitatively the sorts of real economic fluctuations generated by the simple model economy it is necessary to obtain some measure of the productivity shocks. A crude but straightforward method is to follow the example provided by Solow to construct a measure of the state of productivity. Using the data described above and the gross stock of real nonresidential fixed private capital, a Solow technology series is readily constructed.[16] The annual percentage rate of change in technology is plotted in Figure 17.1. The picture corresponds to most observers' impressions that productivity growth was on average higher in the 1960s than the 1970s and 1980s. The growth rate of this 32 year period averages 0.8 percent per year and has a standard deviation of about 1.9 percent. The maximum growth rate is about 4.0 percent and the minimum is about –3.5 percent.

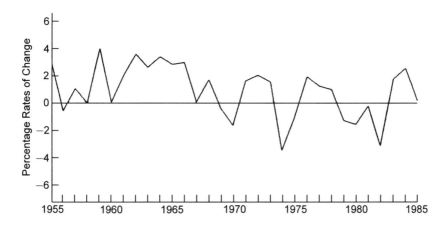

Figure 17.1 Annual growth rate of technology

There is only slight evidence of serial correlation in these growth rates so to a first approximation it seems acceptable to view the level of productivity as a random walk.

These computed productivity disturbances may or may not be very good estimates of the true changes in productivity. However, the real business cycle model delivers explicit and tight restrictions on the behavior of consumption, hours worked, investment, and thus output, conditioned on the disturbances to the model being of a technological source. If the measured technological shocks are poor estimates (that is, if they are confounded by other factors such as 'demand' shocks, preference shocks or change in government policies, and so on) then feeding these values into our real business cycle model should result in poor predictions for the behavior of consumption, investment, hours worked, wages and output.

Real business cycles

Given the form of preferences and technology, the model is used to obtain the responses of the simple neoclassical model to observed productivity shifts.[17] These results are summarized in Panel B of Table 17.1. The model produces sample means that are very close to the data for output, consumption and hours, but is too low for investment and too high for wages. The model generates the same volatility rankings for Y, C, I, but the absolute standard deviation of investment is slightly lower and that for consumption is slightly higher than in the actual data. The major discrepancy appears to be that in the model the growth rate of hours has a standard deviation that is less than one-half of that in the data. In terms of serial correlation properties, the model generates slightly, but perhaps not significantly, more positive autocorrelation than seems present in the data.

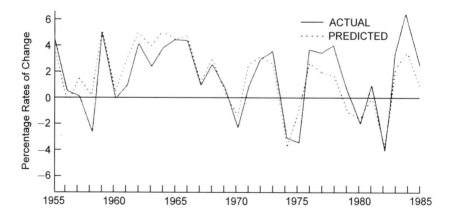

Figure 17.2 Annual growth rate of real output

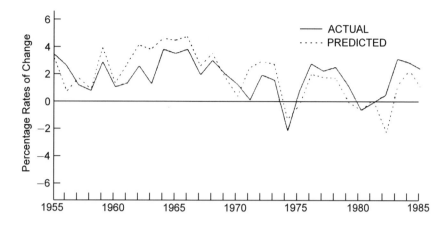

Figure 17.3 Annual growth rate of real consumption

Perhaps the numbers of most interest in the table are those in the last column of Panel B. These are the correlation coefficients of the predicted outcomes with the actual series and range from 0.52 for wages to 0.87 for output. To many economists, the whole idea that such a simple model with no government, no money, no market failures of any kind, rational expectations, no adjustment costs and identical agents could replicate actual experience this well is very surprising. This is especially true given that most macroeconomic research since the late 1930s stressed the importance of one or more of the above factors in explaining business fluctuations.

Figures 17.2 to 17.6 provide a visual impression of these correlations by plotting both the actual and predicted growth rates of each of the five

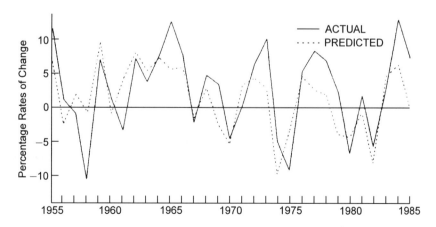

Figure 17.4 Annual growth rate of real investment

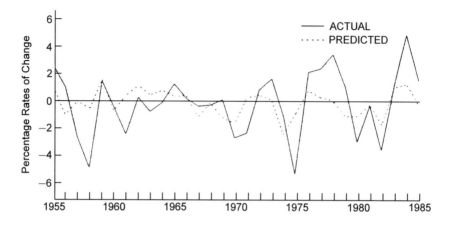

Figure 17.5 Annual growth rate of hours worked

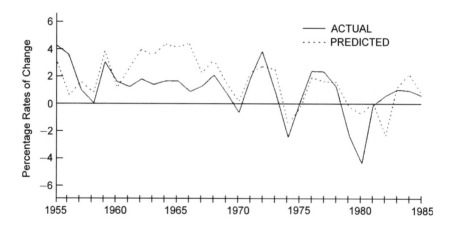

Figure 17.6 Annual growth rate of real wage rate

variables. As expected from the evidence presented in Table 17.1, the growth rate of hours worked exhibits the biggest discrepancy between actual and predicted. Nevertheless, the simple model appears to replicate a significant portion of the behavior of the economy during recessions as well as other periods.

GOVERNMENT POLICIES AND SUBOPTIMAL EQUILIBRIUM

Two key features of the real business cycle model discussed so far are that business cycles are initiated by shocks to technology and that fluctuations are Pareto optimal. Neither of these conditions, however, are necessary features of the real business cycle approach. Many economists, for example, argue that government tax and spending policies are an important source of real disturbances to the economic system. The incorporation of government into the real business cycle models makes it possible to address important questions regarding changes in fiscal policies in the presence of distortionary taxes. Of particular interest is the case where the tax and spending policies are functions of the state of the economy. Variation in government spending introduces a potential source of demand disturbances to the model. The presence of distortionary taxes generally breaks the link between Robinson Crusoe's optimal decisions and Pareto efficiency, since removing the distortions will usually raise welfare. Nevertheless, competitive equilibria can be computed and analyzed that are not Pareto optimal but suboptimal equilibria.

The theoretical underpinning of this line of research draws from earlier work by Arrow (1962), Hall (1971) and Brock (1975) and a series of papers by Romer (1983, 1986, 1987). The basic line of reasoning is that in an economy with many agents, each can take the government's spending and taxing policies as given in their choice problem. The only additional restriction is that aggregate behavior satisfy the government's budget constraint. These models provide an artificial laboratory for answering questions regarding policy changes that is not subject to the criticism of Lucas (1976).

The intuition underlying the effects of unproductive (as assumed in most Keynesian analyses) government purchases in the neoclassical model is basically found in Barro (1981) and Hall (1980).[18] These authors emphasize two sorts of influences. First, raising government purchases induces a negative wealth effect that acts to reduce consumption and raise work effort and output. Second, raising government purchases also induces intertemporal substitution when the increase is temporary. This results in lower consumption, lower investment, higher work effort and higher output. The relative importance of the wealth and intertemporal substitution channels remains unresolved. Barro and Hall assume that the intertemporal substitution channel is quantitatively more important so that temporary changes in government purchases are more important than the wealth channel. Baxter and King (1988) have investigated these effects within a real business cycle model and have concluded that for plausible values of the parameters more persistent changes in government purchases have larger output 'multipliers' than more temporary changes in purchases. Temporary purchases on the other hand, have a more negative impact on investment than more persistent purchases.[19]

The implications of distortionary taxation within the neoclassical model have been a topic in public finance for some time. What distinguishes the more recent work from the earlier efforts, including Hall (1971) and analyses by Abel and Blanchard (1983) and Judd (1985) is that tax rates are assumed to be functions of the state of the economy. King *et al.* (1988b) summarize the implications of a real business cycle model under a period-by-period balanced budget, where tax revenue is based on an output tax and government spending is rebated as lump-sum transfers. In this case a positive productivity shift requires a decline in the tax rate in order to maintain budget balance. This reduction in tax rates reinforces the efforts of the productivity shock on after-tax labor productivity and further increases work effort in response to technology shocks. Thus work effort (and investment, for analogous reasons) are more volatile in this economy.

THE REAL BUSINESS CYCLE RESEARCH AGENDA

The results in the previous sections indicate that the basic neoclassical model of capital accumulation can provide an important framework for developing our understanding of economic fluctuations. The models invest-igated to date, however, are not entirely satisfactory. Indeed, it would be extraordinary if they were. The real business cycle research program is to pursue this class of models to determine how far the approach can take us. In this section, I highlight some of the issues that are likely to be important for developing and evaluating this important class of models.

Multi-sector extensions

The basic neoclassical model has been explored along various dimensions in an effort to expand the scope of the method of analysis. Long and Plosser (1983) explore a model with multiple sectors in order to understand the comovement across sectors in response to shocks that are potentially sector specific. Their interest in multiple sectors is motivated by the observation that many sectors of the economy tend to move together but some sectors lead while other sectors lag the general state of business activity. Multi-sector models are the only way to address this phenomenon and understand it since one-sector models proceed by assuming that the answer is the existence of aggregate or common shocks.[20]

Black (1987) argues that multi-sector models are important, particularly if unemployment is to be explained. Black bases his argument on the notion that both human and physical capital is highly specialized. Shocks to either preferences or technologies will generally require resources in the form of labor and capital to move between sectors. Since these inputs are special-ized, it will be costly to make this adjustment. As a result, unemployment can be expected to rise above its long-run level.

Labor markets

A major thrust of much research in the real business cycle area is to expand and extend the basic model in ways that would result in a better match of the model's predictions for hours and actual hours worked. The source of conflict is that the logarithmic preferences adopted for the purpose of the earlier estimates imply a labor supply elasticity that is much higher than the estimates obtained by labor economists using panel data on prime age males. Thus, the model appears to be incapable of generating sufficient volatility in hours without being in conflict with evidence from detailed microeconomic investigations. This view, however, is unduly pessimistic. Numerous approaches have been pursued (though none has been completely satisfactory to date) that attempt to modify the model in ways that make it compatible with the microeconomic evidence.

One approach pursued by Kydland and Prescott (1982) stresses the importance of preference structures that are not time separable. In their formulation, the current utility of leisure depends on past leisure in an explicit way. This has the effect of permitting an increase in the intertemporal substitutability of leisure which in turn makes hours worked more volatile.

Rogerson (1988) and Hansen (1985) explore the consequences of indivisibilities in the labor supply decision that require agents to work either fulltime or not at all. This is in contrast to the simple model where agents are permitted to vary hours worked continuously. The result is that the volatility of hours worked in response to productivity shifts is significantly increased while estimated labor supply elasticities would remain low for working males.

Another approach to enhancing the response hours worked in the model is to allow for heterogeneity across agents in the economy. Examples of this approach are found in Cho and Rogerson (1988), Kydland (1984), King *et al.* (1988b) and Rebelo (1987). All of these papers suggest that there can be important downward biases in estimates of aggregate labor supply elasticity when there are agents with different skill levels.

Endogenous growth

Another important area for research focuses on the role played by the technology shocks. Solow's view of technological change included anything that shifted the production function other than measurable capital or labor. As an empirical proposition, Solow's results indicate that such shifts, if viewed as exogenous, account for a substantial portion of economic growth. The real business cycle model stresses that these shifts play an important role in economic fluctuations as well. This is not entirely satisfactory. It would be useful if we had a better understanding of the economics of growth that did not rely as heavily on such an exogenous unobservable process.

Work by Uzawa (1965), Romer (1986) and Lucas (1988) modifies the basic neoclassical model to permit growth to be an endogenous outcome of the technology. The key to obtaining such a result is eliminating the diminishing returns in the production process. King and Rebelo (1986, 1988) provide examples of this strategy and explore its implications for economic fluctuations and certain types of fiscal policies. The idea is to permit human capital (labor-augmenting technical change) to be produced using physical capital and human capital as inputs to a constant returns technology. The results are interesting and potentially important. For example, purely temporary productivity shifts can have permanent effects on the level of economic activity. The reason is that a change in productivity that results in more output will generally result in some increased resources being allocated to the production of additional human capital. Thus allocation decisions affect the level of technology and the growth in the economy. These models have the additional implication that such variables as output, consumption and investment are integrated or possess a stochastic trend. This result is appealing because as noted above, Nelson and Plosser (1982) have argued that many economic time series appear to possess stochastic trends or random walk components. Finally, productivity shocks in these models can initiate complex patterns of adjustment to a new growth path. These transition paths generally include complex changes in work effort, investment and consumption. An understanding of these models is likely to be an important part of understanding economic fluctuations, as well as economic development, while reinforcing the concept that growth and fluctuations are intimately connected.

Money

Real business cycle research has focused almost exclusively on models with no role for money. For some economists, this not only doesn't represent progress, but also borders on blasphemy. My view, and that of many other real business cycle researchers, is that the role of money in an equilibrium theory of growth and fluctuations is not well understood and thus remains an open issue. Some researchers, including King and Plosser (1984), Kydland (1987), Eichenbaum and Singleton (1986) and Cooley and Hansen (1988), have explored methods of incorporating money and investigating its implications in a real business cycle model. Unfortunately there is little agreement on what constitutes the most fruitful approach at this time. Nevertheless, without an understanding of the real fluctuations inherent in the basic neoclassical model without money it will be difficult if not impossible to measure the quantitative importance of money in actual business fluctuations. The nature and magnitude, however, of the fluctuations and responses in the real neoclassical model means that real business research poses a challenge to conventional views regarding the relative importance of money. This is particularly true given the difficulties economists have faced in developing a convincing and coherent explanation of the monetary transmission mechanism.

Strategies for estimation and hypothesis testing

A final part of the research agenda relates to empirical assessments of the real business cycle approach. The approach adopted to date takes as given the technological shocks and asks how other variables – such as consumption, work effort and investment – respond over time to these impulses. It would be useful to obtain an independent measure of these shocks or identify observable variables that could proxy for them. Expanding the models to include government, endogenous growth or international trade are important steps in this process.

A closely related topic, and one of intense debate among researchers, is the strategy used to investigate the implications of the model. The traditional way of estimating and testing an economic model is to write down a set of structural equations, estimate the parameters and test any restrictions not necessary to identify parameters. In the context of the real business cycle models described earlier this strategy corresponds to obtaining Robinson Crusoe's optimal decision rules for consumption, work effort and investment, jointly estimating the parameters of technology and preferences and then testing the overidentifying restrictions imposed on these decision rules.[21]

An alternative strategy has been pursued in much of the real business cycle literature. The technique, made popular in this literature by Kydland and Prescott (1982) (but more widely employed in the applied general equilibrium literature like Ballard *et al.* 1985), is called 'calibration'. The strategy is to choose values for certain key parameters of the underlying preferences and technologies using evidence from other empirical studies. This restricts the number of free parameters in the model. Using these parameter values, the stochastic properties (means, variances, autocorrelations and cross-correlations) of certain key variables are constructed. The remaining free parameters are chosen to yield, as closely as possible, a correspondence between the moments predicted by the model and those in the sample data. A formal definition of what constitutes a good fit or the metric along which fit should be judged is not explicitly offered by Kydland and Prescott.[22]

The appropriate empirical strategy for investigating the class of models discussed in this chapter remains an open area of research. Ultimately, this issue must be addressed and real business cycle models will have to face and pass more stringent empirical tests than they have to date.

CONCLUSIONS

The basic framework of real business cycle analysis is the neoclassical model of capital accumulation. This is the natural starting point to begin the study of dynamic fluctuations. While frequently interpreted as a model of economic growth, the neoclassical model generates fluctuations in response to external disturbances that resemble business cycles. While real technology shocks have occupied the central focus in the literature, other shocks arising from preferences, government, terms of trade and eventually money can be included. Thus real business cycle models do not have to be confined to analyzing only technological or productivity shocks. Nevertheless, these real technological disturbances generate rich and neglected dynamics in the basic neoclassical model that appear to account for a substantial portion of observed fluctuations.

Real business cycle theory is still in its infancy and thus remains an incomplete theory of the business cycle. Yet the progress to date has had a significant impact on research in macroeconomics. In particular, simple real business cycle models have demonstrated that equilibrium models are not necessarily inconsistent with many characteristics attributed to the business cycle. In so doing these models have changed the standard by which macroeconomic theories are judged and provided the foundations for an understanding of business cycles that is based on the powerful choice theoretic analysis that is at the core of economic reasoning. The appeal of this line of research is the apparent power of some very simple economic principles to generate dynamic behavior that was heretofore thought to be incompatible with any notion of equilibrium. While the promise is great, much work remains before economists have a real understanding of business cycles.

APPENDIX: SPECIFYING A MODEL OF REAL BUSINESS CYCLES

This appendix presents a more analytical summary of the basic neoclassical model discussed in the second section of the chapter. The first step is to specify the economic environment by describing the preferences, technology and endowments of the model economy.

The neoclassical model

Preferences

The economy is assumed to be populated by many identical agents (households) that live forever.[23] The agents's utility at time t is assumed to be of the form $U_t = \sum_{s=0}^{\infty} \beta_u^{t+s} u(C_{t+s}, L_{t+s})$, where C_t is the level of consumption of the single produced good and L_t is the amount of leisure consumed. The utility discount factor is assumed to be constant. Leisure is included because variation in work effort is an important feature of short-run fluctuations and yet is frequently absent from otherwise similar models encountered in the growth literature. The momentary utility function $u(\cdot)$ is assumed to be concave and twice continuously differentiable.

Production

The single final good, Y_t, is produced by a constant returns to scale production technology given by $Y_t = \Theta_t F(K_t, N_t)$, where K_t is the predetermined capital stock (chosen at $t - 1$) and N_t is labor input in period t. Θ_t is a temporary shift factor that alters total factor productivity. The produced commodity Y can either be consumed or invested. The production function is also assumed to be concave and twice continuously differentiable.

Capital accumulation

The invested commodity becomes part of the capital stock that is available on input to production next period. This capital stock evolves as $K_{t+1} = (1 - \delta)K_t + I_t$, where I_t is gross investment and δ is the depreciation rate of capital.

Resource constraints

Agents also face resource constraints in each period on the use of the commodity and time. These constraints are $L_t + N_t \leq 1$ and $C_t + I_t \leq Y_t$, where the time endowment is normalized to unity. These are non-negativity constraints L_t, C_t, N_t and K_t as well.

The computation of the competitive equilibrium prices and quantities that are implied by this framework is simplified by recognizing that all individuals are alike. Thus, it is easy to imagine a representative agent, Robinson Crusoe, and determine how his optimal choice of consumption, work effort and investment evolve over time. Debreu (1954) and Prescott and Lucas (1972) have shown that we can interpret the utility maximizing choices of consumption, investment and work effort by Robinson Crusoe as the per capita outcomes of a competitive market economy.

Robinson Crusoe's choice problem is to maximize his lifetime (infinite) utility subject to a sequence of resource constraints. The Lagrangian associated with the maximization problem is

$$\mathcal{L} = \sum_{t=0}^{\infty} \beta^t [u(C_t, 1 - N_t)] + \sum_{t=0}^{\infty} \lambda_t [\Theta_t F(K_t, N_t) - C_t - K_{t+1} + (1 - \delta)K_t]$$

where $1 - N_t$ is substituted for L_t, $K_{t+1} - (1 - \delta)K_t$ is substituted for I_t, $\Theta_t F(K_t, N_t)$ is substituted for Y_t, and λ_t is the Lagrange multiplier associated with the period t resource constraint $Y_t - C_t - I_t = 0$.

The first-order efficiency conditions for this problem are obtained by differentiating $\mathcal{L}$ with respect to the variables of choice at each time t, C_t, N_t, K_{t+1} and the multiplier, which yields

$$u_1(C_t, 1 - N_t) - \lambda_t = 0$$
$$u_2(C_t, 1 - N_t) - \lambda_t \Theta_t F_2(K_t, N_t) = 0$$
$$\beta \lambda_{t+1} [\Theta_{t+1} F_1(K_{t+1}, N_{t+1}) + (1 - \delta)] - \lambda_t = 0$$
$$\Theta_t F(K_t, N_t) + (1 - \delta)K_t - K_{t+1} - C_t = 0$$

which must hold for all $t = 1, 2, \ldots \infty$. $F_i(\cdot)$ and $u_i(\cdot)$ denote the partial derivatives of F and u with respect to the ith argument. In addition, it is common to assume that the transversality condition, $\lim_{t \to \infty} \beta^t \lambda_t K_{t+1} = 0$, is satisfied.

Given specific functional forms for $u(\cdot)$ and $F(\cdot)$ the solution to this maximum problem is the time paths of the four unknown choice variables, C, N, K and λ that satisfy these efficiency conditions for some initial condition K_0 and a sequence of productivity disturbances $\{\Theta_s\}_{s=0}^{\infty}$.[24] These time paths can be expressed in the form of time invariant decision rules that take the form

$$C_t = C(K_t, \{\Theta_{t+s}\}_{s=0}^{\infty}),$$
$$N_t = N(K_t, \{\Theta_{t+s}\}_{s+0}^{\infty}),$$
$$K_{t+1} = K(K_t, \{\Theta_{t+s}\}_{s=0}^{\infty}).$$

The competitive market prices implied by these optimal quantities are a real interest rate between t and $t+1$, r_t, and a real wage rate, w. These are readily determined to be $(1+r_t) = \lambda_t/(\lambda_{t+1}\beta)$ and $w_t = \Theta_t F_2(K_t, N_t)$ and are the ones that would prevail in the spot market for labor services and a one-period sequential loan market.[25] Another important feature of this economy is that in the absence of changes in technology (i.e. $\Theta_t = 0$, for all t), and given some initial capital stock, per capita values of consumption, hours, capital and output, converge to constants, referred to as the steady state.

Approximate solutions

Under most specifications of preferences and production functions, the four first-order conditions given earlier constitute a set of nonlinear difference equations. Thus it is usually impossible to solve this maximum problem analytically for the optimal decisions rules of Robinson Crusoe. Consequently, real business cycle researchers find it necessary to compute approximate solutions to Robinson Crusoe's choice problem. These approximation procedures typically result in decision rules that are linear K_t and the Θ's. The details of various procedures available to compute these approximately optimal quantities and competitive prices are beyond the scope of this chapter. Nevertheless, the basic idea pursued in King *et al.* (1988a) is intuitively straightforward and is the method employed in the text.[26]

The first step in the approximation procedure is to choose a point to approximate around. The natural choice is the stationary point or steady state, denoted $[C_s, K_s, N_s, \lambda_s]$. The second step is to express the four first-order conditions in terms of the percentage deviations from the stationary values (defined as $\hat{C}, \hat{K}, \hat{N}$, etc.) and then take a linear approximation to each condition. This results in a set of linear difference equations in percentage deviations from the steady state.

Solving this linear system produces the approximately optimal decision rules that correspond to the three time-invariant decision rules.[27] These decision rules are linear functions of the predetermined capital stock and the sequence of productivity shifts. For example, efficient capital accumulation can be written as

$$\hat{K}_{t+1} = \mu_1 \hat{K}_t + \Psi_1 \hat{\Theta}_t + \Psi_2 \sum_{j=0}^{\infty} \mu_2^{-j} \hat{\Theta}_{t+j+1},$$

where μ_1, μ_2, Ψ_1 and Ψ_2 are complicated functions of the underlying parameters of tastes and technology. Thus next period's capital stock depends on the current capital stock, the current level of productivity $\hat{\Theta}_t$ and the entire future path of shifts discounted by μ_2. The conditions on the problem pretty much guarantee that $\mu_1 < 1$ and $\mu_2 > 1$. The (approximately) optimal decision rules for $\hat{C}_t$ and $\hat{N}_t$ take similar forms.[28]

An example economy

In the text a specific example economy is used to quantitatively measure the responses of a real business cycle model to estimated productivity shifts. As indicated in the text preferences are taken to be logarithmic such that $u(C_t, L_t) = \log(C_t) + \eta_L \log(L_t)$. The production technology is taken to be Cobb-Douglas $Y_t = \Theta_t K_t^{1-\alpha} N_t^\alpha$, or, expressing the technology shift Θ_t as labor-augmenting $Y_t = K_t^{1-\alpha}(\Theta_t^{1/\alpha} N_t)^\alpha$. The technology shifts are computed following Solow and are assumed to follow a logarithmic random walk for purposes of computing the approximate optimal decisions.

The remaining parameters are chosen assuming the time interval is one year and correspond to those used in King *et al.* (1988a, 1988b). Labor's share ($\alpha = 0.58$) is computed as the average ratio of total employee compensation to GNP for the period 1948–85. Depreciation ($\delta = 0.10$) is simply assumed to be 10 percent per annum. The utility discount factor ($\beta = 0.95$) is chosen to yield a return to capital of 6.5 percent per annum, which is the average real return to equity from 1948 to 1981. Finally, the utility parameter η_L is chosen indirectly by specifying that steady state hours work is 0.20 which is based on the average fraction of hours devoted to market work during the 1948–85 period.

ACKNOWLEDGEMENTS

The author has benefited from the comments and suggestions of Marianne Baxter, Fischer Black, Karl Brunner, Thomas Cooley, Robert King, Sergio Rebelo, Carl Shapiro, Joseph Stiglitz and Timothy Taylor. The Bradley Policy Research Center at the W.E. Simon Graduate School of Business Administration provided financial support.

NOTES

1 This interpretation of Friedman's discussion follows Lucas (1977).
2 This view is explicit in the research program initiated by Long and Plosser (1983: 68).

3 Lucas (1980) presents an elegant and clear statement of the importance of our analytical tools in improving our understanding of economic phenomena.

4 Some readers will notice that I have substituted the phrase 'economic fluctuations' for 'business cycle'. I will use these terms interchangeably. My own preference is to use the term 'fluctuations' since 'business cycle' frequently carries the connotation that there is true periodicity present in economic activity. Virtually all of modern macroeconomics dismisses the view that there are actual periodic cycles in economic activity. Instead it follows the important work of Slutsky (1937) and interprets the ups and downs in economic activity as the accumulation of random events or a stochastic process.

5 While the growth theory literature of the 1960s is replete with discussions of dynamic behavior of the models studied, little effort was made to relate this behavior to the characteristics of economies associated with the business cycle. For example, labor supply did not play a particularly important role in the growth theory literature yet it is central to any theory attempting to address the phenomenon of business cycles.

6 See King *et al.* (1988a) or Kydland and Prescott (1982) for further discussion and examples of different methods. The Appendix summarizes the approach followed by the former authors.

7 The economic intuition of how Robinson Crusoe responds to productivity shifts is also discussed in Long and Plosser (1983) and can now be found in intermediate macroeconomic textbooks (e.g. Barro 1987).

8 It is sometimes suggested that evidence of important shifts in 'aggregate demand' is *prima facie* evidence against real business cycle models. As will be argued, this is incorrect and takes an extraordinarily narrow view of this class of models.

9 Abel and Blanchard (1983) illustrate that under certain conditions that government spending shocks can be modelled as negative technology shocks. This further illustrates the potential difficulties of labelling technology shocks as supply or demand.

10 Long and Plosser (1983) provide an example. Unfortunately, their example possesses some special features that limit its usefulness for business cycle research. In particular, they require 100 percent depreciation to obtain the analytical solution. This results in hours worked being invariant to variations in productivity. As suggested by Long and Plosser and demonstrated by King *et al.* (1988a), this result does not hold when the assumption of 100 percent depreciation is relaxed.

11 Increases in computing power are making it possible to move beyond certainty equivalence methods and linear decision rules by computing the equilibrium numerically. For an example see Greenwood *et al.* (1988).

12 Solow suggested a simple way of measuring technological change. Consider any constant returns to scale production function with neutral technological change such as given by $Y_t = \Theta_t F(K_t, N_t)$, where Y_t is output at time t, K is the capital input, N is the labor input and Θ_t measures productivity shifts over time. Solow shows that if labor is paid its marginal product then the percentage change in productivity or technology can be computed as $\Delta \theta_t = \Delta y_t - \Delta k_t -w_l (\Delta n_t - \Delta k_t)$ where lower case letters denote logarithms, Δ denotes first differencing (i.e. $\Delta \theta_t = \theta_t - \theta_{t-1}$) and ω_l is the relative share of the total output going to labor (i.e. $\omega_l = wN/Y$ where w is the real wage rate). Thus, using observable data on y, k, n and an estimate of ω_l estimates of technical change can be computed.

13 There is a large literature on this issue. In addition to Nelson and Plosser (1982), see Nelson and Kang (1981), Campbell and Mankiw (1987) and Stock and Watson (1988).

14 See, for example, Uzawa (1961), Swan (1963) or Phelps (1966).

15 The actual functional forms and parameter values employed in this exercise are given in the Appendix.

16 All data are taken from the CITIBASE data service except the capital stock, which is taken from the August 1986 issue of *Survey of Current Business*. An estimate of labor's share of output is also required (see note 12).

17 The responses are computed using the stochastic version of the model that assumes productivity shifts are known to follow a random walk. Future value of the shifts are not known to the agents in the economy but they form rational expectations of these shifts based on their known stochastic structure.

18 In this discussion government purchases are assumed to be financed by lump-sum taxes or reductions in transfer payments. In this case increase in government purchases can be viewed as negative shocks to production that enter additively. See Abel and Blanchard (1983).

19 Another quantitative example can be found in Wynne (1988), who uses a real business cycle model that includes government purchases to account for the behavior of the US economy during World War II.

20 Baxter (1988) presents a quantitative analysis of a two sector model in the context of an international real trade model.

21 See, for example, Altug (1985) and Christiano (1988).

22 The traditional econometric approach and calibration are not mutually exclusive, however. Singleton (1988) discusses how the calibration approach of Kydland and Prescott might be formulated in the context of the generalized method of moments procedure proposed by Hansen (1982).

23 The use of an infinitely lived agent can also be interpreted as an finite-lived agent with an operative bequest motive that links the current generation's utility with future generations'. See Barro (1974) or Miller and Upton (1974).

24 If these disturbances are known, the equilibrium prices and quantities are a perfect foresight equilibrium. If $\{\Theta_s\}$ is a stochastic process, Robinson Crusoe forms expectations about the future values using all currently available information. In this case the equilibrium is a rational expectations equilibrium.

25 This is but one of the market structures that would support the optimal allocations as a competitive equilibrium. An alternative market structure in the labor market might be that agents are paid a wage rate that corresponds to the annuitized rate based on the present value of their entire future stream of marginal products.

26 For an alternative strategy, see Kydland and Prescott (1982).

27 Solving this system also requires imposing the transversality condition. See King *et al.* (1988a) for more details of this solution technique. Several authors including Christiano (1989) and Rebelo and Rouwenhorst (1989) have studied the accuracy of these linear approximations.

28 Generalizing this approach to handle the case of stochastic variation in productivity is not difficult. The method of certainty equivalence amounts to positing a specific stochastic structure for the $\hat{\Theta}$'s and substituting their conditional expectations for the future values.

REFERENCES

Abel, Andrew B. and Olivier J. Blanchard, 'An Intertemporal Model of Savings and Investment', *Econometrica* May 1983, *51*, 675–92.

Altug, S., 'Gestation Lags and the Business Cycle: An Empirical Investigation', unpublished manuscript, University of Minnesota, 1985.

Arrow, Kenneth, 'The Economic Implications of Learning by Doing', *Review of Economic Studies* June 1962, *29*, 155–73.

Ballard, Charles L., John B. Shoven, and John Whalley, 'General Equilibrium Computations on the Marginal Welfare Costs of Taxes in the United States', *American Economic Review* March 1985, *75*, 128–38.

Barro, Robert J., 'Are Government Bonds Net Wealth?', *Journal of Political Economy* November–December 1974, *82*, 1095–117.

Barro, Robert J., 'Output Effects of Government Purchases', *Journal of Political Economy* December 1981, *89*, 1086–1125.

Barro, Robert J., *Macroeconomics*, New York: John Wiley, 1987.

Baxter, Marianne, 'Dynamic Real Trade Model: New Directions for Open Economy Macroeconomics', Rochester Center for Economic Research, University of Rochester, working paper 167, 1988.

Baxter, Marianne, and Robert G. King, 'Multipliers in Equilibrium Business Cycle Models', unpublished manuscript, University of Rochester, 1988.

Black, F., *Business Cycles and Equilibrium*, New York: Basil Blackwell, 1987.

Brock, William A., 'A Simple Perfect Foresight Monetary Model', *Journal of Monetary Economics* April 1975, *1*, 133–150.

Brock, William A. and Leonard J. Mirman, 'Optimal Economic Growth and Uncertainty: The Discounted Case', *Journal of Economic Theory* June 1972, *4*, 479–513.

Campbell, John, and N. Gregory Mankiw, 'Are Output Fluctuations Transitory?', *Quarterly Journal of Economics* 1987, *102*, 857–80.

Cass, David, 'Optimum Growth in an Aggregative Model of Capital Accumulation', *Econometrica* July 1965, *32*, 223–40.

Cho, F. and Richard D. Rogerson, 'Family Labor Supply and Aggregate Fluctuations', *Journal of Monetary Economics* 1988, *21*, 233–45.

Christiano, L., 'Why Does Inventory Investment Fluctuate So Much?', *Journal of Monetary Economics* 1988, *21*, 247–80.

Christiano, L., 'Solving a Particular Growth Model by Linear Approximation and by Value Function Iteration', Federal Reserve Bank of Minnesota, Discussion Paper 9, 1989.

Cooley, Thomas F. and G. Hansen, 'The Inflation Tax and the Business Cycle', Rochester Center for Economic Research, University of Rochester, working paper 155, 1988.

Debreu, Gerard, 'Valuation Equilibrium and Pareto Optimum', *Proceedings of the National Academy of Sciences of the U.S.*, 1954, *38*, 886–93.

Eichenbaum, Martin, and Kenneth J. Singleton, 'Do Equilibrium Business Cycle Theories Explain Post-war Business Cycles?', in S. Fischer (ed.) *NBER Macroeconomics Annual*, 1986, 91–134.

Friedman, Milton, 'The Role of Monetary Policy', *American Economic Review* March 1968, *58*, 1–17.

Greenwood, J., Z. Hercowitz, and Gregory W. Huffman, 'Investment, Capacity Utilization and the Real Business Cycle', *American Economic Review* June 1988, *78*, 402–17.

Hall, Robert E., 'The Dynamic Effects of Fiscal Policy in an Economy with Foresight', *Review of Economic Studies* April 1971, *38*, 229–44.

Hall, Robert E., 'Labor Supply and Aggregate Fluctuations', in *Carnegie-Rochester Series on Public Policy, 12*, Amsterdam: North Holland, 1980.

Hansen, G., 'Indivisible Labor and the Business Cycle', *Journal of Monetary Economics* 1985, *16*, 309–27.

Hansen, Lars, 'Large Sample Properties of Generalized Method of Moment Estimators', *Econometrica* July 1982, *50*, 1029–54.

Hicks, John, 'Equilibrium and the Cycle', reprinted in John Hicks, *Collected Essay on Economic Theory, Vol. II, Money, Interest and Wages*, Oxford: Basil Blackwell, 1933.

Hicks, John, *Value and Capital*, London: Oxford University Press, 1939.

Hicks, John, *Capital and Growth*, New York: Oxford University Press, 1965.

Judd, Kenneth, 'Short Run Analysis of Fiscal Policy in a Simple Perfect Foresight Model', *Journal of Political Economy* April 1985, *93*, 298–319.

King, Robert G. and Charles Plosser, 'Money, Credit and Prices in a Real Business Cycle,' *American Economic Review* June 1984, *74*, 363–380.

King, Robert G. and Sergio Rebelo, 'Business Cycles with Endogenous Growth', unpublished manuscript, University of Rochester, 1986.

King, Robert G. and Sergio Rebelo, 'Public Policy and Economic Growth', unpublished working paper, University of Rochester, 1988.

King, Robert G., Charles Plosser, James Stock, and Mark Watson, 'Stochastic Trends and Economic Fluctuations', Rochester Center for Economic Research, working paper 79, 1987.

King, Robert G., Charles Plosser, and Sergio Rebelo, 'Production, Growth and Business Cycles I. The Basic Neoclassical Model', *Journal of Monetary Economics* 1988a, *21*, 195–232.

King, Robert G., Charles Plosser, and Sergio Rebelo, 'Production, Growth and Business Cycles II. New Directions', *Journal of Monetary Economics* 1988b, *21*, 309–341.

Koopmans, T., 'On the Concept of Optimal Growth,' in *The Econometric Approach to Development Planning*, Chicago: Rand McNally, 1965.

Kydland, Finn E., 'Labor Force Heterogeneity and the Business Cycle', in *Carnegie-Rochester Conference Series on Public Policy* 1984, *21*, 173–208.

Kydland, Finn E., 'The Role of Money in a Real Business Cycle Model,' unpublished manuscript, Carnegie-Mellon University, 1987.

Kydland, Finn E., and Edward C. Prescott, 'Time to Build and Aggregate Fluctuations', *Econometrica* November 1982, *50*, 1345–70.

Long, John B. and Charles Plosser, 'Real Business Cycles', *Journal of Political Economy* February 1983, *91*, 1345–1370.

Long, John B. and Charles Plosser, 'Sectoral vs. Aggregate Shocks in the Business Cycle', *American Economic Review* 1987, *77*, 333–337.

Lucas, Robert E., 'Econometric Policy Evaluation: A Critique', in *Carnegie-Rochester Conference Series on Public Policy* 1976, *1*, 19–46.

Lucas, Robert E., 'Understanding Business Cycles', in *Carnegie-Rochester Series on Public Policy* 1977, *5*, 7–29.

Lucas, Robert E., 'Methods and Problems in Business Cycle Theory', *Journal of Money, Credit and Banking* November 1980, *12*, 696–715.

Lucas, Robert E., 'On the Mechanics of Economic Development', *Journal of Monetary Economics* 1988, *22*, 3–42.

Miller, Merton H. and Charles W. Upton, *Macroeconomics: A Neoclassical Introduction*, Homewood, IL: Irwin, 1974.

Mitchell, W., *Business Cycles: The Problem and its Setting*, New York: National Bureau of Economic Research, 1927.

Muth, Richard F., 'Rational Expectations and the Theory of Price Movements', *Econometrica* 1961, *29*, 315–35.

Nelson, Charles R. and H. Kang, 'Spurious Periodicity in Inappropriately Detrended Time Series', *Econometrica* 1981, *49*, 741–51.

Nelson, Charles R. and Charles Plosser, 'Trends and Random Walks in Macroeconomic Time Series: Some Evidence and Implications', *Journal of Monetary Economics* September 1982, *10*, 139–67.

Phelps, Edmund S., *Golden Rules of Economic Growth*, New York: Norton, 1966.

Prescott, Edward C., 'Theory Ahead of Business Cycle Measurement', in *Carnegie-Rochester Series on Public Policy* 1986, *25*, 11–66.

Prescott, Edward C. and Robert E. Lucas, 'A Note on Price Systems in Infinite Dimensional Space', *International Economics Review* June 1972, *13*, 416–22.

Rebelo, Sergio, 'Tractable Heterogeneity and Near Steady State Dynamics', unpublished manuscript, University of Rochester, 1987.

Rebelo, Sergio, and G. Rouwenhorst, 'Linear Quadratic Approximations Versus Discrete State Space Methods: A Numerical Evaluation', unpublished working paper, University of Rochester, 1989.

Rogerson, Richard D., 'Indivisible Labor, Lotteries and Equilibrium', *Journal of Monetary Economics* 1988, *21*, 3–16.

Romer, Paul, 'Dynamic Competitive Equilibria with Externalities, Increasing Returns and Unbounded Growth', doctoral dissertation, University of Chicago, 1983.

Romer, Paul, 'Increasing Returns and Long Run Growth', *Journal of Political Economy* 1986, *94*, 1002–73.

Romer, Paul, 'Increasing Returns, Specialization, and External Economies: Growth as described by Allyn Young', Rochester Center for Economic Research, working paper 19, 1987.

Singleton, Kenneth J., 'Econometric Issues in the Analysis of Equilibrium Business Cycle Models', *Journal of Monetary Economics* 1988, *21*, 361–86.

Slutsky, E., 'The Summation of Random Causes as the Source of Cyclical Processes', *Econometrica* 1937, *5*, 105–46.

Solow, Robert, 'A Contribution to the Theory of Economic Growth', *Quarterly Journal of Economics* February 1956, *70*, 65–94.

Solow, Robert, 'Technical Change and the Aggregate Production Function', *Review of Economic Studies* August 1957, *39*, 312–20.

Stock, James H. and Mark H. Watson, 'Variable Trends in Economic Time Series', *Journal of Economic Perspectives* Summer 1988, *2*, 147–74.

Survey of Current Business, United States Department of Commerce/Bureau of Economic Analysis, August 1986.

Swan, T., 'On Golden Ages and Production Functions', in D. Berril (ed.), *Economic Development with Special References to Southeast Asia*, London: Macmillan, 1963.

Uzawa, Hirofumi, 'Neutral Inventions and the Stability of Growth Equilibrium', *Review of Economic Studies* February 1961, *28*, 118–24.

Uzawa, Hirofumi, 'Optimal Technical Change in an Aggregative Model of Economic Growth', *International Economic Review* January 1965, *6*, 18–31.

von Hayek, Friederich August, *Prices and Production*, London: George Routledge & Sons, 1932.

Wynne, Mark A., 'The Aggregate Effects of Temporary Government Purchases', unpublished manuscript, University of Rochester, 1988.

18 Real business cycles

A new Keynesian perspective

N. Gregory Mankiw
Journal of Economic Perspectives (1989) 3, Summer, pp. 79–90

The debate over the source and propagation of economic fluctuations rages as fiercely in the late 1980s as it did in the late 1930s in the aftermath of Keynes's *The General Theory* and in the midst of the Great Depression. Today, as then, there are two schools of thought. The classical school emphasizes the optimization of private economic actors, the adjustment of relative prices to equate supply and demand, and the efficiency of unfettered markets. The Keynesian school believes that understanding economic fluctuations requires not just studying the intricacies of general equilibrium, but also appreciating the possibility of market failure on a grand scale.

Real business cycle theory is the latest incarnation of the classical view of economic fluctuations. It assumes that there are large random fluctuations in the rate of technological change. In response to these fluctuations, individuals rationally alter their levels of labor supply and consumption. The business cycle is, according to this theory, the natural and efficient response of the economy to changes in the available production technology.

My goal in this chapter is to appraise this newly revived approach to the business cycle. I should admit in advance that I am not an advocate. In my view, real business cycle theory does not provide an empirically plausible explanation of economic fluctuations. Both its reliance on large technological disturbances as the primary source of economic fluctuations and its reliance on the intertemporal substitution of leisure to explain changes in employment are fundamental weaknesses. Moreover, to the extent that it trivializes the social cost of observed fluctuations, real business cycle theory is potentially dangerous. The danger is that those who advise policy-makers might attempt to use it to evaluate the effects of alternative macroeconomic policies or to conclude that macroeconomic policies are unnecessary.

WALRASIAN EQUILIBRIUM AND THE CLASSICAL DICHOTOMY

The typical undergraduate course in microeconomics begins with partial equilibrium analysis of individual markets. A market for a good is characterized by a downward sloping demand curve and an upward sloping supply curve. The price of the good is assumed to adjust until the quantity supplied equals the quantity demanded.

The course then builds up to Walrasian general equilibrium. In this Walrasian equilibrium, prices adjust to equate supply and demand in every market simultaneously. The general equilibrium system determines the quantities of all goods and services sold and their relative prices. The most important theoretical result, after the existence of such a Walrasian equilibrium, is the 'invisible hand' theorem: the equilibrium is Pareto efficient.

Courses in microeconomics thus show how employment, production, and relative prices are determined without any mention of the existence of money, the medium of exchange. The simplest way to append money to the model is to specify a money demand function and an exogenous money supply. Money demand depends on the level of output and the price level. The level of output is already determined in the Walrasian system. The price level, however, can adjust to equate supply and demand in the money market.

Introducing money in this way leads to the classical dichotomy (Patinkin 1956). Real variables, such as employment, output, and relative prices, including the real interest rate, are determined by the Walrasian system. Nominal variables, such as the price level, the nominal wage, and the nominal interest rate, are then determined by the equilibrium in the money market. Of course, since nominal variables do not affect real variables, the money market is not very important. This classical view of the economy suggests that, for most policy discussions, the money market can be ignored.

The professor of macroeconomics must in some way deal with the classical dichotomy. Given the assumptions of Walrasian equilibrium, money is largely irrelevant. The macroeconomist must either destroy this classical dichotomy or learn to live with it.

Keynesian macroeconomics destroys the classical dichotomy by abandoning the assumption that wages and prices adjust instantly to clear markets. This approach is motivated by the observation that many nominal wages are fixed by long-term labor contracts and many product prices remain unchanged for long periods of time. Once the inflexibility of wages and prices is admitted into a macroeconomic model, the classical dichotomy and the irrelevance of money quickly disappear.

Much of the early work in the new classical revolution of the 1970s attempted to destroy the classical dichotomy without abandoning the fundamental axiom of continuous market clearing (Lucas 1972; 1973). These models were based on the assumption that individuals have imperfect information regarding prices. These individuals therefore confuse movements in the overall price level (which under the classical dichotomy should not matter) with movements in relative prices (which should matter). An unanticipated decrease in the money supply leads individuals to infer that the relative prices of the goods they produce are temporarily low, which induces them to reduce the quantity supplied. While the fascination with this sort of story was substantial in the 1970s, it has attracted relatively few adherents in the 1980s. It is hard to believe that confusion about the price level is sufficiently great to generate the large changes in quantities observed over the business cycle.

In contrast to both the Keynesian and the early new classical approaches to the business cycle, real business cycle theory embraces the classical dichotomy. It accepts the complete irrelevance of monetary policy, thereby denying a tenet accepted by almost all macroeconomists in the late 1970s. Nominal variables, such as the money supply and the price level, are assumed to have no role in explaining fluctuations in real variables, such as output and employment.

Real business cycle theory thus pushes the Walrasian model farther than it has been pushed before. In evaluating whether it provides a successful explanation of recessions and booms, two questions naturally arise. First, why are there such large fluctuations in output and employment? Second, why do movements in nominal variables, such as the money supply, appear related to movements in real variables, such as output?

CLASSICAL AND KEYNESIAN VIEWS OF ECONOMIC FLUCTUATIONS

The only forces that can cause economic fluctuations, according to real business cycle theory, are those forces that change the Walrasian equilibrium. The Walrasian equilibrium is simply the set of quantities and relative prices that simultaneously equate supply and demand in all markets in the economy. To understand how real business cycle theory explains the business cycle, it is necessary to look into the fundamental forces that change the supplies and demands for various goods and services.

Many sorts of macroeconomic disturbances can in principle generate fluctuations in real business cycle models. For example, changes in the level of government purchases or in the investment tax credit alter the demand for goods and therefore affect the Walrasian equilibrium. Changes in the relative price of oil alter the equilibrium allocation of labor among alternative uses. Many of the macroeconomic disturbances that receive much attention among Keynesian macroeconomists will also have important effects in real business cycle models. There is, however, substantial disagreement between the two schools regarding the mechanisms through which these disturbances work.

Consider the case of a temporary increase in government purchases. Almost all macroeconomists agree that such a change causes an increase in output and employment, and the evidence, mainly from wartime experience, supports this prediction. Yet the explanations of this effect of government purchases differ greatly.

Real business cycle theory emphasizes the intertemporal substitution of goods and leisure (Barro 1987). It begins by pointing out that an increase in government purchases increases the demand for goods. To achieve equilibrium in the goods market, the real interest rate must rise, which reduces consumption and investment. The increase in the real interest rate also causes individuals to reallocate leisure across time. In particular, at a higher real interest rate, working today becomes relatively more attractive than working in the future; today's labor supply therefore increases. This increase in labor supply causes equilibrium employment and output to rise.

While Keynesian theory also predicts an increase in the real interest rate in response to a temporary increase in government purchases, the effect of the real interest rate on labor supply does not play a crucial role. Instead, the increase in employment and output is due to a reduction in the amount of labor unemployed or underutilized. In most Keynesian theory, the labor market is characterized as often in a state of excess supply. In contrast, the Walrasian approach of real business cycle theory does not allow for the possibility of involuntary unemployment.

Both real business cycle theory and Keynesian theory thus conclude that increases in government purchases increase output and employment. This example shows that some of the prominent implications of Keynesian models also come out of intertemporal Walrasian models. Macroeconomists face a problem of approximate observational equivalence: many observed phenomena are consistent with both the classical and Keynesian paradigms.

THE CENTRAL ROLE OF TECHNOLOGICAL DISTURBANCES

While many sorts of macroeconomic disturbances can in principle cause economic fluctuations in real business cycle models, most attention has focused on technological disturbances. The reason is that other sorts of disturbances are unlikely to generate fluctuations in real business cycle models that resemble actual economic fluctuations.

An obvious but important fact is that over the typical business cycle, consumption and leisure move in opposite directions. When the economy goes into a recession, consumption falls and leisure rises. When the economy goes into a boom, consumption rises and leisure falls. Explaining this phenomenon is potentially problematic for real business cycle theory: consumption and leisure would often be expected to move together, since both are normal goods. In the example of a temporary increase in government purchases, both consumption and leisure should fall. Many other changes in the demand for goods, such as a change due to a temporary investment tax credit, also should cause consumption and leisure to move together.

Real business cycle theory must explain why individuals in a recession find it rational to increase the quantity of leisure they demand at the same time they decrease the quantity of goods they demand. The answer must be that the price of leisure relative to goods, the real wage, falls in a recession. Hence, a crucial implication of real business cycle theory is that the real wage is procyclical.[1]

If the production function were unchanging and demand shocks were the source of fluctuations, real business cycle theory would have trouble generating a procyclical real wage. Since labor input is low in a recession, one would expect that the marginal product of labor and thus the real wage should be high. With an unchanging production function, diminishing marginal returns to labor would produce a countercyclical real wage, not the procyclical real wage necessary to explain the fluctuations in consumption and leisure.

Real business cycle theorists therefore assume that there are substantial fluctuations in the rate of technological change. In a recession, the available production technology is relatively unfavorable. The marginal product of labor and thus the real wage are low. In response to the low return to working, individuals reduce consumption and increase leisure.

Since real business cycle theory describes economic fluctuations as a changing Walrasian equilibrium, it implies that these fluctuations are efficient. Given the tastes of individuals and the technological possibilities facing society, the levels of employment, output, and consumption cannot be improved. Attempts by the government to alter the allocations of the private market, such as policies to stabilize employment, at best are ineffective and at worst can do harm by impeding the 'invisible hand'.

Of all the implications of real business cycle theory, the optimality of economic fluctuations is perhaps the most shocking. It seems undeniable that the level of welfare is lower in a recession than in the boom that preceded it. Keynesian theory explains the reduction in welfare by a failure in economic coordination: because wages and prices do not adjust instantaneously to equate supply and demand in all markets, some gains from trade go unrealized in a recession. In contrast, real business cycle theory allows no unrealized gains from trade. The reason welfare is lower in a recession is, according to these theories, that the technological capabilities of society have declined.

THE EVIDENCE ON TECHNOLOGICAL DISTURBANCES

Advocates of real business cycle theories have trouble convincing skeptics that the economy is subject to such large and sudden changes in technology. It is a more standard presumption that the accumulation of knowledge and the concurrent increase in the economy's technological opportunities take place gradually over time. Yet to mimic observed fluctuations, real business cycle theorists must maintain that there are substantial short-run fluctuations in the production function.

Edward Prescott (1986) has offered some direct evidence on the importance of technological disturbances. He examines changes in total factor productivity for the United States economy – the percent change in output less the percent change in inputs, where the different inputs are weighted by their factor shares. This 'Solow residual' should measure the rate of technological progress. Prescott points out that there are substantial fluctuations in the Solow residual, a finding which suggests a potentially important role for technological disturbances as a source of business cycle fluctuations.

Figure 18.1 presents my calculation of the Solow residual and the percent change in output yearly since 1948. (Both variables are for the private economy less agriculture and housing services.) Like Prescott, I find substantial fluctuations in measured total factor productivity. For example, in 1982 total factor productivity fell by 3.5 percent, while in 1984 it rose by 3.4 percent. One might interpret these numbers as showing that the economy's ability to convert inputs into outputs – the aggregate production function – varies substantially from year to year.

Figure 18.1 also shows that measured productivity is highly cyclical. In every year in which output fell, total factor productivity also fell. If the Solow residual is a valid measure of the change in the available production technology, then recessions are periods of technological regress.

The Solow residual need not be interpreted as evidence regarding exogenous technological disturbances, however. The standard explanation of cyclical productivity is that it reflects labor hoarding and other 'off the production function' behavior. Productivity appears to fall in a recession because firms keep unnecessary and underutilized labor. In a boom the hoarded laborers begin to put out greater effort; output increases without a large increase in measured labor input.[2]

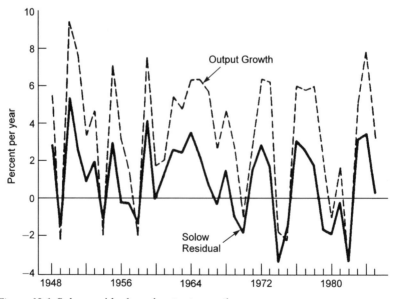

Figure 18.1 Solow residuals and output growth

An examination of the data from the early 1940s appears to support this standard explanation of the cyclical behavior of productivity. The increase in output associated with the World War II build-up is most plausibly a demand-driven phenomenon. Yet from 1939 to 1944 measured total factor productivity grew an average of 7.6 percent per year. (By contrast, the most productivity has grown in any year since then is 5.2 percent in 1950.) One might interpret this finding as showing that the economic boom of the 1940s was in fact driven by supply shocks rather than demand shocks. A more appealing interpretation is that the Solow residual is not a good measure over short horizons of changes in the economy's technological abilities.

Once the Solow residual is rejected as a measure of year-to-year changes in the available production technology, there is no longer any direct evidence for substantial technological disturbances. Yet to generate fluctuations that mimic observed fluctuations, real business cycle models require such disturbances. The existence of large fluctuations in the available technology is a crucial but unjustified assumption of real business cycle theory.

An advocate of real business cycle theory might respond that economic models often rely on assumptions for which there is no formal evidence. Yet more casual evidence also does not give plausibility to the assumption of substantial technological disturbances. Recessions are important events; they receive widespread attention from policy-makers and the media. There is, however, no discussion of declines in the available technology. If society suffered some important adverse technological shock, we would be aware of it. My own reading of the newspaper, however, does not lead me to associate most recessions with some exogenous deterioration in the economy's productive capabilities.

The OPEC energy price changes of the 1970s illustrate that when the economy experiences large real shocks, these shocks are easily identifiable and much discussed. Figure 18.1 indeed shows that the economy experienced large negative Solow residuals in 1974 and 1979, as one might have expected.[3] Yet the five other recessions in the postwar period also exhibit large negative Solow residuals. To explain these Solow residuals as adverse changes in the aggregate production function, one would need to find events with the economic significance of the OPEC price increases. The apparent absence of such events is evidence that these recessions cannot be easily attributed to exogenous real shocks.[4]

LABOR SUPPLY AND INTERTEMPORAL SUBSTITUTION

Real business cycle theorists assume that fluctuations in employment are fully voluntary. In other words, they assume the economy always finds itself on the labor supply curve. Yet over the typical business cycle, employment varies substantially while the determinants of labor supply – the real wage and the real interest rate – vary only slightly. To mimic this observed pattern, real business cycle models require that individuals be very willing to reallocate leisure over time. Individuals must significantly reduce the quantity of labor they supply in response to small temporary reductions in the real wage or in response to small decreases in the real interest rate.

It is unlikely, however, that individuals are so responsive to intertemporal relative prices. Econometric evidence on labor supply typically finds that the willingness of individuals to substitute leisure over time is slight. If leisure were highly intertemporally substitutable, as real business cycle theorists assume, then individuals facing expected increases in their real wage should work little today and much in the future. Individuals facing expected decreases in their real wage should work hard today and enjoy leisure in the future. Yet studies of individual labor supply over time find that expected changes in the real wage lead to only small changes in hours worked (Altonji 1986; Ball 1985). Individuals do not respond to expected real wage changes by substantially reallocating leisure over time.

Personal experience and introspection provide another way to judge the behavioral responses on which real business cycle models rely. One key behavioral response is that quantity of labor supplied reacts substantially to the real interest rate. Without such intertemporal substitution, real business cycle models are unable to explain how a temporary increase in government purchases increases output and employment. Yet such a behavioral response does not seem plausible. The real interest rate is simply not a significant consideration when individuals decide to leave their jobs or to accept new employment. While economists can easily convince non-experts and students that the quantity of apples demanded depends on the price of apples, it is much harder to convince them that labor supply depends on the real interest rate. The implication I draw from this observation is that the intertemporal substitutability of leisure is very likely far too weak to get real business cycle models to work.

REAL BUSINESS CYCLE THEORIES WITH MULTIPLE SECTORS

The real business cycle theories I have been discussing so far treat production as if it takes place in a single industry. This abstraction, however, is not characteristic of all real business cycle theories.

Some real business cycle theories emphasize changes in the technologies of different sectors, rather than economy-wide changes in technology (Long and Plosser 1983). These models highlight the interactions among the sectors. Even if the shocks to the different sectors are independent, the outputs of the different sectors move together. For example, an adverse shock to one sector reduces the wealth of the individuals in the economy; these individuals respond by reducing their demand for all goods. An observer would see an aggregate business cycle, even without a single aggregate shock.

To get these real business cycle models to work, however, the number of independent sectoral shocks cannot be too great. If there were many independent sectoral shocks and labor were mobile between sectors, then the law of large numbers would guarantee that these shocks and their effect on the aggregate economy would average out to zero. To get an aggregate business cycle, these models therefore require that there be only a few sectors and that these sectors be subject to large technological disturbances. These models are therefore similar to the single-sector theories and suffer from the same weaknesses: the absence of any direct evidence for such large technological disturbances and the implausibility of strong intertemporal substitutability of leisure.

A second type of sectoral shock theory emphasizes the costly adjustment of labor among sectors (Lilien 1982). These models, which depart more from the Walrasian paradigm, assume that when a worker moves from one sector to another, a period of unemployment is required, perhaps for job search. In this case, independent shocks across many sectors do not offset each other. Recessions are, according to these theories, periods of more sectoral shocks and thus greater intersectoral adjustment.

This type of real business cycle theory may appear more plausible than those relying on substantial aggregate productivity shocks and intertemporal substitution. It is perhaps easier to imagine that recessions are characterized by an unusually great need for intersectoral reallocation than by some sort of major technological regress that makes leisure unusually attractive. Yet the available evidence appears not to support this intersectoral story. If workers were unemployed voluntarily in recessions because they were moving to new jobs in other sectors, we would expect to find high unemployment coinciding with high job vacancy. Yet observed fluctuations have just the opposite pattern: high unemployment rates coincide with low levels of help wanted advertising (Abraham and Katz 1986). Moreover, in contrast to the prediction of this theory, the measured mobility of workers between sectors is strongly procyclical (Murphy and Topel 1987). This real business cycle theory is also unable to be plausibly reconciled with observed economic fluctuations.

MONEY AND PRICES OVER THE BUSINESS CYCLE

Before real business cycle theory entered the macroeconomic debate in the early 1980s, almost all macroeconomists seemed to agree on one conclusion: money matters. Both historical discussions of business cycles (Friedman and Schwartz 1963) and more formal econometric work (Barro 1977) pointed to the Federal Reserve as an important source of macroeconomic disturbances. While there was controversy as to whether systematic monetary policy could stabilize the economy, it was universally accepted that bad monetary policy could be destabilizing.

It is ironic that real business cycle theory arose in the wake of Paul Volcker's disinflation. Many economists view this experience as clear confirmation of the potency of monetary policy. Volcker announced he was going to slow the rate of money growth to achieve a lower rate of inflation; the rate of money growth in fact slowed down; and one of the deepest postwar recessions followed, as did an eventual reduction in the rate of inflation. This set of events is easy to explain within the context of Keynesian theory with its emphasis on the gradual adjustment of wages and prices. It is less easy to explain within the context of real business cycle theory.[5]

Robert King and Charles Plosser (1984) explain the historical association between money and output by arguing that the money supply endogenously responds to fluctuations in output. Standard measures of the money supply such as M1 are mostly inside money, that is, money created by the banking system. King and Plosser suggest that the transactions services of inside money should be viewed as simply the 'output' of one sector of the economy, the banking sector. Just as one should expect the outputs of different sectors to move together within a multi-sector real business cycle model, one should expect the output of the banking sector to move with the outputs of other sectors. An increase in productivity in any sector will tend to increase the demand for transactions services; the banking system responds by creating more inside money. Hence, the procyclical behavior of standard monetary aggregates cannot necessarily be interpreted as evidence that changes in outside money caused by the monetary authority have real effects.

While the story of King and Plosser can explain the procyclical behavior of money, it cannot explain the procyclical behavior of prices. It is a well-documented fact that, in the absence of identifiable real shocks such as the OPEC oil price changes, inflation tends to rise in booms and fall in recessions. This famous Phillips curve correlation played a central role in the macroeconomic debate of the 1960s, and it was the primary empirical motivation for the early new classical theories in the 1970s (Friedman 1968; Lucas 1972). Yet since the model of King and Plosser generates procyclical money through the demand for transactions services, these fluctuations in money will be associated with fluctuations in real balances not with fluctuations in prices. The short-run Phillips curve has thus been left without an explanation by real business cycle theorists.[6]

THE TRADEOFF BETWEEN INTERNAL AND EXTERNAL CONSISTENCY

A good theory has two characteristics: internal consistency and external consistency. An internally consistent theory is one that is parsimonious; it invokes no *ad hoc* or peculiar axioms. An externally consistent theory is one that fits the facts; it makes empirically refutable predictions that are not refuted. All scientists, including economists, strive for theories that are both internally and externally consistent. Yet like all optimizing agents, scientists face tradeoffs. One theory may be more 'beautiful', while another may be easier to reconcile with observation.

The choice between alternative theories of the business cycle – in particular, between real business cycle theory and new Keynesian theory – is partly a choice between internal and external consistency. Real business cycle theory extends the Walrasian paradigm, the most widely understood and taught model in economics, and provides a unified explanation for economic growth and economic fluctuations. New Keynesian theory, in its attempt to mimic the world more accurately, relies on nominal rigidities that are observed but only little understood. Indeed, new Keynesians sometimes suggest that to understand the business cycle, it may be necessary to reject the axiom of rational, optimizing individuals, an act that for economists would be the ultimate abandonment of internal consistency.

The tension between these two goals of science will undoubtedly continue. Each school of macroeconomic thought will highlight its strengths while trying to improve on its weaknesses. My own forecast is that real business cycle advocates will not manage to produce convincing evidence that there are substantial shocks to technology and that leisure is highly substitutable over time. Without such evidence, their theories will be judged as not persuasive. New Keynesians, however, have made substantial progress in recent years toward providing rigorous microeconomic foundations, the absence of which was the fatal flaw of the Keynesian consensus of the 1960s. While real business cycle theory has served the important function of stimulating and provoking the scientific debate, it will, I predict, ultimately be discarded as an explanation of observed fluctuations.

ACKNOWLEDGEMENTS

I am grateful to Lawrence Ball, Susanto Basu, Marianne Baxter, Mark Bils, Lawrence Katz, Deborah Mankiw, David Romer, Joseph Stiglitz, Lawrence Summers, Timothy Taylor, David Weil, and Michael Woodford for helpful discussions and comments, and to the National Science Foundation for financial support.

NOTES

1 Alternatively, one could explain the observed pattern without a procyclical real wage by positing that tastes for consumption relative to leisure vary over time. Recessions are then periods of 'chronic laziness'. As far as I know, no one has seriously proposed this explanation of the business cycle.
2 A related explanation of the procyclical behavior of the Solow residual has been proposed by Hall (1987). Hall points out that if price exceeds marginal cost because of imperfect competition, then the measured Solow residual will appear procyclical even if the true production technology is unchanging. Alternatively, the Solow residual could reflect endogenous changes in technology due to demand shocks: such endogeneity might arise if, for example, learning-by-doing is important.
3 Whether changes in energy prices affect the Solow residual computed from GNP depends on a variety of issues involving the construction of index numbers like GNP. See Bruno and Sachs (1985: 43) for a discussion.

4 Hamilton (1983) finds oil price changes are also associated with the pre-OPEC recessions. Yet these price changes are much too small to explain plausibly such large declines in productivity.

5 The disinflation is not unusual. Romer and Romer (1989) show that output typically falls after the Fed makes an explicit decision to reduce inflation, which they interpret as evidence against real business cycle theory.

6 Indeed, as King and Plosser (1984) point out, their model makes the counter-factual prediction that the price level should be countercyclical: since the demand for real outside money probably rises in a boom, and it is the outside money stock that pins down the price level, equilibrium in the market for outside money requires that the price level fall in a boom.

REFERENCES

Abraham, Katharine G. and Lawrence F. Katz, 'Cyclical Unemployment: Sectoral Shifts or Aggregate Disturbances?', *Journal of Political Economy* June 1986, *94*, 507–22.

Altonji, Joseph G. 'Intertemporal Substitution in Labor Supply: Evidence from Micro Data', *Journal of Political Economy* June 1986, Part 2, *94*, S176–S215.

Ball, Laurence, 'Intertemporal Substitution and Constraints on Labor Supply: Evidence from Panel Data', manuscript, MIT, 1985.

Barro, Robert J., 'Unanticipated Money Growth and Unemployment in the United States', *American Economic Review* 1977, *67*, 101–15.

Barro, Robert J., *Macroeconomics*, New York: Wiley, 1987.

Bruno, Michael, and Jeffrey Sachs, *Economics of Worldwide Stagflation*, Cambridge, MA: Harvard University Press, 1985.

Friedman, Milton, 'The Role of Monetary Policy', *American Economic Review* 1968, *58*, 1–17.

Friedman, Milton, and Anna Schwartz, *A Monetary History of the United States*, Princeton, NJ: Princeton University Press, 1963.

Hall, Robert E., 'Market Structure and Macroeconomic Fluctuations', *Brookings Papers on Economic Activity* 1987: 1, 285–322.

Hamilton, James D., 'Oil and the Macroeconomy since World War II', *Journal of Political Economy* April 1983, *91*, 228–48.

King, Robert G. and Charles I. Plosser, 'Money, Credit, and Prices in a Real Business Cycle', *American Economic Review* June 1984, *74*, 363–80.

Lilien, David M., 'Sectoral Shifts and Cyclical Unemployment', *Journal of Political Economy* August 1982, *90*, 777–793.

Long, John B. Jr and Charles I. Plosser, 'Real Business Cycles', *Journal of Political Economy* February 1983, *91*, 39–69.

Lucas, Robert E. Jr, 'Expectations and the Neutrality of Money', *Journal of Economic Theory* 1972, *4*, 103–124.

Lucas, Robert E. Jr, 'International Evidence on Output-Inflation Tradeoffs', *American Economic Review* 1973, *63*, 326–334.

Murphy, Kevin M. and Robert H. Topel, 'The Evolution of Unemployment in the United States: 1968–1985', *NBER Macroeconomics Annual* 1987.

Patinkin, Don, *Money, Interest, and Prices: An Integration of Monetary and Value Theory*, Evanston, IL: Row, Peterson, 1956.

Prescott, Edward, 'Theory Ahead of Business Cycle Measurement', *Carnegie-Rochester Conference on Public Policy* Autumn 1986, *25*, 11–44.

Romer, Christina, and David Romer, 'Does Monetary Policy Matter: A New Test in the Spirit of Friedman and Schwartz', *NBER Macroeconomics Annual*, 1989.

Part V
New Keynesian economics

Introduction

The Keynesian propositions of involuntary unemployment, non-neutrality of money and extensive market failures do not rest easily alongside the Walrasian theory of general competitive equilibrium characterized by continuously cleared markets. Although these two strands of economics were brought together during the era of the neoclassical synthesis, the marriage was always potentially explosive. By the early 1970s the Keynesian model was under attack from both monetarists and the newly emerging new classical theorists, the latter being committed to Walrasian formalism with respect to their methodology. This crisis in macroeconomic theory could be reconciled in two ways. Either macroeconomic models could be adapted so as to be consistent with choice-theoretic neoclassical microeconomic theory within a general equilibrium framework, or, alternatively, microeconomic theory could be adapted so as to be consistent with Keynesian propositions. New classical economists chose the former route, new Keynesian economists have followed the latter route (see Greenwald and Stiglitz 1987; Snowdon *et al.* 1994). Hence new Keynesian economists inhabit a brave new world where co-ordination failures and macroeconomic externalities result from market imperfections such as those arising out of imperfect competition, incomplete markets, heterogeneous labour and asymmetric information (see Romer 1996; Dixon 1997).

New Keynesians and new classical/real business cycle theorists differ substantially over the ability and desirability of stabilizing the economy via the use of monetary and fiscal policy. However, new Keynesians fully endorse the call, initiated by Lucas, that macroeconomic models should be based on coherent microfoundations. Beyond this, however, there is little agreement on what constitutes an acceptable model of how markets work. Whereas new classical and real business cycle theorists employ the traditional neoclassical perfectly competitive framework based on a rational representative agent, new Keynesians recognize that whenever information is imperfect or markets are imperfectly competitive and incomplete the economy will fail to be Pareto efficient. Modern Keynesians regard these real world imperfections as the heart of the problem facing business cycle theorists. By incorporating the insights provided by modern market theory where consumers, producers and labour market participants make decisions with incomplete information, new Keynesians argue that they have overcome, to a large extent, the microeconomic deficiencies of orthodox Keynesianism. In addition, by disposing of the fictional Walrasian auctioneer, new Keynesians claim that their models are capable of incorporating features of real economies where co-ordination problems abound (see Phelps 1985: chs 15–20 for an accessible introduction to modern market theory).

Gregory Mankiw, a leading new Keynesian economist, believes that Robert Lucas's wide-ranging criticisms of Keynesian models relating to their inadequate microfoundations have now been met. However, in responding to the new classical critique, the new generation of Keynesian models differ substantially from those which formed the basis of the neoclassical synthesis during the 1960s. In his 1992 *European Economic Review* article 'The Reincarnation of Keynesian Economics' (reprinted on pp. 445–51), Mankiw highlights what he considers to be the essential differences between old and new Keynesian economics by challenging six dubious Keynesian propositions. In doing so Mankiw illustrates how the traditional analysis of the classical economists, modified by the contributions of Friedman and Lucas, has been highly influential in shaping the development of new Keynesian thinking. In particular Mankiw questions the traditional Keynesian emphasis on short-run rather than long-run issues, the downgrading of monetary policy and overemphasis on discretionary policies. Nevertheless Mankiw argues that the reincarnated Keynesianism now has 'firm microeconomic muscle' and is in a far stronger position in explaining economy-wide market failure than the older Keynesian models associated with the neoclassical synthesis.

The views of Gregory Mankiw are further highlighted in the article (reprinted on pp. 452–77) by Brian Snowdon and Howard Vane taken from the Spring 1995 issue of the *American Economist*. Following a brief survey of some of the main features and reasons for the breakdown of the neoclassical synthesis model, Snowdon and Vane present the text of a detailed interview conducted with Mankiw at Harvard University in February 1993. Mankiw's response to a wide range of questions relating to the development and current state of macroeconomics demonstrate that Keynesian economics has been revived. Finally the authors present an assessment of the current state of macroeconomics where they put forward the view that there appears to have taken place a new Keynesian–monetarist synthesis. This now forms the mainstream position in macroeconomics which remains the target of attack from real business cycle theorists who continue to follow the classical tradition of rejecting the idea of economy-wide market failure.

An important problem with new Keynesian economics is that it encompasses an extremely heterogeneous collection of economists and ideas. Numerous elegant theories have been developed which are often unrelated. In a masterful survey entitled 'What is New-Keynesian Economics?', taken from the September 1990 issue of the *Journal of Economic Literature* (reprinted on pp. 478–551), Robert Gordon pulls together the various ideas which make up the main themes identifiable in the modern Keynesian literature. In Gordon's view 'the task of new Keynesian economics is to explain why changes in the aggregate price level are sticky' (see also Gordon 1981). After surveying the evidence on price inertia Gordon goes on to critically examine theories of nominal, and real, wage and price rigidity including those relating to costly price adjustment (menu costs) and efficiency wage theory. Gordon's preference is for what he calls the input-output approach which places the emphasis on co-ordination failure as the main cause of macroeconomic inefficiency. With thousands of firms each buying thousands of components, made up of ingredients supplied by numerous other firms, the typical firm does not know the identity of their complete set of suppliers because 'the input-output table is so broad and deep'. Under such conditions firms are unwilling to index their prices to nominal aggregate demand shocks because marginal cost and marginal revenue are imperfectly correlated with aggregate demand. This is due to the diversity of shocks which can influence a firm's demand and cost conditions. Thus Gordon extends Lucas's two-way distinction between local and aggregate demand shocks to a four-way classification which also includes local and aggregate cost shocks. In effect this magnifies the 'signal extraction' problem raised by Lucas. In such a world 'no *individual* firm has an incentive to take the risk posed by nominal GNP indexation'. Each firm prefers to keep control of its own price – cost relationship 'because they will go bankrupt if costs rise sufficiently in relation to price'.

Bruce Greenwald and Joseph Stiglitz show how there are two broad approaches within new Keynesian economics. The first strand, emphasized by Mankiw and Romer, concentrates on nominal price rigidities as the essential way that actual market economies differ from that depicted in the idealized Walrasian model (see Mankiw 1990; Romer 1993). The second strand explores the path suggested by Keynes (1936) in Chapter 19 of the *General Theory*, namely that increased wage and price flexibility might exacerbate the economy's downturn. In their *Journal of Economic Perspectives* article (reprinted on pp. 552–74) taken from the Winter 1993 issue, Greenwald and Stiglitz explore this second strand of Keynesian analysis and put forward a new Keynesian model where monetary policy has real effects even when wages and prices are flexible. By blending three ingredients, namely, risk averse firms, credit rationing and new labour market theories, Greenwald and Stiglitz demonstrate how in a world of imperfect information, shocks to the macroeconomy have persistent real effects and how greater price flexibility 'might exacerbate the problem of economic fluctuations' (see also Sheffrin 1989; Tobin 1993 – reprinted on pp. 135–55). In the Greenwald-Stiglitz model, because capital markets are imperfect, firms cannot divest themselves of risk via ready access to equity finance. By resorting to debt finance, firms increase the probability that they will face bankruptcy if the economic environment deteriorates. Hence in the face of declining demand, firms prefer, in the first instance, to cut back production rather than reduce the price of their product. Their theory of the risk averse firm thus provides an explanation of why the aggregate supply curve shifts adversely during a recession. The analysis of Greenwald and Stiglitz also suggests that the emphasis of macroeconomic research should shift from the product market to the capital and labour markets (see Stiglitz 1992b).

The work of new Keynesian economists has demonstrated the remarkable resilience of Keynesian economics in the face of the powerful theoretical counter-revolutions launched against its central doctrines. By emphasizing numerous imperfections in labour, product and capital markets new Keynesian analysis has developed robust microfoundations for macro-models which reject continuous market clearing. Since the mid-1970s a 'rich harvest' of non-Walrasian microeconomics has been incorporated into the analysis of aggregate instability (see Benassi *et al.* 1994). Although the new Keynesian research programme is far from complete, the contribution from this 'school' of thought towards the reconstruction of the supply side of macroeconomic models has been highly influential (see Mankiw and Romer 1991).

REFERENCES

*Titles marked with an asterisk are particularly recommended for additional reading.
*Abel, A. B. and B. S. Bernanke (1995) *Macroeconomics*, 2nd edn, Chapter 12, New York: Addison Wesley.
Adnett, N. (1994) 'New Keynesian Economics: Macroeconomics for the 1990s?', *Economics and Business Education* 2, Autumn, pp. 118–20.
Akerlof, G. A. and J. Yellen (eds) (1986) *Efficiency Wage Models and the Labour Market*, Cambridge: Cambridge University Press.
Ball, L., N. G. Mankiw and D. Romer (1988) 'The New Keynesian Economics and the Output Inflation Trade-Off', *Brookings Papers on Economic Activity* 1, pp. 1–65.
Benassi, C., A. Chirco and C. Colombo (1994) *The New Keynesian Economics*, Oxford: Basil Blackwell.
*Colander, D. (1988) 'The Evolution of Keynesian Economics: From Keynesian to New Classical to New Keynesian', in O. F. Hamouda and J. N. Smithin (eds) *Keynes and Public Policy after Fifty Years Vol. 1: Economics and Policy*, Aldershot: Edward Elgar.
*Dixon, H. D. (1997) 'The Role of Imperfect Competition in New Keynesian Economics', in B. Snowdon and H. R. Vane (eds) *Reflections on the Development of Modern Macroeconomics*, Aldershot: Edward Elgar.
Dore, M. H. I. (1993) *The Macrodynamics of Business Cycles: A Comparative Evaluation*, Chapter 7, Oxford: Basil Blackwell.
Dornbusch, R. and S. Fischer (1994) *Macroeconomics*, 6th edn, Chapter 9, New York: McGraw-Hill.
Fischer, S. (1988) 'Recent Developments in Macroeconomics', *Economic Journal* 98, June, pp. 294–339.

*Froyen, R. T. (1996) *Macroeconomics: Theories and Policies*, 5th edn, Chapter 12, London: Prentice-Hall.

*Gerrard, B. (1996) 'Competing Schools of Thought in Macroeconomics: An Ever Emerging Consensus?' *Journal of Economic Studies* 23, pp. 53–69.

*Gordon, R. J. (1981) 'Output Fluctuations and Gradual Price Adjustment', *Journal of Economic Literature* 19, June, pp. 493–530.

Gordon, R. J. (1982) 'Price Inertia and Policy Ineffectiveness in the United States, 1890–1990', *Journal of Political Economy* 90, December, pp. 1087–117.

*Gordon, R. J. (1993) *Macroeconomics*, 6th edn, Chapter 8, New York: Harper-Collins.

*Greenwald, B. C. and J. E. Stiglitz (1987) 'Keynesian, New Keynesian and New Classical Economics', *Oxford Economic Papers* 39, March, pp. 119–32.

*Hall, R. E. and J. B. Taylor (1993) *Macroeconomics*, 4th edn, Chapter 16, New York: W. W. Norton.

Hargreaves Heap, S. P. (1992) *The New Keynesian Macroeconomics: Time, Belief and Social Interdependence*, Aldershot: Edward Elgar.

*Jansen, D. W., C. D. Delorme and R. B. Ekelund, Jr (1994) *Intermediate Macroeconomics*, Chapter 10, New York: West.

Kirman, A. P. (1992) 'Whom or What Does the Representative Individual Represent?', *Journal of Economic Perspectives* 6, Spring, pp. 117–29.

Leslie, D. (1993) *Advanced Macroeconomics: Beyond IS/LM*, Chapter 8, London: McGraw-Hill.

*Mankiw, N. G. (1990) 'A Quick Refresher Course in Macroeconomics', *Journal of Economic Literature* 28, December, pp. 1645–60.

*Mankiw, N. G. (1994) *Macroeconomics*, 2nd edn, Chapter 11, New York: Worth.

Mankiw, N. G. and D. Romer (eds) (1991) *New Keynesian Economics*, 2 vols, Cambridge: MIT Press.

Phelps, E. S. (1985) *Political Economy: An Introductory Text*, New York: W. W. Norton.

Romer, D. (1993) 'The New Keynesian Synthesis', *Journal of Economic Perspectives* 7, Winter, pp. 5–22.

Romer, D. (1996) *Advanced Macroeconomics*, Chapter 6, London: McGraw-Hill.

Rotenberg, J. (1987) 'The New Keynesian Microfoundations', *National Bureau of Economic Research Macroeconomics Annual*.

Sheffrin, S. (1989) *The Making of Economic Policy*, Chapter 5, Oxford: Basil Blackwell.

*Snowdon, B. and H. R. Vane (1992) 'New Classical and New Keynesian Macroeconomics', *Economics* 28, Summer, pp. 54–62.

*Snowdon, B., H. R. Vane and P. Wynarczyk (1994) *A Modern Guide To Macroeconomics: An Introduction to Competing Schools of Thought*, Chapter 7, Aldershot: Edward Elgar.

Stiglitz, J. E. (1992a) 'Methodological Issues and the New Keynesian Economics', in A. Vercelli and N. Dimitri (eds) *Macroeconomics: A Survey of Research Strategies*, Oxford: Oxford University Press.

Stiglitz, J. E. (1992b) 'Capital Markets and Economic Fluctuations in Capitalist Economies', *European Economic Review* 36, pp. 269–306.

Tobin, J. (1993) 'Price Flexibility and Output Stability: An Old Keynesian View', *Journal of Economic Perspectives* 7, Winter, pp. 45–65.

QUESTIONS

1 To what extent have new Keynesian theorists provided more coherent microfoundations for Keynesian models and policies?

2 According to the 1996 Nobel citation, the work of Robert E. Lucas Jr 'transformed macroeconomic analysis and deepened our understanding of economic policy'. In what ways has the influence of Lucas changed Keynesian economics?

3 What is new in new Keynesian economics?

4 'Any satisfactory rehabilitation of Keynesian models requires that the assumption of nominal price stickiness be supported by sound micro-economic reasoning'. How do new Keynesian theorists explain nominal price stickiness and why is this an important issue in macroeconomic analysis?

5 How does the work of new Keynesians differ from that of both Keynes and orthodox Keynesianism?

6 To what extent can efficiency wage and insider-outsider theories provide a coherent explanation of involuntary unemployment as an equilibrium phenomenon?

7 Has the natural rate hypothesis, first put forward by Friedman in 1968, been undermined by hysteresis models of unemployment?

8 'In the Greenwald-Stiglitz (1993) model increased price flexibility is not a solution to demand induced recessions. Indeed such flexibility could make the situation worse'. Why is this the case and to what extent does this conform more closely to the view of Keynes in the *General Theory*?

9 'The real business cycle approach has performed a useful function in raising profound questions relating to the significance and characteristics of economic fluctuations'. How successful have new Keynesian economists been in preserving the view of Keynes that aggregate instability is symptomatic of significant market failure?

10 Critically examine the contribution to the development of modern macroeconomics of any one of the following new Keynesian contributions:

(a) Menu costs
(b) Co-ordination failure
(c) Aggregate demand externality
(d) Staggered wage/price setting
(e) Hysteresis
(f) Near rationality.

19 The reincarnation of Keynesian economics

N. Gregory Mankiw
European Economic Review (1992) 36, April, pp. 559–65

The title of this session, 'Keynesian Economics Today', says much about what has happened in macroeconomics since the early 1980s. When I began graduate school at MIT in 1980, it was not at all clear that Keynesian economics would still be around in the 1990s. Keynes looked as if he were leaving macroeconomics and entering the history of thought. The leading intellectual figure of the day was Robert Lucas, and he had this to say about the state of Keynesian economics:

> One cannot find good, under-forty economists who identify themselves or their work as 'Keynesian'. Indeed, people even take offense if referred to as 'Keynesians'. At research seminars, people don't take Keynesian theorizing seriously anymore; the audience starts to whisper and giggle to one another.

Lucas called his article 'The Death of Keynesian Economics'.

From our current perspective, it is clear that this obituary was premature. Today, Keynesian theorizing does not inspire whispers and giggles from the audience. There are many economists under the age of forty who do not take offense when their work is called 'Keynesian', and I count myself as one of them. If Keynesian economics was dead in 1980, then today it has been reincarnated.

David Romer and I have assembled some of the articles that have been central to this reincarnation in a two-volume collection called *New Keynesian Economics* (Mankiw and Romer 1991a, 1991b). The topics covered in this collection – such as imperfect competition, menu costs, coordination failure, and efficiency wages – are those that have dominated discussions among Keynesians since the early 1980s. It is too early to say there is a consensus about how all these topics fit together. Yet one can say that the new classical challenge has been met: Keynesian economics has been reincarnated into a body with firm microeconomic muscle.

I am careful to call this re-emergence of Keynesian economics a 'reincarnation' rather than a 'resurrection'. My dictionary defines 'reincarnation' as 'the rebirth into another body', and that describes well Keynesian economics today. The Keynesian economics of the 1990s shares the spirit of the Keynesian economics of earlier decades. Like their predecessors, new Keynesians question the relevance of the Walrasian paradigm in explaining economy-wide booms and busts. Old and new Keynesians share a skepticism in the invisible hand's ability to maintain full employment. They both see the business cycle as a type of economy-wide market failure.

Beyond these broad principles, however, old and new Keynesians differ substantially. In many ways, the Keynesian economics of the 1990s does not look like the Keynesian economics of the 1930s, or even that of the 1960s. To some old Keynesians, new Keynesian economics may be hard to recognize as Keynesian at all. Indeed, new Keynesian economics may appear more similar to the classical economics of David Hume, or even to the monetarist economics of Milton Friedman.

My goal today is to highlight some of the differences between old and new Keynesian economics. In particular, I would like to discuss six *dubious Keynesian propositions*. These are propositions that various economists in the past have viewed as basic tenets of Keynesian economics and that, I believe, economists today should discard.

My list of dubious Keynesian propositions is highly personal. I surely would not claim that all new Keynesians view all of these propositions as dubious. Yet my list is not entirely idiosyncratic. I present these dubious Keynesian propositions in part to show the profound impact that monetarism and new classicism has had on the thinking of my generation of Keynesians.

DUBIOUS KEYNESIAN PROPOSITION NO. 1

Learning how the economy works is best achieved by a careful reading of Keynes's *General Theory*

Since Keynesian economics is derived, by definition, from the work of John Maynard Keynes, one might suppose that reading Keynes is an important part of Keynesian theorizing. In fact, quite the opposite is the case. Few young economists – Keynesian or otherwise – concern themselves with the question of what 'Keynes really meant'. New Keynesians view their work as following in the broad tradition that evolved from Keynes, but their goal is to explain the world, not to clarify the views of one particular man. If new Keynesian economics is not a true representation of Keynes's views, then so much the worse for Keynes.

The reason for this attitude is clear. Despite its remarkable contribution, the *General Theory* is an obscure book: I am not sure that even Keynes himself knew completely what he really meant. Moreover, after fifty years of additional progress in economic science, the *General Theory* is an outdated book. The rigor with which we develop economic theories and the data and statistical techniques with which we test our theories were unknown half a century ago. We are in a much better position than Keynes was to figure out how the economy works.

DUBIOUS KEYNESIAN PROPOSITION NO. 2

The lessons of classical economics are not helpful in understanding how the world works

Perhaps for dramatic effect, or perhaps because he was writing in the midst of the Great Depression, Keynes minimized the lessons of classical economics. He called classical economics a 'special case' of his general theory, and he wrote that

> the characteristics of the special case assumed by classical theory happen not to be those of the economic society in which we actually live, with the result that its teaching is misleading and disastrous if we attempt to apply it to the facts of experience.

If the *General Theory* were to have had a subtitle, it might have been 'The Death of Classical Economics'.

Today, few macroeconomists take such a dim view of classical economics. Most accept the natural-rate hypothesis, which interpreted broadly states that classical economics is right in the long run. Moreover, economists today are more interested in the long-run equilibrium. The long run is not so far away that one can cavalierly claim, as Keynes did, that 'in the long run we're all dead'.

The widespread acceptance of classical economics is evidenced by the re-emergence of economic growth as an active area of research. The starting point of all modern growth theory is the Solow growth model. The Solow growth model is eminently classical: it begins by simply assuming that the economy reaches full employment. Although there is continuing debate about whether the Solow model provides an adequate description of economic growth, the model is rarely criticized as being too classical.

DUBIOUS KEYNESIAN PROPOSITION NO. 3

Capitalist economies are threatened by the possibility of excessive saving, which could lead to secular stagnation; deficit spending is, therefore, good for the economy

In 1981 Martin Feldstein wrote an article called 'The Retreat from Keynesian Economics', in which he wrote that

> the most direct effect of Keynesian thinking has been to retard the process of capital formation. Keynes's own writing displayed not only a lack of interest in the potential benefits of capital accumulation but also an outright fear of excessive saving.

More recently, Feldstein (1988) has suggested that Keynes was the 'academic scribbler' who unwittingly inspired Ronald Reagan's decade of budget deficits.

Once again, we see a stark contrast between old and new Keynesians. Feldstein is correct that some early Keynesians feared that the economy might suffer from 'secular stagnation' if the propensity to save were too great. By contrast, few economists today believe that excessive saving threatens the economy. Instead, almost all economists now believe that additional saving will, in the long run, lead to additional investment rather than inadequate aggregate demand. Indeed, rather than being concerned with excessive saving, most American economists fear that the US saving rate is inadequate to maintain the United States' high standard of living.

DUBIOUS KEYNESIAN PROPOSITION NO. 4

Fiscal policy is a powerful tool for economic stabilization, and monetary policy is not very important

The first course I took in macroeconomics used Samuelson's famous textbook. Like many students in my generation, my class was introduced to macroeconomic modelling with the Keynesian cross. Our first lesson was that fiscal policy is a powerful tool that policymakers could (and indeed should) use to control national income. After we learned about the magic of the multiplier, we did study several ancillary topics, such as the role of monetary policy, but we always kept the Keynesian cross as the benchmark model of the economy.

From a modern perspective, it seems most peculiar to begin the study of macroeconomics with the Keynesian cross. The most striking features of this model are what it lacks: any connection to microeconomics, any self-correcting forces returning the economy to the natural rate, and any role for the central bank. Moreover, as an empirical matter, the message of the model is more wrong than right. The numerical examples regularly given to students suggest that the multiplier is indeed quite magical. But, in the world, fiscal policy is not so potent. For example, the quintessentially Keynesian DRI model estimates the government-purchases multiplier (holding the money supply constant) to be only about 0.6 (Eckstein 1983: 169).

For the purpose of analyzing economic policy, a student would be better equipped with the quantity theory of money (together with the expectations-augmented Phillips curve) than the Keynesian cross. In the United States today, fiscal policymakers have completely abdicated responsibility for economic stabilization. Their inability to cope with persistently large government deficits has left them unable even to imagine trying to reach consensus on countercyclical fiscal policy in a timely fashion. All attempts at stabilization are left to monetary policy. When a recession ensues, as it did recently in the United States, fiscal policymakers merely begin discussions about what the Federal Reserve did wrong.

DUBIOUS KEYNESIAN PROPOSITION NO. 5

Policymakers should learn to live with inflation, because it is the cost of low unemployment

In his Presidential Address to the American Economic Association in 1971, James Tobin argued that the 'zero-inflation unemployment rate' is not optimal. What is noteworthy about this fact is not that Tobin reached this conclusion but that he even chose to ask the question. The very phrase 'zero-inflation unemployment rate' presumes the existence of a long-run tradeoff between inflation and unemployment. Most economists today doubt that such a tradeoff exists. On this issue, Milton Friedman (1968) has won the hearts and minds of my generation: in most new Keynesian models, the long-run Phillips curve is vertical.

Perhaps surprisingly, the intellectual victory of the natural-rate hypothesis has not led to consensus among macroeconomists on the relationship between inflation and unemployment. Instead, the debate has shifted focus to the short-run relationship. New Keynesians are the keepers of the faith that policymakers face a short-run tradeoff between inflation and unemployment. New classicals, who have devoted their energy since the early 1980s to real-business-cycle theory, deny the existence of any tradeoff over any time horizon.

Here we can see how misleading the labels have become. Old classical economists, such as David Hume, asserted that money was neutral in the long run but not in the short run. This is exactly the position held by new Keynesians. By contrast, new classical economists claim that money is neutral even in the short run. In advocating this position, they take the classical dichotomy more seriously than did the classical economists themselves.

DUBIOUS KEYNESIAN PROPOSITION NO. 6

Policymakers should be free to exercise their discretion in responding to changing economic conditions and avoid adherence to a rigid policy rule

One striking feature of the economic history since the early 1940s has been high and persistent rates of inflation. Between 1940 and 1990, US inflation averaged 4.6 percent per year. By contrast, between 1870 and 1940, the inflation rate averaged only 0.4 percent per year. In other words, since Keynes wrote the *General Theory*, the US economy has become far more prone to inflation.

This is, I suspect, not merely a coincidence. At its broadest level, the *General Theory* is a call for monetary and fiscal policymakers to control the economy through the management of aggregate demand. In the aftermath of the Great Depression, policymakers were ready to hear this message. The US government accepted the challenge with the Employment Act of 1946, which stated that 'it is the continuing policy and responsibility of the Federal government to... promote full employment and production'. In essence, Keynes ushered in an era of discretionary demand policy.

It was not until the 1980s, however, that economists developed a good understanding of why discretionary policy is intrinsically inflationary. The literature on time inconsistency contains an important warning: at any point in time, policymakers with discretion are tempted to inflate in order to reduce unemployment. Economic actors, however, come to understand this temptation and adjust their expectations of inflation accordingly. Higher expected inflation in turn causes the short-run tradeoff between inflation and unemployment to deteriorate. In the end, discretionary policy yields higher inflation without lower unemployment.

The literature on time inconsistency has, in my view, provided a persuasive case for some sort of commitment to a rule for monetary policy. My own preference would be something like a target for nominal GNP or the nominal wage. Without such a commitment to a policy rule, there is little hope that the modern central bank will achieve the often stated goal of price stability.

DOES MACROECONOMICS MAKE PROGRESS?

In some ways, the history of macroeconomic thought seems like a pendulum swinging between two views of the economy. On the right is the classical view of a well-functioning economy; on the left is the Keynesian view of an economy fraught with market failure. The Great Depression of the 1930s swung the pendulum decisively from the right to the left, and Keynes could plausibly call classical economics 'misleading and disastrous'. The new classical economics of the 1970s swung the pendulum back to the right, and Robert Lucas could plausibly proclaim the 'death of Keynesian economics'. The new Keynesian economics of the 1980s swung the pendulum back toward the left (at least somewhat), and today one can plausibly say that Keynesian economics has been reincarnated.

One might be tempted to conclude from these developments that macroeconomics does not make progress, that it is destined to oscillate between two irreconcilable extremes. Yet one can also take a more sanguine view. The new classical revolution of the 1970s left an indelible mark on the way macroeconomists of all stripes think about the economy, just as the Keynesian revolution of the 1930s did before it. New Keynesian economics is far different from old Keynesian economics – so different, in fact, that today the label 'Keynesian' may generate more confusion than understanding. With new Keynesians looking so much like old classicals, perhaps we should conclude that the term 'Keynesian' has out-lived its usefulness.

Perhaps we need a new label to describe the school of macroeconomics that accepts the existence of involuntary unemployment, monetary non-neutrality, and sticky wages and prices. Until a new label is found, however, we can safely say that Keynesian economics is alive and well.

REFERENCES

Eckstein, Otto (1983) *The DRI Model of the U.S. Economy*, New York: McGraw-Hill.

Feldstein, Martin (1981) 'The retreat from Keynesian economics', *The Public Interest* Summer, 92–105.

Feldstein, Martin (1988) 'Counter-revolution in progress', *Challenge* July/August, 42–6.

Friedman, Milton (1968) 'The role of monetary policy', *American Economic Review* 58 (March), 1–17.

Keynes, John Maynard (1936) *The General Theory of Employment, Interest, and Money*, London: Macmillan.

Lucas, Robert E. Jr (1980) 'The death of Keynesian economics', *Issues and Ideas* Winter (University of Chicago, Chicago, IL) 18–19.

Mankiw, N. Gregory and David Romer (eds) (1991a) *New Keynesian Economics, Vol. 1: Imperfect Competition and Sticky Prices*, Cambridge, MA: MIT Press.

Mankiw, N. Gregory and David Romer (eds) (1991b) *New Keynesian Economics, Vol. 2: Coordination Failures and Real Rigidities*, Cambridge, MA: MIT Press.

Tobin, James (1972) 'Inflation and unemployment', *American Economic Review* 62 (March), 1–18.

20 New-Keynesian economics today

The empire strikes back

Brian Snowdon and Howard Vane
American Economist (1995) 39, Spring, pp. 48–65

> there is no single doctrine taken to be a scientific truth without the
> diametrically opposed view being similarly upheld by authors of high
> repute...in other fields of science these conflicts usually come to an
> end...It is only in the field of economics that the state of war seems to
> persist and remain permanent.[1]
>
> (Knut Wicksell)

INTRODUCTION

In a 'Symposium on Keynesian Economics Today' (*Journal of Economic
Perspectives*, Winter 1993) David Romer, James Tobin, Robert King, Bruce
Greenwald and Joseph Stiglitz offered a variety of perspectives with respect
to the current resurgence of Keynesian ideas which has characterized the
macroeconomics literature since the mid-1980s. In his introduction to the
symposium Gregory Mankiw noted that the 'literature that bears the name
Keynesian is broad and it does not offer a single vision of how the economy
behaves'. However, as a leading new Keynesian he did not present his own
views in the symposium. In February 1993 we interviewed Gregory Mankiw
at Harvard University and here we present his perspective of the current
state of macroeconomics in general and what he has called the 'Reincarnation of Keynesian Economics' (Mankiw 1992a).[2]

We first briefly review the background to the current debate before
presenting Mankiw's assessment of some of the important issues in modern
macroeconomics. In conclusion we compare the varieties of Keynesian
vision presented by some contributors to this debate.

BREAKDOWN OF THE CONSENSUS

In 1977 James Tobin, the United States' most distinguished 'old' Keynesian
economist, asked the question 'How dead is Keynes?' (see Tobin 1977).
That Tobin was even asking this question highlights the turmoil which had
begun to plague macroeconomics in the early 1970s and has continued ever
since. Following the publication of Keynes's *General Theory* macroecono-

mists have been broadly split between those who believe that the price mechanism, unaided by the visible hand of government, is capable of stabilizing a capitalist market economy which is subject to periodic shocks and those, like Tobin, who doubt the capacity of the system to self-equilibrate at a satisfactory level of employment. The synthesis of Keynesian and neoclassical analysis which formed the basis of a consensus in the 1950s and 1960s appeared to have achieved an uneasy reconciliation between these two competing views. The theoretical debate relating to the consistency of macroeconomic equilibrium with an excess supply of labour appeared to have been won by supporters of the invisible hand view, but as a practical matter it was accepted that the self-righting properties of the market were too weak and needed the helping hand of fiscal and monetary policies in order to achieve and maintain the primary stated objective of full employment. Keynesians of all persuasions accepted the possibility of widespread and frequent 'effective' demand failures together with prolonged involuntary unemployment. Nevertheless, apart from a small but highly vocal anti-neoclassical group of heretics centered at Cambridge University, the majority of Keynesians were also adherents, and seminal contributors, to the neoclassical paradigm (Paul Samuelson and Robert Solow are the most obvious examples). This schizophrenia could not last.

During the 1960s the synthesis became increasingly associated with an acceptance of a stable long-run trade-off between inflation and unemployment. With the breakdown of the Phillips curve in the late 1960s and early 1970s it became apparent that the microeconomic underpinnings of the supply side of Keynesian models were fundamentally flawed. The impact of the first OPEC oil shock in 1973 made this even more apparent. As a result Keynesianism was rejected by a growing number of academic economists during the 1970s, especially in the USA, who were increasingly attracted to the work of the emerging new classical school led and inspired by Robert Lucas who for many is 'the leading macro mountaineer of our generation' (Parkin 1992). Lucas's incorporation of John Muth's rational expectations hypothesis into a market clearing setting acted like a siren song to the younger generation of graduate economists (Lucas 1972, 1973). By 1978 Lucas and Sargent were contemplating life 'After Keynesian Macroeconomics'. Soon after Lucas went so far as to claim that 'people even take offense if referred to as "Keynesians". At research seminars, people don't take Keynesian theorizing seriously anymore; the audience starts to whisper and giggle to one another'.[3] In a similar vein, a leading 'younger generation' Keynesian, Alan Blinder, confirmed that by 1980 'it was hard to find an American academic macroeconomist under the age of 40 who professed to be a Keynesian' (Blinder 1988). Lucas's obituary of Keynesian economics can now be seen to have been premature. However, his critiques highlighted the tensions which existed within economics between a flexiprice neoclassical micro world dominated by the fundamental theories of Adam Smith and Leon Walras, and a Keynesian superstructure where arbitrary assumptions relating to nominal price and wage rigidities were the norm. This conflict was in need of resolution as the conventional practice of separating micro from macro analysis was no longer tenable. The new classical solution to this 'crisis' was to adapt macroeconomic theory to neoclassical microeconomics. As Kevin Hoover (1992) has noted, the new classical research programme 'seeks not only to revivify classical modes of equilibrium analysis, but also to secure the euthanasia of macroeconomics'. In contrast the new Keynesian approach has been to set about building new microfoundations for Keynesian macroeconomics which nevertheless remain faithful to the axioms of utility and profit maximization by individual agents. These ground rules relating to optimizing behaviour have been set by new classical economists who insist that no self-respecting model should contain agents who fail to 'exhaust trades that are to the perceived mutual advantage of exchanging parties' (Barro 1979). In the language of Robert Lucas, any acceptable theory must not allow \$100 bills to be left lying on the pavement. Incorporating acceptable microfoundations into macro models has been and remains the principal task facing new Keynesian economists.

THE 'REINCARNATION' OF KEYNESIAN ECONOMICS

New Keynesian economics, conceived in the late 1970s, sprang to life in the 1980s. Since the essential feature of Keynesian macroeconomics is the absence of continuous market clearing, the new Keynesian developments since the mid-1980s have been primarily concerned with the 'search for rigorous and convincing models of wage and/or price stickiness based on maximizing behaviour and rational expectations' (Gordon 1990). In contrast to the new classical monetary surprise and real business cycle models where price taking rational individuals make voluntary choices with respect to quantities, new Keynesian models contain price making, demand taking, risk-averse firms who operate in an imperfectly competitive, uncertain world riddled with imperfect information, transaction costs and asymmetric information (Mankiw and Romer 1991). New Keynesian economics seeks to understand and explain the causes of the imperfections in product, labour and capital markets and to show how these imperfections have macroeconomic consequences. In short 'New Keynesianism throws bucket fulls of grit into the smooth-running neoclassical paradigms' (Leslie 1993). This agenda has led to research into the causes and consequences of:

1 Nominal wage stickiness (see Fischer 1977; Taylor 1979; Laing 1993);
2 Nominal price stickiness (see Mankiw 1985; Akerlof and Yellen 1985; Romer 1993);
3 Real rigidities (see Yellen 1984; Shapiro and Stiglitz 1984; Lindbeck and Snower 1986; Phelps 1994);
4 Co-ordination failures (see Diamond 1982; Cooper and John 1988; Ball and Romer 1991).

Although new Keynesian theory is still at a rudimentary stage and there are various strands to this diverse school, one of the leading advocates, Gregory Mankiw (1992a) has claimed that 'the new classical challenge has been met. Keynesian economics has been reincarnated into a body with firm micro-economic muscle.' Mankiw also argues that this reincarnation was necessary because 'the new classical revolution seriously wounded the once prevailing Keynesian consensus.' In the development of Mankiw's brand of new Keynesianism it is evident that dissatisfaction with older style Keynesian models emphasizing nominal wage rigidity played a crucial role. A combination of price-taking firms, neoclassical production technology and sticky nominal wages imply that aggregate demand contractions will be associated with a rise in real wages during a recession i.e. real wages will move *countercyclically*. By 1980 Mankiw had concluded that such models made little sense even if modified to allow for rational expectations (e.g. Fischer 1977) since they imply

> that recessions must be quite popular. Sure, a few people get laid off. But most people get to enjoy the higher real wages that result when prices fall and their nominal wages do not.... If high real wages accompanied low employment, as the *General Theory* and my professors had taught me, then most households should welcome economic downturns.
>
> (Mankiw 1991: 129–30)

Since the weight of evidence suggests that real wages do not move counter-cyclically over the business cycle and the assumption of nominal wage rigidity seems to imply substantial departures from rationality, many economists sympathetic to the old neoclassical synthesis view shifted their attention from the labour market to the goods market in their search for *nominal* rigidities. As Mankiw notes 'In fact, it was thinking about the real-wage puzzle that originally got me interested in thinking about imperfections in goods markets and, eventually, about monopolistically competitive firms facing menu costs' (Mankiw 1991: 132). When aggregate supply is derived from inflexible goods prices, rather than from inflexible nominal wages, then real wages can move procyclically or acyclically. Furthermore, new Keynesians argue that price rigidities do not imply gross departures from rationality given the existence of 'near rational behaviour' and 'menu costs' (see Akerlof and Yellen 1985; Mankiw 1985). In new Keynesian models the reason why firms lay off workers during a recession is not because labour costs are too high but for the intuitively appealing reason that sales are too low (Mankiw 1991: 106). Accordingly the new breed of Keynesian models share the spirit of the old Keynesian economics in viewing the business cycle as evidence of economy-wide market failure. This also implies accepting the existence of involuntary unemployment, the non-neutrality of money, sticky prices and wages, and non-clearing markets. However, it is important not to assume that new Keynesians are protagonists in the monetarist–Keynesian debate because new Keynesians do not hold a unified view with respect to the relative potency of fiscal and monetary policy nor do they 'necessarily believe that active government policy is desirable' (Mankiw and Romer 1991). The work of Edmund Phelps has also inspired the emergence of a 'structuralist' branch to the new Keynesian school where non-monetary models are given emphasis (see Phelps 1991: vol. III; Phelps 1994).

What progress has been made? What are the likely directions of further research? How does new Keynesian analysis differ from old Keynesian and new classical varieties? We sought answers to these and other questions from Gregory Mankiw. In what follows, where appropriate, we have provided references where the substance of Gregory Mankiw's answers are developed more fully or where some of the ideas discussed have been applied.

GENERAL ISSUES

Why do you think we have so much controversy in macroeconomics compared to microeconomics?

That is a hard question. It is certainly true that there is more agreement among microeconomists as to how they approach things. That is, most microeconomists start off with utility and profit maximization as the underlying motives and go from there. Macroeconomics is in some ways harder since you are dealing with the whole economy; the field therefore requires more simplifying assumptions to make anything manageable, to make the problem simpler than it really is in the world. I think there is disagreement as to which simplifying assumptions are the most natural or the most useful.

How important do you think it is for macroeconomics to have neoclassical choice theoretic foundations?

Well it is certainly true that all macro phenomena are the aggregate of many micro phenomena; in that sense macroeconomics is inevitably founded on microeconomics. Yet I am not sure that all macroeconomics necessarily has to start off with microeconomic building blocks. To give an analogy, all of biology is in some sense the aggregate of particle physics, because all biological creatures are made up of particles. That doesn't mean that the natural place to start in building biology is to start with particle physics and aggregate up. Instead I would probably start with theory at the level of the organism or the cell, not the level of the sub-atomic particle. We have a lot of models like the IS-LM model in macroeconomics that are very useful for studying the macroeconomy, even though those models don't start off with the individual unit and build up from there.

Which papers or books do you feel have had the biggest impact on the development of macroeconomics over the last 25 years?

The biggest impact has undoubtedly come from Lucas. He put the cracks into the Keynesian consensus that existed in the 1960s. He really pulled macroeconomics apart by proposing new and intriguing ideas. The disagreements today among macro economists have largely arisen from the critiques of Lucas and of his followers. As you know, I don't agree with Lucas's solutions, but I take the problems that he pointed out very seriously. A lot of the work that I and other new Keynesians have done are a response to the problems that he pointed out in the old Keynesian ideas.

(See Mankiw 1990.)

To some extent you've answered our next question. Where did you draw inspiration for your own work?

It's been a combination of influences. Part comes from the older generation of macroeconomists. I view a lot of the work I do as building on the work of Tobin, Modigliani and Friedman. I see a lot of truth in the views they were pushing. I also take the problems that Lucas pointed out very seriously. A lot of new Keynesian work is trying to reformulate the 1960s Friedman–Tobin view of the world. What is now called the neoclassical synthesis had a large element of truth in it. On the other hand, it had problems, and Lucas pointed those problems out very forcefully. We need to fix those problems and address the concerns that Lucas had while still maintaining the element of truth in the neoclassical synthesis.

(See Mankiw 1992a.)

ON KEYNES AND THE GENERAL THEORY

One interpretation of the neoclassical synthesis which emerged at the end of the 1950s suggested that the General Theory *was a special case of a more general classical model. Would you agree with that interpretation?*

I would say that the classical model and the Keynesian model make different assumptions about adjustment of prices. I think of the classical model as being the model that assumes complete price flexibility, and therefore describes a horizon over which it is plausible to make such an assumption. Probably a period of years, rather than a period of months. The Keynesian model applies over a horizon where wages and prices are relatively inflexible or sluggish. Both models are special cases of a more general model which allows a varying degree of flexibility and sluggishness in prices depending on the horizon we want to study. When we study the effect of policies over a quarter or a decade, we want to make a different assumption about the degree of flexibility of prices.

Why do you think there are so many conflicting interpretations of the General Theory?

There are a lot of conflicting interpretations because Keynes had a lot of different ideas. The ideas don't necessarily have to be packaged all together, so some people grab on to one set of ideas and say that this is really what is central to what Keynes was saying and other people grab onto other sets of ideas. The question is, when we look at the market imperfection that we call the business cycle, which set of general ideas from the *General Theory* are the most important? There is so much in the *General Theory* that it is hard to comprehend it all at once. Some is very important, but some is not particularly important. Disagreements come by choosing different pieces of Keynes's world view and emphasizing those.

(See Mankiw 1992a.)

Do you think that if Keynes had still been living in 1969 he would have received the first Nobel Prize in Economics?

Oh undoubtedly. I think there are a few very very important economists of the century, and there is no question that Keynes has got to be on anybody's shortlist.

NEW CLASSICAL MACROECONOMICS

Do you regard new classical macroeconomics as a separate school of thought from monetarism?

I think so. My impression is that monetarism is a school of thought that says fluctuations in the money supply are the primary cause of fluctuations in aggregate demand and income, whereas new classicism is a particular theory as to why fluctuations in aggregate demand might matter through an unanticipated price surprise. This price surprise view proposed by Lucas is, I think, the next step after monetarism. More recently, new classical economists have turned their attention to real business cycle theory, which is the antithesis of monetarism.

Do you think that overall the new classical contributions have had a beneficial effect on the development of macroeconomics?

Debate is healthy, and the new Keynesian school arose largely in response to the new classical school. In that sense it is a debate leading to greater truths, and it has been helpful. A lot of the specific contributions, especially real business cycle theory, are probably not going to survive the test of time. The literature on the time inconsistency of policy is a contribution that will survive and has probably been one of the most important contributions to policy analysis in the past two decades.

(See Mankiw 1988a: 441–3; 1992a: 563–4.)

How important is the rational expectations hypothesis?

It is important in the sense that it has now become the working hypothesis of all practicing macroeconomists. Economists routinely assume that people are rational when they make decisions: they maximize utility, they rationally maximize profits, and so on. It would be peculiar for us to assume that people are rational except when they come to form expectations and then they act irrationally. I don't think the rational expectations hypothesis is important in the sense of having all the sweeping implications as was at first believed. At first people thought that it had all sorts of properties about policy being ineffective.

(See Mankiw *et al.* 1987; Mankiw 1990.)

Isn't that more to do with the market clearing assumption?

Exactly. People have come to realize that it is other assumptions, like the market clearing assumption, that are really important and that rational expectations in itself doesn't have implications as sweeping as was once thought.

You have questioned the argument that the disinflation experience of the early 1980s both here and in Britain has provided decisive evidence against the new classical claim of painless disinflation. Is this because the deflation was unanticipated?

There are two new classical views. The first is the price surprise theory of Lucas. The second is real business cycle theory. This second view says that money anticipated or unanticipated doesn't matter. My view of that is that it is completely at variance with the evidence. Larry Ball has a paper that shows systematically for a large number of countries that whenever you have a major disinflation it is associated with a period of low output and high unemployment (see Ball 1994). So I think that the evidence is completely clear on that. The evidence is more favourable to early new classical theory. You're right that to a large extent the disinflation was unanticipated even in the United States where Volcker said he was going to disinflate. I don't think people believed he was going to disinflate as fast as he did. Most measures of expectations of inflation did not come down until after the recession was well under way. I am sympathetic to the view that credibility is one determinant of how costly a disinflation will be.

(See Mankiw 1986a: 218–20.)

ON KEYNESIANISM AND THE NEW KEYNESIANS

Do you regard yourself as a Keynesian?

I do but I'm always nervous about the term because the term Keynesian can mean different things to different people, just as different people will read the *General Theory* and pull out different elements as being important. People use the word Keynesian in so many different ways that recently I have actually tried to avoid using the term at all on the grounds that it is more confusing than illuminating. I think of myself as a Keynesian in the sense of believing that the business cycle represents some sort of market imperfection on a grand scale. In that sense I think of myself as a Keynesian. Milton Friedman was also a Keynesian in that sense. My own views emerged as much from Milton Friedman as they have from John Maynard Keynes. Some people take the word Keynesian as meaning a belief in fine tuning the economy so that the government controls every wiggle of ups and downs. Other people take it as a belief that deficit spending is not a bad thing. I don't subscribe to either of those views. I think that the broad theme of the *General Theory* is that the business cycle is something that we really need to worry about because it is a sign of a market imperfection. In that way I am a Keynesian, but as I said so is Milton Friedman.

(See Mankiw 1987; 1992a.)

Was the breakdown of the Phillips curve fatal for Orthodox Keynesianism?

It highlighted the absence of a good theory of aggregate supply. What orthodox Keynesians had was a pretty good theory of aggregate demand. The IS-LM model has held up pretty well as a general structure for thinking about how aggregate demand is determined. The problem is once you've got aggregate demand – a downward sloping curve in P-Y space – you still need a good story for the aggregate supply curve. The Phillips curve came out of nowhere. It is really just an empirical description of what was true in the data without any particularly good theories as to why it should look that way, how it would change in response to policy, and what might make it unstable. So we never had a good theory of that, and the breakdown of the Phillips curve made that very apparent and provided room for the more general critique that Lucas put forward. The deficiency on the supply side was always a weakness, but it wasn't given attention until the Phillips curve broke down.

(See Mankiw 1990: 1647–8.)

What would you summarize as being the central propositions of new Keynesian macroeconomics?

The central propositions are largely theoretical rather than policy oriented. New Keynesians accept the view of the world summarized by the neoclassical synthesis: the economy can deviate in the short term from its equilibrium level, and monetary and fiscal policy have important influences on real economic activity. New Keynesians are saying that the neoclassical synthesis is not as flawed as Lucas and others have argued. The purpose of the new Keynesian school has been largely to try to fix those theoretical problems raised by Lucas and also accept Lucas's argument that we need models supported by better microeconomic foundations.

(See Ball *et al.* 1988: 149–61; Mankiw and Romer 1991, vol. 1: 1–26.)

So you wouldn't subscribe to arguments in favour of incomes policies advocated by Post-Keynesians?

No, not at all. When the government gets in the business of setting wages and prices it is not very good at it. The setting of wages and prices should be left to free markets.

So you are no Galbraithian?

Absolutely not (*laughter*).

How important is the theory of imperfect competition to new Keynesian macroeconomics?

A large part of new Keynesian economics is trying to explain why firms set and adjust prices over time in the way they do. Firms in a perfectly competitive environment don't have any choice over what their prices are going to be. Competitive firms are price takers. If you want to even talk about firms setting prices you have to talk about firms that have some ability to do so, and those are firms that have some market power: they are imperfectly competitive. So I think imperfect competition is central to thinking about price setting and therefore central to new Keynesian economics.
(See Mankiw 1985; 1988b; Ball *et al.* 1988: 156–8.)

This is strange, because if you think of the 1930s, you had Keynes and Joan Robinson at Cambridge. Joan Robinson developed the theory of imperfect competition and Keynes developed his General Theory. *Why did it take so long to bring these two ideas together?*

I don't think that Keynes was as worried about building his model based on microfoundations as we are today. Joan Robinson was building the microeconomics that would later prove to be very useful for addressing the macroeconomics of Keynes, but Keynes, not having read Robert Lucas yet, wasn't worried about building the microeconomics of aggregate supply (*laughter*).

In a sense haven't the Post-Keynesians been ahead of you here? People like Paul Davidson have for years taken imperfect competition as their microfoundation. So are the new Keynesians simply catching up on what the Post-Keynesians did quite a while ago?

They have a broad theme of imperfect competition, but the details are not very similar. My impression is that the new Keynesian economics is much more in line with the neoclassical synthesis than with the Post-Keynesians.

You will obviously be very familiar with Alan Blinder's recent surveys. Are they supporting the new Keynesian views? (See Blinder 1991.)

Alan is providing a way of judging a variety of different new Keynesian views. There are a lot of new theories about wage and price rigidities. He is trying to sort out which is right and wrong using a fairly novel perspective of asking firms how they set wages and prices. This is terrific work, but what we are going to learn in the end is still unclear. He is still producing the papers and we haven't seen all the results yet. The goal is to provide one way of deciding which theories we like and which we don't. It's a very exciting project.

An important distinction seems to be made by new Keynesians between real rigidities and nominal rigidities. Why is it important to make this distinction?

The reason is that a real rigidity, which is a rigidity in a relative price, is not a reason for monetary non-neutrality. Unions, for example, could set rigid real wages away from equilibrium. A rigid real wage is not going to provide any reason to believe that money is not neutral, since it does not create any nominal lever for money to work on. It would cause unemployment but not monetary non-neutrality. To get monetary non-neutrality, which is a central challenge for macro theorists, you need some nominal rigidity such as sticky prices. Having said that, there do seem to be a variety of real rigidities in the world; unions setting wages way above equilibrium levels for example. The question is whether nominal and real rigidities interact. One of the big themes of this literature, mainly due to Larry Ball and David Romer, is that real and nominal rigidities seem to reinforce each other. The real rigidity is actually going to make the nominal rigidity a lot more important than it would be otherwise.

(See Ball *et al.* 1988: 153–6; Ball and Romer 1990; Mankiw and Romer 1991, vol. 2: 2).

Critics of the menu cost literature, Robert Barro for example, have suggested that this is a small peg on which to hang an explanation of the business cycle. How can small menu costs have such large real effects on the macro economy? (See Barro 1989.)

It is clear that menu costs are quite small. Firms don't bear huge costs when they change their prices. Yet it also is clear that recessions are very costly events. The question is whether these relatively small menu costs can be a key part of understanding this relatively costly business cycle. This literature shows that price adjustment by firms has external effects. When a firm decides to keep prices sticky, this could well be costly for the economy in a way that is not costly for the firm who is making the decision.

(See Mankiw 1985; Ball *et al.* 1988.)

How do efficiency wage and insider/outsider theories fit into new Keynesian thinking?

Both of those theories provide a particular explanation for real rigidities, such as why real wages don't move to the equilibrium level in labour markets. As I said before, real rigidities and nominal rigidities can complement each other. That is, the insider/outsider and efficiency wage explanations for rigid real wages in some senses complement the menu cost story of rigid prices.

(See Mankiw 1990: 1658.)

Is the idea of hysteresis crucial to new Keynesian macroeconomics?

Actually I don't think of it as being crucial. It is an interesting idea, that a recession can have long-lived effects on the economy and leave permanent scars after the initial cause of the recession has gone. For example, the high unemployment in Europe in the 1980s persisted far longer than anyone could explain with standard models. But if this idea turned out to be wrong it would not bring down the rest of our theories. This has been an interesting, but relatively separate question.

Do you see the concept of NAIRU, and Friedman's natural rate, as being the same idea or are they different?

I have always thought of them as being basically the same. Most new Keynesian models involve some sort of natural rate; in that sense Milton Friedman has won the debate. Most new Keynesians believe in the natural rate hypothesis except for a small group of people working with hysteresis. The natural rate hypothesis is pretty well entrenched.

(See Mankiw 1992a: 563; 1992b: 483–4.)

What about the concept of full employment? It was difficult to think of doing macroeconomics 15–20 years ago without the concept of full employment being central. What do we do about issues like involuntary unemployment? Lucas suggests that we should abandon this concept, what are your views on this? (See Lucas 1978.)

I think there is involuntary unemployment. Part of the new Keynesian literature has come up with models of the labour market to explain why involuntary unemployment exists, why real wages don't adjust to equilibrate labour markets. There is a lot of truth to the efficiency wage theories and the insider/outsider theories, for example.

Do new Keynesians think of full employment as the natural rate?

I avoid the term full employment because it suggests that the natural rate is in some sense desirable. I think there is some natural rate which is the long-run unemployment rate that the economy tends to, that can't be influenced by monetary policy in the long run. That doesn't mean that it is immutable in response to any policy intervention. There are things that have been done to the labour market that either increase or decrease the natural rate, things like the minimum wage, unemployment insurance laws, labour training policies. There are all sorts of things that the government can do to change the natural rate. I don't like calling it full employment because good labour market policies might well raise employment beyond that level.

(See Mankiw 1992b: 118–39.)

How important do you think it is to take into account fairness when looking at the labour market? We are thinking here of the work of George Akerlof, Janet Yellen and Robert Solow who have stressed the idea of fairness. Doesn't this work suggest that perhaps new Keynesians should start looking more closely at the psychology and sociology literature? (See Akerlof and Yellen 1990; Solow 1990.)

Some of the papers that they have written have been extremely interesting. I don't think there is a lot of compelling evidence yet that we need to abandon neoclassical assumptions. I'm not doing so yet in my work, but I'm certainly happy to read the work of others who are doing so (*laughter*).

In your edited volumes of collected papers on new Keynesian economics you say that 'new Keynesian macroeconomics could just as easily be labelled new monetarist economics'. What exactly did you mean? (See Mankiw and Romer 1991.)

The challenge raised by the real business cycle school is the question of whether money is neutral and, if not, why not? Twenty years ago, when Friedman and Tobin were debating, there were some things they agreed on. They agreed on the proposition that the Federal Reserve was an important player in the economy, that what it did really mattered. The real business cycle school has challenged that by writing down models without any real effects of monetary policy. What the new Keynesian models have tried to do is establish why money is not neutral, what microeconomic imperfections are necessary to explain monetary non-neutrality at the macro level. In this sense, these models are trying to support both traditional Keynesian and monetarist views.

Would you agree with Stanley Fischer that the views of Friedman, Brunner and Meltzer are closer to those of Keynesians than they are to equilibrium business cycle theorists? (See Fischer 1988.)

Oh yes absolutely. The essence of real business cycle models is the absence of any role for the Federal Reserve, whereas I think Brunner, Meltzer and Friedman would agree with Tobin that the Fed is very important. None of them would ever argue that money is neutral in the way that real business cycle theorists have.
(See Mankiw 1986b.)

James Tobin has suggested that good papers in economics contain surprises. What surprises have new Keynesian papers uncovered? (See Tobin 1988.)

One of the big surprises is that one can go a lot further with menu cost models than people once thought. A lot of people used to see these models as a silly way of thinking about price rigidity. What the new literature is trying to do is to say no, maybe we should take menu cost models seriously. I think the complementarity between real and nominal rigidities is a surprise. As I mentioned earlier one of the disappointing features so far of the new Keynesian literature is that it hasn't been as empirical as I would have liked. That is a problem being remedied right now in some research. Ultimately that is where the literature should go. More empirical work is needed.

(See Mankiw 1987; Ball *et al.* 1988: 161–201; Ball and Mankiw 1992a.)

Peter Howitt has talked about a Keynesian recovery, Alan Blinder about a Keynesian restoration, you seem to prefer the term reincarnation. Is there something important in the different terms used? (See Howitt 1990; Blinder 1992a; Mankiw 1992a.)

I chose the term reincarnation because it means rebirth into another body. While there are many similarities between new and old Keynesian economics, there are also a lot of differences as well, and I wanted to emphasize that. In some senses the spirit of Keynes has been brought back, but it doesn't look like the old Keynes. In fact Keynes might not recognize the new Keynesians as Keynesians at all. In general, people might not recognize themselves after they have been reincarnated. So that is why I used the term reincarnation (*laughter*).

Would you say that your work is, with respect to Keynes, faithful in spirit, but critical in detail?

I think that is fair. It tries to go beyond Keynes in a sense of taking microfoundations more seriously. Alan Blinder wrote a paper 'Keynes after Lucas' and I think that title pretty much describes new Keynesians. It takes some of Keynes's ideas seriously, and it also takes some of the critiques of Lucas seriously as well.

(See Blinder 1986.)

Do you think Keynes would have been a new Keynesian?

I don't know, I think Keynes was a very unpredictable fellow. I guess he would see some things in it he would like, and some things in it he wouldn't.

REAL BUSINESS CYCLE THEORY

You've argued that real business cycle theory has served an important function in stimulating and provoking scientific debate, but you predict that the approach will eventually be discarded. What are your main objections to real business cycle theory? What are the weaknesses, theoretical, empirical or both?

My objections are mainly empirical. Theoretically they are very elegant models and that is a large part of their appeal. They are very parsimonious models. But when I look at the real world I see the same things that Milton Friedman and James Tobin do, which is a very powerful Federal Reserve board in the United States or the Bank of England in the UK. There is a lot of evidence across countries that periods of disinflation are periods of low output and high unemployment. Those effects are completely absent in real business cycle models. I think the central driving forces for the business cycle that those models highlight – technology shocks – aren't very important.

(See Mankiw 1989; 1994; Campbell and Mankiw 1989).

Isn't the pro-cyclical behaviour of the real wage a strong feature of these theories? How do new Keynesians explain the movement of real wages over the business cycle?

The theories do predict pro-cyclical wages. Although I've not looked at the models carefully on this question, my understanding is that they predict very pro-cyclical, real wages. While it is true that real wages are pro-cyclical, my reading of the evidence is that they are only mildly procyclical. Therefore, the fact that these theories predict very pro-cyclical real wages, and the data show that they are only mildly pro-cyclical, makes it hard to reconcile this model with the evidence. I think the real wage evidence is not that hard to explain. If you believe in a world where wages and prices are sluggish over time, the cyclical behaviour of the real wage is really a question of whether wages or prices are more sluggish. The fact that real wages are roughly a-cyclical, maybe slightly pro-cyclical, is some indication to me that wages and prices are simply equally sticky. This is consistent with Alan Blinder's evidence which says that prices change on average once a year, and we know a lot of wages change on average once a year. So I think that explanation is consistent with a lot of the evidence.

(See Blinder and Mankiw 1984; Mankiw *et al.* 1985; Mankiw 1991).

How do we explain pro-cyclical productivity? Some Keynesians seem to suggest that it is due to labour hoarding.

The pro-cyclical behaviour of productivity is a puzzle for people who don't believe in technology shocks. The traditional explanation for why productivity is pro-cyclical is labour hoarding. In recessions firms keep on workers they don't really need so that they can have the workers still available when the next boom comes, and that tends to give the appearance of pro-cyclical productivity. These theories make a lot of sense to me. I know I work my secretary harder when I have more work to be done; therefore her productivity is pro-cyclical. I know I work harder when there is more work to be done (*laughter*). I think there is a lot of causal evidence that labour hoarding and pro-cyclical effort are important.

(See Mankiw 1989: 83–5.)

ON MACROECONOMIC POLICY

One of the central ideas of Keynesian economics is that an increase in aggregate demand will stimulate the economy. Under what circumstances do you think a government should actually stimulate demand?

There are a couple of questions. First, when should it act? Second, how should it act? That is, should it use monetary or fiscal policy? On the first question, one should stimulate aggregate demand when it is too low to maintain full employment – that is when you observe very high unemployment or when there is reason to believe that unemployment is going to rise. The policy implications of a lot of new Keynesian theories really go back to a lot of the policy implications of the neoclassical synthesis of the 1960s. Some of the limitations on policy that were then debated are still relevant today. Even if you accept everything that new Keynesians say about prices being sluggish and so on, there is still the question of how good the government is at responding in a timely fashion to the shocks? In that debate, I side to a large extent with Milton Friedman. The government is very bad at recognizing shocks in a timely fashion, and when they do respond to shocks they often do so quite late and often counter-productively. So while I see the business cycle as a sign of market failure I also think it is a kind of market failure that a government is very limited in its ability to fix. If we have a very deep persistent recession, certainly something on the lines of the Great Depression, there is room for the government to do something. For the relatively minor wiggles that we have experienced in the post-war economy, it is not clear that the government can do a lot better than it has.
(See Mankiw 1992b: 322–41.)

Do you think Keynes was politically naive in thinking that politicians would be advised by technocrats and take the correct action? We are thinking here of the public choice literature and the political business cycle literature. Can we actually trust politicians once they have their hands on the fiscal and monetary levers to use them in the right way?

I think that is a serious concern but there are a lot of ways of fixing that problem. For example, there is a large literature showing that countries with more independent central banks have a lower inflation on average. With less independence in the central bank, there is more political pressure and therefore a greater possibility of following a policy of inflating too much. There are ways around the political problem, like making independent central banks, which to some extent are staffed by technocrats. For that reason an independent central bank would be better at fine-tuning the economy, to the extent we fine tune it at all, compared to fiscal policy which is always run by politicians.
(See Mankiw 1992b: 331–3; 1994.)

You've said that the literature on time inconsistency has provided a persuasive case for a commitment to some sort of rule for monetary policy, do you also support fiscal rules?

Fiscal rules have to be well crafted. A balanced budget amendment that is too strict could be a disaster. At certain times, like recessions and wars, it is appropriate to run budget deficits. So any fiscal rule has to take into account those special situations where budget deficits are the appropriate policy response. A fiscal rule by itself wouldn't be a bad idea, but it has to be well crafted and so far I haven't seen one that is.

Isn't one of the problems with devising rules that if the economy is hit by an unforeseen shock then the government really has to renege on that rule and take some discretionary action? It is difficult to think of a rule which really would be binding.

There are two parts to the question. First, how might you make the rule binding? Second, do you want to make the rule binding? One way to make the rule binding is reputational. Many rules are rules just because long tradition has established them as rules and people don't want to break tradition. Another more legalistic way of imposing rules is by writing them into the constitution. I think the harder question you raise is do you want to make rules binding? The question is whether you can write a rule that works well even in response to unforeseen events. If it becomes too costly to be tied by the rule people will stop abiding by it. What we want to do is write down a rule that will be good in response to normal kinds of shocks. That is, you don't know what the shocks are going to be, but you know what kind of shocks are possible. You've got oil shocks, monetary demand shocks and so on. You write down a rule that is good in response to the kinds of shocks you expect the economy to experience, based on the shocks experienced in the past. Therefore, unless something completely unforeseeable happens, you stick by the rule.

Leijonhufvud once argued that the economy can be thought of as travelling along a corridor, as long as it stays in the corridor leave it alone, but if it gets out of this corridor into a severe recession that is the time for intervention. Is that what you are saying? (See Leijonhufvud 1981.)

Well no, because recessions are reasonably foreseeable. Although you don't necessarily know when a recession is going to occur, you know that one will occur eventually. A recession is one of the contingencies that you want your rule to deal with. So I don't think a recession *per se* is one of those extraordinary events that make you want to break the rule. A recession is something you can plan for in advance. I'm talking about an event that not only can you not predict when it is going to happen, but you have never even thought that it might happen. For example, before 1973 people never imagined an OPEC supply shock. The whole idea of OPEC never even crossed anybody's mind. That is the type of situation where you might want to rethink the rule. Now that we know what OPEC is capable of, we can write down a rule that takes oil shocks into account.

What is the role of fiscal policy in new Keynesian macroeconomics?

To a large extent new Keynesian economics has been about the theory of aggregate supply and why it is that prices adjust slowly. It has been relatively neutral on the question of what determines aggregate demand, in particular whether monetary or fiscal policy levers are most useful. As I mentioned a moment ago, I am skeptical personally about the usefulness of fiscal policy in fine tuning the economy because, at least in the United States, the Congress acts very slowly. Even as we are doing this interview (18 February 1993) the Congress is debating a fiscal stimulus, even though the recovery has been going on for about a year now. By the time this fiscal stimulus actually has an effect on the economy, my guess is that we will be pretty close to the natural rate again. This is the perfect example of how the lags can be very long in fiscal policy. Monetary policy is a more useful tool for stabilizing aggregate demand.

(See Mankiw and Summers 1986.)

Do budget deficits matter?

I think they matter a lot. The main way they matter is not for short-run macroeconomic reasons but for long-run reasons – reasons that are best described not by Keynesian models but by growth models. The evidence as I see it is that large budget deficits reduce national saving. And the lesson from growth theory and growth experience across countries is that low saving leads to low growth. This is a big problem for the United States today.

(See Mankiw 1992b: 423–35.)

If you were advising President Clinton about macroeconomic policy for the next three or four years what would be the kinds of policies you feel are necessary?

My reaction to President Clinton's speech (17 February 1993) is that I don't think we need the fiscal stimulus that he is proposing. Recovery is already on its way. It wasn't a very deep recession to start off with, so I'm not terribly shocked that there is a mild recovery. It will take the fiscal stimulus a while to get people employed. I am happy that he is worried about the budget deficit, as low national saving is an important macro problem in the long term in the United States. Yet I am disappointed that he is putting so much emphasis on tax increases rather than spending cuts. That is really a view not so much about macroeconomics as about the size of government. I am also disappointed that he is giving no attention to the low rate of private saving in the United States. I would recommend tax reforms to remove the present disincentives toward saving. So I give him a mixed review.

CURRENT AND FUTURE PROGRESS IN MACROECONOMICS

Much research in the 1980s, your own included, was directed at providing more rigorous microeconomic foundations for the central elements of Keynesian economics. Taking an overview of the last decade how successful do you think that research has been in providing a more substantial micro foundation for Keynesian economics?

It has been successful at the theoretical level in the sense that one can now say that Keynesian economics, the economics of wage and price rigidities, is well founded on microeconomic models. There are now several microeconomic models that people can pull off the shelf. The theoretical challenge of Lucas and his followers has been met. It is less clear whether this line of research is going to be successful as an empirical matter. That is, to what extent does it yield new insights to help us understand actual economic fluctuations? Does it give us new ways to look at data and policies? The jury is still out on that one. There is a small empirical literature, but I can probably count the number of empirical papers on the fingers of two hands. I hope it is a growth area, but so far the literature has not been as empirically oriented as I would like.

(See Ball *et al.* 1988; Ball and Mankiw 1992a, 1992b; Mankiw 1985.)

Do you think there is some truth to the view that at the moment we have too many theories?

Yes, I have a lot of sympathy with that view. There is too big a premium for coming up with clever new theories in the profession. Yet I don't know of any way to solve this problem. Obviously I believe the things I believe, and I can't tell people that they should believe what I believe, just because there are too many theories (*laughter*). It would be nice if macroeconomists reached a consensus and they could do more work on details and less work on creating brand new theories of the business cycle. Until we do naturally reach a consensus, there is no way to enforce that by fiat.

Do you see any signs of an emerging consensus in macroeconomics?

That is a good question. I change my mind on that a lot depending on what conference I go to (*laughter*). I think there are certainly groups within the profession that are agreeing with each other. There is much agreement among new Keynesian people like Olivier Blanchard, Larry Ball, David Romer, George Akerlof, Alan Blinder and so on. Whether we as a group are coming to agreement with some of the real business cycle group is hard to say. I'm delighted that some of the people who previously worked closely with the real business cycle models are now trying to incorporate monetary effects into those models. That provides a hope that somewhere down the line the new Keynesian models and the real business cycle models are going to merge to some grand synthesis that incorporates the strengths of both approaches. That hasn't happened yet; that is just a hope.

(See Mankiw 1989: 88–9.)

MANKIW'S REINCARNATED KEYNESIANISM

Gregory Mankiw provides a relatively optimistic vision of the future of Keynesian macroeconomics which in his view has been 're-incarnated' since the mid-1980s rather than 'resurrected' in its old form. His Keynesian vision shares the spirit of Keynes in seeing economy-wide market failures caused by the inability of the invisible hand to maintain full employment. However, following the new classical critiques Mankiw, like many other Keynesians, accepts that the fatal defect of the neo-Keynesian synthesis model was the lack of an adequate theory of aggregate supply. To Mankiw and other new Keynesians the wage and price rigidities characteristic of Keynesian models could no longer remain as an assumption but required theoretically rigorous foundations. The vitality of the new classical revolution in the 1970s was attributable as much, if not more, to theoretical flaws in the supply side of the Keynesian model as it was to empirical dissatisfaction (see Mankiw 1988a). To remedy those theoretical flaws by building a Keynesian theory of aggregate supply which can rationally account for wage and price rigidities and hence the non-neutrality of money is for Mankiw the paramount job facing Keynesian theorists today. Indeed Mankiw goes further and argues that the reconstruction appears to be well on the way and that Lucas's criticisms relating to the microfoundations of Keynesian models have been met.

OLD V NEW KEYNESIANS

Although they share the spirit of Keynes, and Mankiw's work has in part been inspired by older Keynesian views, the difference between James Tobin's 'unreconstructed old Keynesian' views and Mankiw's reincarnation are striking. For Mankiw (and Romer) nominal aggregate demand disturbances have real effects because wages and prices are rigid (see Romer 1993). In sharp contrast Tobin argues that 'Keynesian macroeconomics neither asserts nor requires nominal wage and/or price rigidity' (Tobin 1993a). Indeed that Keynesian economics is defined by price rigidities is especially misleading if it suggests that such an assumption is necessary to generate Keynesian results. For Tobin the empirical fact that markets do not clear *instantaneously* leaves room, for 'flexibility in any common sense meaning of the word' and the resulting excess supply regimes allow quantities to determine quantities with output and employment constrained by deficient effective demand. Tobin also argues that the classical equilibrating mechanisms are 'weak' or 'possibly non existent or perverse' and certainly require help from activist government fiscal and monetary policy. According to Tobin (1993b) the suggestion that 'Keynesian economics is doomed without new theories to explain price and wage rigidities is to misunderstand Keynes himself and old Keynesian economics'. It is evident from Mankiw's answers to our questions that his brand of new Keynesianism has been heavily influenced by the theoretical and empirical contributions of Friedman (1968), Lucas (1972) and Kydland and Prescott (1977). In particular he questions the desirability of activist discretionary fiscal policy as a stabilizing weapon and following the new classical work on the dynamic inconsistency of monetary policy he has also been persuaded by the arguments in favour of a monetary rule, something old (and some new) Keynesians would never subscribe to.

Bruce Greenwald and Joseph Stiglitz, both leading new Keynesians, appear to occupy an intermediate position somewhere between that of Tobin and Mankiw. Greenwald and Stiglitz support Tobin's old Keynesian position that increasing wage and price flexibility might well exacerbate a recession. This alternative new Keynesian view suggests 'that natural economic forces can magnify economic shocks that may seem small and that existing price rigidities may *reduce* the magnitude of the fluctuations as Keynes argued' (see Greenwald and Stiglitz 1993a). Hence for Greenwald and Stiglitz the single-minded focus by Mankiw and others on wage and price rigidities would appear to be somewhat misguided. With respect to the policy implications of new Keynesian economics Stiglitz supports a more interventionist stance than Mankiw. Most recently Stiglitz has noted that new Keynesians 'disagree with virtually every one of the presumptions underlying non-interventionist theories' (see Stiglitz 1993: ch. 39). He argues that the government on balance has done more to stabilize than destabilize the economy and should certainly not bind itself to fixed rules of the kind advocated by Milton Friedman (1968), Robert Barro (1986), Finn Kydland and Edward Prescott (1977). Like Tobin, Stiglitz favours discretionary policies because 'changing economic circumstances require changes in economic policy, and it is impossible to prescribe ahead of time what policies would be appropriate'. Indeed Stiglitz questions whether it would ever be possible for a government to stick by a rule because 'if the unemployment rate becomes high, government must and will do something regardless of what is said' (Stiglitz 1993). However Stiglitz, like Mankiw, is not as optimistic as old Keynesians on the ability of government to *fine tune* the economy. Here the monetarist and new classical arguments have modified all new Keynesian views (and no doubt some old ones also). Stiglitz, like Mankiw, accepts that 'by attempting to do too much the government may do worse than it would if it were less ambitious' (Stiglitz 1993).

Old and new Keynesians alike are united in their view that the traditional IS-LM model remains the best way to think about the demand side of the macro models although Tobin gives emphasis to real rather than nominal demand shocks (see Tobin 1993a). Their more unified position here differs considerably from that of equilibrium business cycle theorists. For example in Robert King's contribution to the Symposium on Keynesian Economics Today, he criticizes new Keynesians like Mankiw for maintaining their faith in the textbook IS-LM model (see King 1993; Mankiw 1990). This is because 'of its treatment of expectations the IS-LM model, as traditionally constructed and currently used, is a hazardous base on which to build positive theories of business fluctuations and to undertake policy analysis'

(King 1993). However, even if Keynesians old and new agree on the IS-LM interpretation of aggregate demand a further complication arises in connection with the recent work of Greenwald and Stiglitz on financial market imperfections and business cycles (see Greenwald and Stiglitz 1993a; 1993b; Stiglitz 1993). The Greenwald and Stiglitz model shows how a negative aggregate demand shock could translate itself into a leftward shift of the aggregate supply schedule due to firms' increased perception of risk during an economic downturn. Due to financial market imperfections generated by asymmetric information equity rationed firms can only partially diversify out the risks they face. Their resultant dependence on debt rather than new equity issues to finance investment makes firms more vulnerable to bankruptcy the higher the level of their output. Hence any changes in a firm's net worth position or in their perception of the risks they face will have a negative effect on their willingness to produce. Risk-averse firms will be less willing to supply at every price when the environment becomes less favourable and increasingly uncertain. When in an economic downturn firms observe a shift in their demand curve they must either reduce their output or their price. Risk-averse firms prefer to adjust their output because the 'uncertainties associated with changing prices may be much greater' (Stiglitz 1993). In such a world the Greenwald-Stiglitz model suggests that wage and price flexibility may well be destabilizing and exacerbate any economic downturn. The important implication is that the resultant *risk-based aggregate supply curve* will shift leftwards following an economic downturn initiated by an aggregate demand shock. This results in the non-neutrality of money even if prices are perfectly flexible.

A NEW KEYNESIAN–MONETARIST SYNTHESIS?

Not all Keynesian economists are as convinced as Gregory Mankiw and other new Keynesians that real progress has been made since the mid-1970s. Alan Blinder has questioned whether the 'prodigious amounts of labour and capital devoted to macroeconomic research since 1972 have been allocated correctly' and Olivier Blanchard has criticized the readiness of macroeconomists to adopt the new classical 'quasi-religious insistence on microfoundations' which has led to the construction of 'too many monsters with few interesting results' (see Blinder 1986; Blanchard 1992). Certainly the new Keynesian developments have been criticized for their lack of attention to empirical research, a criticism Mankiw accepts. However, given that the new classical critique was launched mainly from a theoretical rather than an empirical base it is perhaps understandable that younger Keynesians, at least initially, have concentrated their efforts on providing 'fort Keynes' with more solid microfoundations rather than giving continuing emphasis to empirical work (see Snowdon *et al.* 1994: ch. 7).

So where does macroeconomics go from here? David Laidler, Olivier Blanchard and Alan Blinder have made it abundantly clear that in their view a monetarist augmented mainstream macroeconomics, circa 1972, although not perfect, 'had solid foundations and was basically right' (see Blanchard 1992; Laidler 1992; Blinder 1992b). By the mid-1970s the impact of supply shocks had been successfully incorporated into the mainstream model and as a result it has, in their view, proved capable of withstanding the new classical challenge. Thus the current debate is now mainly between a small but very influential group of equilibrium business cycle theorists (Robert Barro's 'good guys') and a larger group of mainstream macroeconomists who adhere to what could justifiably be called a new Keynesian – monetarist synthesis (Robert Barro's 'bad guys': see Barro 1989). However, as we have noted above, an important implication of the work of Greenwald and Stiglitz is that the traditional distinction between aggregate demand and aggregate supply disturbances, although useful as an organizing principle, may be misleading. In a similar vein Benjamin Friedman has recently argued that 'Many occurrences that initially seem to represent disturbances to aggregate supply likewise cause disturbances to aggregate demand and vice versa' (Friedman 1992). Indeed Greenwald and Stiglitz even suggest that their theory of risk-averse firms if combined with market clearing flexible wages and prices can be viewed as a special case of real business cycle theory. This requires that the financial disorganization and risk associated with recessions can be thought of as representing a form of negative shock to technology and capital. Perhaps here there is some hope that this line of research could lead to some future collaboration between the 'good guys' and the 'bad guys'.

CONCLUDING REMARKS

The remarkable versatility of Keynesian economics guarantees that it will continue to serve as a relevant research programme which will influence both theoretical developments and policy proposals. It remains to be seen if Gregory Mankiw's optimism with respect to the usefulness of the burgeoning new Keynesian microfoundations literature significantly improves our understanding of macroeconomic phenomena. We share Mankiw's optimism. Keynesian economics, in resurrected or reincarnated form, is alive and well. Recent controversies surely confirm the observation made by Sir Denis Robertson (1954) many years ago when he noted that:

> Highbrow opinion is like a hunted hare; if you stand in the same place, or nearly the same place, it can be relied upon to come round to you in a circle.

So it's back to the future!

NOTES

1 Taken from 'Ends and Means in Economics,' in *Selected Papers on Economic Theory* (ed. E. Lindahl, London: Allen and Unwin, 1958).

2 This interview was one in a series held in connection with the preparation of a book published by Edward Elgar (see Snowdon, Vane and Wynarczyk 1994).
3 Cited in Mankiw (1992a).

REFERENCES

Akerlof, G. A. and Yellen, J. L. (1985) 'A Near-Rational Model of the Business Cycle, with Wage and Price Inertia', *Quarterly Journal of Economics*, Supplement.

Akerlof, G. A. and Yellen, J. L. (1990) 'The Fair Wage-Effort Hypothesis and Unemployment', *Quarterly Journal of Economics* May.

Ball, L. (1994) 'What Determines the Sacrifice Ratio?', In *Monetary Policy* (ed. N.G. Mankiw), Chicago: University of Chicago Press.

Ball, L. and Mankiw, N. G. (1992a) 'Asymmetric Price Adjustment and Economic Fluctuations', *Harvard Institute of Economic Research*, Discussion Paper no. 1602, July.

Ball, L. and Mankiw, N. G. (1992b) 'Relative-Price Change As Aggregate Supply Shocks', *National Bureau of Economic Research*, Working Paper no. 4168, September.

Ball, L. and Romer, D. (1990) 'Real Rigidities and the Non-Neutrality of Money', *Review of Economic Studies* April.

Ball, L. and Romer, D. (1991) 'Sticky Prices as Coordination Failure', *American Economic Review* June.

Ball, L., Mankiw, N. G. and Romer, D. (1988) 'The New Keynesian Economics and the Output–Inflation Trade-Off', *Brookings Papers on Economic Activity*.

Barro, R. J. (1979) 'Second Thoughts on Keynesian Economics', *American Economic Review* May.

Barro, R. J. (1986) 'Recent Developments in the Theory of Rules Versus Discretion', *Economic Journal* Supplement.

Barro, R. J. (1989) 'New Classicals and Keynesians, or the Good Guys and the Bad Guys', *Schwiez Zeitschrift für Volkswirtschaft und Statistik*.

Blanchard, O. J. (1992) 'For a Return to Pragmatism', in *The Business Cycle: Theories and Evidence* (eds M. Belongia and M. Garfinkel), London: Kluwer Academic.

Blinder, A. S. (1986) 'Keynes After Lucas', *Eastern Economic Journal* July/September.

Blinder, A. S. (1988) 'The Fall and Rise of Keynesian Economics', *Economic Record* December.

Blinder, A. S. (1991) 'Why Are Prices Sticky? Preliminary Results from an Interview Study', *American Economic Review* May.

Blinder, A. S. (1992a) 'A Keynesian Restoration is Here', *Challenge*, September/October.

Blinder, A. S. (1992b) 'Déjà Vu All Over Again', in *The Business Cycle: Theories and Evidence* (eds M. Belongia and M. Garfinkel), London: Kluwer Academic.

Blinder, A. S. and Mankiw, N. G. (1984) 'Aggregation and Stabilization Policies in a Multi-Contract Economy', *Journal of Monetary Economics* January.

Campbell, J. Y. and Mankiw, N. G. (1989) 'International Evidence on the Persistence of Economic Fluctuations', *Journal of Monetary Economics* March.

Cooper, R. and John, A. (1988) 'Coordinating Coordination Failures in Keynesian Models', *Quarterly Journal of Economics* August.

Diamond, P. A. (1982) 'Aggregate Demand Management in Search Equilibrium', *Journal of Political Economy* October.

Fischer, S. (1977) 'Long-Term Contracts, Rational Expectations, and the Optimal Money Supply Rule', *Journal of Political Economy* February.

476 *Brian Snowdon and Howard Vane*

Fischer, S. (1988) 'Recent Developments in Macroeconomics', *Economic Journal* June.

Friedman, B. (1992) 'How Does It Matter?', in *The Business Cycle: Theories and Evidence* (eds M. Belongia and M. Garfinkel), London: Kluwer Academic.

Friedman, M. (1968) 'The Role of Monetary Policy', *American Economic Review* March.

Gordon, R. J. (1990) 'What Is New-Keynesian Economics?', *Journal of Economic Literature* September.

Greenwald, B. and Stiglitz, J. (1993a) 'New and Old Keynesians', *Journal of Economic Perspectives* Winter.

Greenwald, B. and Stiglitz, J. (1993b) 'Financial Markets, Imperfections and Business Cycles', *Quarterly Journal of Economics* February.

Hoover, K. D. (ed.) (1992) *The New Classical Macroeconomics*, Aldershot: Edward Elgar.

Howitt, P. W. (1990) *The Keynesian Recovery*, Oxford: Philip Allan.

King, R. G. (1993) 'Will the New Keynesian Macroeconomics Resurrect the IS-LM Model?', *Journal of Economic Perspectives* Winter.

Kydland, F. E. and Prescott, E. C. (1977) 'Rules Rather than Discretion: The Inconsistency of Optimal Plans', *Journal of Political Economy* June.

Laidler, D. E. W. (1992) 'The Cycle Before New Classical Economics', in *The Business Cycles: Theories and Evidence* (eds M. Belongia and M. Garfinkel), London: Kluwer Academic.

Laing, D. (1993) 'A Signalling Theory of Nominal Wage Inflexibility', *Economic Journal* November.

Leijonhufvud, A. (1981) *Information and Coordination: Essays in Macroeconomic Theory*, Oxford: Oxford University Press.

Leslie, D. (1993) *Advanced Macroeconomics Beyond IS-LM*, Maidenhead: McGraw-Hill.

Lindbeck, A. and Snower, D. (1986) 'Wage Setting, Unemployment, and Insider–Outsider Relations', *American Economic Review* May.

Lucas, R. E. Jr (1972) 'Expectations and the Neutrality of Money', *Journal of Economic Theory* April.

Lucas, R. E. Jr (1973) 'Some International Evidence on Output–Inflation Trade-offs', *American Economic Review* June.

Lucas, R. E. Jr (1978) 'Unemployment Policy', *American Economic Review* May.

Lucas, R. E. Jr and Sargent, T. J. (1978) 'After Keynesian Macroeconomics', in *After the Phillips Curve: Persistence of High Inflation and High Unemployment*, Boston; Federal Reserve Bank of Boston.

Mankiw, N. G. (1985) 'Small Menu Costs and Large Business Cycles: A Macroeconomic Model of Monopoly', *Quarterly Journal of Economics* May.

Mankiw, N. G. (1986a) 'Issues in Keynesian Macroeconomics: A Review Essay', *Journal of Monetary Economics* September.

Mankiw, N. G. (1986b) 'The Allocation of Credit and Financial Collapse', *Quarterly Journal of Economics* August.

Mankiw, N. G. (1987) 'Comment' on J. J. Rotemberg, 'The New Keynesian Microfoundations', *NBER Macroeconomics Annual*.

Mankiw, N. G. (1988a) 'Recent Developments in Macroeconomics: A Very Quick Refresher Course', *Journal of Money, Credit and Banking* August.

Mankiw, N. G. (1988b) 'Imperfect Competition and the Keynesian Cross', *Economic Letters*.

Mankiw, N. G. (1989) 'Real Business Cycles: A New Keynesian Perspective', *Journal of Economic Perspectives* Summer.

Mankiw, N. G. (1990) 'A Quick Refresher Course in Macroeconomics', *Journal of Economic Literature* December.

Mankiw, N. G. (1991) 'Comment on J. J. Rotemberg and M. Woodford "Markups and the Business Cycle"', *NBER Macroeconomics Annual*.

Mankiw, N. G. (1992a) 'The Reincarnation of Keynesian Economics', *European Economic Review* April.

Mankiw, N. G. (1992b) *Macroeconomics*, New York: Worth.

Mankiw, N. G. (ed.) (1994) *Monetary Policy*, Chicago: University of Chicago Press.

Mankiw, N. G. and Romer, D. (eds) (1991) *New Keynesian Economics*, 2 vols, Cambridge, MA: MIT Press.

Mankiw, N. G. and Summers, L. H. (1986) 'Money Demand and the Effect of Fiscal Policies', *Journal of Money, Credit and Banking* November.

Mankiw, N. G., Rotemberg, J. J. and Summers, L. H. (1985) 'Intertemporal Substitution in Macroeconomics', *Quarterly Journal of Economics* February.

Mankiw, N. G., Miron, J. A. and Weil, D. N. (1987) 'The Adjustment of Expectations to a Change in Regime: A Study of the Founding of the Federal Reserve', *American Economic Review* June.

Parkin, M. (1992) 'Where Do We Stand?', in *The Business Cycle: Theories and Evidence* (eds M. Belongia and M. Garfinkel), London: Kluwer Academic.

Phelps, E. S. (ed.) (1991) *Recent Developments in Macroeconomics*, Aldershot: Edward Elgar.

Phelps, E. S. (1994) *Structural Slumps: The Modern Equilibrium Theory of Unemployment, Interest and Assets*, Cambridge, MA: Harvard University Press.

Robertson, D. H. (1954) 'Thoughts on Meeting Some Important Persons', *Quarterly Journal of Economics* May.

Romer, D. (1993) 'The New Keynesian Synthesis', *Journal of Economic Perspectives* Winter.

Shapiro, C. and Stiglitz, J. (1984) 'Equilibrium Unemployment as a Discipline Device', *American Economic Review* June.

Snowdon, B., Vane, H. R. and Wynarczyk, P. (1994) *A Modern Guide to Macroeconomics: An Introduction to Competing Schools of Thought*, Aldershot and Vermont: Edward Elgar.

Solow, R. M. (1990) *The Labour Market as a Social Institution*, Oxford: Basil Blackwell.

Stiglitz, J. (1993) *Economics*, New York: W. W. Norton.

Taylor, J. B. (1979) 'Staggered Wage Setting in a Macro Model', *American Economic Review* May.

Tobin, J. (1977) 'How Dead is Keynes?', *Economic Inquiry* October.

Tobin, J. (1988) 'Comment' on David Romer's paper on 'What Are the Costs of Excessive Deficits?', *NBER Macroeconomics Annual*.

Tobin, J. (1993a) 'Price Flexibility and Output Stability: An Old Keynesian View', *Journal of Economic Perspectives* Winter.

Tobin, J. (1993b) 'Price Flexibility and the Stability of Full Employment Equilibrium', in *Monetary Theory and Thought* (eds H. Barkai, S. Fischer and N. Livitian), London: Macmillan.

Yellen, J. L. (1984) 'Efficiency Wage Models of Unemployment', *American Economic Review* May.

21 What is new-Keynesian economics?

Robert J. Gordon

Journal of Economic Literature (1990) 28, September, pp. 1115–71

1 INTRODUCTION

Background

In the late 1970s it appeared that the US macroeconomic landscape was being swept by a new-classical tide, and that Keynesian economics had become an isolated backwater. In fact there is still a widespread impression that the best and brightest young macroeconomists almost uniformly marched under the new-classical banner as the decade of the 1980s began.[1] Yet it is now apparent that the rumours of the death of Keynesian economics were greatly exaggerated. Building on foundations laid in the late 1970s by Stanley Fischer (1977a) and Edmund Phelps and John Taylor (1977), a large number of authors, young and middle-aged alike, since the late 1970s have produced an outpouring of research within the Keynesian tradition that attempts to build the microeconomic foundations of wage and·price stickiness. The adjective *new-Keynesian* nicely juxtaposes this body of research with its arch-opposite, the new-classical approach.[2]

This chapter extracts the essential elements of new-Keynesian economics for an audience of professional economists who are not specialists in the microeconomic foundations of macroeconomics. There is no intention to survey comprehensively every notable paper in the field, but rather to sift the literature for the most important ideas and themes. One commentator has asserted that the new-Keynesian literature has provided *too many* explanations of wage and price stickiness, and so we apply tough standards to the major contributions, asking whether they make an essential contribution to an understanding of the adjustment of wages and prices. In short, our intent is to ask what is new and what is convincing in the large literature that collectively has become known as the new Keynesian economics.

Main themes

Like its precursor a decade previously (R. Gordon 1981), this chapter differs from conventional surveys not just in its intent to sift and criticize rather than to provide a broad and evenhanded overview. It also contains a substantial empirical prologue before reaching the core material on new-Keynesian theory. The prologue (sections 1 and 2) argues that there are three different dimensions of price stickiness (which we will label the *inertia*, *rate-of-change*, and *level effects*). A brief survey of the emerging literature in the new empirical industrial organization, together with a new empirical time-series investigation of price adjustment across time and countries, reveals the essential fact that any satisfactory theory of price adjustment must explain the *variability* of price adjustment parameters across industries, across countries, and across historical intervals. We ultimately reach the verdict that much of new-Keynesian theory does not succeed in explaining these facts.

The prologue (Sections 2 and 3) is followed by the core of the chapter, the critical review of theoretical contributions in the new-Keynesian literature. The review is organized by recognizing two central distinctions, the first between price setting in product markets and wage setting in labor markets, and the second between nominal rigidity and real rigidity. The theoretical analysis in the chapter is organized into a treatment of main themes and issues (Section 4), and discussions of nominal rigidity in the product market (Section 5), real rigidity in the product market (Section 6), and models of labor market rigidity (Section 7), followed by a conclusion (Section 8).

The task of new-Keynesian economics is to explain why changes in the aggregate price level are sticky, that is, why price changes do not mimic changes in nominal GNP. Sticky prices imply that real GNP is not an object of choice by individual workers and firms but rather is cast adrift as a residual. Thus new-Keynesian economics is about the choices of monopolistically competitive firms that set their individual prices and accept the level of real sales as a constraint, in contrast to new-classical economics in which competitive price-taking firms make choices about output.

Why do changes in the aggregate price level fail to mimic changes in nominal GNP? Two main themes emerge from the theoretical review, (1) the reasons for the absence of nominal GNP indexation of individual prices, and (2) the reasons why, in the absence of such indexation, individual prices fail fully to reflect changes in nominal GNP. Underlying the first theme is an essential element of any industrial economy – the role of idiosyncratic elements of cost and demand. Firms care about the relation of their own price to their own marginal cost. But because idiosyncratic shocks cause their own costs and demand to evolve differently than nominal aggregate demand, firms have no reason to accept the risk involved in indexing their price to nominal aggregate demand. The absence of nominal GNP indexation opens the way for theories of real rigidity to explain the sources of nominal price stickiness.

The second theme is that, in the absence of nominal GNP indexation, changes in individual prices will respond to changes in individual marginal costs, not changes in nominal GNP. Thus the aggregate price level will be sticky unless firms expect changes in their own marginal costs to mimic changes in nominal GNP. Yet they have no such expectation. In the framework that I label the *input-output* approach, each of thousands of heterogeneous firms is enmeshed in a web of intricate supplier–demander relationships. The input-output element helps to explain why firms do not simply assume that marginal costs will move in parallel with aggregate nominal demand: most firms do not know the identity of all of their suppliers, their suppliers' suppliers, and so on. The input-output approach places equal emphasis on the purchase-material and labor-cost components of marginal cost and points to models of real rigidities in the labor market, including the efficiency wage and insider-outsider models, to help explain why prices are less flexible in some industries than in others.

An important empirical finding in Section 3 is that prices were sticky not just in the Great Depression and the postwar era, but long before World War I. This fact casts doubt on institutional sources of price and wage rigidity, for example, labor unions, and reinforces our emphasis on universal features of microeconomic structure. In our treatment, price and wage stickiness emerges from a core set of microeconomic elements that are timeless and placeless: a technology of transactions, heterogeneity of goods and factor inputs, imperfect competition, imperfect information, and imperfect capital markets. Because these core elements remove any incentive for individual agents to focus on nominal demand in making their own price-setting decisions, their presence supports the traditional view that Keynesian economics is fundamentally about the macroeconomic externalities of individual decisions and the coordination failure inherent in a free-market economy.

The dichotomy between supply and demand

With much ground to cover, there are many interesting topics in macroeconomics that cannot be treated here. The coverage is limited to the determinants of aggregate supply behavior, roughly, the division of a change in nominal GNP growth between changes in prices and output, and the role of wage stickiness (if any) in contributing to price stickiness. The entire demand side of the economy is omitted as beyond the scope of the chapter. In particular, we pay no attention to the reasons why aggregate demand fluctuations exhibit positive serial correlation, nor to the respective role of monetary and nonmonetary demand disturbances in causing these fluctuations, nor to the significance of changes in the behavior of money demand and velocity that have occurred in the 1980s, nor to the merits of monetary rules, nor to the relative merits of monetary rules versus nominal GNP rules. These topics on the demand side can be omitted, simply because they are not at the heart of the conflict between new-Keynesian and new-classical macroeconomics.

Omission of the demand side from the scope of the chapter leads us to skip over those contributions, sometimes classified as new-Keynesian, which emphasize credit rationing as a source of fluctuations in commodity demand and as a channel through which the influence of monetary policy is transmitted (see Blanchard and Fischer 1989: 478–88).[3] We also omit any treatment of feedbacks from changes in the parameters of aggregate price stickiness to the variance of aggregate nominal demand (see the debate between Taylor 1986, and DeLong and Summers 1986).[4] We take as a precedent for imposing a dichotomy between supply and demand, and for assuming nominal GNP to be exogenous, Robert Lucas' famous paper on the international output–inflation trade-off (1973), which assumed that nominal GNP was an exogenous random walk. In short, we are interested here in the price times output side of the quantity equation ($MV \equiv PQ$), to the exclusion of the money times velocity side.

However, our focus here on nominal GNP rather than money helps to clarify one source of frequent misunderstanding in this area. New-Keynesian macroeconomics is not limited to the question 'Why does money affect output?'[5] If prices are sticky, then any change in nominal GNP will affect real output, no matter whether its source is a change in the nominal money supply or some autonomous movement of spending on consumption, investment, government purchases, or net exports. Further, nominal price stickiness opens the way for supply shocks, for example, a change in the relative price of oil, to create macroeconomic externalities that supplement the initial impact on output of the shock by induced demand feedbacks. The microeconomic theories surveyed in this chapter apply equally to the broad question as to why demand disturbances in money and autonomous spending, as well as supply shocks, cause changes in real output.[6]

2 THE THREE DIMENSIONS OF WAGE AND PRICE STICKINESS

Price stickiness in the presence of policy feedback

A prerequisite for any theory purporting to explain wage and/or price stickiness is a demonstration that the phenomenon of stickiness exists in realworld data. In this section we begin by defining three different dimensions of price stickiness and distinguish between the essential role of price stickiness and the peripheral role of wage stickiness. The exposition is carried out insofar as possible with a set of identities, which clarify issues without imposing any theory at all.

By definition, the log of nominal GNP (X) must be divided between the log of the GNP deflator (P) and the log of real GNP (Q):

$$X \equiv P + Q. \tag{1}$$

Reserving uppercase letters for logs of levels and lowercase letters for percentage changes per unit of time, we take the time derivative of (1) and obtain:

$$x \equiv p + q, \tag{2}$$

which states that any change in nominal GNP must be divided between a change in the aggregate price level and a change in real GNP. Next, we subtract from both sides of (2) the long-run equilibrium or natural growth rate of real GNP (q^*), and use a 'hat' ($\hat{\ }$) to designate variables defined net of that trend growth rate of real output:

$$x - q^* \equiv p + (q - q^*);$$
$$\hat{x} \equiv p + \hat{q}. \tag{3}$$

This states that an excess of nominal GNP growth over the long-run growth rate of real output ($\hat{x}$) must be accompanied by some combination of inflation (p) and a deviation of real output from that same long-run growth rate ($\hat{q}$).

In many recessions and depressions over the course of the industrial era the economy has experienced a decline in output and employment that appears to have constrained employees to work fewer hours than they wished at the current real wage, and firms to produce less output than they wished at the current price. These episodes admit the possibility that actual output and long-run equilibrium output are two distinct concepts, implying in turn that the way is open to consider the meaning of price stickiness. For instance, if the rate of change of prices over the business cycle is always equal to some constant fraction (α) of the excess nominal GNP movement, then business-cycle movements in real output ($\hat{q}$) must soak up the remaining fraction ($1 - \alpha$):

$$p = \alpha\hat{x},$$
$$\hat{q} = \hat{x} - p = (1 - \alpha)\hat{x}. \tag{4}$$

One concludes from (4) that an economy with relatively sticky prices (a small α) must exhibit correspondingly large fluctuations in real output, as long as fluctuations in nominal demand ($\hat{x}$) are independent of the price stickiness parameter α.

It is tempting to estimate a regression equation like either line of (4) to determine the degree of price stickiness (α). But four crucial features of the economy – level effects, inertia effects, policy feedback, and supply shocks – are ignored in (4) and may invalidate any interpretation of an estimated value of α as representing a structural price-stickiness coefficient. The first problem is that (4) ignores level or Phillips-curve effects. It is possible for actual output to be growing at its long-run equilibrium *growth rate* (i.e. $\hat{x} = 0$) while being off its equilibrium *growth path*, that is, when there is a gap between the levels of actual and equilibrium output. The second problem is the possible presence of price inertia, as occurs when lagged variables (especially lagged inflation) enter into the determination of current inflation. We defer the introduction of level and inertia effects until the next section in order to concentrate on the other two basic problems with (4), which concern policy feedback and supply shocks.

The third problem is the possible presence of policy feedback from inflation to excess nominal GNP growth, as would occur with a policy of monetary accommodation to price changes. Such feedback would be implied when the central bank attempts to peg or stabilize interest rates, or with a real bills doctrine in which bank loans automatically expand to meet the needs of trade. The fourth problem arises in the presence of autonomous supply shocks which shift the rate of price change up and down relative to that predicted by (4). We now consider a model in which the interaction between policy feedback and supply shocks becomes crucial in estimating the coefficient of price adjustment (α) in an equation like (4). The subsequent results on coefficient bias apply to literally every empirical study that has attempted to relate price or output change to such endogenous variables as nominal or real GNP, the money supply, or unemployment.

Consider the two-equation model:

$$p = \alpha\hat{x} + z$$
$$\hat{x} = \theta p + e, \tag{5}$$

where z is the supply-shock term and e is the demand shock. The coefficient of policy feedback (θ) would be positive if growth in the money supply responds positively to a contemporaneous change in the inflation rate.

It is easy to see that in a world with no supply shocks ($z = 0$), policy accommodation makes no difference. Here we relegate the algebra to the source note in Table 21.1 and consider a numerical example with a 10 percent positive realization of e, a price-adjustment parameter $\alpha = 0.5$, and a policy accommodation parameter $\theta = 1.0$. Then (5) is satisfied with the values $p = 10$, $\hat{x} = 20$, and $\hat{q} = 10$. A regression of p on $\hat{x}$ for a sample period with no supply shocks will recover the correct value of α, $0.5 = 10/20$. Despite policy feedback, we would correctly infer that the smaller the price adjustment coefficient, the larger the amplitude of output fluctuations in $\hat{q}$. Intuitively, because in the absence of supply shocks price change depends *only* on nominal demand ($\hat{x}$), and any policy feedback simply 'blows up' price and nominal demand change by the same proportion.

We cannot, however, recover the correct value of α in the presence of supply shocks. With a supply shock $z = 10$ but no demand shock ($e = 0$), and with the same values of α and θ, (5) is satisfied for $p = \hat{x} = 20$ and $\hat{q} = 0$. If no 'z' variable is included to capture the supply-shock effect, a simple regression of p on $\hat{x}$ will recover an incorrect value of $\alpha = 1$. In general, as shown in the notes to Table 21.1, a regression of p on $\hat{x}$ in a sample containing both demand and supply shocks will yield an upward biased estimate of the price-adjustment parameter α, the larger is the accommodation parameter (θ) and the larger is the variance of supply shocks relative to demand shocks ($\sigma^2 z / \sigma^2 e$). The problem cannot be avoided by replacing nominal GNP change ($\hat{x}$) by real GNP change ($\hat{q}$) in the first equation in (5), because this would introduce a negative bias that works in reverse and is larger, the *smaller* the extent of policy accommodation.

Table 21.1 provides examples of the bias that will result in estimating the price-stickiness coefficient (α), when excess nominal GNP growth ($\hat{x}$) or excess real GNP growth ($\hat{q}$) are used as the alternative explanatory demand growth variables. Columns 3 and 4 show that there is no bias in using $\hat{x}$ with any degree of policy feedback or any importance of supply shocks, as long as both do not occur together. Using $\hat{q}$ as the explanatory variable introduces a downward bias when there are supply shocks, even if there is no policy feedback. In intermediate situations, as on lines 4 and 5, estimates using alternatively $\hat{x}$ and $\hat{q}$ bracket the true value. Using $\hat{q}$ retrieves the correct coefficient only when policy feedback is complete, that is, when policy fully accommodates the supply shock, as in lines 6 and 7.

We reach five important conclusions from this analysis. First, to the extent that demand shocks have been substantially more important than supply shocks (at least prior to the oil-shock decade of the 1970s), the degree of price stickiness can be measured by the coefficient on excess nominal GNP change ($\hat{x}$) in a regression equation explaining price change, even if policy has partially or wholly accommodated price changes. Second,

Table 21.1 Range of estimated price stickiness coefficients when the true coefficient is $\alpha = 0.25$

Line	Policy response coefficient (θ)	Relative importance of supply shocks (r)	Estimated value of α when regressor is	
			$\hat{x}$	$\hat{q}$
	(1)	*(2)*	*(3)*	*(4)*
1	0	0	0.25	0.25
2	0	0.25	0.25	0.06
3	0	1	0.25	−0.50
4	0.5	0.25	0.35	0.12
5	0.5	1	0.60	−0.15
6	1	0.25	0.40	0.25
7	1	1	0.63	0.25

Sources by column: With reference to the model in equation (5) in the text, the estimated coefficient $E(\alpha)$ in column (3) is the true coefficient (α) plus the ratio of the covariance of $\hat{x}$ with z divided by the variance of $\hat{x}$:

$$E(\alpha) = \alpha + [\theta(1 - \alpha\theta)r]/[1 + \theta^2 r],$$

where $r = \sigma^2 z/\sigma^2 e$. When $\hat{q}(= \hat{x} - p)$ is used as an alternative explanatory variable in the first equation of (5), instead of $\hat{x}$, the equation estimated is $p = \beta\hat{q}$, and the estimated coefficient $E(\beta)$ is

$$E(\beta) = \beta - \{(1 - \theta)[1 + \beta(1 - \theta)]\}/[1 + (1 - \theta)^2 r].$$

The coefficient shown in column (4) is the value of α that would be calculated on the assumption that β is true, $\alpha = \beta/(1 + \beta)$.

in view of the widespread view of Milton Friedman and Anna Schwartz (1963) and most commentators that monetary policy has been accommodative (i.e. procyclical rather than countercyclical), the price-adjustment coefficient is more likely to be upward than downward biased when the demand variable is $\hat{x}$, thus overstating the extent of price flexibility and tilting the conclusions *against* the new-Keynesian view that prices are sticky and *toward* the new-classical view that prices are flexible. Third, in the presence of partial policy accommodation, equations with nominal and real GNP changes ($\hat{x}$ and $\hat{q}$) as alternative demand variables will bracket the true coefficient of price stickiness. Fourth, any empirical study of price adjustment should attempt to find proxies for the supply shocks themselves, rather than allowing such shocks to remain hidden in the error term, in order to minimize these biases that occur in the presence of policy accommodation. Fifth, any study that does not control for supply shocks is likely to reach unreliable conclusions regarding the extent and/or secular change in price stickiness. For instance, a conclusion that prices had become more sticky since World War II could be subject to the criticism that prewar price adjustment coefficients are upward biased because of some combination of (*a*) greater prewar policy accommodation and (*b*) a higher prewar variance of unmeasured supply shocks.

Where the Phillips curve and price inertia fit in

One reason different authors disagree on historical changes in the extent of price stickiness is that authors have focused on different dimensions of stickiness. Thus far we have characterized price stickiness by a single parameter (α), which denotes the marginal response of the rate of price change to a change in the excess growth rate of nominal GNP. Yet this relation between the *change* in prices and the *change* in demand stands in contrast to the relation between the *change* in prices and the *level* of demand, that is, the Phillips curve, that may come first to mind in connection with price adjustment. While the Phillips curve was originally developed (Phillips 1958) as an association between the change in nominal wage rates and the level of unemployment, it has become common to use the Phillips-curve terminology to label any relation between the *rate of change* of nominal prices or wages and the *level* of a utilization variable like the unemployment rate or detrended output. Here we focus on detrended output rather than unemployment and, because our interest is primarily in price rather than wage stickiness, we write a Phillips-curve relation for price change:[7]

$$p_t = \gamma \hat{Q}_t + z_t, \tag{6}$$

where $\hat{Q}_t$ is the log ratio of actual to natural output, and we indicate explicitly the time subscript that previously has been suppressed. The supply-shock term from (5) is included here in each subsequent price adjustment equation, in view of our previous conclusion that adjustment coefficients will be biased unless a careful attempt is made to control for supply shocks.

A third dimension of price stickiness is serial correlation, sometimes simply called *inertia*. A frequent specification of the postwar US inflation process combines the Phillips curve and inertia.[8]

$$p_t = \lambda p_{t-1} + \gamma \hat{Q}_t + z_t. \tag{7}$$

When the lagged inflation term is interpreted as a proxy for the expected rate of inflation (p_t^e), then (7) is called an *expectational Phillips curve*. Friedman's (1968) natural rate hypothesis (NRH) states that the coefficient on p_t^e in an expectational Phillips curve is unity,

$$p_t = p_t^e + \gamma \hat{Q}_t + z_t. \tag{8}$$

This expression is compatible with steady fully anticipated inflation when actual and natural output are equal ($\hat{Q}_t = 0$) and implies that inflation steadily accelerates whenever the log output ratio is positive.

But, as originally pointed out by Sargent (1971), the NRH does *not* imply that the coefficient λ in (7) must be unity. The coefficient on p_t^e in (8) could be unity, while at the same time rational agents could form their expectations of inflation by applying a coefficient λ below unity to lagged inflation, if this provided the best possible predictor. For instance, if inflation were a random walk the optimal predictor would be $\lambda = 1$, but if inflation were white noise, the optimal predictor would be $\lambda = 0$. By expressing the Phillips curve in form (7) rather than (8), we recognize that the coefficient λ may vary in different times and places, depending on the nature of the inflation process. Further, (7) recognizes, as (8) does not, that there may be many reasons for serial dependence in the inflation rate, of which expectation formation is only one, and overlapping wage and price contracts may be among the others.

Blanchard (1987b) has stressed that there are two dimensions of price adjustment, corresponding to the two parameters λ and γ in (7).[9] An equation like (7) implies that shocks to nominal aggregate demand cause the economy to travel through loops on a diagram plotting inflation (p) against the output ratio ($\hat{Q}$), and an economy with low values of λ and γ has 'fat loops'; that is, it exhibits relatively large output fluctuations and only a slow incorporation of the change in nominal demand growth into the rate of inflation.

However, in addition to the two adjustment parameters in (7), we have already introduced a third parameter (α) in (4) and (5), which measures the fraction of current excess nominal GNP change ($\hat{x}_t$) taking the form of price change. How are these parameters related? The connection when we add the explanatory variable contained in (4) to those already present in (7):

$$p_t = \lambda p_{t-1} + \alpha \hat{x}_t + \gamma \hat{Q}_t + z_t. \tag{9}$$

While the $\alpha \hat{x}_t$ term may appear to drop from the sky, in fact equation (9) can be interpreted simply as loosening the artificial restriction in (7) that allows only the current value of the log output ratio to enter. The more general form (9) allows both the current and one lagged value of the output ratio to enter as explanatory variables, as becomes transparent when we use the identity that $\hat{Q}_t \equiv \hat{Q}_{t-1} + \hat{x}_t - p_t$ to rewrite (9) in either of two equivalent forms:[10]

$$p_t = [1/(1 - \alpha)][\lambda p_{t-1} \\ + (\alpha + \gamma)\hat{Q}_t - \alpha\hat{Q}_{t-1} + z_t], \text{ or,} \tag{10a}$$

$$p_t = [1/(1 - \alpha)][\lambda p_{t-1} \\ + \alpha\hat{q}_t + \gamma\hat{Q}_t + z_t]. \tag{10b}$$

Note that either (10a) or (10b) reduces to (7) when the α parameter is set equal to zero.[11] If both the current and one lagged output term matter for the rate of price change, as in (10a), this implies in (10b) that the rate of change of prices is related to both the *rate of change* ($\hat{q}_t$) and the *level* ($\hat{Q}_t$) of output. The generalization of the Phillips-curve hypothesis contained in (9) and (10) illustrates that the same hypothesis of price adjustment can be expressed in several alternative forms, and that the extent of price change in response to a change in nominal demand depends not on a single parameter, but on the three parameters λ, α, and γ.[12]

Where wages fit in

Keynesian economics has traditionally been more concerned with wage rigidity than price rigidity. Yet our discussion to this point has made no mention of wages. This is fitting, because only price stickiness, not wage stickiness, is a necessary condition for business cycles in real output, given a particular path of nominal aggregate demand. There are no arithmetically necessary implications of nominal wage rigidity for the cyclical behavior of output or employment, because sufficient flexibility in profits could allow prices to be flexible (so that p mimics $\hat{x}$), even if the nominal wage rate were absolutely fixed. Yet a world of highly flexible profits with completely rigid wages would have economic, if not arithmetic, implications. High profit volatility for any given firm would shift the firm's securities out along the mean-variance schedule and raise the average cost of capital, thus creating pressure in two directions, toward an increase in the flexibility of wages and toward a decrease in the flexibility of prices, both of which would reduce the volatility of profits. In new-Keynesian economics there is no primacy to wage rigidity as contrasted with price rigidity, and thus no presumption that wages are less cyclically sensitive than prices. In fact, much of the research since 1985 has been directed toward the microfoundations of price rigidity.

The nature of cyclical flexibility in real wages has always played a role in discussions of Keynesian economics, dating back to the debate involving John Dunlop (1938), Lorie Tarshis (1938), and John Maynard Keynes (1939). Even though these authors are known for the criticism of the countercyclical real wage assumption implicit in the *General Theory*, resulting from its assumption of price flexibility combined with nominal wage rigidity, it is less well known that Tarshis in 1939 soon recanted and provided evidence of a relatively strong negative correlation between average hourly earnings and total hours worked.[13] Subsequently we shall examine new evidence on the cyclicality of real wages.

Rate of change or hysteresis effects

Equations (9) and (10) imply that there may be three quite different types of price stickiness, indicated respectively by a relatively high value of the λ parameter, and by relatively low values of the α and γ adjustment parameters. The role of the inertia parameter λ is straightforward, with a higher value of λ prolonging the duration of adjustment to changes in nominal demand, for any given values of the α and γ parameters, and increasing the importance of overshooting and dynamic adjustment loops. The distinction between rate-of-change adjustment (α) and level or Phillips-curve adjustment (γ) is clarified by examining extreme cases in which one or the other is absent. When there is no rate-of-change effect ($\alpha = 0$) we are back in the simple Phillips-curve framework in which only the level of output matters. For any given values of the λ and γ parameters, the acceleration of inflation implied by an output ratio of +5 percent is the same, regardless of whether the output ratio is rapidly rising or rapidly falling.

The opposite extreme is of more interest, because it has been the focus of so much attention in the context of high European unemployment in the 1980s. An economy lacking a level effect ($\gamma = 0$) is said to be characterized by hysteresis. Considerable theoretical work has emerged to explain hysteresis phenomena, particularly in the context of the insider-outsider model of employment reviewed in Section 7 (pp. 524–5). Whatever the theoretical explanation, the presence of hysteresis would have profound implications for both economic doctrine and policy.[14] Friedman's NRH posits a self-correction or level effect that automatically stabilizes output at its equilibrium value in the presence of steady nominal demand growth. With no level effect, the economy could settle down at any arbitrary distance from its equilibrium output path (with $\hat{q}_t = 0$) and experience a constant rate of inflation, with no tendency for self-correction. And, if the NRH were abandoned, it would cast stabilization policy adrift from its previous mooring, the task of steering the economy toward a fixed natural rate ($\hat{Q}_t = 0$), and open to the central implication of hysteresis that any level of detrended output or rate of unemployment, no matter how low or high, would be consistent with steady inflation (at a rate that depends on the history of both inflation and unemployment).

As we see below, the pattern of price adjustment described by hysteresis is not a novel phenomenon isolated to Europe in the 1980s, for the Phillips curve or 'level effect' also vanished in the United States, the United Kingdom, and Germany during the interwar period.[15] A key implication of (9) is that with hysteresis ($\gamma = 0$) and with $\lambda = 1 - \alpha$, the acceleration or deceleration of inflation, as well as the change in detrended output, depends only on the difference between $\hat{x}_t$ and p_{t-1}, that is, whether or not excess nominal GNP growth ratifies the inherited inflation rate:

$$p_t - p_{t-1} = \alpha(\hat{x}_t - p_{t-1}) + z_t, \text{ and} \tag{11}$$

$$\hat{Q}_t - \hat{Q}_{t-1} = (1 - \alpha)(\hat{x}_t - p_{t-1}) - z_t. \tag{12}$$

In short, hysteresis implies that changes in both inflation and output are completely independent of the *level* of detrended output, and that an economy in the depths of a great depression can experience an acceleration of inflation, no matter how high the level of unemployment or low the level of detrended output, if excess nominal GNP growth exceeds last period's inflation rate.

Empirical estimates of the general price-adjustment model in (9) and (10) can reveal the size of the three adjustment parameters (λ, α, and γ) in different countries and historical eras. There remains the issue of which alternative specification in (9) and (10) is preferable for estimation. As argued earlier, in the presence of policy feedback and unmeasured supply shocks, the α adjustment parameter is likely to be overstated when nominal GNP change ($\hat{x}$) is included as in (9) and understated when real GNP change ($\hat{q}$) is used instead as in (10b). This suggests that estimates based alternatively on both forms are preferable, because they will 'bracket' the true parameter.

We conclude from this discussion that three parameters are required to measure the degree of price stickiness: λ measuring the extent of inertia, α measuring the rate-of-change or hysteresis effect, and γ measuring the level or Phillips-curve effect. Any attempt to measure changes in the degree of stickiness over time, or differences among countries, may be flawed if it omits any of these three parameters from empirical testing. Further, we have seen that policy accommodation of supply shocks can bias coefficients of price adjustment, and thus any adequate empirical investigation must make a careful attempt to control for supply shocks as well.

Section 2 began by stressing the most obvious implication of the identity linking changes in nominal demand, real output, and the price level. Changes in the price level must exactly mimic changes in nominal demand if business cycles in real output are to be avoided. Thus the requirements for perfect price flexibility are highly restrictive: in the context of equation (10) price changes can mimic changes in nominal demand only if $\alpha = 1$, $\lambda = 0$, and $\gamma = 0$. Thus any combination of a rate-of-change coefficient below unity, the presence of Phillips-curve level effects ($\gamma > 0$), or the presence of inertia effects is sufficient to generate business cycles. However, Lucas (1973) showed that Phillips-curve level effects could be derived in a business-cycle model in which markets clear; thus the absence of perfect price flexibility is not sufficient to distinguish between new-classical market-clearing models and new-Keynesian sticky-price models. Instead, the presence of price inertia ($\theta > 0$) is crucial for rejecting the new-classical interpretation and demonstrating the existence of price stickiness.[16]

3   THE VARIETY OF HISTORICAL EXPERIENCE

Diversity of response across industries

Since well before the publication of Keynes' *General Theory*, for example, Mills (1927), industrial economists have been aware that the responsiveness of prices to changes in demand differs sharply across industries. The contrast between the flexibility of the prices of agricultural products, and the inflexibility of the prices of complex manufactured goods, was the point of departure of Gardiner Means' (1935) administered price hypothesis. In the Great Depression every farmer knew what Table 21.2 shows.

Table 21.2   Decline in Price and Production, various US industries, 1929–33

Industry	Percentage decline in price	Percentage decline in production
Agricultural implements	6	80
Motor vehicles	16	80
Textile products	45	30
Petroleum	56	20
Agricultural products	63	6

Source: Gardiner Means (1935: 8)

In an economic downturn the farmer was the victim of a highly unfavorable twist in relative prices, because the prices of agricultural products fell much more than those of many manufactured goods, especially the agricultural implements listed on the first line that represent one of the main purchased inputs in the farm sector. Within the spectrum of manufactured goods, crude products like textiles tended to exhibit more price flexibility than more finished products like tractors and automobiles.

Unfortunately, there are few empirical studies that document these differences systematically. Stigler and Kindahl (1970) collected prices from buyers for a large number of products, and these data were analyzed by Carlton (1986) to determine if there were any structural relations between seller and buyer characteristics and the degree of price rigidity. Carlton concludes that there is a significant degree of price rigidity: 'It is not unusual in some industries for prices to individual buyers to remain unchanged for several years' (1986: 638). Unfortunately, however, neither Stigler and Kindahl nor Carlton show that, as Means suggested, the degree of 'complexity' of a product is related to price rigidity. Although Carlton did try to measure complexity as well as other structural variables, he was able to find a significant positive correlation only between the concentration ratio for a product and the duration of its price rigidity (i.e. the number of months a price remains unchanged).[17]

But it is important to stress another of Carlton's findings that may be of substantial importance in assessing the theories reviewed below. By no means are all prices rigid or do they remain unchanged for substantial periods of time: 'The fixed costs of changing price at least to some buyers may be small. There are plenty of instances where small price changes occur' (Carlton 1986: 638). Specifically, 'there are a significant number of price changes that one would consider small (i.e., less than 1 percent) for most commodities and transaction types.' Industries where frequent price changes are common include plywood and nonferrous metals, and commodities with relatively long spells of rigid prices include steel, paper, chemicals, cement, and glass. Carlton's evidence that spells of price rigidity can be both short and long calls into question the generality of the oft-cited study by Cecchetti (1986) which provides evidence that newsstand prices of magazines can remain unchanged for years (see also Kashyap 1990). Carlton's finding that spells are sometimes short and price changes sometimes small would appear to call into question the theories of new-Keynesian economists based on 'menu costs' of price changes, reviewed in Section 5 (pp. 511–14). However, this apparent implication is subject to the caveat that if demand and/or supply shift permanently, then small price adjustments can produce large benefits and will be observed even if fixed costs are large (Carlton 1989a: 932).

There has been remarkably little interaction between new-Keynesian theory and the evidence provided in the emerging literature of the new empirical industrial organization (NEIO) surveyed by Bresnahan (1989). The overall conclusion is that there is 'a great deal of market power, in the sense of price-cost margins, in some concentrated industries' (Bresnahan 1989: 1052). One could emphasize the words a great deal as supporting the emphasis by new-Keynesian theorists on models of monopolistic rather than perfect competition. Or one could emphasize the word 'some' to point out that the world is made up of both monopolistic and competitive industries. But the matter is even more complex: one important theme of recent NEIO work is that pricing behavior can alternate between collusive monopolistic behavior and price wars in which a cartel temporarily collapses, implying that a given industry is characterized neither by exclusively monopolistic nor competitive behavior.

The theme of heterogeneity extends along other dimensions. Product differentiation is so pervasive that 'there is almost no industry for which the position that there are more than 100 products is untenable: without putting more structure on the problem, the analyst could need to estimate literally thousands of elasticities' (Bresnahan 1989: 1045).[18] Heterogeneity extends to pricing behavior across firms in a single industry. For instance, a study of airline competition found not only that concentration affects price in airline city-pair markets, but also that the identity of the competitors matters. Carlton stresses that a given seller can charge different prices to different customers and change them at different times, based on 'a seller's knowledge of his customers and on the optimality of non-price rationing' (Carlton 1989a). In a cross-section of industries, numerous dimensions of structure appear to vary together, including mass production, large-scale facilities, unionization, capital intensity, concentration, and cyclical price rigidity, all of which are more pronounced in the cyclically sensitive sectors of the economy, particularly durable goods.[19]

As we shall see below, new-Keynesian theory has contributed relatively little to understanding these differences across industries, and as yet there has been virtually no research that attempts to test theories on a diversity of industrial data. We emphasize the numerous aspects of heterogeneity across and within industries to support several themes that emerge below, including the importance of idiosyncratic elements of product cost and demand that prevent firms from assuming, as in so many simple models, that their costs and product demand will mimic the behavior of nominal aggregate demand. Even so basic a distinction as Arthur Okun's (1975, 1981) dichotomy between auction and customer markets rarely surfaces in new-Keynesian writing, much less in new-classical contributions. And the seminal work in understanding the coexistence of auction and customer markets has been contributed by microeconomists, especially Carlton (e.g. 1989b), who stresses that, because of the high costs of establishing auction markets, 'there is no incentive for the efficient creation of markets' (p. 7).[20]

Diversity of response across time and space

Just as challenging for theorists as the diversity of responses across industries at a particular time in a particular country is the diversity of responses across time and countries. Much of the empirical work in this area has been within the context of a debate over whether prices, wages, or both have become less flexible in the postwar USA as contrasted with various periods before the Great Depression (among these studies are Allen 1989; Mitchell 1985; Sachs 1980; Schultze 1981, 1986; Taylor 1986; R. Gordon 1980, 1982b). In related work Charles Schultze and others have examined differences in response coefficients over both time and space for the USA and several other major industrialized nations (see Alogoskoufis and Smith

1989; Backus and Kehoe 1988; Coe 1989; Schultze 1981, 1986; R. Gordon 1982a, 1983).

It is beyond the scope of this chapter to track all the differences in data and specification that contribute to the variety of conclusions that these studies have reached; that would require a separate survey on this issue alone. Some of the disagreements, particularly about changes in cyclical behavior for the USA, arise because authors often do not recognize that there are three dimensions to price and wage rigidity, as demonstrated in Section 2. These are the degree of inertia or serial correlation (λ), the rate-of-change or hysteresis coefficient (α), and the level or Phillips-curve coefficient (γ). Here we provide a link between that classification scheme and historical data by presenting estimates of the three parameters based on price-adjustment equations (9) and (10) developed above. We address two issues, differences in the responsiveness of prices and wages over US history, and differences in the responsiveness of prices over the period since 1870 for five major industrial nations (USA, UK, France, Germany and Japan).

The empirical equations summarized in this chapter are estimated only for nominal and real output data corresponding to the $\hat{x}_t$ and $\hat{Q}_t$ variables in the theoretical price-adjustment equation (9). There is no attempt to estimate alternative versions for other possible nominal and real demand variables, for example, the money supply or unemployment. Annual output data extend back much further than unemployment data – to 1855 for the UK, 1870 for France, Germany, and the USA, and 1885 for Japan. Wage-adjustment equations are illustrated only for the USA, pending a careful study to determine whether wage data for other countries are consistent over time.[21]

Numerous decisions must be made in the development of tests covering such a long span of history for these nations. These include the method of detrending and the development of proxy variables for the major supply shocks, a critical issue in view of the likely bias in coefficient estimates when supply shocks are left unmeasured. Another issue is the estimation of parameter shifts over subintervals of a long historical sample period. Details on the methodology and the regression estimates are provided in Appendix A, which shows that it is desirable to conduct the estimation with slightly transformed versions of (9) and (10b). This allows us to proceed directly to Tables 21.3 and 21.4, where the underlying parameters are unscrambled from the transformed equations and presented for different countries and historical eras.

The estimated parameters are provided for changes in prices, nominal wages, and real wages for the USA in Table 21.3. We are interested in the nature of changes in the three price- and wage-adjustment parameters over time, and also evidence on the hotly debated issue of the cyclical sensitivity of real wages. Following our analysis in Section 2, two estimates of each parameter are provided. The left-hand element in each column is based on

Table 21.3 Estimated price and wage adjustment parameters for the USA, 1873–1987

	Inertia effect (λ)		Rate-of-change effect (α)		Level effect (γ)	
	(1)		*(2)*		*(3)*	
Price change						
1873–1914, 1923–29	0.29	(0.37)	0.17	(0.03)	0.28	(0.28)
1915–22	0.29	(0.43)	0.69	(0.43)	0.28	(0.17)
1930–53	0.25	(0.37)	0.29	(0.03)	0.09	(0.08)
1954–87	0.87	(1.01)	0.17	(0.03)	0.28	(0.28)
Nominal wage change						
1873–1914, 1923–29	0.46	(0.51)	0.20	(0.07)	0.43	(0.40)
1915–22	0.46	(0.44)	0.73	(0.49)	0.43	(0.22)
1930–53	0.32	(0.37)	0.44	(0.33)	−0.01	(0.02)
1954–87	0.67	(0.86)	0.20	(0.07)	0.43	(0.40)
Real wage change						
1873–1914, 1923–29	0.17	(0.14)	0.03	(0.04)	0.15	(0.12)
1915–22	0.17	(0.01)	0.04	(0.06)	0.15	(0.05)
1930–53	0.05	(0.00)	0.15	(0.30)	−0.10	(−0.06)
1954–87	−0.20	(−0.15)	0.03	(0.04)	0.15	(0.12)

Notes: Equation specifications and details are provided in Appendix A. The left parameter in each column comes from unscrambling the coefficients of equation (9′) in Appendix A, the version containing excess nominal GNP growth ($\hat{x}_t$) as the rate-of-change variable; the right parameter in parentheses ( ) comes from unscrambling the coefficients of equation (9″), the version containing excess real GNP growth ($\hat{q}_t$) as the rate-of-change variable.

an adjustment equation in which excess nominal GNP growth is included, and this is likely to yield an upward biased value of the rate-of-change parameter (α) in the presence of supply shocks and policy feedback. The right-hand element in each column replaces excess nominal GNP growth with excess real GNP growth, and this will tend to yield a downward-biased estimate of α. The two estimates should bracket the true value. The parameters listed in Tables 21.3 and 21.4 are allowed to change across time periods and are recorded when parameter-shift coefficients are statistically significant, and identical parameters across time periods indicate that such shift coefficients are insignificant (for details and the significance of the shift coefficients themselves, see Tables 21.5 and 21.6 in Appendix A).

The single most striking finding in Table 21.3 is that neither prices nor wages were more sticky in 1954–87 than 1873–1914, as measured by the rate-of-change (α) and level (γ) coefficients.[22] The sole change between pre-World War I and post-World War II was an increase in the inertia (λ) coefficient, and this increase was much greater for prices than wages. Between 1915 and 1953, however, there were substantial changes. The α parameter rose substantially during World War I, while the α parameter virtually disappeared during 1930–53. When the estimated price-change parameters are subtracted from the wage-change parameters, the results before 1930 and after 1953 suggest that real wages have a negligible rate-of-

Table 21.4 Estimated price adjustment parameters for five countries, 1873–1986

	Inertia effect (λ)		Rate-of-change effect (α)		Level effect (γ)	
	(1)		*(2)*		*(3)*	
USA						
1873–1914, 1923–29	0.29	(0.37)	0.17	(0.03)	0.28	(0.28)
1915–22	0.29	(0.43)	0.69	(0.43)	0.28	(0.17)
1930–53	0.25	(0.37)	0.29	(0.03)	0.09	(0.08)
1954–87	0.87	(1.01)	0.17	(0.03)	0.28	(0.28)
UK						
1858–1914	0.24	(0.23)	0.43	(−0.06)	0.35	(0.38)
1915–22	0.24	(0.15)	0.60	(0.33)	0.35	(0.56)
1923–38	0.20	(0.18)	0.26	(0.17)	0.09	(0.07)
1960–86	0.57	(1.00)	0.43	(−0.06)	0.35	(0.38)
France						
1873–1913	−0.20	(−0.38)	0.47	(0.10)	0.26	(0.03)
1925–38	0.15	(0.09)	0.47	(0.26)	0.26	(0.65)
1960–86	0.55	(0.40)	0.47	(0.10)	0.26	(0.03)
Germany						
1873–1913	0.00	(0.30)	0.66	(−0.11)	0.21	(0.12)
1925–38	0.00	(0.00)	0.40	(0.38)	0.07	(0.07)
1960–86	0.73	(1.08)	0.33	(−0.11)	0.21	(0.12)
Japan						
1888–1914, 1923–38	0.15	(0.70)	0.64	(0.02)	0.39	(0.34)
1915–22	0.15	(0.18)	0.87	(0.75)	0.39	(0.09)
1960–86	0.15	(0.50)	0.64	(0.29)	0.39	(0.24)

Notes: Sample period for the UK begins in 1958, for Japan begins in 1888, and for the USA ends in 1987. Equation specifications and details are provided in Appendix A. The left parameter in each column comes from unscrambling the coefficients of equation (9′) in the appendix, the version containing excess nominal GNP growth ($\hat{x}_t$) as the rate-of-change variable; the right parameter in parentheses ( ) comes from unscrambling the coefficients of equation (9″), the version containing excess real GNP growth ($\hat{q}_t$) as the rate-of-change variable.

change effect but a substantial procyclical level effect. That is, a persistent economic boom causes steady upward pressure on the real wage, and a persistent recession does the reverse. However, this finding is subject to the qualification that the manufacturing wage data used here exaggerate the cyclical sensitivity of economy-wide rates. When the equations are re-estimated for the postwar 1954–87 period alone with the fixed-weight nonfarm wage index replacing the manufacturing wage index, the cyclical sensitivity of real wages drops to zero.[23]

Table 21.4 compares the results for US prices with similar price equations for the other countries. Again the most striking finding is that the α and γ parameters were the same before World War I and after World War II in the UK, France, and Japan, with a decline in the α coefficient only in Germany (and one may question the linking of German data over periods when its borders were so different). In every country but Japan the inertia effect was much higher after World War II than before World War I. The

UK and Japan duplicate the jump in the α coefficient already observed for the USA during the 1915–22 interval, and both the UK and Germany exhibit a substantial decline in the γ coefficient during the interwar period.

Implications

Is the aggregate price level highly flexible, mimicking changes in excess nominal GNP growth? Or does the aggregate price level live a life of its own, bearing little relation to excess nominal GNP growth and thus allowing those nominal changes to create business cycles in real output? The conclusion from Tables 21.3 and 21.4 is that both these statements are true. And many in-between responses have been observed as well.

At one extreme is the very high rate-of-change coefficient for Japan throughout, and for the USA and the UK during World War I and its aftermath. Figure 21.1 plots the 1886–1914 data for Japan and shows how closely price changes track excess nominal GNP changes. The figure also exhibits cycles in the log output ratio that are small relative to the large amplitude of nominal GNP changes. We have argued above that the best

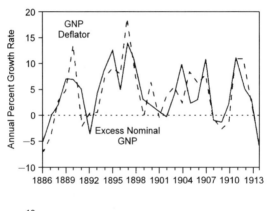

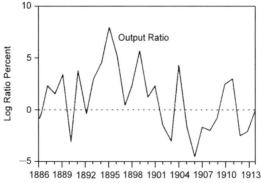

Figure 21.1 Inflation, Adjusted Nominal GNP Growth, and the Output Ratio, Japan, 1886–1914

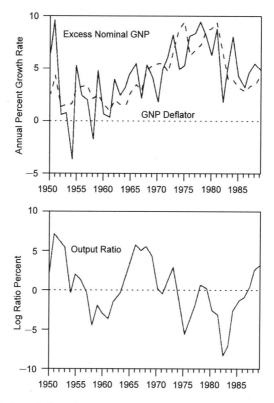

Figure 21.2 Inflation, Adjusted Nominal GNP Growth, and the Output Ratio, United States, 1950–89

estimates of the adjustment parameters are given by the average of the two estimates shown in each column in Tables 21.3 and 21.4. On the basis of these averages, it is quite apparent in Table 21.4 that the USA has the smallest rate-of-change parameter (α) and Japan the largest, both before World War I and after World War II, with the other countries arrayed in between. The postwar USA also contrasts starkly with Japan in its strong inertia effect. The top frame of Figure 21.2 shows how loose is the relation between inflation and excess nominal GNP growth in the postwar USA, and how large is the amplitude of output cycles relative to nominal GNP growth cycles. Again basing conclusions on the average of the two figures in each column, inertia effects in all countries were negligible before World War II.

These results demonstrate the strong diversity of aggregate price-adjustment behavior that has occurred across time and across countries. The variety of historical responses of price changes to nominal demand changes raises questions that new-Keynesian theorists have barely begun to address. Perhaps the most widely noted empirical test thus far devised by new-Keynesian economists (Ball *et al.* 1988) takes as its point of departure Lucas' (1973) demonstration that the Phillips curve becomes steeper with a higher variance of the growth rate of nominal demand. Ball *et al.* show that menu-cost theory supports the Lucas correlation but also makes the additional prediction that increases in the *mean* growth rate of nominal demand should steepen the Phillips curve, because with staggered price setting an increase in the mean inflation rate increases the frequency of price changes. Thus far, their empirical work in support of this theoretical prediction has been subject to substantial criticism.[24] In relation to our empirical results of Tables 21.3 and 21.4, either the Lucas or the Ball *et al.* approach can help to explain why prices became more flexible during World War I but contribute little or nothing to an understanding of the other main findings: the similar level and rate-of-change effects before World War I and after World War II, despite the higher variance of nominal demand in the earlier period; the disappearance of the level effect in the Depression years; the emergence of inertia after World War II; and the differences in price flexibility among the five countries.

Empirical research and the revival of Keynesian economics

Theories are often judged on their ability to explain time-series data on aggregate variables. This is clearly evident in the interaction of events and ideas since 1970. Theories have risen and fallen in acceptance in accord with the correspondence of their predictions with the evolution of actual events in the macroeconomy. To gain perspective on the development of new-Keynesian economics, we need to understand what went wrong with the old-Keynesian economics. Our emphasis here is the empirical failure of the Keynesian paradigm of the 1960s, and the elements that contributed to the empirical revival of the Keynesian approach in the 1980s. We concentrate on empirical aspects of the contest between new-classical and new-Keynesian economics, and we limit the scope of the chapter by omitting any theoretical critique of either the Lucas imperfect-information (Mark I) approach or the real-business-cycle (Mark II) variant of new-classical macroeconomics.[25]

In the 1960s Keynesian economists incorporated into their theoretical and econometric models an exploitable negative long-run Phillips-curve trade-off between inflation and unemployment. The acceleration of inflation after 1965, together with the positive correlation between inflation and unemployment observed during much of the 1970s, caused the mid-1960s Keynesian orthodoxy to unravel. In flowery language that amounted to a simultaneous declaration of war and announcement of victory, Lucas and Sargent (1978: 49–50) described 'the task which faces contemporary students of the business cycle [as] that of sorting through the wreckage ... of that remarkable intellectual event called the Keynesian Revolution'.

It is not widely recognized that the empirical reconstruction of Keynesian economics occurred prior to the wave of theoretical work that is now most commonly associated with the term *new-Keynesian economics.* Lucas and Sargent were only partly right. Yes, the predictions of the late 1960s were incorrect, but incorrect forecasts do not provide de facto proof that a doctrine's theoretical underpinnings are fundamentally flawed. The essential element of Keynesian doctrine is non-market-clearing, which in turn requires the gradual adjustment of prices. The 1960s version of the Phillips relation combined three elements, (1) gradual price adjustment, (2) a long-run trade-off, and (3) a closed-economy, demand-only approach with no role for import prices or supply shocks. Yet only (1) is necessary to maintain the essence of the Keynesian paradigm, non-market-clearing. The other two elements, (2) and (3), were ephemeral empirical results, based mainly on the 15 or 20 years of US postwar data, that revealed more of the short time horizon and closed-economy mentality of the first generation of econometric model builders than any fundamental weakness of the non-market-clearing approach.

The long-run trade-off result was abandoned within five years of Friedman's presidential address.[26] This allowed the gradual-adjustment property of the 1960s-style wage and price equations to be combined with the long-run neutrality property advocated by Friedman. The effects of supply shocks, including the relative prices of oil and imports, were absorbed into the US Phillips-curve framework in my work of the mid-1970s, which was developed alongside the work by David Laidler, Michael Parkin, and their collaborators in the open-economy setting of the UK.[27] The result was an econometric analogy to the dynamic aggregate demand and supply model that was introduced with the 1978–9 publication of a new generation of economic principles and intermediate macro textbooks.[28] Now a single reduced-form econometric equation for price change, like those summarized in Tables 21.3 and 21.4 could incorporate the effects of gradual adjustment, of demand shocks that created a temporary positive correlation between inflation and output, and of supply shocks that created a temporary negative correlation. By the end of the 1970s the supply side of the economy had been opened up to outside influences, and the list of relevant supply shocks for the USA had grown to include not only price controls and oil shocks, but also changes in non-oil import prices, exchange rates, tax rates, and the minimum wage.[29]

This so-called gradual-adjustment price-change equation is completely non-structural and as such is in principle highly vulnerable to the Lucas (1976) critique. We have seen in Tables 21.3 and 21.4 that coefficients of price adjustment are subject to substantial change when there are major changes in the economic environment, as in World War I or the Great Depression. The sharp US disinflation of the 1980s posed a formidable challenge which the empirical price-adjustment equation could have failed but did not. A central implication of the resuscitated 1980-vintage empirical Phillips curves, the value of the sacrifice ratio of lost output required to achieve a permanent deceleration of inflation, turned out to be surprisingly close to predictions made in advance. This suggests that, at least in the USA, the substantial changes in price-adjustment parameters observed in Tables 21.3 and 21.4 to have occurred in previous historical eras have been largely absent in the postwar US setting.[30]

The empirical stability and predictive success of the resuscitated US Phillips curve is highly ironic in view of the inflammatory language used by Lucas and Sargent. If anything lay smoldering in 'wreckage' in the mid-1980s, it was the few abortive attempts to estimate price equations within the framework of Mark I new-classical macroeconomics, particularly those by Barro (1977a, 1978; Barro and Rush 1980). So strongly was price inertia embedded in the US data that Barro could explain price movements only by entering a distributed lag of between four and six years of monetary surprises that themselves lasted only a single quarter. Why agents should be reacting with a four-year lag to a one-quarter monetary surprise was never explained. The attraction for the economics profession of the empirical versions of Mark I new-classical macro, like the theoretical versions, was undermined by the discrepancy between the time lags involved in data dissemination, measured in days or weeks, as contrasted to the lags of price changes in response to nominal demand shocks, measured in years or half-decades.

4 NEW-KEYNESIAN THEORY: COMMON FEATURES

Essential features of Keynesian economics

The essential feature of Keynesian macroeconomics is the absence of continuous market clearing. Thus a Keynesian model is by definition a non-market-clearing model, one in which prices fail to adjust rapidly enough to clear markets within some relatively short period of time. Common to almost all Keynesian models is the prediction that in response to a decline in nominal demand, the aggregate price level will decline less than proportionately over a substantial time period, during which the actual price level is above the equilibrium price level consistent with the maintenance of the initial equilibrium level of real output. The fact that the price level is too high means that the subequilibrium level of output actually produced is not chosen voluntarily by firms and workers, but rather is imposed on them as a constraint. It is the decline in nominal demand together with the absence of full price adjustment that causes the economic system itself to impose the constraint on each agent; nominal demand is insufficient to generate adequate real sales at the actual price level. Each agent faces a constraint that is indirectly a result of its own failure to reduce sufficiently its price and this points to a coordination failure as a central ingredient in the description of Keynesian price stickiness.

So many people now refer to new-classical models as *equilibrium business-cycle models* that the word *equilibrium* has been co-opted as meaning the opposite of the term *Keynesian*. This leads some commentators to label an approach that is the opposite of equilibrium economics as *disequilibrium economics*. In one sense this is mere semantics; it does not matter whether we describe the USA in 1932 or Europe in the mid-1980s as being in a state of disequilibrium or low-employment equilibrium. However, the adjective *disequilibrium* is not helpful, as it conveys 'a failure of agents to realize perceived gains from trade' (to use Barro's provocative 1979 phrase). Rather, it is best to regard the core feature of Keynesian economics as the gradual adjustment of prices and its corollary, that output and employment are not choice variables.

In contrast to new-classical equilibrium models, with their price-taking firms ('yeoman barbers') making voluntary choices of the output level, Keynesian non-market-clearing models turn the role of prices and output on their head, with demand-taking firms making voluntary choices of the price level. Thus price-setting behavior is the essence of Keynesian economics. Any attempt to embed it in microeconomic foundations must begin from monopolistic or imperfect competition, not perfect competition, because Keynesian agents are inherently price setters, not price takers.

A central theme of both new-classical and new-Keynesian macroeconomics is that accurate empirical predictions are necessary but not sufficient conditions of an acceptable theory. In addition, a theory must have microeconomic foundations in the behavior of utility-maximizing and profit-maximizing individual agents. The search for tractable analytic models to form the micro foundations often leads analysts astray, causing them to lose sight of the forest as they construct their single exquisitely proportioned tree. Almost all new-classical theory is conducted in the analytically convenient setting of 'representative agent models', where one can move back and forth between the individual agent and the aggregate economy simply by adding or removing i subscripts, without having to consider such analytically inconvenient issues as coordination failures or the speed of price adjustment. Professional microeconomists, as distinguished from macroeconomists who dabble in microeconomic modeling, find the failure to confront aggregation seriously to be the most critical flaw of representative agent modeling.[31] A surprising number of new-Keynesian models share in common the neglect of aggregation; the aggregate economy is simply the representative agent multiplied by n. Accordingly, we shall find unsatisfactory those new-Keynesian models that neglect aggregation issues, and we shall emphasize the central role of interactions among agents, including coordination failures, macroeconomic externalities, and producer–supplier relations.

Micro agents, macro spillovers, and coordination failures

The development of new-Keynesian economics since 1980 has primarily involved the search for rigorous and convincing models of wage and/or price stickiness based on maximizing behavior and rational expectations. The ground rules of this search are commonly accepted. The key ingredient in the now-abandoned Mark I new-classical approach was not rational expectations, but rather the assumption of continuous market clearing, as is evident in the labels *new-classical macroeconomics* or *equilibrium macro-economics*. Most new-Keynesian models combine rational expectations with maximizing behavior at the level of the individual agent. Any attempt to build a model based on irrational behavior or submaximizing behavior is viewed as cheating. No new-Keynesian wants to build a model with agents that Barro (1979) could criticize as failing 'to realize perceived gains from trade.' So the game is to tease a failure of macro markets to clear from a starting point of rational expectations and the maximization of profits and individual welfare at the micro level. In short, effects of changes in nominal aggregate demand on real output and employment are derived in models characterized by equilibria in which all individual agents take only those actions that make them better off and in which no agent foregoes an opportunity to take advantage of a 'gain from trade'.

The development of microfoundations for wage and price stickiness does not, of course, represent the first attempt to develop micro underpinnings for Keynesian economics. The work of Friedman and Franco Modigliani on consumption, Dale Jorgenson on investment, and William Baumol and James Tobin on the demand for money were all based on profit-maximizing behavior at the micro level. But all this work was carried out within a partial equilibrium framework, assuming in particular that both real income and the price level were given. A useful distinction can be made between micro theorizing at the level of individual demand and supply functions, and micro analysis of the market mechanisms (especially the price system) whereby the actions of maximizing agents are coordinated.[32] Even before the advent of new-classical economics, the work of Clower (1965) and Leijonhufvud (1968) stressed interactions and spillovers among markets and argued that the nexus of research should shift from a partial to a general equilibrium setting.

An interesting aspect of US new-Keynesian research is the near-total lack of interest in the general equilibrium properties of non-market-clearing models. That effort is viewed as having reached a quick dead end after the insights yielded in the pioneering work of Barro and Grossman (1971, 1976), building on the earlier contributions of Patinkin (1965), Clower, and Leijonhufvud. Explaining sticky wages and/or prices is viewed as a tough task, and no one is prepared to anticipate its achievement by examining broader theoretical implications.[33] The disdain shown by new-Keynesian theorists for the work of Barro and Grossman, and the latter evolution of that line of research in the hands of Malinvaud, Muellbauer and Portes, Benassy, Grandmont, and others – notably all Europeans – is understand-able in light of the primacy of microfoundations models as the prerequisite for macro discourse.[34] Nevertheless I find that even the most perceptive new-Keynesian commentators tend to forget the central message of these models.

This message is that spillovers between markets imply that the failure of one market to clear imposes constraints on agents in other markets. Most notably, when firms in a recession experience a decline in sales at the going price, this excess supply of commodities 'spills over' into a decline in labor demand at the going real wage. In this light, I am sometimes surprised to read otherwise sensible commentators refer to the inconsistency of one or another new-Keynesian explanation with microeconomic evidence on the elasticity of labor supply. Such evidence is simply irrelevant for Keynesian macroeconomics. In a genuinely Keynesian model, agents are not in a position to choose the amount they work or produce as output varies over the cycle, and so the constrained amount that they do work or produce cannot be interpreted as tracing movements along a choice-theoretic labor supply curve or production function.

Much existing new-Keynesian theorizing is riddled with inconsistencies as a result of its neglect of constraints and spillovers, and its focus on single markets, one at a time, in a partial equilibrium framework. For instance, several of the most prominent models of price determination in the presence of adjustment costs limit the source of price stickiness to the product market; they often assume a perfectly competitive labor market in which workers slide up and down their labor supply curves, indifferent between economic states that offer relatively large and small amounts of leisure. Such models stand Keynesian economics on its head, because any satisfactory explanation of business cycles that warrants the label *Keynesian* must incorporate not just price stickiness, but in addition some element that explains the evident unhappiness of the employed in recessions and depressions. Further, such models fail to explain why the adjustment costs that lead to price stickiness do not in parallel imply wage stickiness.

One important exception to this neglect of macroeconomic constraints and spillovers is the seminal work of Cooper and John (1988) on macroeconomic coordination failures. In several new-classical models in which agents set output, they show that spillovers and strategic complementarities can arise at the levels of preferences and technology or in the organization of transactions. They reach the same conclusion as Barro and Grossman (without making the connection) that macroeconomic quantities belong in microeconomic choice functions. Almost alone among recent American authors in the new-Keynesian tradition, Cooper and John cite Jean-Pascal Benassy's fixed-price models (1975, 1982) and conclude for such models that 'strategic complementarity is a distinguishing element of models with Keynesian features' (1988: 461).

The contribution of Cooper and John reaffirms the traditional view (see particularly Leijonhufvud 1981) that coordination failures represent the core problem in macroeconomics. In response to a nominal demand change, no single private agent has an incentive to move its price exactly in proportion unless it believes that all other agents will do likewise, and will do so without delay. In Tobin's example,

> No one can see the spectacle in the theater or stadium if everyone stands, but who has the incentive to obey a general admonition to sit down. When the teacher tells her grade school class there will be no picnic unless all gum-chewing ceases, would any rational child who shares the general liking of gum stop? Threats against everybody in general addressed to nobody in particular rarely work.
>
> (Tobin 1989: 15)

The same point can be put differently: rational microeconomic agents care about the relation of their own price to their own costs, not to aggregate nominal demand. Unless a single agent believes that the actions of all other agents will make its marginal costs mimic the behavior of nominal demand with minimal lags, the aggregate price level cannot mimic nominal demand, and Keynesian output fluctuations result.

A notable limitation of most formal models related to coordination failures, including Cooper and John (1988) and Durlauf (1989: esp. p. 110), is a classical setting of competitive output setters, rather than a Keynesian world of monopolistic price setters. In Durlauf's words,

> the hallmark of this class of theories is the compatibility of different levels of real activity with the same microeconomic specification of individual firms and consumers. The key source of the multiplicity of long-run equilibriums is the positive effect that high production by some set of agents has on the decision of others to produce.

This approach, based in part on seminal research by Diamond (1982, 1984), essentially concerns the cyclical behavior of productivity, the positive response of which is claimed to reflect 'thick markets' as a result of 'positive complementarities'. However, this has little to do with the essential Keynesian coordination failure, the absence of incentives for price-setting agents to move their individual prices in tandem with aggregate nominal demand rather than individual marginal cost.[35]

Real rigidities, nominal rigidities, and the indexation puzzle

Two central distinctions are required as a preliminary to any summary of new-Keynesian work. The first is between price setting in product markets and wage setting in labor markets. The second distinction is between nominal rigidity and real rigidity.

The necessary condition for non-market-clearing is a barrier to the full adjustment of nominal prices, that is, something that prevents movements in nominal prices that are equiproportionate to movements in nominal demand. However, some of the new-Keynesian theories explain real rigidities as the stickiness of a wage relative to another wage, of a wage relative to a price, or of a price relative to another price. Explanations of real rigidities in product markets include customer markets, inventory models, and theories of markups under imperfect competition, while those of labor markets include implicit contracts, efficiency wages, and insider-outsider models. But theories of real rigidities are subject to the criticism that they do not explain nominal rigidity, because nothing prevents each individual agent from indexing its nominal price to nominal aggregate demand.

There is surprisingly little discussion in new-Keynesian papers of optimal indexation nor of the relation between the absence of full indexation and the sources of nominal rigidities. Gray (1976), Fischer (1977b), and others showed in the mid-1970s that full CPI indexation is not optimal in the presence of supply shocks. Intuitively, no agent can afford an indexed contract that rigidifies real wages and relative prices if supply disturbances continuously shift the optimal relative price. However, Gray's argument supports only indexation to a mix of price indexes preferred by firms and workers, not zero indexation. Failing to index is tantamount to linking the prices and wages of individual agents to a price index whose value is constant, and this becomes increasingly irrational as the inflation rate increases.[36]

Further, full indexation of the wage rate to nominal GNP escapes most of the theoretical objections to CPI indexation, because nominal GNP indexation leaves the price level free to move to equate the real wage to the marginal product of labor. Adopting our previous notation with lower-case letters representing growth rates, the condition necessary for labor's share in national income to remain constant is that the growth rate of the real wage $(w - p)$ equals the growth rate of labor's average product $(q - n)$:

$$w - p = q - n, \text{which occurs if}$$
$$w = p + q - n = x - n.$$

Thus the growth rate of the nominal wage rate should be indexed to the growth rate of nominal GNP per unit of labor input $(x - n)$. If an adverse supply shock reduces labor's average product, then such indexation allows the needed reduction in the real wage, whether nominal GNP growth remains constant and the rate of inflation increases, or whether the inflation rate remains constant and the growth rate of nominal GNP decelerates.

Fischer (1986: 152–3, 263–9) has pondered why indexation to the price level is so often incomplete, and why we so rarely observe indexed contracts contingent on other variables (whether economy-wide like nominal GNP or idiosyncratic variables like firm sales or profits). The primary barrier to indexation may be the costs of making contracts more complicated, particularly when it is recognized that there are conflicts along at least two dimensions. First is the Gray-Fischer point that the presence of aggregate supply shocks makes incomplete indexation optimal, and second is the presence of firm-specific shocks that create a conflict between the general market basket to which workers would prefer to index, and the firm-specific variables to which firms would prefer to index. Parties to a contract may differ not only in their objective functions, but also in their perceptions of the relative importance of aggregate demand shocks, aggregate supply shocks, and firm-specific shocks, and these perceptions may change continuously, requiring that the form of indexation in each new contract be negotiated from scratch.

As we review sources of rigidities in Keynesian models, we shall return to the issue of nominal GNP indexation. Are the nominal rigidities adequate to explain the real-world absence of such indexation? How are the two distinctions, product versus labor market and real versus nominal rigidities, related to each other? We begin our inquiry by reviewing models of nominal price rigidity in product markets, beginning with the elementary example of a textbook monopolist. This example implies that the response of price to a shift in demand is conditional not just on the elasticity of demand and the shape of the marginal cost curve, but crucially on the shift (if any) of marginal cost in response to demand. Thus product and labor market rigidities are complementary and may be of equal importance.

5 THE SEARCH FOR STRUCTURE: NOMINAL PRICE RIGIDITY IN THE PRODUCT MARKET

The textbook monopolist and the behavior of marginal cost

The behavior of a textbook monopolist is part of relative price theory, and therefore would appear to belong in our subsequent discussion of real rigidities. However, the monopolist model has been used to derive the conditions under which costs of adjustment create a barrier to changes in nominal prices. This explains the connection between theories of nominal price stickiness and the traditional partial equilibrium analysis of a price-setting monopolist illustrated in Figure 21.3. Note that two special assumptions are made in drawing Figure 21.3, that the demand curves are linear and that the marginal cost curve is horizontal. Implications of dropping both of these assumptions are discussed shortly.

In response to a shift in the demand curve from D_0 to D_1, quantity will change unless there is an equiproportionate shift in nominal marginal revenue and nominal marginal cost at the original level of real output. The implied marginal cost curve that maintains a constant level of output (Q_0) is labeled 'Required' MC_1. If, following the decline in demand, marginal cost drops instantly to the 'Required' MC_1 line, then the intersection of MR and MC will drop from E to G, and the price will fall by exactly the vertical displacement of the demand curve, from P_0 to P_2. Any source of incomplete adjustment in marginal cost can then explain an incomplete adjustment of price. For instance, if the marginal cost schedule remains

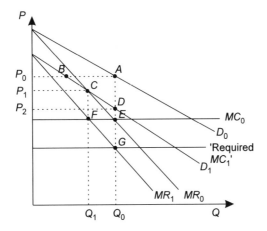

Figure 21.3

fixed at MC_0, the intersection of MR and MC occurs at point F, the new price is P_1, and the new quantity is Q_1.

When we loosen the two special assumptions incorporated into Figure 21.3, we alter the path of the price level at output levels away from the initial level Q_0 but not the basic conclusion about the required drop in marginal cost for the economy to remain at Q_0. For instance, replacing the special assumption of a linear demand curve with a demand curve of constant elasticity, while retaining the assumption of a horizontal MC schedule, point C would lie directly to the left of point A, and the price level would remain fixed in the presence of any leftward movement of the demand curve. Second, replacing the horizontal MC schedule with a positively sloped MC schedule going through point D would move points C and F down and to the right, thus increasing the response of the price level to the decline in demand and correspondingly reducing the output response.

This analysis suggests that the primary reason for sticky price adjustment is the sticky adjustment of marginal cost. This would appear to place the analysis of cost stickiness at the top of the new-Keynesian research agenda. From the standpoint of the aggregate economy, the most important cost component is labor cost, suggesting the familiar idea from the old Keynesian economics that wage inflexibility is the key element in price stickiness. However, from the standpoint of the individual firm, labor cost may be less important than purchased materials as a component of cost, and this recognition elevates to the top of the research agenda, along with wage determination, the formation of expectations by individual producers about the prices of purchased materials.

While Figure 21.3 identifies the rigidity of marginal cost as the key ingredient in price stickiness, it also leaves open a role for direct barriers to the adjustment of price to the profit-maximizing level for the monopolist, that is, to point *C* in the case of a fixed *MC* schedule or to point *D* in the case of a fully flexible *MC* schedule. Point *B* represents a price above the profit-maximizing levels *C* or *D*, and could be explained by costs of adjustment of the price level emphasized by new-Keynesian theorists under the general heading of menu costs or by old-Keynesian economists who emphasized rules of thumb like fixed markups of price over long-run average cost. If the price level is predetermined at point *B*, while marginal costs are predetermined along the schedule MC_0, output and employment may vary up and down in response to variation in product demand without a change in the real product wage.

This analysis of Figure 21.3 helps to organize our treatment of new-Keynesian research on the sources of price stickiness. First we examine the studies of direct barriers to price adjustment, independent of the behavior of marginal cost, which cause the price to deviate from the price that would be set by a profit-maximizing monopolist who has no costs of adjustment to consider. These direct barriers may be subdivided into two categories, (1) state-dependent rules, which call for price changes if the optimal price strays outside of boundaries determined by menu costs of price adjustment, and (2) time-dependent rules, which call for price changes at fixed and predetermined intervals written into contracts and are in turn presumably based on the costs of negotiating new contracts at more frequent intervals. This branch of new-Keynesian economics reinterprets these rules as profit-maximizing when menu-type or negotiation-type costs of adjustment are taken into account. Then we turn to sources of stickiness in marginal cost, both in prices of purchased materials and in wages.

It should be clear from this analysis that the labor market and product market may be equally important in contributing sources of price rigidity. There has been some tendency to stress product markets relatively more in recent research and to search for some source of nominal rigidity for prices in the form of state-dependent or time-dependent rules. Yet it is clear from the monopolist example that any source of nominal rigidity will do: a menu cost for wage adjustment will make marginal cost sticky and indirectly create a source of nominal price stickiness, even if costs of adjusting prices are completely absent.

The representative-agent model of monopolistic competition

It is clear from Figure 21.3 that the mere presence of monopolistic competition does not create a presumption of price stickiness. Some ingredient must be introduced either as a direct barrier to instantaneous price adjustment or as a source of sticky marginal cost. In new-Keynesian literature this point is most often made in the context of a simple model of a representative-agent monopolist developed by Blanchard and Kiyotaki (1987) and described as the canonical model of monopolistic competition by Fischer (1988).[37] There are n identical producer-consumers producing goods that are imperfect substitutes, and there are no purchased materials. Nominal aggregate demand depends only on the nominal money supply. Marginal cost consists of the marginal disutility of production for each producer-consumer. The canonical model describes the determinants of output and of the desired relative price (P_i/P). With constant returns in production and a constant marginal disutility of work, the model is equivalent to Figure 21.3 with a flat *MC* schedule and a constant-elasticity demand curve. The producer reacts to changes in demand by changing output while leaving the relative price constant.

Only with an upward sloping *MC* schedule (due either to decreasing returns to labor in production or to an increasing marginal disutility of work) does the producer desire to change the relative price in response to a shift in demand. However, because there is complete symmetry across producers, relative prices must all be equal to unity. An attempt to decrease relative price in response to a decline in demand leads to a decrease in all nominal prices and in the aggregate price level, and this adjustment of the aggregate price level continues until all relative prices are back to unity. Money is completely neutral. The only element introduced by monopolistic competition is a declining marginal revenue schedule, which means that in equilibrium (with $P_i/P = 1$) price is above marginal cost rather than equal to marginal cost, and output is lower than in competitive equilibrium.

There is no role for sticky marginal cost in the Blanchard and Kiyotaki 'pure' model of monopolistic competition, because the imposition of symmetry across identical representative-agent producers has the effect of implicitly indexing both the relative price (P_i) and marginal cost to the aggregate price level, which in turn depends only on the nominal money supply. Thus the new-Keynesian theorists recognize that they must go beyond the mere introduction of monopolistic competition in order to locate the sources of price stickiness. One route is to study direct barriers to nominal price adjustment in the form of state-dependent or time-dependent rules. The other direction is to study the sources of sticky marginal cost.

S,s state-dependent pricing rules

The new menu-cost literature owes its origins to a paper by Barro (1972) on the *S,s* approach to price adjustment by a profit-maximizing monopolist who faces a lump-sum cost of adjusting prices. The common theme linking the older *S,s* literature and the newer menu-cost literature is that price setters do not change price every time the desired price level changes, but only when the desired level deviates by more than a particular percentage from the current price. In the *S,s* literature the width of the percent band is arbitrarily given, while in the menu-cost literature the width, while also given, is presumed to be 'small' and ultimately capable of being explained by particular adjustment costs. For expository purposes these contributions may be discussed together, because they both concern barriers to the adjustment of nominal prices and share the common theme of a percentage band within which the price remains fixed.

The basic S,s result is derived for a monopolist facing a stochastic additive shift in its demand curve taking the form of a random walk without drift. The optimal strategy for the monopolist is shown to be the selection of 'floor' and 'ceiling' bands, with the price remaining constant when the shift is within the bands and changing fully to the new desired level when the shift is outside the bands. The width of the band, expressed as a percentage of the current price, depends positively on the cost of a price change and inversely on the opportunity cost of not changing, which in turn depends on the slopes of the demand and cost functions.[38]

This result is specific to a demand disturbance that is modeled as a random walk, so that changes in the disturbance are serially independent, and as yet optimal rules have not been derived for more general processes in which the changes in the disturbance are serially correlated (as surely they must be in view of serial correlation in changes in nominal demand evident in Figures 21.2 and 21.3). Instead, most of the extensions of the S,s approach concern inflation which is at a sufficiently rapid rate that the price level cannot decrease, so the choice problem is simplified to choosing the timing of price increases. Sheshinski and Weiss (1977, 1983) show that the S,s approach carries over to inflation; now the price is increased at any point when it sinks below the optimal price by an amount exceeding a lower s band.

Caplin and Spulber (1987) have investigated the implications of aggregating S,s behavior from the level of the individual to the aggregate economy. Their striking result is that one-sided S,s rules (as are appropriate in an economy with an inflationary bias) do not lead to price stickiness or the non-neutrality of money. If firms face both local and aggregate shocks, their price changes will be independent and staggered across time. But when they do increase their individual price, they will raise it sufficiently to boost the aggregate price level by the full amount of the aggregate shock. For example, if demand increases in a series of one-unit steps, and adjustment costs limit individual firms to a price increase every fourth step, then that individual price increase will be four units and will increase the aggregate price level by one unit.

The Caplin-Spulber result is contingent on an unrealistic assumption, that the desired price follows a continuous and monotone path. A more general model, which reverses their main conclusion, has been developed by Caplin and Leahy (1989). Their main point is that when the monetary shocks are two-sided, that is, when money can go both up and down, without any monotonic tendency in a single direction, there can be long periods in which the aggregate price level does not change in response to monetary disturbances. Intuitively, money is neutral only when the economy continuously hits an upper S or lower s band, but a more general stochastic process for money may leave it inside both bands for substantial periods during which there is no incentive for any agent to change its nominal price.

A difficulty in the S,s literature is that for analytical tractability all firms are identical, and thus have price increases of equal size that differ only in timing. This is belied by virtually all evidence on cross-section pricing behavior, including the differing cyclical responsiveness of prices across industries in the Great Depression (shown in Table 21.2). This evidence suggests that elements beyond simple state-dependent pricing rules must lie behind observed price behavior at the micro level.

The menu-cost insight and its limitations

Taking the S,s literature as a point of departure, what new insights have been contributed by the menu-cost literature developed in the mid-1980s? The menu-cost approach began defensively in response to those critics who argued that costs of changing nominal prices are much too small to justify output fluctuations of the size observed in the USA. Its key insight is that second-order adjustment costs may have first-order social consequences, simply because profit functions are flat on top.[39] Following a change in demand there may be little difference in the firm's profit if it does or does not adjust its price, and thus even small menu costs may potentially dissuade the firm from price adjustment. Yet the social consequence of such a failure to adjust price may be large swings in output.

The proponents of the menu-cost approach are quick to admit that this widely used label is misleading. Included among the nominal costs of price adjustment are not just the literal application of the label to changing prices on menus, lists, catalogs, and other printed material, but more generally the entire range of costs that managers must incur whenever nominal prices are changed. Meetings, phone calls, and trips to renegotiate with suppliers all fall under the rubric of menu costs. Included in this more general definition of menu costs is Okun's (1981) analysis of the product market. Okun explains the reluctance of firms to shift from FIFO (first in first out) pricing policies to the more economically rational behavior of replacement cost pricing as a consequence of the perceived costs of delegating pricing authority to lower levels of management, in contrast to general FIFO-type rules of thumb that save these costs of delegation even if they lead to pricing decisions that may be otherwise suboptimal. All these physical costs of printing, negotiating, and delegating are doubtless present in the real world of business, although one can quibble with their importance. Costs of negotiating are also a key ingredient that motivates staggered contracting, a time-dependent rule considered in the next section.

Whatever the nature of the menu costs, the analysis may be presented in terms of Figure 21.3 which already provides the ingredients necessary to illustrate the point initially made by Akerlof and Yellen (1985) and Mankiw (1985). Following Mankiw, we examine the situation in which demand has declined in Figure 21.3 from D_0 to D_1 and marginal cost has declined from MC_0 to 'Required MC_1'. The optimal price-output point is at D, and we ask what difference is made if the firm leaves its price unchanged at P_0. Figure 21.4 copies the new demand curve and shows the same points B and D as in Figure 21.3. The difference between profits at points D and B is shown by the rectangles $T - R$. However, at point B total surplus is smaller by the area $S + T$ than at point D. But the firm will reduce price only if the extra profit $T - R$ exceeds the menu cost. Mankiw shows that as the price elasticity of demand varies from ten to two, the ratio of the social cost to the profit increment varies from 23 to 200. His results, as do Figures 21.3 and 21.4, assume that the marginal cost schedule is flat. In general, the flatter is the marginal cost schedule, the smaller are the menu costs needed to make the firm's fixed-price decision optimal and hence to create an output response from a change in nominal aggregate demand.

At least four important criticisms of the menu-cost approach may be offered. Taken together, they make a strong case against this core contribution of the new-Keynesian macroeconomics.

First, a consideration of symmetry brings the basic conclusion into question. If the failure to reduce price in response to a demand reduction makes output too low, then the failure to raise price in response to a demand increase makes output too high. Yet, starting from an initial profit-maximizing equilibrium level of output like Q_0 under monopolistic competition, society gains from additional output because price is above marginal cost. Hence the menu-cost model fails to prove its point: social costs in recessions are balanced by social gains in booms. Any cost from price rigidity must involve

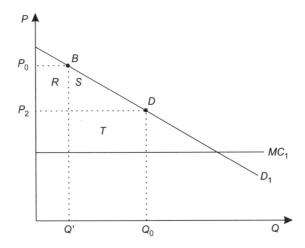

Figure 21.4

increasing the variance of output, not changing its mean, and hence are likely to be second-order, just as the costs of changing price are second-order. One cannot conclude that sticky prices necessarily reduce welfare, for the comparison of two second-order effects turns on model-dependent comparisons of parameter values.[40] This argument of Ball and Romer (1989a) greatly weakens the appeal of the menu-cost approach, although their own model implies that the second-order social costs can be much larger than the costs of changing price.

Second, but independent of the Ball-Romer symmetry argument, the menu-cost approach seems flawed from the start, because it considers only costs of price adjustment and totally ignores costs of output adjustment. This places its assumptions in diametric opposition to other important branches of macroeconomics, such as Tobin's q theory of investment based on time-dependent physical costs of changing the capital stock, or the production-smoothing theory of inventory behavior based on the assumption that a smooth rather than variable production minimizes cost. Costs of output adjustment raise the cost of not changing price and tilt the firm's decision toward price flexibility; whether costs of output adjustment raise the social costs of aggregate output fluctuations depends on the relative size of the private and social costs.

Third, the two-period comparison of Figure 21.4 neglects the calculus of costs and benefits in future periods. The proper setting is dynamic, as with the analogous question of the 'sacrifice ratio' in the form of a temporary aggregate output loss required to achieve a permanent reduction of the aggregate inflation rate. The proper comparison is between the one-shot menu cost and the present value of the infinite stream of losses by maintaining the price (and output) levels at different values than the social optimum. The Ball-Romer symmetry argument vitiates the force of this criticism, because the infinite stream of losses when the price is set too high is balanced by a similar stream of gains when the price is set too low.

Fourth, like the S,s approach, the menu-cost approach fails to explain why prices of some products are more flexible than others over the business cycle. The failing of the Mankiw version illustrated in Figure 21.4 is in this regard similar to that of the canonical Blanchard-Kiyotaki model described earlier; marginal cost is simply assumed to move in proportion with demand. Once we consider the many layers of heterogeneity of products and industries studied in the industrial organization literature of Section 3 (pp. 490–92), we recognize that no individual firm can assume its marginal cost will be perfectly correlated with aggregate demand. Subsequently this will lead us to the input-output table as an essential component in the description of price stickiness and will reinforce our previous point that the failure to consider heterogeneity and aggregation issues is a central flaw in representative agent modeling.

Thus we return to the original objection to models of nominal rigidity based on adjustment costs. Any satisfactory model of price rigidity must be able to cope with the Great Depression, yet the magnitude of demand shifts between 1929 and 1933 would seem to swamp any reasonable guess as to the magnitude of S,s bands or menu costs. And one does not have to dip into history to doubt the relevance of such adjustment costs. Everyone has witnessed the fast-changing price tags in the produce section of the neighborhood supermarket: There seems to be nothing to prevent the price of a pint of strawberries from moving from $1.89 to $0.59 to $1.89 in successive weeks. Carlton's evidence shows that prices can jump not just by large amounts in successive weeks, but by small amounts in successive months. Roberts *et al.* (1989) have found in time-series data for 20 two-digit US industries over 1958–83 that the adjustment of nominal prices to nominal labor and materials costs takes place extremely rapidly. For four industries, 90 percent of price adjustment occurs *within the month*, and for no industry is the first-month adjustment lower than 45 percent. This provides strong evidence that the menu-cost approach is on the wrong track, and that the key issues concern the stickiness of both wages and materials costs, not final goods prices. The mere fact of imperfect competition and price tags appears to be quite compatible with nominal flexibility.

Time-dependent rules and staggered contracts

The last element to be considered in new-Keynesian explanations of nominal price rigidity is the staggered contract model. As noted above, new-Keynesian economics can be said to begin with the Fischer (1977a) and Phelps-Taylor (1977) models of staggered contracts, which emphasized wage contracts. More recently, models of staggered price contracts have been developed by Blanchard (1983, 1986) and Ball and Romer (1989b), among others. These models investigate the implications of staggered overlapping price-setting intervals of constant length, and in the case of Ball-Romer investigate the conditions necessary for firms to engage in staggering.

The staggering and overlapping of intervals in which individual prices or wages are fixed introduces a critical element of realism into new-Keynesian economics. As shown by Blanchard (1983), a change in nominal demand can affect output for a period that exceeds the length of the interval during which prices are predetermined, which we will call the *contract interval* even though there is no necessity that explicit or implicit contracts be involved. Consider contracts of n months, with a fraction $1/n$ of agents resetting contracts each month. The firms that reset their price in the first month following a demand shift move their price not to the optimum given the level of nominal demand, but to the optimum contingent on the fact that the other outstanding contracts cause a fraction $(n-1)/n$ of the aggregate price level to be preset. Any firm adjusting all the way would cause a suboptimal divergence of its *relative* price from the optimum level, given the stickiness of other prices.

The study of staggered prices takes as its point of departure that the length of predetermination of prices reflects a balancing of the costs of adjusting prices and the opportunity costs of nonadjustment, just as in the *S,s* model. Because this decision need be made only by the profit-maximizing price-setting monopolist, there is no need for an actual contract with another agent. There has been little attention to the nature of the adjustment costs or in particular their variation across industries or over time, which is unfortunate as this might provide the element that is missing in so many new-Keynesian models, the ability to explain cross-time and cross-industry differences in price behavior. In particular, there is no element in the theory that would explain why the rate-of-change (α) coefficient of price adjustment increased in most countries during World War I, or why the inertia (λ) effect increased in most countries except Japan after World War II. As a separate criticism, there has been no attempt to introduce explicit indexation into these staggered contract models, which contain no element to explain why firms do not predetermine *real* prices for a time interval (presumably to save on management decision costs) and then index the nominal price to nominal GNP.

Instead, attention has been concentrated on the question of why there is staggering rather than complete synchronization. Ball and Romer (1989b) show that staggering is a stable equilibrium if there are firm-specific shocks that arrive at different times for different firms. However, they show that synchronization can also be an equilibrium: 'Multiple equilibria are possible because there is an incentive for synchronized price setters to remain bunched, but not for staggered price setters to move toward synchronization' (1989b: 193). There seems to be a debate as to whether firm-specific shocks are sufficient to guarantee a staggering equilibrium, but only in the context of simple models in which firms can choose only to change price at odd or even dates. A more general setting in which some prices are changed weekly and others yearly, and in which the yearly price changers have 365 possible dates on which to change, destroys the argument that each individual price setter still has an incentive to 'bunch' price changes at the same time, because there is no such thing as the 'same time'.[41]

6 SOURCES OF REAL RIGIDITY IN THE PRODUCT MARKET

Customer markets

The analysis of nominal price rigidity in Section 5 treats only the first quadrant of our two-by-two matrix defined along the dimensions of product versus labor market and nominal versus real rigidity. We turn now to models of real rigidity, that is, models that explain why real wages or prices are unresponsive to changes in economic activity. In the product market, a model of real rigidity explains why a firm would choose to hold its relative price or price-cost margin constant. In the context of the canonical

Blanchard-Kiyotaki monopoly model, this occurs with a constant marginal disutility of work and constant returns to labor. In the textbook monopoly model of Figure 21.3, the price-cost margin is fixed if the marginal cost schedule is horizontal and the elasticity of demand is constant.

Recall that our discussion of indexation in Section 4 (pp. 504–6) introduced a basic objection to all models of real rigidity. No matter how rigid is the real wage or real price, what prevents the nominal price and wage from being indexed to nominal GNP? At that point we asked whether nominal rigidities were sufficiently important to be able to explain the absence of nominal GNP indexation. Thus far we have concluded that nominal rigidities based on S,s or menu-cost models are not convincing, while time-dependent rules in the form of staggered price-setting intervals are completely compatible with any form of indexation. Thus a critical test for the theories of real price and wage rigidity is whether they stand up to the indexation criticism.

Perhaps the earliest prominent model of real rigidity in product markets explains why customers do not respond instantaneously to changes in real prices, that is, in the price charged by one firm relative to others. Okun (1975), building on the work of Alchian (1969) as well as Phelps and Winter (1970), popularized the distinction between auction and customer markets. The former are perfectly competitive. But, in the latter, costly search makes customers willing to pay a premium to do business with customary suppliers, and intertemporal comparison shopping discourages firms from changing prices in response to short-run changes in demand in order to avoid giving customers an incentive to begin exploring. Okun argues that his customer-search model explains markup pricing practices based on full costs. Customers appear willing to accept as fair an increase in price based on a permanent increase in cost, whereas transitory events, whether an increase in demand or a reduction in productivity, are not generally expected to last long enough to justify price increases.

Okun's approach has several critical defects. He argues that price increases based on cost are perceived as fair, while cost increases based on demand are not so perceived. The case for customer dissatisfaction is difficult to argue, because any loss of goodwill created by a price increase in a boom would be balanced by a gain of goodwill created by a price decrease in a recession. Okun seems to be thinking of an inflationary world in which price changes are one-sided, as in the trend-inflation S,s literature. Further, the fairness explanation leaves open the determination of fair behavior, and in fact what is perceived to be fair may just reflect whatever behavior may be normal, for whatever reason. Thus Okun's approach has an element of circularity.

Okun's approach also seems vulnerable to the same criticism often directed at Lucas-type new-classical models: why should a firm be afraid to lose customers when raising prices in response to higher nominal demand if information on higher nominal demand is instantly available? What prevents all firms from indexing to nominal demand and advertising price specials on items priced lower than would be warranted by the indexation formula? As we have seen already, the elementary theory of monopoly pricing behavior by itself suggests little for price flexibility. Everything depends on the response of marginal cost to aggregate demand shocks.

The independence of costs and demand

Nevertheless, there is a deeper insight in Okun's distinction between cost and demand. Firms raise price in response to an upward shift in the marginal cost schedule not just because it is optimal in a textbook model, but because they will go bankrupt if cost rises sufficiently in relation to price. There is no such economic necessity of raising price in response to an increase in demand when cost is fixed, and for a monopolist such a price increase is not even optimal with a constant-elasticity demand curve and a flat MC schedule. When OPEC raises the price of oil sharply in relation to the level of nominal aggregate demand, everybody understands why the local service station raises the price of gasoline at the pump, but they do not understand why an increase in aggregate demand requires any such response of the gasoline price if the costs of service station inputs are fixed.

This distinction hinges on the possibility that shifts in marginal cost can be independent of shifts in aggregate demand. Our historical study of price adjustment in Sections 2 and 3 stressed the theoretical and empirical importance of supply shifts. Ball and Romer's (1989b) study of staggering emphasizes the critical role of idiosyncratic firm-specific shocks. Bertola and Caballero (1990) emphasize the role of idiosyncratic uncertainty in explaining infrequent price adjustment at the micro level. New-classical Mark I macroeconomics was built on Lucas' distinction between local and aggregate shocks. Okun's emphasis on cost-based pricing leads us to broaden Lucas' two-way distinction between local and aggregate *demand* shocks and suggest a four-way distinction between local and aggregate demand shocks, and local and aggregate cost shocks.[42]

This four-way distinction creates two complementary sets of reasons why firms may rationally expect marginal cost to move differently from marginal revenue. First, marginal revenue may move with aggregate nominal demand but marginal costs may not. This would occur if a firm believes that its costs depend not just on nominal demand but on local supply factors (e.g. harvests, strikes, price changes for imported materials). Second, in a situation with nominal aggregate demand fixed, a firm might face a local shift in demand (e.g. a decline in beer drinking in response to drunk-driving laws) that reduces marginal revenue, while marginal cost is fixed, tied to aggregate nominal demand. More generally, any set of covariances among the four shock concepts is possible.

The role of the input-output table

To be a credible explanation of real price rigidity, the distinction among local and aggregate cost and demand shocks must be embedded in a world with many heterogeneous firms interacting within a complex input-output table. With only two firms, each supplying the other, information would be cheap enough to permit both firms to disentangle the local versus aggregate component of their costs. But with thousands of firms buying thousands of components, containing ingredients from many other firms, the typical firm has no idea of the identity of its full set of suppliers when all the indirect links within the input-output table are considered. Because the informational problem of trying to anticipate the effect of a currently perceived nominal demand change on the weighted-average cost of all these suppliers is difficult to formulate and probably impossible to solve, since (as Bresnahan emphasizes) thousands of elasticities are involved, the sensible firm just waits by the mailbox for news of cost increases and then, Okun-like, passes them on as price increases.

The input-output table approach provides a critical contribution not just to understanding real price rigidity, but also nominal rigidity. The standard accusation against all theories of real rigidity, made often above, is that they are consistent with nominal flexibility achieved through indexation to nominal demand. Yet the input-output table approach emphasizes the high fraction of a firm's costs that is attributable to suppliers of unknown identity, with some unknown fraction producing in foreign countries under differing aggregate demand conditions. This environment would give pause to any firm considering nominal demand indexation of the product price, because the failure of all suppliers to adopt similar indexation could lead to bankruptcy when nominal demand declines. Thus the input-output approach borrows one element that is basic to Keynesian economics, the coordination failure that arises from the lack of private incentives to solve a social problem, with another element inherited from Lucas, the distinction between aggregate and idiosyncratic shocks.

One criticism of the input-output approach claims that with perfect information about aggregate variables, the only equilibrium of the economy would be for immediate adjustment of all prices to nominal shocks. Yet this ignores the fundamental assumption that marginal cost and marginal revenue are imperfectly correlated with aggregate demand. Under these conditions each firm would be unwilling to index price to nominal GNP both because marginal cost may not move with nominal GNP even if marginal revenue were to do so, and vice versa.

A good reason for every domestic firm to refuse to index its product price to domestic nominal demand would occur to any economist from, say, Belgium or Chile. Because we know that purchasing power parity (PPP) fails and that real exchange rates are volatile, why would any firm adopt indexation of its price to domestic Belgian or Chilean nominal GDP, which would disconnect its price from the large share of its costs that are imported? The input-output approach, by stressing the independence of marginal cost and aggregate demand, provides an understanding of the lack of indexation to domestic nominal GNP and thus the critical link that converts a theory of real rigidity into a theory of nominal rigidity.[43]

A firm's viability depends on the relation of price to cost, not price to nominal GNP. Aggregate macroeconomic stability is a public good subject to a free-rider problem. No individual firm has an incentive to take the risk posed by nominal GNP indexation, which would take away from the firm the essential control required of the relation of price to cost. In this sense, the input-output explanation of nominal rigidity requires capital markets that are imperfect enough to penalize the profit volatility that would result if a firm tried to index its prices to nominal demand without being sure in advance that its suppliers would do likewise.

There is another sense in which the input-output table explains nominal rigidity. It creates a technological environment for staggered price setting, similar to but more complex than Taylor's staggered wage setting. Today's product price is based on costs set at many different dates in the past as product components weave their way through the input-output table. This may appear to violate the maxim that prices should be based on replacement cost. But there are too many links in the input-output table for the producer even to guess what the replacement cost may be. The automobile firm may receive a notice from the headlight maker of a price increase, but no warning of a price-increase notice that is already in the mail from the filament maker to the headlight maker or from the copper maker to the filament maker. Blanchard (1987b) uses the term *cumulation hypotheses* to describe the role of the input-output table in translating prompt price adjustment at the individual level to gradual price adjustment at the aggregate level. He provides suggestive supporting evidence that in disaggregated data prices adjust faster than in aggregate data. The automobile, headlight, filament, and copper maker may all respond to cost increases within a day, but months can separate the effects of a change in the price of copper from the ultimate change in the price of automobiles.

The input-output table approach dominates menu costs in explaining why the price of strawberries is more volatile than the price of automobiles (because strawberries are not physically transformed from farm to market). It explains the different rate-of-change adjustment coefficient (α) across industries by two auxiliary assumptions. First, auction markets are distinct from customer markets and are limited mainly to crude and intermediate goods. Thus products like strawberries and plastics that appear relatively early in the input-output chain have relatively flexible auction-like prices. But what is it that creates more price rigidity for more complex products later in the chain? Partly it is the law of large numbers that cancels out idiosyncratic supply shocks for final products incorporating large numbers of different purchased materials. But there also may be a role for wage rigidity, as the prices of products embodying relatively large amounts of embodied labor, like automobiles, tend to be more rigid than that of products embodying large amounts of embodied land, like wheat or strawberries. Thus the input-output approach is complementary to theories of rigidity in the labor market.

A safe compromise place to end the discussion of product-market rigidities is to admit that the input-output approach is complementary as well to at least one of the new-Keynesian approaches based on nominal rigidities. The input-output approach needs some additional element to explain why we do not observe in the real world extremely frequent small price changes every day as firms react to each tiny cost change as it arrives in the mail through the input-output table (while Carlton documents some such small changes, long intervals of complete rigidity are common as well).

The core element that needs to be added to the input-output approach is a cost to making price changes every day that causes rational managers to concentrate price-setting decisions at discrete intervals. There is no need to force this sort of nominal rigidity into a single semantic category; the core factor for some firms may best be described as staggered time-dependent rules and for others as state-dependent rules based on menu-type costs. Undoubtedly these categories overlap because many firms face both time-dependent and state-dependent costs. Some firms that routinely hold price-setting meetings once a week or month to save on managerial time costs may decide at those periodic meetings to leave some or all prices unchanged when the difference between the current and optimal price does not yet exceed the perceived cost of printing new menus and catalogs.

7 THE SEARCH FOR STRUCTURE: LABOR MARKET BEHAVIOR

The relation of wage and price behavior

The dominant new-Keynesian view is that nominal rigidities originate in the product market, not the labor market. The path of wages, to use the words of Mankiw, is 'completely indeterminant and completely irrelevant' (1988: 446). Yet surely this goes too far. Mankiw follows earlier writing, notably by Barro (1977b) and Hall (1980), who have argued that wage rigidity is irrelevant for employment determination. In the context of a long-term or even lifetime job, there is no reason for the wage in a given time period to be equal to the marginal product of labor. The wage can be an installment payment on a lifetime contract.

However, the claim that sticky wages are irrelevant to allocation calls for prices to be perfectly flexible, as is required for perfect market clearing, while wages are sticky. We have already observed in Section 2 (pp. 487–88) that capital markets are likely to impose a tax on the resulting profit variability. Further, the monopolist example shows that prices will not be perfectly flexible unless all elements of marginal cost are perfectly flexible. This brings us back to indexation: The sticky wages that are installment payments for lifetime jobs must be fully indexed to nominal demand for Barro, Hall, and Mankiw to be correct that sticky wages are irrelevant to allocation.

Just as it is implausible for wages to be sticky while prices are perfectly flexible, so is the reverse, for wages to be perfectly flexible while prices are sticky. Yet this is just what is assumed in much of the menu-cost literature reviewed in Section 5. When menu costs lead rational firms to avoid price changes and meet demand through changes in output, corresponding fluctuations in labor input are required. In menu-cost models the real wage adjusts to make workers willing to change the amount they work; that is, the nominal wage rate is perfectly flexible. In the Blanchard-Kiyotaki canonical model of monopolistic competition, the representative agents set their relative price to minimize the marginal disutility of work; that is, they slide along their voluntary labor supply curve. As Rotemberg has noted, 'both of these approaches have the very un-Keynesian implication that in recessions workers are close to indifferent between working and not working'.

For new-Keynesian models to avoid inconsistency, their distinction between small menu costs of price changes and large social costs of output changes must apply equally in the labor and product markets. The same costs of adjustment that inhibit price changes must apply equally to wages, which are just another price. Sticky prices cause changes in nominal aggregate demand to be transmitted directly to shifts in the demand curves facing not just individual firms, but also individual workers. The Barro-Grossman spillover model discussed in Section 4 (pp. 501–4) achieves the desired symmetric treatment, in which sticky wages and prices cause both firms and workers to face constraints on the amount they can sell.

Blanchard and Fischer (1989: 427) state that the key issue in new-Keynesian economics is explaining why 'labor and output supply functions [are] relatively flat.' They intend this phrase to mean real rigidities.[44] Yet their choice of words is unfortunate, because it ignores the distinction between aggregate and individual supply curves, as well as between notional and effective supply functions. The labor supply function of an individual head of household may be vertical, but any mechanism that rigidifies the real wage will cause the individual to be pushed off this notional supply function. Actual behavior traces shifts in the effective labor demand schedule and tells us nothing about the shapes of notional functions. In our interpretation the key issue is the explanation of wage and price rigidity, not the explanation of why labor and output supply curves are flat.[45] And at a deeper level, as argued in Section 4 (pp. 501–4), the really central element is the coordination failure that underlies wage and price rigidity.

Early theories of real rigidity: search models and implicit contracts

Just as theories of price stickiness can usefully be divided between theories of nominal versus real rigidity, so can theories of wage stickiness. Reflecting the chronological development of the field, we begin with models of real wage rigidity and then turn to models of nominal wage rigidity.

Widely recognized as the first attempt to build structural models of labor market behavior as the outcome of maximizing behavior was the new microeconomics of the famous volume edited by Phelps (1970). Most of the papers in the Phelps volume, including Phelps' own desert island parable, yielded market-clearing conclusions and as such should be regarded as part of the development of new-classical rather than new-Keynesian ideas. In the parable, workers are on isolated islands and react to a wage cut by boarding rafts to sample wage offers on other islands. Variations in employment during business cycles are due solely to the voluntary response of workers to changes in the expected real wage. The parable ignores the prompt availability of aggregate information, fails to explain layoffs and "no help wanted" signs, and yields the counterfactual implication that voluntary quits vary countercyclically (see Okun 1981: ch. 2).

The main contribution of the new microeconomics volume was not to business cycle theory but rather to explain why the natural unemployment rate is greater than zero, due chiefly to the work of Mortensen (1970a, 1970b). In a world of costly information and heterogeneous jobs and workers, workers sample from an array of job offers and firms sample from an array of workers. Unemployment is a voluntary activity, but all voluntary unemployment is not socially beneficial, and government unemployment benefits tend to stretch out the interval between searches, imposing a social cost through the taxes levied on some to support the extended search interval of others. The new microeconomics volume also contained the important Phelps-Winter (1970) theory of customer markets, based also on the assumption of imperfect information. We have seen that this was later picked up and developed by Okun in a new-Keynesian rather than new-classical setting.

While the new microeconomics was explicitly classical in approach, the next wave of contributions under the heading of implicit contract theory was the first to develop what some initially thought was a microeconomic explanation for Keynesian wage stickiness. In the simultaneously written and independent contributions by Azariadis (1975), Baily (1974), and Donald F. Gordon (1974), employees were assumed to be relatively more risk averse than their employers, mainly because of self-selection of individuals to become entrepreneurs. Firms maximized profits by minimizing the variability of income to their workers, who disliked variability, in effect providing a compensation package that consisted partly of pecuniary wage payments and partly of insurance services.

It was soon recognized that this approach provides no satisfactory explanation of Keynesian unemployment; it justifies only a fixed-income contract (i.e. tenure) rather than the fixed-wage variable-employment contracts actually observed. Variable employment is explained only by a gratuitous element patched onto the theory, government side-payments during periods of unemployment. Even when these variable employment fixed-wage contracts are generated by the theory, they have the unKeynesian implication that workers are equally happy when employed and unemployed.[46] Further, workers are shown to care about stability in *real* income, not nominal income, so implicit contract theory has no explanation for the failure of workers to insist on full indexation of wage contracts.

Labor unions

The effects of labor unions have been extensively analyzed by labor economists. Bargaining models have been developed in which firms and unions, which in turn act on behalf of their member workers, bargain over wages and employment. Some models characterize the employment decision as a unilateral decision of management, as it is in many contracts. These models that are concerned only with wage setting are sometimes called the *right-to-manage* model and fall between two extremes. At one extreme firms are all powerful and are able to pay the minimum wage possible, that is, the competitive wage. Because firms have complete control of both employment and the wage, this subclass of models does not warrant the label *bargaining* model at all; the efficiency wage models discussed in Section 7 (pp. 525–7) fall into this class. At the other extreme is the union-monopoly model dating back to Dunlop (1944); here too there is no bargaining, because firms set employment and unions set the wage.

A more general model is developed by McDonald and Solow (1981), who show that a bilateral monopoly between a firm and a union can lead to relatively large employment fluctuations and relatively small real-wage fluctuations, thus contributing a source of real-wage rigidity. In an extension, McDonald and Solow (1985) examine the impact of business-cycle fluctuations on a labor market segmented into a union primary sector and a competitive secondary sector. Reflecting the small real-wage fluctuations in the union sector, they show that either permanent or temporary changes in real aggregate demand widen sector wage differentials in recession and cause greater fluctuations in primary sector than secondary sector employment.

Yet the formal theory of unions does not provide a general explanation of Keynesian wage rigidity. If union members care about stability of employment, it is difficult to understand why they are willing to tolerate a wage rate that is set for a substantial interval, while the decision on the amount of employment is left to the firm.[47] Obviously if the wage rate is predetermined as part of a union contract, this rigidifies marginal cost and hence prices, and nominal demand fluctuations are transmitted to output and employment. But, overall, the union literature leaves open the question why the wage rather than the level of employment is set by contracts, and why the wage rate is not indexed to nominal demand so as to stabilize employment.

Another problem is raised by the empirical evidence of Table 21.3 (p. 494). Unions became important in the USA only after the mid-1930s, yet the estimated rate-of-change (α) and level (γ) effects for the USA are the same during 1873–1914 and 1954–87. Some factor other than unions must account for the price stickiness evident in US data for the nineteenth century. The main contribution of unionization may have been the particular US phenomenon of the three-year staggered wage contract, which has doubtless contributed to the higher inertia parameter for both wages and prices. Yet here too there are problems, because inertia in price change seems to have increased more than for wage change (Table 21.3), and, further, inertia increased substantially for price change in the postwar period in the UK, France, and Germany (Table 21.4), nations in which the three-year contract is not prevalent.

Insider-outsider theory

Another body of work that deals with the existence and persistence of unemployment is the insider-outsider theory. The insiders are experienced incumbent employees whose jobs are protected by a variety of labor turnover costs which make it costly for firms to replace them. The outsiders, who are either unemployed or work in the casual or secondary labor market, have no such protection. Lindbeck and Snower (1986, 1988) argue that, owing to these turnover costs, the insiders gain market power, which they use to their own advantage, without necessarily taking fully into account the interests of the outsiders. Further, the insiders often can influence the turnover costs themselves by agreeing to cooperate among themselves but not with outsiders should the latter attempt to gain employment by underbidding the insider wage. This structure causes unemployment for the outsiders, who cannot find jobs even though they would be willing to work for less than the prevailing insider wage.

Although the insider-outsider theory contributes to our understanding of union behavior, it is not primarily a contribution to the union literature. A wide variety of labor turnover costs may well be significant even in the absence of unions, for example, hiring, training, negotiation, litigation, and firing costs, as well as costs that can be directly imposed by the insiders when they shirk or fail to cooperate in the presence of underbidding outsider entrants. Nevertheless, the insider-outsider theory does suggest a rationale for unionization by showing how unions can organize and coordinate insiders' rent-seeking activities.

The insider-outsider theory sheds light on a variety of labor market phenomena, such as the persistence of unemployment, differences in variability of employment across industries and countries, labor market segmentation, the duration and composition of unemployment, and the interindustry wage structure. The theory has been applied to the puzzle of persistently high unemployment in Europe in the 1980s by Blanchard and

Summers (1986) and Lindbeck and Snower (1988) and has become one of several explanations of the hysteresis hypothesis (see Section 2, pp. 488–90), in which the rate of unemployment depends on the history of actual unemployment rather than, as in Friedman's original version, being 'ground out' by the microeconomic structure of the economy. The insider-outsider approach explains the emergence of high unemployment in the 1980s as an indirect consequence of the oil shocks of the 1970s, which created a temporary adverse reduction in labor demand and caused the insider work force to contract. When labor demand recovered the remaining insiders set wages to maximize their own welfare, thereby discouraging employment and making the high unemployment persist.[48] The best evidence in support of this approach is the work of Layard and Nickell (1987) which shows that the demand pressure variable entering the Phillips-curve wage equation is not total unemployment, but rather total unemployment minus the long-term unemployed. However, to the extent that it explains the persistence of high European unemployment by high insider real wages, it is subject to the criticism (R. Gordon 1988) that high unemployment was immune to the moderation of real wage growth and the disappearance of the European wage gap in the 1980s.

Efficiency wage theory

If any development in the microeconomics of labor markets could be called the 'rage of the 1980s', it is efficiency wage theory, based on the hypothesis that worker productivity depends on the level of the real wage. When there is such a link between the wage rate and worker efficiency, firms may rationally pay a real wage rate that exceeds the market-clearing level. Firms may refuse to reduce the wage to hire members of a pool of unemployed workers who may be available at a lower wage, fearful that a reduction in real wages for existing workers may reduce productivity by more than the gain in lower wages. The appearance of an excess supply of labor in such a setting can be shown to be consistent with maximizing behavior of both firms and workers. There is substantial overlap between the insider-outsider and efficiency wage models, as they both focus on barriers to underbidding by unemployed outsiders. While the insider-outsider approach emphasizes the market power of incumbent workers, the efficiency wage approach stresses the choice problem of firms that have imperfect information about the productivity of their employees.[49]

The reasons for the response of productivity to the real wage vary across models and include effort, reduced shirking, lower turnover and training costs, the ability of high-wage firms to screen and obtain a higher-quality labor force, and improved morale and loyalty.[50] Virtually all the literature with implications for macroeconomics dates from the 1980s. Although most surveys trace the germ of the idea back three decades to early work on less-developed countries that posited a linkage among wages, nutrition, and health (e.g. Leibenstein 1957), the terms *efficiency wages* and *efficiency earnings* appear in Alfred Marshall's *Principles* (1920: 456–69). Another precursor of the idea is the negative relationship between wages and quit rates embedded in Phelps' (1970) desert island parable and other early models in the new microeconomic literature. Efficiency wage theory provides a rare common meeting ground for mainstream and radical economists, because the far left in US economics has taken the lead in developing theories of dual labor markets and for setting out policy proposals for higher minimum wages based on the assumed validity of the efficiency wage approach.[51]

The basic efficiency wage result is obtained in a simple model with identical, perfectly competitive firms and a production function in which labor input is multiplied by an efficiency factor e that depends on the real wage. Because the elasticity of e with respect to the real wage declines as the real wage increases, the first-order conditions require the firm to choose an optimal real wage rate (w^*) at which this elasticity is unity. Workers are hired up to the point where their marginal product equals the optimal wage (w^*). The intuition of the unit elasticity result is that firms forgo efficiency gains that yield more than they cost when they pay below w^*, while a wage above w^* would cost more than it yields in efficiency gains. Stated another way, effective labor cost is minimized at w^*.

Because w^* is completely fixed by whatever factors of taste and technology that determine the e function, the firm's reaction to any change in its relative price (i.e. a demand shock) is to cut employment while maintaining the wage rate at w^*. Firms have no incentive to cut the actual wage, because this would actually increase their wage bill per unit of output. The extreme result of a fixed real wage in this model stems from the assumption that a worker's efficiency depends on the absolute level of the real wage rather than on the real wage *relative* to something else, whether some measure of economy-wide real earnings or real wages in a perceived peer group or comparison group. A variant of this approach, in which effort depends on the relative real wage and on the unemployment rate (a high value of which raises effort by increasing the cost of job loss), allows the real wage to regain some flexibility and to depend inversely on the unemployment rate (Shapiro and Stiglitz 1984; Summers 1988).

Several criticisms of the efficiency wage approach have been offered.[52] One line is to propose that job applicants should 'buy' high-wage jobs either by offering lump-sum payments or performance bonds to employers, or by offering to work in low-wage apprentice status for an initial period. Efficiency wage proponents point out, however, that unemployed workers lack sufficient wealth and are risk averse, and that the same monitoring problems that generate the efficiency wage result also make it unlikely that banks or other financing sources will come forth to provide finance for the initial lump-sum payments or performance bonds. This defense does not rule out low-wage apprenticeships, which are in fact observed, but these can be interpreted alternatively as a means of sharing the cost of training rather than as the 'sale' of a job by a firm. A second criticism is that the efficiency wage model is dominated by direct payments to workers in proportion to their efficiency, whether through piece-rate contracts or through 'tournaments' that pay workers according to their ranking by performance. The defense against this criticism is similar to the first. Piece rates and tournaments are subject to information problems. Workers involved in joint production do not often have a unique claim to a 'piece', while payments to a team invite shirking by some members of the team. Tournaments are also difficult to implement; there are rarely many workers in a firm doing exactly the same tasks and no way to rank across tasks.

Overall, the efficiency wage approach seems to be an essential ingredient in explaining numerous aspects of microeconomic labor market behavior, including segmented labor markets, persistent wage differentials for similar workers that are not equalizing differences, queues for high-paid jobs, and procyclical fluctuations of the quit rate.[53] Variations on the model can explain why firms sometimes dismiss workers instead of cutting their wage. However, as a theoretical underpinning of the new-Keynesian paradigm, it suffers from the same defect as all models of real rigidities. If workers gear their effort to the real wage, there appears to be no barrier to full wage indexation that allows firms simultaneously to maintain worker effort through maintenance of the optimal real wage w^*, while changing the nominal wage in tandem with the nominal price in order to achieve macroeconomic self-correction. Further, the efficiency wage theory has little to say about the sources of variations in wage and price responsiveness over time and across countries that were identified in Section 3.

This negative verdict applies only if a new-Keynesian explanation of nominal wage and price rigidity is erected on the sole base of the efficiency wage theory. However, once the input-output approach and the independence of local and aggregate costs and demand are accepted as the underlying reason why actual economies do not index to nominal demand, the way is open to accept the efficiency wage approach as another source of cost rigidity within the input-output table, of potentially equal importance with the uncertain evolution of the prices of purchased materials. Once again, we find that the new-Keynesian approach is most convincing when sources of real and nominal rigidity are combined rather than when either one or the other is proposed as the sole explanation.[54]

Nominal rigidities: wage contract models

Theories of wage stickiness can be based on real rigidities, as in the approaches outlined above, or on nominal rigidities. The most influential work that rationalizes nominal rigidities in new-Keynesian labor market analysis is the staggered-contract approach of Fischer (1977a) and Taylor

(1980). The classification of contract rigidities as nominal is subject to the preceding criticism – that the negotiation costs that rationalize the existence of contracts do not rule out fully indexed contracts. The costly negotiations set the real wage, while the nominal wage is costlessly indexed, preferably to nominal GNP.

The Fischer-Taylor contract literature is set up entirely in nominal terms and does not discuss the option of full nominal demand indexation, so we will discuss it on those terms, as a source of nominal rigidity. In Fischer's version the wage for half the workers is set for two periods at the beginning of period t and for the other half at $t + 1$. The wage set for the first group can respond to any change in the money supply in the first period but not in the second. The greater flexibility of nominal money than of nominal wages is an assumption rather than a result and leads to real effects of perceived monetary disturbances that cannot occur within the new-classical framework. Fischer's version assumes no barriers to price flexibility and market clearing in product markets. The unemployment his model generates during a period when money has declined but wages have not declined is classical (because of an excessive real wage), not Keynesian.

In the setting of an n-period rather than two-period contract model, Taylor (1980) makes the nominal wage fixed over the life of the contract (at a level that depends on the expected price and expected output) and setting the price as a simple markup over the average wage rate. A monetary disturbance falls fully on output during the period until the next contract renegotiation. Then wages can adjust quite rapidly, because the dependence of the negotiated wage on expected future output creates a strong feedback loop between unemployment and wage behavior. Nevertheless, because prices depend on wages set in any previous contract still in force, the duration of the real output response to a nominal monetary shock can last for much longer than the length of the contract, the same result as was subsequently derived by Blanchard (1983) for the product market (see Section 5, pp. 514–15).

Taylor's approach is sufficiently plausible and important to take seriously. Yet it is subject to at least two criticisms. First, the assumptions of staggering and of fixed contract length are arbitrary. In some places (especially Japan) contract expiration dates among firms in the union sector are nearly simultaneous. If contract length depends on a balancing of negotiation costs and the allocative costs of infrequent adjustment, one would expect changes in contract length in response to the variability of either local or aggregate shocks. A more general statement of this first criticism is that the existence of nominal wage contracts is not explained from the first principles of microeconomics. Models of optimal contracting do not produce the nominal stickiness generated by the Taylor-type contracting models. The Taylor approach needs to be supplemented by an extension to wage setting of work on staggered price setting by Ball and Romer (1989b) and others, as reviewed above.

The second problem is that, once the contract expires, the adjustment of the wage in response to expected future output is not complete but is bounded in Taylor's model by an arbitrary Phillips-type adjustment coefficient. As argued by Blanchard (1987a), Taylor's results require this adjustment coefficient to be relatively 'small' and, if a cyclical response of the markup of prices over wages is allowed, that must be 'small' as well. While Blanchard's point suggests that Taylor's wage adjustment may be too slow, I would argue the opposite. In particular, Taylor (1983) has claimed that it is possible for the monetary authorities to engineer a disinflation with no output loss. However, this result depends heavily on Taylor's assumption that the effect of real demand on wage-setting decisions works through *expected future real demand* rather than *past and current real demand*. For wage setters to use a model to calculate the implications of their current wage-contract decisions on future real demand requires not only a universal belief that the announced disinflationary path of nominal demand will be maintained on target, but also a universal ability to forecast the response of actual prices to the path of nominal demand, as is required for future real demand to be predicted.

Where then do staggered wage contracts fit in? We have seen that full price flexibility for a monopolist requires full flexibility of marginal cost, and staggered contracts eliminate that full flexibility in the absence of instantaneous nominal GNP indexation. Barro, Hall, and Mankiw have argued that it is possible for firms to adjust their prices in proportion to a change in nominal aggregate demand if wages do not adjust. But this is not profit maximizing. In almost any model of monopolistic price setting, an incomplete adjustment of wages implies less than full adjustment of profit-maximizing prices. In this sense, new-Keynesian theorists have gone overboard in shifting the emphasis from the labor to the product market.

CONCLUSION

We have stressed throughout the need for new-Keynesian theory to address the most important elements of *variability* in the adjustment of prices along three dimensions, the inertia effect (λ), the rate-of-change effect (α), and the level effect (γ). The industrial organization literature contributes ample evidence of differences in rate-of-change effects across industries. It also shows that intervals of fixed prices lasting months or years in some industries can coexist with frequent small price changes in other industries. It stresses that some industries are competitive, some are monopolistic, and some industries combine monopolistic cartels with competitive price wars. Within industries, all firms do not exhibit the same price behavior, and given firms do not even charge the same prices to all customers. Heterogeneity is rampant, with hundreds of products common in many industries, and many products combine labor with hundreds or thousands of purchased components.

The time-series evidence shows a wide variety of price adjustment patterns across time and countries. The inertia (λ) effect has become more prevalent since World War II in every country but Japan. The rate-of-change (α) and level (γ) effects were remarkably similar before World War I and after World War II in most countries, but exhibited sharp divergences in between. The rate-of-change effect increased sharply during and after World War I, while the level effect virtually disappeared during the interwar period in the US, UK and Germany. The inertia-prone post-war USA is at one extreme, and Japan throughout most of its history is at the other extreme of relative flexibility.

A convenient image for understanding the desirable direction of new-Keynesian theory is a small 1×1 box set next to a gigantic $n \times n$ matrix, where n is measured in the thousands, if not the millions. The small box represents the identical representative agents of both new-classical models and the canonical monopolistic competition model, with their i subscripts, and the practice of treating the macro economy as identical to the representative agent with the subscripts removed. The gigantic matrix represents the real world, full of heterogeneous firms enmeshed in a web of intricate supplier–demander relationships. This $n \times n$ matrix suggests two main themes of the theoretical review in this chapter.

First, the key to introducing theories of real rigidity as a source of nominal price stickiness is to find a good reason why we do not observe nominal GNP indexation. That reason is simple, and is at the heart of all good microeconomics. Individual firms maximize profit by setting *their own* marginal cost equal to *their own* marginal revenue. They have no reason whatsoever to care about nominal GNP unless it provides useful information to supplement what they can learn from observing their 'local' cost and demand. There are many reasons for firms to expect their nominal marginal costs and local demand to contain idiosyncratic elements that cause them to evolve independently from nominal demand. The most straightforward argument, which is enough to make the case, is that firms in a small open economy know that their costs are determined outside the national boundaries within which domestic nominal demand applies. This principle generalizes to firms in large open economies, because we know that even under flexible exchange rates purchasing power parity does not hold over long periods, so costs of imports and domestically produced import substitutes can evolve independently of domestic aggregate demand.

The independence of cost and demand, and the input-output table approach, represent two separate components in the required (but as yet missing) new-Keynesian analysis that can come to grips with the industry, cross-time, and cross-country facts summarized here. The idea of independent cost and demand shocks seems crucial to come to grips with the time-series evidence. Just as Lucas (1973) argued that Argentina had a more vertical Phillips curve because agents knew that aggregate demand shocks dominated local shocks, so we can argue in parallel that the increase in the rate-of-change coefficient (α) in Table 21.4 for the USA, UK and Japan during 1915–22 reflected a recognition by price setters that the increasing importance of aggregate disturbances created a greater than usual correlation between changes in marginal costs and changes in aggregate demand. Similarly, the increase in persistence (the λ parameter) observed almost everywhere after World War II reflects a widespread belief that government full-employment policies and the end of the gold standard created an upward drift in prices, leading to the expectation that marginal costs would have an upward drift and would no longer be a stationary process.

The input-output component is complementary to the independent shocks idea, and helps to explain why firms do not simply assume that marginal costs will move in parallel with aggregate nominal demand: Most firms do not know the identity of their suppliers, their suppliers' suppliers, and so on, because the input-output table is so broad and so deep. The input-output component of the proposed explanation is required to grapple with the industry evidence. Prices of corn and wheat on auction markets exhibit sharp daily swings, subject to administered limits. Prices of strawberries exhibit frequent sharp weekly swings. Prices of many crude materials exhibit frequent changes, both small and large. Yet prices of newspapers and many finished goods can remain unchanged for more than a year. A unified explanation that explains the degree of volatility of fixity for every product may be impossible to achieve, but the basic idea that crude materials are relatively volatile and finished goods relatively fixed seems compatible with the input-output approach which stresses the number of steps and number of purchased components that are mixed together with labor input in each final good. The input-output approach also leaves open a role for a theory of real wage rigidity, once it is admitted that nominal GNP indexation is unlikely. The input-output approach emphasizes the time lags in transmitting news of cost and demand changes back and forth within the input-output table. However, to explain why prices do not change by small amounts every day, this approach needs to be supplemented with a plausible mixture of time-dependent and state-dependent costs of daily price changes.

Once the independence of local costs, local demand, and aggregate demand is admitted as the fundamental explanation for the lack of nominal demand indexation, the way is open to take seriously new-Keynesian research on real rigidities in the labor market. Work on union behavior and on nominal contracting in the labor market does not appear promising, in light of the similarity of the α and γ coefficients in most countries before World War I and after World War II. However, the efficiency wage model has strong persuasive power as to why firms resist real wage cuts, and the independence of shocks and input-output table explanations contribute the needed supplementary explanation of why real wage rigidity becomes translated into nominal wage rigidity. The other most promising development in the labor market literature is the insider-outsider approach, if only because the disenfranchisement of outsiders holds up the best available ray of hope that we have for understanding why the Phillips-curve level (λ) effect disappeared in the USA, UK and German interwar periods, and perhaps in some European countries in the 1980s.

Our perspective that emphasizes independent shocks and the input-output approach reinforces the view that coordination failures are the essence of macroeconomic inefficiency in new Keynesian models. Should the government attempt to intervene to provide the missing coordination of microeconomic wage and price decisions, or should its activities be limited to the traditional Keynesian use of monetary and fiscal policy to manipulate aggregate demand directly? Clearly, traditional forms of internalization through tax and subsidy policy are infeasible in light of pervasive heterogeneity among products and decision makings in the millions; to go in this direction would mean slipping into the quagmire from which Eastern Europe is trying to emerge. Even mandatory indexation to domestic nominal demand may be suboptimal in many countries where an important component of nominal marginal cost is set in foreign currencies and responds more to foreign than to domestic aggregate demand. This shifts the ultimate weapon for fighting business cycles back to the traditional instrument, aggregate demand policy, but not in the form of any old-fashioned Keynesian bias in favor of fiscal policy. If prices respond slowly to fluctuations in nominal GNP growth, then the optimal objective of stabilization policy should be to stabilize the growth rate of nominal GNP growth. Whether and how this can be achieved is beyond the scope of this chapter.[55]

Some commentators (particularly Blanchard 1987a) have lamented that, far from being a set of facts looking for a theory, the new-Keynesian paradigm suffers from *too many* unrelated theoretical explanations. Yet the essential features emphasized here, the independence of shocks, and the input-output table, embody a core set of realistic microeconomic elements: a technology of transactions, heterogeneity of goods and factor inputs, imperfect competition, imperfect information, and imperfect capital markets. Unlike time-dependent or place-dependent factors like unions, these essential features are timeless and placeless. They lead us to expect that the degree of price flexibility in the early nineteenth century would not be much greater than today, except insofar as the $n \times n$ matrix was smaller, with fewer steps from primary producer to final consumer, and indeed we find a basic similarity within each country in the α and γ parameters before World War I and after World War II.

Recognition of the universality of these imperfections in economic life is overdue – perhaps a campaign can be started to change economic language so that these features will be considered the norm, rather than some aberrant or exotic flower. Rather than thinking of basic aspects of transaction and capital-market technology as imperfections, perhaps we could all start recognizing that these features are part of the way that markets function.

But these suggestions represent only the beginning of a needed research program. At the truly micro-micro level of relations between individual firms and customers, imperfections go far beyond anything that the independence of shocks, input-output, or efficiency wage approaches can explain by themselves. The evidence presented by Carlton that firms charge different prices to different customers for the same product, and apply nonprice allocation rules differently across customers, opens up a whole new dimension of heterogeneity that future theorists will need to consider. The ultimate merger of the new empirical industrial organization and the new Keynesian macroeconomics (it is hoped not by leveraged buyout) seems a long way off, but it is a worthy goal to support.

APPENDIX A: THE VARIETY OF HISTORICAL EXPERIENCE: REGRESSION METHODOLOGY AND ESTIMATES

Specification of regression equations

The aim is to estimate the three parameters λ, α, and γ in equation (9) in the text, which is repeated here for convenience:

$$p_t = \lambda p_{t-1} + \alpha \hat{x}_t + \gamma \hat{Q}_t + z_t \qquad (9)$$

There may be some concern regarding the close resemblance of (9) to an identity obtained by rearranging (3):

$$p_t \equiv \hat{x}_t - \hat{Q}_t + \hat{Q}_{t-1} \qquad (a)$$

Comparing (9) and (a), the former includes p_{t-1} and excludes $\hat{Q}_{t-1}$. Because inertia may be absent in some historical eras ($\lambda = 0$), the difference between (9) and (a) boils down to the exclusion of $\hat{Q}_{t-1}$. Thus if (9) is a true structural equation, the identity (a) provides the value of the missing variable, $\hat{Q}_{t-1}$. This argument is more transparent when (9) is transformed to include $\hat{Q}_{t-1}$ but to exclude $\hat{Q}_t$:

$$p_t = [1/(1+\gamma)][\lambda p_{t-1} + (\alpha + \gamma)\hat{x}_t + \gamma \hat{Q}_{t-1} + z_t]. \qquad (9')$$

If (9) is a structural relation, so is (9'). Given the values of the right-hand variables in (9'), two of which are predetermined (p_{t-1} and $\hat{Q}_{t-1}$) and one of which is endogenous ($\hat{x}_t$), the role of the identity (a) is to determine output as $\hat{Q}_t \equiv \hat{Q}_{t-1} + \hat{x}_t - p_t$. In short, the identity shows how output must change, given the structural price equation (9'). This just restates the basic point about Keynesian economics: if the current price is predetermined by an equation like (9'), then the current output level $\hat{Q}_t$ is determined as a residual.

The main estimation problem is not the fact that there is an identity linking some of the variables in (9'), but rather the endogeneity of $\hat{x}_t$, which we have discussed above in the context of policy feedback. Because the essence of the problem is policy feedback, there can be no escape by replacing nominal GNP by the money supply, or by using money as an instrument for nominal GNP. And alternative versons with real GNP or unemployment are also subject to bias if policy feedback is not complete, as illustrated in Table 21.1. Our solution, which is to bracket the α parameter by estimating alternative versions of (9′) with $\hat{x}_t$ and $\hat{q}_t$ as alternative explanatory variables, seems to be the best alternative.

To do this, we provide a pair of estimates for each dependent variable (price change, nominal wage change, and real wage change for the USA, and price change for the UK, France, Germany, and Japan). The specification for the first member of each pair is (9′). The specification for the second member of each pair is the transformation of (9′) that results when identity (a) is used to replace $\hat{x}_t$ by $\hat{q}_t$:

$$p_t = [1/(1-\alpha)][\lambda p_{t-1} + (\alpha + \gamma)\hat{q}_t + \gamma \hat{Q}_{t-1} + z_t]. \qquad (9'')$$

The values of the three parameters λ, α, and γ can be easily unscrambled. If in (9′) a_1 is the estimated coefficient on $\hat{x}_t$, a_2 is the estimated coefficient on p_{t-1}, and a_3 is the estimated coefficient on $\hat{Q}_{t-1}$, then the parameters resulting from the estimation of (9′) are $\gamma = [a_3/(1-a_3)]$, $\alpha = a_1 - \gamma(1-a_1)$, and $\lambda = a_2(1+\gamma)$. If in (9″) b_1 is the estimated coefficient on $\hat{q}_t$, b_2 is the estimated coefficient on p_{t-1}, and b_3 is the estimated coefficient on $\hat{Q}_{t-1}$, then the parameters resulting from the estimation of (9″) are $\alpha = (b_1 - b_3)/(1 + b_1 - b_3)$, $\gamma = b_3(1-\alpha)$, and $\lambda = b_2(1-\alpha)$.

Data, detrending, and parameter shifts

Postwar data are taken from standard US and OECD sources, and data prior to World War II are based on Balke and R. Gordon (1989) for the USA, Feinstein (1972) for the UK, Ohkawa and Shinohara (1979) for Japan, and national sources as summarized by Maddison (1982) for France and Germany. Data for Japan, the UK and the US measure nominal GNP, real GNP, and the GNP deflator. Data for Germany and France prior to World War II measure real GNP, the CPI, and a hybrid concept of nominal GNP equal to the CPI times real GNP. The nominal wage equations for the USA are based on Rees' data on average hourly earnings in manufacturing linked in 1960 to the BLS index of average hourly earnings in manufacturing. The real wage is this nominal wage series divided by the GNP deflator. Data sources are given in Appendix B.

The use of output data in estimating (9′) and (9″) requires a detrending procedure to define the $\hat{x}$, $\hat{q}$, and $\hat{Q}$ variables. Significant variations in population and productivity growth over the past century prevent the use of a single trend and require the choice of benchmark years to separate multiple piecewise log-linear output trends. The choice of the wrong benchmark years would introduce measurement error into all three of these variables. To avoid the possible criticism that benchmark years might have been selected to support or refute a particular hypothesis, all are copied from previous research directed at other issues.[56] The main control for supply shocks is a set of dummy variables to proxy the effects of government intervention both in the form of price controls (as during World War II) and intervention to raise prices and wages, as during the National Recovery Act period in the US Great Depression. Also for the USA we include a variable to measure the effect on aggregate inflation of changes in the relative prices of food and energy.[57] The specific values of the supply-shock dummy variables are given in Appendix B.

The key issue of changing cyclical responsiveness can be addressed by two alternative methods. One obvious way of providing information on parameter shifts would be to estimate separate versions of (9') and (9'') for each major subperiod within the available data set. An alternative method, carried out previously in R. Gordon (1983), involves estimating a single equation for the entire period for which data are available, and then searching for parameter shifts. If additional variables are defined as the product of the three economic variables of interest (p_{t-1}, $\hat{x}_t$ or $\hat{q}_t$, and $\hat{Q}_{t-1}$) and '0, 1' dummy variables for each subperiod, then the t ratios on the additional variables provide estimates of the statistical significance of parameter shifts. In developing the results displayed in Tables 21.5 and 21.6, a search procedure was followed in an attempt to locate parameter shifts during the following subperiods: first year through 1914, 1915–22, 1923–38 (1930–53 for the US), and 1960–86 (1954–87 for the US). All of the statistically significant parameter shifts are listed separately in Tables 21.5 and 21.6. Because of severe declines in output during wartime and postwar recovery periods, the following years are omitted from the regression equations: 1914–24 for France and Germany, and 1939–59 for the UK, France, Germany and Japan. No years were omitted for the USA.

Regression Results

Table 21.5 addresses the issue of changing cyclical responsiveness of prices, nominal wage rates, and real wage rates in the USA.[58] Six columns of results are shown for the entire 1873–1987 sample period, with equations for price, nominal wage, and real wage changes presented in pairs. The first member of each pair uses specification (9') in which nominal GNP change ($\hat{x}_t$) appears and the second member uses (9'') in which real GNP change ($\hat{q}_t$) appears as an alternative. The separate lines within each group of explanatory variables report several extra effects, that is, the coefficients on the product of the variable concerned and a 0,1 dummy variable for the period shown. A parallel presentation of results for price-change equations only is provided in Table 21.6 for the other four countries. The parameters are unscrambled in Tables 21.3 and 21.4 of the text, and the results are interpreted in Section 3.

Table 21.5 Equations explaining annual changes in the GNP deflator, the nominal wage rate, and the real wage rate in the USA, 1873–1987

Variable	Price		Nominal wage		Real wage	
	(1)	*(2)*	*(3)*	*(4)*	*(5)*	*(6)*
Lagged inflation (p_{t-1})						
Basic effect	0.23*	0.38*	0.32*	0.55*	0.09	0.18**
Extra effects:						
1915–22	—	0.38**	—	0.31	—	−0.07
1954–87	0.45*	0.66*	0.15	0.37**	−0.31*	−0.29**
Excess nominal GNP growth ($\hat{x}_t$)						
Basic effect	0.35*	—	0.44*	—	0.09**	—
Extra effects:						
1915–22	0.40*	—	0.37*	—	−0.04	—
Excess real GNP growth ($\hat{q}_t$)						
Basic effect	—	0.32*	—	0.51*	—	0.19*
Extra effects:						
1915–22	—	0.73*	—	0.89*	—	0.16
Detrended log output ($\hat{Q}_{t-1}$)						
Basic effect	0.22*	0.29*	0.30*	0.43*	0.08	0.14**
Extra effects:						
1930–53	−0.16*	−0.21**	−0.31*	−0.41*	−0.16**	−0.20*
Supply-shock variables (z_t)						
World War I controls	−4.97*	−6.98**	2.00	−1.85	6.99*	5.13**
NRA	7.21*	9.52**	13.12*	17.53*	5.91**	8.01*
World War II controls	−16.68*	−20.19*	−2.13	−8.87**	14.54*	11.32*
Nixon controls	−2.94	−3.60	−2.47	−3.81	0.46	−0.21
Food-energy effect	0.63	0.97	0.39	0.81	−0.24	−0.16
$\bar{R}^2$	0.85	0.52	0.83	0.58	0.36	0.43
SEE	2.02	3.59	2.45	3.80	2.53	2.38
Durbin-Watson	2.10	2.09	2.08	2.11	2.23	2.15

Notes: Supply-shock variables are defined in Appendix B
* indicates statistically significant at 1 percent level, ** at 5 percent level

Table 21.6 Equations explaining the annual inflation rate, five countries, 1873–1986

Country (years omitted)	UK 1939–59		France 1914–24, 1939–59		Germany 1914–24, 1939–59		Japan 1939–59	
Lagged inflation (p_{t-1})								
Basic effect	0.18*	0.22*	−0.15**	−0.42*	0.00	0.27**	0.11*	0.71*
Extra effects:								
1923–38	—	—	0.27*	0.69*	—	−0.27**	—	—
1960–86	0.24*	0.72*	0.59*	1.41*	0.60*	0.70*	—	—
Excess nominal GNP growth ($\hat{x}_t$)								
Basic effect	0.58*	—	0.61*	—	0.72*	—	0.74*	—
Extra effects:								
1915–22	0.12**	—	—	—	—	—	0.17*	—
1923–38	−0.26**	—	—	—	−0.28*	—	—	—
1960–86	—	—	—	—	−0.27**	—	—	—

Country (years omitted)	UK 1939–59		France 1914–24, 1939–59		Germany 1914–24, 1939–59		Japan 1939–59	
Excess real GNP growth ($\hat{q}_t$)								
Basic effect	—	0.30*	—	0.14	—	0.01	—	0.37
Extra effects:								
1915–22	—	1.33*	—	—	—	—	—	2.91
1923–38	—	—	—	1.23*	—	0.72*	—	—
1960–86	—	—	—	—	—	—	—	0.38
Detrended log output ($\hat{Q}_{t-1}$)								
Basic effect	0.26*	0.36*	0.36*	0.03	0.27*	0.11*	0.28*	0.34*
Extra effects:								
1915–22	—	0.83*	—	—	—	—	—	—
1923–38	−0.18*	−0.27*	—	0.88*	−0.21*	—	—	—
Supply-shock variables (z_t)								
UK World War I	−10.16*	−23.48*	—	—	—	—	—	—
UK 1972–3 controls	−6.37*	−10.24*	—	—	—	—	—	—
UK 1976–7 Social Contract	−4.38*	−7.55*	—	—	—	—	—	—
France Poincare	—	—	10.48*	26.69*	—	—	—	—
France Popular Front	—	—	16.76*	44.37*	—	—	—	—
Hitler controls	—	—	—	—	−3.82**	−5.97	—	—
Japan oil shock	—	—	—	—	—	—	6.63*	13.54**
$\bar{R}^2$	0.96	0.85	0.94	0.82	0.86	0.60	0.95	0.45
SEE	1.28	2.46	1.51	2.65	1.27	2.15	1.72	5.44
Durbin-Watson	1.99	2.03	1.88	2.35	1.73	1.88	1.55	1.62

Notes: Sample period for UK begins in 1958, and for Japan begins in 1888
Supply-shock variables are defined in Appendix B
* Indicates statistically significant at 1 percent level, ** at 5 percent level

APPENDIX B: DATA APPENDIX

United States

GNP, deflator, and food-energy effect

1929–87

Output and prices from *National Income and Product Accounts*, Tables 1.1 and 7.4., US Department of Commerce. Food-energy effect (1959–87 only) is the difference between the growth rates of the fixed-weight consumption deflator and the fixed-weight deflator for consumption expenditures net of food and energy, from National Income and Product Accounts, Table 7.1.

1869–1928

Balke and Gordon (1989: Table 10).

Nominal wage rate

1960–87

BLS average hourly earnings in manufacturing, *Economic Report of the President* (1989: Table B-44).

1888–1959

Rees' series on real CPI-deflated average hourly earnings in manufacturing, series B-70 in *Long-term Economic Growth, 1860–1970*, US Department of Commerce, 1973, divided by CPI, series B-69.

Output trend

The output trend is calculated as a log-linear trend between the benchmark years 1869, 1873, 1884, 1891, 1900, 1910, 1924, and the quarterly data for the quarters 1949:Q1, 1954:Q1, 1957:Q3, 1963:Q3, 1970.Q2, 1974:Q2, 1979:Q3, and 1987:Q3. For further details, see R. Gordon (1990: Appendix C).

Dummy variables

World War I: 1918 = 1.0, 1919–20 = 0.5. NRA: 1933–34 = 0.5, 1935–36 = –0.5. World War II: 1943–44 = 0.5, 1946–47 = –0.5. Nixon: 1972–73 = 0.5, 1974 = –0.3, 1975 = –0.7.

France and Germany

GNP and prices

1960–86

Real GNP and deflator from OECD Statistics Paris (1988).

1870–1959

Real GNP and CPI from Maddison (1982: Appendices A and E).

Output trend

The output trend is calculated as a log-linear trend between the following benchmark years. For France: 1870, 1875, 1882, 1892, 1899, 1904, 1912, 1924, 1939, 1951, 1964, 1972, and 1979. For Germany: 1870, 1874, 1884, 1890, 1900, 1907, 1913, 1925, 1928, 1938, 1952, 1961, 1972, and 1979. For both countries, growth in 1979–86 is calculated by applying the 1972–79 growth in the capital-output ratio to the observed growth of the capital stock, as in Schultze (1987).

Dummy variables

France Poincare: 1926 = 1.0.
France Popular Front: 1936–38 = 0.33.
Hitler controls: 1937–38 = 0.5.

United Kingdom

GNP and deflator

1960–86 OECD Statistics Paris (1988).

1870–1959 Feinstein (1972).

Output trend

The output trend is calculated as a log-linear trend between the following benchmark years: 1856, 1865, 1873, 1882, 1889, 1907, 1913, 1920, 1940, 1951, 1961, 1972, 1979, and 1987.

Dummy variables

UK World War I: 1915–18 = 0.25, 1919–20 = −0.5. UK 1972–3 Controls: 1972–3 = 0.5, 1974–75 = −0.5. UK 1976–7 Social Contract: 1976 = 1.0, 1980 = −1.0.

Japan

GNP and deflator

1960–86 OECD Statistics Paris (1988).

1870–1940 Ohkawa and Shinohara (1979: Tables A9 and A50).

Output trend

The output trend is calculated as a log-linear trend between the following benchmark years: 1885, 1890, 1903, 1914, 1919, 1929, 1938, 1953, 1961, 1972, 1979, and 1987.

Dummy variable

Japan Oil Shock: 1974 = 1.0.

ACKNOWLEDGEMENTS

This research was supported by the National Science Foundation. I am grateful to George Williams for help with the data and to Steven Allen, Laurence Ball, Olivier J. Blanchard, Timothy Bresnahan, Charles Calomiris, Dennis Carlton, Robert Chirinko, Russell Cooper, Stanley Fischer, Herschel Grossman, R. Glenn Hubbard, David Laidler, John Leahy, Assar Lindbeck, N. Gregory Mankiw, David Romer, Julio Rotemberg, Dennis Snower, John Taylor, Andrew Weiss, and two anonymous referees for comments on one or more earlier drafts. I am also indebted to Michael Parkin and Edmund S. Phelps for helping to establish the etymology of the phrase 'new-Keynesian'.

NOTES

1 The strongest written statement of the dominance of new-classical macroeconomics among the younger generation is by Alan Blinder: 'By about 1980, it was hard to find an American academic macroeconomist under the age of 40 who professed to be a Keynesian. That was an astonishing intellectual turnabout in less than a decade – an intellectual revolution for sure ... the young were recruited disproportionately into the new classical ranks ... By 1980 or so, the adage "there are no Keynesians under the age of 40" was part of the folklore of the (American) economics profession' (1988: 278).
2 The label *new-Keynesian* should be attributed to Michael Parkin (1982), who has offered me the opinion that he originated the term *new-Keynesian theory*, not *new-Keynesian macroeconomics*. The term *new-Keynesian theory* was incorporated into a chapter subsection in Phelps (1985: 562) and 'new-Keynesian model' in a chapter title in the fourth edition of my textbook (Gordon 1990), written in 1986. One of the first uses of the label *new-Keynesian economics* in a scholarly article is by Laurence Ball, N. Gregory Mankiw, and David Romer (1988). The word *new* rather than *neo* to describe the recent work in the classical tradition distinguishes it from what Paul Samuelson in the early postwar period called the *neoclassical synthesis* of old-Keynesian macroeconomics and classical microeconomics. In turn, the word *new* rather than *neo* is used for the recent work in the Keynesian tradition, so that it can be properly juxtaposed to the new-classical approach.
3 I accept David Laidler's objection in correspondence that Keynesian economics is about more than wage and price stickiness and includes a treatment of 'how the monetary system interferes with the coordination of inter-temporal choices'. The new-Keynesian analysis of credit rationing and other failings of the monetary system is recognized as a legitimate research activity but falls outside the scope of this chapter, which is delimited by the supply–demand dichotomy.
4 Nevertheless, we recognize the importance of feedback from price behavior to nominal GNP for the econometric estimation of price adjustment coefficients and devote considerable emphasis in Section 2 to the treatment of econometric bias that results from such feedback.
5 This is the title of the survey by Blanchard (1987a).
6 For convenience, this introduction concludes with some references to the many available surveys that overlap with this chapter, or that treat particular issues in more detail. Fischer (1988) provides a broadbrush survey of macroeconomics, including demand, supply, and policy; while Michael Bruno (1988) assesses the

classical Keynesian debate from the perspective of high-inflation countries designing stabilization policies. Olivier Blanchard (1987a) provides an extended treatment of some of the supply-side issues that concern us here, whereas Assar Lindbeck (1988) provides a briefer treatment from a European perspective. Blanchard and Fischer (1989: chs 8–9) provide a relatively technical exposition of several new-Keynesian models. At the level of specific topics within the general new-Keynesian rubric, surveys are available on labor market developments in general (Stiglitz 1986; Katz 1988), implicit contract theory (Rosen 1985), efficiency wage theory (Katz 1986; Weiss 1990), new-Keynesian product-market theory (Rotemberg 1987), and the interrelations between industrial organization theory and macroeconomic price stickiness (Carlton 1989a).

7 The Okun's law relation between detrended output and the unemployment rate holds very closely in the postwar USA, ensuring that any conclusions developed here for the relationship between inflation and detrended output carry over to the relation between inflation and the unemployment rate. For plots of output, trend output, and the unemployment rate, see R. Gordon (1990: 14) for the twentieth century and p. 324 for 1964–88.

8 In practice, the first-order autoregression on p_{t-1} in (7) is too simple to capture the dynamics in quarterly data, and higher-order autoregressive terms must be included in regression estimation. In annual data one or two lagged inflation terms are sufficient.

9 Blanchard (1987b) presents an equation like (7) in which the rate of wage change also appears, because he is interested in the speed of transmission of cost changes into price changes. But the same point applies to (7), where we are interested in the division of nominal demand changes between price changes and output changes.

10 The identity in the text, $\hat{Q}_t \equiv \hat{Q}_{t-1} + \hat{x}_t - p_t$, is identical to the identity written as equation (3) above, in view of the fact that $\hat{q}_t$ (the rate of change of detrended output) is the same as $\hat{Q}_t - \hat{Q}_{t-1}$ (the change in the log ratio of actual to trend output).

11 Early precursors of (10a) and (10b), developed and originally published in 1972–3, are reprinted in David Laidler (1975: 127, 140) and differ only in assuming that $\theta = 1$ and that $z_t = 0$.

12 The inclusion of both level and rate-of-change effects dates back to Richard Lipsey (1960), who aggregated a model with heterogeneous micro labor markets characterized by limited labor mobility between markets and showed that the rate of change of wages would depend on both the level and rate of change of the aggregate unemployment rate. In Lipsey's model the economy exhibits counter-clockwise loops in a diagram plotting wage change against the level of unemployment, while an alternative model emphasizing the inertia ($\lambda = 1$) effect generates clockwise loops. Barro and Grossman (1976: ch. 5) derive both types of loops as special cases, as well as the condition for one or the other type of loop to dominate.

13 I am grateful to Robert Chirinko for providing me with a copy of the Tarshis (1939) note.

14 A valuable compendium of papers on hysteresis, including a fascinating introduction that traces the history of the term *hysteresis* in both economics and science, is Cross (1988). The first use of hysteresis-based models of inflation was by Phelps (1972).

15 I have emphasized the disappearance of the level effect in the US Great Depression in several of my papers, especially R. Gordon and Wilcox (1981: 86–92) and R. Gordon (1983: 93–6).

16 R. Gordon (1982b) shows that the Lucas (1973) model can be nested in a general model of price adjustment like (9) and can be rejected in the presence of price inertia.

17 I am grateful to Dennis Carlton for suggesting the wording of the last two sentences.

18 Further evidence on the extent of product differentiation comes in detailed studies of international trade, showing the countries at the same stage of development both import and export goods within the same industrial categories. See Blomstrom *et al.* (1989).

19 This point was suggested in a letter from Bresnahan, who describes these common features of cyclically sensitive industries as 'some famous coincidences about industry structure.'

20 Particularly striking is Carlton's example of the costs of running the futures markets in Chicago, consisting of large office buildings, expensive real estate, elaborate record keeping, and the large time cost of the many people involved. 'A significant fraction of the economy of the city of Chicago is devoted to the making of markets. If a magic spell could be cast to make transactions costless, the Chicago economy would be devastated, at least in the short run. This emphasizes how far from costless the making of markets really is' (1989b: 6).

21 As we have been reminded by Allen (1989), the standard prewar series on US wages are for production workers in manufacturing and must be linked with a postwar series on manufacturing wages, not the wage index for the nonfarm private economy that is most often used in studies limited to the postwar period. Allen concludes after an exhaustive study that differences in measurement methods in either wage or output series do not change his conclusion that the cyclical sensitivity of wages was the same in the prewar and postwar periods.

22 This finding is consistent with that of Allen's careful (1989) study, which examines only wage behavior, not price behavior. Allen's specification is similar to mine and uses both unemployment and output gap data, but no nominal GNP data or supply shock proxies, and is thus subject to a bias in the unemployment or output coefficients toward zero. Allen's conclusion claims that his study finds similar behavior prewar and postwar, but his text reveals that he finds the same increase in the inertia effect (coefficients on lagged inflation) as is shown in Table 21.3.

23 The respective parameter estimates for 1954–87 in an equation for the change in the real wage are, with manufacturing wage data, $\lambda = -0.33$, $\alpha = 0.12$, $\gamma = -0.12$. With the fixed-weight nonfarm wage index (spliced to the employment cost index in 1975), the parameters are $\lambda = 0.01$, $\alpha = -0.07$, $\gamma = -0.02$.

24 See the numerous criticisms of the paper by Ball *et al.* (1988) contained in the discussant comments by George Akerlof, Andrew Rose, and Janet Yellen, as well as by Christopher Sims.

25 The Lucas (1972, 1973) imperfect information approach (Mark I) is now widely viewed as unconvincing, because it is undermined by the availability of information on the aggregate price level and money supply over a much shorter time period than the duration of the average business cycle. Major contributions to real-business-cycle theory (Mark II) include Kydland and Prescott (1982) and Prescott (1986). A generally supportive survey is provided by Plosser (1989), and critical surveys include Mankiw (1989) and McCallum (1989).

26 Simultaneous work by me (R. Gordon 1972) and by Eckstein and Brinner (1972) showed how postwar wage and price data could be made consistent with long-run neutrality.

27 My two papers were R. Gordon (1975, 1977). See Laidler and Parkin (1975: esp. pp. 759–74) for a comprehensive survey of research on wage and price equations in the late 1960s and early 1970s. Nordhaus (1972) presents a survey of US work on econometric price markup equations.

28 As author Alan Blinder described the aggregate demand and supply model as developed in his own textbook, 'now the Marshallian scissors come in a giant economy size.'

29 These additional supply-shock factors are omitted in Tables 21.3 and 21.4, as their effects are hard to discern in century-long annual data samples and instead require the finer discrimination possible with postwar quarterly data and with the improved fixed-weight price and wage indexes available only in the postwar period.

30 Depending on the exact price index used and the criterion of what constitutes a permanent slowdown in the inflation rate, the US sacrifice ratio observed during the disinflation of the 1980s was between 5 and 7. An estimate of 6.2 was calculated on the basis of data through 1980 in R. Gordon and King (1982: Table 5, line 3); reasons for preferring this version were given in that paper (pp. 236–7). Blanchard (1984) also provides evidence from a quite different specification that the Phillips curve remained relatively stable during the Volcker disinflation.

31 John Pencavel suggests to me that this critical view by microeconomists is wide-spread.

32 I am grateful to David Laidler for suggesting this distinction.

33 In defense of the new-Keynesian approach, Andrew Weiss has suggested to me that 'we have to solve the partial equilibrium problems first; these also are the most interesting.'

34 Research on general disequilibrium or fixed-price models appears to have become a specialized European activity in macroeconomics, with near-total invisibility in a recent survey I conducted of first-year graduate macro reading lists at the top ten American economics departments.

35 In related work Howitt (1986) calls this effect a 'thin market externality.'

36 McCallum (1986: 409) argues that linking to a constant price index instead of to the CPI would be chosen only by those agents whose most preferred index is negatively correlated to the CPI.

37 The model is presented in slightly simplified form in Blanchard and Fischer (1989: 376–81) and Fischer (1988: 321–3). An even simpler version with constant marginal cost is presented by Rotemberg (1987: 78–80).

38 The original result was derived by Barro (1972) and is restated by Blanchard and Fischer (1989: 402–5).

39 Laurence Ball disputes this interpretation and claims that 'the central point [of recent work] is that nominal rigidity has negative externalities because it exacerbates fluctuations in real aggregate demand.' But this is clear as a matter of definition (see equation (4) on p. 482), is common to any theory of price stickiness, and has nothing to do with the particular contributions of recent work.

40 This important point credited to Ball and Romer, whose paper was written in 1986, is summarized and endorsed by Rotemberg (1987: 83–5).

41 For this reason I find unconvincing the skepticism of Blanchard and Fischer (1989: 401) that it is possible to derive stable staggered contracting, as when they write 'the introduction of stochastic idiosyncratic shocks does not make staggering more likely.' Their argument is carried out entirely within an either-or choice between even and odd dates of price changing, and they show that a 50–50 equilibrium with the same number of firms choosing each date is unstable, because the slightest tilt in either direction gives all the other firms an incentive to shift. But with uneven frequency of shocks and a large number of possible dates of changing, the incentive to shift disappears. If my optimal frequency of price change is weekly, the fact that there is bunching with more price changes on 1 January than any of the other 364 days of the year does not lead me to limit my price changes to once a year on 1 January.

42 I have previously (1981: 520ff.) suggested a distinction between aggregate and local components of both cost and demand with explicit reference to Lucas' original two-way classification.

43 Cooper (1989) provides an analysis of the interdependence between wage and price indexation; the likelihood of wage indexation depends on whether prices are indexed, and vice versa.

44 Blanchard has written to me that what he means by flat labor supply is 'the set of real wages and employment traced out as the marginal product of labor shifts' and not 'the competitive labor supply curve.' The issue here is the possibly misleading choice of words, not any substantive difference between my interpretation and that of Blanchard and Fischer.

45 Thus I concur with Barsky and Solon (1989: 29–30), who find that procyclical real wage behavior at the individual level in micro data is consistent with noncyclical behavior in aggregate data. This pattern reflects a cyclical variation in the 'employment opportunities' (read 'constraints') that face both 'stayers' at firms who face changing opportunities to work overtime, and 'switchers' who face cyclicality in opportunities for across-firm career advancement.

46 More technically, as pointed out to me by Blanchard, it is the marginal utility of consumption that is equalized between the employed and unemployed. The ranking of utility depends on the form of the utility function.

47 This point is made by Blanchard and Fischer (1989: 453).

48 To this point the discussion of the insider-outsider model is largely based on several paragraphs of text kindly contributed by Assar Lindbeck and Dennis Snower.

49 An excellent comparison of the two approaches is provided by Lindbeck and Snower (1988: ch. 3).

50 Two surveys of the literature that identify those authors and papers who have studied particular channels of efficiency wage effects are Katz (1986) and Weiss (1990).

51 On dual labor markets, see especially Doeringer and Piore (1971) and David Gordon et al. (1982). More evidence by mainstream economists is provided by Dickens and Lang (1985). For policy proposals based on efficiency wage assumptions, see Bowles et al. (1983). Their policy proposal to raise the minimum wage assumes implicitly that the current wage is below the optimum efficiency wage, whereas all the work in the new-Keynesian tradition examines the implications of assuming that the actual wage is already at the optimum efficiency wage level.

52 This paragraph summarizes Weiss (1990: 6–10).

53 The most controversial item on this list is persistent wage differentials, as argued by Katz and Summers in a series of papers, including Katz (1986) and Katz and Summers (1989). For a sample of a dissenting view, see Robert Topel's comment which appears after the latter paper.

54 In this important conclusion we fully endorse the basic message of Akerlof and Yellen (1985) and Ball and Romer (1987).

55 Advantages, problems, and techniques relevant to the targeting of nominal GNP growth are discussed in Tobin (1983), Hall (1984), McCallum (1988) and R. Gordon (1985).

56 For the postwar USA, benchmark years are taken from my macroeconomics textbook (1990) and for the other four countries from R. Gordon (1988); for the pre-World War II period, US benchmarks are taken from Romer (1989), for France, Germany, and the UK from Solomou (1987), and for Japan from R. Gordon (1983). Inconsistency may result from the use of benchmark years originally selected by varying criteria – peak output in some cases, average output in others, and the level of output consistent with a particular unemployment rate in still others. For the European countries, where the benchmark years before World War I are all peaks (thus eliminating any positive values of $\hat{Q}_t$), the resulting $\hat{Q}_t$ series is adjusted by subtracting its (negative) mean and converting the mean to zero. This results in a mix of positive and negative values. No such adjustments are carried out in the interwar or postwar periods.

57 The larger number of such supply-shock variables for the USA than for other countries may indicate that supply shocks have been more important in the USA, or they may simply indicate that I am more familiar with the history of the USA than of the other countries. However, the extra attention given to the USA is largely due to the inclusion of wartime data for the USA but not for the other countries, where the years of World War II and its aftermath are excluded for all four of the other countries, while World War I and its aftermath are excluded for France and Germany.

58 Here the wage data are adjusted for the trend in productivity growth (using piecewise linear trends between benchmarks), so that the dependent variable in the columns labeled *Nominal Wage* is actually the change in trend unit labor cost, and in the columns labeled *Real Wage* is actually the change in labor's income share adjusted for cyclical fluctuations in productivity.

REFERENCES

Akerlof, George and Yellen, Janet, 'A Near-rational Model of the Business Cycle with Wage and Price Inertia', *Quarterly Journal of Economics* 1985 suppl., *100*(5), pp. 823–38.

Alchian, Armen, 'Information Costs, Pricing, and Resource Unemployment', *Western Economic Journal* June 1969, *7*(2), pp. 109–28.

Allen, Steven G., 'Changes in the Cyclical Sensitivity of Wages in the United States, 1891–1987', working paper without number, North Carolina State University, Aug. 1989.

Alogoskoufis, George and Smith, Ron, 'The Phillips Curve and the Lucas Critique: Some Historical Evidence', working paper without number, Birkbeck College, London, Mar. 1989.

Azariadis, Costas, 'Implicit Contracts and Underemployment Equilibria', *Journal of Political Economy* Dec. 1975, *83*(6), pp. 1183–1202.

Backus, David K. and Kehoe, Patrick J., 'International Evidence on the Historical Properties of Business Cycles', working paper without number or place, May 1988.

Baily, Martin Neil, 'Wages and Unemployment under Uncertain Demand', *Review of Economic Studies*. Jan. 1974, *41*(1), pp. 37–50.

Balke, Nathan and Gordon, Robert J., 'The Estimation of Prewar Gross National Product: Methodology and New Evidence', *Journal of Political Economy* Feb. 1989, *97*(1), pp. 38–92.

Ball, Laurence, Mankiw, N. Gregory and Romer, David, 'The New Keynesian Economics and the Output-Inflation Trade-off', *Brookings Papers on Economic Activity* 1988 (1), pp. 1–65.

Ball, Laurence and Romer, David, 'Real Rigidities and the Non-Neutrality of Money', NBER Working Paper no. 2476, Oct. 1987.

—— 'Are Prices Too Sticky?', *Quarterly Journal of Economics* Aug. 1989a, *104*(3), pp. 507–24.

—— 'The Equilibrium and Optimal Timing of Price Changes', *Review of Economic Studies* 1989b, *56*(2), pp. 179–98.

Barro, Robert J. 'A Theory of Monopolistic Price Adjustment', *Review of Economic Studies* Jan. 1972, *39*(1), pp. 17–26.

—— 'Unanticipated Money Growth and Unemployment in the United States', *American Economic Review* Mar. 1977a, *67*(2), pp. 101–15.

—— 'Long-term Contracting, Sticky Prices, and Monetary Policy', *Journal of Monetary Economics* July 1977b, *3*(3), pp. 305–16.

—— 'Unanticipated Money, Output, and the Price Level in the United States', *Journal of Political Economy* Aug. 1978, *86*(4), pp. 549–80.

—— 'Second Thoughts on Keynesian Economics', *American Economic Review* May 1979, *69*(2), pp. 54–9.

Barro, Robert J. and Grossman, Herschel, 'A General Disequilibrium Model of Income and Employment', *American Economic Review* Mar. 1971, *61*(1), pp. 82–93.

—— *Money, Employment, and Inflation*, Cambridge: Cambridge University Press, 1976.

Barro, Robert J. and Rush, Mark, 'Unanticipated Money and Economic Activity', in *Rational Expectations and Economic Policy*, Stanley Fischer (ed.), Chicago: University of Chicago Press for NBER, 1980, pp. 23–48, 72–3.

Barsky, Robert and Solon, Gary, 'Real Wages over the Business Cycle', NBER Working Paper no. 2888, Mar. 1989.

Benassy, Jean-Pascal, 'Neo-Keynesian Disequilibrium Theory in a Monetary Economy', *Review of Economic Studies* Oct. 1975, *42*(4), pp. 503–23.

—— *The Economics of Market Disequilibrium* New York: Academic Press, 1982.

Berndt, Ernst R. and Wood, David O., 'Engineering and Econometric Interpretations of Energy-Capital Complementarity', *American Economic Review* June 1979, *69*(3), pp. 342–54.

Bertola, Giuseppe and Caballero, Ricardo J., 'Kinked Adjustment Costs and Aggregate Dynamics', paper presented at Fifth Annual NBER Conference on Macroeconomics, 9–10, Mar. 1990.

Blanchard, Olivier J., 'Price Asynchronization and Price Level Inertia', in *Inflation, Debt, and Indexation*, Rudiger Dornbusch and Mario Henrique Simonsen (eds), Cambridge: MIT Press, 1983, pp. 3–24.

—— 'The Lucas Critique and the Volcker Deflation', *American Economic Review* May 1984, *74*(2), pp. 211–15.

—— 'The Wage-Price Spiral', *Quarterly Journal of Economics* Aug. 1986, *101*(3), pp. 543–65.

—— 'Why Does Money Affect Output? A Survey', NBER Working Paper no. 2285, June 1987a, in *Handbook of Monetary Economics*, B. Friedman and F. Hahn (eds), Amsterdam: North-Holland, June 1990.)

—— 'Aggregate and Individual Price Adjustment', *Brookings Papers on Economic Activity* 1987b, (1), pp. 57–122.

Blanchard, Olivier J. and Fischer, Stanley, *Lectures on Macroeconomics*, Cambridge: MIT Press, 1989.

Blanchard, Olivier J. and Kiyotaki, Nobuhiro, 'Monopolistic Competition and the Effects of Aggregate Demand', *American Economic Review* Sept. 1987, 77(4), pp. 647–66.

Blanchard, Olivier J. and Summers, Lawrence H., 'Hysteresis and the European Unemployment Problem', *NBER Macroeconomics Annual*, 1986, Cambridge: MIT Press, pp. 15–78.

Blinder, Alan S., 'The Fall and Rise of Keynesian Economics', *Economic Record*. Dec. 1988, *64*, pp. 278–94.

Blomstrom, Magnus, Lipsey, Robert E. and Ohlson, Lennart, 'What Do Rich Countries Trade with Each Other? R & D and the Composition of U.S. and Swedish Trade', NBER Working Paper no. 3140, Oct. 1989.

Bowles, Samuel, Gordon, David M. and Weisskopf, Thomas, *Beyond the Waste Land*, New York: Doubleday, 1983.

Bresnahan, Timothy F., 'Industries with Market Power', in *Handbook of Industrial Organization*, Richard Schmalensee and Robert Willig (eds), Amsterdam: North-Holland, 1989, ch. 17, pp. 1011–57.

Bruno, Michael, 'Theoretical Developments in the Light of Macroeconomic Policy and Empirical Research', NBER Working Paper no. 2757, Nov. 1988.

Caplin, Andrew S. and Leahy, John, 'State-dependent Pricing and the Dynamics of Money and Output', working paper without number or place, Oct. 1989.

Caplin, Andrew S. and Spulber, Daniel F., 'Menu Costs and the Neutrality of Money', *Quarterly Journal of Economics* Nov. 1987, *102*(4), pp. 703–25.

Carlton, Dennis W. 'The Rigidity of Prices', *American Economic Review* Sept. 1986, *76*(4), pp. 637–58.

——'The Theory and the Facts of How Markets Clear: Is Industrial Organization Valuable for Understanding Macroeconomics?' in *Handbook of Industrial Organization*, vol. I, R. Schmalensee and R. D. Willig (eds), Amsterdam: North-Holland 1989a, pp. 909–46.

——'The Theory of Allocation and Its Implications for Marketing and Industrial Structure', unnumbered working paper, University of Chicago Graduate School of Business, May 1989b.

Cecchetti, Stephen, 'The Frequency of Price Adjustment: A Study of the Newsstand Prices of Magazines, 1953 to 1979', *Journal of Econometrics* 1986, *31*(3), pp. 255–74.

Clower, Robert W. 'The Keynesian Counterrevolution: A Theoretical Appraisal', in *The Theory of Interest Rates*, F. H. Hahn and F. Brechling (eds), London: Macmillan, 1965, pp. 103–25.

Coe, David T., 'Hysteresis and Insider–Outsider Influences on Industry Wages', working paper without number or place, Mar. 1989.

Cooper, Russell, 'Predetermined Wages and Prices and the Impact of Expansionary Government Policy', working paper without number or place, Sept. 1989.

Cooper, Russell and John, Andrew, 'Coordinating Coordination Failures in Keynesian Models', *Quarterly Journal of Economics* Aug. 1988, *100*(3), pp. 441–63.

Cross, Rod (ed.) *Unemployment, Hysteresis, and the Natural Rate Hypothesis*, Oxford and New York: Basil Blackwell, 1988.

DeLong, J. Bradford and Summers, Lawrence H., 'The Changing Cyclical Variability of Economic Activity in the United States', in *The American Business Cycle: Continuity and Change*, Robert J. Gordon, (ed.) Chicago: University of Chicago Press for NBER, 1986, pp. 679–734.

Diamond, Peter A., 'Aggregate Demand Management in Search Equilibrium', *Journal of Political Economy* Oct. 1982, *90*(5), pp. 881–94.

——*A Search Equilibrium Approach to the Micro Foundations of Macroeconomics*, Cambridge: MIT Press, 1984.

Dickens, William T. and Lang, Kevin, 'A Test of Dual Labor Market Theory', *American Economic Review* Sept. 1985, *75*(4), pp. 792–805.

Doeringer, Peter B. and Piore, Michael J., *Internal Labor Markets and Manpower Analysis*, Lexington, MA: D.C. Heath, 1971.

Dunlop, John T., 'The Movements of Real and Money Wage Rates', *Economic Journal* Sept. 1938, *48*(191), pp. 413–34.

——*Wage Determination under Trade Unions*, New York: Macmillan, 1944.

Durlauf, Steven N., 'Output Persistence, Economic Structure, and the Choice of Stabilization Policy', *Brookings Papers on Economic Activity* 1989, *20*(2), pp. 69–116.

Eckstein, Otto and Brinner, Roger, *The Inflation Process in the United States*, A Study Prepared for the use of the Joint Economic Committee, 92 Cong. 2 session, 1972.

——*Economic Report of the President 1989*, Washington, DC: US GPO, 1989.

Feinstein, C. H. *National Income Expenditure and Output of the United Kingdom, 1855–1965*, Cambridge: Cambridge University Press, 1972.

Fischer, Stanley. 'Long-term Contracts, Rational Expectations, and the Optimal Money Supply Rule', *Journal of Political Economy*. Feb. 1977a, *85*(1), pp. 191–205.

——'Wage Indexation and Macroeconomic Stability', in *Stabilization of the Domestic and International Economy*, Karl Brunner and Allan Meltzer (eds), *Carnegie-Rochester Conference Series on Public Policy*, vol. 5. Amsterdam: North-Holland 1977b, pp. 107–47.

——*Indexing, Inflation, and Economic Policy*, Cambridge: MIT Press, 1986.

548   *Robert J. Gordon*

—— 'Recent Developments in Macroeconomics', *Economic Journal.* June 1988, *98*(391), pp. 294–339.

Friedman, Milton, 'The Role of Monetary Policy', *American Economic Review* Mar. 1968, *58*(1), pp. 1–17.

Friedman, Milton and Schwartz, Anna, *A Monetary History of the United States, 1867–1960*, Princeton, NJ: Princeton University Press for NBER, 1963.

Gordon, David M., Edwards, Richard and Reich, Michael, *Segmented Work, Divided Workers: The Historical Transformation of Labor in the United States*, New York: Cambridge University Press, 1982.

Gordon, Donald F., 'A Neo-Classical Theory of Keynesian Unemployment,' *Economic Inquiry* Dec. 1974, *12*(4), pp. 431–59.

Gordon, Robert J., 'Wage-Price Controls and the Shifting Phillips Curve', *Brookings Papers on Economic Activity* 1972 (2), pp. 385–421.

—— 'The Impact of Aggregate Demand on Prices', *Brookings Papers on Economic Activity* 1975 (3), pp. 613–62.

—— 'Can the Inflation of the 1970s Be Explained?', *Brookings Papers on Economic Activity* 1977 *8*(1), pp. 253–77.

—— 'A Consistent Characterization of a Near-Century of Price Behavior', *American Economic Review* May 1980, *70*(2), pp. 243–49.

—— 'Output Fluctuations and Gradual Price Adjustment', *Journal of Economic Literature* June 1981, *19*(2), pp. 493–530.

—— 'Why U.S. Wage and Employment Behavior Differs from that in Britain and Japan', *Economic Journal* Mar. 1982a, *92*(365), pp. 13–44.

—— 'Price Inertia and Policy Ineffectiveness in the United States, 1890–1980', *Journal of Political Economy* Dec. 1982b, *90*(6), pp. 1087–1117.

—— 'A Century of Evidence on Wage and Price Stickiness in the United States, the United Kingdom, and Japan', in *Macroeconomics, Prices, and Quantities*, James Tobin (ed.), Washington, DC: Brookings Institution, 1983, pp. 85–121.

—— 'The Conduct of Domestic Monetary Policy', in *Monetary Policy in Our Times*, Albert Ando *et al.* (eds), Cambridge: MIT Press, 1985, pp. 45–81.

—— 'Wage Gaps vs. Output Gaps: Is There a Common Story for All of Europe?', in *Macro and Micro Policies for More Growth and Employment: Keil Symposium*, Herbert Giersch (ed.), Tubingen: J. C. B. Mohr [Paul Siebeck] 1988, pp. 97–151.

—— *Macroeconomics*, 5th edn Glenview, IL: Scott, Foresman, 1990.

Gordon, Robert J. and King, Stephen R., 'The Output Cost of Disinflation in Traditional and Vector Autoregressive Models', *Brookings Papers on Economic Activity* 1982 *13*(1), pp. 205–42.

Gordon, Robert J. and Wilcox, James, 'Monetarist Interpretations of the Great Depression: An Evaluation and Critique', in *The Great Depression Revisited*, Karl Brunner, (ed.) Boston, MA: Martinus Nijhoff, 1981, pp. 49–107.

Gray, Jo Anna, 'Wage Indexation: A Macroeconomic Approach', *Journal of Monetary Economics* Apr. 1976, *2*(2), pp. 221–35.

Hall, Robert E., 'Employment Fluctuations and Wage Rigidity', *Brookings Papers on Economic Activity* 1980 (1), pp. 91–123.

—— 'Monetary Policy with an Elastic Price Standard', in *Price Stability and Public Policy*, Federal Reserve Bank of Kansas City, 1984, pp. 137–59.

Howitt, Peter, 'The Keynesian Recovery', *Canadian Journal of Economics* Nov. 1986, *19*(4), pp. 626–41.

Kashyap, Anil. 'Sticky Prices: New Evidence from Retail Catalogs', Finance and Economics Discussion Series Working Paper no. 112, Federal Reserve Board, Washington, DC, Mar. 1990.

Katz, Lawrence F., 'Efficiency Wage Theories: A Partial Evaluation', *NBER Macroeconomics Annual*, 1986, *1*, Cambridge: MIT Press, pp. 235–75.

—— 'Some Recent Developments in Labor Economics and Their Implications for Macroeconomics', *Journal of Money, Credit, Banking* Aug. 1988, *20*(3), pp. 507–22.

Katz, Lawrence F. and Summers, Lawrence H., 'Industry Rents: Evidence and Implications', *Brookings Papers on Economic Activity.: Microeconomics 1989*, 1989, 51, pp. 209–90.

Keynes, John M., 'Relative Movements of Real Wages and Output', *Economic Journal.* Mar. 1939, *49*(193), pp. 34–51.

Kydland, Finn E. and Prescott, Edward C. 'Time to Build and Aggregate Fluctuations', *Econometrica* Nov. 1982, *50*(6), pp. 1345–70.

Laidler, D. E. W. *Essays on Money and Inflation*, Manchester: Manchester University Press, 1975.

Laidler, D. E. W. and Parkin, J. Michael, 'Inflation – A Survey', *Economic Journal* Dec. 1975, *85*(340), pp. 741–809.

Layard, Richard and Nickell, Stephen, 'The Labour Market', in *The Performance of the British Economy*, Rudiger Dornbusch and Richard Layard (eds), Oxford: Clarendon Press, 1987, pp. 131–79.

Leibenstein, Harvey, 'The Theory of Underemployment in Backward Economies', *Journal of Political Economy.* Apr. 1957, *65*(2), pp. 91–103.

Leijonhufvud, Axel, *On Keynesian Economics and the Economics of Keynes*, New York: Oxford University Press, 1968.

—— *Information and Coordination: Essays in Macroeconomic Theory*, New York: Oxford University Press, 1981.

Lindbeck, Assar, 'Remaining Puzzles and Neglected Issues in Macroeconomics', Institute for International Economic Studies (University of Stockholm), Seminar Paper no. 424, Dec. 1988.

Lindbeck, Assar and Snower, Dennis, 'Wage Setting, Unemployment, and Insider-Outsider Relations', *American Economic Review.*, May 1986, *76*(2), pp. 235–39.

—— *The Insider–Outsider Theory of Employment and Unemployment*, Cambridge: MIT Press, 1988.

—— 'Remaining Puzzles and Neglected Issues in Macroeconomics', *Scandinavian Journal of Economics* 1989, *91*(2), pp. 495–516.

Lipsey, Richard G., 'The Relation between Unemployment and the Rate of Change of Money Wage Rates in the United Kingdom, 1862–1957: A Further Analysis', *Economica* n.s., Feb. 1960, *27*, pp. 1–31.

Long-term Economic Growth, 1860–1970, Washington, DC: US Dept. of Commerce, 1973.

Lucas, Robert E. Jr. 'Expectations and the Neutrality of Money', *Journal of Economic Theory* Apr. 1972, *4*(2), pp. 103–24.

—— 'Some International Evidence on Output–Inflation Tradeoffs', *American Economic Review* June 1973, *63*(3), pp. 326–34.

—— 'Econometric Policy Evaluation: A Critique', in *The Phillips Curve and Labor Markets*, Karl Brunner and Allan Meltzer (eds), Amsterdam: North-Holland, *Carnegie-Rochester Series on Public Policy*, a supplementary series to *Journal of Monetary Economics* Jan. 1976, *1*, pp. 19–46.

Lucas, Robert E. Jr and Sargent, Thomas J. 'After Keynesian Macroeconomics', in *After the Phillips Curve: Persistence of High Inflation and High Unemployment*, Boston, MA: Federal Reserve Bank of Boston, 1978, pp. 49–72.

Maddison, Angus, *Phases of Capitalist Development*, Oxford: Oxford University Press, 1982.

Mankiw, N. Gregory, 'Small Menu Costs and Large Business Cycles: A Macroeconomic Model', *Quarterly Journal of Economics* May 1985, *100*(2), pp. 529–38.

—— 'Recent Developments in Macroeconomics: A Very Quick Refresher Course', *Journal of Money, Credit and Banking* Aug. 1988, *20*(3, part 2), pp. 436–49.

—— 'Real Business Cycles: A New Keynesian Perspective', *Journal of Economic Perspectives*, Summer 1989, *3*(3), pp. 79–90.

Marshall, Alfred, *Principles of Economics*, London: Macmillan, 1920.

McCallum, Bennett T., 'On "Real" and "Sticky-Price" Theories of the Business Cycle', *Journal of Money, Credit and Banking* Nov. 1986, *18*(4), pp. 398–414.

—— 'Postwar Developments in Business Cycle Theory: A Moderately Classical Perspective', *Journal of Money, Credit, and Banking* Aug. 1988, *20*(3, Part 2), pp. 459–71.

—— 'Real Business Cycle Theory', in *Modern Business Cycle Theory*, Robert J. Barro (ed.), Cambridge: Harvard University Press, 1989, pp. 16–50.

McDonald, Ian and Solow, Robert M., 'Wage Bargaining and Employment', *American Economic Review* Dec. 1981, *71*(5), pp. 896–908.

—— 'Wages and Employment in a Segmented Labor Market', *Quarterly Journal of Economics* Nov. 1985, *100*(4), pp. 1115–41.

Means, Gardiner C., 'Industrial Prices and their Relative Inflexibility', US Senate Document 13, 74th Congress, 1st session, Washington, DC, 1935.

Mills, Frederick C. *The Behavior of Prices* NBER General Series, no. 11. New York: Arno Press, 1927.

Mitchell, Daniel J. B. 'Wage Flexibility: Then and Now', *Industrial Relations* Spring 1985, *24*, pp. 266–79.

Mortensen, Dale T, 'A Theory of Wage and Employment Dynamics', in Phelps, 1970, pp. 167–211.

—— 'Job Search, the Duration of Unemployment, and the Phillips Curve', *American Economic Review* Dec. 1970b, *60*(5), pp. 847–62.

National Income and Product Accounts of the United States, 1929–82. Washington, DC: US Dept. of Commerce, 1986. (Updated beyond 1982 from *Survey of Current Business*, various issues)

Nordhaus, William D., 'Recent Developments in Price Dynamics', in *The Econometrics of Price Determination*, Otto Eckstein (ed.), Washington, DC: Board of Governors of the Federal Reserve System, 1972, pp. 16–49.

OECD Statistics. Paris, 1988. (Data obtained from data diskette.)

Ohkawa, Kazushi, and Shinohara, Mihohei (eds) *Patterns of Japanese Economic Development: A Quantitative Appraisal*. New Haven: Yale University Press, 1979.

Okun, Arthur M., 'Inflation: Its Mechanics and Welfare Cost', *Brookings Papers on Economic Activity*, 1975 (2), pp. 351–401.

—— *Prices and Quantities: A Macroeconomic Analysis*. Washington, DC: Brookings Institution, 1981.

Parkin, Michael, *Macroeconomics*. Scarborough, Ontario: Prentice-Hall, 1984.

Patinkin, Don, *Money, Interest, and Prices*, 2nd edn, New York: Harper & Row, 1965.

Phelps, Edmund S., *Microeconomic Foundations of Employment and Inflation Theory*, New York: Norton, 1970.

—— *Inflation Policy and Unemployment Theory: The Cost-benefit Approach to Monetary Planning*, New York: Norton, 1972.

—— *Political Economy: An Introductory Text*, New York: W. W. Norton, 1985.

Phelps, Edmund S. and Taylor, John B., 'Stabilizing Powers of Monetary Policy Under Rational Expectations', *Journal of Political Economy* Feb. 1977, *85*(1), pp. 163–90.

Phelps, Edmund S. and Winter, Sidney G. Jr, 'Optimal Price Policy Under Atomistic Competition', in Phelps, 1970, pp. 309–37.

Phillips, A. W., 'The Relation between Unemployment and the Rate of Change of Money Wage Rates in the United Kingdom, 1861–1957', *Economica* Nov. 1958, *25*, pp. 283–99.

Plosser, Charles I., 'Understanding Real Business Cycles', *Journal of Economic Perspectives*, Summer 1989, *3*(3), pp. 51–77.

Prescott, Edward C., 'Theory Ahead of Business Cycle Measurement', *Carnegie-Rochester Conference Series on Public Policy*, Autumn 1986, *25*, pp. 11–44.

Roberts, John M., Stockton, David J. and Struckmeyer, Charles S., 'An Evaluation of the Sources of Aggregate Price Rigidity', Working Paper 99, Economic Activity Section, Division of Research and Statistics, Board of Governors of the Federal Reserve System, May 1989.

Romer, Christina, 'The Prewar Business Cycle Reconsidered: New Estimates of Gross National Product, 1869–1908', *Journal of Political Economy* Feb. 1989, *97*(1), pp. 1–37.

Rosen, Sherwin, 'Implicit Contracts: A Survey', *Journal of Economic Literature* Sept. 1985, *23*(3), pp. 1144–75.

Rotemberg, Julio, 'The New Keynesian Microfoundations', *NBER Macroeconomics Annual* 1987, *2*, pp. 69–104.

Sachs, Jeffrey D., 'The Changing Cyclical Behavior of Wages and Prices: 1890–1976', *American Economic Review.*, Mar. 1980, *70*(1), pp. 78–90.

Sargent, Thomas J., 'A Note on the "Accelerationist" Controversy,' *Journal of Money, Credit and Banking* Aug. 1971, *3*(3), pp. 721–25.

Schultze, Charles, 'Some Macro Foundations for Micro Theory,' *Brookings Papers on Economic Activity* 1981, (2), pp. 521–76.

—— *Other Times Other Places: Macroeconomic Lessons from U.S. and European History* Washington, DC: Brookings Institution, 1986.

—— 'Real Wages, Real Wage Aspirations, and Unemployment in Europe', in *Barriers to European Growth: A Transatlantic View*, Robert Z. Lawrence and Charles L. Schultze (eds), Washington, DC: Brookings Institution, 1987, pp. 230–91.

Shapiro, Carl and Stiglitz, Joseph, 'Equilibrium Unemployment as a Discipline Device', *American Economic Review* June 1984, *64*(3), pp. 433–44.

Sheshinski, Eytan and Weiss, Yoram, 'Inflation and Costs of Price Adjustment', *Review of Economic Studies* June 1977, *44*(2), pp. 287–303.

—— 'Optimum Pricing Policy under Stochastic Inflation', *Review of Economic Studies.* July 1983, *50*(3), pp. 513–29.

Solomou, Solomos, *Phases of Economic Growth, 1850–1973*, Cambridge: Cambridge University Press, 1987.

Stigler, George and Kindahl, James K., *The Behavior of Industrial Prices*, New York: Columbia University Press for the NBER, 1970.

Stiglitz, Joseph, 'Theories of Wage Rigidity', in *Keynes' Economic Legacy: Contemporary Economic Theories*, James L. Butkiewicz, Kenneth J. Koford, and Jeffrey B. Miller (eds), New York: Praeger, 1986, pp. 153–206.

Summers, Lawrence H., 'Relative Wages, Efficiency Wages, and Keynesian Unemployment', *American Economic Review* May 1988, *78*(2), pp. 383–8.

Tarshis, Lorie, 'Real Wages in the United States and Great Britain', *Canadian Journal of Economics* Aug. 1938, *4*(3), pp. 362–76.

—— 'Changes in Real and Money Wages', *Economic Journal* Mar. 1939, *49*(193), pp. 150–54.

Taylor, John, 'Aggregate Dynamics and Staggered Contracts', *Journal of Political Economy* Feb. 1980, *88*(1), pp. 1–24.

—— 'Union Wage Settlements', *American Economic Review* Dec. 1983, *73*(5), pp. 981–93.

—— 'Improvements in Macroeconomic Stability: The Role of Wages and Prices', in *The American Business Cycle: Continuity and Change*, Robert J. Gordon (ed.), Chicago: University of Chicago Press for NBER, 1986, pp. 639–77.

Tobin, James, 'Monetary Policy: Rules, Targets, and Shocks', *Journal of Money, Credit and Banking*, Nov. 1983, *15*(4), pp. 506–18.

—— 'On the Theory of Macroeconomic Policy', Cowles Foundation Discussion Paper no. 931, Dec. 1989.

Weiss, Andrew, *Efficiency Wages: Models of Unemployment, Layoffs, and Wage Dispersion*, Princeton, NJ: Princeton University Press, 1990.

22 New and old Keynesians

Bruce Greenwald and Joseph Stiglitz
Journal of Economic Perspectives (1993) 7, Winter, pp. 23–44

All Keynesians, whether new or old, would agree on three propositions. First, during some periods – often extended – an excess supply of labor exists at the prevailing level of real wages (and expectations concerning future wages and prices).

Second, the aggregate level of economic activity fluctuates markedly, whether measured by capacity utilization, GDP, or unemployment. These fluctuations are greater in magnitude and different in pattern from any that might be accounted for by short-run changes in technology, tastes, or demography.

Third, money matters, at least most of the time, although monetary policy may be ineffective in some periods (like the Great Depression).

From these three propositions follow certain important policy conclusions; while old and new Keynesians may disagree upon the exact form of their policy recommendations, they would agree generally that government intervention is at least sometimes (many would argue frequently) desirable to stabilize the level of economic activity.

Agreement upon these three propositions, and the associated policy perspective, sets old and new Keynesians apart from advocates of other major schools of macroeconomic thought, including new classical and real business cycle theorists. Both of these, for instance, believe that the labor market and other markets essentially always clear, with wages and prices adjusting quickly to any disturbances; that shifts in the demand or supply curves for labor can explain fluctuations in observed levels of employment; and that the economy's (presumably efficient) responses to shocks can explain these fluctuations in output. In the case of real business cycles, the focus is on shocks to technology; for many new classical theories, the focus is shocks to the money supply.

Despite the fundamental differences in views between these different schools, they have agreed upon two methodological premises: that macroeconomics should be grounded in microeconomic principles, and that understanding macroeconomic behavior requires the construction of a (simple) general equilibrium model. The real difference arises here: real business cycles and (to a lesser extent) new classical economists base their theories on simple (we would say simplistic) models of markets that employ perfect information, perfect competition, the absence of transactions costs, and the presence of a complete set of markets. They also often employ a representative agent model.[1] These assumptions often interact: the absence of risk markets is of no import in a world in which all individuals are identical – since there is no one to whom a representative agent can transfer risk. Problems of asymmetric information cannot arise if all individuals are identical. Moreover, the strong assumptions allow market results to be Pareto efficient, despite the fact that economies with imperfect information and incomplete markets are generally not constrained Pareto efficient (Greenwald and Stiglitz 1986, 1988a).[2] In contrast, modern Keynesians have identified these real world 'imperfections' as the source of the problem: leaving them out of the model is like leaving Hamlet out of the play.

The insistence on micro-foundations enhances the ability of economists to distinguish among alternative theories, and helps to set the research agenda. Statistical analyses based on variances and covariances of the principle aggregate time series simply do not have enough power to distinguish among many of the alternative theories. Good macro-theories should do more. A host of other facts clamor to be explained; for instance, good macro-theories must explain why variations in the number of hours worked should take the form of layoffs rather than work-sharing; why layoffs tend to be concentrated among certain parts of the labor force; why investment in general, and inventories and construction in particular, should be so volatile; and more. Beyond that, the micro-foundations from which the aggregate behavior is derived can often be tested directly. A rejection of the underlying micro-hypotheses should suffice to cast doubt on the validity of the derived macro-theory.

Incorporating the newer micro-foundations is the principal task ahead of new Keynesians.[3] The challenge is to choose between the myriad of ways in which markets can be imperfect, and to decide on the central questions and puzzles to be explained.

Different strands of research within new Keynesian economics have taken two broadly different approaches.[4] The first argues that nominal price rigidities are the essential way in which market economies differ from the Walrasian Arrow-Debreu model. Without such rigidities, the argument goes, flexible prices would allow the economy to adjust quickly to whatever shocks it experiences, maintaining all the while full employment and economic efficiency. Early work in this area focused on constructing general equilibrium models with price rigidities.[5] More recent work has been concerned with explaining the sources of those price rigidities, as discussed by Romer (1993).

The second strand of new Keynesian literature explores another path suggested by Keynes: that increased flexibility of wages and prices might exacerbate the economy's downturn. This insight implies that wage and price rigidity are not the only problem, and perhaps not even the central problem. This view holds that even if wages and prices were perfectly flexible, output and employment would be highly volatile. It sees the economy as amplifying the shocks that it experiences, and making their effects persist. It identifies incomplete contracts, and, in particular, imperfect indexing, as central market failures, and it attempts both to explain the causes and consequences of these market failures.

Clearly, these two new Keynesian approaches have different implications for how the economy works. The first holds that the classical dichotomy breaks down, allowing monetary policy to have effects other than on the price level, because nominal prices are at least somewhat rigid throughout the economy. The second approach, however, holds that monetary policy has real effects even when wages and prices are flexible.

In addition, the nominal price rigidity theories describe how the economy will recover from a recession as wages and prices *eventually* fall enough that consumption recovers, or as capital goods wear out to the point where gross investment is required to replace even the small amount of capital required for the low level of output. However, neither the sources of the shocks, nor the mechanisms by which falling prices and wages would restore the economy to equilibrium, have received extensive attention; implicitly, in most of the models, it appears as a hidden real balance effect – as wages and prices fall, the real value of individuals' holdings of money increases, and this induces them to consume more.

The new Keynesian view that emphasizes price flexibility suggests an alternate and more complex perspective: first, that natural economic forces can magnify economic shocks that may seem small, and second, that existing price rigidities may *reduce* the magnitude of the fluctuations, as Keynes argued.[6] Since even with perfectly flexible wages and prices, the economy could experience substantial variations in employment, they believe the single-minded focus on price and wage rigidities is misguided. And since small disturbances can give rise to large effects, there is less concern about identifying the source of the disturbance: in one case, it may be a supply shock (the oil price shocks of 1973 and 1979), in another case it may be a monetary shock (the Volcker recession).

BASIC INGREDIENTS

The purpose of this chapter is to describe the second strand of new Keynesian literature and to contrast it both with the alternative strand of new Keynesian literature based on price rigidities as well as with other points of view. The models described here contain three basic ingredients, each playing a different role in explaining aspects of the underlying macroeconomic quandaries, but all based on problems which arise in economies with imperfect information and incomplete contracts. The ingredients are: risk averse firms; a credit allocation mechanism in which credit-rationing, risk-averse banks play a central role; and new labor market theories, including efficiency wages and insider-outsider models. These building blocks should help to explain how price flexibility contributes to macroeconomic fluctuations and to unemployment. In particular, the first two building blocks will explain why small shocks to the economy can give rise to large changes in output, while the new labor market theories will explain why those changes in output (with their associated changes in the demand curve for labor) result in unemployment.

RISK AVERSE FIRMS

Much of the macroeconomic behavior of firms can be explained by the fact that firms are risk averse. Let us first explore several alternative theories as to why firms are risk averse, and then examine the consequences of that finding.[7]

A first explanation for risk averse firms has to do with imperfections in the equity market. In traditional Keynesian theory, whether finance came from equity or debt was not important. In our view, it is central. With equity, the firm shares risk with those who provide finance, and the firm has no fixed obligation to repay. With debt, the firm has a fixed obligation, and if it fails to meet those obligations, it can be forced into bankruptcy. Thus, firms will tend to be risk averse if they do not have ready access to equity finance, and are therefore pushed to debt finance.

In fact, despite the seeming advantages of equity, firms finance a relatively small fraction of their investment with new equity issues. One obvious explanation is when firms do issue new equities, their market values tend to decline markedly, because the market interprets issuing new shares as a negative signal. Think of it this way: assume the owner of a firm knew the value of the company. Then auctioning off shares in the firm is no different from auctioning off dollar bills. If I know the number of dollar bills in my back pocket, and auction off 1 percent shares, what is the equilibrium price? Zero! And for an obvious reason. If there are $100,000 in my back pocket, and you offer me less than $1000 for a 1 percent share, then I will not accept the offer; if you offer me more, I will. The only price at which you will not lose is a price of zero.

So how can markets for issuing new equity exist at all, in the presence of asymmetric information? Owners of firms are risk averse, and do not have perfect information about the value of their firm. Provided it is not too costly, they would like to sell some of their shares and diversify their risk. But the adverse selection effect still works with a vengeance. Those who know that the market overvalues their shares are most anxious to sell additional shares. Accordingly, in a rational expectations equilibrium, the 'worst firms' (most overvalued, or least undervalued) are most willing to issue equities; and, given that, issuing equity will be treated as a negative signal and the equity market will be thin.

Investors may also be generally leery of equity because of its effect on incentives. An early version of this argument, using principal-agent theory, pointed out that equity means that management must share the returns of its efforts with others (Ross 1973; Stiglitz 1974). A more recent, probably more important effect is what Robert Hall refers to as the 'backs to the wall theory' of corporate finance, or what Jensen (1986) refers to as the 'free cash flow' hypothesis. In these theories, the fixed obligations entailed by high debt obligations can provide strong managerial incentives.

The literature offers a number of other reasons why firms may be risk averse; the discussion here is not meant as exhaustive.[8] For example, one major strand of literature emphasizes that modern corporations are controlled by managers who act in a risk averse manner. While managerial incentive schemes may attempt to reduce this behavior, they do so only imperfectly.

At this juncture, many a macroeconomist may ask: while all of this is interesting micro-theory, what does it have to do with macroeconomics? To answer this challenge, we have to describe a bit more how risk aversion affects firm behavior.

A risk averse firm will be sensitive to the risk associated with any action (including inaction). Production itself is risky; it takes time and there are no future markets for the sale of goods. Firms are often uncertain about the consequences of their actions (so-called 'instrument uncertainty') and their uncertainty grows with the size of the change. In general, firms know more about the status quo than about what things might be like if they changed their actions.

The risk averse nature of firms under these conditions of uncertainty is the basis of the 'portfolio theory' of the firm, in which firms simultaneously choose all of their actions – prices, wages, employment, production, and so on – taking into account the risk (covariances as well as variances) and expected returns with each 'portfolio' of decisions. In assessing the consequences of various actions, firms look at the effects that those actions will have on the firm's assets, which include cash, a set of machines, a group of employees, a set of customers, and so on. Changes in economic circumstances – either the firm's willingness to bear risks, or its perceptions concerning the riskiness or value of various assets, will lead it to want to change that portfolio; for instance, increased uncertainty about the value of inventories will lead it to want to hold smaller inventories.

Changes in the economic environment will in general necessitate changes in some actions of the firm. Thus, if the demand curve for the firm's product shifts to the left, it must either change the price it charges, the quantity it sells, or the inventories it holds. If it holds price constant, the quantity sold must adjust, and conversely. Evaluating what it should do entails an evaluation of the risks associated with each of these changes and the costs of adjustment.

The actions of firms are affected by their perceptions of risks, both through instrument uncertainty (the uncertainty concerning the consequences of any actions), and the uncertainty associated with the value of various assets. At least three factors influence the risks firms face and their willingness to bear those risks. One key factor is the overall state of the economy. When the economy goes into a recession, and firms talk about their pessimism or uncertainty, these perceptions have real consequences. A second factor is the firm's cash (or liquid asset) position. Changes in a firm's cash position affect how much it must borrow to maintain its production activities. A firm's cash position is affected by profits, and since profits are a residual, small changes in prices may have large effects on profits, and thus on firm liquidity, particularly for highly leveraged firms. Of course, the lower profits also adversely affect the firm's net worth. A third important factor is changes in the price level. Since almost all debt is denominated in nominal terms, such changes have large effects on firm real liquidity and real wealth.[9]

The theory of the risk averse firm can thus provide an explanation of why each firm's supply curve, and hence the aggregate supply curve – the amount that they are willing to produce at each level of prices (given wages) – should shift markedly as the economy goes into a recession. The riskiness of production has increased, and firm's willingness and ability to bear that risk has decreased.

To maintain the same level of economic activity, with the reduced cash flow from lower profits, firms must borrow more. But increased debt creates a higher probability that future returns will not be sufficient to meet these fixed obligations. As the firm expands its production, it must borrow more, increasing its fixed obligations; there is an increased chance of not being able to meet those increased fixed obligations. The expected extra costs associated with bankruptcy are what is meant by the 'marginal bankruptcy cost'. Normally, the necessity to borrow more resulting from lower cash flow (lower profits) not only increases the probability of bankruptcy (at any fixed level of economic activity) but also the marginal bankruptcy costs. Once bankruptcy costs are taken into account, we need to modify the standard theory of the firm, where, as a firm expands, it compares price (marginal revenue) with marginal cost.

Thus, the aggregate supply curve shifts to the left. The shift in the firm (and aggregate) supply curve means that the amount firms are willing to produce, at each level of prices and wages, is reduced; conversely, it also means that at each level of output the firm's mark-up of price over marginal costs (largely determined by the wage) is increased. Moreover, the same reasoning provides an explanation of why the aggregate demand curve should shift to the left in this situation: the firm's demand for investment may shift down markedly.

The theory also explains why large redistributions, like those stemming from large price changes (like the oil price shocks of the 1970s) should have a negative effect on the economy. While increases in wealth lead to increasing production and investment in the sectors which benefit from the price change, there are diminishing returns; the increases of, say, production from those who benefit are more than offset by the reductions from those who lose.

The theory of the risk averse firm explains a number of other aspects of the cyclical behavior of the economy. For instance, imperfections in equity markets and the extent of leveraging on equity differ across sectors. Construction, for instance, is an industry dominated by small firms, most of whom do not have access to the equity market; and construction firms typically borrow heavily to finance their construction activities. Such sectors one would expect to be particularly volatile.

To illustrate how the risk averse theory of the firm can explain why shocks to the economy, whether real or monetary, can have real, large, and persistent effects, let's trace through an example. Say that a decrease in export prices (to lower than expected levels) reduces exporters' net worth, leading them to reduce their supply, and their demand for inputs from other producers. This unexpected change in the demand curve for others' products leads to lower prices than expected in other sectors, with adverse effects on their asset and liquidity position and on what they want to produce, and their demand for inputs (including investment).

Inventory adjustments exacerbate the process: with greater perceived risk and lower wealth, and hence reduced willingness to bear risk, firms cut back on their desired level of inventories; this translates into a further reduction in production. Note that the theory of risk averse firm thus offers an answer to one of the long-standing puzzles of macroeconomics: why inventories do not seem to perform the production smoothing role they should, with concave production functions: if anything, inventories seem to exacerbate economic fluctuations (Blinder and Maccini 1991).

We thus have a mechanism for the transmission, amplification, and persistence of the effects of shocks, *even with complete flexibility of wages and prices.* Such a model can explain volatility, and also provide answers to the two other questions posed in the beginning of this chapter. If one adopts a standard model of money demand, say with constant velocity, then unanticipated changes in the money supply lead to unanticipated changes in the price level, which will set off the process described above. Remember, changes in the price level affect the value of firm debt, since that debt is usually denominated in nominal terms.

Moreover, hiring workers is an investment. As the economy goes into a recession, the optimal portfolio of assets for a firm includes less 'human capital'. Beyond that, the shadow cost of capital – taking into account, for instance, the increased risks of bankruptcy that follow from the increased borrowing required to finance the hiring and training costs of new employees – is high in a recession, and thus, even if firms eventually wanted to increase their stock of employees, the depths of a recession is not the time to make that investment. Thus, new hires are reduced.[10] This gives rise to unemployment, which results when the rate of separations exceeds the rate of new hires. As this theory would predict, the rate of new hires shows greater cyclical volatility than the rate of separations.

CREDIT MARKETS AND RISK AVERSE BANKS

The theory of risk averse firms takes us a considerable distance, but effects that operate through the banking system and credit markets provide yet another process by which shocks to the economy are amplified and their effects propagated, and another set of reasons why monetary policy will work, even in a world with flexible prices and wages.[11]

Recent economic work has emphasized that credit is not allocated in an auction process, with whoever is willing to pay the highest interest rate receiving the loan. Instead, lenders must face the risk that a loan will not be repaid, and institutions, like banks, have arisen for screening loan applicants and monitoring loans. Banks are highly leveraged; with fixed obligations (the deposits they hold) and risky assets, banks must worry about the risk of bankruptcy. It is now well-known that increasing interest rates may have adverse effects both on the mix of loan applicants and on the incentives of borrowers to undertake risky activities, and that these adverse incentive and selection effects can be so strong that lenders' expected returns may actually decrease as the interest rate charged increases. This can lead to credit rationing, with the interest rate charged being that which maximizes the expected return to lenders, and at that interest rate, there is an excess demand for credit.

Greenwald and Stiglitz (1990a) have extended that analysis to embrace risk averse lenders. Like the equity-constrained firms described earlier, banks, who must worry about the risk of bankruptcy, act in a risk averse manner. There will still be credit rationing, with interest rates chosen to maximize the 'expected utility' of the lender, or the expected returns minus the costs of bankruptcy. But with risk averse banks, the same kinds of factors which affect firm behavior – changes in risk perceptions and changes in net worth, affecting the willingness to bear risk – affect bank behavior, too.

This risk averse behavior of banks will magnify an initial negative economic shock, and make recessions deeper and longer. The banks' portfolio of activities can usefully be divided into recruiting and processing new customers; making (and monitoring) loans to existing customers; and buying a safe asset, like Treasury bills. When economic conditions worsen, banks' perceptions of the relative risk of loans increases; and since bad economic conditions are often accompanied by high default rates, banks' net worth decreases, along with their willingness to bear risks. On both accounts, banks respond to bad conditions by shifting their portfolio towards the safer activity: investing in Treasury bills. Equilibrium in the loan markets would be attained only at a higher real interest rate, which would also discourage investment activity. And banks will often be unwilling to raise interest rates, because of a fear that higher rates will have the adverse selection effect of chasing away credit-worthy borrowers and adverse incentive effects, inducing them to undertake greater risks (Stiglitz and Weiss 1981).

Monetary policy still works (at times) in this situation, but not in the accustomed way. The conventional monetary policy story has the Federal Reserve driving down interest rates, which stimulates investment. In this situation, though, while monetary policy may succeed in lowering the rate of interest on Treasury bills, the change in interest rates charged by banks may well be minimal. It may also result in little change, if any, in the supply of loans: while there is a substitution effect associated with loans being relatively more attractive, there is an income effect which goes the other way (if banks have decreasing absolute risk aversion). And in the credit rationing regime, it is the supply of loans which is critical; firms are limited in their investment activities, and possibly even in their production activities (if they rely on bank credit for working capital) by the lack of credit.[12]

However, monetary policy also works through another set of mechanisms. Reserve requirements (when reserves are kept in accounts that bear little or no interest) act as a tax on deposits. Higher reserve requirements raise that tax, and reduce the wealth of banks; lower reserve requirements have the reverse effect. Lowering the discount rate has the effect of reducing one cost facing the bank – the cost of obtaining funds from the central bank. This change increases the real wealth of banks, making them more willing to bear risks and make loans. Since the ratio of loans to net worth for banks is typically very large, relatively small changes in bank net worth can give rise to large changes in credit availability.[13]

Although monetary policy can have potent effects through these channels, it will also be relatively impotent at times. If the economy is very weak, so that expected returns on bank loans are very low, relative to the risks associated with them, then raising the wealth of banks may still not make lending money look profitable.[14]

LABOR MARKETS

One peculiar aspect of old Keynesian analysis was that while its main concern was unemployment, it offered little discussion of the labor market. However, a consensus is growing that an understanding of the labor market must be at the center of any macroeconomic theory (Lindbeck 1992).

The basic empirical puzzle in the labor market is that employment levels change markedly, with little change in real wages. One explanation is that the supply curve for labor is horizontal, but that would run counter to all the microeconomic evidence, as well as introspection. Another explanation is that, by some miracle of coincidence, shifts in the demand and supply curves have been perfectly offsetting. A recession, for example, is marked by a leftward shift in the labor supply schedule, just as the demand schedule moved left. But why should labor supply fall so fortuitously? Changes in real interest rates and expectations concerning future wages could, of course, through intertemporal substitution, induce shifts in the labor supply schedule; but micro-evidence suggests that these intertemporal substitution effects are far too small to obtain the desired effects. A further problem is presented by the contradictory movements in real interest rates: in the Great Depression they rose markedly; during the recessions of the 1950s, 1960s and early 1970s, they changed hardly at all.

New Keynesians offer an alternate interpretation. They have explored reasons why real wages are not likely to move. As a result, shifts in demand for labor can create a situation where people are willing to work at the going wage, but cannot find jobs; in other words, there is involuntary unemployment. Some of the possible reasons for sticky real wages include efficiency wages, insider-outsider theory, imperfect competition, and implicit contracts. Let us say a few words about each; the reader interested in a thorough evaluation of these theories might begin with Stiglitz (1992a) or Newbery and Stiglitz (1987).

Efficiency wage theories argue that productivity often increases with real wages; as a result, it does not pay firms to cut wages. High wages may raise productivity either because they attract higher quality labor; or because they result in increased effort; or because they reduce labor turnover and save on hiring and training costs.[15] Efficiency wage theories can be used to explain why firms do not lower wages even in the presence of an excess supply of workers, and also why they avoid two-tier wage systems, under which new workers are hired at lower wages than existing workers.

Insider-outsider theories and bargaining theories begin with the presence of turnover costs, and then argue that trained 'inside' workers are not a perfect substitute for untrained 'outside' workers. This situation gives rise to a bargaining problem. Since 'inside workers' control the training process, they would react negatively to hiring workers at lower wages who could potentially replace them. Moreover, the fact that new workers cannot commit themselves not to demand higher wages once trained provides a further reason that firms do not hire 'cheap' new workers.

When imperfect competition exists in labor and product markets, firms set wages, prices, and employment. Given the risk averse nature of the firm, as described earlier, and efficiency wage and insider-outsider effects just mentioned, a firm that is considering lower wages must face considerable uncertainty about the possible effects on the effort, quality, and turnover of its labor force.

To this point, the discussion has focused on the 'supply side' of the labor market. But the demand side offers a puzzle as well. The demand for labor at any real product wage can be derived in a straightforward way from the production function. The fact that employment varies considerably with small variations in real product wages presents a puzzle.

With given technology and capital stock, if firms operate along their supply function (with concave production functions), then a reduction in output should be associated with an increase in real product wages, contrary to what is observed. There are several possible explanations. One is that, somehow, there has been a large negative change in technology. The implausibility of this hypothesis, and the empirical evidence against it, are matters taken up elsewhere. Second, there could be a change in the degree of competition, and hence in the mark-up over marginal costs. Third, firms could simply be off their supply curve. (For a critique of these alternative explanations, see Stiglitz 1992b.)

We prefer a fourth theory, provided by the theory of the risk averse firm. Earlier, we explained why the firm and aggregate supply curve of output shifts as the economy goes into a recession. One can easily translate this into a shift in the firm and aggregate demand curves for labor.

The new Keynesian research program in labor economics followed traditional macroeconomics in seeking to explain the observed patterns of real wages and employment. But it has also tested those explanations against a number of other key aspects of the labor market, like why reductions in the demand for labor take the form of layoffs rather than reduced hours for everyone and why unemployment seems to be so concentrated in certain groups in the population. Focusing on these characteristics of unemployment is important, because if the reduction in the demand for labor took the form of an equi-proportionate reduction in the hours worked by each individual, the social and economic consequences of unemployment would be much less than they in fact are. The labor market theories described above are able to explain these phenomena.[16]

PERSPECTIVES ON ALTERNATIVE THEORIES

Our main objective in this chapter is to describe this emerging strand of new Keynesian literature in broad terms. To this point, we have described how theories based on informational imperfections can explain the main puzzles mentioned at the start of the chapter: the presence and persistence of unemployment, the variability of output, and why money matters. In fact, the theories described here go farther, and offer an explanation of why certain sectors of the economy exhibit greater volatility than others; why the variability in hours worked takes the form of layoffs; and the logic behind the cyclical patterns of inventories, hours worked and employment.

In this section, we describe the kinds of arguments that persuade us that alternative theories are at best incomplete, at worse wrong. None of the theories discussed in this chapter, including our own, have been fully embodied in a large macro-econometric model. We believe that constructing such models, together with conducting the kind of simulation exercises that have provided much of the support for real business cycles, should be on the agenda for future research. But before subjecting a model to that sort of extensive testing, we believe it must be shown that it can at least display the critical basic observed facts about the economy. Thus, our discussion will seek to identify key observations which, in our judgment, cast serious doubt on the major competing theories.[17]

NEW KEYNESIAN PRICE RIGIDITIES

As mentioned earlier, one strand of new Keynesian economics has emphasized nominal price rigidity, and used explanations that go under the name of 'menu costs' to explain that rigidity.

A number of facts imply that price rigidities are, at a minimum, not the only source of economic problems like volatility and unemployment. For example, Keynesian-like unemployment problems seem to arise even in economies which are experiencing inflationary pressures, and thus where the *nominal* wages do not need to fall, but only to rise more slowly. Moreover, nominal wages and prices did fall in the Great Depression, as well as in other economic downturns. We agree with Keynes that had prices fallen even faster, the economy would have degenerated farther, rather than improving more quickly.

Indeed, in most new Keynesian models the mechanism by which wage and price flexibility would *eventually* restore the economy to full employment is the old real balance effect. The enormous attention that the real balance effect has received over the years hardly speaks well for the profession. Quantitatively, it is surely an nth order effect; one calculation put it that, even at the fastest rate at which prices fell in the Great Depression, it would take more than two centuries to restore the economy to full employment. And in the short run even its sign is ambiguous, as intertemporal substitution effects may (depending on expectations) more than offset the wealth effects (Neary and Stiglitz 1982; Grandmont 1983).

But while price rigidities may not be at the center of phenomena like fluctuations and unemployment, and one does not have to assume price rigidities to establish that monetary policy has real effects, the relative rigidity of wages and prices remains a phenomenon which needs to be explained.

The menu cost literature has attempted to argue that the costs of adjustment, like the costs of printing new menus, results in firms only adjusting prices periodically, which is another way of saying that price stickiness exists. From a tactical point, the advocates of menu costs beat their critics to the punch by choosing a name – 'menu costs' – which would seem to belittle the importance of the subject. Indeed, these costs are small, and have become smaller as computer programs allow the printing of menus on a daily basis at a marginal cost of pennies.

Two arguments were necessary to give these seemingly small effects any plausible relevance (Akerlof and Yellen 1985). First, if firms are already choosing their prices optimally, then the cost of not adjusting was of second order. Thus, while the costs of adjusting may be small, so were the benefits of adjusting. Second, in spite of the small (second order) losses to the firm, the losses to society could be first order.[18] While both of these propositions are correct, they are not sufficient to justify paying much attention to the menu cost literature. Both propositions apply to *any* decision of the firm: they offer no reason to single out pricing decisions.

By contrast, we have emphasized that firms must view all their decisions together; that the costs of adjusting prices must be put in juxtaposition with the costs of adjusting (or not adjusting) quantities. Since there is a strong presumption that costs of adjusting outputs and inputs will be much greater than those associated with simply adjusting prices, this would seem to argue for quantity rigidities, and against price stickiness. But when focusing on risk, as we have done, the conclusion changes. When a firm considers the various ways it might react, it will perceive greater uncertainty about the consequences of price and wage adjustments – because those consequences depend on the uncertain responses of rival firms, customers, and workers – than about the consequences of output adjustments. In fact, for those goods which can be put into inventory, the only risk associated with producing too little is the risk associated with higher production costs next period, when any inventory deficiency must be made up. (Of course, boom times may create a risk of running out of stock, but that risk is not important in recessionary periods.) This portfolio theory of firm adjustment does provide an explanation of price and wage rigidity, at least in the short run; though in the long run, the theory suggests that prices and wages eventually do adjust.[19]

To be sure, *if* agents in the economy perfectly anticipated changes in the money supply and *if* it was common knowledge that all agents in the economy responded to changes in the money supply by changing all prices proportionately, then money might be neutral. But since the money supply is not perfectly observed by all agents, not all agents change prices proportionately, and so there is no reason that they should all believe that price changes will perfectly offset changes in the money supply. Given the uncertainty about whether other agents will increase prices proportionately to observed changes, it will not generally be optimal for any firm to increase its price proportionately; thus, the beliefs about non-proportional responses to price changes are consistent.

Thus, there is a presumption that as long as risk markets are incomplete and firms and individuals are risk averse, and debt is imperfectly indexed, then an expansion of the money (credit) supply will have real effects. Also, there are distributional consequences of the manner in which the money (credit) supply is increased. A credit expansion affects some individuals, firms, and industries more than others. In short, money (credit) matters, but not just because of nominal rigidities.

In fact, our theory can be seen as a particular kind of menu cost theory – a theory which emphasizes the riskiness of adjusting prices, rather than the actual adjustment costs. But while our theory does provide a theory of price stickiness, it argues that price stickiness is only one element, and not the most important one, in understanding macroeconomic phenomena. And nothing that we have said would be substantially altered if, in addition to the risk costs which we have emphasized, fixed costs of price adjustment were significant.[20]

Another major distinction between the two strands of new Keynesian literature is whether nominal or real price rigidities are emphasized. One strand uses nominal rigidities as an important step in explaining why money matters. But in the alternative theory, based on the risk averse theory of the firm with incomplete contracting and indexing, money matters more as prices become more flexible. By contrast, to explain unemployment, it focuses on real rigidities in the labor market (such as associated with the efficiency wage theory). It argues that whatever happens to the product market, unless one has a theory of real wage rigidity, one cannot explain unemployment. For even if there were large shifts in the demand curve for labor, if the real wage were flexible, demand and supply for labor would equilibrate.[21]

There is, however, an important difference between the two approaches for policy purposes. A menu cost theorist would focus efforts at structural macroeconomic reform on reducing the costs and speeding the implementation of price changes. Anti-inflation measures like those considered in the 1970s, which penalized price changers, would have potentially destructive consequences for overall economic welfare. A menu cost theorist would to the contrary advocate measures which would provide incentives for rapid nominal price adjustments. In contrast, in our model rapid price adjustment is a two-edged sword. On the one hand, it reduces the reliance of firms on quantity adjustment and hence might stabilize aggregate levels of employment and output. On the other hand, greater overall price changes would mean greater wealth transfers to and from firms, exacerbating the financing imbalances which act to amplify the original macroeconomic disturbances. On balance, therefore, we would regard price and wage rigidity more as a symptom of underlying financial and labor market failures and not as a fundamental cause of business cycles. We, therefore, would focus structural reform on those fundamental areas rather than directly on price and wage setting by firms.

OTHER KEYNESIAN THEORIES

Of course, there are other strands of Keynesian and new Keynesian thought besides those focused on price rigidities. One strand which enjoyed considerable popularity in the 1970s and 1980s was that of Tobin, which, like our theory, emphasized the importance of risk. It used a portfolio theory to explain the demand and supply of assets; and related firm investment to the price of (existing) capital goods, as reflected in the price of equity, which emerged in the market equilibrium. Monetary policy affected this price, and hence the level of investment.

The theory has had limited empirical success. One possible reason is that firms raise little of their funds for investment through equity. What success it has had may be due to a spurious correlation: when a firm's future prospects are good, firm managers invest more, and the firm's stock is high. There is not (necessarily) the causal connection suggested by that theory.

That theory, as well as most other Keynesian theories, explain the effect of monetary policy by looking at the demand for money by households. Our theory focuses more on the effects on the banking system, and on the implications through the credit mechanism, both as a result of credit rationing and the behavior of the risk averse firm.[22]

REAL BUSINESS CYCLE THEORIES

Real business cycle theory addresses two of the three puzzles with which we began this chapter by denying their existence: proponents of this school deny either that (involuntary) unemployment exists or that money matters. (The fact that monetary policy is ineffective is of little moment, since in any case the economy is, in this view, efficient, with resources being fully used.) This school of thought focuses on the second problem, that of economic volatility, and proposes exogenous technology shocks as the source of that volatility. The most telling criticisms of this view is the difficulty it has explaining the large negative shocks that mark recession: was there a loss in technological competence?[23]

Of course, if one includes economic organization in 'technology', and in the information embodied in the various firms within the economy in 'capital', then the financial disorganization and risk associated with recessions discussed in this chapter represents both a negative technology and capital shock. With this expanded vocabulary, the basic model of risk averse firms and banks, together with flexible wages and prices, and market clearing in the labor market, can be viewed as a version of real business cycle theory – but one with fundamentally different predictions and policy presumptions than the standard version of the theory.

NEW CLASSICAL THEORIES

The branch of new Keynesian theory emphasized here shares a methodological premise with at least some versions of new classical theories: the importance of imperfect information in explaining observed deviations from the predictions of neoclassical theory. But new classical theories have tended to focus on the consequences of imperfect information for the inferences firms make – say, about the desirability of changing price or quantity. We think the difficulties firms have in inferring whether a shift in the demand curves which they face is due to a real or nominal shock may play a role in explaining 'why money matters', but surely it is not the only reason, nor even perhaps the most important one. While accepting the importance of looking at these issues, we also emphasize the implications of imperfect information for how markets function – the causes and consequences, for instance, of credit rationing, limited equity markets, and efficiency wages.

Another ingredient in new classical models attempts to explain why unanticipated increases in prices (presumably following from an unanticipated increase in the money supply) might elicit a larger than normal output. Our theory provides an alternative explanation: larger-than-anticipated increases in prices increase firms' net worth, and this increases the amount they are willing to supply. Our theory is not based on misperceptions: at the time the loan contract was made, it was anticipated that, with some probability, prices would be high.

New classical economists have also emphasized the importance of expectations (as does King 1993), and particularly rational expectations. Thinking about expectations is hardly new. Keynes invoked a variety of assumptions concerning expectations, and in this, he was only reflecting the common practice of the time.[24] Today, most Keynesians believe that whether expectations are 'rational' is an empirical question – one which, in important instances, will surely be answered in the negative. For example, the stock market crashes of 1929 or 1987 seem very difficult to reconcile with 'rational' expectations.

At the same time, many new Keynesians are not adverse to using the rational expectation assumption when it is convenient to do so (for example, Greenwald and Stiglitz 1986). One especially interesting result is that the basic results of the models which lead to the conclusion that government policy is ineffective do not depend on the assumptions of rational expectations, but rather on even less realistic assumptions concerning instantaneous market clearing. For instance, Nearly and Stiglitz (1983) supply a model with price and wage rigidities where rational expectations actually increased the multipliers from government action. The multipliers were *larger* for an obvious reason: consumers with rational expectations recognized that the 'leakage' of increased income into savings would be translated into higher consumption in future periods; and the expectation of this higher future income 'spilled over' into higher current consumption.

To be sure, rational expectations of policy changes may sometimes lead individuals to act in a manner which undoes those policy changes, but this is surely not the case when the government imposes taxes or subsidies which change intertemporal prices, nor when the government engages in redistributions which have aggregate effects. Obviously, in models with a representative agent, redistributions make no sense, and cannot have any effects. But this just illustrates how such models may be of little use in addressing fundamental issues of macroeconomics.

SUMMARY

The economy is a complex organization, requiring coordination of decisions of the millions of households and firms. Unemployment and other macro-economic problems can be viewed as a failure of society to solve the necessary coordination problem efficiently. The focus of our research program has been to understand why markets and other social institutions sometimes do not work as well as we would like. Given the complexity of the economy, no one should expect to find a single explanation of any of the macroeconomic phenomena under study. There is no Holy Grail. But new Keynesian economists, whether of the first or the second type as described in this chapter agree on two broad propositions.

First, they agree that the Walrasian auctioneer does not really exist, and that 'as if' stories about the auctioneer are a fiction that has too long misled the profession. Instead, firms set prices and wages in an un-coordinated fashion, facing considerable uncertainties about the consequences of their actions. As a result, it will often be true that wages, prices, and interest rates are not at market clearing levels (and will not adjust rapidly to those levels), so that large parts of the economy will not be in equilibrium.

Second, they agree that problems of coordinating prices and wages simply cannot be studied in the context of a macroeconomy consisting only of an aggregated representative agent, like Robinson Crusoe. It is not even clear that an island with Robinson Crusoe and Friday provides a fertile basis for studying macroeconomic problems, though at least this opens the possibility of problems such as those associated with asymmetric information. Indeed, at the core of the models discussed here is the notion that redistributions of wealth across firms and between households and firms matter, and they matter because there is a corporate veil created by imperfect information. Aggregate approaches using representative agent models are not of much use in studying these macroeconomic phenomena.

The strand of new Keynesian literature discussed and advocated here attempts to shift the focus of the research program in two ways. It argues for shifting the analysis of these issues from the product market to the capital and labor markets. In addition, it argues for shifting away from a single-minded pursuit of the consequences and causes of price rigidities; in fact, the analysis here suggests that greater price flexibility might exacerbate the problem of economic fluctuations.[25, 26] Instead, we believe that the focus should be on how imperfections in information limit, and sometimes even eliminate, the markets which distribute risk in modern economies; how these market imperfections serve to amplify the shocks facing the economy and make their effects persist; and how, when translated to the labor market and combined with information and other problems there, they can give rise to high levels of unemployment.

NOTES

1 For a devastating attack on the underlying methodological premises of the representative agent approach, see Kirman (1992).

2 The term 'constrained' in the concept of 'constrained Pareto efficiency' is simply inserted to remind readers that the constraints – absence of a complete set of markets, the imperfections of information, and so on – were indeed taken into account. Even when the government faces these constraints, when the economy is not constrained Pareto efficient, there exist interventions in the market which can make all individuals better off. There are, to be sure, innumerable papers in the literature showing that with incomplete markets and imperfect information, the economy may be constrained Pareto efficient. The point of the Greenwald-Stiglitz (1986) paper was to show that these papers all entail special assumptions; and that in general, the market economy is not constrained Pareto efficient.

3 Some new Keynesians are wont to claim that this insistence on micro-foundations is what distinguishes them from Keynes and the older Keynesians. Though much macroeconomic analysis in the Keynesian tradition in the 1950s and 1960s did stray from a solid grounding in micro-foundations, Keynes himself clearly argued each of his macroeconomic relations on the basis of microeconomic analysis. In fact, we would argue that Keynes did the best he could with the micro-foundations which were available at the time. Macroeconomists of the 1950s and 1960s faced a dilemma: the microeconomics that was fashionable at that time – assuming perfect information, complete markets, and so on – was obviously inconsistent with the spirit of the Keynesian model. It made sense for them to ignore that kind of microeconomics.

4 There are still other strands emphasizing, for example, imperfect competition or coordination failures.

5 For example, Hansen (1951), Solow and Stiglitz (1968), Barro and Grossman (1971), and the large subsequent literature surveyed in Benassy (1982).

6 In taking this approach, this second strand of new Keynesian thought addresses one of the major criticisms of real business cycle theory – that real shocks to the economy are simply not large enough to account for the magnitude of the observed fluctuations. Standard neoclassical models have strong forces working to stabilize the economy: price adjustments act like shock absorbers; savings and inventories act as buffers; lags mean that even a major new innovation will take years to be absorbed into the economy; and many shocks have offsetting effects in different sectors, implying limited aggregative impacts.

7 For a more detailed discussion of the arguments presented in this section, and the empirical evidence in its support, as well as a more complete list of references, see Greenwald and Stiglitz (1987, 1988b, 1988c, 1989, 1990a, 1990b, 1991a, 1993), Stiglitz (1992a), and Greenwald *et al.* (1984).

8 One explanation for why firms do not issue equities upon which we do not put much credence is the costly state verification model, which notes that using equity requires verifying the state (the firm's profits), so the costs of implementing equity contracts thus exceed that of debt contracts. While this argument has some relevance for small businesses, firms that have already issued equity have little or no marginal cost of verifying their state when they seek to issue additional equity.

9 A major lacuna in this theory is the failure to explain why debt contracts are denominated in nominal terms. However, there are models, such as Cooper (1990), which show that there may be Nash equilibrium with imperfect indexing; that is, given that all other contracts are not indexed, firms would not want to just index debt contracts.

10 The story, as presented thus far, is not quite complete: Why don't workers cut the wages at which they are willing to work, and thus make it worthwhile for the firm to hire them even though costs of capital are high? There are several answers: the required reductions in wages are so large that workers prefer to wait (what they expect to be the short time) until the costs of hiring are lowered; workers are not willing to put up the cost of being hired for a whole variety of reasons, from lack of capital, worker risk aversion, and firm moral hazard; workers cannot reduce the firm's risk of hiring by making wages contingent upon the performance of the firm, for that would entail, in effect, workers taking an equity share in the firm, and all the arguments for why equity markets fail apply with equal force here; and workers cannot even commit themselves to charging only a low wage, once they are trained, as insider-outsider theories have emphasized.

11 For a more extensive development of these ideas, see Stiglitz (1988, 1992a) and Stiglitz and Weiss (1992a, 1992b).

12 Of course, this story raises the question of why firms facing credit constraints from their banks do not turn to other sources of funds. We have explained why equity is not a viable alternative. Other sources of funds are even less informed about creditworthiness; they are likely to make credit available only under much less favorable terms, or not at all. Adverse selection works to exacerbate other sources of credit, too; the firms that avail themselves of these alternative supplies are those in dire straits.

13 Open market operations will have a similar net wealth effect on banks. However, this will occur only to the extent that rates of interest paid on demand deposit are held below their competitive levels, by either direct legal fiat or limitations on interbank competition. With zero interest on demand deposits, increases in deposits (if believed to be permanent) represent equal increases in effective bank equity; thus money supply expansions represent a particularly powerful wealth transfer from households to banking firms. (Letting W = bank wealth derived from deposits, r = interest rate, D = deposits, $W = r (D / r) = D$). If the monetary policy is believed to be temporary, then there may be no significant wealth effect ($\Delta W = \Delta M \cdot r + \Delta r \cdot M$; when r is near zero, this is near zero). However, if rates paid on demand deposits are competitive either because, as recently, they are deregulated or because, as in the Depression, a zero nominal rate is close to the competitive rate of interest, increases in demand deposits through open market operations will have no significant effect on bank wealth.

14 At one level of analysis, the insights of this model can be viewed as a mild modification of standard IS-LM theory. The LM curve is now derived not as the equilibrium in the money market – the locus of interest rates and income levels at which the demand for money equals the supply of money; but rather as the equilibrium in the capital market – the locus of interest rates and income levels at which the capital market is in equilibrium; for the capital market to be in equilibrium the demand for reserves must be equal to the supply (otherwise banks would change their behavior) and the demand for Treasury bills held by the public must be equal to the supply.

Operationally, the standard IS-LM curves differ in two fundamental ways from the ones implicit in our analysis. First, we have identified a set of variables – balance sheet variables of firms and banks, and the dispersion in those variables – which affect both the IS and LM curves, and can cause them to shift markedly. Second, monetary policy may shift the IS curve: firm investment depends on the interest rates charged by banks and the credit they make available. The interest rate charged by banks is not just the government interest rate. There may be marked changes in the spread (for instance, they increased in 1991, so that bank loan rates fell much less than did government interest rates).

Monetary policy may affect not only the Treasury bill rate, but also the spread, so that monetary policy, in effect, shifts the IS curve as well.

15 Workers' efforts may be reduced if they receive less than what they perceive to be a fair wage; while they may respond to higher wages with higher effort as part of a 'gift exchange' (Akerlof 1982).

16 The precise mechanism differs among the different theories. For instance, in the Shapiro and Stiglitz (1984) efficiency wage theory, it is the risk of being fired, and with it loss of total rents which provides workers incentives not to shirk. But part-time workers, with the same surplus per hour, have a lower total level of surplus. Certain changes in the economic environment which necessitate an increase in the wages to induce workers not to shirk will necessitate a larger increase in the wages of part-time workers, and thus, these workers become less attractive – their costs, adjusted for quality, increase.

17 One group of theories not discussed here, which should be mentioned briefly, are those focusing on imperfect competition. For many of the central issues with which macroeconomics is concerned, we do not believe that imperfect competition is central. For example, imperfect competition can hardly explain the cyclical movements in output and employment. While prices might be different from what they would be in perfect competition, imperfect competition in the product market cannot explain why the labor market does not clear. While the classical dichotomy has traditionally been couched in terms of models with perfect competition, one can prove analogous results from general equilibrium models with imperfect competition. However, we do view imperfect competition as important to the extent that it allows firms to set prices and wages. As explained earlier, the price and wage setting behavior of risk averse firms has important macroeconomic consequences.

18 This result can also be seen as a direct corollary of the Greenwald and Stiglitz (1986) analysis of the welfare economics of economies with imperfect information and incomplete markets. We show there that under those conditions the economy is not (constrained) Pareto efficient, and that whenever this is true, pecuniary externalities matter.

19 In some important cases, however, the economy exhibits nominal rigidities even in the long run. In effect, these are cases of multiple equilibria. If each firm believes other firms are going to keep their nominal wages rigid, it pays each firm to keep its own nominal wages unchanged. There are thus equilibrium exhibiting nominal wage rigidities (Stiglitz 1985). Similarly, if each firm believes other firms are going to keep their nominal prices unchanged, it pays each firm to keep his nominal prices unchanged. There are thus Nash equilibrium nominal price rigidities (Stiglitz 1987).

20 One empirical objection to standard menu cost theory (which is addressed by our theory) is that while the theory would seem to explain rigidities in the adjustments in the level of prices; it has a hard time explaining inflation inertia – that is, rigidities in adjustments of the rate of change of prices.

21 Of course, nominal rigidities in wages *and* prices give rise to real wage rigidities. See Solow and Stiglitz (1968) for a model incorporating explicitly stickiness in both. Of course, if the costs of adjusting wages and prices differ, one would not expect the same degree of stickiness in both markets, and thus, one would expect systematic changes in real wages in response to particular economic disturbances.

22 For a more extended critique of the standard theory of the household's demand for money, see Greenwald and Stiglitz (1991b).

23 For an introduction to the claims and difficulties of real business cycle theory, see the exchange between Plosser and Mankiw in the Summer 1989 issue of *Journal of Economic Perspectives*. Other criticisms, besides those mentioned in the text, include the lack of correlation across countries of the implied shocks to

different industries (which one would expect if the shocks were really technology shocks), compared to the correlation of industries within a country. Also, this school has failed to identify large positive shocks of the required magnitude. (Remember that once one takes into account the shock absorbers, buffers, and lags, and that much of technology is 'embodied', then the implied shocks to technology must indeed be large.) Furthermore, negative technology shocks move the factor price frontier inward; that would imply that if real product wages remain unchanged, real interest rates would have to fall markedly. But in fact, while real interest rates vary little in many recessions, in other recessions, like the Great Depression and the 1982 recession, real interest rates rose.

24 At times, Keynes seems inconsistent in his discussion of expectations. For example, in discussions of the liquidity trap, it was argued that the value of long-term bonds – consols – was inversely proportional to the short-term interest rate, a result which can be justified on the basis of *static* expectations concerning interest rates (that is, the expectation that future interest rates will, on average, be equal to current interest rates) and risk neutrality. It was then argued that, when interest rates were very low, investors were worried that the interest rate would rise, giving rise to a fall in the price of consols. But if investors expect interest rates to fall, then the price of consols will not be inversely proportional to the short-term interest rate, and changes in the short-term interest rate will have negligible effects on the price of consols.

25 Thus, the work described in this chapter can be thought of as providing the theoretical underpinnings of one of the standard interpretations of the Great Depression and other major economic downturns, the debt-deflation theories. See for example, Calomiris (1993) and the papers cited there. (Of course, the effects we describe do not require actual deflation, only a slowdown in the rate of inflation relative to that anticipated.)

26 Keynes seemed to be of that view when he concluded, 'In the light of these considerations, I am now of the opinion that the maintenance of a stable general level of money wages is, on balance of considerations, the most advisable policy for a closed system.' Clearly, Keynes did not consider the central problem one of lack of wage (and price) flexibility.

REFERENCES

Akerlof, G. A., 'Labor Contracts as Partial Gift Exchange', *Quarterly Journal of Economics*, 97:4, November 1982, 543–69.

Akerlof, G. A. and J. Yellen, 'A Near-Rational Model of the Business Cycle with Wage and Price Inertia', *Quarterly Journal of Economics* 1985, *100*, 823–38.

Barro, R. J. and H. I. Grossman, 'A General Disequilibrium Model of Income and Employment', *American Economic Review* 1971, *61*, 82–93.

Benassy, Jean-Pascal, *The Economics of Market Disequilibrium*, New York: Academic Press, 1982.

Blinder, A. S. and L. J. Maccini, 'Taking Stock: A Critical Assessment of Recent Research on Inventories', *Journal of Economic Perspectives* Winter 1991, 5:1, 73–96.

Calomiris, Charles W., 'Financial Factors in the Great Depression', *Journal of Economic Perspectives* Spring 1993, 7:2.

Cooper, Russell, 'Predetermined Wages and Prices and the Impact of Expansionary Government Policy', *Review of Economic Studies* April 1990, *57*, 205–14.

Grandmont, Jean-Michel, 'Money and Value: A Reconsideration of Classical and Neoclassical Monetary Theories', Cambridge: Cambridge University Press, 1983.

Greenwald, B. and J. E. Stiglitz, 'Externalities in Economies with Imperfect Information and Incomplete Markets', *Quarterly Journal of Economics* 101:2, May 1986, 229–64.

Greenwald, B. and J. E. Stiglitz, 'Imperfect Information, Credit Markets and Unemployment', *European Economic Review* February/March 1987, 31:2, 444–56.

Greenwald, B. and J. E. Stiglitz, 'Pareto Inefficiency of Market Economies: Search and Efficiency Wage Models', *American Economic Review* 78:2, May 1988a, 351–55.

Greenwald, B. and J. E. Stiglitz, 'Examining Alternative Macroeconomic Theories', *Brookings Papers on Economic Activity* 1988b, no. 1, 207–70.

Greenwald, B. and J. E. Stiglitz, 'Imperfect Information, Finance Constraints and Business Fluctuations', in Meir Kohn and S. C. Tsiang (eds) *Finance Constraints, Expectations and Macroeconomics*, Oxford: Oxford University Press, 1988c, 103–40.

Greenwald, B. and J. E. Stiglitz, 'Toward a Theory of Rigidities', *American Economic Review* May 1989, 79:2, 364–69.

Greenwald, B. and J. E. Stiglitz, 'Macroeconomic Models with Equity and Credit Rationing', in R. Glenn Hubbard (ed.) *Information, Capital Markets and Investments*, Chicago: University of Chicago Press, 1990a, 15–42.

Greenwald, B. and J. E. Stiglitz, 'Asymmetric Information and the New Theory of the Firm: Financial Constraints and Risk Behavior', *American Economic Review* May 1990b, 80:2, 160–65.

Greenwald, B. and J. E. Stiglitz, 'Capital Market Imperfections and Labor Market Adjustments', paper presented at NBER/CEPR Conference on Labor Market Dynamics, Cambridge, Massachusetts, October 1991a, in *Conference Proceedings*.

Greenwald, B. and J. E. Stiglitz, 'Towards a Reformulation of Monetary Economics', Caffee Lectures presented to the University of Rome and the Bank of Italy, April 1991b, Cambridge: Cambridge University Press, 1992.

Greenwald, B. and J. E. Stiglitz, 'Financial Market Imperfections and Business Cycles', *Quarterly Journal of Economics* 108:1, 1993, 77–114.

Greenwald, B. and J. E. Stiglitz and A. Weiss, 'Informational Imperfections in the Capital Markets and Macroeconomic Fluctuations', *American Economic Review* May 1984, 74:1, 194–99.

Hansen, Bent, *A Study on the Theory of Inflation*, London: Allen Press, 1951.

Jensen, Michael C., 'Agency Costs of Free Cash Flow, Corporate Finance and Takeovers', *American Economic Review* May 1986, 76, 323–29.

King, R. G., 'Will the New Keynesian Macroeconomics Resurrect the IS-LM Model?', *Journal of Economic Perspectives* Winter 1993, 7:1, 67–82.

Kirman, A., 'Whom or What does the Representative Consumer Represent?', *Journal of Economic Perspectives* Spring 1992, 6:2, 117–36.

Lindbeck, Assar, 'Macroeconomic Theory and Labor Markets', *European Economic Review* 1992, 36:2/3, 209–36.

Mankiw, N. Gregory, 'Real Business Cycles: A New Keynesian Perspective', *Journal of Economic Perspectives* Summer 1989, 3:3, 79–90.

Neary, P. and J. E. Stiglitz, 'Expectations, Asset Accumulation and the Real Balance Effect', Presented at the Dublin Meetings of the Econometric Society, September 1982.

Neary, P. and J. E. Stiglitz, 'Toward a Reconstruction of Keynesian Economics: Expectations and Constrained Equilibria', *Quarterly Journal of Economics* Supplement 1983, 98: 3, 199–228.

Newbery, D. and J. E. Stiglitz, 'Wage Rigidity, Implicit Contracts, Unemployment and Economic Efficiency', *Economic Journal* June 1987, 97:386, 416–30.

Plosser, C. I., 'Understanding Real Business Cycles', *Journal of Economic Perspectives* Summer 1989, 3:3, 51–77.

Romer, D., 'The New Keynesian Synthesis', *Journal of Economic Perspectives* Winter 1993, 7:1, 5–22.

Ross, S. A., 'The Economic Theory of Agency: The Principal's Problem', *American Economic Review* May 1973, *63*:2, 134–39.

Shapiro, C. and J. E. Stiglitz, 'Equilibrium Unemployment as a Worker Discipline Device', *American Economic Review* June 1984, *74*:3, 433–44. Reprinted in N. G. Mankiw and D. Romer (eds) *New Keynesian Economics, 2*, Cambridge: MIT Press, 1991, 123–42.

Solow, R. and J. E. Stiglitz, 'Output, Employment and Wages in the Short Run', *Quarterly Journal of Economics* XLXXXII, November 1968, 537–60.

Stiglitz, J. E., 'Incentives and Risk Sharing in Sharecropping', *Review of Economic Studies* April 1974, *41*:2 219–55.

Stiglitz, J. E., 'Equilibrium Wage Distribution', *Economic Journal* September 1985, *95*:379, 595–618.

Stiglitz, J. E., 'Competition and the Number of Firms in a Market: Are Duopolies More Competitive than Atomistic Markets?', *Journal of Political Economy* October 1987, *95*:5, 1041–61.

Stiglitz, J. E., 'Money, Credit and Business Fluctuations', *Economic Record* December 1988, 307–22.

Stiglitz, J. E., 'Methodological Issues and the New Keynesian Economics', in A. Vercelli and N. Dimitri (eds) *Macroeconomics: A Survey of Research Strategies* Oxford: Oxford University Press, 1992a.

Stiglitz, J. E., 'Capital Markets and Economic Fluctuations in Capitalist Economies', *European Economic Review* North-Holland, *36*, 1992b, 269–306. (Marshall Lecture prepared for the European Economic Association Annual Meeting, Cambridge, UK, August 1991.)

Stiglitz, J. E. and A. Weiss, 'Credit Rationing in Markets with Imperfect Information, *American Economic Review* June 1981, *71*:3, 393–410.

Stiglitz, J. E. and A. Weiss, 'Banks as Social Accountants and Screening Devices and the General Theory of Credit Rationing' in *Essays in Monetary Economics in Honor of Sir John Hicks*, Oxford: Oxford University Press, 1992a.

Stiglitz, J. E. and A. Weiss, 'Asymmetric Information in Credit Markets and Its Implications for Macroeconomics', *Oxford Economic Papers*, October 1992b (Special Issue), *44*.4. Reprinted in A. S. Courakis (ed.) *Financial Markets, Institutions, and Policy*, Oxford: Oxford University Press, 1993.

Part VI

The renaissance of economic growth analysis

Introduction

In 1987 the Nobel Prize for Economics was awarded to Robert Solow for his contributions to the theory of economic growth, the most important of which were made in the 1950s (see Solow 1956; 1957). Solow's research proved to be highly influential and led to the development of the neoclassical growth model which following the demise of the Harrod-Domar approach, has remained the most popular basic framework for studying economic growth (for an introduction to neoclassical growth theory see Gordon 1993; Barro and Grilli 1994; Jansen *et al.* 1994; Mankiw 1994; Abel and Bernanke 1995; Froyen 1995).

As we noted in Chapter 1 of this volume, there has been a reawakening of economists' interest into the long-run issue of growth since about the mid-1980s. This work, known as *endogenous* growth theory, has sought to provide a better understanding of the growth process and in so doing holds out the prospect of providing insights which may be invaluable in helping to design policies which could make a significant difference to the long-term growth rate (see Crafts 1996). Solow's neoclassical model shows how capital accumulation could raise an economy's growth rate in the medium term but generates the prediction that the long-run (steady state) rate of growth is constrained by the rate of growth of the labour force if the production function exhibits diminishing returns to the variable factor, constant returns to scale and zero technical progress. Hence technical progress which is assumed exogenous in the Solow model came to be seen as the main driving force of long-run growth. Following Solow's (1957) article, where he showed how the aggregate production function could be decomposed so that the contribution of the various factor inputs towards the growth of output could be calculated, it was discovered that a large part of measured growth was left unexplained. This 'Solow residual', representing the growth of total factor productivity, was viewed as a measure of technical progress. But since technological change was exogenous, it meant that a large part of economic growth remained unexplained in the neoclassical model. The Solow residual, extracted by growth accounting procedures, was in Abramovitz's words a 'measure of our ignorance about the causes of growth' (see Abramovitz 1956; Fagerberg 1994). Endogenous growth theory has attempted to get round some of these difficulties by reasserting the importance of capital accumulation, proposing various ways of endogenizing technological change, emphasizing the role of human capital and stressing the importance of research and development. As a result endogenous growth theory raises the prospect that *sustained* differences in the levels and growth rates of national income are possible. This is in contrast to the Solow model where (conditional) *convergence* across countries is implied with respect to either growth rates or income levels (see Mankiw *et al.* 1992; Mankiw 1995). The large observed differences in income between countries which persist is a problem for the Solow model, where a country's growth rate of per capita income should be inversely related to its initial or starting level of income per head. In the absence of shocks poor countries should tend to converge with rich countries in terms of levels of per capita income.

The first article reprinted in this final part is the classic 1986 article by Moses Abramovitz first published in the *Journal of Economic History*. In it Abramovitz examines the catch-up hypothesis which asserts that 'being backward in the level of productivity carries a *potential* for rapid advance'. Hence *productivity growth rates* across countries should be inversely related to initial *levels* of productivity. Given that the United States is the world leader in terms of productivity levels, other countries have the opportunity to catch up providing they utilize unexploited technology. Providing the low productivity countries have the 'social capability' to exploit the opportunities available to them converging incomes and productivity should be observed. Abramovitz examines the experience of a group of industrialized countries over the past 100 years and finds support for the convergence of productivity levels implied by the catch-up hypothesis particularly in the quarter century following the Second World War.

Steve Dowrick's article from the May 1992 issue of the *Economic Journal* (reprinted on pp. 604–15) draws attention to the diverging growth paths of the world's economies which have led to a widening of income disparities. Dowrick's growth accounting exercise isolates the main features and patterns of world economic growth. In particular they show that there is supporting evidence for the technological spillover hypothesis and that the poorest countries have tended to experience faster growth in total factor productivity. However, this has not prevented income divergence due to lower rates of investment and labour force participation in the poorest countries compared to richer countries (see also Baumol 1986; Baumol *et al.* 1994).

As noted above, the neoclassical growth model, relying as it does on exogenous population growth and technological change to explain long-run growth, leaves little room for government intervention to enhance growth performance. Keith Shaw's 1992 *Economic Journal* paper (reprinted on pp. 616–27) examines the policy implications implied by the new endogenous theories of growth. After first reviewing traditional and new growth theories, Shaw goes on to discuss how differences in public policy can influence the '*incentives* to acquire capital in both physical and human forms'. This is particularly important in less advanced economies where protectionist activity could lead to the transfer of skilled labour resources from the knowledge-creating sector to the manufacturing sector leading to a decline in growth-enhancing innovation. Also important is tax policy which by affecting decisions to invest can have 'real and permanent effects on the level and growth rate of income' (see also Stern 1991).

Paul Romer is widely acknowledged to be the leading figure in the new growth economics. In his 1994 *Journal of Economic Perspectives* article (reprinted on pp. 628–48) Romer traces the origins of the new ideas which have dominated this branch of macroeconomic analysis during recent years. Romer recounts two explanations which have been put forward to account for the origin of these new theories. The first explanation, primarily empirical in character, relates to the convergence controversy (discussed earlier). The second is linked to the various theoretical attempts to replace the model of perfect competition at the aggregate level. With respect to the former issue of convergence Romer argues that this controversy 'captures only part of what endogenous growth has been all about' and in many respects 'represents a digression from the main story behind endogenous growth theory'. Romer argues that a significant factor driving the new literature has been the desire to accommodate the fact that technological change comes from what people actually do and that many individuals and firms have market power and do not operate as price takers as in perfect competition. In order to understand the important growth enhancing processes of discovery, diffusion and technological advance, Romer argues that economists must incorporate models of imperfect competition into the analysis of economic growth. Such models are more consistent with the empirical evidence and also call into question traditional perfectly competitive neoclassical models where market incentives and government policies have little impact on the crucial growth enhancing activities (see Nelson and Romer 1996).

The final article is by Robert Solow and is also taken from the 1994 *Journal of Economic Perspectives* symposium on the analysis of economic growth (reprinted on pp. 649–59). Solow seeks to place the new ideas on endogenous growth in historical perspective. To do this Solow divides the history of modern growth analysis into three waves, namely the Harrod-Domar impulse, the neoclassical response and newer alternatives, i.e. endogenous growth theories. Solow endorses the attempts made by endogenous growth theorists to incorporate imperfect competition into their models and also their emphasis on modelling the endogenous component of technological change. However, he is also critical of some of the assumptions arbitrarily introduced by new growth theorists. Solow concludes with a plea for more research into developing workable hypotheses which may throw light on 'good ways to model the flow of productivity-increasing innovations and improvements' (see Grossman and Helpman 1994).

REFERENCES

*Titles marked with an asterisk are particularly recommended for additional reading.

*Abel, A. B. and B. S. Bernanke (1995) *Macroeconomics*, 2nd edn, Chapter 6, New York: Addison Wesley.

Abramovitz, M. (1956) 'Resource and Output Trends in the United States since 1870', *American Economic Review*, 46, May, pp. 5–23.

Abramovitz, M. (1986) 'Catching Up, Forging Ahead, and Falling Behind', *Journal of Economic History* 46, June, pp. 385–406.

Barro, R. J. and V. Grilli (1994) *European Macroeconomics*, Chapter 14, London: Macmillan.

Barro, R. J. and X. Sala-i-Martin (1995) *Economic Growth*, New York: McGraw-Hill.

*Baumol, W. J. (1986) 'Productivity Growth, Convergence and Welfare: What the Long Run Data Show', *American Economic Review* 76, December, pp. 1072–85.

Baumol, W. J., R. R. Nelson and E. N. Wolff (eds) (1994) *Convergence of Productivity: Cross-National Studies and Historical Evidence*, New York: Oxford University Press.

Boltho, A. and G. Holtham (1992) 'New Approaches to Economic Growth', *Oxford Review of Economic Policy* 8, Winter, pp. 1–14.

*Crafts, N. (1996) 'Post-Neoclassical Endogenous Growth Theory: What are its Policy Implications?', *Oxford Review of Economic Policy* 12, pp. 30–47.

Crafts, N. and G. Toniolo (eds) (1996) *Economic Growth in Europe since 1945*, Cambridge: Cambridge University Press.

*Fagerberg, J. (1994) 'Technology and International Differences in Growth Rates', *Journal of Economic Literature* 32, September, pp. 1147–75.

*Froyen, R.T. (1995) *Macroeconomics: Theories and Policies*, 5th edn, Chapter 17, London: Prentice Hall.

*Gordon, R. J. (1993) *Macroeconomics*, 6th edn, Chapter 12, New York: HarperCollins.

Grossman, G. and E. Helpman (1994) 'Endogenous Innovation in the Theory of Growth', *Journal of Economic Perspectives* 8, Winter, pp. 23–44.

*Jansen, D. W., C. D. Delorme and R. B. Ekelund, Jr (1994) *Intermediate Macroeconomics*, Chapter 18, New York: West.

Lucas, R.E. Jr (1993) 'Making a Miracle', *Econometrica* 61, March, pp. 251–72.

*Mankiw, N. G. (1994) *Macroeconomics*, 2nd edn, Chapter 4, New York: Worth.

*Mankiw, N. G. (1995) 'The Growth of Nations', *Brookings Papers on Economic Activity* pp. 275–326.

Mankiw, N. G., D. Romer and D. N. Weil (1992) 'A Contribution to the Empirics of Economic Growth', *Quarterly Journal of Economics* 107, May, pp. 407–37.

*Nelson, R. R. and P. M. Romer (1996) 'Science, Economic Growth and Public Policy', *Challenge* March–April, pp. 9–21.

Rebelo, S. (1991) 'Long Run Policy Analysis and Long Run Growth', *Journal of Political Economy* 99, June, pp. 500–21.

Solow, R. (1956) 'A Contribution to the Theory of Economic Growth', *Quarterly Journal of Economics* 70, February, pp. 65–94.

Solow, R. (1957) 'Technical Change and the Aggregate Production Function', *Review of Economics and Statistics* 39, August, pp. 312–20.

Stern, N. (1991) 'The Determinants of Growth', *Economic Journal* 101, January, pp. 122–33.

QUESTIONS

1 'Differences among countries in productivity levels create a strong potentiality for subsequent convergence of levels, provided that countries have a social capability adequate to absorb more advanced technologies' (Abramovitz 1986). Explain and discuss.

2 Does convergence of productivity levels extend beyond the convergence club of free market industrialized countries?

3 'One strength of Solow's version of the neoclassical growth model is that, despite its simplicity, it has many predictions' (Mankiw 1995). What are the predictions of the neoclassical growth model?

4 What are the main sources of growth in the Solow neoclassical growth model?

5 To what extent have endogenous growth theories been successful in accounting for the long-run growth of per capita incomes without the need to invoke exogenous technological progress?

6 'Better supply-side policies tend to have their pay-off in the far distant future' (Crafts 1996). Does this mean that the short-termism of politicians will always provide an obstacle to faster long-run growth?

7 What are the policy implications of endogenous growth theory?

8 'The main engine of growth is the accumulation of human capital – of knowledge – and the main source of differences in living standards among nations is differences in human capital. Physical capital accumulation plays an essential but decidedly subsidiary role' (Lucas 1993). Is this the essential message of recent research into the growth process?

9 What factors led to the reawakening of economists' interest into the long-run issue of growth in the mid-1980s? What progress has been made?

10 'Economic growth is the part of macroeconomics that really matters' (Barro and Sala-i-Martin 1995). Critically examine this view.

23 Catching up, forging ahead, and falling behind

Moses Abramovitz
Journal of Economic History (1986) 46, June, pp. 385–406

A widely entertained hypothesis holds that, in comparisons among countries, productivity growth rates tend to vary inversely with productivity levels. A century of experience in a group of presently industrialized countries supports this hypothesis and the convergence of productivity levels it implies. The rate of convergence, however, varied from period to period and showed marked strength only during the first quarter-century following World War II. The general process of convergence was also accompanied by dramatic shifts in countries' productivity rankings. This chapter extends the simple catch-up hypothesis to rationalize the fluctuating strength of the process and explores the connections between convergence itself and the relative success of early leaders and latecomers.

Among the many explanations of the surge of productivity growth during the quarter-century following World War II, the most prominent is the hypothesis that the countries of the industrialized 'West' were able to bring into production a large backlog of unexploited technology. The principal part of this backlog is deemed to have consisted of methods of production and of industrial and commercial organization already in use in the United States at the end of the war, but not yet employed in the other countries of the West. In this hypothesis, the United States is viewed as the 'leader', the other countries as 'followers' who had the opportunity to 'catch up'. In conformity with this view, a waning of the opportunity for catching up is frequently advanced as an explanation of the retardation in productivity growth suffered by the same group of followers since 1973. Needless to say, the size of the initial backlog and its subsequent reduction are rarely offered as sole explanations of the speedup and slowdown, but they stand as important parts of the story.

These views about postwar following and catching up suggest a more general hypothesis that the productivity levels of countries tend to converge. And this in turn brings to mind old questions about the emergence of new leaders and the historical and theoretical puzzles that shifts in leadership and relative standing present – matters that in some respects fit only awkwardly with the convergence hypothesis.

The pertinence of all these questions to an understanding of modern economic growth obviously demands their continued study. The immediate occasion for this chapter, however, is the appearance of Angus Maddison's compilation of historical time series of the levels and growth of labor productivity covering sixteen industrialized countries from 1870 to 1979.[1] These data enable us to observe the catch-up process in quantitative terms over a much longer span of time than was possible hitherto. At the same time, the evidence of Maddison's tables raises again the historical puzzles posed by productivity leadership and its shifts.

THE CATCH-UP HYPOTHESIS

The hypothesis asserts that being backward in level of productivity carries a *potential* for rapid advance. Stated more definitely the proposition is that in comparisons across countries the growth rates of productivity in any long period tend to be inversely related to the initial levels of productivity.

The central idea is simple enough. It has to do with the level of technology embodied in a country's capital stock. Imagine that the level of labor productivity were governed entirely by the level of technology embodied in capital stock. In a 'leading country', to state things sharply, one may suppose that the technology embodied in each vintage of its stock was at the very frontier of technology at the time of investment. The *technological* age of the stock is, so to speak, the same as its *chronological* age. In an otherwise similar follower whose productivity level is lower, the technological age of the stock is high relative to its chronological age. The stock is obsolete even for its age. When a leader discards old stock and replaces it, the accompanying productivity increase is governed and limited by the advance of knowledge between the time when the old capital was installed and the time it is replaced. Those who are behind, however, have the potential to make a larger leap. New capital can embody the frontier of knowledge, but the capital it replaces was technologically superannuated. So – the larger the technological and, therefore, the productivity gap between leader and follower, the stronger the follower's potential for growth in productivity; and, other things being equal, the faster one expects the follower's growth rate to be. Followers tend to catch up faster if they are initially more backward.

Viewed in the same simple way, the catch-up process would be self-limiting because as a follower catches up, the possibility of making large leaps by replacing superannuated with best-practice technology becomes smaller and smaller. A follower's potential for growth weakens as its productivity level converges towards that of the leader.

This is the simple central idea. It needs extension and qualification. There are at least four extensions:

1 The same technological opportunity that permits rapid progress by modernization encourages rapid growth of the capital stock partly because of the returns to modernization itself, and partly because technological

progress reduces the price of capital goods relative to the price of labor. So – besides a reduction of technological age towards chronological age, the rate of rise of the capital–labor ratio tends to be higher. Productivity growth benefits on both counts. And if circumstances make for an acceleration in the growth of the capital stock its chronological age also falls.[2]

2 Growth of productivity also makes for increase in aggregate output. A broader horizon of scale-dependent technological progress then comes into view.

3 Backwardness carries an opportunity for modernization in disembodied, as well as in embodied, technology.

4 If countries at relatively low levels of industrialization contain large numbers of redundant workers in farming and petty trade, as is normally the case, there is also an opportunity for productivity growth by improving the allocation of labor.

Besides extension, the simple hypothesis also needs qualification.

First, technological backwardness is not usually a mere accident. Tenacious societal characteristics normally account for a portion, perhaps a substantial portion, of a country's past failure to achieve as high a level of productivity as economically more advanced countries. The same deficiencies, perhaps in attenuated form, normally remain to keep a backward country from making the full technological leap envisaged by the simple hypothesis. I have a name for these characteristics. Following Kazushi Ohkawa and Henry Rosovsky, I call them 'social capability'.[3] One can summarize the matter in this way. Having regard to technological backwardness alone leads to the simple hypothesis about catch-up and convergence already advanced. Having regard to social capability, however, we expect that the developments anticipated by that hypothesis will be clearly displayed in cross-country comparisons only if countries' social capabilities are about the same. One should say, therefore, that a country's potential for rapid growth is strong not when it is backward without qualification, but rather when it is technologically backward but socially advanced.

The trouble with absorbing social capability into the catch-up hypothesis is that no one knows just what it means or how to measure it. In past work I identified a country's social capability with technical competence, for which – at least among Western countries – years of education may be a rough proxy, and with its political, commercial, industrial, and financial institutions, which I characterized in more qualitative ways.[4] I had in mind mainly experience with the organization and management of large-scale enterprise and with financial institutions and markets capable of mobilizing capital for individual firms on a similarly large scale. On some occasions the situation for a selection of countries may be sufficiently clear. In explaining postwar growth in Europe and Japan, for example, one may be able to say with some confidence that these countries were competent to absorb and exploit then existing best-practice technology. More generally, however, judgments about social capability remain highly problematic. A few comments may serve to suggest some of the considerations involved as well as the speculative nature of the subject.

One concerns the familiar notion of a trade-off between specialization and adaptability. The content of education in a country and the character of its industrial, commercial, and financial organizations may be well designed to exploit fully the power of an existing technology; they may be less well fitted to adapt to the requirements of change. Presumably, some capacity to adapt is present everywhere, but countries may differ from one another in this respect, and their capacities to adapt may change over time.

Next, the notion of adaptability suggests that there is an interaction between social capability and technological opportunity. The state of education embodied in a nation's population and its existing institutional arrangements constrains it in its choice of technology. But technological opportunity presses for change. So countries learn to modify their institutional arrangements and then to improve them as they gain experience. The constraints imposed by social capability on the successful adoption of a more advanced technology gradually weaken and permit its fuller exploitation. Thorstein Veblen said it this way:

> There are two lines of agency visibly at work shaping the habits of thought of [a] people in the complex movements of readjustment and rehabilitation [required by industrialization]. These are the received scheme of use and wont and the new state of the industrial arts; and it is not difficult to see that it is the latter that makes for readjustment; nor should it be any more difficult to see that the readjustment is necessarily made under the surveillance of the received scheme of use and wont.[5]

Social capability, finally, depends on more than the content of education and the organization of firms. Other aspects of economic systems count as well – their openness to competition, to the establishment and operation of new firms, and to the sale and purchase of new goods and services. Viewed from the other side, it is a question of the obstacles to change raised by vested interests, established positions, and customary relations among firms and between employers and employees. The view from this side is what led Mancur Olson to identify defeat in war and accompanying political convulsion as a radical ground-clearing experience opening the way for new men, new organizations, and new modes of operation and trade better fitted to technological potential.[6]

These considerations have a bearing on the notion that a follower's potential for rapid growth weakens as its technological level converges on the leader's. This is not necessarily the case if social capability is itself endogenous, becoming stronger – or perhaps weaker – as technological gaps close. In the one case, the evolution of social capability connected with catching up itself raises the possibility that followers may forge ahead of even progressive leaders. In the other, a leader may fall back or a follower's pursuit may be slowed.

There is a somewhat technical point that has a similar bearing. This is the fact, noticed by Kravis and Denison, that as followers' levels of per capita income converge on the leader's, so do their structures of consumption and prices.[7] R.C.O. Matthews then observed that the convergence of consumption and production patterns should make it easier, rather than more difficult, for followers to borrow technology with advantage as productivity gaps close.[8] This, therefore, stands as still another qualification to the idea that the catch-up process is steadily self-limiting.

The combination of technological gap and social capability defines a country's *potentiality* for productivity advance by way of catch-up. This, however, should be regarded as a potentiality in the long run. The pace at which the potentiality is realized depends on still another set of causes that are largely independent of those governing the potentiality itself. There is a long story to tell about the factors controlling the rate of realization of potential.[9] Its general plot, however, can be suggested by noting three principal chapter headings:

1 The facilities for the diffusion of knowledge – for example, channels of international technical communication, multinational corporations, the state of international trade and of direct capital investment.
2 Conditions facilitating or hindering structural change in the composition of output, in the occupational and industrial distribution of the workforce, and in the geographical location of industry and population. Among other factors, this is where conditions of labor supply, the existence of labor reserves in agriculture, and the factors controlling internal and international migration come in.
3 Macroeconomic and monetary conditions encouraging and sustaining capital investment and the level and growth of effective demand.

Having considered the technological catch-up idea, with its several extensions and qualifications, I can summarize by proposing a restatement of the hypothesis as follows.

Countries that are technologically backward have a potentiality for generating growth more rapid than that of more advanced countries, provided their social capabilities are sufficiently developed to permit successful exploitation of technologies already employed by the technological leaders. The pace at which potential for catch-up is actually realized in a particular period depends on factors limiting the diffusion of knowledge, the rate of structural change, the accumulation of capital, and the expansion of demand. The process of catching up tends to be self-limiting, but the strength of the tendency may be weakened or overcome, at least for limited periods, by advantages connected with the convergence of production patterns as followers advance towards leaders or by an endogenous enlargement of social capabilities.

HISTORICAL EXPERIENCE WITH CATCHING UP

I go on now to review some evidence bearing on the catch-up process. The survey I make is limited to the sixteen countries covered by the Maddison estimates of product per worker hour for nine key years from 1870 to 1979.[10] The estimates are consistently derived as regards gross domestic product and worker hours and are adjusted as regards levels of product

Table 23.1 Comparative levels of productivity, 1870–1979 means and relative variance of the relatives of fifteen countries compared with the United States
(US GDP per manhour = 100)[a]

	(1) *Mean*	*(2)* *Coefficient of variation*[b]
1870	77 (66)	0.51 (0.51)
1890	68 (68)	0.48 (0.48)
1913	61	0.33
1929	57	0.29
1938	61	0.22
1950	46	0.36
1960	52	0.29
1973	69	0.14
1979	75	0.15

Notes: [a] 1870 and 1890. Figures in parentheses are based on relatives with the United Kingdom = 100
[b] Standard deviation divided by mean
Source: Calculated from Angus Maddison, *Phases of Capitalist Development* (New York, 1982), Tables 5.2 and C.10

Table 23.2 The association (rank correlation) between initial levels and subsequent growth rates of labor productivity
(GDP per manhour in sixteen countries, 1870–1979)

	Shorter periods		Lengthening periods since 1870	
	(1)	*(2)*		*(3)*
1870–1913	−0.59		1870–1890	−0.32
1870–1890		−0.32	−1913	−0.59
1890–1913		−0.56	−1929	−0.72
			−1938	−0.83
1913–1938	−0.70		−1950	−0.16
1913–29		−0.35	−1960	−0.66
1929–38		−0.57	−1973	−0.95
			−1979	−0.97
1938–1950	+0.48			
1950–1979	−0.92			
1950–60		−0.81		
1960–73		−0.90		
1973–79		−0.13		

Source of underlying data: Maddison, *Phases*, Tables 5.1, 5.2, and C.10

per worker hour by the Kravis estimates of purchasing power parities for postwar years. I have compressed the message of these data into three measures (see Tables 23.1 and 23.2).

1 Averages of the productivity levels of the various countries relative to that of the United States, which was the leading country for most of the period. (For 1870 and 1890, I have also calculated averages of relatives based on the United Kingdom.) I calculate these averages for each of the nine key years and use them to indicate whether productivity levels of followers, *as a group*, were tending to converge on that of the leader.[11]
2 Measures of relative variance around the mean levels of relative productivity. These provide one sort of answer to the question of whether the countries that started at relatively low levels of productivity tended to advance faster than those with initially higher levels.
3 Rank correlations between initial levels of productivity and subsequent growth rates. If the potential supposedly inherent in technological backwardness is being realized, there is likely to be some inverse correlation; and if it works with enough strength to dominate other forces the coefficients will be high.

The data I use and the measures I make have a number of drawbacks. The data, of course, have the weaknesses that are inherent in any set of estimates of GDP and manhours, however ably contrived, that stretch back far into the nineteenth century. Beyond that, however, simple calculations such as I have made fail, in a number of respects, to isolate the influence of the catch-up hypothesis proper.

To begin with, my measures do not allow for variation in the richness of countries' natural resources in relation to their populations. Labor productivity levels, therefore, are not pure reflections of levels of technology. In the same way, these levels will also reflect past accumulations of reproducible capital, both physical and human, and these may also be independent of technological levels in one degree or another. Further, the measured growth rates of labor productivity will be influenced by the pace of capital accumulation. As already said, differences in rates of accumulation may reflect countries' opportunities to make advances in technology, but rates of capital formation may also be independent, to some degree, of countries' potentials for technological advance. Finally, my measures make no allowance for countries' variant abilities to employ current best-practice technology for reasons other than the differences in social capability already discussed. Their access to economies of scale is perhaps the most important matter. If advanced technology at any time is heavily scale-dependent and if obstacles to trade across national frontiers, political or otherwise, are important, large countries will have a stronger potential for growth than smaller ones.

There are many reasons, therefore, why one cannot suppose that the expectations implied by the catch-up hypothesis will display themselves clearly in the measures I present. It will be something if the data show some systematic evidence of development consistent with the hypothesis. And it will be useful if this provides a chance to speculate about the reasons why the connections between productivity levels and growth rates appear to have been strong in some periods and weak in others.

Other countries, on the average, made no net gain on the United States in a period longer than a century (Table 23.1, col. 1). The indication of very limited, or even zero, convergence is really stronger than the figures suggest. This is because the productivity measures reflect more than gaps in technology and in reproducible capital intensity, with respect to which catch-up is presumably possible. As already said, they also reflect differences in natural resource availabilities which, of course, are generally favorable to the United States and were far more important to the United States and to all the other countries in 1870 than they are today. In 1870, the agricultural share of United States employment was 50 percent; in 1979, $3\frac{1}{2}$ percent. For the other fifteen countries, the corresponding figures are 48 and 8 percent on the average. The declines were large in all the countries.[12] So the US advantage in 1870 depended much more on our favorable land–person ratio than it did in 1979. Putting it the other way, other countries on the average must have fallen back over the century in respect to the productivity determinants in respect to which catch-up is possible.

In other respects, however, one can see the influence of the potential for catching up clearly. The variance among the productivity levels of the fifteen 'follower' countries declines drastically over the century – from a coefficient of variation of 0.5 in 1870 to 0.15 in 1979. Not only that: the decline in variance was continuous from one key year to the next, with only one reversal – in the period across World War II. In the same way, the inverse rank correlation between the initial productivity levels in 1870 and subsequent growth rates over increasingly long periods becomes stronger and stronger, until we reach the correlation coefficient of –0.97 across the entire 109 years.[13] (Again there was the single reversal across World War II when the association was actually – and presumably accidentally – positive.)

I believe the steadily declining variance measures and the steadily rising correlation coefficients should be interpreted to mean that initial productivity gaps did indeed constitute a potentiality for fast growth that had its effect later if not sooner. The effect of the potentiality became visible in a very limited degree very early. But if a country was incapable of, or prevented from, exploiting that opportunity promptly, the technological growth potential became strong, and the country's later rate of advance was all the faster. Though it may have taken a century for obstacles or inhibitions to be fully overcome, the net outcome was that levels of productivity tended steadily to even out – at least within the group of presently advanced countries in my sample.

This last phrase is important. Mine is a biased sample in that its members consist of countries all of whom have successfully entered into the process of modern economic growth. This implies that they have acquired the educational and institutional characteristics needed to make use of modern technologies to some advanced degree. It is by no means assured – indeed, it is unlikely – that a more comprehensive sample of countries would show the same tendency for levels of productivity to even out over the same period of time.[14]

This is the big picture. How do things look if we consider shorter periods? There are two matters to keep in mind: the tendency to convergence *within* the group of followers; and the convergence – or lack of it – of the group of followers *vis-à-vis* the United States. I take up the second matter in the next section. As to the convergence *within* the follower group, the figures suggest that the process varied in strength markedly from period to period. The main difference was that before World War II it operated weakly or at best with moderate strength. For almost a quarter-century following the war it apparently worked with very great strength. Why?

Before World War II, it is useful to consider two periods, roughly the decades before 1913, and those that followed. In the years of relative peace before 1913 I suggest that the process left a weak mark on the record for two reasons, both connected with the still early state of industrialization in many of the countries. First, the impress of the process was masked because farming was still so very important; measured levels of productivity, therefore, depended heavily on the amount and quality of farmland in relation to population. Productivity levels, in consequence, were erratic indicators of gaps between existing and best-practice technology. Second, social competence for exploiting the then most advanced methods was still limited, particularly in the earlier years and in the more recent latecomers. As the pre-World War I decades wore on, however, both these qualifying circumstances became less important. One might therefore have expected a much stronger tendency to convergence after 1913. But this was frustrated by the irregular effects of the Great War and of the years of disturbed political and financial conditions that followed, by the uneven impacts of the Great Depression itself and of the restrictions on international trade.

The unfulfilled potential of the years 1913–38 was then enormously enlarged by the effects of World War II. The average productivity gap behind the United States increased by 39 percent between 1938 and 1950; the poorer countries were hit harder than the richer. These were years of dispersion, not convergence.

The post-World War II decades then proved to be the period when – exceptionally – the three elements required for rapid growth by catching up came together.[15] The elements were large technological gaps; enlarged social competence, reflecting higher levels of education and greater experience with large-scale production, distribution, and finance; and conditions favoring rapid realization of potential. This last element refers to several matters. There was *on this occasion* (it was otherwise after World War I) a strong reaction to the experience of defeat in war, and a chance for political reconstruction. The postwar political and economic reorganization and reform weakened the power of monopolistic groupings, brought new men to the fore, and focused the attention of governments on the tasks of recovery and growth, as Mancur Olson has argued.[16] The facilities for the diffusion of technology improved. International markets were opened. Large labor reserves in home agriculture and immigration from Southern and Eastern Europe provided a flexible and mobile labor supply. Government support, technological opportunity, and an environment of stable international money favored heavy and sustained capital investment. The outcome was the great speed and strength of the postwar catch-up process.[17]

Looking back now on the record of more than a century, we can see that catching up was a powerful continuing element in the growth experience of the presently advanced industrial countries. The strength of the process varied from period to period. For decades it operated only erratically and with weakened force. The trouble at first lay in deficient social capability, a sluggish adaptation of education and of industrial and financial organization to the requirements of modern large-scale technology. Later, the process was checked and made irregular by the effects of the two world wars and the ensuing political and financial troubles and by the impact of the Great Depression. It was at last released after World War II. The results were the rapid growth rates of the postwar period, the close cross-country association between initial productivity levels and growth rates, and a marked reduction of differences in productivity levels, among the follower countries, and between them and the United States.

Looking to the future, it seems likely that this very success will have weakened the potentiality for growth by catching up among the group of presently advanced countries. The great opportunities carried by that potential now pass to the less developed countries of Latin America and Asia.

FORGING AHEAD AND FALLING BEHIND

The catch-up hypothesis in its simple form does not anticipate changes in leadership nor, indeed, any changes in the ranks of countries in their relative levels of productivity. It contemplates only a reduction among countries in productivity differentials. Yet there have been many changes in ranks since 1870 and, of course, the notable shift of leadership from Britain to the United States towards the end of the last century.[18] This was followed by the continuing decline of Britain's standing in the productivity scale. Today there is a widely held opinion that the United States is about to fall behind a new candidate for leadership, Japan, and that both Europe and the United States must contemplate serious injury from the rise of both Japan and a group of still newer industrializing countries.

Needless to say, this chapter cannot deal with the variety of reasons – all still speculative – for the comparative success of the countries that advanced in rank and the comparative failure of those that fell back.[19] I focus instead on a few matters that help illustrate the ramifications of the catch-up process and reveal the limitations of the simple hypothesis considered in earlier sections.

The congruity of technology and resources: United States as leader

Why did the gap between the United States and the average of other countries resist reduction so long? Indeed, why did it even appear to become larger between 1870 and 1929 – before the impact of World War II made it larger still? I offer three reasons:

1 The path of technological change which in those years offered the greatest opportunities for advance was at once heavily scale-dependent and biased in a labor-saving but capital-and resource-using direction. In both respects the United States enjoyed great advantages compared with Europe or Japan. Large-scale production was favored by a large, rapidly growing, and increasingly prosperous population. It was supported also by a striking homogeneity of tastes. This reflected the country's comparative youth, its rapid settlement by migration from a common base on the Atlantic, and the weakness and fluidity of its class divisions. Further, insofar as the population grew by immigration, the new Americans and their children quickly accepted the consumption patterns of their adopted country because the prevailing ethos favored assimilation to the dominant native white culture. At the same time, American industry was encouraged to explore the rich possibilities of a labor-saving but capital- and resource-using path of advance. The country's resources of land, forest, and minerals were particularly rich and abundant, and supplies of capital grew rapidly in response to high returns.[20]

2 By comparison with the United States and Britain, many, though not all, of the 'followers' were also latecomers in respect to social capability. In the decades following 1870, they lacked experience with large-scale production and commerce, and in one degree or another they needed to advance in levels of general and technical education.

3 World War I was a serious setback for many countries but a stimulus to growth in the United States. European recovery and growth in the following years were delayed and slowed by financial disturbances and by the impact of territorial and political change. Protection, not unification, was the response to the new political map. The rise of social democratic electoral strength in Europe favored the expansion of union power, but failed to curb the development and activities of industrial cartels. Britain's ability to support and enforce stable monetary conditions had been weakened, but the United States was not yet able or, indeed, willing to assume the role of leadership that Britain was losing. In all these ways, the response to the challenge of war losses and defeat after World War I stands in contrast to that after World War II.

Points (2) and (3) were anticipated in earlier argument, but Point (1) constitutes a qualification to the simple catch-up hypothesis. In that view, different countries, subject only to their social capability, are equally competent to exploit a leader's path of technological progress. That is not so, however, if that path is biased in resource intensity or if it is scale-dependent. Resource-rich countries will be favored in the first instance, large countries in the second. If the historical argument of this section is correct, the United States was favored on both counts for a long time; it may not be so favored in the future. Whether or not this interpretation of American experience is correct, the general proposition remains: countries have unequal abilities to pursue paths of progress that are resource-biased or scale-dependent.

Interaction between followers and leaders

The catch-up hypothesis in its simple form is concerned with only one aspect of the economic relations among countries: technological borrowing by followers. In this view, a one-way stream of benefits flows from leaders to followers. A moment's reflection, however, exposes the inadequacy of that idea. The rise of British factory-made cotton textiles in the first industrial revolution ruined the Irish linen industry. The attractions of British and American jobs denuded the Irish population of its young men. The beginnings of modern growth in Ireland suffered a protracted delay. This is an example of the negative effects of leadership on the economies of those who are behind. Besides technological borrowing, there are interactions by way of trade and its rivalries, capital flows, and population movements. Moreover, the knowledge flows are not solely from leader to followers. A satisfactory account of the catch-up process must take account of these multiple forms of interaction. Again, there is space only for brief comment.

Trade and its rivalries

I have referred to the sometimes negative effects of leading-country exports on the economies of less developed countries. Countries in the course of catching up, however, exploit the possibilities of advanced scale-dependent technologies by import substitution and expansion of exports. When they are successful there are possible negative effects on the economies of leaders. This is an old historical theme. The successful competition of Germany, the United States and other European countries is supposed to have retarded British growth from 1870 to 1913 and perhaps longer.[21] Analogous questions arise today. The expansion of exports from Japan and the newer industrializing countries has had a serious impact on the older industries of the United States and Europe, as well as some of the newer industries.

Is there a generalized effect on the productivity growth of the leaders? The effect is less than it may seem to be because some of the trade shifts are a reflection of overall productivity growth in the leader countries themselves. As the average level of productivity rises, so does the level of wages across industries generally. There are then relative increases in the product prices of those industries – usually older industries – in which productivity growth is lagging and relative declines in the product prices of those industries enjoying rapid productivity growth. The former must suffer a loss of comparative advantage, the latter a gain. One must keep an eye on both.

Other causes of trade shifts that are connected with the catch-up process itself may, however, carry real generalized productivity effects. There are changes that stem from the evolution of 'product cycles', such as Raymond Vernon has made familiar. And perhaps most important, there is the achievement of higher levels of social capability. This permits followers to extend their borrowing and adaptation of more advanced methods, and enables them to compete in markets they could not contest earlier.

What difference does it make to the general prospects for the productivity growth of the leading industrial countries if they are losing markets to followers who are catching up?

There is an employment effect. Demand for the products of export- and import-competing industries is depressed. Failing a high degree of flexibility in exchange rates and wages and of occupational and geographical mobility, aggregate demand tends to be reduced. Unless macroeconomic policy is successful, there is general unemployment and underutilization of resources. Profits and the inducements to invest and innovate are reduced. And if this condition causes economies to succumb to protectionism, particularly to competitive protectionism, the difficulty is aggravated.

International trade theory assures us that these effects are transitory. Autonomous capital movements aside, trade must, in the end, balance. But the macroeconomic effects of the balancing process may be long drawn out, and while it is in progress, countries can suffer the repressive effects of restricted demand on investment and innovation.

There is also a Verdoorn effect. It is harder for an industry to push the technological frontier forward, or even to keep up with it, if its own rate of expansion slows down – and still harder if it is contracting. This is unavoidable but tolerable when the growth of old industries is restricted by the rise of newer, more progressive home industries. But when retardation of older home industries is due to the rise of competing industries abroad, a tendency to generalized slowdown may be present.

Interactions via population movements

Nineteenth-century migration ran in good part from the farms of Western and Southern Europe to the farms and cities of the New World and Australia. In the early twentieth century, Eastern Europe joined in. These migrations responded in part to the impact on world markets of the cheap grains and animal products produced by the regions of recent settlement. Insofar they represent an additional but special effect of development in some members of the Atlantic community of industrializing countries on the economies of other members.

Productivity growth in the countries of destination was aided by migration in two respects. It helped them exploit scale economies; and by making labor supply more responsive to increase in demand, it helped sustain periods of rapid growth. Countries of origin were relieved of the presence of partly redundant and desperately poor people. On the other hand, the loss of population brought such scale disadvantages as accompany slower population growth, and it made labor supply less responsive to industrial demand.

Migration in the postwar growth boom presents a picture of largely similar design and significance. In this period the movement was from the poorer, more slowly growing countries of Southern Europe and North Africa to the richer and more rapidly growing countries of Western and Northern Europe.[22] There is, however, this difference: The movement in more recent decades was induced by actual and expected income differences that were largely independent of the market connections of countries of origin and destination. There is no evidence that the growth boom of the West itself contributed to the low incomes of the South.

Needless to say, migrations are influenced by considerations other than relative levels of income and changing comparative advantage. I stress these matters, however, because they help us understand the complexities of the process of catch-up and convergence within a group of connected countries.

Interaction via capital flows

A familiar generalization is that capital tends to flow from countries of high income and slow growth to those with opposite characteristics or, roughly speaking, from leaders to followers. One remembers, however, that that description applies to gross new investments. There are also reverse flows that reflect the maturing of past investments. So in the early stages of a great wave of investment, followers' rates of investment and productivity growth are supported by capital movement while those of leaders are retarded. Later, however, this effect may become smaller or be reversed, as we see today in relations between Western leaders and Latin American followers.

Once more, I add that the true picture is far more complicated than this idealized summary. It will hardly accommodate such extraordinary developments as the huge American capital import of recent years, to say nothing of the Arabian–European flows of the 1970s and their reversal now underway.

Interactions via flows of applied knowledge

The flow of knowledge from leader to followers is, of course, the very essence of the catch-up hypothesis. As the technological gaps narrow, however, the direction changes. Countries that are still a distance behind the leader in average productivity may move into the lead in particular branches and become sources of new knowledge for older leaders. As they are surpassed in particular fields, old leaders can make gains by borrowing as well as by generating new knowledge. In this respect the growth potential of old leaders is enhanced as the pursuit draws closer. Moreover, competitive pressure can be a stimulus to research and innovation as well as an excuse for protection. It remains to be seen whether the newly rising economies will seek to guard a working knowledge of their operations more closely than American companies have done, and still more whether American and European firms will be as quick to discover, acquire, and adapt foreign methods as Japanese firms have been in the past.

Development as a constraint on change: tangible capital

The rise of followers in the course of catching up brings old leaders a mixed bag of injuries and potential benefits. Old leaders, however, or followers who have enjoyed a period of successful development, may come to suffer disabilities other than those caused by the burgeoning competitive power of new rivals. When Britain suffered its growth climacteric a century ago, observers thought that its slowdown was itself due in part to its early lead. Thorstein Veblen was a pioneer proponent of this suggestion, and Charles Kindleberger and others have picked it up again.[23] One basis for this view is the idea that the capital stock of a country consists of an intricate web of interlocking elements. They are built to fit together, and it is difficult to replace one part of the complex with more modern and efficient elements without a costly rebuilding of other components. This may be handled efficiently if all the costs and benefits are internal to a firm. When they are divided among different firms and industries and between the private and public sectors, the adaptation of old capital structures to new technologies may be a difficult and halting process.

What this may have meant for Britain's climacteric is still unsettled. Whatever that may be, however, the problem needs study on a wider scale as it arises both historically and in a contemporaneous setting. After World War II, France undertook a great extension and modernization of its public transportation and power systems to provide a basis for later development of private industry and agriculture. Were the technological advances embodied in that investment program easier for France to carry out because its infrastructure was technically older, battered, and badly maintained? Or was it simply a heavy burden more in need of being borne? There is a widespread complaint today that the public capital structure of the United

States stands in need of modernization and extension. Is this true, and, if it is, does it militate seriously against the installation of improved capital by private industry? One cannot now assume that such problems are the exclusive concern of a topmost productivity leader. All advanced industrial countries have large accumulations of capital, interdependent in use but divided in ownership among many firms and between private and public authorities. One may assume, however, that the problem so raised differs in its impact over time and among countries and, depending on its importance, might have some influence on the changes that occur in the productivity rankings of countries.

Development as a constraint on change: intangible capital and political institutions

Attention now returns to matters akin to social capability. In the simple catch-up hypothesis, that capability is viewed as either exogenously determined or else as adjusting steadily to the requirements of technological opportunity. The educational and institutional commitments induced by past development may, however, stand as an obstacle. That is a question that calls for study. The comments that follow are no more than brief indications of prominent possibilities.

The United States was the pioneer of mass production as embodied in the huge plant, the complex and rigid assembly line, the standardized product, and the long production run. It is also the pioneer and developer of the mammoth diversified conglomerate corporation. The vision of business carried on within such organizations, their highly indirect, statistical, and bureaucratic methods of consultation, planning and decision, the inevitable distractions of trading in assets rather than production of goods – these mental biases have sunk deep into the American business outlook and into the doctrine and training of young American managers. The necessary decentralization of operations into multiple profit centers directs the attention of managers and their superiors to the quarterly profit report and draws their energies away from the development of improved products and processes that require years of attention.[24] One may well ask how well this older vision of management and enterprise and the organizational scheme in which it is embodied will accommodate the problems and potentialities of the emerging computer and communications revolution. Or will that occur more easily in countries where educational systems, forms of corporate organization, and managerial outlook can better make a fresh start?

The long period of leadership and development enjoyed by the United States and the entire North Atlantic community meant, of course, a great increase of incomes. The rise of incomes, in turn, afforded a chance to satisfy latent desires for all sorts of non-market goods ranging from maintenance in old age to a safeguarded natural environment. Satisfying these demands, largely by public action, has also afforded an ample opportunity for special interest groups to obtain privileges and protection in a process that Mancur Olson and others have generalized.

The outcome of this conjuncture of circumstances and forces is the mixed economy of the West, the complex system of transfers, taxes, regulations, and public activity, as well as organizations of union and business power, that had its roots long before World War II, that expanded rapidly during the growth boom of the 1950s and 1960s, and that reached very high levels in the 1970s. This trend is very broadly consistent with the suggestion that the elaboration of the mixed economy is a function of economic growth itself. To this one has to add the widely held idea advanced by Olson and many others that the system operates to reduce enterprise, work, saving, investment, and mobility and, therefore, to constrict the processes of innovation and change that productivity growth involves.

How much is there in all this? The answer turns only partly on a calculation of the direct effects of the system on economic incentives. These have proved difficult to pin down, and attempts to measure them have generally not yielded large numbers, at least for the United States.[25] The answer requires an equally difficult evaluation of the positive roles of government activity. These include not only the government's support of education, research, and information, and its provision of physical overhead capital and of the host of local functions required for urban life. We must remember also that the occupational and geographical adjustments needed to absorb new technology impose heavy costs on individuals. The accompanying changes alter the positions, prospects, and power of established groups, and they transform the structure of families and their roles in caring for children, the sick, and the old. Technical advance, therefore, engenders conflict and resistance; and the Welfare State with its transfers and regulations constitutes a mode of conflict resolution and a means of mitigating the costs of change that would otherwise induce resistance to growth. The existing empirical studies that bear on the economic responses to government intervention are, therefore, far from meeting the problem fully.

If the growth-inhibiting forces embodied in the Welfare State and in private expressions of market power were straightforward, positive functions of income levels, uniform across countries, that would be another reason for supposing that the catch-up process was self-limiting. The productivity levels of followers would, on this account, converge towards but not exceed the leader's. But these forces are clearly not simple, uniform functions of income. The institutions of the Welfare State have reached a higher degree of elaboration in Europe than in the United States. The objects of expenditure, the structures of transfers and taxes, and people's responses to both differ from country to country. These institutional developments, therefore, besides having some influence on growth rates generally, may constitute a wild card in the deck of growth forces. They will tend to produce changes in the ranks of countries in the productivity scale and these may include the top rank itself.

A sense that forces of institutional change are now acting to limit the growth of Western countries pervades the writings of many economists – and, of course, of other observers. Olson, Fellner, Scitovsky, Kindleberger, Lindbeck, and Giersch are only a partial list of those who see these economies as afflicted by institutional arthritis or sclerosis or other metaphorical malady associated with age and wealth.

These are the suggestions of serious scholars, and they need to be taken seriously. One may ask, however, whether these views take account of still other, rejuvenating forces which, though they act slowly, may yet work effectively to limit and counter those of decay – at least for the calculable future. In the United States, interregional competition, supported by free movement of goods, people, and capital, is such a force. It limits the power of unions and checks the expansion of taxation, transfers, and regulation.[26] International competition, so long as it is permitted to operate, works in a similar direction for the United States and other countries as well, and it is strengthened by the development in recent years of a more highly integrated world capital market and by more vigorous international movements of corporate enterprise.

In the ranking of countries within the group of presently advanced industrial economies, their variant responsiveness to competition may be still another influence making for change in rank and relative level of productivity. As this group competes with the newly industrializing countries of the East and South, however, the pressures of competition on their institutional development, as distinct from their impact on particular industries, should help the older group maintain a lead. There are, however, still more solid grounds for a renewal of productivity advance in both Europe and the United States and for the maintenance of a substantial lead over virtually all newcomers. These are their high levels of general and technical education, the broad bases of their science, and the well-established connections of their science, technology, and industry. These elements of social capability are slow to develop but also, it seems very likely, slow to decay.

Finally, it is widely recognized that the process of institutional aging, whatever its significance, is not one without limits. Powerful forces continue to push that way, and they are surely strong in resisting reversal. Yet it is also apparent that there is a drift of public opinion that works for modification both in Europe and North America. There is a fine balance to be struck between productivity growth and the material incomes it brings and the other dimensions of social welfare. Countries are now in the course of readjusting that balance in favor of productivity growth. How far they can go and, indeed, how far they should go are both still in question.

CONCLUDING REMARKS

This chapter points in two directions. It shows that differences among countries in productivity levels create a strong potentiality for subsequent convergence of levels, provided that countries have a 'social capability' adequate to absorb more advance technologies. It reminds us, however, that the institutional and human capital components of social capability develop only slowly as education and organization respond to the requirements of technological opportunity and to experience in exploiting it. Their degree of development acts to limit the strength of technological potentiality proper. Further, the pace of realization of a potential for catch-up depends on a number of other conditions that govern the diffusion of knowledge, the mobility of resources and the rate of investment.

The long-term convergence to which these considerations point, however, is only a tendency that emerges in the average experience of a group of countries. The growth records of countries on their surface do not exhibit the uniformly self-limiting character that a simple statement of the catch-up hypothesis might suggest. Dramatic changes in productivity rankings mark the performance of a group's individual members. Some causes of these shifts in rank are exogenous to the convergence process. The state of a country's capability to exploit emerging technological opportunity depends on a social history that is particular to itself and that may not be closely bound to its existing level of productivity. And there are changes in the character of technological advance that make it more congruent with the resources and institutional outfits of some countries but less congruent with those of others. Some shifts, however, are influenced by the catch-up process itself – for example, when the trade rivalry of advancing latecomers makes successful inroads on important industries of older leaders. There are also the social and political concomitants of rising wealth itself that may weaken the social capability for technological advance. There is the desire to avoid or mitigate the costs of growth, and there are the attractions of goals other than growth as wealth increases. A reasonably complete view of the catch-up process, therefore, does not lend itself to simple formulation. Its implications ramify and are hard to separate from the more general process of growth at large.

ACKNOWLEDGEMENTS

The author acknowledges with thanks critical comments and suggestions by Paul David and Knick Harley. This chapter is the revision of a draft read to the Economic History Association at its New York meeting in September 1985. This, in turn, was a greatly abbreviated version of a longer paper since published. See 'Catching Up and Falling Behind', Fackföreningsrörelsens Institut für Ekonomisk Forskning (Trade Union Institute for Economic Research), Economic Research Report no. 1 (Stockholm, 1986).

NOTES

1 Angus Maddison, *Phases of Capitalist Development* (New York, 1982). Maddison's estimates of productivity levels are themselves extrapolations of base levels established for most, but not all, countries by Irving B. Kravis, Alan Heston, and Robert Summers in their *International Comparisons of Real Product and Purchasing Power* (Baltimore, 1978) and in other publications by Kravis and his associates.

2 W.E.G. Salter, *Productivity and Technical Change* (Cambridge, 1960) provides a rigorous theoretical exposition of the factors determining rates of turnover and those governing the relation between productivity with capital embodying best practice and average (economically efficient) technology.

3 K. Ohkawa and H. Rosovsky, *Japanese Economic Growth: Trend Acceleration in the Twentieth Century* (Stanford, 1973), especially ch. 9.

4 Moses Abramovitz, 'Rapid Growth Potential and its Realization: The Experience of the Capitalist Economies in the Postwar Period', in Edmond Malinvaud (ed.) *Economic Growth and Resources*, Proceedings of the Fifth World Congress of the International Economic Association, vol. 1 (London, 1979), pp. 1–30.

5 Thorstein Veblen, *Imperial Germany and the Industrial Revolution* (New York, 1915), p. 70.

6 Mancur Olson, *The Rise and Fall of Nations: Economic Growth, Stagflation and Social Rigidities* (New Haven, 1982).

7 Kravis *et al.*, *International Comparisons*; Edward F. Denison, assisted by Jean-Pierre Poullier, *Why Growth Rates Differ, Postwar Experience of Nine Western Countries* (Washington, DC, 1967). pp. 239–45.

8 R.C.O. Matthews, Review of Denison (1967), *Economic Journal* (June 1969), pp. 261–8.

9 My paper cited in note 4 describes the operation of these factors in the 1950s and 1960s and tries to show how they worked to permit productivity growth to rise in so many countries rapidly, in concert and for such an extended period ('Rapid Growth Potential and Its Realization', pp. 18–30).

10 The countries are Australia, Austria, Belgium, Canada, Denmark, Finland, France, Germany, Italy, Japan, Netherlands, Norway, Sweden, Switzerland, United Kingdom and United States.

11 In these calculations I have treated either the United States or the United Kingdom as the productivity leader from 1870 to 1913. Literal acceptance of Maddison's estimates, however, make Australia the leader from 1870–1913. Moreover, Belgium and the Netherlands stand slightly higher than the United States in 1870. Here are Maddison's relatives for those years (from *Phases*, Table 5.2):

	1870	1890	1913
Australia	186	153	102
Belgium	106	96	75
Netherlands	106	92	74
United Kingdom	114	100	81
United States	100	100	100

Since Australia's high standing in this period mainly reflected an outstandingly favorable situation of natural resources relative to population, it would be misleading to regard that country as the technological leader or to treat the productivity changes in other countries relative to Australia's as indicators of the catch-up process. Similarly, the small size and specialized character of the Belgian and Dutch economies make them inappropriate benchmarks.

12 Maddison, *Phases*, Table C5.

13 Since growth rates are calculated as rates of change between standings at the terminal dates of periods, errors in the estimates of such standings will generate errors in the derived growth rates. If errors at both terminal dates were random, and if those at the end-year were independent of those at the initial year, there would be a tendency on that account for growth rates to be inversely correlated with initial-year standings. The inverse correlation coefficients would be biased upwards. Note, however, that if errors at terminal years were random and independent and of equal magnitude, there would be no tendency *on that account* for the variance of standings about the mean to decline between initial and end-year dates. The error bias would run against the marked decline in variance that we observe. Errors in late-year data, however, are unlikely to be so large, so an error bias is present.

14 See also William J. Baumol, 'Productivity Growth, Convergence and Welfare: What the Long-run Data Show', C. V. Starr Center for Applied Economics, New York University, Research Report no. 85–27, August 1985.

15 See Abramovitz, 'Rapid Growth Potential and its Realization'.

16 Olson, *Rise and Fall*.

17 Some comments on the catch-up process after 1973 may be found in Abramovitz, 'Catching Up and Falling Behind' (Stockholm, 1986), pp. 33–9.

18 If one follows Maddison's estimates (*Phases*, Table C.19), the long period from 1870 to 1979 saw Australia fall by 8 places in the ranking of his 16 countries, Italy by $2\frac{1}{2}$, Switzerland by 8, and the United Kingdom by 10. Meanwhile the United States rose by 4, Germany by $4\frac{1}{2}$, Norway by 5, Sweden by 7, and France by 8.

19 The possibility of overtaking and surpassing, however, was considered theoretically by Edward Ames and Nathan Rosenberg in a closely reasoned and persuasive article, 'Changing Technological Leadership and Industrial Growth', *Economic Journal*, 72 (1963), pp. 13–31. They conclude that the troubles connected with leadership and industrial "aging" that doom early leaders to decline in the productivity scale are not persuasive. They hold that outcomes turn on a variety of empirical conditions, the presence of which is uncertain and not foreordained.

20 These arguments are anticipated and elaborated in Nathan Rosenberg's fertile and original chapter, 'Why in America?', in Otto Mayr and Robert Post (eds) *Yankee Enterprise: The Rise of the American System of Manufactures* (Washington, DC, 1981).

21 See also R.C.O. Matthews, Charles Feinstein and John Odling-Smee, *British Economic Growth, 1856–1973* (Stanford, 1983), chs. 14, 15, 17. Their analysis does not find a large effect on British productivity growth from 1870 to 1913.

22 The migration from East to West Germany in the 1950s was a special case. It brought to West Germany educated and skilled people strongly motivated to rebuild their lives and restore their fortunes.

23 Charles P. Kindleberger, 'Obsolescence and Technical Change', *Oxford Institute of Statistics Bulletin* (Aug. 1961), pp. 281–97.

24 These and similar questions are raised by experienced observers of American business. They are well summarized by Edward Denison, *Trends in American Economic Growth, 1929–1982*, (Washington, DC, 1985), ch. 3.

25 Representative arguments supporting the idea that social capability has suffered, together with some quantitative evidence, may be found in Olson, *Rise and Fall*; William Fellner, 'The Declining Growth of American Productivity: An Introductory Note', in W. Fellner (ed.) *Contemporary Economic Problems, 1979*

(Washington, DC, 1979); and Assar Lindbeck, 'Limits to the Welfare State', *Challenge* (Dec. 1985). For argument and evidence on the other side, see Sheldon Danzigar, Robert Haveman, and Robert Plotnick, 'How Income Transfers Affect Work, Savings and Income Distribution', *Journal of Economic Literature*, 19 (Sept. 1982), pp. 975–1028; and E. F. Denison, *Accounting for Slower Economic Growth* (Washington, DC, 1979), pp. 127–38.

26 See R. D. Norton, 'Regional Life Cycles and US Industrial Rejuvenation', in Herbert Giersch (ed.) *Towards an Explanation of Economic Growth* (Tübingen, 1981), pp. 253–80; and R. D. Norton, 'Industrial Policy and American Renewal', *Journal of Economic Literature*, 24 (March 1986).

24 Technological catch up and diverging incomes

Patterns of economic growth 1960–88

Steve Dowrick

Economic Journal (1992) 102, May, pp. 600–10

INTRODUCTION

The pattern of worldwide economic growth since the early 1960s displays diverging growth paths. Most economies shared the experience of high growth rates in the 1950s and 1960s, reverting in the 1970s and 1980s to rates which are more normal by historical standards. At the same time, however, income disparities across the national economies of the world have been widening. The richer economies have, in per capita terms, been growing faster than the middle-income economies, which in turn have out-paced the poorest economies. Moreover, within each of these broadly defined groups, income levels have been diverging.

The divergence of growth paths of GDP per capita is perhaps surprising. The post-war period has witnessed an explosion in world trade, commun-ications and the dissemination of information – all factors which might be supposed to both encourage and enable the technologically backward economies to learn from and adopt the production techniques of the more advanced. At the same time, the integration of capital markets, the emer-ging dominance of transnational corporations and the development of both transport and communications technology might be expected to lead to growth-enhancing investment in the poorer, low-wage economies.

The first of these conjectures is supported by an analysis of the sources of economic growth. There is indeed evidence to support the technological spillover hypothesis: the less advanced economies have tended to experience faster growth in multi-factor productivity (although not necessarily with respect to manufacturing technology in the poorest economies). It appears, therefore, that income divergence has occurred in spite of technological catching up. The proximate causes are lower rates of investment in the poorer countries allied to declining rates of labour force participation in the poorer countries and rising participation in the richer countries.

There are several explanations for the divergence of the growth paths of capital and labour inputs. Employment growth, relative to total population, is strongly enhanced in the medium term by the demographic transition from high to low rates of population growth. The poorest group of countries have tended to experience, however, either stable or even increasing rates of population growth since the early 1960s. Population has tended to decelerate only in those countries which already had higher income levels by 1960.

There is some weak statistical evidence that aggregate rates of return on capital investment across poorer countries may be higher than in richer countries, in which case their low investment rates might be attributable to capital barriers and an inability to generate substantial domestic savings out of near-subsistence incomes. Moreover, it seems likely that complementarities between private capital investment on the one hand and human capital and public infrastructure on the other, lower the private returns to investment in the poorer economies.

THE PATTERN OF GROWTH 1960–4 TO 1984–8 FOR 113 COUNTRIES

Summers and Heston (1991) continue to feed the ongoing analysis of worldwide economic growth with improved estimates of real GDP and its principal components for an ever increasing number of countries. The sample of countries used here consists of 113 out of their total of 138. The 25 exclusions were made either because of lack of data on key variables before 1965, or because a country belongs to OPEC. The sample breaks down into 42 African countries, 25 American, 20 Asian, 22 European and 4 Southern Pacific.

I take as the base for measurement of economic growth the annual average value of real GDP (1985 US$) over the period 1960–4. The end-point is the average for the period 1984–8. The purpose of taking these five-year averages is to remove cyclical variation from the cross-country comparisons. Real output is deflated either by population or by the workforce to give approximate indicators of per capita incomes and labour productivity. Examination of the ranked productivity measure reveals natural breaks which divide the sample into three (in a similar way to Baumol's 1986 divisions). The high productivity group, with 1960–4 output per worker above $6,500 contains most of the European economies and the richer American and Asian economies. The low productivity group, with output per worker below $2,800 contains most of the African economies and the poorer Asian economies. The middle group contains mostly Asian and Latin American countries. Since output per head of population and output per worker are very highly correlated ($r = 0.98$), I also refer to these groups as the rich, poor and middle-income economies – although such descriptions ignore variations in average incomes which may be due to foreign ownership and the terms of trade.

Table 24.1 displays some of the key statistics for the sample and for each of the three groups. Rows 4 and 5 reveal that while the average growth rates of GDP per worker are very similar for the three groups (ranging from 1.90

Table 24.1 Average values of principal variables

	Entire sample	Poor	Middle	Rich
1 Sample size	113	42	32	39
2 RGDP per capita (pc) 1962[a]	2,330	736	1,481	4,744
3 RGDP per worker (pw) 1962	6,019	1,658	4,231	12,183
4 Growth of RGDP pc (% pa)[b]	1.98	1.36	2.16	2.49
5 Growth of RGDP pw (% pa)	2.00	1.90	2.03	2.06
6 Dispersion of RGDP pc 1962[c]	0.88	0.44	0.24	0.48
7 Dispersion of RGDP pc 1986[a]	1.07	0.59	0.62	0.57
8 Dispersion of RGDP pw 1962	0.96	0.48	0.26	0.37
9 Dispersion of RGDP pw 1986	1.06	0.62	0.62	0.42
10 Investment 1960–88 (% GDP)	18.1	12.4	20.1	22.6
11 Population growth (% pa)	2.05	2.60	2.22	1.32
12 Workforce growth (% pa)	2.03	2.06	2.34	1.75

Notes:
[a] 1962 is the average for the period 1960–4 and 1986 is the average for 1984–8
[b] Growth rates are annual averages of logarithmic growth rates 1962–86
[c] Dispersion is the standard deviation of the logarithm

to 2.06 per cent per annum for the poor and rich groups respectively), growth of GDP per capita is substantially lower in the poor group (1.36 per cent per annum) than in the middle group (2.16 per cent) and the rich group (2.49 per cent). In other words, although average labour productivity across the three groups displays only a weak tendency towards divergence, this tendency is amplified strongly when output is measured per head of population. The proximate reason is given in rows 11 and 12 of Table 24.1: the workforce has, on average, grown slower than population in the poorer countries, and vice versa in the rich countries.

The dispersion of income and productivity levels within each group can be read from rows 6–9 of Table 24.1. In each case within group dispersion increased between 1960–4 and 1984–8. Divergence appears to be somewhat stronger in output per capita than in output per worker. The overall picture is one of increasing dispersion in incomes and productivity both within and between the three income groups. Since the early 1960s it appears that the world's economies have been on divergent growth paths, leading to increasing inequality, especially in per capita output.

This divergence in world income levels can be seen in Figure 24.1 which plots the growth of per capita GDP against the logarithm of 1960–4 real GDP for the 113 countries. First, it is evident that growth rates have varied tremendously, within a range of −2 to +7 per cent per annum for all but the richest 20 countries (where the range has been between 1 and 4 per cent). Second, a weak upward drift in the per cent scatter points is just about discernible, at least with the aid of a least squares regression line as displayed. Average incomes in the richer countries are tending to pull away

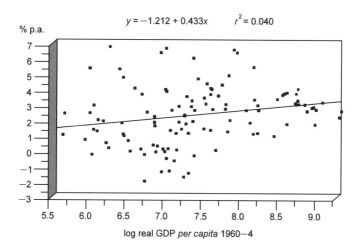

Figure 24.1 Growth of real GDP per capita 1960–4 to 1984–8 for 113 countries

from the levels in the poorer countries. Closer examination also reveals a tendency for income convergence amongst the very richest group of countries – at the extreme right of Figure 24.1 – roughly speaking the OECD group.

Evidence such as this has been taken by some commentators, for example DeLong (1988) to refute arguments that there has been a tendency for poorer economies to catch up on the richer. Nevertheless, Dowrick and Nguyen (1989) have shown that at least within the OECD group of countries there has been a strong and consistent tendency since 1950 for technological catch up to occur, even though income levels have not been converging since 1973. In other words, after taking account of the rate of growth of labour and capital, the poorer OECD countries have tended to experience faster growth in the residual (multi-factor productivity).

If we repeat this growth accounting exercise on the 113 economies in our sample, we reach a similar conclusion. There is a strong tendency, at least within the upper and lower ends of the world income distribution, for multi-factor productivity growth to be inversely related to the starting level of productivity. Simple regression of GDP growth ($\hat{Y}$) on initial labour productivity (ln Y/L_0), the growth of the workforce ($\hat{W}$) and average investment rates (INV) gives estimates of the growth accounting parameters within each of the three income groupings. The first parameter captures the extent of technological catch up (if negative); the second parameter measures the elasticity of output with respect to employment; the third is an estimate of the marginal productivity of gross capital investment. The regression results are summarized below, omitting the constant terms, with heteroscedasticity-consistent *t*-statistics in parentheses.

Poor economies

$$\hat{Y} = -0.013 \ln Y/L_0 + 0.89 \hat{W} + 0.15 \text{ INV} \tag{1}$$
$$(-2.2) \qquad\qquad (2.3) \qquad (4.0) \quad (n = 42, \ R^2 = 0.33, \ \text{s.e.} = 1.87)$$

Middle income economies

$$\hat{Y} = 0.019 \ln Y/L_0 + 0.48 \hat{W} + 0.05 \text{ INV} \tag{2}$$
$$(1.4) \qquad\qquad (0.9) \qquad (0.9) \quad (n = 42, \ R^2 = 0.13, \ \text{s.e.} = 1.88)$$

Rich economies

$$\hat{Y} = -0.014 \ln Y/L_0 + 0.95 \hat{W} + 0.13 \text{ INV} \tag{3}$$
$$(-3.1) \qquad\qquad (5.9) \qquad (5.6) \quad (n = 39, \ R^2 = 0.63, \ \text{s.e.} = 0.94)$$

It is only within the middle-income group that we fail to find evidence of technological catch up. Within this group, however, the standard errors are large, due to collinearity amongst the explanatory variables. The coefficients estimated on the other two groups are well defined and remarkably similar. The hypothesis that the parameters are in fact the same across all three samples is not rejected at even the 20 per cent level ($F_{8,101} = 1.38$) – so it is legitimate on statistical criteria to pool the samples. Pooling the three samples gives weight to the inter-group variation in the data, as well as the intra-group variation, so these are the preferred estimates.

All economies

$$\hat{Y} = -0.006 \ln Y/L_0 + 0.88 \hat{W} + 0.11 \text{ INV} \tag{4}$$
$$(-3.1) \qquad\qquad (4.6) \qquad (4.2) \quad (n = 113, \ R^2 = 0.28, \ \text{s.e.} = 1.63)$$

Technological catch-up is strongly significant across the whole sample. So too are the growth of the workforce and the rate of gross investment although nearly three-quarters of the variance in growth rates remains

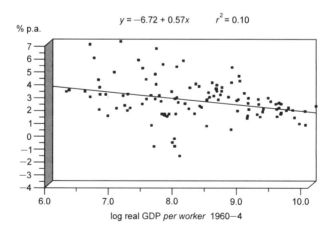

Figure 24.2 Growth of multi-factor productivity, 1960–88

Table 24.2 Decomposition of relative growth performance for four groups of countries

Country group	Relative growth of RGDP per capita	= Catching up	+ Employment deepening	+ Capital deepening	+ Residual
Poorest					
Average	−0.6	0.6	−0.5	−0.7	0.0
SD	2.1	0.3	0.4	0.8	1.8
Middle income					
Average	0.2	0.0	0.1	0.2	−0.1
SD	2.2	0.2	0.5	1.0	1.9
Richest					
Average	0.5	−0.6	0.4	0.6	0.1
SD	1.3	0.2	0.4	0.7	1.0
Five NICs					
Average	4.0	−0.1	0.8	0.9	2.4
SD	0.5	0.3	0.5	0.5	0.6

Note: The contribution of each factor is derived from the regression parameters in (4) and the deviation of variables for each country from the overall mean. See Appendix for details.

unexplained.[1] Figure 24.2 illustrates the technological catch-up tendency by plotting growth in multi factor productivity against productivity levels.[2] We can discern the tendency for a negative correlation, with dispersion around the regression line most pronounced for the middle-income countries.

Using these parameter estimates it is possible to decompose observed rates of growth of per capita GDP into four elements: the amount attributable to technological catch up; the amount due to the growth of the workforce relative to the total population; the amount due to investment; and the unexplained residual. The decomposition method is explained in Dowrick and Nguyen (1989: 1025). Results for each of 113 countries are available from the author on request. Table 24.2 gives the average values for each of the three income groups. The decomposition is also given for a group of five rapidly growing Asia-Pacific economies consisting of Japan, Korea, Taiwan, Singapore and Hong Kong. Their exceptional growth record makes study of this group of newly industrializing countries (NICs) of particular interest.

Output per capita in the poorest group of countries grew at 0.6 percentage points per annum below the sample average. This performance occurred despite the 'advantage of backwardness', or catching up effect, which afforded them 0.6 points in above average productivity growth. Overall, then, these economies underperformed, relative to the world average, by 1.2 points. This underperformance is, on average, attributable to two factors: the decline in employment relative to population and the poor rate of growth of the capital stock, which contributed −0.5 and −0.7 points respectively. The employment shallowing effect reflects the fact that the workforce failed to grow at the same rate as population. The capital shallowing effect reflects the fact that investment rates were only just over one-half of average investment rates in the rich economies, despite much higher population growth in the poor countries.

When this growth accounting exercise is repeated for the rich group of countries it presents an almost exact mirror image. Above average per capita growth of 0.5 points, on top of the slower productivity growth due to less opportunity for technological catch up, implies that the richer countries' growth performance was some 1.1 percentage points per annum above what might have been expected. This performance is partly due to employment deepening, which contributed 0.4 points, but is mainly due to capital deepening which contributed 0.6 points.

The five rapidly growing Asian economies have each outperformed the world economy by over four percentage points per annum, with the exception of Japan whose growth rate has been only 3.1 points above average. These exceptional growth rates imply that per capita output in each of these countries is now more than double what it would have been if they had grown at the world average rate of 2 per cent per annum. The growth decomposition in Table 24.2 suggests that nearly half of this exceptional performance can be attributed to faster than average growth in factor inputs relative to population. It is particularly interesting to note that employment deepening, i.e. raising the ratio of the workforce to the population, has been relatively more important than capital deepening in three of these five countries. It is only in Japan that capital deepening has substantially outweighed the employment deepening effect.

Increasing the ratio of workers to population has also made significant contributions to the growth record of a number of other countries, notably the USA and Portugal (in each case contributing an average of 0.7 percentage points per annum) and Iceland and Malta (1.1 points). Capital deepening has been particularly important in contributing to above average annual growth rates in Norway (1.9 points), West Germany, Denmark, France, Israel, Italy, Spain, Cyprus, Malaysia, Malta and Yugoslavia (above 1 point in each case).

The relationship between divergence of world incomes on the one hand and both employment deepening and capital deepening on the other hand is illustrated in Figures 24.3 and 24.4. Figure 24.3 plots the growth in the workforce to population ratio against the logarithm of real GDP per capita. The simple regression line highlights the moderately strong positive correlation in the data ($r = +0.53$). Since the early 1960s, the richer countries have tended to experience a rise in the ratio of workers to population, whilst in the poorer countries the ratio has tended to decline. Note also that some of the middle-income countries (including Singapore, Hong Kong and South Korea) have experienced particularly large rises in this aggregate participation ratio.

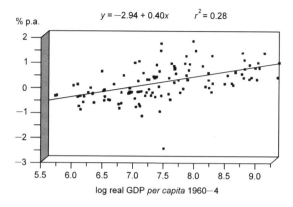

Figure 24.3 Growth of ratio of workers to population, 1962–86

Figure 24.4 presents a corresponding plot of investment rates against 1960–4 levels of per capita GDP. There is again a clear positive correlation ($r = +0.58$). Richer countries tend to devote a greater proportion of their output to physical investment than do the poorer countries. Allied with employment deepening, it is this relative capital deepening in the more advanced economies which provides a proximate explanation for the divergence of world per capita GDP despite technological catch up.

EXPLANATIONS AND POLICIES

The growth-accounting exercises of the previous section are important in isolating the immediate features and patterns of world economic growth. They do not necessarily provide much depth of explanation, nor much guide for constructive policies by either national governments or development

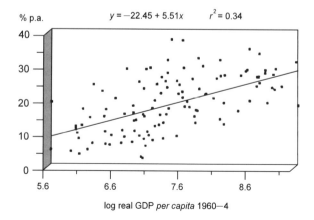

Figure 24.4 Investment rates, 1960–88

agencies, except to add weight to 'motherhood' prescriptions such as that more investment and employment will promote economic growth! I will discuss in turn some of the mechanisms that may underlie the three sources of growth that have been identified: catch up, employment deepening and capital deepening.

The most obvious explanation of observed productivity catch up is technological spillover, or the ability of less advanced economies to imitate and copy the techniques of production used by more advanced economies. Abramovitz (1986) warns, however, that such spillovers may not be effective if a country lacks the technical and social capability to absorb and implement new ideas. This hypothesis is supported by several studies which suggest reasons why catch up may be limited in the poorest economies of the world. Dowrick and Gemmell (1991) report evidence that although the poorest countries of sub-Saharan Africa have managed some catch-up in agricultural productivity, they have tended to fall behind in industrial productivity, where complementarities with human capital and infrastructural development are likely to be particularly strong. Barro (1991) finds that low levels of educational enrolment are a substantial impediment to growth.[3]

We have seen in the previous section that the contribution of employment deepening to the faster economic growth of the richer economies is substantial. This does not reflect, however, any systematic increase in the rate of participation by adults in the workforce. Although rising participation is important in a number of individual countries, on average it is offset by increasing aged dependency. The average ratio of workers to adults (over 15 years of age) in the richer economies has barely increased at all since the early 1960s. The major demographic change affecting the aggregate participation ratio in the richer countries has been the decline in youth dependency. This in turn reflects declining birth rates in most advanced economies. Brander and Dowrick (1990) argue that even though economic growth is independent of steady-state birth rates, declining birth rates provide a temporary but substantial stimulus through this labour supply effect.

There is evidence to support this view in Figure 24.5 where the growth of the worker to population ratio is plotted against the change in rates of population growth between the beginning and end of the sample period. A strong negative correlation ($r = -0.69$) supports the idea that declining fertility raises, albeit temporarily, the ratio of adults to total population which in turn raises the ratio of workers to population for a given adult participation rate. Moreover, to the extent that female participation in the labour force is a substitute for child-rearing, declining fertility may have an additional positive participation effect.

The importance of demographic change for the five fastest growing Asian economies is illustrated in Table 24.3. With the exception of Japan, all countries experienced a sharp rise in the ratio of workers to population.

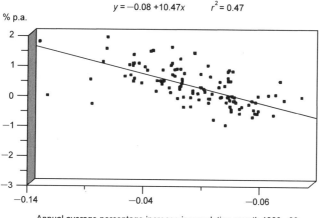

$$y = -0.08 + 10.47x \qquad r^2 = 0.47$$

Annual average percentage increase in population growth 1960–88

Figure 24.5 Growth in the ratio of workers to population

In each of these four cases the main impetus was a rise in the ratio of adults to population, i.e. a decline in youth dependency rates. In the case of Japan, the fall in youth dependency more than offset a fall in the adult participation rate. In all five cases, the rising ratio of adults to population was associated with a sharp fall in the rate of growth of population.

We can infer from these figures that the halving of population growth over three decades, and the consequent maturing of the population age structure, has increased substantially the supply of labour relative to total population.[4] The labour supply effect of demographic change has contributed substantially to the rapid increase in per capita output in these countries, and it is probable that the rapid increase in per capita incomes has also contributed to the demographic change.

Turning to investment, and referring back to Figure 24.4, the pattern to be explained here is the strong tendency for rates of investment to rise with income levels. In the absence of international capital movements, where investment has to be funded entirely out of domestic savings, this pattern might simply reflect sharply diminishing marginal utility of consumption, i.e. if the cost of forgoing present consumption is higher, the nearer a person is to a subsistence income. This would imply, however, that real rates of return to investment should be substantially higher in the poorer countries and that internationally mobile capital should flow to these economies. The simple regression estimates (1)–(3) of gross returns to investment are difficult to interpret because of the large standard error on the estimate for the middle-income countries. There is some weak evidence that rates of return are slightly higher in the low income countries, although the differences are not statistically significant. It is possible then that it is barriers to capital mobility which are holding back investment rates in the poorer countries.

Table 24.3 Demographic change in five NICs

	Population growth rate	Adult/population ratio	Worker/adult ratio	Worker/population ratio
Hong Kong				
Av. 1960–5	3.2	60.4	64.1	38.7
Av. 1984–8	1.4	76.4	68.9	52.6
Growth % p.a.		1.0	0.3	1.3
Japan				
Av. 1960–5	1.0	71.8	67.7	48.7
Av. 1984–8	0.5	78.8	63.0	49.6
Growth % p.a.		0.4	−0.3	0.1
South Korea				
Av. 1960–5	2.8	58.2	58.9	34.2
Av. 1984–8	1.3	69.0	59.8	41.2
Growth % p.a.		0.7	0.1	0.8
Singapore				
Av. 1960–5	2.7	58.4	56.4	32.9
Av. 1984–8	1.2	74.5	63.4	47.2
Growth % p.a.		1.0	0.5	1.5
Taiwan				
Av. 1960–5	3.1	56.5	58.1	32.9
Av. 1984–8	1.2	71.0	57.1	40.6
Growth % p.a.		1.0	−0.1	0.9

A more likely general explanation of the pattern of investment rates would seem to be concerned with complementarities between physical investment and human and social capital. Simple neo-classical growth models based on diminishing returns to capital imply that real rates of return should be highest in those countries with the lowest capital stock. It seems to be the case, however, that backward infrastructure and low levels of education and training substantially reduce rates of return to physical investment. Whilst investment in the physical and social infrastructure might generate a higher return, these returns would not generally be captured by private investors. The problem then becomes one of directing international investment and aid into infrastructural development and education and training.

NOTES

1 The magnitude of the factor input parameters might be taken to imply that there are increasing returns to scale since the output–labour elasticity is almost 0.9 and the output–capital elasticity is approximated by multiplying the coefficient 0.11 by the capital–output ratio which is typically between two and three. Some of the unexplained variance in the regression is due to differences in openness to world trade, as in Romer (1990), and variance in industrial structure, as in Dowrick and Gemmell (1991) as well as a multiplicity of country-specific policies and natural events. Government consumption is not a significant explanatory variable; however there is evidence that government consumption crowds out investment, which

would explain Barro's (1991) result. The addition of dummy variables for Asia, Africa, Europe and Latin America raises the R^2 to 0.35, statistically significant at the 5 % level but not at the 1 % level. The parameter estimates are not affected significantly by these additions, except that the coefficient on investment falls from 0.11 to 0.09. A further test of the regression model has been carried out by dividing the observations for each country into two periods, 1960–75 and 1975–88. The hypothesis that the regression coefficients are stable over the two periods is accepted ($F_{3,218} = 0.4$) and the coefficient estimates for the pooled samples are very similar to those reported here.

2 Multi-factor productivity is defined here as the growth in GDP minus the contribution of the growth of the workforce and of investment (relative to the sample averages) calculated using the coefficients of equation (4).

3 Note however that measurement of technological catch-up in these broad cross-section studies is fraught with difficulties. First, we have to rely on gross investment rates to capture changes in capital stocks and gross employment to capture aggregate labour input. Second, there are substantial gaps in standard national accounting techniques which may lead to systematic mismeasurement of GDP growth due to the omission of domestic production and the omission of production externalities such as pollution and the maintenance of environmental standards.

4 This is the immediate consequence of lowering birth rates. There will in future, however, be a rebound effect due to increases in the aged dependency rate.

REFERENCES

Abramovitz, M. (1986) 'Catching up, forging ahead and falling behind', *Journal of Economic History* 46, pp. 385–406.

Barro, Robert J. (1991) 'Economic growth in a cross-section of countries', *Quarterly Journal of Economics* 106, pp. 407–43.

Baumol, William J. (1986) 'Productivity growth, convergence and welfare: what the long-run data show', *American Economic Review* 76, pp. 1072–85.

Brander, James A. and Dowrick, Steve (1990) 'The role of fertility and population in economic growth: new results from aggregate cross-national data', Centre for Economic Policy Research Discussion Paper no. 232, Australian National University, Canberra.

DeLong, J. Bradford (1988) 'Productivity growth, convergence and welfare: comment', *American Economic Review* 78, pp. 1138–54.

Dowrick, Steve and Gemmell, Norman (1991) 'Industrialisation, catching up and economic growth: a comparative study across the world's capitalist economies', *Economic Journal* 101, pp. 263–75.

Dowrick, Steve and Nguyen, Duc-Tho (1989) 'OECD comparative economic growth 1950–85: catch up and convergence', *American Economic Review* 79, pp. 1010–30.

Romer, Paul (1990) 'Endogenous technological change', *Journal of Political Economy* 98, pp. S71–S102.

Summers, Robert and Heston, Alan (1991) 'The Penn World Table (Mark 5): an expanded set of international comparisons, 1950–88', *Quarterly Journal of Economics* 106, pp. 327–68.

25 Policy implications of endogenous growth theory

G. K. Shaw
Economic Journal (1992) 102, May, pp. 611–21

INTRODUCTION

Harrod-Domar Growth Theory sanctioned the overriding importance of capital accumulation in the quest for enhanced growth. Since budgetary surpluses could substitute for domestic savings, fiscal policy became identified as the primary growth instrument. Government had a role to play.

The influence of Harrod-Domar economics was far reaching. Development agencies gave great prominence to the need to raise savings ratios. In doing so, they were reflecting the spirit of contemporary development doctrine. Lewis (1954, 1958), Rostow (1960) and Fei and Ranis (1964) had pinpointed the raising of the savings ratio as the key to understanding the process of development and the 'take-off' into sustained growth. In advanced market economies concerned with the apparent success of Soviet economic growth, similar sentiments were expressed and the 'strict fiscal – easy money' prescription for economic growth was frequently advocated.

The introduction of the neo-classical growth model, especially in the contributions of Solow (1956) and Swan (1956) provided the necessary antidote to the excessive claims made for capital accumulation. In neo-classical one sector models, the ultimate determinant of the growth rate is shown to be the autonomously determined rate of population expansion. Fiscal policy is thus rendered an irrelevancy in the pursuit of higher growth *per se*, although it may still have a part to play in the more esoteric pursuit of Golden Rules to achieve Golden Ages.

What the early Harrod-Domar and neo-classical formulations of growth theory possessed in common was the belief that the third ingredient in growth, namely technical progress, was an exogenously determined, fortuitous and costless occurrence – descending like manna from the heavens. Even though it was recognized that technical progress could be the dominant element in the growth equation, especially following the publication of Solow (1957), there was no satisfactory account of the determinants of technical change. Indeed, in the neo-classical growth model with exogenous population expansion and exogenous technical change there was virtually no role for government to play. Discussion turned to the rather sterile issue of whether government intervention could speed up the process of adjustment in the event of some temporary disturbance from the steady state path. But there was no growth policy as such.

This essentially unsatisfactory position has continued until very recent times. The present paper offers an attempt to detail recent contributions which seek to rectify this situation and to draw out the more important implications for economic policy.

THE SOLOW GROWTH FORMULA

Solow (1957) devised a framework for distinguishing the contributions of labour, capital and technical change to economic growth. This pioneering contribution formed the basis of growth accounting exercises pursued by growth specialists such as Denison (1962, 1967) in order to derive important implications for policy as well as to explain international differences in actual recorded growth rates. Whilst critics have questioned the validity of the aggregate production function approach (Hicks 1960) and others have pointed to inconsistencies (Hall 1991) it remains none the less a useful conceptual starting point.

Given a production function of the form

$$Y_t = A_t F(N_t K_t), \tag{1}$$

where A is an index of overall productivity, N and K inputs of labour and capital respectively and the subscript t denotes the time period, the growth rate of output, $\Delta Y/Y$ can be approximated as the *sum* of the growth rate of technology, $\Delta A/A$ and the growth rate of factor inputs $\Delta F(N,K)/F(N,K)$. Since the contribution stemming from the augmentation of factor inputs is indicated by the marginal product of the factor multiplied by the finite change in factor employment, we obtain

$$\Delta Y/Y = \Delta A/A + \partial F \partial N \cdot dN/Y + \partial F \partial K \cdot dK/Y. \tag{2}$$

Assuming factors are paid according to their marginal product so that $\partial F \partial N = W/P$ and $\partial F \partial K = R/P$ where W is the nominal wage, R the nominal rental cost and P the general price index, we have

$$\Delta Y/Y = \Delta A/A + W/P \cdot \Delta N/Y + R/P \cdot \Delta K/Y. \tag{3}$$

Rearranging gives

$$\Delta Y/Y = \Delta A/A + WN/PY \cdot \Delta N/N + RK/PY \cdot \Delta K/K. \tag{4}$$

But WN/PY is simply the share of income paid to wage labour and RK/PY is the share accruing to the owners of employed capital. Empirically, in the context of the United States, these shares are in the order of 0.7 and 0.3 respectively. Consequently, we obtain as a general growth formula the conclusion

$$\Delta Y/Y = \Delta A/A + 0.7\Delta N/N + 0.3\Delta K/K. \tag{5}$$

The initial implications are as startling as perhaps they are misleading. Stated simply and without qualification, they suggest that a 1 per cent increase in output growth could be achieved by *either* a 1 per cent increase in productivity growth, *or* a 1.4 per cent increase in employment, or a 3.3 per cent increase in the capital stock. Even more dramatically, Solow concluded from US time series data over the period 1909 to 1949 that gross output per man had doubled with 87.5 per cent of the increase being attributable to technical change and the remaining 12.5 per cent stemming from the increased use of capital.

Abramovitz (1956) and later Kendrick (1973) were to confirm these general findings; it now became clear that at least 50 per cent of United States growth stemmed from the increased efficiency of productive inputs rather than the mere augmentation of those inputs. And yet there existed no adequate theory to account for such efficiency gains. Indeed, technical progress measures were derived as a *residual* after determining the contribution obtained from augmenting factor inputs. To all intents and purposes the determinants of technical progress lay outside the scope and concern of mainstream economics. This was clearly an unsatisfactory and untenable position for the economics profession and research agendas were modified accordingly.

Finally, it will be noted, that although the Solow growth formula had indicated a comparatively minor role to the capital input in overall growth, it must be recalled that productivity growth may not be independent of the rate of investment activity. That is to say that technical progress may be embodied in the act of investment.

The Solow growth formula, regardless of its limitations, focused attention firmly upon the role of technical progress. If the sources of technical progress could be identified, then the implications for government policy could be profound. Advocates of technical progress pointed to the possible role of education and training where government policy might be expected to exert a major impact. The role of multi-national enterprise as a vehicle for the transmission of technical progress to the less advanced economies also took on new meaning. The distinction between embodied and disembodied technical progress was also brought into sharp focus.[1]

KENNETH ARROW AND LEARNING BY DOING MODELS

One of the first attempts to render technical progress endogenous in growth models was the seminal paper by Arrow (1962) incorporating the concept of learning by doing. Arrow's approach has been generalized and extended by Levhari (1966) and Sheshinski (1967) without departing from Arrow's general well-known conclusion that socially too little is invested and produced. This derives from the spillover effects of increased knowledge benefiting the economy in general over and above those benefits internal to the firm.

In this framework, the level of knowledge is itself a productive factor which depends upon past levels of investment. Moreover, each firm learns from the investment activity of other firms as well as from its own investment behavior. The productivity of a given firm is thus assumed to be an increasing function of cumulative aggregate investment for the industry. More broadly, knowledge acquired by labour is accordingly a function of the total capital stock; learning at any date reflects the integral of capital output to that date.

The essence of these early learning models can be summarized quite simply. Each firm within the economy is assumed to operate with constant returns to scale. A doubling of labour and capital inputs with a given state of knowledge (assumed constant by the firm) will double output. However, the very act of increasing the capital stock through investment by the firm raises the level of knowledge elsewhere. The economy as a whole, therefore, is operating subject to increasing returns. This, of course, is perfectly consistent with decreasing marginal productivity of the intangible capital good, knowledge.

The concept of knowledge being a factor in the production function renders increasing returns inevitable. This follows because a doubling of all tangible factor inputs and productive processes should double output *in an environment with a constant level of knowledge*. When knowledge is permitted to vary as well in consequence of enlarging the capital input, increasing returns follows automatically. The notion of increasing returns being essentially external to individual firms stems from such knowledge being public knowledge. It is this feature, that of increasing returns being external to the firm in the tradition of Marshall (1920) and Young (1928) which allows competitive equilibrium to exist. In doing so, it reconciles increasing returns with the marginal productivity theory of distribution which would otherwise imply total factor payment being in excess of total output (if factors are paid their marginal product). In essence, equilibrium is possible because only labour and capital are actually compensated financially – knowledge being treated as a public good.

Although the Arrow-Levhari-Sheshinski models rendered technical progress endogenous and explained economic growth in the context of aggregate increasing returns being consistent with competitive equilibrium, the steady state solution remains, growth of the economy being equated with the autonomously determined rate of growth of the labour force. Whilst the Arrow model had pointed to sub-optimal levels of investment, the ultimate determinant of economic growth remained non-amenable to policy action. A permanent increase in the share of national income devoted to investment, whether attained through a raising of the private sector savings ratio or by fiscal intervention, cannot influence the ultimate long run growth path. In other words, within these models endogenous technological change is reflected in a *level* effect (via an upward raising of the production function) as opposed to a *growth* effect – to adopt the terminology of Lucas (1988).

It is for this reason that a recent model in this tradition, linking productivity growth directly to investment, takes on special interest. King and Robson (1989) invoke a technical progress function which emphasizes 'learning by watching'. This is the idea that new investment projects in one sector of the economy have a demonstration effect or contagion effect upon the efficiency of other sectors, permitting a raising of their output from the employment of existing factors. The significance of the King and Robson analysis, however, lies in its conclusion that multiple steady state growth paths exist, even for economies which have similar initial endowments, and that tax policy can influence the ultimate growth path attained by the economy. Tax policy can accordingly have real and permanent effects upon the level and growth rate of income.

THE ROMER VERSION

A striking variant on these learning by doing models was provided by the work of Romer (1986, 1989). Again, knowledge is taken as an input in the production function and competitive equilibrium is rendered consistent with increasing aggregate returns owing to externalities. However, the essential feature of Romer's analysis is that knowledge displays increasing marginal productivity. Traditional growth models had postulated diminishing returns; the rate of return upon investment and the rate of growth of income per capita was shown to be a decreasing function of the level of capital per capita. In these models, in the absence of technological change, per capita income attains a constant value in steady state equilibria with no per capita income growth. Moreover, in two sector models or international trade models, rates of return upon capital investment and wage compensation to labour will ultimately converge over time.

In contrast, Romer's model offers a totally different prospect. Even whilst retaining a fully specified competitive equilibrium, per capita income can grow without limit and the rate of return to capital may increase. It is important to note that in Romer's model *new knowledge*, the ultimate determinant of long-run growth, is produced by investment in research technology which exhibits *diminishing returns*. That is to say, a doubling of investment in research technology will not double knowledge. Moreover, the increase in knowledge will not be appropriated solely by the firm undertaking the investment. The creation of new knowledge by one firm raises production possibilities of other firms owing to the inadequacy of patent protection. But – and here is the crucial point of departure – the production of goods from increased knowledge demonstrates *increasing returns*. In other words, knowledge displays increasing marginal productivity.

Romer demonstrates that the three key elements of his model namely externalities, increasing returns in the production of output and decreasing returns in the production of new knowledge are consistent with competitive equilibrium. Moreover, the assumption of diminishing returns to research technology imposes an optimal (from the viewpoint of the private investor) upper limit to the amount of knowledge creating investment activity. Thus, endogenous technical change is explained in terms of the acquisition of knowledge by rational profit maximizing economic agents. It follows that they should respond to appropriate tax and fiscal incentives.

The striking implications of Romer's analysis however, are far more dramatic than the immediate policy implications. The assumption of increasing marginal productivity questions the entire conclusions of traditional growth models. There is no longer any presupposition to converging incomes per capita in two sector or international trade models. Less advanced economies may experience slower rates of growth than advanced economies thus widening the gap between rich and poor countries. Indeed, capital and investment might well flow from poor to rich economies given the increasing marginal productivity of capital in the latter – an analysis reminiscent of Myrdal's (1970) thesis of cumulative causation. Small economies would appear to be placed at a disadvantage in the growth process. Returns to knowledge would appear to carry positive implications for economic integration, economic unions and common markets.

The relevance of Romer's model turns upon the empirical question of whether increasing marginal productivity does or does not apply to the intangible asset knowledge. Romer claims that the conclusion of the model analysis is consistent with the stylized facts as insisted upon by Kaldor (1961) especially the problematic wide dispersion of growth rates across countries.

R & D MODELS

An alternative attempt to explain technological change endogenously is provided in the approach of Uzawa (1965), Lucas (1988) and Romer (1990). The essential feature of these models, as Stern (1991) has highlighted, lies in identifying a sector specializing in the production of ideas. The research sector invokes human capital together with the existing stock of knowledge to produce new knowledge. New knowledge enhances productivity and is available to other sectors at virtually zero marginal cost.

What these models possess in common is an emphasis upon the importance of human capital as being the crucial determinant in the growth process. Production of human capital is more important than the production of physical capital. Learning by doing, or on the job training is, of course a part of human capital formation and may be as important as formal education. Lucas (1988) stresses the distinction between the *internal* effects of human capital where the return accrues to the individual undergoing training and the *external* effects which spill over into output changes. Romer (1990) has a similar emphasis. His formal model separates the rival component of knowledge from the non-rival technological component. Technology is a non-rival input; its use by one firm does not preclude its use by another. Treating knowledge as a non-rival good explains knowledge spillovers and denies a constant returns to scale production function since it is not necessary to replicate the non-rival inputs.

Specifically, the research sector produces ideas – or improved designs for the production of producer durables available for final goods production. In the Romer model, knowledge enters into production in two distinct ways. A new design (idea) allows the production of a new intermediate input. But also, a new design increases the total stock of knowledge and accordingly increases the productivity of human capital employed in the research sector. The owner of a new idea has certain property rights over its use in the production of a new producer durable but not over its use in research. To quote Romer directly: 'If an inventor has a patented design for widgets, no one can make or sell widgets without the agreement of the inventor. On the other hand, other inventors are free to spend time studying the patent application for the widget and learn knowledge that helps in the design of a wodget'.

The clear implication of this distinction is that the benefits of new design inputs are *partially* excludable and retainable to the party initiating the new design. This consideration points to an important difference between the Romer and Lucas papers. In the latter, it is assumed that the production of human capital generates a non-rival non-excludable good. As in the case of Arrow (1962), the production of a non-rival non-excludable good is shown to be the side effect of the production of a conventional good. In effect, knowledge emerges as a public good whose production cannot be explained in terms of firm investment in research and development. By introducing partial excludability, investment in research and development is accounted for in terms of rational profit maximizing behaviour upon the part of firms able to enjoy quasi-rents.

All these models conclude that research produced by the research sector will be suboptimal because of those benefits arising which are freely available to all. This would suggest a possible role for government in subsidizing research. The difficulty here would lie in the adequate identification of the relevant R & D sectors. A second best option might lie in the subsidization of the acquisition of human capital generally.

Romer's formal model goes further in terms of its policy implications. Since research is explained in terms of profit maximizing behaviour, and involves making current outlays in the anticipation of future returns, then a clear role emerges for the rate of interest. More importantly, it suggests that countries with greater stocks of human capital will enjoy a faster rate of economic growth. Low levels of human capital would help to explain the comparative lack of growth in certain underdeveloped economies. Finally, it points to the advantages to be gained from greater involvement in international trade and economic integration.

Brief mention may be made of the paper by King and Rebelo (1990) which like the contribution of King and Robson (1989) stresses the role of tax policy. Essentially King and Rebelo build upon approaches of Uzawa (1965) and Lucas (1988). Their concern is with the observed disparity in international growth rates and they suggest in the context of a two sector endogenous growth model, built upon explicit microeconomic foundations, that differences in public policy can affect the *incentives* to acquire capital in both physical and human forms. In consequence taxation policy can have adverse effects reinforced in open economies having access to international capital markets. Comparatively small changes in tax rates can generate development traps (zero-growth steady states) as well as growth miracles. This emphasis upon the incentive effects of policy on investment in human capital is reminiscent of Schultz (1961).

SOME IMPLICATIONS FOR LESS ADVANCED ECONOMIES

From the policy perspective the most important and arguably the most urgent considerations turn upon the implications for the developing economies. Recent growth accounting exercises have suggested that the percentage of growth accounted for by the 'unexplained residual', is much smaller for the less advanced economy. Estimates by Chenery (1983) suggest ratios exceeding half and less than a quarter for advanced and less advanced economies respectively. This may of course simply reflect the greater stock of human capital in the former. Alternatively, it may reflect other considerations generally excluded from growth theory but which possess particular relevance for the developing economies. Stern (1991) for example, has stressed the importance of management, organization, infrastructure, and sectorial transfer as key elements in the growth process of third world economies.

The implications for Third World economies is probably of greatest moment in terms of international trade and trade policy. This is an area of research explored in considerable detail by Grossman and Helpman (1989, 1990, 1991*a*, 1991*b*) and Helpman (1984). *Potentially*, it is the less advanced economy which stands to gain the most from the freeing of international trade since by doing so it can draw upon the stock of world knowledge. But technological flows from rich to poor economies are by no means automatic (see for example Lucas 1990) which raises the issue of the role of multinational corporations and how they respond to incentives for technological transfer.

This leads naturally into the question of policy. The essence of modern statements of endogenous growth is that the technical progress residual is accounted for by endogenous human capital formation. But if the latter can be influenced by government policy world growth may be changed accordingly. For example, if a country possessed of a comparative advantage in R & D activity were to subsidize research, world growth would increase. Equally, a similar subsidy introduced by an economy relatively more efficient in manufacturing as opposed to innovating *may* cause world growth to decline.

With regard to trade policy, clearly protectionist activity can influence the allocation of resources into the knowledge creating sector. Trade policies which afford protection to the manufacturing sector may promote the transfer of skilled labour from research activity into manufacturing which will retard innovation. *Ceteris paribus*, trade policy will effect a shift of resources from research to manufacturing in policy active countries and in the opposite direction in policy inactive countries. However, the issue is by no means clear cut. If the profit motive governs investment in research activities, returns to research will rise when the sector incorporating the resulting technology is promoted by trade policy. In a three sector model (research, manufacturing and services) research and manufacturing may advance together when the latter is protected at the expense of contraction within the service sector.

Other complications emerge. Different economies will possess different ratios of skilled human capital to unskilled labour. The opening up of trade will then be expected to change relative prices of human capital and labour. The sudden appearance of cheap labour available to high ratio countries may reduce incentives to produce non-rival inputs and thus slow down the growth process for the high ratio country – the example afforded here being the United States *vis-à-vis* Mexico. Again, on reasonable assumptions concerning the required ratio of human capital per unskilled worker for R & D activity as compared to that for the production of industrial goods, these models are able to predict the emergence of international licensing and multinational investment and also to account for the growth of world trade as a percentage of world GNP over time.

Implications also emerge for the international product cycle. Traditionally, invention and new products occur in the advanced economy where R & D activity is well developed. Later, either by imitation or technology transfer they will be produced in the less advanced country and ultimately production of these goods will migrate to the low wage economy. Accordingly, trade in manufactured products takes place on the basis of exchange between the latest innovative goods produced only in the advanced economy and the more traditional goods now produced predominantly by the less advanced. The product cycle accounts for an ever evolving pattern of international trade with the advanced economy importing the very same goods that initially it exported.

In the context of the product cycle model, international trade always emerges as a contributor to faster economic growth in both advanced and less advanced economies. In the former, the migration of production from the advanced to the less advanced economy frees resources for use in growth enhancing product development activity. At the same time, growth occurs faster in the less advanced economy since the resources needed for learning and adapting the techniques imported from the advanced economy are far fewer than those needed for autonomous new product development. In both cases, the subsidization of learning activities (innovation in the advanced economy, imitation in the less advanced) may be expected to enhance long run growth rates.

In conclusion, it would appear clear that trade policy has the potential for influencing long run growth paths for the world economy. However, it would be unwise to suggest that the future is one of unlimited optimism. Numerous difficulties present themselves. The identification of growth influencing knowledge sectors is itself a major difficulty *ex ante* if not *ex post*. Second, the fact that conclusions deriving from the model analysis can be so easily overturned by the alteration of the conditions or assumptions underlying the analysis – which for the most part are unlikely to be resolved empirically – weakens one's confidence in growth prescription. Moreover, in the context of international trade and the world economy, the outcome and effects of policy measures are themselves interdependent with the policy actions of others. This would point to the need for the coordination of national policies or at least the consideration of second best outcomes. None the less, and despite these caveats one might reasonably endorse the policy proposal of Lucas (1990), namely that economic aid programmes to developing economies might well be tied to the recipients' willingness and openness to accept foreign investment upon competitive terms.

NOTE

1 Disembodied technical progress is that which is able to be exploited by the *existing* stock of capital employing the same kind of labour. In contrast, embodied technical change does not benefit older machinery; rather it is embodied in the very act of new investment.

REFERENCES

Abramovitz, M. (1956) 'Resource and output trends in the United States since 1870', *American Economic Review* 46, Papers and Proceedings, May, pp. 5–23.
——(1986) 'Catching up, forging ahead, and falling behind', *Journal of Economic History* 46, pp. 385–406.
Arrow, K. J. (1962) 'The economic implications of learning by doing', *Review of Economic Studies* 29, pp. 155–73.
Arthar, W. B. (1989) 'Competing technologies: increasing returns and lock-in by historical events', *Economic Journal* 99, March, pp. 116–31.
Baumol, W. J. (1986) 'Productivity growth, convergence and welfare: what the long-run data show', *American Economic Review* 76, pp. 1072–85.
Blitch, Charles P. (1983) 'Allyn Young on increasing returns', *Journal of Post-Keynesian Economics* 5, pp. 359–72.
Chenery, H. B., Robinson, S. and Syrquin, M. (1986) *Industrialization and Growth: A Comparative Study*, Washington DC: World Bank.
Cohen, W. M. and Levinthal, D. A. (1989) 'Innovation and learning: the two faces of R & D', *Economic Journal* 99, pp. 569–96.
Denison, Edward F. (1961) *The Sources of Economic Growth in the United States*, Committee for Economic Development, New York.
——(1962) 'How to raise the high-employment growth rate by one percentage point', *American Economic Review*, Papers and Proceedings, May, pp. 67–75.

Denison, Edward F. (Assisted by J. Poullier) (1967) *Why Growth Rates Differ: Postwar Experience in Nine Western Countries*, Washington, DC: Brookings.

Domar, E. (1947) 'Expansion and employment', *American Economic Review* 37, pp. 34–55.

Dowrick, Steve and Nguyen, Duc-Tho (1989) 'OECD comparative economic growth 1950–85: catch-up and convergence', *American Economic Review* 79, pp. 1010–30.

Feder, Gershon (1983) 'On exports and economic growth', *Journal of Development Economics* 12, pp. 59–73.

Fei, J. C. H. and Ranis, G. (1964) *Development of the Labor Surplus Economy: Theory and Policy*, Homewood, IL: Irwin.

Grossman, G. M. and Helpman, E. (1989) 'Product development and international trade', *Journal of Political Economy* 97, pp. 1261–83.

——(1990) 'Trade innovation and growth', *American Economic Review* 80, Papers and Proceedings, pp. 86–91.

——(1991 *a*) 'Endogenous product cycles', *Economic Journal* 101, pp. 1214–29.

——(1991 *b*) *Innovation and Growth: In The Global Economy*, pp. 359 Cambridge, MA: MIT Press.

Hall, Robert (1991) 'Invariance properties of Solow's productivity residual', *Growth/ Productivity/Unemployment: Essays in Honor of Robert Solow's 65th Birthday* (ed. P. Diamond), Cambridge, MA: MIT Press.

Harrod, R. F. (1939) 'An essay in dynamic theory', *Economic Journal* 49, pp. 14–33.

Helpman, E. (1984) 'A simple theory of international trade with multinational corporations', *Journal of Political Economy* 92, pp. 451–71.

Hicks, J. R. (1960) 'Thoughts on the theory of capital: The Corfu Conference', *Oxford Economic Papers* 12, pp. 123–32.

Kaldor, N. (1957) 'A model of economic growth', *Economic Journal* 67, pp. 591–624.

——(1961) 'Capital accumulation and growth', In *The Theory of Capital* (ed. F. A. Lutz and D. C. Hague), London: Macmillan.

Kendrick, J. (1973) *Postwar Productivity Trends in the United States 1948–1969*, New York: National Bureau of Economic Research.

King, Mervyn (1989) 'Economic growth and the life-cycle of firms', *European Economic Review* 33, pp. 325–34.

King, Mervyn and Robson, Mark (1989) *Endogenous Growth and the Role of History*, London: LSE Financial Markets Group, Discussion Paper no. 63.

King, Robert G. and Rebelo, Sergio (1990) 'Public policy and economic growth: developing neo-classical implications', *Journal of Political Economy* 98, pp. S126–50.

Levhari, David (1966*a*) 'Further implications of "learning by doing"', *Review of Economic Studies* 33, pp. 31–9.

——(1966 *b*) 'Extensions of "Arrow's learning by doing"', *Review of Economic Studies* 33, pp. 117–32.

Levin, R. C., Cohen, W. M. and Mowery, D. C. (1985) 'R & D appropriability, opportunity and market structure: new evidence on some Schumpeterian hypotheses', *American Economic Review* 75, pp. 20–4.

Lewis, W. A. (1954) 'Economic development with unlimited supplies of labour', *Manchester School* 22, pp. 139–91.

Lucas, Robert E. Jr (1988) 'On the mechanics of economic development', *Journal of Monetary Economics* 22, pp. 3–22.

——(1990) 'Why doesn't capital flow from rich to poor countries?', *American Economic Review*, Papers and Proceedings, vol. 80, pp. 92–6.

Marshall, A. (1920) *Principles of Economics*, 8th edn, London: Macmillan.

Mokyr, Joel (1991) 'Evolutionary biology, technological change and economic history', *Bulletin of Economic Research* 43, pp. 127–49.

Myrdal, Gunnar (1970) *The Challenge of World Poverty*, New York: Pantheon.

Norsworthy, J. R. (1984) 'Growth accounting and productivity measurement', *Review of Income and Wealth* 30, pp. 309–29.

Romer, Paul M. (1986) 'Increasing returns and long-run growth', *Journal of Political Economy* 94, pp. 1002–37.

—— (1987) 'Growth based on increasing returns due to specialization', *American Economic Review* 77, Papers and Proceedings, pp. 56–62.

—— (1990) 'Endogenous technical change', *Journal of Political Economy* 98, pp. S71–102.

—— (1990) 'Are non-convexities important for understanding growth', *American Economic Review*, Papers and Proceedings, vol. 80, pp. 97–103.

Rostow, W. W. (1960) *The Stages of Economic Growth: A Non-Communist Manifesto*, Cambridge: Cambridge University Press.

Schultz, Theodore W. (1961) 'Investment in human capital', *American Economic Review* 51, pp. 1–17.

Scott, Morris (1989) *A New View of Economic Growth*, Oxford: Oxford University Press.

Segerstrom, Paul S. (1991) 'Innovation, imitation and economic growth', *Journal of Political Economy* 99, pp. 807–27.

Sheshinski, E. (1967) 'Optimal accumulation with learning by doing', in *Essays on the Theory of Optimal Economic Growth* (ed. K. Shell), Cambridge, MA: MIT Press.

Solow, R. M. (1956) 'A contribution to the theory of economic growth', *Quarterly Journal of Economics* 70, pp. 65–94.

—— (1957) 'Technical change and the aggregate production function', *Review of Economics and Statistics* 31, pp. 312–20.

—— (1970) *Growth Theory: An Exposition*, Oxford: Oxford University Press.

Stern, N. H. (1989) 'The economics of development: a survey' *Economic Journal* 99, pp. 597–685.

—— (1991) 'The determinants of growth', *Economic Journal* 101, pp. 122–33.

Stokey, Nancy L. (1988) 'Learning by doing and the introduction of new goods', *Journal of Political Economy* 96, pp. 701–17.

Swan, T. W. (1956) 'Economic growth and capital accumulation', *Economic Record* 32, pp. 334–61.

—— (1964) 'Growth models of golden ages and production functions', in *Economic Development with Special Reference to East Asia* (ed. K. Berrill), London: Macmillan.

Uzawa, H. (1965) 'Optimum technical change in an aggregative model of economic growth', *International Economic Review* 6, pp. 18–31.

Young, Allyn A. (1928) 'Increasing returns and economic progress', *Economic Journal* 38, pp. 527–42.

26 The origins of endogenous growth

Paul M. Romer
Journal of Economic Perspectives (1994) 8, Winter, pp. 3–22

The phrase 'endogenous growth' embraces a diverse body of theoretical and empirical work that emerged in the 1980s. This work distinguishes itself from neoclassical growth by emphasizing that economic growth is an endogenous outcome of an economic system, not the result of forces that impinge from outside. For this reason, the theoretical work does not invoke exogenous technological change to explain why income per capita has increased by an order of magnitude since the industrial revolution. The empirical work does not settle for measuring a growth accounting residual that grows at different rates in different countries. It tries instead to uncover the private and public sector choices that cause the rate of growth of the residual to vary across countries. As in neoclassical growth theory, the focus in endogenous growth is on the behavior of the economy as a whole. As a result, this work is complementary to, but different from, the study of research and development or productivity at the level of the industry or firm.

This chapter recounts two versions that are told of the origins of work on endogenous growth. The first concerns what has been called the convergence controversy. The second concerns the struggle to construct a viable alternative to perfect competition in aggregate-level theory. These accounts are not surveys. They are descriptions of the scholarly equivalent to creation myths, simple stories that economists tell themselves and each other to give meaning and structure to their current research efforts. Understanding the differences between these two stories matters because they teach different lessons about the relative importance of theoretical work and empirical work in economic analysis and they suggest different directions for future work on growth.

VERSION 1: THE CONVERGENCE CONTROVERSY

The question that has attracted the most attention in recent work on growth is whether per capita income in different countries is converging. A crucial stimulus to work on this question was the creation of new data sets with information on income per capita for many countries and long periods of time (Maddison 1982; Heston and Summers 1991).

In his analysis of the Maddison data, William Baumol (1986) found that poorer countries like Japan and Italy substantially closed the per capita income gap with richer countries like the United States and Canada in the years from 1870 to 1979. Two objections to his analysis soon became apparent. First, in the Maddison data set, convergence takes place only in the years since World War II. Between 1870 and 1950, income per capita tended to diverge (Abramovitz 1986). Second, the Maddison data set included only those economies that had successfully industrialized by the end of the sample period. This induces a sample selection bias that apparently accounts for most of the evidence in favor of convergence (De Long 1988).

As a result, attention then shifted to the broad sample of countries in the Heston-Summers data set. As Figure 26.1 shows, convergence clearly fails in this broad sample of countries. Income per capita in 1960 is plotted on the horizontal axis. The average annual rate of growth of income per capita from 1960 to 1985 is plotted on the vertical axis.[1] On average, poor countries in this sample grow no faster than the rich countries.

Figure 26.1 poses one of the central questions in development. Why is it that the poor countries as a group are not catching up with the rich countries in the same way that, for example, the low income states in the United States have been catching up with the high income states? Both Robert Lucas (1988) and I (Romer 1986) cited the failure of cross-country convergence to motivate models of growth that drop the two central assumptions of the neoclassical model: that technological change is exogenous and that the same technological opportunities are available in all countries of the world.

To see why Figure 26.1 poses a problem for the conventional analysis, consider a very simple version of the neoclassical model. Let output take the

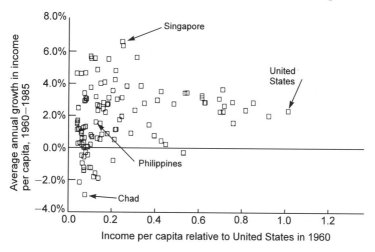

Figure 26.1 Testing for convergence

simple Cobb-Douglas form $Y = A(t)K^{1-\beta}L^\beta$. In this expression, Y denotes net national product, K denotes the stock of capital, L denotes the stock of labor, and A denotes the level of technology. The notation indicating that A is a function of time signals the standard assumption in neoclassical or exogenous growth models: the technology improves for reasons that are outside the model. Assume that a constant fraction of net output, s, is saved by consumers each year. Because the model assumes a closed economy, s is also the ratio of net investment to net national product. Because we are working with net (rather than gross) national product and investment, sY is the rate of growth of the capital stock. Let $y = Y/L$ denote output per worker and let $k = K/L$ denote capital per worker. Let n denote the rate of growth of the labor force. Finally, let a ``$\hat{\ }$'' over a variable denote its exponential rate of growth. Then the behavior of the economy can be summarized by the following equation:

$$\hat{y} = (1 - \beta)\hat{k} + \hat{A}$$
$$= (1 - \beta)[sA(t)^{1/(1-\beta)}y^{(-\beta)/(1-\beta)} - n] + \hat{A} \tag{1}$$

The first line in this equation follows by dividing total output by the stock of labor and then calculating rates of growth. This expression specifies the procedure from growth accounting for calculating the technology residual. Calculate the growth in output per worker, then subtract the rate of growth of the capital–labor ratio times the share of capital income in total income from the rate of growth of output per worker. The second line follows by substituting in an expression for the rate of growth of the stock of capital per worker, as a function of the savings rate s, the growth rate of the labor force n, the level of the technology $A(t)$, and the level of output per worker, y.

Outside of the steady state, the second line of the equation shows how variation in the investment rate and in the level of output per worker should translate into variation in the rate of growth. The key parameter is the exponent β on labor in the Cobb-Douglas expression for output. Under the neoclassical assumption that the economy is characterized by perfect competition, β is equal to the share of total income that is paid as compensation to labor, a number that can be calculated directly from the national income accounts. In the sample as a whole, a reasonable benchmark for β is 0.6. (In industrialized economies, it tends to be somewhat larger.) This means that in the second line of the equation, the exponent $(-\beta)/(1 - \beta)$ on the level of output per worker y should be on the order of about -1.5.

We can now perform the following calculation. Pick a country like the Philippines that had output per worker in 1960 that was equal to about 10 percent of output per worker in the United States. Because $0.1^{-1.5}$ is equal to about 30, the equation suggests that the United States would have required a savings rate that is about 30 times larger than the savings rate in the Philippines for these two countries to have grown at the same rate. If we use $\frac{2}{3}$ instead of 0.6 as the estimate of β, the required savings rate in the United States would be 100 times larger than the savings rate in the Philippines. The evidence shows that these predicted saving rates for the United States are orders of magnitude too large.

A key assumption in this calculation is that the level of the technology $A(t)$ is the same in the Philippines and the United States. (The possibility that $A(t)$ might differ is considered below.) If they have the same technology, the only way to explain why workers in the Philippines were only 10 percent as productive as workers in the United States is to assume that they work with about $0.1^{1/(1-\beta)}$ or between 0.3 percent and 0.1 percent as much capital per worker. Because the marginal product of capital depends on the capital stock raised to the power $-\beta$, the marginal product of an additional unit of capital is $0.1^{-\beta/(1-\beta)}$ times larger in the Philippines than it is in the United States, so a correspondingly higher rate of investment is needed in the United States to get the same effect on output.

Figure 26.2 plots the level of per capita income against the ratio of gross investment to gross domestic product for the Heston-Summers sample of countries. The correlation in this figure at least has the correct sign to explain why poor countries on average are not growing faster than the rich countries – that is, a higher level of income is associated with a higher investment rate. But if β is between 0.6 and 0.7, the variation in investment between rich and poor countries is at least an order of magnitude too small to explain why the rich and poor countries seem to grow at about the same rate. In concrete terms, the share of investment in the United States is not 30 or 100 times the share in the Philippines. At most, it is twice as large.

Of course, the data in Figures 26.1 and 26.2 are not exactly what the theory calls for, but the differences are not likely to help resolve the problem here. For example, the display equation depends on the net

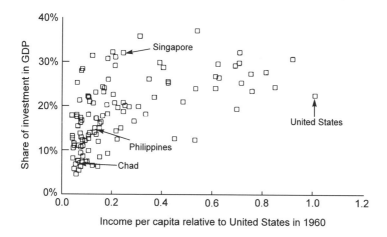

Figure 26.2 Per capita income and investment

investment rate instead of the gross investment rate. Because we do not have reliable data on depreciation for this sample of countries, it is not possible to construct a net investment ratio. A reasonable conjecture, however, is that depreciation accounts for a larger share of GDP in rich countries than it does in poor countries, so the difference between the net investment rate in rich and poor countries will be even smaller than the difference between the gross investment rates illustrated in the figure. The display equation also calls for output per worker rather than output per capita, but for a back-of-the-envelope calculation, variation in income per capita should be close enough to variation in output per worker to show that a simple version of the neoclassical model will have trouble fitting the facts.

The way to reconcile the data with the theory is to reduce β so that labor is relatively less important in production and diminishing returns to capital accumulation set in more slowly. The theoretical challenge in constructing a formal model with a smaller value for β lies in justifying why labor is paid more than its marginal product and capital is paid less. To explain these divergences between private and social returns, I proposed a model in which A was determined locally by knowledge spillovers (Romer 1987a). I followed Arrow's (1962) treatment of knowledge spillovers from capital investment and assumed that each unit of capital investment not only increases the stock of physical capital but also increases the level of the technology for all firms in the economy through knowledge spillovers. I also assumed that an increase in the total supply of labor causes negative spillover effects because it reduces the incentives for firms to discover and implement labor-saving innovations that also have positive spillover effects on production throughout the economy.

This leads to a functional relationship between the technology in a country and the other variables that can be written as $A(K, L)$. Then output for firm j can be written as $Y_j = A(K, L)K_j^{1-\alpha}L_j^{\alpha}$, where variables with subscripts are ones that firm j can control, and variables without subscripts represent economy-wide totals. Because the effect that a change in a firm's choice of K or L has on A is an external effect that any individual firm can ignore, the exponent α measures the private effect of an increase in employment on output. A 1 percent increase in the labor used by a firm leads to an α percent increase in its output. As a result, α will be equal to the fraction of output that is paid as compensation to labor. Suppose, purely for simplicity, that the expression linking the stock of A to K and L takes the form $A(K, L) = K^{\gamma}L^{-\gamma}$ for some γ greater than zero. Then the reduced form expression for aggregate output as a function of K and L would be $Y = K^{1-\beta}L^{\beta}$ where β is equal to $\alpha - \gamma$. This exponent β represents the aggregate effect of an increase in employment. It captures both the private effect α and the external effect $-\gamma$. In the calculation leading up to the equation displayed above, it is this aggregate or social effect that matters. According to this model, β can now be smaller than labor's share in national income.

Using a simple cross-country regression based on an equation like the display equation, I found that the effect of the investment rate on growth was positive and the effect of initial income on growth was negative. Many other investigators have found this kind of negative coefficient on initial income in a growth regression. This result has received special attention, particularly in light of the failure of overall convergence exhibited in Figure 26.1. It suggests that convergence or regression to the mean would have taken place if all other variables had been held constant.

After imposing the constraint implied by the equation, I estimated the value of β to be in the vicinity of 0.25 (Romer 1987a: Table 4). With this value, it would take only a doubling of the investment rate – rather than a 30- or 100-fold increase – to offset the negative effect that a ten-fold increase in the level of output per worker would have on the rate of growth. These figures are roughly consistent with the numbers for the United States and the Philippines. For the sample as a whole, the small negative effect on growth implied by higher levels of output per worker are offset by higher investment rates in richer countries.

Robert Barro and Xavier Sala i Martin (1992) subsequently showed that the conclusions about the size of what I am calling β (they use different notation) were the same whether one looked across countries or between states in the United States. They find that a value for β of the order of 0.2 is required to reconcile the convergence dynamics of the states with the equation presented above. Convergence takes place, but at a very slow rate. They also observe that this slow rate of convergence would be even harder to explain if one introduced capital mobility into the model.

As a possible explanation of the slow rate of convergence, Barro and Sala i Martin (1992) propose an alternative to the neoclassical model that is somewhat less radical than the spillover model that I proposed. As in the endogenous growth models, they suggest that the level of the technology $A(t)$ can be different in different states or countries and try to model its dynamics. They take the initial distribution of differences in $A(t)$ as given by history and suggest that knowledge about A diffuses slowly from high A to low A regions. This would mean that across the states, there is underlying variation in $A(t)$ that causes variation in both k and y. As a result, differences in output per worker do not necessarily signal large differences in the marginal product of capital. In fact, free mobility of capital can be allowed in this model and the rate of return on capital can be equalized between the different regions. Because the flow of knowledge from the technology leader makes the technology grow faster in the follower country, income per capita will grow faster in the follower as diffusion closes what has been called a technology gap.[2] The speed of convergence will be determined primarily by the rate of diffusion of knowledge, so the convergence dynamics tell us nothing about the exponents on capital and labor.

The assumption that the level of technology can be different in different regions is particularly attractive in the context of an analysis of the state data, because it removes the prediction of the closed-economy, identical-technology neoclassical model that the marginal productivity of capital can be many times larger in poorer regions than in rich regions.[3] According to the data reported by Barro and Sala i Martin (1992), in 1880, income per capita in states such as North Carolina, South Carolina, Virginia, and Georgia was about one-third of income per capita in industrial states such as New York, Massachusetts, and Rhode Island. If β is equal to 0.6, $-\beta/(1-\beta)$ is equal to -1.5 and $(\frac{1}{3})^{-1.5}$ is equal to about 5. This means that the marginal product of capital should have been about five times higher in the South than it was in New England. It is difficult to imagine barriers to flows of capital between the states that could have kept these differences from rapidly being arbitraged away. In particular, it would be difficult to understand why any capital investment at all took place in New England after 1880. But if there were important differences in the technology in use in the two regions, the South may not have offered higher returns to capital investment.

In a third approach to the analysis of cross-country data, Greg Mankiw, David Romer, and David Weil (1992) took the most conservative path, showing that it is possible to justify a low value for β even in a pure version of the closed economy, neoclassical model which assumes that the level of technology is the same in each country in the world. The only change they make is to extend the usual two-factor neoclassical model by allowing for human capital H as well as physical capital K. They use the fraction of the working age population that attends secondary school as a measure of the rate of investment in human capital that is analogous to the share of physical capital investment in total GDP.

They conclude from their cross-country growth regressions that $Y = A(t)K^{\frac{1}{3}}H^{\frac{1}{3}}L^{\frac{1}{3}}$ is a reasonable specification for aggregate output. In this model, the exponent β on the fixed factor of production L has been reduced from 0.6 to 0.33. This lower value of β is consistent with the data on income shares because total wage payments consist of payments to both human capital and unskilled labor. If K and H vary together across countries, this specification implies that it takes about a three-fold increase in investment (an increase by the factor $0.1^{-0.5}$ to be precise) to offset a ten-fold increase in output per worker in a comparison across nations. Once one takes account of variation in investment in schooling as well as in investment in physical capital, a factor of three is roughly consistent with the variation in total investment rates observed in the Summer-Heston sample of countries.

Although Mankiw *et al.* (1992) do not examine the state data, it is clear what their style of explanation would suggest. They would assume that the same technology was available in the North and the South. Suppose that Northern states had levels of both human capital and physical capital that were higher than those in the Southern states in the same ratio. A value of β equal to $\frac{1}{3}$, together with the fact that output per capita was about one-third as large in the South in 1880, would imply that rate of return on physical capital and the wage for human capital were both about $(\frac{1}{3})^{-0.5}$ (or about 1.7) times higher in the Southern states than they were in the New England states. Compared to the factor of 5 implied by the model without human capital, these parameters would imply much smaller incentives to shift all capital investment to the South. (They would imply, however, that human capital would tend to migrate from the North to the South.)

The implication from this work is that if you are committed to the neoclassical model, the kind of data exhibited in Figures 26.1 and 26.2 cannot be used to make you recant. They do not compel you to give up the convenience of a model in which markets are perfect. They cannot force you to address the complicated issues that arise in the economic analysis of the production and diffusion of technology, knowledge, and information.

AN EVALUATION OF THE CONVERGENCE CONTROVERSY

The version of the development of endogenous growth theory outlined above skips lots of detail and smooths over many complications that made this seem like a real controversy at the time. In retrospect, what is striking is how little disagreement there is about the basic facts. Everyone agrees that a conventional neoclassical model with an exponent of about one-third on capital and about two-thirds on labor cannot fit the cross-country or cross-state data. Everyone agrees that the marginal product of investment cannot be orders of magnitudes smaller in rich countries than in poor countries. The differences between the different researchers concern the inferences about models that we should draw from these facts. As is usually the case in macroeconomics, many different inferences are consistent with the same regression statistics.

This history has many elements in common with other stories about the development of economics. The story starts with the emergence of new data. These present anomalies that lead to new theoretical models, some of which differ markedly from previous, well-accepted models. Then a more conservative interpretation emerges that accommodates the new evidence and preserves much of the structure of the old body of theory. In the end, we have refined the set of alternatives somewhat, but seem to be left in about the same position where we started, with too many theories that are consistent with the same small number of facts.

But economists who accept this interpretation come to the conclusion that we do not have enough data only because they restrict attention to the kind of statistical evidence illustrated in Figures 26.1 and 26.2. They fail to take account of all the other kinds of evidence that are available. My original work on growth (Romer 1983, 1986) was motivated primarily by the observation that in the broad sweep of history, classical economists like Malthus and Ricardo came to conclusions that were completely wrong about prospects for growth. Over time, growth rates have been increasing, not decreasing.[4] Lucas (1988) emphasized the fact that international patterns of migration and wage differentials are very difficult to reconcile with a neoclassical model. If the same technology were available in all countries, human capital would not move from places where it is scarce to places where it is abundant and the same worker would not earn a higher wage after moving from the Philippines to the United States.

The main message of this chapter is that the convergence controversy captures only part of what endogenous growth has been all about. It may encompass a large fraction of the recently published papers, but it nevertheless represents a digression from the main story behind endogenous growth theory. The story told about the convergence controversy also tends to reinforce a message that I think is seriously misleading – that data are the only scarce resource in economic analysis.

VERSION 2: THE PASSING OF PERFECT COMPETITION

The second version of the origins of endogenous growth starts from the observation that we had enough evidence to reject all the available growth models throughout the 1950s, 1960s and 1970s. What we lacked were good aggregate-level models. This version of the origins of endogenous growth is therefore concerned with the painfully slow progress we have made in constructing formal economic models at the aggregate level. It suggests that progress in economics does not come merely from the mechanical application of hypothesis tests to data sets. There is a creative act associated with the construction of new models that is also crucial to the process.

The evidence about growth that economists have long taken for granted and that poses a challenge for growth theorists can be distilled to five basic facts.

Fact 1: There are many firms in a market economy

The fact is so obvious that we often do not bother to state it, but it clearly will not do to have a model in which there are overwhelming forces that tend to concentrate all output in the hands of a single, economy-wide monopolist.

Fact 2: Discoveries differ from other inputs in the sense that many people can use them at the same time

The idea behind the transistor, the principles behind internal combustion, the organizational structure of a modern corporation, the concepts of double entry bookkeeping – all these pieces of information and many more like them have the property that it is technologically possible for everybody and every firm to make use of them at the same time. In the language of public finance, ordinary goods are rival goods, but information is nonrival.

Fact 3: It is possible to replicate physical activities

Replication implies that the aggregate production function representing a competitive market should be characterized by homogeneity of degree one in all of its conventional (that is, rival) inputs. If we represent output in the form $Y = AF(K, H, L)$, then doubling all three of K, H, and L should allow a doubling of output. There is no need to double the nonrival inputs represented by A because the existing pieces of information can be used in both instances of the productive activity at the same time. (The assumption that the market is competitive means that the existing activity already operates at the minimum efficient scale, so there are no economies of scale from building a single plant that is twice as large as the existing one.)

If farming were the relevant activity instead of manufacturing, we would clearly need to include land as an input in production, and in the economy as a whole, it is not possible to double the stock of land. This does not change the fundamental implication of the replication argument. If aggregate output is homogeneous of degree 1 in the rival inputs and firms are price takers, Euler's theorem implies that the compensation paid to the rival inputs must exactly equal the value of output produced. This fact is part of what makes the neoclassical model so simple and makes growth accounting work. The only problem is that this leaves nothing to compensate any inputs that were used to produce the discoveries that lead to increases in A.

Fact 4: Technological advance comes from things that people do

No economist, so far as I know, has ever been willing to make a serious defense of the proposition that technological change is literally a function of elapsed calendar time. Being explicit about the issues here is important nevertheless, because it can help untangle a link that is sometimes made between exogeneity and randomness. If I am prospecting for gold or looking for a change in the DNA of a bacterium that will let it eat the oil from an oil spill, success for me will be dominated by chance. Discovery will seem to be an exogenous event in the sense that forces outside of my control seem to determine whether I succeed. But the aggregate rate of discovery is endogenous. When more people start prospecting for gold or experimenting with bacteria, more valuable discoveries will be found. This will be true even if discoveries are accidental side effects of some other activity (finding gold as a side effect of ditch-digging) or if market incentives play no role in encouraging the activity (as when discoveries about basic molecular biology were induced by government research grants). The aggregate rate of discovery is still determined by things that people do.

Fact 5: Many individuals and firms have market power and earn monopoly rents on discoveries

Even though the information from discoveries is nonrival (as noted in fact 2), economically important discoveries usually do not meet the other criterion for a public good; they typically are partially excludable, or excludable for at least some period of time. Because people and firms have some control over the information produced by most discoveries, it cannot be treated as a pure public good. This information is not like a short-wave radio broadcast that everyone can access without the permission of the sender. But if a firm can control access to a discovery, it can charge a price that is higher than zero. It therefore earns monopoly profits because information has no opportunity cost.

The neoclassical model that was developed and applied by Robert Solow (1956, 1957) and others constituted a giant first step forward in the process of constructing a formal model of growth. The discussion of the convergence controversy, framed as it was almost entirely in terms of the neoclassical model, illustrates the model's power and durability. Like any model, the neoclassical model is a compromise between what we would like from a model and what is feasible given the state of our modeling skills. The neoclassical model captured facts 1, 2, and 3, but postponed consideration of facts 4 and 5. From a theoretical point of view, a key advantage of the model is its treatment of technology as a pure public good. This makes it possible to accommodate fact 2 – that knowledge is a nonrival good – in a model that retains the simplicity of perfect competition. The public good assumption also implies that knowledge is nonexcludable, and this is clearly inconsistent with the evidence summarized in fact 5 – that individuals and firms earn profits from their discoveries. This assumption was useful, nevertheless, as part of an interim modeling strategy that was adopted until models with nonrivalry and excludability could be formulated.

Endogenous growth models try to take the next step and accommodate fact 4. Work in this direction started in the 1960s. For example, Karl Shell (1966) made the point about replication noted above, showing that it left no resources to pay for increases in A. He proposed a model in which A is financed from tax revenue collected by the government. Endogenous growth models have tended to follow Arrow (1962) and emphasize the private sector activities that contribute to technological advance rather than public sector funding for research. A subset of these models has tried to incorporate both fact 4 (that technological advance comes from things people do) and fact 5 (the existence of monopoly rents). These are sometimes referred to as neo-Schumpeterian models because of Schumpeter's emphasis of the importance of temporary monopoly power as a motivating force in the innovative process.[5] In addition, there are two other distinct kinds of endogenous growth models. Spillover models have already been mentioned. Linear models will be described below.[6]

With the benefit of hindsight, it is obvious that growth theorists would eventually have to do what economists working at the industry and firm level have done: abandon the assumption of price-taking competition. Otherwise, there is no hope of capturing fact 5. Even at the time, the point received at least some attention. In his 1956 paper, Solow remarked in a footnote on the desirability of extending the model to allow for monopolistic competition. One of his students, William Nordhaus (1969), subsequently outlined a growth model that did have patents, monopoly power, and many firms. For technical reasons, this model still invoked exogenous technological change, so it is not strictly speaking a model of endogenous growth – but it could have been extended to become one. Because a general formal treatment of monopolistic competition was not available at the time, little progress in this direction took place for the next 20 years.

Even though it is obvious in retrospect that endogenous growth theory would have to introduce imperfect competition, this was not the direction that the first models of the 1980s pursued. Both my model (Romer 1986) and Robert Lucas's model (1988) included fact 4 without taking the final step and including step 5. In both of these models, the technology is endogenously provided as a side effect of private investment decisions. From the point of view of the users of technology, it is still treated as a pure public good, just as it is in the neoclassical model. As a result, firms can be treated as price takers and an equilibrium with many firms can exist.

This technique for introducing a form of aggregate increasing returns into a model with many firms was first proposed by Alfred Marshall (1890). To overturn the pessimistic predictions of Malthus and Ricardo, he wanted to introduce some form of aggregate increasing returns. To derive his downward sloping supply curve from an industry with many firms, Marshall introduced the new notion of increasing returns that were external to any individual firm. External effects therefore entered into economics to preserve the analytical machinery of supply and demand curves and price taking in the presence of increasing returns. The analysis of other kinds of external effects – smoke, bees, and so on – came later.[7]

As noted in the previous discussion of spillover models, Arrow (1962) constructed a model along these lines. In a simplified form, output for firm j in his model can be written as $Y_j = A(K)F(K_j, L_j)$, where (as before) K without a subscript denotes the aggregate stock of capital. For technical reasons, Arrow, like Nordhaus, did not emphasize the fact that his model could lead to sustained, endogenous growth. For the parameter values that he studies, if the size of the population is held constant, growth eventually comes to a halt.

Lucas's model has a very similar underlying structure. There, it is investments in human capital rather than physical capital that have spillover effects that increase the level of the technology. It is as if output for firm j takes the form $Y_j = A(H)F(K_j, H_j)$. Both of these models accommodated facts 1–4 but not fact 5.[8]

In my first paper on growth (Romer 1986), I assumed in effect that aggregate output could be written as $Y = A(R)F(R_j, K_j, L_j)$ where R_j stands for the stock of results from expenditure on research and development by firm j.[9] I assumed that it is spillovers from private research efforts that lead to improvements in the public stock of knowledge A. This seemed appealing because it recognized that firms did research and development on purpose and that the relevant spillovers or incomplete property rights were associated with the results from research and development. (In the microeconomic analysis of research and development at the industry level, Zvi Griliches (1979) used this same kind of formulation.) But to make this model fit within the framework of price-taking with no monopoly power, I assumed that the function F was homogeneous of degree one in all of its inputs, including R. This, unfortunately, violates fact 2, that research is a nonrival good and fact 3, that only rival goods need to be replicated to double output. If I had admitted that R_j was nonrival, the replication argument would have implied that the firm faced increasing returns in the inputs R_j, K_j, and L_j that it controlled, because output would double merely by replicating K_j and L_j.

My sleight of hand in treating R_j as a rival good and making F homogeneous of degree 1 in all three of K, L, and R may seem like a trifling matter in an area of theory that depends on so many other short cuts. After all, if one is going to do violence to the complexity of economic activity by assuming that there is an aggregate production function, how much more harm can it do to be sloppy about the difference between rival and nonrival goods? Unfortunately, quite a bit. The distinctions between rival and nonrival inputs, and the distinction between excludable and nonexcludable goods, are of absolutely fundamental importance in modeling and in policy formulation.

For years, the economic analysis of science and technology policy consisted of little more than a syllogism. The major premise was that the government should provide public goods and the private sector should provide private goods. The minor premise was that basic research is a public good and applied research is a private good. Once you think carefully about nonrivalry and excludability, it is clear that the major premise is misleading because it understates the possible role for collective action. Governments can usefully provide goods that are nonrival but are not true public goods, because they are potentially excludable. The minor premise is simply wrong. Applied research is not an ordinary private good. Discussion in policy circles is now taking place using new terms – critical technologies, generic research, and pre-competitive research – that are only vaguely defined but that take the discussion outside of the simple dichotomy between public goods and private goods. This is probably useful, but it would lend needed structure to this discussion if participants paid more attention to the distinction between the two different aspects of publicness (nonrivalry and nonexcludability) and looked more formally at the different kinds of policy challenges that nonrivalry and nonexcludability present.

The linear model branch of endogenous growth theory pursued even more aggressively the strategy I used.[10] If I could treat the part of knowledge that firms control as an ordinary input in production – that is, as an input that is rival and hence is not associated with increasing returns – why bother to allow for any nonrival inputs at all? In effect, these models assumed that output could be written as $Y = F(R, K, H)$ for a homogenous of degree 1 production function F. These models assumed that research R, physical capital K, and human capital H were like ordinary inputs. If there are no nonrival goods, there are no increasing returns. It is then a relatively simple matter to build a perfectly competitive model of growth. To simplify still further, these models often aggregate R, K, and H into a single broad measure of capital. Suppose we call it X. Then we can write $F(X)$ as a linear function: $Y = F(X) = aX$, hence the name linear models. If we assume that a constant fraction of output Y is saved and used to produce more X, the model generates persistent, endogenous growth. Relative to the neoclassical model, these models capture fact 4 – that technological change comes from investments that people make – at the cost of abandoning fact 2, that technology or knowledge is a nonrival good.

Proponents of the linear model and the neoclassical model have sometimes been drawn into pointless arguments about which model is worse. Proponents of the linear growth models point out that the neoclassical model fails to capture fact 4. Proponents of the neoclassical model observe that the linear model cannot capture fact 2. This dispute is partly an outgrowth of the convergence controversy. Both sides specify that output takes the form $Y = K^{1-\beta}L^{\beta}$ and then argue about whether β is bigger than zero (as the proponents of the neoclassical model claim) or close to zero (as some versions of the linear growth model suggest).

This is not a very useful debate. There are circumstances in which each model can be a useful expositional device for highlighting different aspects of the growth process, but presumably the agenda for the profession ought to be to capture both facts 2 and 4 and pick up fact 5 to boot.

NEO-SCHUMPETERIAN GROWTH

Two steps were required for the neo-Schumpeterian models of growth to emerge. The first was that after struggling for years to preserve perfect competition, or at least price-taking in the presence of external effects, growth theorists had to decide to let go. It helped that economists working on industrial organization had given them something else to hang onto. By the late 1970s, there were aggregate models with many firms (fact 1), each of which could have market power (fact 5). The most convenient such model was developed by Dixit and Stiglitz (1977). Ethier (1982) subsequently showed how their model of preferences over many goods could be interpreted as a production function that depended on a large number of inputs in production.

Once people who were interested in growth recognized that this approach offered the alternative to a competitive market structure, there was only one technical detail that remained to be resolved, the detail that had kept both Nordhaus and Arrow from producing models of endogenous growth. All models of growth need at least one equation which describes the evolution of something like $A(t)$.[11] This equation usually takes the form

$$\dot{A} = -A^\phi, \tag{2}$$

where A with a dot denotes the time derivative of A. Models that produce steady state growth fill in the blank with a constant and set the exponent ϕ equal to 1. For example, if we set ϕ equal to 1 and insert a constant g in the blank, we have the driving equation behind the neoclassical model with exogenous technological change.

Mathematically, this kind of formulation is not robust. If ϕ turns out to be even slightly greater than 1, the equation implies that the stock of technology will go to infinity in finite time. When we use this same kind of model to study population growth, this lack of robustness does not raise any particular difficulties. We understand that functional forms are always approximations, and that a linear differential equation leading to exponential growth is a particularly convenient approximation. But Nordhaus and Arrow both worked at a time when there was real concern about the knife-edge character of the assumptions about ϕ.[12] If it was less than one, growth eventually stopped. If it was even slightly greater than one, everything blows up. As a result, economists stayed well away from the edge and assumed that ϕ had to be strictly less than 1. In a model like Nordhaus's, growth can be kept going only by adding a second kind of knowledge A_2 that grows exogenously. (Formally, bringing in exogenous technological change amounts to bringing in a new equation in which the exponent corresponding to ϕ has already been set to 1, and it only takes one equation with this property to keep things going.)

I devoted a great deal of attention to this robustness problem in my analysis of the spillover models. I modified other functional forms elsewhere in the model to construct robust models of endogenous growth in which the level of output and its rate of growth stayed finite for all time for a range of values of ϕ that were strictly bigger than 1 (Romer 1983, 1986). For values slightly less than 1, growth eventually stopped but could persist, nevertheless, for a very long time. The mathematical analysis in this more complicated robust model was much harder than the analysis that is possible when ϕ is equal to 1. The difference between the two models is the difference between studying the phase plane of a nonlinear differential equation system and solving a simple linear differential equation. Once it is clear that we could build a complicated model that is robust, there is every reason to work with the simple special case whenever possible.

By the late 1980s, economists like Judd (1985) and Grossman and Helpman (1989) were working out models of growth with monopolistic competition. Like Nordhaus and Arrow, they stayed well away from the case where ϕ was equal to 1. Judd invoked exogenous technological change to keep his economy growing. Grossman and Helpman were investigating the connection between trade and growth, and settled for an analysis of transitional dynamics of the model as it converged to a steady state level of income where growth stopped. In each model, monopoly profits motivate discovery.

I took what I had learned about generating sustained growth from my analysis of spillover models and applied it to the monopolistic competition model. I constructed two very simple models of sustained growth that accommodated all five of the facts cited above. One of these did not invoke any spillover effects at all (Romer 1987b). The other combined both monopoly power and spillovers – that is, incomplete intellectual property rights (Romer 1990). In each of these models I set the analog of ϕ equal to 1. I knew that by repeating my analysis of the spillover model, it would be possible to construct more complicated robust models with the same qualitative implications.

Research on endogenous growth models in which monopoly profits motivate innovation has progressed rapidly since then and has uncovered a number of unexpected connections between market size, international trade, and growth, as Grossman and Helpman (1994) explain.

CONCLUSIONS

The economics profession is undergoing a substantial change in how we think about international trade, development, economic growth and economic geography.[13] In each of these areas, we have gone through a progression that starts with models based on perfect competition, moves to price-taking with external increasing returns, and finishes with explicit models of imperfect competition. It is likely that this pattern will repeat itself in other areas like the theory of macroeconomic fluctuations.

The effects of this general trend may be far-reaching. Ultimately, it may force economists to reconsider some of the most basic propositions in economics. For example, I am convinced that both markets and free trade are good, but the traditional answer that we give to students to explain why they are good, the one based on perfect competition and Pareto optimality, is becoming untenable. Something more interesting and more complicated is going on here.[14]

In each of the areas where our understanding has changed, evidence that challenged the models of perfect competition and supported the models with imperfect competition had been apparent all along. Everyone knew that there was lots of intra-industry trade between developed nations and little trade between the North and the South. Everyone knew that some developing countries grew spectacularly while others languished. Everyone knew that people do the things that lead to technological change. Everyone knew that the number of locally available goods was limited by the extent of the market in the city where someone lives and works.

In evaluating different models of growth, I have found that Lucas's (1988) observation, that people with human capital migrate from places where it is scarce to place where it is abundant, is as powerful a piece of evidence as all the cross-country growth regressions combined. But this kind of fact, like the fact about intra-industry trade or the fact that people make discoveries, does not come with an attached t-statistic. As a result, these kinds of facts tend to be neglected in discussions that focus too narrowly on testing and rejecting models.

Economists often complain that we do not have enough data to differentiate between the available theories, but what constitutes relevant data is itself endogenous. If we set our standards for what constitutes relevant evidence too high and pose our tests too narrowly, we will indeed end up with too little data. We can thereby enshrine the economic orthodoxy and make it invulnerable to challenge.[15] If we do not have any models that can fit the data, the temptation will be to set very high standards for admissible evidence, because we would prefer not to reject the only models that we have.

When I look back on my work on growth, my greatest satisfaction comes from having rejected the first round of external effects models that I tried. I am glad that I was able to learn something about robustness and nonrivalry from struggling with these models, but was still able to let go when a better alternative became apparent. My greatest regret is the shift I made while working on these external effects models, a shift that took me away from the emphasis on research and knowledge that characterized my 1986 paper and toward the emphasis on physical capital that characterized the empirical work in the paper cited in the discussion of convergence (1987a). This paper contributed to the convergence controversy and to an emphasis on the exponents on capital and labor in aggregate production. I am now critical of this work, and I accept part of the blame. Looking back, I suspect that I made this shift toward capital and away from knowledge partly in an attempt to conform to the norms of what constituted convincing empirical work in macroeconomics. No international agency publishes data series on the local production of knowledge and inward flows of knowledge. If you want to run regressions, investment in physical capital is a variable that you can use, so use it I did. I wish I had stuck to my guns about the importance of evidence like that contained in facts 1 through 5.

If macroeconomists look only at the cross-country regressions deployed in the convergence controversy, it will be easy to be satisfied with neoclassical models in which market incentives and government policies have no effect on discovery, diffusion, and technological advance. But if we make use of all of the available evidence, economists can move beyond these models and begin once again to make progress toward a complete understanding of the determinants of long-run economic success. Ultimately, this will put us in position to offer policy-makers something more insightful than the standard neoclassical prescription – more saving and more schooling. We will be able to rejoin the ongoing policy debates about tax subsidies for private research, antitrust exemptions for research joint ventures, the activities of multinational firms, the effects of government procurement, the feedback between trade policy and innovation, the scope of protection for intellectual property rights, the links between private firms and universities, the mechanisms for selecting the research areas that receive public support, and the costs and benefits of an explicit government-led technology policy. We will be able to address the most important policy questions about growth: In a developing country like the Philippines, what are the best institutional arrangements for gaining access to the knowledge that already exists in the rest of the world? In a country like the United States, what are the best institutional arrangements for encouraging the production and use of new knowledge?

ACKNOWLEDGEMENTS

I have benefited from comments by Jeffrey Frankel, Alan Krueger, David Romer, Carl Shapiro, and Timothy Taylor on early drafts of this chapter. This work was supported by NSF Grant SES 9023469 and by the Canadian Institute for Advanced Research.

NOTES

1 The data here are taken from version IV of the Penn World Table. The income measure is RGDP2. See Summers and Heston (1988) for details.
2 Nelson and Phelps (1966) give a theoretical model that allows for diffusion of the technology between countries. Fagerberg (1987) interprets cross-country growth regressions in the context of a technology gap model instead of a neoclassical model or a spillover model. For further discussion of diffusion, see also Barro and Sala i Martin (1994) and Jovanovic and Lach (1993).
3 See King and Rebelo (1993) for a fuller discussion of both the price and quantity implications of the neoclassical model.
4 See Kremer (1993) for a stimulating look at this question from a very long-run point of view.
5 Of course, Stigler's law applies in this case: the person that any result is named after was not the first person to derive or state the result. It just helps to have a label so that you can keep track of the players without a scorecard.
6 Nelson and Winter (1982) developed an alternative evolutionary model of growth. Their verbal, descriptive style of theory, which they label appreciative theory, was flexible enough to accommodate facts 1–5. This style of work can be thought of as a complement to formal theory, not a substitute for it. It leaves open the problem of constructing a formal theory that could accommodate these facts.

7 For an explicit treatment showing that Marshallian external increasing returns is ultimately an untenable way to model any process involving learning or knowledge, see Dasgupta and Stiglitz (1988).

8 Lucas actually makes A depend on per capita H rather than total H. The difference between these two formulations is not relevant for the discussion here, but is important for some of the other implications of the model.

9 For consistency with the rest of the discussion, I distinguish here between R and K. In the paper, I actually dropped physical capital from consideration so that I have only one state variable to deal with. This leads to a potential confusion because I also used the symbol K for knowledge instead of R.

10 One of the early linear models was Uzawa (1965). Important papers in this line of work include Becker *et al.* (1990), Jones and Manuelli (1990) and Rebelo (1991).

11 Sometimes other variables like H or K are used in place of A, but the basic issues are the same.

12 See Stiglitz (1990) for a discussion of how people working on growth at the time perceived this problem.

13 Paul Krugman has made influential contributions in all of these areas. See Krugman (1990, 1991, 1993) for a discussion of the changes in these fields.

14 Romer (1994) offers a demonstration that, for example, the costs of trade restrictions in a developing country can be far greater in the context of a model with imperfect competition than they are in a model with perfect competition.

15 In their discussion of real business cycle theories and the kind of evidence used to test them, Greg Mankiw (1989) and Robert Solow (1988) have both made a similar point about explicit statistical versus broader kinds of evidence.

REFERENCES

Abramovitz, Moses, 'Catching Up, Forging Ahead, and Falling Behind', *Journal of Economic History* June 1986, *46*:2, 385–406.

Arrow, Kenneth J., 'The Economic Implications of Learning by Doing', *Review of Economic Studies* June 1962, *29*, 155–73.

Barro, Robert J. and Xavier Sala i Martin, 'Convergence', *Journal of Political Economy* April 1992, *100*:2, 223–51.

Barro, Robert J. and Xavier Sala i Martin, 'Chapter 8: Diffusion of Technology'. In R. J. Barro and X. Sala-i-Martin (eds) *Economic Growth*, New York: McGraw Hill, 1994.

Baumol, William J., 'Productivity Growth, Convergence, and Welfare: What the Long-run Data Show', *American Economic Review* December 1986, *76*:5, 1072–85.

Becker, G., K. Murphy and R. Tamura, 'Economic Growth, Human Capital, and Population Growth', *Journal of Political Economy* October 1990, *98*:5 Part 2, S12–S137.

Dasgupta, P. and J. Stiglitz, 'Learning-by-Doing, Market Structure, and Industrial and Trade Policies', *Oxford Economic Papers* June 1988, *40*:2, 246–68.

De Long, J. Bradford, 'Productivity Growth, Convergence and Welfare: Comment', *American Economic Review* December 1988, *78*:5, 1138–54.

Dixit, A. and J. Stiglitz, 'Monopolistic Competition and Optimum Product Diversity', *American Economic Review* June 1977, *67*:3, 297–308.

Ethier, W. J., 'National and International Returns to Scale in the Modern Theory of International Trade', *American Economic Review* June 1982, *72*:3, 389–405.

Fagerberg, Jan, 'A Technology Gap Approach to Why Growth Rates Differ', *Research Policy* 1987, *16*, 87–99.

Griliches, Zvi, 'Issues in Assessing the Contribution of Research and Development to Productivity Growth', *Bell Journal of Economics* Spring 1979, *10*, 92–116.

Grossman, Gene, and Elhanan Helpman, 'Product Development and International Trade', *Journal of Political Economy* December 1989, *97*:6, 1261–83.

Grossman, Gene, and Elhanan Helpman, 'Endogenous Innovation in the Theory of Growth', *Journal of Economic Perspectives* Winter 1994, 8: 1, 23–44.

Heston, Alan, and Robert Summers, 'The Penn World Trade (Mark 5): An Expanded Set of International Comparisons, 1950–1988', *Quarterly Journal of Economics* May 1991, *106*, 327–68.

Jones, Lawrence, and Rodolfo Manuelli, 'A Convex Model of Equilibrium Growth: Theory and Policy Implications', *Journal of Political Economy* October 1990, *98*:5 Part 1, 1008–38.

Jovanovic, Boyan, and Saul Lach, 'Diffusion Lags and Aggregate Fluctuations', mimeo, New York University, August 1993.

Judd, K. L., 'On the Performance of Patents', *Econometrica* May 1985, *53*:3, 567–85.

King, Robert G. and Sergio Rebelo, 'Transitional Dynamics and Economic Growth in the Neoclassical Model', *American Economic Review* September 1993, *83*:4, 908–31.

Kremer, Michael, 'Population Growth and Technological Change: One Million B.C. to 1990', *Quarterly Journal of Economics* August 1993, *108*:3, 681–716.

Krugman, Paul, *Rethinking International Trade*, Cambridge: MIT Press, 1990.

Krugman, Paul, *Geography and Trade*, Cambridge: MIT Press, 1991.

Krugman, Paul, 'Towards a Counter-Counter Revolution in Development Theory', *Proceedings of the Annual World Bank Conference on Development 1992*, Supplement, Washington, DC, *World Bank Economic Review* 1993, 15–38.

Lucas, Robert E., Jr, 'On the Mechanics of Economic Development', *Journal of Monetary Economics* July 1988, *22*:1, 3–42.

Maddison, A., *Phases of Capitalist Development*, Oxford: Oxford University Press, 1982.

Mankiw, N. Gregory, 'Real Business Cycles: A New Keynesian Perspective', *Journal of Economic Perspectives* Summer 1989, *3*:3, 79–90.

Mankiw, N. Gregory, David Romer, and David N. Weil, 'A Contribution to the Empirics of Economic Growth', *Quarterly Journal of Economics* May 1992, *107*, 407–37.

Marshall, Alfred, *Principles of Economics*, London: Macmillan, 1890.

Nelson, Richard R. and Edmund S. Phelps, 'Investment in Humans, Technological Diffusion, and Economic Growth', *American Economic Review* May 1966, *56*, 69–75.

Nelson, Richard R. and Sidney G. Winter, *An Evolutionary Theory of Economic Change*, Cambridge: Belnap Press of Harvard University Press, 1982.

Nordhaus, William D., 'An Economic Theory of Technological Change', *American Economic Review* May 1969, *59*:2, 18–28.

Rebelo, Sergio, 'Long Run Policy Analysis and Long Run Growth', *Journal of Political Economy* June 1991, *99*:3, 500–21.

Romer, Paul M., 'Dynamic Competitive Equilibria with Externalities, Increasing Returns and Unbounded Growth', Ph.D. dissertation, University of Chicago, 1983.

Romer, Paul M., 'Increasing Returns and Long-Run Growth', *Journal of Political Economy* October 1986, *94*:5, 1002–37.

Romer, Paul M., 'Crazy Explanations for the Productivity Slowdown', in S. Fischer (ed.) *NBER Macroeconomics Annual*, Cambridge: MIT Press, 1987a, 163–202.

Romer, Paul M., 'Growth Based on Increasing Returns Due to Specialization', *American Economic Review* May 1987b, *77*:2, 56–62.

Romer, Paul M., 'Endogenous Technological Change', *Journal of Political Economy* 1990, *98*, S71–102.

Romer, Paul M., 'Two Strategies for Economic Development: Using Ideas and Producing Ideas', *Proceedings of the Annual World Bank Conference on Development 1992*, Supplement, Washington, DC, *World Bank Economic Review*, 1993.

Romer, Paul M., 'New Goods, Old Theory and the Welfare Costs of Trade Restrictions', *Journal of Development Economics* February 1994, *43*:1.

Shell, Karl, 'Toward a Theory of Inventive Activity and Capital Accumulation', *American Economic Review* May 1966, *56*, 62–68.

Solow, Robert, 'A Contribution to the Theory of Economic Growth', *Quarterly Journal of Economics* February 1956, *70*, 65–94.

Solow, Robert, 'Technical Change and the Aggregate Production Function', *Review of Economics and Statistics* August 1957, *39*, 312–20.

Solow, Robert, 'Growth Theory and After', *American Economic Review* June 1988, *78*:3, 307–17.

Stiglitz, Joseph, 'Comments: Some Retrospective Views on Growth Theory', in Peter Diamond (ed.) *Growth, Productivity, and Unemployment*, Cambridge: MIT Press, 1990, 50–68.

Summers, Robert, and Alan Heston, 'A New Set of International Comparisons of Real Product and Price Levels Estimates for 130 Countries, 1950–1985', *Review of Income and Wealth* March 1988, *34*:1, 1–25.

Uzawa, Hirofumi, 'Optimum Technical Change in an Aggregative Model of Economic Growth', *International Economic Review* January 1965, *6*, 18–31.

27 Perspectives on growth theory

Robert M. Solow

Journal of Economic Perspectives (1994) 8, Winter, pp. 45–54

The current wildfire revival of interest in growth theory was touched off by articles from Romer (1986, from his 1983 thesis) and Lucas (1988, from his 1985 Marshall Lectures). This boom shows no signs of petering out. The time is not yet ripe for stock-taking and evaluation. My goal is not nearly so ambitious. All I want to do is to place the new thinking in some sort of historical perspective, and perhaps sprinkle a few idiosyncratic judgments along the way.

There have been three waves of interest in growth theory during the past 50 years or so. The first was associated with the work of Harrod (1948) and Domar (1947); Harrod's greater obscurity attracted more attention at the time (and earlier, in 1939), although Domar's way of looking at things is more relevant to some of the current ideas.[1] The second wave was the development of the neoclassical model. I think – probably inevitably – that some misconceptions remain about what that was all about, and why. The third wave began as a reaction to omissions and deficiencies in the neoclassical model, but now generates its own alternation of questions and answers.

THE HARROD-DOMAR IMPULSE

Suppose aggregate output is for some reason – technological or any other – proportional to the stock of (physical) capital. There is a warrant for this in the almost-trendlessness of the observed ratio. Suppose that realized saving and investment (net, for simplicity) is proportional to output and income. There is similar warrant for this assumption. It follows that investment is proportional to the stock of capital, and this fixes the trend rate of growth of both capital and output, unless the rate of capacity utilization is allowed to go wild. That rate of growth is the product of the investment–output ratio and the output–capital ratio. If we think entirely in *ex post* terms, the saving–income ratio and the investment–output ratio are the same thing. One of the defining characteristics of growth theory as a branch of macroeconomics is that it tends to ignore all the difficult economics that is papered over by that sentence.

Now suppose that the required labor input per unit of output is falling at the rate m (which is to say that labor productivity is rising at the rate m), again for whatever reason. If the labor force is increasing at the rate n, a sort of impasse arises. Total output must grow at the rate $m + n$ on average, or else the unemployment rate will rise indefinitely (if output growth is too slow) or the economy will run out of labor (if growth is too fast). But we have just seen that the growth rate must satisfy a quite independent condition: it must be equal to the product of the saving–investment quota (s) and the output–capital ratio (a). The two conditions can be reconciled only if $sa = m + n$. But there is no reason why this should ever happen, because the four parameters come from four wholly unrelated sources.

This construction seemed to have two unpalatable consequences. The first is that observed economies should spend most of their time experiencing either prolonged episodes of increasing or falling unemployment rates and/or prolonged periods of rising or falling capacity utilization. There is no reason to expect these movements to be confined to minor business-cycle dimensions or to be quickly reversed. But that is not what the record of the main capitalist economies looks like.

The second apparent consequence is this. Suppose the first problem can be evaded. This might happen, for instance, in a developing country with a large pool of rural labor. It could then have an industrial labor force growing at whatever the required rate, *sa-m*, happens to be; the consequences of a mismatch would be seen only in the waxing or waning of the rural population. Such an economy could jack up its long-term rate of industrial growth merely by increasing its investment quota. Under the influence of this model, that policy was sometimes prescribed. It makes general sense. But if economic development were that easy, it would be hard to understand why more poor countries did not follow that route to rapid growth. Even rich countries would surely want to take advantage of this possibility sometimes. Something seems to be wrong with this way of looking at long-run economic growth.

The straightforward way to avoid the first of these awkward conclusions is to recognize that at least one of the four underlying parameters is likely to be endogenous. Then the condition $sa = m + n$ may have a solution most or all of the time; and there may be a plausible adjustment process that will realize the solution and allow uninterrupted growth to take place. Obviously the investment–income ratio quota s and the output-capital ratio a are the natural candidates for endogeneity.[2] Kaldor (1956) and others tried to use s in this way, usually by emphasizing its interpretation as a saving rate, introducing different saving rates applying to different categories of income, especially wages and profits, and then focussing on changes in the functional distribution of income as the mechanism causing the aggregate saving rate to vary endogenously. (Bertola 1992 is an interesting modern treatment of this line of thought.) It is fair to say that this way of resolving the problem did not catch on, partly for empirical reasons and partly because the mechanism seemed to require that factor prices be completely divorced from productivity considerations.

THE NEOCLASSICAL RESPONSE

The standard neoclassical model, of course, resolves the problem by making the output–capital ratio a the endogenous variable. Then labor productivity growth m will have an endogenous component too, as capital-intensity changes; but there may remain an exogenous component, loosely identified as technological progress. This has several related advantages. It fits in well with the rest of economics; the possibility of increasing the output–capital ratio by substituting labor for capital is a comfortable and sensible device, especially on a longish time scale. The implied adjustment mechanism is plausible and familiar. If $sa - m > n$, so that labor is getting scarce relative to capital, one might naturally expect the wage–rental ratio to rise; cost-minimizing firms would naturally substitute capital for labor. The output–capital ratio would fall and the economy would move closer to satisfying the consistency condition. Similarly in reverse. (There the habit of ignoring aggregate-demand considerations might grate a little. In periods of high unemployment firms face weak product markets; lower wages could make things worse.) The assumptions about diminishing returns that are required to make this mechanism work come easily to most economists. Substitution along isoquants is routine stuff. That does not count as evidence in favor of the traditional assumptions, but it explains why the model feels comfortable to economists. Besides, there is quite a bit of evidence to support the traditional assumptions, considerably more than there is in the opposite direction.

Notice that I have not mentioned constant returns to scale. That is because the model can get along perfectly well without constant returns to scale. The occasional expression of belief to the contrary is just a misconception. The assumption of constant returns to scale is a considerable simplification, both because it saves a dimension by allowing the whole analysis to be conducted in terms of ratios and because it permits the further simplification that the basic market-form is competitive. But it is not essential to the working of the model nor even overwhelmingly useful in an age of cheap computer simulation.

Everybody knows that fixing up the first awkward implication in this way (the implication that economies should be experiencing prolonged swings in unemployment and capacity utilization) also takes care of the second awkward implication (that growth by raising an investment quota seems somehow too easy an approach). Diminishing returns to capital implies that the long-run rate of growth is completely independent of the saving-investment quota. A closed economy that manages to raise or lower the fraction of output invested, and sticks to the program, will experience a rise or fall in its aggregate rate of growth, but only temporarily. Eventually the rate of growth relapses back to its long-run value. This underlying rate of growth is the sum of n and the technological-progress component of m. The only permanent effect of the maintained change in investment will be an upward or downward shift in the level of the trend path, but not in its slope. Increasing the rate of per capita growth is not only not easy in this model, but also impossible unless the rate of technological progress can be altered deliberately.

This reversal of conclusions has led to a criticism of the neoclassical model: it is a theory of growth that leaves the main factor in economic growth unexplained. There is some truth in that observation, but also some residual misconception. First of all, to say that the rate of technological progress is exogenous is not to say that it is either constant, or utterly erratic, or always mysterious. One could expect the rate of technological progress to increase or decrease from time to time. Such an event has no explanation within the model, and may have no apparent explanation at all. Or else it might be entirely understandable in some reasonable but after-the-fact way, only not as a systematic part of the model itself.

Second, no one could ever have intended to deny that technological progress is at least partially endogenous to the economy. Valuable resources are used up in pursuit of innovation, presumably with some rational hope of financial success. The patent system is intended to solidify that hope, and thus attract more resources into the search for new products and processes. It would be very odd indeed if all that activity had nothing to do with the actual achievement of technological progress. The question is whether one has anything useful to say about the process, in a form that can be made part of an aggregative growth model. I will suggest later on that this is probably the most promising aspect of the current third wave of growth theory, even if much that has been written on the subject so far seems simplistic and unconvincing.

NEWER ALTERNATIVES

The direction taken at first by the newer growth-theoretic models was not toward a direct approach to the economics of technological progress. It was something much simpler: a straightforward abandonment of the idea of diminishing returns to 'capital' (now interpreted as the whole collection of accumulatable factors of production, one of which might be labelled human capital or even the stock of knowledge). This stage of the revival could be described as a return to generalized Domar, but with sophisticated bells and whistles. Among the bells and whistles were allowance for substitutability between capital and labor and between various forms of capital, allowance for only asymptotic absence of diminishing returns, the adoption of a representative-agent set-up with infinite-horizon intertemporal optimization to determine investment (in everything), and the introduction of monopolistic competition as the underlying market form.

Here I would like to interject two comments. The modelling of imperfect competition was made necessary by the appearance of increasing returns to scale. I have already mentioned that the presence of increasing returns to scale is not the essence of these newer approaches. It is perfectly possible to have increasing returns to scale and preserve all the standard neoclassical results. What *is* essential is the assumption of constant returns to capital. The presence of increasing returns to scale is then inevitable, because otherwise the assumption of constant returns to capital would imply negative marginal productivity for non-capital factors. Anyway, I register the opinion that the incorporation of monopolistic competition into growth theory is an unambiguously good thing, for which the new growth theory can take a bow (along with a derived curtsey to Dixit and Stiglitz).

I cannot say the same about the use made of the intertemporally optimizing representative agent. Maybe I reveal myself merely as old-fashioned, but I see no redeeming social value in using this construction, which Ramsey intended as a representation of the decision-making of an idealized policy-maker, as if it were a descriptive model of an industrial capitalist economy. It adds little or nothing to the story anyway, while encumbering it with unnecessary implausibilities and complexities.

Now I return to the question of constant returns to capital. It may not be generally recognized how restrictive this assumption is. There is no tolerance for deviation. Lucas emphasized in his 1988 article that a touch of diminishing returns to capital (human capital in his case) would change the character of the model drastically, making it incapable of generating permanent growth. He did not notice that a touch of increasing returns to capital would do the same, but in a quite different way. Since I have not seen this acknowledged in the literature I will spell it out here.

Suppose that the production function is $f(K, L)$, with non-decreasing returns to capital. Treat L as constant for the moment, so we can think of this as just $f(K)$. Let net investment be the fraction s of output so that the time path of K is determined by $dK/dt = sf(K)$. It is obvious on the face that there is potential for fairly explosive behavior if $f(K)$ increases more and more rapidly with K. For instance, if $f(K)/K$ increases with K, the rate of growth of K gets faster as K gets larger. Then the time path for this growth model has the property that the stock of capital becomes infinite in finite time. (It is one thing to say that a quantity will eventually exceed any bound. It is quite another to say that it will exceed any stated bound before Christmas.) It takes a little calculus to show that 'fairly explosive' puts it mildly.[3]

The fragility of the constant-elasticity case is worth pursuing further. I will choose $h = 0.05$ to represent a fairly small degree of increasing returns to capital. If $Y = K^{1.05}$, increasing K by 20 percent will increase Y by a bit more than 21 percent. This is already a fairly weak dose of increasing returns, and might even be empirically undetectable. Anything more would have even more drastic consequences. The capital–output ratio is of order of magnitude about one, to be conservative. A straightforward calculation shows that output will be infinite in about $(1/sh)$ years.[4] If s is about 0.1 and h is as small as 0.05, a country like Germany or France will achieve infinite output in about 200 years, or even a shorter time from 'now'. They should live so long, one is inclined to say.

Of course this kind of calculation should never be taken literally, but it teaches an important lesson. The knife-edge character of the constant-returns model can not be evaded by the obvious dodge: oh, well, so it blows up in finite time – that time could be a million years from now, by which time we will have evolved into God knows what. For the Land of Cockaigne to be a million years away, $1 + h$ would have to be so close to 1 that we would never be able to discern the difference. The conclusion has to be that this version of the endogenous-growth model is very un-robust. It can not survive without *exactly* constant returns to capital. But you would have to believe in the tooth fairy to expect that kind of luck.

This branch of the new growth theory seems unpromising to me on straight theoretical grounds. If it found strong support in empirical material, one would have to reconsider and perhaps try to find some convincing reason why Nature has no choice but to present us with constant returns to capital. On the whole, however, the empirical evidence appears to be less than not strong; if anything, it goes the other way.

A particular style of empirical work seems to have sprung from the conjunction of growth theory and the immensely valuable body of comparative national-accounts data compiled by Summers and Heston (1991). It rests on international cross-section regressions with the average growth-rates of different countries as the dependent variable and various politico-economic factors on the right-hand side that might easily affect the growth rate if the growth rate were easily affected. I had better admit that I do not find this a confidence-inspiring project. It seems altogether too vulnerable to bias from omitted variables, to reverse causation, and above all to the recurrent suspicion that the experiences of very different national economies are not to be explained as if they represented different 'points' on some well-defined surface. These weaknesses are confirmed by Levine and Reinelt (1992) and Levine and Zervos (1992), who find that these cross-section regressions are not robust to the choice of explanatory variables and are otherwise statistically unprepossessing. More strictly focussed studies – I am thinking especially of Mankiw *et al.* (1992) and Islam (1992) – seem to favor some extended version of the neoclassical model.

The temptation of wishful thinking hovers over the interpretation of these cross-section studies. It should be countered by cheerful skepticism. The introduction of a wide range of explanatory variables has the advantage of offering partial shelter from the bias due to omitted variables. But this protection is paid for. As the range of explanation broadens, it becomes harder and harder to believe in an underlying structural, reversible relation that amounts to more than a sly way of saying that Japan grew rapidly and the United Kingdom grew slowly during this or that period.

I think that the real value of endogenous growth theory will emerge from its attempt to model the endogenous component of technological progress as an integral part of the theory of economic growth. Here too the pioneer was Romer (1990). Many others have followed his lead: my short list includes Grossman and Helpman (1991), Aghion and Howitt (1992), Stokey (1991) and Young (1991, 1993), but there are others.

This is a very hard problem for a number of reasons. For one thing, there is probably an irreducibly exogenous element in the research and development process, at least exogenous to the economy. Fields of research open up and close down unpredictably, in economics as well as in science and technology. This is reflected, for instance, in the frequency with which research projects end up by finding something that was not even contemplated when the initial decisions were made. There is an internal logic – or sometimes non-logic – to the advance of knowledge that may be orthogonal to the economic logic. This is not at all to deny the partially endogenous character of innovation but only to suggest that the 'production' of new technology may not be a simple matter of inputs and outputs. I do not doubt that high financial returns to successful innovation will divert resources into R&D. The hard part is to model what happens then.

A second difficulty, no doubt related to the first, is the large uncertainty surrounding many research projects. It is possible that some of this uncertainty is not probabilistic: if 'Knightian uncertainty' shows up anywhere, it could be here. If so, then appropriate analytical techniques are lacking. Third, it is not clear how you would know if you had a promising model. Surface plausibility is one criterion, but hardly a sufficient one. The best source of empirical material may be historical case studies, but then the test of truth is bound to be fuzzy.

There are, of course, historians and sociologists, as well as economists, who study the R&D process in contextual detail. Their insights and conclusions are usually not in a form that can be used by a macroeconomic model-builder, and they may even regard the necessary abstraction and codification as a kind of violation. Even so, there is no excuse for ignoring the generalizations that emerge from other styles of work. Models of innovation can be constructed out of thin air, but it is surely better to use more durable materials if they are available. The best bet, no doubt, would be collaboration between model-builders and those who use informal methods, to compromise between one side's need for definiteness and the other side's sense of complexity.

All the difficulties notwithstanding, it seems to me that the body of work I have just cited has an air of promise and excitement about it. Aghion and Howitt (1992) manage to give some precision to Schumpeter's vague notions about 'creative destruction'. They make a formal model in which each innovation kills off its predecessors. It is obvious that some innovations reduce or wipe out the rents that might otherwise have accrued to previous innovations, and this fact of life has to be taken into account in any understanding of the process. But sometimes – who knows, maybe just as often – innovations are complementary with predecessors and add to their rents. This possibility matters too. Is there any non-mechanical way to take both contingencies into account? (Schumpeter is a sort of patron saint in this field. I may be alone in thinking that he should be treated like a patron saint: paraded around one day each year and more or less ignored the rest of the time.)

It seems to me that there is great merit in Alwyn Young's (1993) project of treating learning-by-doing as one mode of productivity increase, but not the only one. It is an important fact of life that many instances of product improvement and cost reduction have little to do with the R&D activity, but originate in some other way, for instance from the cumulation of small suggestions coming from production workers, process engineers, and even customers. Categorical R&D spending may be an inadequate measure of the resources devoted to increasing productivity. How to understand and model that other way is an important question. Growth theorists might profit from picking the brains of informed observers of industry.

This is a good place for me to insert a few more idiosyncratic criticisms of the new wave. Much of the advanced literature uses the 'new product' as a universal metaphor for innovation. Even cost reduction is often supposed to come about via the invention of new intermediate goods. The development of new products is certainly a prominent feature of the technological landscape, but one is permitted to wonder if that is the only way to go, or even the best way. Any particular metaphor can impose a bias on subsequent trains of thought.

The idea of endogenous growth so captures the imagination that growth theorists often just insert favorable assumptions in an unearned way; and then when they put in their thumb and pull out the very plum they have inserted, there is a tendency to think that something has been proved. Suppose that the production function is $Af(K, L)$ where A carried (Hicks-neutral) technological progress. (The neutrality is just for clarity; it is inessential.) Successful innovations make A larger. But how much larger?

For this purpose, take it for granted that there is something meaningful called 'an innovation' and a stream of these innovations occurs as a result of decisions made by firms. It is easy to agree that the flow of innovations per unit time depends on the amount of resources devoted to creating them. If an innovation generates a proportionate increase in A, then we have a theory of easy endogenous growth. Spend more resources on R&D, there will be more innovations per year, and the growth rate of A will be higher. But suppose that an innovation generates only an absolute increase in A: then greater allocation of resources to R&D buys a one-time jump in productivity, but not a faster rate of productivity growth. I do not know which is the better assumption, and these are only two of many possibilities.

But merely to adopt the more powerful assumption is no more than to assume the more powerful conclusion.

Ideally, such modelling decisions should be made in the light of facts. Unfortunately there are not a lot of usable facts to be digested. One could hope for some enlightment from case studies of industries, technologies, and R&D decisions. Even that is not easy: it takes two to tango and the authors of case studies do not like to see their insights reduced to terms in a highly-simplified equation. Nevertheless I think the best candidate for a research agenda right now would be an attempt to extract a few workable hypotheses from the variegated mass of case studies, business histories, interviews, expert testimony, anything that might throw light on good ways to model the flow of productivity-increasing innovations and improvements. Finally I would like to call attention to an interesting paper by Caballero and Jaffe (1993) who made an ingenious start on exploiting whatever data there are. I am not necessarily endorsing all their conclusions, but rather their willingness to sift through a lot of data looking for reasonable generalizations.

NOTES

1 Harrod's exposition tended to rest on incompletely specified behavioral and expectational hypotheses. Domar focussed more straightforwardly on the requirements for equilibrium of demand and supply in steady growth.

2 In principle there is no reason to exclude the endogeneity of m and n. But induced changes in population growth, although an important matter in economic development, seemed not to figure essentially in the rich countries for which these models were devised. The idea of endogenous technological progress was never far below the surface. In those days it would have seemed rash to conjure up some simple connection between the allocation of resources and the *rate of growth* of productivity. Kaldor and Mirrlees' 'technical progress function' (1962) was an attempt that apparently did not seem plausible. I would recommend Karl Shell's papers (1966, 1967, 1973) as an indication of how far a technically-sophisticated and well-read economist of the time would have been willing to go. There has been some progress since those papers, but not a whole lot.

3 The solution of this differential equation is given by $\int_{K(t_0)}^{K(t)} dx/f(x) = s(t - t_0)$. Now suppose that the improper integral $\int_{K(t_0)}^{\infty} dx/f(x)$ converges to a number J (which will depend on $K(t_0)$ though this is not significant). Indeed the capital stock approaches infinity as t gets closer and closer to $t_0 + (J/s)$. If the production function will generate infinite output from infinite capital (as with Cobb and Douglas or a better-than-unit elasticity of substitution between labor and capital) then aggregate output and income become infinite at that time too. Allowing employment to increase can only hasten the date of the Big Bang. If output is finite even with infinite capital, the economy will achieve its maximal output in finite time. That is what I meant by saying that the model changes its character in a different way. What will make that improper integral converge? Clearly it is more likely to do so if $f(K)$ increases very rapidly with K. It can not do so if $f(K)$ is concave or linear. There are convex functions $f(K)$ for which the integral diverges. But increasing returns to capital helps a lot. It is easy to see that the integral converges if $f(K) = K^{1+h}$ for any positive h, no matter how small.

4 When $f(K) = K^{1+h}$, the number J is, $\int_{K(t_0)}^{\infty} x^{-(1+h)} dx$, which is $K(t_0)^{-h}/h$. Since $Y(t_0) = K(t_0)^{1+h}, K(t_0)^{-h} = K(t_0)/Y(t_0)$. Thus the date of the Big Bang satisfies $s(t - t_0) = h^{-1} K(T_0)/Y(t_0)$. Solving for t shows that the date of the Big Bang (the end of scarcity as we know it) occurs at $t_0 + (K(t_0)/Y(t_0))(sh)^{-1}$.

REFERENCES

Aghion, P. and P. Howitt, 'A Model of Growth through Creative Destruction', *Econometrica* March 1992, *60*:2, 322–52.

Bertola, G., 'Wages, Profits and Theories of Growth', International Economic Association Conference Paper, Varenna, Italy, 1992. In L. Pasinetti and R. Solow (eds) *Economic Growth and the Structure of Long-Term Development*, New York: St Martin's Press, 1994.

Caballero, R. and A. Jaffe, 'How High are the Giant's Shoulders: An Empirical Assessment of Knowledge Spillovers and Creative Destruction in a Model of Economic Growth', *NBER Macroeconomics Annual, 1993*, Cambridge and London: MIT Press, 1993, 15–74.

Dixit, Avinash, and Joseph E. Stiglitz, 'Monopolistic Competition and Optimum Product Diversity', *American Economic Review* June 1977, *67*: 3, 297–308.

Domar, E., 'Expansion and Employment', *American Economic Review*, March 1947, *37*:1, 343–55.

Grossman, G. and E. Helpman, *Innovation and Growth in the World Economy*, Cambridge: MIT Press, 1991.

Harrod, R. F., *Towards a Dynamic Economics*, London: MacMillan, 1948.

Islam, N., 'Growth Empirics: A Panel Data Approach', unpublished paper, Harvard University, 1992.

Kaldor, Nicholas, 'Alternative Theories of Distribution', *Review of Economic Studies* 1956, *23*:2, 83–100.

Kaldor, Nicholas and J. Mirrlees, 'A New Model of Economic Growth', *Review of Economic Studies* June 1962, *29*:3, 174–92.

Levine, R. and D. Reinelt, 'A Sensitivity Analysis of Cross-Country Growth Regressions', *American Economic Review* September 1992, *82*:4, 942–63.

Levine, R. and S. Zervos, 'Looking at the Facts: What We Know about Policy and Growth from Cross-Country Analysis', Unpublished paper prepared for International Economic Association Conference on 'Economic Growth and the Structure of Long-Term Development', Varenna, Italy, 1–3, October 1992.

Lucas, R., 'On the Mechanics of Economic Development', *Journal of Monetary Economics* July 1988, *22*:1, 3–42.

Mankiw, N. G., D. Romer, and D. Weil, 'A Contribution to the Empirics of Economic Growth', *Quarterly Journal of Economics* May 1992, *107*:2, 407–37.

Romer, P., 'Increasing Returns and Long-Run Growth', *Journal of Political Economy* October 1986, *94*:5, 1002–37.

Romer, P., 'Endogenous Technological Change', *Journal of Political Economy* October 1990, *985*:2, S71–102.

Shell, Karl, 'Toward a Theory of Inventive Activity and Capital Accumulation', *American Economic Review* May 1966, *56*:2, 62–68.

Shell, Karl, 'A Model of Inventive Activity and Capital Accumulation', in K. Shell (ed.) *Essays on the Theory of Optimal Economic Growth*, Cambridge: MIT Press, 1967, 67–85.

Shell, Karl, 'Inventive Activity, Industrial Organization and Economic Growth'. In J. A. Mirrlees and N. Stern (eds) *Models of Economic Growth*, Macmillan: London, 1973, 77–100.

Stokey, N., 'Human Capital, Product Quality, and Growth', *Quarterly Journal of Economics* May 1991, *106*, 587–616.

Summers, Robert, and Alan Heston, 'The Penn World Table (Mark 5: An Expanded Set of International Comparisons, 1950–1988)', *Quarterly Journal of Economics* May 1991, *106*:2, 327–68.

Young, A., 'Learning by Doing and the Dynamic Effects of International Trade', *Quarterly Journal of Economics* May 1991, *106*:2 369–406.

Young, A., 'Invention and Bounded Learning by Doing', *Journal of Political Economy* June 1993, *101*:3, 443–72.

Index

A Macroeconomics Reader brings together in a single volume a collection of key articles on developments and current debates in modern macroeconomics. The articles have been selected to provide the reader with an accessible and informative overview of a number of the most significant issues and controversies in macroeconomics.

Areas covered include:

Keynesian Economics and the Keynesian Revolution

The Monetarist Counter-Revolution

The Challenge of Rational Expectations and
New Classical Macroeconomics

The Real Business Cycle Approach to Economic Fluctuations

New Keynesian Economics

The Renaissance of Economic Growth Analysis

Brian Snowdon is Principal Lecturer in Economics at the University of Northumbria. His previous books include *Markets, Intervention and Planning* (1987) and (with Howard Vane and P. Wynarczyk) *A Modern Guide to Macroeconomics* (1994).

Howard R. Vane is Reader in Economics at Liverpool John Moores University. His previous books (with J. Thompson) include *Current Controversies in Macroeconomics* (1992) and *An Introduction to Macroeconomic Policy* (1993).

Economics/History of Economic Thought

ROUTLEDGE

11 New Fetter Lane
London EC4P 4EE

29 West 35th Street
New York NY 10001

Printed in Great Britain

ISBN 0-415-15716-1

9 780415 157162